Ethiopia & Eritrea

Frances Linzee Gordon
Jean-Bernard Carillet

LONELY PLANET PUBLICATIONS
Melbourne • Oakland • London • Paris

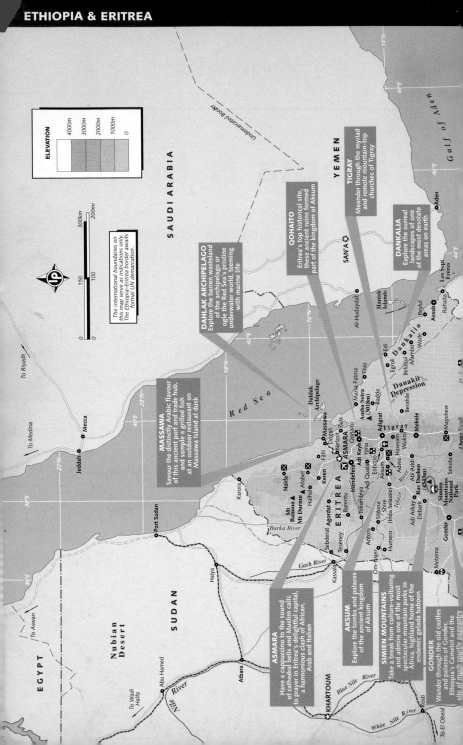

ETHIOPIA & ERITREA

ELEVATION

4000m
3000m
2000m
1000m
0

The international boundaries on this map serve as indications only. The Ethiopia-Eritrea border awaits formal UN demarcation.

DAHLAK ARCHIPELAGO
Explore the barren wasteland of this ancient archipelago or ogle the Red Sea's pristine underwater world, teeming with marine life

QOHAITO
Eritrea's top historical site, these ancient ruins formed part of the kingdom of Aksum

TIGRAY
Meander through the myriad and remote mountain-top churches of Tigray

DANKALIA
Explore the surreal landscapes of one of the most desolate areas on earth

MASSAWA
Savour the distinctly Arabic flavour of this ancient port and trade hub, and sample a grilled fish at an outdoor restaurant on Massawa Island at dusk

ASMARA
Have a cappuccino to the sound of cathedral bells and Muslim calls to prayer in Eritrea's delightful capital, a harmonious clash of African, Arab and Italian

AKSUM
Explore the tombs and palaces of the ancient kingdom of Aksum

SIMIEN MOUNTAINS
Take a break from culture-vulturing and admire one of the most spectacular mountain parks in Africa, highland home of the endemic gelada baboon

GONDER
Wander through the old castles and palaces of Gonder, Ethiopia's Camelot and the site of much courtly pageantry

EGYPT

SUDAN

Nubian Desert

SAUDI ARABIA

YEMEN

ERITREA

Tigray

Red Sea

Gulf of Aden

Danakil Depression

Dankalia

Simien Mountains National Park

KHARTOUM

To Riyadh
To Medina
To Aswan
To Wadi Halfa

Mecca
Jeddah
Medina
Port Sudan
Abu Hamed
Atbara
Haya
Kassala
Karora
Teseney
Agordat
Sebderat
Barentu
Tokombiya
Om Hajer
Humera
Metema
Gonder
Sekota
Maychew
Mekele
Berahile
Adigrat
Badda
Wukro
Adwa
Aksum
Adi Addi
Debark
Ras Dashen (4543m)
Simien
Amba Soira (3018m)
Marsa Fatma
Thio
Edi
Egoli
Beilul
Afambo
Wade
Assab
Beylul
Rahaita
Les Sept Frères
Aden
Al-Hudaydah
Hanish Islands
SAN'A
Dahlak Archipelago
Massawa
Nefasit
Zula
Dogali
Ghinda
Filfil
Keren
Nakfa
Halhal
Afabet
Mt Bizen
Mt Durmu
Mendefera
Adi Quala
Senafe
Qohaito
Adi Keyh
ASMARA
Yeha
Adwa
Enticcio
Shire
(Inda Selassie)
Sistona
Antoro
Abi Adi
Adi Arkay
Debark

Barka River
Gash River
Nile River
Blue Nile River
White Nile River

To El Obeid
Kosti

Nile River

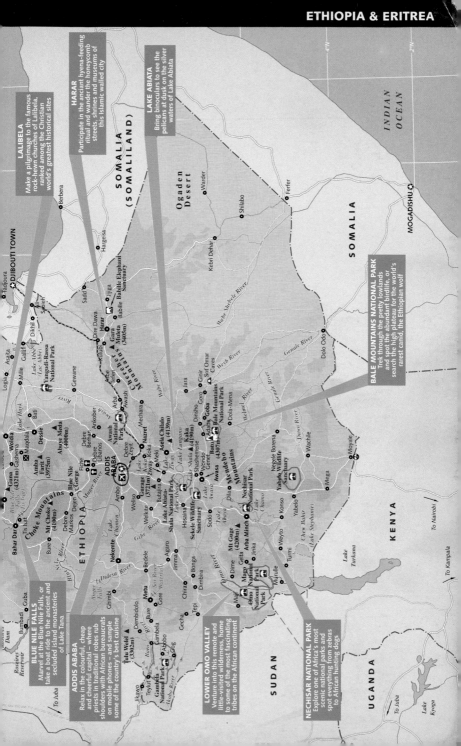

LALIBELA
Make a pilgrimage to the famous rock-hewn churches of Lalibela, ranked among the Christian world's greatest historical sites

HARAR
Participate in the ancient hyena-feeding ritual and wander the honeycomb streets, shrines and museums of this Islamic walled city

LAKE ABIATA
Bring binoculars to see the pelicans at dusk on the silver waters of Lake Abiata

BALE MOUNTAINS NATIONAL PARK
Trek through the pretty lowlands and spot the abundant birdlife, or search the high plateau for the world's rarest canid, the Ethiopian wolf

BLUE NILE FALLS
Marvel at the Blue Nile Falls, or take a boat ride to the ancient and secluded island monasteries of Lake Tana

ADDIS ABABA
Relax in the colourful, cheap and cheerful capital – where priests in traditional robes rub shoulders with African bureaucrats on mobile phones – and sample some of the country's best cuisine

LOWER OMO VALLEY
Venture into this remote and little-visited wilderness, home to some of the most fascinating tribes on the African continent

NECHISAR NATIONAL PARK
Explore one of Africa's most scenic national parks and spot everything from zebras to African hunting dogs

INDIAN OCEAN

SOMALIA (SOMALILAND)

Ogaden Desert

SOMALIA

MOGADISHU

KENYA

SUDAN

UGANDA

ETHIOPIA

To Nairobi

To Kampala

To Juba

Contents – Text

2 Contents – Text

NORTHERN ETHIOPIA   133

SOUTHERN ETHIOPIA   188

EASTERN ETHIOPIA   226

WESTERN ETHIOPIA   250

ERITREA   267

FACTS ABOUT ERITREA   269

Contents – Maps

The Authors

Frances Linzee Gordon

Frances wrote her first travel article following a school scholarship to Venice aged 17. Since then she has travelled in over 50 countries, and has contributed travel articles, books and photos to a variety of international publications. Other work includes radio and television appearances (including a slot as 'travel advisor' to BBC News 24), as well as lectures and interviews on travel and tourism around the world.

In 2003, she will present a series of films on Africa, as well as completing an MA in African and Asian History (with Arabic and Amharic).

Frances believes passionately in the benefits of travel for the tourist as well as for the country. She also encourages women to travel, considering her gender 'a help not a hindrance', particularly when negotiating hurdles on the road!

Jean-Bernard Carillet

After a degree in translation and in international relations from La Sorbonne in Paris, Jean-Bernard joined Lonely Planet's French office in 1995 as an editor before donning the hat of full-time author. A diving instructor and incorrigible traveller, he will decamp at the slightest opportunity to travel, photograph and dive around the world. Jean-Bernard is the coauthor of numerous LP titles in French and in English, including *Tahiti & French Polynesia*, *South Pacific*, *Corsica*, *Provence*, *Marseilles* and diving and snorkelling guides to French Polynesia and the Red Sea. He also contributes to various publications in France, including *Zurban*, the Parisian equivalent of *Time Out*. When not travelling, Jean-Bernard has a weird passion for industrial architecture.

FROM THE AUTHORS
Frances Linzee Gordon

Various travellers and researchers shared information while on the road, including Lena Merleert, Petra Kellermann, Ben Tunstall, Lucy Tallents and Deborah Randall.

In Ethiopia, many thanks to the following: Aster Wohabe, Zewdu Mekonen, Wondwossen Addisu, Tadessa Daba, Kebede Zewdie, Mahmood Kadeto, Murimiri Mathai, Aman Dadesa, Getachew Yehuala, Tsehay Kebede Molla, Abdul Ahmed, Zewdie Giji, Major Muluken Zegeye, Sisay Asrat, Mesele Asfaw, Zeleke Zulas, Negussie Tadesse, Girma Mengesha, Mohammed Abdi, Temesghen Maekele, Oguta Adiw, Teyib Abafogi, Gudissa Lafe, Alo Aydihas, Teshome Seleshi Shawel, Mekonen Gashaw, Mustafa Osman and Mulugeta Alemu.

Special thanks to: Fisseha Zibelo, Head of Tourism, Aksum; Fasil Ayehu, Head of Tourism, Bahar Dar; Bisrat Weldu, Ghion Hotel; Dario Morello and Adege Eshetu, Greenland Tours; Abdullah Hussein, Edriss Ebu and Tilahun Tameru, Park Headquarters, Bale;

Dinote Kasia Shenkere, Tourist Office, Konso; Kapo Kansa, Tourist Office, Arba Minch; Tegenu Gebrewold, Head of Immigration; Bekele Negussie, Head of Planning, Road Mapping Authority (and Tilahun Abera and John Hine); and Abdunasir Edris, Tourism, Harar.

And special, special thanks (for generously agreeing to check and comment on my work) to: Tesfaye Hundessa, Director of EWCO; Professor Richard Pankhurst and Mrs Rita Pankhurst; Kebede Amare, Commissioner of Tourism, Tigray; Habteselassie Asmare, Gonder; Chemere Zewdie, Park Warden, Nechisar; Professor David Phillipson, leader of digs at Aksum; Bekele Negussie, Ethiopian Roads Authority; Yasmin Mohammed and John Summers, Ethiopian Airlines; Tony Hickey; Solomon Maereg and Kassa Haile in Lalibela; Dr Yonas Berhane, Archaeology Department; Jara Haile-Maryam, General Manager CRCCH; and Ahmed Zekaria, Curator Ethnological Museum.

Above all, thanks to HE, Yusuf Sukkar, Tourism Commissioner, who lent me his staff and his encouragement, and whose conviction, passion and hope for Ethiopian tourism I share. Of his staff, thanks must go to the efficient, hardworking (and uncomplaining!) Menbere Girma, Weizero Almaz, Habtamu Bekele and particularly to Sisay Getachew.

In Eritrea, particular thanks to Solomon Abraha and Tedros Kebbede for their help and support with the whole project (and for assisting JB); to Mike Street, for his architectural knowledge, expertise and passion (and to whom the architectural section is largely owed); and to Marianne Scott for her architectural contribution on Massawa.

At Lonely Planet, a big thank you to my excellent coauthor, Jean-Bernard Carillet, as well as the unsung editors and cartographers in Australia, particularly Shahara Ahmed. Above all, thanks to Hilary Rogers and Virginia Maxwell. It was a pleasure to work with them all.

Finally, at SOAS, London, thanks to my long-suffering and patient professors when I missed class after class when in the field, and in particular to Dr Ben Fortna (History), Fattima Rawan (Arabic), Dr David Appleyard and Yoseph Mengistu (Amharic).

This book is dedicated to Nicholas Linzee Gordon, a courageous man and a wonderful brother.

Jean-Bernard Carillet

First off, warmest and fervent *teanastellen* and gratitude to Frances Linzee Gordon, coauthor of this book, for her ongoing support, encouragement and guidance. Frances has also introduced me to the special ambience of the Horn of Africa. *Mauruuru roa également* to Hilary Rogers at LP Australia, who trusted a true-blue Frenchman.

In Addis, I'd like to express my deepest gratitude to HE Yusuf Sukkar, Tourism Commissioner, for opening doors; Messeletch Tsige; Maurizio Melloni; Paul Mandl, for being so English and for the wonderful time spent together; Engineer Solomon Kassaye,

NUPI; Guy Delisle and Nadege; Bruno Pardigon for a home away from home; Isabelle Chipot, Vincente; Ayele, Tigabu and Gebeneysh for the good mood.

In Eritrea, ardent thanks to Tedros Kebbede and Solomon Abraha for help and assistance, as well as for a superb day trip to Gash Barka; Pierre Montaigne; Mathieu; Suzanne Wendel and Karl-Heinz Kolb; Abraham Ghebrezghi; Amanuel Sahle for philosophical discussions; Dominique Lommatzsch; and Marie-France Simeone-Senelle.

In Paris, I'm also grateful to Annabel Hart and Thomas Fitzsimmons.

This Book

Frances Linzee Gordon wrote the first edition of *Ethiopia, Eritrea & Djibouti*. This edition was updated by Frances, who worked on the Ethiopia chapters, and Jean-Bernard Carillet, who wrote the Addis Ababa and Eritrea chapters.

From the Publisher

This edition of *Ethiopia & Eritrea* was produced in Lonely Planet's Melbourne office. Hilary Rogers commissioned and developed this title. Andrew Weatherill was the project manager. Production was coordinated by Will Gourlay and Barbara Delissen (editorial), Sarah Sloane (mapping), and Sonya Brooke and Cris Gibcus (layout). Assisting with editing were Suzannah Shwer, Charlotte Keown, Jocelyn Harewood and Nick Tapp; with mapping Helen Rowley, Julie Sheridan, Valentina Kremenchutskaya and Huw Fowles; and with layout Sally Darmody and Yvonne Bischofberger.

The illustrations were drawn by Ethiopian artist Dawit Abebe. Thanks go to Sonya Brooke for designing the colour pages, Quentin Frayne for producing the language chapter and Brendan Dempsey for designing the cover.

Ethiopia title page: An ornate Axumite-style cross inside Bet Amanuel Church, Lalibela (Photograph by Patrick Ben Luke Syder).

Eritrea title page: Traditionally dressed all in white, women celebrate the festival of Timkat (Photograph by Frances Linzee Gordon)

THANKS
Many thanks to the travellers who used the last edition and wrote to us with helpful hints, advice and interesting anecdotes. Your names appear in the back of this book.

Foreword

ABOUT LONELY PLANET GUIDEBOOKS

The story begins with a classic travel adventure: Tony and Maureen Wheeler's 1972 journey across Europe and Asia to Australia. There was no useful information about the overland trail then, so Tony and Maureen published the first Lonely Planet guidebook to meet a growing need.

From a kitchen table, Lonely Planet has grown to become the largest independent travel publisher in the world, with offices in Melbourne (Australia), Oakland (USA), London (UK) and Paris (France).

Today Lonely Planet guidebooks cover the globe. There is an ever-growing list of books and information in a variety of media. Some things haven't changed. The main aim is still to make it possible for adventurous travellers to get out there – to explore and better understand the world.

At Lonely Planet we believe travellers can make a positive contribution to the countries they visit – if they respect their host communities and spend their money wisely. Since 1986 a percentage of the income from each book has been donated to aid projects and human rights campaigns, and, more recently, to wildlife conservation.

Although inclusion in a guidebook usually implies a recommendation we cannot list every good place. Exclusion does not necessarily imply criticism. In fact there are a number of reasons why we might exclude a place – sometimes it is simply inappropriate to encourage an influx of travellers.

UPDATES & READER FEEDBACK

Things change – prices go up, schedules change, good places go bad and bad places go bankrupt. Nothing stays the same. So, if you find things better or worse, recently opened or long-since closed, please tell us and help make the next edition even more accurate and useful.

Lonely Planet thoroughly updates each guidebook as often as possible – usually every two years, although for some destinations the gap can be longer. Between editions, up-to-date information is available in our free, monthly email bulletin *Comet* (W www.lonelyplanet.com/ newsletters). You can also check out the *Thorn Tree* bulletin board and *Postcards* section of our website which carry unverified, but fascinating, reports from travellers.

Tell us about it! We genuinely value your feedback. A well-travelled team at Lonely Planet reads and acknowledges every email and letter we receive and ensures that every morsel of information finds its way to the relevant authors, editors and cartographers.

Everyone who writes to us will find their name listed in the next edition of the appropriate guidebook. The very best contributions will be rewarded with a free guidebook.

We may edit, reproduce and incorporate your comments in Lonely Planet products such as guidebooks, websites and digital products, so let us know if you don't want your comments reproduced or your name acknowledged.

How to contact Lonely Planet:
Online: e talk2us@lonelyplanet.com.au, W www.lonelyplanet.com
Australia: Locked Bag 1, Footscray, Victoria 3011
UK: 72-82 Rosebery Ave, London, EC1R 4RW
USA: 150 Linden St, Oakland, CA 94607

Introduction

Jutting tusk-like into the Indian Ocean at the eastern tip of the African continent, Ethiopia and Eritrea make up part of the region known alluringly as the Horn of Africa. The Horn has long attracted visitors – sea- and land-borne merchants and explorers have for centuries fought and jostled for the riches of the region, but it is only quite recently that the tourist has set food here. Yet Ethiopia and Eritrea hold remarkable – and astonishingly little known – attractions

Ethiopia, almost the only African country to have escaped European colonialism, has kept firm hold of its cultural identity. With its complex traditions, ancient history and long connection with Christianity, Ethiopia is

a fascinating country to visit. Known above all for its exceptional historical attractions, its sites include centuries-old rock-hewn churches and grandiose castles. Home to several famous archaeological finds, Ethiopia is also known as the Cradle of Humanity. Archaeologically and historically speaking, Ethiopia is to East Africa what Egypt is to North Africa.

In contrast to its international image as a land of desert and famine, Ethiopia is in fact striking for its diversity. Diverse in geography, diverse in peoples and diverse in wildlife, it offers correspondingly varied attractions. The Simien and Bale Mountains offer trekking in beautiful landscapes, the country's parks offer good wildlife and

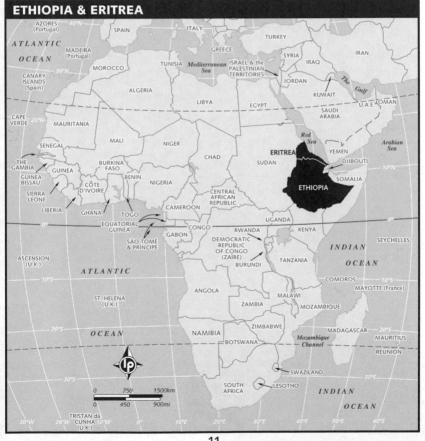

ETHIOPIA & ERITREA

exceptional bird-watching and the southwestern regions offer encounters with tribes described as among the most fascinating on the continent. With its 'little bit of everything' but in fact much of each, Ethiopia turns out to be a country richer in tourism potential than many might have imagined.

Though it long formed part of the area now known as Ethiopia, Eritrea is very different from her larger neighbour. Colonised by the Italians, Eritrea's European heritage is still much in evidence. Beautiful Asmara, safe and clean and with outstanding Art Deco architecture, ranks among the most attractive capital cities on the continent.

Eritrea is also home to some interesting archaeological finds: from the ruins of the ancient kingdom of Aksum, right up to the poignant war relics of the 30-year Struggle for Independence. Though arid, Eritrea's landscape can be starkly beautiful, and its Red Sea coral reefs remain rich, pristine and undiscovered. The Eritrean people – proud, independent and enterprising – welcome the visitor warmly to the country they fought so hard to free.

Providing a rarely encountered combination of diverse and impressive attractions, Ethiopia and Eritrea make for a deeply rewarding visit. Once mythicised by the ancients for their exotic allure and rich resources, the countries today yet barely register on the tourism map – and that's just one more of their attractions.

Ethiopia

Ethiopia

How can it be that a country with such outstanding historical and cultural attractions, remains so little known? How can it be that a country with such remarkable natural attractions remains so little visited?

It seems that Ethiopia still has an image problem. Pigeonholed as a land of desert, famine and war, misconceptions are so rife that Ethiopian Airlines - one of Africa's most successful commercial airlines - regularly fields inquiries as to whether its passengers will get anything to eat on their planes!

Poor it may be materially, but the fact remains that Ethiopia boasts outstanding historical and natural wealth. In historical terms, it has the longest archaeological record of any country on Earth; in religious terms, it was only the second country in the West to adopt Christianity, and in natural terms, it boasts an exception number of endemic species and more birds than any other country on the continent except South Africa.

Among its attractions are 2000-year-old Aksum, described as 'one of the last of the great civilisations of antiquity to be revealed to modern knowledge'; the beautiful 13th-century rock-hewn churches of Lalibela; and the 17th-century castles of Gonder.

Yet right up until the latter half of the 19th century, the country remained almost unknown to outsiders and it wasn't until the latter half of the 20th century that visitors began to set foot here. Even today, the attractions of Ethiopia remain little known. A land still visited by very few, a trip here will afford the traveller a real sense of discovery.

Ethiopia is also remarkable culturally. The country's isolation, along with its unique political independence (it was almost the only country on the continent to avoid colonisation), has ensured that its culture has remained remarkably intact, untainted and undiluted by outside influences. The country retains its own distinctive language and script, its own food and drink, its own church and saints, even its own calendar and clock.

Though modernising slowly, much about Ethiopian life continues as it has for millennia, apparently heedless of the modern world. Priest still thumb the parchment in the centuries-old churches, ancient ceremonies are faithfully re-enacted and ancestral traditions are rigidly adhered to. There are men who claim to receive visions directly from God, priests with a gift for prophecy and wandering minstrels who recite verses of praise and flattery.

Isolated from within as well as from without, Ethiopia's rugged terrain has also seen the development of great cultural diversity. Some of the ethnic groups that inhabit the southwest, such as the Mursi lip stretchers, have been described as 'among the most fascinating on the African continent'.

Despite the apparent indifference to Ethiopia as a tourist destination, facilities for travellers are not found wanting. The country boast an excellent national airline, enterprising tour operators, and some good hotels (including one ranked as the most luxurious on the continent). For the budget traveller, hotels and food are cheap, buses are reasonably comfortable and safe, and the dollar goes on forever.

With a history as rich as anything found in North Africa, with birds and animals as interesting as anything in East Africa, with tribal groups as fascinating as any in West Africa and with climate and scenery as pleasant as that in Southern Africa, Ethiopia turns out to be a country far richer than many might imagine.

Ethiopia is Africa's best-kept secret; get there before it's discovered.

Facts about Ethiopia

HISTORY

Ethiopia absolutely negates the Western misconception that sub-Saharan Africa is lacking in culture. This country is home to one of the oldest Christian civilisations in the world, and with the longest archaeological record of any country on Earth, it is also credited with being the 'cradle of humanity'.

Having a little knowledge of Ethiopia's long, rich and colourful history will greatly enhance your travels around the country.

Cradle of Humanity (4,500,000 BC)

During the last 40 years, some extraordinary prehistoric finds have been unearthed in the region. The most famous, Lucy (see the boxed text 'Lucy in the Sky') has earned Ethiopia the prestigious title of 'Cradle of Humanity'.

In December 1992, another find rocked the world of palaeoanthropology. At Aramis, close to Hadar, a joint American–Japanese team unearthed over 50 tooth and bone fragments. These remains not only belonged to a whole new group (numbering around 17 to 20 individuals), but also to a whole new species. Dating from some 4.4 million years ago, Lucy looked positively modern by comparison. Christened *Australopithecus ramidus*, the creature's ape-like features combined with the typical hominid characteristics (such as smaller teeth), has led to the suggestion that the ape was Darwin's famous 'missing link' – a crucial transitional point from ape to human.

Yet more excitement came in 1992–94 with the American–Ethiopian excavations in the Gona Valley, southwest of Hadar. Several thousand stone tools were discovered, thought to date back between 2.5 to 2.6 million years. They were the oldest tools yet found in the world.

Meanwhile, similar finds of a comparable age are being unearthed in another very rich palaeoanthropological site, the Omo Valley in southern Ethiopia. In 1998, a US team began investigating the region. The area is thought to be brimming with animal and human fossils.

Palaeoanthropology is still in its infancy in Ethiopia and it's very likely that more finds – perhaps just as sensational as Lucy – await discovery. Although finds in southern Africa have recently challenged Ethiopia's claims to being the cradle of humanity, the Ethiopian

Ethiopia at a Glance

Capital City: Addis Ababa

Population: 64 million (estimate for 2004)

Time: 3 hours ahead of GMT

Land Area: 1,098,000 sq km

International Telephone Code: ☎ 251

GDP/Capita: US$94

Currency: Birr (Birr8 = US$1 approx)

Languages: Amharic (national language)

Rift Valley remains an extremely important source of information on this still very obscure period in our early history.

Stone Age (4500 BC)

Other important prehistoric remains include recently discovered paintings and engravings dating to the Late Stone Age. Evidence of cereal cultivation has also been found. Some cereals, such as *tef*, are thought to be indigenous; others such as wheat and barley may have come down the Nile from Egypt several millennia earlier.

Land of Punt (3500–2000 BC)

Though this period of Ethiopia's history is still shrouded in darkness, the region now comprising Ethiopia and Eritrea is believed to have formed part of the ancient Land of Punt, an area on the southern Red Sea coast, which had attracted the trading ships of the Egyptian Pharaohs for millennia.

Many valuable commodities such as gold, myrrh, ivory and slaves issued from the interior of the region and were exported from the coast (see also the boxed text 'Land of Punt').

ETHIOPIA

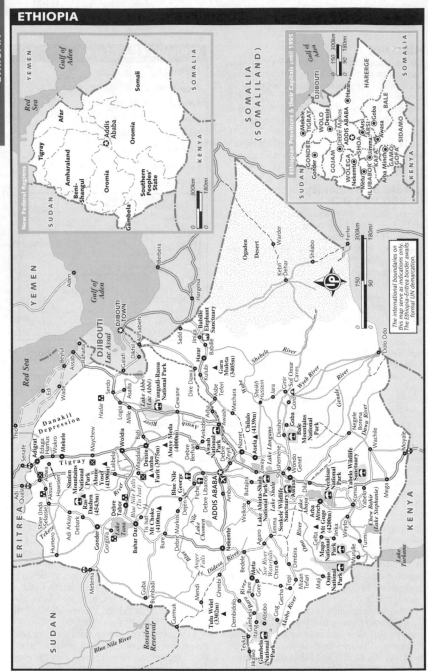

New Federal Regions

YEMEN
Gulf of Aden
Red Sea
SOMALIA
Tigray
Afar
Amharaland
Beni-Shangul
Addis Ababa
Oromia
Oromia
Somali
Southern Peoples' State
Gambela
SUDAN
KENYA

Ethiopian Provinces & their Capitals until 1995

SUDAN
GONDER
GONDER
Gonder
WOLO
Mekele
TIGRAY
Dessie
Debre Markos
GOJAM
WOLEGA
Nekemte
ADDIS ABABA
Metu
Jimma
ILLUBABOR
KAFA
GAMO GOFA
Arba Minch
SIDAMO
Avasa
BALE
Goba
ARSI
Asela
HARERGE
Harar
Dire Dawa
SHOA
SOMALIA
DJIBOUTI
Gulf of Aden
KENYA

The international boundaries on this map serve as indications only. The Ethiopia-Eritrea border awaits formal UN demarcation.

YEMEN
Red Sea
Gulf of Aden
Aden

SOMALIA (SOMALILAND)

Ogaden Desert
Warder
Ferfer
Shilabo
Kebri Dehar
Dolo Odo

Berbera
Hargesa

DJIBOUTI
DJIBOUTI TOWN
Lac Assal
Ali-Sabieh
Dikhil

Assab
Beylul
Edi
Wade

Red Sea

Thio
Senafe
Adigrat
Edaga Hamus
Wukro
Mekele
Maychew
Woldia

ERITREA
Adi Quala
Adi Arkay
Debark
Shire (Inda Selassie)
Aksum
Adwa
Hawzien
Simien Mountains National Park
Ras Dashen (4543m)
Abuna Yosef (4190m)
Lalibela

Danakil Depression

Serdo
Hadar
Logia
Mille
Gewane

Afar

Tendaho
Asaita

Galafi

Tadjoura

YEMEN

Djibouti
Lake Abbe (Lac Abbé)
Yangudi-Rassa National Park

Dire Dawa
Harar
Babille
Elephant Sanctuary
Babille
Jinica
Kulubi
Gara Muleta (3405m)

Awash
Arba
Nazret
Adama

Sheikh Hussein
Jara
Mechara
Sof Omar Caves
Ginir
Goro
Goba
Bale Mountains National Park
Dinsho

Shebele River
Wabe
Wyeb River
Genale River

Nagele Borena
Dawa River
Wachile
Moyale

KENYA

Gorgora
Gonder
Lake Tana
Bahar Dar
Tis Isat (Tis Isat)
Blue Nile Falls
Debre Tabor
Mt Choke (4100m)
Debre Markos
Dejen

Metema
Guba
Bumbadi
Gurmuk

Roseires Reservoir
Blue Nile River

SUDAN

Tulu Welel (3302m)
Mendi
Ghimbi
Bedele
Metu
Gore

Dembidolo
Gambela National Park
Itang
Jikawo
Teylut
Akobo
Alobo
Gog
Gecha
Tepi
Maji
Mizan Tefari

Omo National Park
Murulle
Turmi
Lake Turkana

Jinka
Mago National Park
Mt Guge (4200m)
Gelta
Weyto
Chew Bahir (Lake Stephanie)
Konso
Yabelo
Yabelo Wildlife Sanctuary
Mega

Arba Minch
Dila
Awasa
Wondo Genet
Shashemene
Lake Shala
Lake Abiata-Shala National Park
Senkele Wildlife Sanctuary
Lake Langano
Nechisar National Park
Lake Chamo
Lake Abaya

Ziway
Butajira
Weliso
Ambo
Debre Zeyit
ADDIS ABABA
Fiche
Debre Libanos
Bure
Bahir
Nekemte
Agaro
Jimma
Sor River Waterfalls
Chira
Dimbira

Blue Nile (Abay) River
Didesa River
Anger Falls
Lake Chomen
Bure
Debre Markos

Danakil
Abuye Meda (4000m)
Debre Berhan
Ankober
Awash National Park
Debre Zeyit
Chilalo (4139m)
Asela
Awash River

Woldia
Bati
Dessie
Amba Farit (3975m)
Magdala
Kombolcha

Gondar

SUDAN

KENYA

Lucy in the Sky

On 30 November 1974, a dried-up lake near Hadar in the far northeast of Ethiopia was the scene of an international sensation when the fossilised remains of a very remote human ancestor were found. Named Lucy or, more evocatively, *Denkenesh* or *Birkinesh* ('You are wonderful' in Ethiopian Amharic), she was then the oldest and most complete hominid in the world, dated at least 3.2 million years old. Today, her remains are conserved in the National Museum In Addis Ababa.

Darwin was right, and Lucy seemed to prove it: man's 'nearest ally' was the ape, and its orlglnal home was in Africa. Belonging to the group *Australopithecus afarensis*, Lucy was a hominid: a kind of half-human–half-ape, distinguished above all by her erect walk. Hominids represent a major step on the evolutionary ladder towards modern man.

But Lucy was special, not just for her incredible age, but for her anatomy, too. Her skeleton seemed to suggest that our ancestors – contrary to previous theories – began to walk *before* they developed bigger brains. Standing just over a metre high, and weighing no more than 30kg, the little creature had a tiny brain, yet her other features were unmistakably human: the pelvis, legs and above all her V-shaped jaw. Similar to our own, it differed entirely from the box-like, parallel-tooth formation of her ape ancestors.

Named after the Beatles' song *Lucy in the Sky with Diamonds*, which happened to be playing in the archaeologists' camp at the moment of discovery, Lucy continues to intrigue. According to her discoverer, Donald Johanson, many aspects about her still provide ongoing riddles. In 2003, Lucy will go on tour in the United States.

Very little is known about the area at this time (c. 3500 BC), but it is thought that the northern region saw much migration from surrounding areas. By around 2000 BC, strong contacts had been established between the people of what is now northern Ethiopia and Eritrea and the inhabitants of southern Arabia across the Red Sea.

Pre-Aksumite Civilisation (1500–400 BC)

The cultural significance of the meeting of the southern Arabians and the East Africans was enormous. One of the consequences was the emergence of a number of Afro-Asiatic languages, including an early Ge'ez (like a kind of Ethiopian Latin and forerunner of modern Amharic), which is studied by Christian priests in Ethiopia and Eritrea to this day.

Most significant was the rise, in the first millennium BC, of a remarkable civilisation in the Horn. The fact that the influence of southern Arabia was so clear (in the Semitic language, the Sabaean script and in the worship of Sabaean gods); that the civilisation appeared to mushroom overnight and was confined to a few very small settlements; and that it benefited from specialist crafts, skills and technologies previously unknown in the area, made it appear that the civilisation was spawned by settlers who brought their own specialist knowledge.

Noting this, and disinclined to believe that such a civilisation could be African, scholars for years concluded that the culture was Arabian, transplanted from across the Red Sea by Sabaean settlers migrating between 1000 to 400 BC. However in the last few years, scholars have argued with great conviction

Rock Art – The Uncracked Code

Rock art is notoriously difficult to date; nevertheless, some Ethiopian rock paintings are thought to date back at least 10,000 years. Still very little studied, the paintings provide an invaluable glimpse into the social, economic, religious and artistic life of Stone Age man.

Rock art is found particularly in the old provinces of Tigray (north), Harerge (east) and Gamo-Gofa (southwest), and varies from simple engravings to beautifully executed carvings and delicate colour paintings. Depictions include domestic and wild animals (such as zebu cattle, lions and elephants) and human subjects with bows and arrows, spears and shields. Various enigmatic and abstract signs and symbols have also been found. The latter, difficult to interpret, may well come to reveal much information about the period.

Travellers From Heaven

Ethiopia, meaning 'Land of the Burnt Faces', was named by the Greeks, who saw the country as a far-off realm, populated by remarkable people and extraordinary animals. According to the Greek historian Diodorus Siculus, Ptolemy II used to return from hunting expeditions in Ethiopia in the 3rd century BC with wild and exotic animals, which were objects of amazement to the Greeks.

The Greek poet Homer (writing in 800 BC) spoke of the people as the 'blameless Ethiopians'. In the *Iliad*, he writes that some of the Greek gods even deigned to visit the remote land. The celestial travellers purportedly included Zeus himself, the king of the gods; the goddess Iris, who fancied taking part in some sacrificial rites there; and Poseidon the sea god, who 'lingered delighted' at the sumptuous Ethiopian feasts.

that this civilisation was indeed African and while undoubtedly influenced by Sabaean ideas, it developed from within from local effort and initiative. If proved correct, histories of the Horn will have to be completely rewritten.

Whatever the origin, the civilisation was a very important one. The most famous relic of the times is the extraordinary stone 'temple' of Yeha, lying to the north of Aksum. Thought to date to between 800 and 500 BC, it was probably Ethiopia's very first capital.

The remains of many other buildings also exist, including the large and remarkable sites of Metera, Tocanda and Keskese in southern Eritrea.

Kingdom of Aksum (AD 1–700)

At the beginning of the first millennium AD, there arose in the highlands of present-day Ethiopia and Eritrea a unique African civilisation. Over seven centuries, it grew to rank among the most powerful kingdoms of the ancient world.

Aksum is thought to have owed its importance to its position, lying at the pivot of an important commercial crossroads. To the northwest lay Egypt, and to the west, near the present-day Sudanese border, were the rich, gold-producing lowlands. To the northeast, in present-day Eritrea, was the Aksumite port of Adulis, positioned at the crux of an extensive trading route that stretched from Egypt and the Mediterranean, all the way to India and Sri Lanka. Trade flourished and the Aksumite kingdom boomed.

Aksum also benefited from its well-watered agricultural lands, which were further exploited by the use of well-designed dams, wells and reservoirs.

The kingdom's greatest assets and those that made up the bulk of its exports, were its natural resources: frankincense, grain, animal skins, rhino horn, apes and particularly ivory. Wildlife at this time was abundant and tens of thousands of elephants were reported to roam the region. Ivory was one of the most highly prized nonprecious products in the Egyptian world.

The *Periplus of the Erythraean Sea*, written by a Greek-speaking Egyptian sailor or merchant around the 1st century AD, describes Aksum's imports. Most came from Egypt, Arabia and India, and ranged from dyed cloaks and cheap unlined coats to glassware, and iron for making spears, swords and axes. Syrian and Italian wine and olive oil (then considered a luxury) were also imported, as was much gold and silver plate for the king.

During its heyday between the 3rd and 6th centuries, the kingdom of Aksum stretched east across the Red Sea into large parts of southern Arabia, and west into the Sudanese Nile Valley. Aksumite society was rich, well organised and technically and artistically advanced. During this era, an unparalleled coinage in bronze, silver and gold was produced, extraordinary monuments were built and, exerting the greatest influence of all on the future of Ethiopia, Christianity was introduced.

The Coming of Christianity (AD 300–600)

The Ethiopian church claims that Christianity first reached Aksum at the time of the Apostles. According to the Byzantine ecclesiastical historian, Rufinus, it arrived on Ethiopian shores by accident rather than by design, when a Christian merchant from Syria, returning from a long voyage to India with his two young students, stopped for water on the coast of Africa.

What is certain is that Christianity did not become the state religion until around the beginning of the 4th century. King Ezana's stone inscription makes reference to Christ, and his famous coins bear the Christian Cross – the first in the world to do so.

The end of the 5th century AD saw the arrival of the famous Nine Saints, a group of Greek-speaking missionaries who established well-known monasteries in the north of the country, including Debre Damo. At this time, the Bible was first translated from Greek into Ge'ez, the early language of Ethiopia.

The arrival of Christianity was a major turning point in Ethiopian history. The religion was to have an enormous influence on the country, shaping not just its spiritual and intellectual life, but also its cultural and social life, including its art and literature. Today around half the population of Ethiopia is Orthodox Christian.

Soon to account for the other half, and hot on the heels of Christianity, came a new religion to Ethiopian shores: Islam.

The Coming of Islam (AD 700)

According to Muslim tradition, the Prophet Mohammed was nursed by an Ethiopian woman. Later, the Muslim Hadith (collection of traditions about Mohammed's life) recounts that Mohammed sent some of his followers to Ethiopia in AD 615, to avoid persecution in Arabia. Among the group was the Prophet's own daughter and son-in-law and future successor, Uthman.

At Aksum, the refugees were shown hospitality and, it is said, King Armah liked them so much that he didn't wish to let them go. However, at the end of the persecution the refugees were allowed to return safely to Arabia.

Good relations between the two religions continued until at least the death of King Armah. Thereafter, as Islam's fortunes waxed and those of Christian Aksum began to wane, a clash of interests became inevitable.

The Demise of Aksum (AD 700)

Islam's expansion in the area went hand in hand with the rise in the fortunes of the Arabs, fast becoming the new masters of the Red Sea. Little by little, Aksum became isolated: trade and the economy slumped, coins ceased to be minted and hard times set in. Aksum's commercial domination of the region was over.

Nevertheless, to this day, Aksum occupies a very special position in Ethiopian history and consciousness. From its decline, beginning in AD 700 right up to the present day, Aksum has remained a religious and spiritual capital in the eyes of Ethiopia's Christian population.

The Zagwe Dynasty (1137–1270)

After the decline of Aksum, political power began to shift southwards. In the early 12th century, a new capital was established under a new power: the Zagwe dynasty. Based in the mountains of Lasta not far from Lalibela, the Zagwe capital was initially known as Adafa.

The dynasty reigned from around AD 1137 to 1270, yet the period is one of the most obscure in Ethiopian history. Seemingly, no stones were inscribed, no chronicles written, and no coins minted.

Unlike the kingdom of Aksum, no accounts of the dynasty by foreign travellers have survived. Positioned further from the coast, the Zagwe capital has revealed far fewer imported items – objects that might have provided clues to this enigmatic period. In addition, the dynasty is traditionally treated as a kind of embarrassment in Ethiopian history. The Zagwes were seen as usurpers of power from the Aksumite rulers.

Nevertheless, the period is an extremely important one in the cultural history of Ethiopia. During the reign of three of its kings, Yemrehanna Kristos, Lalibela and Na'akuto La'ab, the astonishing rock-hewn churches of Lalibela were constructed. Today they number among Ethiopia's top attractions.

It is not certain what brought the Zagwe dynasty to an end; it is likely it was a combination of infighting within the ruling dynasty and local opposition from the clergy. In 1270 the dynasty was overthrown. Political power shifted once again, this time to the province of Shoa. There, Yekuno Amlak set himself on the throne and established a new dynasty that would come to reign for the next 500 years.

Known as the 'Solomonic Dynasty' (after Yekuno Amlak's claims to descend from King Solomon and the Queen of Sheba), the king's claims (and the dynasty's legitimacy) were soon to be reaffirmed by the country's national epic *Kebra Negast* (see boxed text 'Kebra Negast' later in this chapter) written during the reign of his grandson, Amda Seyon (1312–42).

The Ethiopian Middle Ages (1270–1450)

Medieval Ethiopia is quite well documented, thanks to the royal chroniclers of the court and to various reports made by foreign travellers.

The Middle Ages were both a continuation of the past (with its all-powerful monarchy and influential clergy) and a break with it. Trade was now conducted by barter with pieces of iron, cloth or salt rather than with a minted currency. The kingdom's capitals also became 'itinerant'; little more than vast, moving military camps.

Culturally, the period was important for the significant output of Ge'ez literature, including the nation's epic, the *Kebra Negast* (see under Arts later in this chapter). It was also at this time that contacts with European Christendom began to increase. With the increasing threat of well-equipped Muslim armies in the East, Europe was seen as a Christian superpower.

Europe, for its part, dreamed of winning back Jerusalem from the 'Saracens', and realised the important strategic position occupied by Ethiopia. At the time, it was almost the only Christian kingdom outside Europe. Ethiopia even became a candidate for the location of the legendary Kingdom of Prester John. According to this legend, an immensely wealthy and powerful Christian monarch reigned in a far-off land in the East; it was hoped that one day, he would join the kings of Europe in a mighty crusade against the infidel.

In the early 15th century, the first European embassy arrived in Ethiopia, sent by the famous French aristocrat Duc de Berry. Ethiopians in their turn began to travel to Europe, particularly to Rome, where many joined churches already established there.

The Muslim–Christian Wars (1500–50)

The first decades of the 16th century were plagued by some of the most costly, bloody and wasteful fighting in Ethiopian history, in which the empire, its institutions and its culture came close to being wiped out.

From the 13th century, relations with the Muslim Ethiopian emirates of Ifat and Adal were showing signs of strain. With the increasing competition for control of the valuable trade routes connecting the Ethiopian highlands with the Red Sea, tension was growing.

In the 1490s, animosities came to a head. Establishing himself at the port of Zeila in present-day Somalia, a skilled and charismatic Muslim named Mahfuz arrived on the scene. From his new base, he declared a *jihad* (holy war) against Christian Ethiopia and made twenty-five annual raids into the highlands of Shoa. Emperor Lebna Dengel finally halted Mahfuz's incursions, but not before he had carried off huge numbers of Ethiopian slaves and cattle.

An even more legendary figure was Ahmed Ibn Ibrahim al Ghazi, nicknamed Ahmed Gragn the Left-Handed. After overthrowing Sultan Abu Bakr of Harar, Ahmed declared his intention: to continue the jihad of Mahfuz. Carrying out several raids into Ethiopian territory, he managed in March 1529 to defeat Emperor Lebna Dengel himself.

Ahmed then embarked on the conquest of all of Christian Ethiopia. Well supplied with firearms from Ottoman Zeila and southern Arabia (which he pragmatically exchanged for captured Christian slaves), the Muslim leader had, by 1532, overrun almost all of eastern and southern Ethiopia.

In 1535 the Emperor Lebna Dengel appealed in desperation to Portugal – already active in the region. In 1541, an army of 400 well-armed musketeers arrived in Massawa (in present-day Eritrea), led by Dom Christovão da Gama, son of the famous mariner Vasco da Gama. Ahmed met the Portuguese army near Lake Tana. There he not only defeated the Portuguese, but also captured and beheaded the young and foolhardy commander, Dom Christovão.

By 1543, the new Ethiopian emperor, Galawdewos, had assembled a new army. Joining ranks with the surviving Portuguese force, he met Mohammed at Wayna Daga in the west. This time, the huge numbers proved too much for Ahmed: he was killed and his followers fled. Keen to follow up his victory, Galawdewos turned his attention to the rich trading Muslim city of Harar. But advancing too hastily and without the back-up of his main army, the emperor also lost his life.

The Muslim–Christian Wars had been terribly costly. Thousands of people lost their lives, the Christian monarchy was nearly wiped out, and the once mighty Muslim state of Adal lay in ruins. Many of the most beautiful churches and monasteries in Ethiopia – along with their precious manuscripts, church relics and regalia – lay in ashes.

Oromo Migrations (1550–1750)

Following the imam's death, and filling the power vacuum left behind, a new threat to the Ethiopian empire arose. A Cushitic people, the Oromos (then known as the Gallas), originating from the south and present-day Kenya, began a great migration northwards.

For the next 200 years intermittent armed conflict raged between the empire and the Oromos. For the empire, the expansion meant loss of territory and vital tax revenue.

The Jesuits (1600–29)

At the beginning of the 17th century, the Oromo threat led several emperors to seek an alliance with the Jesuits, who were backed in their cause by the well-armed Portuguese. Two emperors, Za-Dengel and Susenyos, even went as far as conversion to Catholicism. However, in attempting to impose this faith on the state, the emperors provoked widespread rebellion. Za-Dengel was overthrown and, in 1629, Susenyos' draconian measures to convert his people incited civil war.

Much bloodshed followed – 32,000 peasants are thought to have lost their lives at the hands of the emperor's army. Susenyos was forced to back down, and the Orthodox faith was re-established.

On Susenyos' death, his son Fasiladas expelled the meddling Jesuits, and forbade all foreigners to set foot in his empire. For nearly 130 years only one European, a French doctor Charles Poncet (see the boxed text 'The Barge He Sat In...', later), was allowed to enter Ethiopia.

Though the Jesuits' interference had caused great suffering and bloodshed in Ethiopia, they left behind one useful legacy: books. Pero Pais wrote the first serious history of

Itinerant Courts

During the Ethiopian Middle Ages, the business of most monarchs consisted of waging wars, collecting taxes and inspecting the royal domains.

Obliged to travel continuously throughout their far-flung empire, the kings led a perpetually nomadic existence. And with the rulers went their armies, courtiers and servants; the judges, prison officers and priests; the merchants, prostitutes and a whole entourage of artisans: butchers and bakers, chefs, tailors and blacksmiths. The camps could spread over 20km; for transportation up to 100,000 mules were required.

The retinue was so vast that it rapidly exhausted the resources of the location. Four months was usually the maximum possible length of stay, and ten years had to pass before the spot could be revisited.

The put-upon peasantry were said to dread the royal visits as they dreaded the swarms of locusts. In both cases, everything that lay in the path of the intruders was consumed.

the country. Other writings included detailed accounts of Ethiopia's cultural, economic and social life.

With the Ottoman hold in the east, and the Oromo entrenchment in the south, the political authority of Shoa had become increasingly circumscribed. It was time to relocate – once again – the centre of power.

The Rise & Fall of Gonder (1636–1855)

In 1636, following the old tradition of his forefathers, the Emperor Fasiladas, decided to found a new capital. But Gonder – the chosen site – proved to be different from its predecessors. The town, situated near Lake Tana, became a permanent capital, the first in Ethiopian history since the days of the ancient kingdoms of Aksum and Lalibela. Gonder was to flourish for the next 200 years.

Indeed, by the end of the 17th century, the city boasted magnificent palaces, beautiful gardens and extensive plantations. The site also of sumptuous feasts and extravagant court pageantry, it attracted visitors from around the world. The town also hosted a thriving market, which drew rich Muslim merchants from across the country.

Under the ample patronage of church and state, the arts and crafts flourished. Impressive churches were built – among them the famous Debre Berhan Selassie, which can be seen to this day. Outside Gonder, building projects included the remarkable island churches of Lake Tana.

But Gonder's sumptuous court proved to be rotten to the core and, in 1706, Emperor Iyasu was assassinated. In the struggle for succession over the next 24 years, no less than four monarchs held power. The royal bodyguard, the clergy, the nobles, even the ordinary citizens, all tried their hand at conspiracy. Assassination, plotting and intrigue became the order of the day, and the ensuing chaos reads like something out of Shakespeare's *Macbeth*, or the worst excesses of the late Roman Empire. Emperor Bakaffa's reign (1721–30) briefly restored stability, during which time new palaces and churches were built, and literature and the arts once again thrived.

However, by the time of Iyasu II's death in 1755, the Gonder kingdom was back in turmoil. The provinces started to rebel. Ethnic rivalries surfaced at court and came eventually to a head in a power struggle between the Oromo people, who had become increasingly absorbed into the court, and the

The Barge He Sat In...

...A great emerald glitter'd on his forehead and added majesty to him...[the emperor was clad] with a vest of blue velvet, flower'd with gold, which trail'd upon the ground. His head was cover'd with a muslin, strip'd gold, which fram'd a sort of crown after the manner of the ancients, and which left the middle of his head bare. His shoes were wrought, after the Indian fashion, with flowers beset with pearls...The throne, of which the feet were of massy silver, was plac'd at the bottom of a hall, in an alcove cover'd with a dome all shining with gold and azure.

French traveller Charles Poncet describing the Emperor Iyasu, in *A Voyage to Ethiopia* (trans), 1709, republished by the Hakluyt Society, 1949

Tigrayan ruler, Ras Mikael Sehul. Assassination and murder again followed and central government fell apart.

The emperors soon became little more than puppets in the hands of the rival feudal lords and their powerful provincial armies. The country disintegrated and civil war became the norm. After a renaissance of sorts during the beginning of the Gonder era, Ethiopia had stepped right back into the dark ages.

Ethiopian historians later referred to the time after Iyasu II's death as the period of the *masafent* or judges, after the reference in the Book of Judges 21:25 when 'every man did that which was right in his own eyes'.

Emperor Tewodros (1855–69)

Right up until the middle of the 19th century, what is now Ethiopia existed only as a cluster of separate fiefdoms. In the mid-19th century, however, there arose from among the feuding lords one who dreamed of unity.

Kassa Haylu had a curious background. The son of a western chief, he was brought up in a monastery. Later, he became a *shifta* (bandit), then a Robin Hood figure, looting the rich to give to the poor.

Quickly attracting followers, he began to defeat the rival princes, one after another, until in 1855 he had himself crowned Emperor Tewodros. The new monarch soon began to show himself not just as a capable leader and strong ruler but as a unifier, innovator and reformer as well.

Choosing as his base the natural fortress of Maqdala, about 112km east of Debre Tabor, Tewodros began to formulate mighty plans. Among the emperor's many projects were the establishment of a national army, an arms factory and a great road network. His policies included a major programme of land reform, the abolition of the slave trade and the promotion of Amharic (the vernacular) in place of the classical written language, Ge'ez.

But these reforms met with deep resentment and opposition from his people: the land-holding clergy, the rival lords and even the common faithful. Tewodros' response, however, was ruthless and sometimes brutal. Like a tragic Shakespearean hero, the emperor suffered from some fatal flaws: an intense pride, a fanatical belief in his cause and an inflated sense of destiny. This would eventually bring him into conflict with other forces too.

Frustrated by failed attempts to enlist European, and particularly British, support for his modernising programmes, Tewodros impetuously imprisoned some British functionaries present at his court. Initially successful in extracting concessions, Tewodros overplayed his hand, and his plan badly miscarried. In 1867, Sir Robert Napier set out from Britain at the head of 32,000 men. His mission was to free the hostages held at Maqdala. Far better equipped, far superior in numbers and better backed by rival Ethiopian lords, the British army inflicted appalling casualties on Tewodros' men, many of them armed with little more than shields and spears.

Refusing to surrender and with his offer of peace rebuffed, Tewodros – playing the tragic hero to the last – penned a final dramatic and bitter avowal, put a pistol in his mouth and shot himself. The British, with their mission accomplished, looted Maqdala's royal treasures, set it in flames and rode away.

Tewodros' defeat gravely weakened Ethiopia. This did not escape the watchful eyes of others: the colonial powers, now hungry for expansion.

Emperor Yohannes (1872–89)

In the trail of destruction left by the British, there arose another battle for succession. After winning weaponry from the British in exchange for support of their expedition to Maqdala, Kassa Mercha of Tigray rose to the fore. In 1871 at the battle of Assam, he managed to defeat his opponent, the newly crowned Emperor Tekla Giorgis.

After proclaiming himself Emperor Yohannes the following year, Kassa reigned for the next 17 years. In contrast to Tewodros, Yohannes staunchly supported the church and recognised the independence of the local lords. With the latter, he struck a bargain: in exchange for keeping their kingdoms, they were obliged to recognise the emperor's overall power, and to pay taxes to his state. In this way, Yohannes secured the religious, political and financial backing of his subjects.

Yohannes also proved himself a skilful soldier. In 1875, after the Egyptians had advanced into Ethiopia from the coastal area, Yohannes drew them into battle. The Emperor beat them resoundingly, once at Gundat in 1875 and again at Gura in 1876. His victories not only ended any Egyptian designs on the territory, but brought much captured weaponry – turning his army into the first well-equipped force in Ethiopian history.

But soon another power threatened: the Italians. The opening of the Suez Canal in 1869 greatly increased the strategic value of the Red Sea, which again became a passageway to the East and beyond.

In 1885, the Italians arrived in Massawa, (in present-day Eritrea), and soon blockaded arms to Yohannes. Furious at their failure to impede the arrival of the Italians, Yohannes accused the British of contravening the Hewett Treaty, signed in 1884. Though protesting otherwise, the British privately welcomed the Italians, both to counter French influence on the Somali coast (in present-day Djibouti), and to deter Turkish designs on the coast.

In the meantime in the West, the Mahadists (or Dervishes) were raising their heads. Dislodging the Egyptians and the British, they overran Sudan. In 1888, a large Dervish army arrived in Ethiopia. Defeating the army sent against them, they sacked Gonder, and torched many of its churches.

Yohannes rushed to meet the Dervishes at Qallabat in 1889 but, at the close of yet another victory, he fell, mortally wounded by a sniper's bullet.

Emperor Menelik (1889–1913)

Menelik, King of Shoa since 1865, had long aspired to the imperial throne. Confined at Maqdala for ten years by Tewodros, he was yet reportedly much influenced by his captor, and dreamt like Tewodros of the unification and modernisation of his country.

After his escape from Maqdala and his ascendancy in Shoa, Menelik concentrated on consolidating his own power, and embarked on an aggressive, ruthless and sometimes brutal campaign of expansion. He occupied territories to the south, southwest and southeast, forcing the various ethnic groups under the yoke of his empire.

Relations with the Italians were at first good; Menelik had been seen as a potential ally against Yohannes. On Yohannes' death, the Italians recognised Menelik's claim to the throne and, in 1889, the Treaty of Wechale was signed. In exchange for granting Italy the region that was later to become Eritrea, the Italians recognised Menelik's sovereignty and gave him the right to import arms freely through Ethiopian ports.

However, a dispute over a discrepancy in the purportedly identical Amharic and Italian texts – the famous Article 17 – led to disagreement. According to the Italian version, Ethiopia was obliged to approach other foreign powers through Italy – in effect reducing Ethiopia to the status of an Italian protectorate. Relations rapidly began to sour.

In the meantime, the Italians continued their expansion in their newly created colony of Eritrea. Soon, they were spilling into territory well beyond the confines agreed to in both treaties.

Despite the Italians' attempts to subvert the local chiefs of Tigray, the latter instead chose to assist Menelik. Nevertheless, the Italians still managed to defeat Ras Mangasha and his Tigrayan forces and were soon in occupation of the Ethiopian town of Mekele in 1895.

Provoked at last into marching north, Menelik assembled his forces and met the Italians in Adwa in 1896. To international shock and amazement, the Italian armies were resoundingly defeated (see the boxed text 'The Battle of Adwa' in the Northern Ethiopia chapter). In the following months, diplomatic missions were sent to Ethiopia from across the world and international boundaries were formally drawn up. Ethiopia as an independent country was born.

The Battle of Adwa was one of the biggest and most significant battles in African history – numbering among the very few occasions when a colonial power was defeated by a native force. To the rest of Africa, Ethiopia became a beacon of independence in a continent almost entirely enslaved by colonialism.

Menelik was responsible for another great achievement, too: the modernisation of his

ETHIOPIA

country. During his reign, the old Shoan capital of Ankober was abandoned and the new capital of Addis Ababa was founded. Electricity and telephones were introduced, bridges, roads, schools and hospitals built, banks and industrial enterprises established.

The greatest technological achievement of the time was undoubtedly the construction of Ethiopia's railway, which reached Addis Ababa in 1915. Linking Addis Ababa to Djibouti, it contributed greatly to the growth of Addis Ababa and the expansion of Ethiopian trade (see the boxed text 'A Dream Come True' in the Eastern Ethiopia chapter).

Iyasu (1913–21)
Menelik managed to die a natural death in 1913. Iyasu, his raffish young grandson and nominated heir, proved to be very much a product of the 20th century. Continuing with Menelik's reforms, he also showed a 'modern' secularist, nonsectarian attitude.

The young prince built mosques as well as churches, took several Muslim as well as Christian wives, and took steps to support the empire's peripheral populations, which had for years suffered at the oppressive hands of the Amharic settlers and governors.

Iyasu and his councillors attempted to push through a few reforms, including improving the system of land tenure and taxation, but they faced ever-deepening opposition from the church and nobility.

Finally, after also upsetting the allied powers with his dealings with Germany, Austria and the Ottoman Empire, a pretext for his removal was found. Accused by the nobles of 'abjuring the Christian faith', the prince was deposed, Zewditu, Menelik's daughter, was proclaimed empress, and Ras Tafari (the son of Ras Makonnen, Menelik's cousin) was proclaimed the prince regent.

Ras Tafari (1921–30)
Upon coming to power, Ras Tafari boasted both more experience and greater maturity than Iyasu, particularly in the field of foreign affairs. In an attempt to improve the country's international image, he at last abolished the Ethiopian slave trade.

In 1923 Tafari pulled off a major diplomatic coup: Ethiopia was granted entry into the League of Nations. Membership not only firmly placed Ethiopia on the international political map, but also gave it some recourse against the grasping designs of its European, colonial neighbours.

Memories of His Majesty

It was a small dog, a Japanese breed... During various ceremonies, he would run away from the Emperor's lap and pee on dignitaries' shoes. The august gentlemen were not allowed to flinch ... when they felt their feet getting wet. I had to walk among the dignitaries and wipe the urine from their shoes with a satin cloth.

From *The Emperor* by Ryszard Kapucinski (Vintage International, 1989)

Continuing the tradition begun by Menelik, Tafari showed himself to be an advocate of reform. A modern printing press was established as well as several secondary schools and an air force. In the meantime, Tafari was steadily outmanoeuvring his rivals. In 1930, the last rebellious noble was defeated and killed in battle. A few days later the sick empress also died. Ras Tafari assumed the throne.

Emperor Haile Selassie (1930–74)
On 2 November 1930, Tafari was crowned Emperor Haile Selassie. The extravagant spectacle that was staged was attended by representatives from around the world and proved a terrific public relations exercise. It even led indirectly to the establishment of a new faith (see the boxed text 'Rastafarians' in the Southern Ethiopia chapter).

The following year, the country's first written constitution was introduced. It granted the emperor virtually absolute power, and his body was declared sacred. The two-house parliament consisted of a senate, which was nominated by the emperor from among his nobles; and a chamber of deputies, which was elected from the landholders. It was thus little more than a chamber for self-interested debate.

Even since the day of his regency, the emperor had been bringing the country under centralised rule. For the first time, the Ethiopian state was unambiguously unified.

Italian Occupation (1933–41)
By the early 20th century, Ethiopia was the only state in Africa to have survived the European Scramble (see the boxed text 'Scramble for Africa' in the Eritrea chapter). However, Ethiopia's position – between the two Italian colonies of Eritrea and Somalia –

made her an enticing morsel. Any attempt by the Italians to link or develop its two colonies would require expansion into Ethiopia. When Mussolini seized power in 1922, the inevitable happened.

From 1933, in an effort to undermine the Ethiopian state, Italian agents, well heeled with funds, were dispatched to subvert the local chiefs, as well as to stir up ethnic tensions. Britain and France, nervous of pushing Mussolini further into Hitler's camp, refrained from protests and turned a blind eye.

In 1934, a minor skirmish known as the Wal Wal incident took place between Italian and Ethiopian forces. Italy had found its pretext. Though the export of arms was banned to both countries, in Italy's case (a major arms manufacturer), the embargo was almost meaningless. France and the USA in the meantime declared themselves 'neutral'.

Growing Italian Interest in Ethiopia

On 3 October 1935, the invasion began. An Italian army, overwhelmingly superior in both ground and air forces, invaded Ethiopia from Eritrea. First the northern town of Aksum fell, then Mekele.

Following the complete contravention of its covenants, the League of Nations was obliged to issue sanctions against Italy. However, these proved to be little more than a slap on the wrist. Although the sanctions' effect was eventually felt on Italy's domestic economy, the measures were wholly ineffectual in either deterring or slowing down Italy's aggression abroad.

More pro-Italy still was the Hoare-Laval proposal of 1936. It proposed that Ethiopia should cede to Italy all territory then occupied, as well as many economic rights – all in return for a 'passageway to the sea'.

Italy's Dirty War

During the Italian campaign in Ethiopia, hundreds of tons of bombs were dropped on civilian as well as military targets including international Red Cross hospitals and ambulances. The countryside was set on fire with incendiary devices, and vast quantities of the internationally banned mustard gas were used. The campaign cost Italy 4350 men. An estimated 275,000 Ethiopians lost their lives. It wasn't until 1996 that the Italian Ministry of Defence finally admitted to the use of mustard gas in this war.

If, as should have happened, the Suez Canal had been closed to the Italians, or an oil embargo put in place, the Italian advance – as Mussolini was later to admit – would have been halted within weeks. The lives of tens of thousands of innocent men, women and children would have been spared.

Campaigning Mussolini was in a hurry. Terrified that the international community would come to its senses and impose more serious embargoes, and keen to keep Italian morale high, Il Duce pressed for a swift campaign.

Impatient with progress made, he soon replaced De Bono, his first general. Pietro Badoglio, his replacement was authorised 'to use all means of war – I say all – both from the air and from the ground'. Implicit in the instructions was the use of mustard gas – then strictly banned according to the 1926 Geneva Convention.

Ethiopian resistance was stiff. Despite overwhelming odds, they succeeded in launching a major counter offensive, known as the Christmas Offensive, at the Italian position at Mekele at the end of 1935.

Following the first Battle of Tembien, however, the Italians were soon on the offensive again. Backed by hundreds of planes, cannons and weapons of every type, the Italian armies swept across the country. In May 1936, Mussolini triumphantly declared: 'Ethiopia is Italian'.

Emperor Haile Selassie in the meantime had fled Ethiopia to escape the invader (some Ethiopians never forgave him for it) as well as to present the cause of Ethiopia to the world. On 30 June 1936, he made his famous speech to the League of Nations in Geneva. The league responded by lifting sanctions in the same year – against Italy. Despite the injustice of this, the emperor's appeals and the widespread popular opposition to Italy's conquest, the invasion was recognised by most of the world; barring only the USSR, USA, Haiti, Mexico and New Zealand.

Occupation & Resistance Soon Ethiopia was merged with Eritrea and Somalia to become the new colonial territory of 'Africa Orientale Italiana' (or Italian East Africa). During this time, the Aksum stele was famously removed to Rome – its return is still under discussion.

Hoping to turn Abyssinia (Ethiopia) into an important economic base, the Italians were prepared to invest heavily in their new colony.

From 1936, as many as 60,000 Italian workers poured into the territory and were put to work on the country's infrastructure.

Ethiopia kept up a spirited resistance to Italian rule throughout its brief duration. Italy's response was famously brutal. Mussolini personally ordered all rebels to be shot, and insurgencies were put down using large-scale bombing, poison gas and machine-gunning from the air.

Ethiopian resistance, however, reached a peak in the attempt on the life of the much-hated Italian viceroy, Graziani, in February 1937. In reprisal, the Fascists carried out a three-day massacre in Addis Ababa, in which several thousand Ethiopians were shot, beheaded or disembowelled.

The 'patriot's movement' (the resistance fighters) was mainly based in Shoa, Gojam and Gonder, but drew support from all parts of the country; many fighters were women. Small underground movements worked in Addis Ababa and other towns; its members were known as *wist arbagna* (insider patriots).

Graziani's response was simple: 'Eliminate them, eliminate them, eliminate them', (a statement that echoes uncannily Kurtz's 'Exterminate all the brutes' in Conrad's *Heart of Darkness*). But Ethiopian resolve stiffened and resistance grew. The Italians, though in control of the major towns, never succeeded in conquering the whole country.

The outbreak of WWII in 1939, however, changed the course of events. Italy's declaration of war against Britain in 1940 caused Britain at last to reverse its policy of tacit support of Italian expansion in East Africa. Britain initially offered assistance on the Sudan–Ethiopia border. Later, at the beginning of 1941, the British launched three major attacks.

Though not then widely recognised, the Ethiopian patriots played a major role in the campaign for liberation, both before, during and after the liberation of Addis Ababa. On 5 May 1941, the emperor and his men entered Addis Ababa. The Italian occupation was over.

Post-Liberation Ethiopia & the Derg (1941–91)

The British, who had entered the country as liberators, seemed at first to have replaced the Italians as occupiers. However, two Anglo-Ethiopian treaties (one signed in 1942, the other in 1944) finally marked the resumption of Ethiopian independence.

The 1940s and '50s saw much post-war reconstruction, including – with US assistance – the establishment of a new government bank, a national currency, and the country's first national airline, Ethiopian Airlines, in 1946.

New schools were also developed and, in 1950, the country's first institution of higher education was established: the University College of Addis Ababa (later the Haile Selassie I University, and now Addis Ababa University).

In 1955, the Revised Ethiopian Constitution was introduced. Although for the first time, the legislature included a fully elected chamber of deputies, the government remained autocratic and real power continued to lie with the emperor.

Ethiopia's long-standing independence, untarnished but for the brief Italian occupation, also gave it a new-found diplomatic authority vis-à-vis other African states. In 1962, Addis Ababa became the headquarters of the Organisation of African Unity (OAU) and, in 1958, of the United Nations Economic Commission for Africa (ECA).

Discontent Despite the modernisation, dissatisfaction began to grow. The country's slow pace of development during the 1950s, as well as the autocratic rule of the emperor began to breed disaffection. Finally, taking advantage of a state visit to Brazil in December 1960, the emperor's imperial bodyguard staged a coup d'etat. Though put down by the army and air force, it signalled the beginning of the end of imperial rule in Ethiopia.

After 1965, discontent simmered among the students too, who protested in particular against land tenure, corruption and the appalling famine of 1972–74 in which an estimated 200,000 peasants died.

The emperor, now an old man in his eighties, seemed more preoccupied with foreign affairs than with internal ones. Additionally, his government was slow and half-hearted in its attempts at reform.

Meanwhile, international relations had also been deteriorating. The newly established state of Somalia claimed the Somali-inhabited region of the Ogaden in Ethiopia. In 1964, war broke out between Somalia and Ethiopia.

Additionally, in 1962, Ethiopia had abrogated the UN-sponsored federation with Eritrea and unilaterally annexed the Eritrean state. Separatist Eritreans launched a bitter guerrilla war.

Cause of Death Unknown

No one knows for certain how the emperor met his end. The most accepted theory is that he was smothered with a pillow as he slept in his bed. The alleged perpetrator of this crime against the Chosen One of God was the man who had engineered his downfall: Lieutenant-Colonel Mengistu Haile Mariam.

Evidence for the crime? A certain ring spotted on Mengistu's middle finger; the ring of Solomon – as it was said to be – was rumoured to have been plucked from the murdered emperor's hand.

In the capital that day, the news ran as follows:

Addis Ababa, August 28, 1975. Yesterday Haile Selassie I, the former Emperor of Ethiopia, died. The cause of death was circulatory failure.

The Ethiopian Herald, 29 August 1975

The Fall of the Emperor During 1974, an unprecedented wave of teacher, student and taxi strikes broke out in Addis Ababa. Even army mutinies began to be reported. At crisis point, the prime minister and his cabinet resigned and a new one was appointed with the mandate to carry out far-reaching constitutional reforms. But it was too late. By this time an increasingly powerful and radical military group had emerged, which would replace the new prime minister with their own.

Gaining in power, this group (known as the *Derg,* or Committee) arrested ministers, nobles and close confidants of the emperor. Finally, using the media with consummate skill, it began to undermine the authority of the emperor himself. On 26 August 1975, footage was used from Jonathan Dimbleby's well-known BBC TV report on the Wolo famine. Scenes of starving people were famously flashed in between clips of sumptuous palace banquets.

The following day the emperor was deposed, unceremoniously bundled into the back of a Volkswagen, and driven away. The absolute power of the emperor and the divine right of rule of the century-old imperial dynasty were finished forever.

The 1974 Revolution The radicals soon dissolved parliament and established a provisional military government: the Provisional Military Administrative Council (PMAC). It was to become known as the Derg (Committee).

However, bitter power struggles and clashes of ideology soon splintered the Derg, culminating in the famous Death of the Sixty in which, in a single night on 23 November 1974, 57 high-ranking civilian and military officials were executed.

Emerging from the chaos was a certain Colonel Mengistu Haile Mariam who conveniently piggy-backed on the wave of popular opposition to the old regime, as well as the Marxist–Leninist ideology of left-wing students. But the political debate soon degenerated into violence. In 1977, the Red Terror campaign was launched to suppress all political opponents. At a conservative estimate, 100,000 people were killed and several thousand more fled abroad.

The Socialist Experiment On 20 December 1974, a socialist state was declared. In 1975, the Derg carried out a series of revolutionary reforms. Under the adage *Ityopya Tikdem* or 'Ethiopia First', banks, businesses and factories were nationalised as was the rural and urban land. Over 30,000 peasant associations were also set up. Raising the status of the Ethiopian peasants, the campaign was initially much praised internationally, particularly by Unesco.

In the meantime, the external threats posed by Somalia and secessionist Eritrea were increasing. In July 1977, Somalia invaded Ethiopia. Thanks to the intervention of the Soviet Union, which flooded socialist Ethiopia with Soviet state-of-the-art weaponry, Somalia was beaten back. In Eritrea, however, the secessionists continued to thwart Ethiopian offensives.

The End of Music

Since the revolution, every song, old or new, has been censored. Some are played with verses deleted, some have been shelved permanently. Love songs have been banned from radio and TV for good. Now during listener-choice programmes, one hears people dedicating martial music to their loved ones.

Alem Mezgebe, *Ethiopia: The Deadly Game*, writing on the Derg in Aug 1978

ETHIOPIA

The Fall of Mengistu Opposition to the Derg had existed since at least the Death of the Sixty in 1974, and had culminated in an unsuccessful coup d'etat in May 1989. Opposition parties during this time included the Marxist EPRP, and later, various ethnically based regional liberation movements, including those of the Afar, Oromo, Somali and particularly Tigrayan peoples.

In 1984–85, another appalling famine followed a drought, in which hundreds of thousands more people died. Failed government resettlement campaigns, communal farms and 'villageisation' programmes aggravated the disaster.

The different opposition groups eventually united to form the Ethiopian People's Revolutionary Democratic Front (EPRDF), which in 1989, began its historic march towards Addis Ababa.

Mengistu's time was up. Doubly confronted by the EPRDF in Ethiopia and the EPLF in Eritrea; with the fall of his allies in Eastern Europe; and with his state in financial ruin as well as his own military authority in doubt, Mengistu decided to flee the country. On 21 May 1991, he boarded a plane probably first to Kenya, and then to Zimbabwe, where he remains to this day. Seven days later, the EPRDF entered Addis Ababa.

The Road to Democracy (1991–95)

After the war of liberation from the Derg, the leaders of both Ethiopia and Eritrea showed a similar determination and zeal in their battle to rebuild their countries.

In July 1991, a transitional charter was endorsed, which gave the EPRDF-dominated legislature a four-year, interim rule under the executive of the TPLF leader, Meles Zenawi. First and foremost, Mengistu's failed socialist policies were abandoned, and de facto independence granted to Eritrea.

In 1992, extensive economic reforms began. These were demarked along mainly linguistic-ethnic lines. See the insets on the country map.

In August 1995, the Federal Democratic Republic of Ethiopia was proclaimed, a series of elections followed, and the constitution of the second republic was inaugurated. Meles Zenawi formed a new government. Soon the leaderships of both Ethiopia and Eritrea were hailed, in US President Clinton's words, as belonging to a 'new generation of African leaders'.

Old Dogs & New Tricks

After 17 years of fighting for freedom, Ethiopia's leaders emerged well schooled in the art of warfare, but less well versed in the skills of modern government. After deciding that you can teach old dogs new tricks, twenty senior government officials enrolled for an MBA at the well-known British distance-learning institution, the Open University.

When the final exams came around, a certain Meles Zenawi was gripped by a bout of nerves. On spying the 'no smoking' sign in the examination room, he exclaimed, 'I have spent the last 17 years fighting a civil war but I have never been so frightened as I am now. There's no way I'll sit the exam without a fag!'

Declaiming the newly learnt philosophy of 'participative decision making', the prime minister insisted on a vote and smoking was permitted during the exam.

Fourteen of the 20 government officials graduated with an MBA, and Meles – demonstrating true leadership by example – took third place in one of the exams out of 1400 candidates worldwide.

The Ethiopia–Eritrea War (1998–2000)

Unfortunately, much of the progress made by Ethiopia and Eritrea in the decade since independence was undermined and even reversed at the end of 1997. In November, Eritrea introduced its own currency to replace the old Ethiopian birr. The new currency, the nakfa, represented not just an historic break with Ethiopia, but an economic one too – annulling the de facto currency union that had been in operation until then.

A dispute over Eritrea's whole exchange-rate system followed, and in early 1998 bickering began over bilateral trade relations. Resulting tensions between the countries escalated into a major military conflict that erupted in May-June 1998 over a disputed border post near Badme.

Eritrea then occupied the town of Badme, followed in June by the towns of Shiraro, Zala Ambassa and Tsorena. An interim settlement proposed by the OAU was accepted by Ethiopia. At the same time, a much-criticised mass deportation of people of Eritrean origin began from Ethiopia. After Ethiopia's recapture of Badme in February 1999, Eritrea agreed to accept the plan. However, the fighting continued with major battles occurring on the Tsorena–Zala Ambassa front.

In June 2000, after a further ten months of failed international diplomacy in which Eritrea refused to approve the changes to the peace plan proposed by the UN and OAU envoys, Ethiopia launched a major offensive that recaptured all territory. It went on to occupy parts of central and western Eritrea as well. An amended settlement was then accepted by Eritrea which implemented a ceasefire and the installation of a OAU–UN buffer zone on Eritrean soil.

In December 2000, a formal peace settlement was signed in Algiers. In April 2001, a 25km-deep demilitarised strip, which ran the length of the internationally recognised border on the Eritrean side, was set up under UN supervision.

Ethiopia Today

The economies of both Ethiopia and Eritrea suffered gravely during the war. Additionally, much international credibility was lost, and many aid organisations temporarily broke off assistance. Tens of thousands of troops lost their lives on both sides (123,000 in Ethiopia alone according to Ethiopian press reports).

Following the creation of the Temporary Security Zone (TSZ) between the two countries in April 2001, the UN Mission in Ethiopia and Eritrea (UNMEE) was charged with three objectives as part of the peace process: to determine the root causes of the war, to establish a Claims Commission (investigating deportations and damaged property) and above all, to establish a neutral Boundary Commission charged with the demarcation of the disputed border. At the time of writing, the mandate of the UNMEE looked likely to be extended again by the UN Security Council when it expires in mid-September 2003, and remain in place until well into 2004.

In April 2002, the Boundary Commission announced its decision on the demarcation of the border, which was accepted by both sides. However, progress has been stalled by a lack of funding pledged for the project. Also, until full arbitration between the two sides takes place, bad blood between the two countries will continue. Nevertheless, surveying has commenced and the construction of boundary posts began in May 2003. Relations with Eritrea will remain tense until the border demarcation is completed probably sometime in 2004.

In the meantime, the loss of Ethiopian access to Eritrean ports has brought about closer relations with neighbouring Djibouti (although recent tensions have arisen over port fees and regulations, as well as differences in foreign policy towards Somalia).

Relations with Egypt remain strained because of disagreements over Ethiopia's right to harness the waters of the Blue Nile for irrigation and hydroelectric projects. Relations with Sudan are currently stable.

In December 2002, Prime Minister Meles Zenawi met American President George Bush in Washington DC. Since 11 September 2001, Ethiopia has been put under pressure to co-operate with the USA (mainly in the exchange of intelligence). Neighbouring Somalia continues to be viewed by the USA as a possible base and refuge of Islamic militants.

At the same time, Ethiopia has used this mandate as an excuse to increase its surveillance and interference in the affairs of its neighbours and to quash the domestic insurgencies of anti-government Ethiopian Somali and Oromo armed factions. In mid-April 2003, skirmishes between government troops and armed factions were reported in the Ogaden region.

GEOGRAPHY

With a land area of 1,098,000 sq km, Ethiopia measures five times the size of Britain or about twice the size of Texas. Ethiopia's topography is remarkably diverse ranging from 20 mountains peaking above 4000m to one of the lowest points on the Earth's surface: the infamous Danakil Depression, which lies up to 120m below sea level.

Two principal geographical zones can be found in the country: the cool highlands and the hot lowlands that surround them.

Ethiopia's main topographical feature is the vast central plateau (the Ethiopian highlands) with an average elevation of between 1800m and 2400m. It is here that the country's major peaks are found including Ras Dashen at 4543m (4620m according to some estimates and maps), Ethiopia's highest mountain and the fourth highest in Africa.

The mountains are also the source of four large river systems, the most famous of which is the Blue Nile. Rising in Lake Tana and joined later by the White Nile in Sudan, it supplies a massive 90% of the Nile's water, which nurtures the fertile Nile Valley of Egypt to the north. The other principal rivers are the Awash, the Omo and the Wabe Shebele.

Southern Ethiopia is bisected diagonally by the Rift Valley. Averaging around 50km wide, it runs all the way down to Mozambique. Several lakes can be found on the valley floor, including the well-known chain lying due south of Addis Ababa.

The northern end of the East African Rift Valley opens into the Danakil Depression, one of the hottest places on Earth.

CLIMATE

Ethiopia's climate reflects its topography.

The highlands are classed as temperate with an average daytime temperature of 16°C. Most rain occurs between mid-June and mid-September when around 1000mm falls. Rainstorms can be violent. In the notoriously drought-susceptible areas in the northeast, however, rainfall is much more erratic. Rainfall in the lowlands is around half that of the highlands, but some areas also experience small rains between March and April.

The southern Rift Valley, with an average elevation of around 1500m, is classed as moderate to hot, and shares a similar rainfall pattern to the highlands. In the Bale Mountains in the south, snow sometimes falls. At the other end of the scale, temperatures in the Danakil Depression can touch 50°C, and rainfall in the region is practically zero.

The far south and the eastern lowlands are hot and dry. The western lowlands are hot and humid. In the southwest the main rains fall from March to June and the small rains in November.

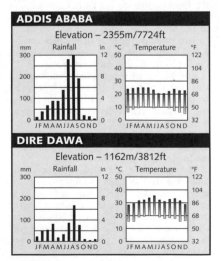

ECOLOGY & ENVIRONMENT

The farmer who eats his chickens as well as all their eggs will have a bleak future

Tigrayan proverb

Biodiversity & Endemism

Reflecting the diversity of Ethiopia's geography is the diversity of her ecosystems – from high peaks and semitropical forest to salt lakes and desert. For details of the range of Ethiopia's habitats see Flora & Fauna later.

The highlands in particular are an unusual habitat. Rising like a vast natural fortress above the surrounding lowlands, the Ethiopian central plateau is home to a unique assemblage of plants and animals. Isolated for millions of years within this 'fortress environment' and unable to cross the inhospitable terrain surrounding it, much highland wildlife evolved on its own. Many species are found nowhere else in the world.

Of the 277 mammal species in the country, no less than 31 are endemic, 11.2% of the total number. In 1919, the last large mammal species on Earth to be named by science was declared: it was Ethiopia's mountain nyala. Endemism is rife not just among Ethiopia's mammals but among other creatures too: amphibians (24 species; 38.1%), birds (16 species; 1.9%), reptiles (9 species; 4.5%), insects and even fish (4 species; 2.7%).

Among the endemic mammals are the mountain nyala, the walia ibex, the Ethiopian wolf, the gelada baboon, and fifteen species of rodent including the mole rat. Swayne's hartebeest and Menelik's bushbuck are endemic races of mammals.

Ethiopia's highland flora is no less exceptional for the same reason. The country is classed as one of the 12 Vavilov centres in the world for crop plant diversity, and is thought to possess extremely valuable pools of crop plant genes. Between 600 and 1400 plants species are thought to be endemic; an enormous 10–20% of Ethiopia's flora.

Environmental Problems

Like many sub-Saharan African countries, three factors above all have taken their toll on Ethiopia's environment: war, famine (see also the boxed text 'Famine' later in this chapter) and demographic pressure. Additionally, Ethiopia has not benefited from the investment and development of wildlife conservation that has occurred in some colonised countries of Africa.

Funny Frogs

No less than 32% of frog species are endemic to Ethiopia. During a recent scientific expedition to the Harenna Forest in the Bale Mountains, biologists discovered four entirely new species in the space of just three weeks. Many of the frogs appear to have made peculiar adaptations to their environment. One species swallows snails whole, another has forgotten how to hop and a third has lost its ears!

Although limited conservation has long been practised – the Aksumite state itself set aside designated areas for hunting – national legitimised conservation programmes are still in their infancy and have been long delayed by war.

In recent years, however, the government has shown signs of a growing awareness of the importance of conservation. A National Conservation Action Plan has been launched by the government (though it still awaits enactment), which includes a reforestation programme. An Environmental Protection Agency has also been established, and a biodiversity strategy is planned for the future. Major ongoing obstacles include a lack of funding, trained personnel and a clear government agenda.

For more information on wildlife and wildlife conservation, contact the **Ethiopian Wildlife Conservation Organisation** (☎ 51 79 22; PO Box 386, Addis Ababa).

War During the civil war in Ethiopia, whole forests were torched to smoke out rebel forces. Additionally, large armies, hungry and with inadequate provisions, turned their sights on the land's natural resources; much wildlife was wiped out.

The armed conflict that continues between warring tribes in the Omo and Mago National Parks also impedes wildlife conservation efforts.

Demographic Pressures Ethiopia's population has quadrupled in the last 65 years, and is growing at a rate of nearly 2.5%. As living space, firewood, building materials, agricultural land, livestock grazing and food is increasingly sought, more pressure is put on the land and its resources, and larger and larger areas of wildlife habitat are lost.

Harmful Practices About 95% of Ethiopia's original forest is believed to have been lost to agriculture and human settlement. The highlands are the worst affected area. Here, for seven millennia, farming has been practised and land cleared. Today, 85% of Ethiopia's population gain their livelihood from agriculture. A direct result of deforestation, soil erosion represents an extremely serious threat to Ethiopia, and exacerbates the threat of famine (see the boxed text 'Famine' later in this chapter).

Hunting and poaching over the centuries have decimated the country's once large populations of elephant and rhino. Today, hunting is controlled by the government and may even provide the most realistic and pragmatic means of ensuring the future survival of Ethiopia's large mammals. Poaching, however, continues to pose a serious threat to animals. Ivory and particularly rhino horn still fetch astronomical prices in Asia. The black rhino was last recorded twenty years ago. Most probably, it is now extinct in Ethiopia.

Protective Measures

Ethiopia's national parks were set up during the time of Emperor Haile Selassie. In order to create Western-style conservation projects, land was forcefully taken from the peasants – a measure much resented by the local people. When the Derg government fell in 1991, there was a brief period of anarchy, when park property was looted and wildlife killed.

Wildlife authorities are now actively trying to encourage the participation of the local people in the conservation of wildlife: educational programmes are on the agenda.

Future efforts to preserve wildlife will include the captive breeding and re-introduction of animals and possibly the establishment of private wildlife ranches, which will provide not just wildlife protection, but local employment and revenue for the government, which can then be reinvested in conservation projects.

FLORA & FAUNA

Although Ethiopia lacks the large and spectacular animal herds found in Kenya, its wildlife is no less remarkable. In some ways it's more remarkable, since many animals and birds are unique to Ethiopia. (See Biodiversity & Endemism under Ecology & Environment earlier in this chapter for more information on endemic flora and fauna. See also the special section 'Birds in Ethiopia'.)

Spot the Endemic Flora

Ethiopia has more unique species of flora than any other country in Africa. In September and October, look out particularly for the famous yellow daisy known as the Meskel flower, which carpets the highlands; it belongs to the Bidens family, six members of which are endemic.

In towns and villages, the endemic yellow-flowered *Solanecio gigas* is commonly employed as a hedge. Around Addis Ababa, the tall endemic *Erythrina brucei* tree can be seen. In the highlands, such as in the Bale Mountain and Simien Mountain National Parks, the indigenous Abyssinian rose is quite commonly found. Also in the Bale Mountains, look out for the endemic species of globe thistle *(Echinops longisetus)*.

Major Habitats

Eight major habitats can be found in Ethiopia. The following guide will give you a brief description of the habitats along with the flora and fauna you can expect to see there.

Desert & Semidesert Scrubland

The Dankalia region, Omo delta and Ogaden Desert all fall into this category. Vegetation is typically characterised by highly drought-resistant plants such as small trees, shrubs and grasses, including acacia. Succulent species include euphorbia and aloe. Larger mammals include the (extremely rare) African wild ass, Grevy's zebra, Soemmering's gazelle and beisa oryx. Birds include the ostrich, secretary bird, Arabian, Kori and Heuglin's bustards, Abyssinian roller, red-cheeked cordon bleu and crested francolin.

Small-leaved Deciduous Forest

These woodlands can be found all over the country apart from the western regions, at an altitude of between 900m and 1900m. Vegetation consists of drought-tolerant shrubs and trees with either leathery persistent leaves or small deciduous ones. Trees include various type of acacia. Herbs include *Acalypha* and *Aerva*.

Large mammals include Grevy's zebras, hartebeests, greater and lesser kudus and beisa oryx. Birds include the white-bellied go-away bird, superb starling, red-billed quelea, helmeted guinea fowl, secretary bird and Ruppell's long-tailed starling.

Broad-leaved Deciduous Forest

These forests occur mainly in western and north-western parts of the country. Bamboo is also found in the western valleys. Wildlife includes hartebeests, greater and lesser kudus, gazelles, buffaloes, common elands, elephants and De Brazza's monkeys. Bird species include the gambaga flycatcher, red-cheeked cordon bleu, bush petronia and black-faced firefinch.

Moist Evergreen Forest

Found in the southwestern and western parts of the country, these forests consist of tall and medium-sized trees and understorey shrubs. Wildlife includes Menelik's bushbucks, bushpigs, forest hogs and De Brazza's monkeys. The very colourful birdlife includes the Abyssinian black-headed oriole, Abyssinian hill babbler, white-cheeked turaco, scaly throated honeyguide, scaly francolin, emerald cuckoo and the yellow-billed coucal.

Lowland Semi-Evergreen Forest

These can be found in western Ethiopia around Gambela. Vegetation consists of semi-evergreen tree and shrub species as well as grasses. Wildlife includes elephants, giraffes, lions and the white-eared kob. Birds include the openbill and Adim's storks, pelicans and egrets. The shoebill has not been seen since 1973.

Dry Evergreen Montane Forest & Grassland

Covering much of the highlands, and the north, northwest, central and southern parts of the country, this habitat is home to a large number of endemic plants. Tree species include various types of acacia, olive and Euphorbia. Africa's only rose the *Rosa abyssinica* is here. Wildlife includes leopards, gazelles, jackals and hyena. Birds include the Abyssinian longclaw, black-headed siskin, yellow-fronted parrot, black-winged lovebird, blue-winged goose, half-collared kingfisher and wattled ibis.

Afro-Alpine Vegetation

This habitat is found in the national parks of the Bale and Simien Mountains. In the Bale Mountains, the endemic giant lobelia *(Lobelia rhynchopetalum)*, an endemic species of globe thistle and the so-called 'soft thistle' are found. Heather grows into large trees of up to 10m. On the high plateaus at around 4000m, many varieties of gentian can be found. For wildlife

Injera baskets, Addis Ababa

Traditional raincoat, Simien Mountains

Young boy near Wondo Genet

Young girl, market day at Dila

Ethiopian wolf

Pelicans, Lake Abiata-Shala

Gelada baboon

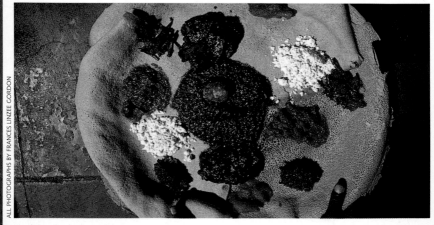
Traditional Ethiopian dishes served on *injera*

and bird species, see National Parks later in this chapter.

Wetlands In Ethiopia wetlands occur along the Baro River and around Gambela in the west as well as in the highlands and the northwest. Look out for fig and tamarind trees along river banks or *wadis* (seasonal rivers). Crocodiles and hippos inhabit many rivers. Birdlife is particularly abundant and includes Rouget's rails and white-winged flufftails in the swamps, and the Senegal thick-knee and red-throated bee-eater in riverbank habitats.

Endangered Species

According to the accounts of early travellers, Ethiopia was once home to vast numbers of animals. In AD 525, Cosmos Indicopleustes of Byzantium reported tame giraffes and elephants at the kingdom of Aksum. They were kept apparently for the amusement of the court and to pull the royal chariots!

The Byzantine writer and traveller, Nonosus, claimed to have seen 5000 elephants in a single herd near Adwa in the north of the country. Even as late as the turn of the 19th and 20th centuries, the game hunter Harrison reported a herd of 100 elephants in the Middle Awash area.

Flora and fauna today is much reduced. Currently 151 flowering species, 21 mammal species and 17 species of birds are classed by the International Union for the Conservation of Nature and Natural Resources (IUCN) as endangered.

Among them are the Ethiopian wolf, the walia ibex, the dibatag (a type of antelope), the African wild ass, Swayne's hartebeest, the Tora hartebeest and Grevy's zebra. Endangered birds include the Prince Ruspoli's turaco, the Sidamo long-clawed lark and the Ankober serin (see also the special section 'Birds of Ethiopia').

NATIONAL PARKS

There are ten national parks (NP) and three wildlife sanctuaries (WS) in Ethiopia. The latter await the awarding of full national park status.

A new World Bank–funded project, the Global Environmental Facility (GEF), is currently reviewing the national parks. Around US$8 million dollars will be used to review the design, redefine borders, perhaps establish new parks and downgrade others. In December 2002, the French government approved a plan to fund a major new biodiversity wildlife project in the mid and northern Afar region.

Awash NP (827 sq km; see the Eastern Ethiopia chapter) Habitats include arid and semi-arid woodland and some riverine forest. Wildlife includes greater and lesser kudus, Soemmering's gazelles, beisa oryx, Swayne's hartebeests, lions (rare) and kori bustards. There are 63 species of large mammals recorded here and 392 species of bird. Established for its range of large mammals (easily seen), the national park is easily accessible (210km east of Addis Ababa).

The Bleeding Heart Baboon

The gelada baboon *(Theropithecus gelada)* is one of Ethiopia's most fascinating endemic mammals. In fact not a baboon at all, it makes up its own genus of monkey.

Of all the nonhuman primates, it is by far the most dexterous. It also lives in the largest social groups (up to 800 have been recorded), and is the only primate that feeds on grass and has its 'sexual skin' on its chest and not on its bottom – a convenient adaptation, given that it spends most of its time sitting on its bottom whilst grazing!

The gelada also has the most complex system of communication of any nonhuman primate and the most sophisticated social system: the females decide who's boss, the young males form bachelor groups, and the older males perform a kind of grandfather role looking after the young.

Although the males sport magnificent leonine manes, their most striking physical feature is the bare patch of skin on their chest. This has given rise to their other popular name: the 'bleeding heart baboon'. The colour of the patch indicates the sexual condition not just of the male (his virility), but also his female harem (their fertility), like a kind of communal sexual barometer.

Unfortunately, the gelada is gravely threatened, and because of climatic changes its habitat (precipitous mountain pockets at up to 4200m) is fast disappearing. It will almost certainly become extinct – one of the first victims of global warming. See also the boxed text 'Monkey Trouble' in the Northern Ethiopia chapter.

Babille Elephant Sanctuary (6982 sq km; see the Eastern Ethiopia chapter) The sanctuary was established to protect the indigenous elephant subspecies *Loxodonta africana oreleansi*. Disrupted badly by incursions of Somali refugees and livestock, elephants are very rare. Habitats include semi-arid open woodland. The sanctuary is definitely not worth a special visit; it's also difficult to reach (570km east of Addis Ababa).

Bale Mountains NP (2471 sq km; see the Southern Ethiopia chapter) Established to protect the mountain nyala and the Ethiopian wolf (both endemic and both commonly seen), this park is also a good spot to see other mammals such as Ethiopian wolves, Menelik's bushbucks, mountain nyalas and giant mole rats. Habitats include Afro-alpine, high mountain and montane vegetation. There are 64 species of large mammals recorded here and 270 birds, as well as beautiful scenery and great trekking. It's a must for birders with many endemics easily seen. It's fairly accessible (400km southeast of Addis Ababa).

Gambela NP (5060 sq km; see Western Ethiopia chapter) This park was established for large mammal species typical of Sudan. It suffers from Sudanese poaching and an influx of refugees and has yet to be developed. Habitats include semi-arid woodland and deciduous woodland. Wildlife includes savanna Nile lechwe, white-eared kobs, elephants, roan antelopes, tiangs and shoebills. There are 41 recorded species of large mammals and 41 recorded bird species here. Difficult to get to (lying 700km west of Addis Ababa), this park is not worth a special trip.

Kuni-Muktar WS Habitats here include two small hills with forested peaks with 20 recorded species of large mammals and 24 species of bird. Wildlife includes mountain nyalas and Menelik's bushbucks. Difficult to get to (350km east of Addis Ababa), the sanctuary was established to protect the mountain nyala. It's not worth a special visit.

Lake Abiata-Shala NP (887 sq km; see Southern Ethiopia chapter) Easily accessible (208km south of Addis Ababa) and with attractive scenery, this park boasts good numbers of aquatic birds. Habitats include savanna and acacia woodland. There are 31 species of large mammal recorded here as well as 299 species of bird, among them the great white pelican, lesser flamingo, whitenecked cormorant and Grant's gazelle.

Mago NP (2162 sq km; see the Southern Ethiopia chapter) This national park is worthwhile if you have the time and patience, although it's difficult to get to and the animals are not easily seen. With habitats including semi-arid open woodland and savanna and wildlife such as the elephant, cheetah, giraffe, lelwel, hartebeest, buffalo and tiang, the park is home to 56 recorded large mammal species and 153 species of bird. There are also local tribes here. It was

established to protect large mammals of the plains (elephants, buffaloes, giraffes etc) and lies 785km southwest of Addis Ababa.

Nechisar NP (514 sq km; see the Southern Ethiopia chapter) The savanna habitat of Nechisar is home to Swayne's hartebeest, Burchell's zebra, greater kudu, crocodile, the Nechisar nightjar, hippos and kori bustard. Thirty-seven large mammal species and 188 bird species have been recorded here. There is plentiful wildlife on the plains, especially Burchell's zebras and Swayne's hartebeests. The park boasts very beautiful scenery; it's easily accessible from Arba Minch and it's 500km south of Addis Ababa.

Omo NP (4068 sq km; see the Southern Ethiopia chapter) This inaccessible park rewards a lengthy stay. Its savanna and deciduous woodland habitats are home to common elands, elephants, cheetahs, giraffes and buffaloes. There are 57 large mammal species and 306 bird species here. Local tribes are colourful. Although established to protect wilderness and prolific plains wildlife, the park suffers from poaching by the Surma people. It's 886km southwest of Addis Ababa.

Senkele NP (54 sq km; see the Southern Ethiopia chapter) While probably not worth a special trip, this national park is quite accessible (320km southwest of Addis Ababa). There are 13 recorded species of large mammal, including Swayne's hartebeests which the park was established to protect, and 91 recorded species of bird. The main habitat is savanna.

Simien Mountains NP (179 sq km; see the Northern Ethiopia chapter) With spectacular mountain scenery this is a rewarding place for trekking. Afro-alpine, high mountain habitats are home to 21 species of large mammal and 63 species of bird, including the walia ibex, Ethiopian wolf, gelada baboon and lammergeyer (quite easily seen). It's quite easily accessible (around 750km north of Addis Ababa).

Yabelo WS (2496 sq km; see the Southern Ethiopia chapter) The savanna of Yabelo is home to Streseman's bushcrow, the white-tailed swallow and Swayne's hartebeest. There are 20 large mammals species recorded and 194 species of bird. Established to protect the Swayne's hartebeest (now greatly reduced) it is now an important sanctuary for endemic birds. It's quite difficult to get to (500km south of Addis Ababa) and probably not worth a special trip.

Yangudi-Rassa NP (4731 sq km; see the Eastern Ethiopia chapter) This park is not well developed or maintained. African wild ass, oryx, gerenuk, Soemmering's gazelle, cheetah and ostrich live in the semidesert habitat. There are 36 large mammal species on record and 136 bird species. The park was established to protect the African wild ass, but lying around 200km northeast of Addis Ababa, it's not worth a special trip.

GOVERNMENT & POLITICS

The second Ethiopian republic, formally known as the Federal Democratic Republic of Ethiopia, came into being in August 1995. It consists of a federation of regional states governed by two assemblies: the 548-member Council of Peoples' Representatives (CPR), which is the legislative arm, and the smaller 108-member Federal Council (FC), which serves as the senate, with a merely supervisory role. The president has a mainly ceremonial role. The prime minister is the head of state and appoints the 18-member cabinet.

Under the new republic's principle of 'ethnic federalism', the nine newly-created regional states (among them the city-state of Harar) and two metropolitan regions (Addis Ababa and Dire Dawa) have their own autonomous councils and hold their own elections. The regions are demarked largely along linguistic lines, and five of Ethiopia's largest ethnic groups (the Amhara, Oromo, Tigrayan, Afar and Somali) now have their own regional states.

The ruling party, the EPRDF (originally a coalition of armed groups responsible for overthrowing Mengistu in May 1991 – see History earlier), holds 90% of the CPR's seats, and dominates all the major regional state councils and principal state institutions.

The main ministries are also headed by leading EPRDF loyalists, but in accordance with the new republic's principle of 'ethnic federalism', cabinet members are drawn from the main ethnic groups. This has led both to accusations of 'political appointee-ism' on the one hand, and empty political appeasement on the other.

Within the EPRDF, however, the real power, especially in foreign and economic affairs, is said to lie with party staff outside the cabinet – in particular with the ex-Tigrayan People's Liberation Front (TPLF; prominent in the overthrow of Mengistu). Nevertheless, the effort to acknowledge its multicultural and multiethnic society makes Ethiopia stand almost alone in Africa.

In the late 1990s, cracks within the Tigrayan core of the government were felt. They showed up visibly during the lead up to war with Eritrea. In March 2001, they came to a head with an open rebellion. It took the Prime Minister, Meles Zenawi, along with his foreign affairs minister, Seyoum Mesfin, seven months to allay the crisis, reassert authority and put down the rebellion. No fewer than 11 members of the 30-strong central committee were suspended. Many of the rebels were imprisoned – and silenced – on corruption charges. It was the most serious crisis to face the government since coming to power in 1991, and undoubtedly damaged its credibility at home and abroad.

Various opposition groups to the government, though vociferous, have proved largely ineffectual, unable to unite or mobilise much support and lacking in clear political agendas. Among them are the Addis Ababa–based Coalition of Alternative Forces for Peace and Democracy in Ethiopia (CAFPDE), and the various regional factions including Afar, Oromo, Ogaden Somali and Amhara groups. Armed conflict continues between the government and various Oromo factions including the Oromo Liberation Front (OLF).

Since 1991, the government has undoubtedly come a long way from the repressive regime of the Derg: the oppressive security apparatus is being dismantled and there is greater freedom of speech, expression and political organisation. Nevertheless, oppression of both the press and political opponents continue.

In the May 2000 elections, Meles Zenawi the incumbent prime minister and his EPRDF party convincingly won another term in office. The current president, Girma Wolde-Giorgis, was appointed in October 2001. The next elections are due in May 2005.

Human Rights

Compared with many African countries, Ethiopia's human rights record isn't bad, and the government seems keen to improve it further. In May 1998, an international council was called to consider the establishment of a National Human Rights Commission, and in June 1998, Ethiopia acceded to the African charter on Human and People's Rights.

But there's still room for improvement: more than 10,000 political detainees are thought to be held, most without charge or trial. 'Disappearances' of government opponents are still reported; prison conditions are grim, with medical treatment either delayed or denied; and freedom of the press is notoriously restricted, with at least 20 journalists languishing in jail for criticism of the government.

ETHIOPIA

ECONOMY

The Ethiopian economy suffers from two major and persistent weaknesses: food insecurity and a near total dependency on coffee for foreign exchange earnings.

Agriculture provides the livelihood of 85% of the population, but drought, pests and severe soil erosion have all kept agricultural yields notoriously erratic and low. Per capita income is estimated at around US$670 (according to a 2000 UNDP report) – making Ethiopia one of three poorest countries in the world.

Agriculture accounts for a huge 45% of Ethiopia's GDP. During the 1980s and '90s, however, food imports to feed Ethiopia's population sometimes exceeded 1 million tonnes per year. Recent measures to improve productivity include the increased use of fertilisers, pesticides, and irrigation systems.

Though not officially promoted by the government, one plant that has proved lucrative is the notorious chat plant (see the boxed text 'Chat Among the Pigeons' in the Eastern Ethiopia chapter), which earned Ethiopia over US$61m in 2000–01. Remarkably, it is now the second largest export earner. Most of it is exported to Djibouti and Somalia, where it meets the steady and high demand from locals. In recent years, farmers particularly in eastern Ethiopia, have been replacing coffee plants grown on ancient sites with chat plants, which offer far faster returns.

Placing the Ethiopian economy in a particularly vulnerable position is the notoriously volatile international price of coffee. Up to 60% of the country's foreign earnings come from coffee. However, between 1997 and 2001, earnings dropped by 62%. Diversification into horticulture, such as the production of fresh flowers or spices, is among the initiatives currently encouraged. Other hopes lie in the country's rich, and as yet unexploited, mineral deposits including gold, iron ore and potassium.

Attempts have also been made to bolster manufacturing (particularly food processing), which accounts for just 5% of GDP, particularly in the area of food processing. In 1999,

Famine

From time immemorial, Ethiopia has been prone to cyclical drought. Since the early 1970s, the country's name has become synonymous in the West with drought, disaster and famine. In May 2000 and in 2002, horrifying pictures of famine again shocked the world.

In the past, the causes have had less to do with environmental factors – Ethiopia has abundant natural resources – and more to do with economic mismanagement and inequitable and oppressive government. More recently, however, failed rains over consecutive seasons, given Ethiopia's near total dependence on rain-fed agriculture, have been the main cause. Additionally, serious soil erosion, inefficient production methods and low fertiliser and pesticide use have all contributed to poor and erratic yields, thus aggravating the problem.

Severe food shortages are currently a continent-wide threat with eight countries in East and southern Africa most acutely affected. Of these, Ethiopia and Eritrea face among the worst problems. In 2003, up to 14 million people in Ethiopia were estimated to face famine (two-thirds of the population faced shortages). In Eritrea a further one million faced famine. This required a huge 1.44 million tonnes and 400,000 tonnes of cereal food aid to each country. They faced the worst drought since 1984–85.

In recent years, the problem has been confounded by a new problem: the AIDS epidemic. AIDS, which particularly effects the 16- to 40-year-old age bracket, is decimating the labour force, the sector of the population required to re-establish agricultural production. Weakened by hunger, AIDS sufferers are less able to combat the disease.

It is hoped that, in the future, a combination of improved agriculture, land reform, measures to combat soil erosion and the development of irrigation systems will help make Ethiopia self-sufficient at last. The prime minister, himself from the notoriously famine-prone region of Tigray, has made the fight against famine something of a personal crusade. Recent measures to establish early-warning systems for famine and the foundation of food security reserves have had a measure of success, but they are short-term solutions only.

In the meantime, the image of Ethiopia as a desertified land wracked by drought and famine has widespread economic repercussions. It is perhaps the single greatest obstacle to the development of its tourism industry – the one sector that could earn it millions of dollars.

French and South African companies began building new breweries in the country.

Despite inheriting a Marxist economy in 1991 that was particularly badly damaged by years of war, and despite having very little experience in economic management, the government hasn't done at all badly in its attempts at reform (see the boxed text 'Old Dogs & New Tricks' earlier in this chapter). The transition, albeit very cautious and slow, has been reasonably successful and steady. Real GDP growth averaged 4.4% between 1997 and 2001.

Wholesale privatisation of hotels, state farms, restaurants, shops and factories is happening apace, and in recent years foreign investment has been encouraged.

In 2002, the government began to offer incentives to nonresident Ethiopians to invest in the country. By far the biggest foreign investor to date is the Midroc group, controlled by the half-Ethiopian entrepreneur, Sheikh Alamoudi of Saudi Arabia. Alamoudi's many ventures range from the ultra-luxurious Sheraton Hotel in Addis Ababa to a travel agency, and gold prospecting at Lega Dembi. Along with the current wave of tax reforms, VAT was introduced in January 2003.

At present government expenditure is principally directed towards three things: education, health and the development of infrastructure (and particularly roads – see the Getting Around chapter). However, tourism is thought to have the greatest growth potential of any economic activity in Ethiopia. Civil war, famine, state socialism, the border conflict with Eritrea and more recently the American-led war on Iraq have dealt a severe blow to the growth of the industry which, in the 1970s, counted 75,000 visitors a year. Currently the largest group of visitors is Ethiopians living abroad, followed by northern Europeans, then business and diplomatic visitors and aid workers.

Although the government allocates a minuscule 0.08% of its budget to the tourist industry, the private sector has proved much more proactive and visionary. This is evidenced in the rash of hotels and travel agencies mushrooming in Addis Ababa and some of the provincial capitals. In April 2003, the go ahead was given to at last amend the 1995 investment code in order to allow for the first time non-Ethiopians to invest in the travel and tour operation sector.

Due to the failure of harvests in 2002, the economic forecast for 2003–04 was not so rosy, with growth forecast at between zero and 2%. Growth was expected to return to between 3% and 4% from 2004.

By the end of 2003, Ethiopia should be certified officially as a producer of organic coffee, which should allow it to increase significantly the revenue gained from organic coffee exports.

POPULATION & PEOPLE

In the past, war, slavery, epidemic diseases and famine have all taken their toll on Ethiopia's population. The 20th century saw the abolition of slavery (in 1917), and the introduction of modern medicine and foreign food aid. Due to these factors the population increased from 15 million in 1935 to an estimated 64 million in 2004.

Today Ethiopia is the second most populous nation in sub-Saharan Africa (Nigeria is most populous). Growing by a hefty rate of up to 2.4% per year, the Ethiopian population is predicted to reach a huge 113 million by 2025. However, AIDS, which at the beginning of 2000 affected an estimated 10.6% of the population, will inevitably slow future growth. Life expectancy is currently 49 years.

AIDS in Africa

Sub-Saharan Africa is home to two-thirds of the world's 33.4 million people infected with AIDS; some 5000 die daily on the continent. It is estimated that by 2005, the figure will have increased to 13,000 daily – a number that will bring the AIDS death toll in the region to above that of the two world wars combined.

Ethiopia is now second only to South Africa in numbers of HIV infections and deaths from AIDS. In 2001, the Ministry of Health estimated there were three million HIV-infected people in Ethiopia, though there may be many more. By 2009, it is estimated that the mortality rate for the age group 15 to 49 years old will have increased by a staggering 57%.

AIDS is now the single greatest threat to economic development in Ethiopia and Africa. In the last few years, the government has at last taken stock: hard-hitting warnings on television and radio, as well as the ubiquitous poster around the country ('Give Your Life a Price' in Amharic), reflect the drive to educate the population.

ETHIOPIA

Peoples of Ethiopia

The 83 languages and 200 dialects spoken in Ethiopia give an indication of the country's remarkable ethnic diversity. See also the boxed texts 'Peoples of the Lower Omo Valley' and 'The People of Konso' in the Southern Ethiopia chapter. The major tribal groups include the following:

The Oromo

Thought to originate from the south and from present-day Kenya, the Cushitic Oromo were once nomadic pastoralists and skilful warrior horsemen (see Oromo Migrations under History earlier in this chapter). Today, most are sedentary, making a living as farmers or cattle breeders. The Oromo are Muslim, Christian and animist in religion, and are known for their egalitarian society, which is based on the *gada* or age-group system. A man's life is divided into age-sets of eight years. In the fourth set (between the ages of 24 and 32), men assume the right to govern their people. The Oromo are estimated to form the largest ethnic group (around 54%). For more on the Oromo see the Eastern Ethiopia chapter.

The Amharas & Tigrayans

In the centre and north of the country live the Semitic Amharas and Tigrayans, traditionally tillers of the soil. Their staple cereal is the famous *tef*, an indigenous type of millet, which is made into the Ethiopian *injera* or pancake (see Food in the Facts for the Visitor chapter).

In the past, the Amharas and to a lesser extent the Tigrayans proved themselves as great warriors, skilful governors and astute administrators. This century-old domination was always much resented by other tribal groups, who saw it as little more than a kind of colonialism.

Fiercely independent, devoutly Christian and fanatically attached to their land, the Amhara and Tigrayans disdain all manual labour with the single exception of agriculture – DIY is a notion completely lost on the average highlander! The Amhara form the second largest ethnic group (24%), and the Tigrayans the third largest (5%).

The Gurage

The Gurage are Semitic–Cushitic in origin. Most practise herding or farming, and the *enset* plant is their favoured crop (see boxed text 'Enduring Enset' in the Southern Ethiopia chapter). Known as great workers, clever improvisers – even counterfeiters – and skilled craftspeople, the Gurage will apply themselves to any task. Many work as seasonal labourers for the highlanders. Their faith is Christian, Muslim or animist, depending on the area from which they originate.

The population is still largely rural with 85% of the people living in the countryside. Only Addis Ababa has a population of over one million. Several hundred thousand Ethiopians are believed to have immigrated to the USA (with large communities in Washington and Los Angeles in particular). There are also quite large Ethiopian communities in the EU.

Amharic, the indigenous language of Ethiopia, is Semitic (like Arabic) in origin, and is the national language. Twelve million or so Amharas speak Amharic and it is the second language of around one-third of the population. It is also the official language of the media and the government.

EDUCATION

Providing education for Ethiopia's youth is a major challenge (over half the population is under 16, and many inhabit rural areas), and along with the improvement of the nation's health, is a top government priority. New schools can be seen mushrooming across the country.

Only 38.5% (World Bank figures) of the adult population is literate (compared to 75% in neighbouring Kenya). Currently, school attendance is also well below other African countries: just 52% of children attend primary school; only 12% of children make it to secondary school.

Students are also encouraged to take vocational training; some of the regional technical colleges are now flourishing. Other schools include missionary and church schools, and 'community' schools (such as the British, French, German, American, Indian and Italian schools in Addis Ababa).

The Addis Ababa University was founded by Emperor Haile Selassie in 1961. Since then,

Peoples of Ethiopia

ETHIOPIA

The Harari
Also Semitic in origin are the Harari people (sometimes known as Adare), who have long inhabited the walled Muslim city of Harar in the east of the country. The people are particularly known for their distinct two-storey houses known as *gegar* (see the boxed text 'Traditional Adare Houses' in the Eastern Ethiopia chapter) and for the very colourful traditional costumes still worn by many Harari women today. In the past, the Harari were known as great craftspeople – as weavers, basket-makers and bookbinders – as well as renowned Islamic scholars.

The Somali
The arid lowlands of the southeast dictate a nomadic or seminomadic existence for the Somali, a Cushitic people. Somali society is Muslim, strongly hierarchical, tightly knit and based on the clan system, which requires intense loyalty from its members. In the harsh environment in which they live, fierce competition for the scant resources leads to frequent and sometimes violent disputes over grazing grounds and sources of water.

The Afar
The Afar, formerly also known as the Danakils, are a Cushitic people inhabiting the famous Dankalia region, which stretches across Ethiopia's east, Djibouti's west and into Eritrea's southeast. It is considered one of the most inhospitable environments in the world. The people are famously belligerent and proud, and in the past won social prestige for themselves and their clan through the murder and castration of a member of an opposing tribe (see the boxed text 'The Dreaded Danakils' in the Eastern Ethiopia chapter). For more information on the Afars and Somalis, see the special section 'A Museum of Peoples'.

The Sidama
The Sidama, a heterogeneous Cushitic people, originate from the southwest, and can be divided into five different groups: the Sidama proper, the Derasa, Hadiya, Kambata and Alaba. Most Sidama are farmers who cultivate cereals, tobacco, *enset* and coffee. The majority are animists and many ancient beliefs persist, including a belief in the reverence of spirits. Pythons are believed to be reincarnations of ancestors and are sometime kept in houses as pets. The Sidama social organisation, like the *gada* system of the Oromo, is based on an age-group system.

---

six other universities have opened around the country (Alemaya in the east, Bahar Dar and Mekele in the north, Debub in the south and Jimma in the west). Additionally, 12 private institutions of higher learning are now accredited by the Ministry of Education.

Many better-off Ethiopians (both boys and girls) go abroad for secondary education, particularly to Europe, Canada and the US, traditionally returning and joining the state's civil service or becoming part of the new breed of entrepreneurs.

Where previously Amharic (the language of the historically dominant ethnic group) was compulsory in schools, regions are now free to teach children in their own ethnic languages. Whilst the theory is welcomed by the majority, some claim that the practice is likely to hinder children rather than help them in the long term (such as when seeking employment outside their home regions). English is taught in secondary schools and is being accorded increasing importance.

See also the Language chapter, and under Books in Facts for the Visitor.

ARTS
Encompassed on all sides by the enemies of their religion, the Aethiopians slept near a thousand years, forgetful of the world, by whom they were forgotten.
Edward Gibbon, *The History of the Decline and Fall of the Roman Empire,* **1776–88**

More than perhaps any other country in sub-Saharan Africa, Ethiopia is known for its ancient and rich culture. Furthermore, as almost the only country on the continent to escape colonialism, its culture has been less exposed to modern outside influence.

The development of Ethiopia's culture has been profoundly influenced by three things: the dominance of the Amhara people, the country's historical, geographical and political isolation, and by its nature as an enclave of Christianity within a wholly Islamic area (though five strong sultanates did exist in Ethiopia in the 9th century).

Dominating the country's history since 1270, as well as its politics and society, the Amhara have imposed their own language and their own culture on the country. All but one of the Ethiopian emperors (Yohannes) were wholly or largely Amhara, and it was under their aegis that the country's most famous monuments were built.

The church – traditionally enjoying almost as much authority as the state – is responsible both for inspiring Ethiopia's art forms and stifling them with its great conservatism and rigorous adherence to convention.

Firmly moulded by the church, some Ethiopian art has been accused of 'sterility', and lack of innovation. However, there is much in Ethiopian art that is both original and innovative.

Long neglected and ignored, the cultural contributions of Ethiopia's other ethnic groups are only now receiving due credit and attention. Their contribution to dance, for example, and to the country's vast and rich oral literary tradition is very significant.

For further information on arts, see also the National Museum and the Ethnological Museum in the Addis Ababa chapter as well as the boxed text: 'Oral Literature - Tales Tall & True' later in this chapter.

Dance

Dance forms an extremely important part of the lives of most Ethiopians, and almost every ethnic group has its own distinct variety. Although the *iskista* (see boxed text 'Dancing the Iskista') movement is the best known, there are myriad others.

Dance traditionally serves a variety of important social purposes: from celebrating religious festivities (such as the *shibsheba* or priestly dance), to celebrating social occasions such as weddings and funerals and, in the past, to motivating warriors before departing for battle.

Still found in rural areas are dances in praise of nature, such as after a good harvest or when new sources of water are discovered, and dances that allow the young 'warriors' to show off their agility and athleticism. Look out for the *fukara* or 'boasting' dance, which is often performed at public festivals. A leftover from less-peaceful times, it involves a man holding a spear, stick or rifle horizontally above his shoulders while moving his head from side to side and shouting defiantly at the 'enemy'.

Among the tribes of the Omo Valley in the south, many dances incorporate jumping and leaping up and down, a little like the dances of the Maasai of Kenya. All dancing is in essence a social, communal activity, and you'll often be expected to join in. If you do give it a go, you'll win a lot of friends! Note also that declining to dance can infer a slight.

Music

Amharic traditional music consists largely of a continual repetition of a series of limited musical themes. However, the music was designed to suit the subject matter and occasion – usually solemn religious rites and, though simple, it can be very beautiful. With the exception of the music of the Hararis, traditional Ethiopian music is usually pentatonic.

Church Music Yared the Deacon is traditionally credited with inventing church music, with the introduction in the 6th century of a system of musical notation.

Church music known as *aquaquam* uses just the drum, in particular the *kabaro*, as well as the *tsinatseil* or sistrum, a kind of sophisticated rattle, thought to be directly descended from an ancient Egyptian instrument used in the worship of Isis. Only percussion instruments are used since their function is to mark the beat for chanting and dancing. The *maquamia* (prayer stick) also plays an essential role in church ceremony and, with hand-clapping, is used to mark time. Very occasionally a *meleket* or trumpet is used, such as to lead processions.

Dancing the Iskista

When dancing the famous *iskista*, the shoulders are juddered up and down, backwards and forwards, in a careful rhythm, while the hips and legs are kept motionless. Sometimes the motion is accompanied by a sharp intake of breath, making a sound like the word 'iskista', or alternatively by a *zefen*, a loud, high-pitched and strident folk song. If you're not in practice, the dance is surprisingly strenuous!

You'll get plenty of opportunities to hear church music in Ethiopia. In the solemn and sacred atmosphere of the old churches, with the colour of the priestly robes, and the heady perfume of incense, it can be quite mesmerising.

Secular Music Strongly influenced by church music, secular music usually combines song and dance, emphasises rhythm, and often blends both African and Asian elements. The music of the Amharas and Tigrayans in the highlands, as well as that of the peoples living near the Sudanese border, is much influenced by Arab music, and is very strident and emotive.

Wind as well as percussion instruments are used for secular music. The *begenna* is a type of harp similar to that played by the ancient Greeks and Romans. The most popular instrument in the country is the *krar*, a kind of five or six-stringed lyre, which is often heard at weddings, or to attract customers to traditional pubs or bars. The *masenko* is a single-stringed fiddle and is the instrument of the *azmaris* or wandering minstrels (see the boxed text 'Mincing Minstrels' in the Addis Ababa chapter).

In the highlands, particularly the Simien and Bale Mountains, shepherd boys can be found with reed flutes. The *washint* is about 50cm long, with four holes, and makes a bubbling sound which is said to imitate running water. It is supposed to keep the herds close by and to have a calming effect on the animals.

Modern composers and performers include Tesfaye Lemma, Mulaku Astatike and Tefera Abunewold.

Song Traditionally passed down from generation to generation, every ethnic group has their own repertoire of songs, from *musho* (household songs) and *lekso* (laments for the dead) to war songs, hunting songs and lullabies for the cradle and caravan.

Ethiopian male singing in the highlands is often in falsetto. The most characteristic element of female singing is the high-pitched trilling – a kind of tremulous and vibrating ululation (again, similar to that heard in the Arab world), which can be heard on solemn, religious occasions.

Modern, traditional singers to look out for include Habtemikael Demissie, Yirga Dubale, Tadesse Alemu and the female singer Maritu Legeese.

Modern Music Ethiopian modern music is both diverse and affected by outside influences, and ranges from classical Amharic to jazz and blues. Modern classical singers and musicians include the late Assefa Abate, Kassa Tessema and the female vocalist, Asnakech Worku. The latter two are known for their singing and *krar* playing. Girma Achanmyeleh, who studied in England, is known for his piano playing. The composer Mulatu Astatike is well known for his jazz.

Amharic popular music boasts a great following with the young. Unlike many other African countries, it is generally much preferred to the Western variety, and can be heard in all the bars and discos of the larger towns. For visitors, it can take a little time to get used to, particularly when played at full volume through unsympathetic speakers on buses.

The most famous Ethiopian pop singers have huge followings both in Ethiopia and among the expat populations abroad. Many record and live or spend time in America. Among the best known (and those to listen out for) are Ephrem Tamiru, Tsehaye Yohannes, Berhane Haile, Argaw Bedasso and Ali Bira, as well as the old-timers Tilahun Gessesse and Mohammed Ahmud. Particularly popular at the time of writing were Tewodros Tadesse (also known as 'Teddy', who incorporates Reggae) and Neway Debebe.

Among the female vocalists are Aster Aweke, Chachi Tadesse and a current favourite, Ejigaheyehu Shibabaw (popularly known as 'Gigi'). Other up and coming singers to keep an ear out for include Tewedros Kassahun, Gossaye Alemayehu, and Alemayehu Hirpo.

Literature

Inscriptions in Ge'ez (the ancestor of modern Amharic) date from Aksumite times. During the Aksumite period, the Bible was translated from Greek into Ge'ez.

The year 1270 is considered to mark the golden age of Ge'ez literature, in which many works were translated from Arabic, as well as much original writing produced. It is thought that in the early 14th century the Kebra Negast was written.

During the Muslim–Christian wars of the 16th century, book production ground to a halt and a huge amount of literature was destroyed. By the 17th century Ge'ez was in decline as a literary language and had long ceased to serve as the vernacular.

Amharic, today the official language of Ethiopia, is the national language of the

Kebra Negast

Written during the 14th century by an unknown author(s), the *Kebra Negast* or Glory of Kings, is considered Ethiopia's great national epic. But it is more than a literary work – like the Quran to Muslims or the Old Testament to the Jews: it is a repository of Ethiopian national, religious and cultural sentiment.

Of the collection of legends, the story of Solomon and Sheba is the most important. Though based on a biblical passage in the Book of Kings, the Ethiopian version goes much further, claiming not only that Sheba (known as Makeda) was Ethiopian, but that she had a son by Solomon. Menelik, their offspring, is then said to have later stolen the Ark of the Covenant from Jerusalem and taken it to Ethiopia (where it apparently resides to this day in Aksum; see the boxed text 'The Ark of the Covenant' later in this chapter).

The epic is notoriously shrouded in mystery – perhaps deliberately so. It may even represent a kind of massive propaganda stunt to legitimise the rule of the so-called 'Solomonic kings', who came to power in the 13th century and who, the book claims, were direct descendants of the kings of Israel.

Amharas. It was Emperor Tewodros who first gave encouragement to the local language in an attempt to promote national unity. The chronicles of his reign were written in Amharic. In a continuation of the trend begun in the 14th century, even during the days of Haile Selassie, the last emperor, many compositions and poetic laudatory songs were written to praise the ruler's qualities and munificence.

Under the Derg, both writing and writers were suppressed. Be'alu Girma is a well-known example of one of the many artists who disappeared at the hands of the Derg.

See also under 'Books' in the Facts for the Visitor chapter for recommended books on Ethiopian arts.

Poetry Written in Amharic as well as other Ethiopian languages, poetry, along with dance and music, is used on many religious and social occasions, such as weddings or funerals. Rhymed verse is almost always chanted or sung in consonance with the rhythm of music.

Poetry places great stress on meaning, metaphor and allusion. In Ge'ez poetry, the religious allusions demand an in-depth knowledge of Ethiopian religious legends and the Bible.

Folk Literature Perhaps the source of the greatest originality and creativity is the vast folk literature of Ethiopia – most of it in oral form and existing in all languages and dialects. It encompasses everything from proverbs, tales and riddles, to magic spells and prophetic statements.

Theatre

Ethiopia boasts one of the most ancient, prolific and flourishing theatrical traditions in Africa. Addis Ababa is home to no less than five state-owned theatre companies, and state-supported *kinet* (performance arts) groups are found throughout the regions. The University of Addis Ababa also has a special drama department.

Ethiopian theatre has also played an important part in the country's history. Because Ethiopian theatre is written mainly in Amharic, however, it is practically unknown outside the country. Having largely resisted European influence, it has also preserved its own very local flavour and outlook.

Ethiopian Eloquence

The Amharas, like the ancient Romans, place great value on eloquence. Considered the mark of a cultured and refined man, eloquence cannot, unlike other status symbols, be bought. A good speaker employs clear and measured expression, and makes ample use of metaphor, allusion and double meaning – a kind of literary gymnastics.

Ambiguity, thought to originate from centuries of political instability and courtly intrigue, has become an art in itself and is valued above all. The skilled speaker is said to be able to answer any question put to them in the most eloquent and beautiful, but entirely vague, manner possible. It is also said that a litigant can win a point or even a legal case with an apt poetic reference or witty innuendo.

The Ethiopian love of wordplay can be seen today in the innumerable and often weird and wonderful marketing slogans and quips of travel agencies, businesses and even banks. Keep a look out for them.

Oral Literature - Tales Tall & True

Every time an old person passes away, it's as if a whole library were lost.

Ethiopian–Somali saying

In the West, culture is usually defined in terms of grandiose monuments, works of art and sophisticated customs. In some countries, however, and particularly where the climate dictates a nomadic existence for its people, culture manifests itself not in enduring buildings and great writings, but in the spoken word, passed down from generation to generation.

Many languages in Africa are in the process of disappearing along with the cultures that support them. And while vast amounts of time, effort and money continue to be invested in excavating tangible evidence of past civilisations, the intangible evidence – the oral patrimony, which is just as important and certainly as fragile – is allowed to disappear forever.

The oral tradition of many African societies is rich, and particularly so in East Africa, including Ethiopia and Eritrea. Here, literally thousands of proverbs, maxims and tales are in circulation, having been told and retold for centuries by nomads, cattle herders and traders.

Among the nomadic people of East Africa, the tale serves as a kind of bedtime story. After the heat and work of the day, when the animals have been fed, watered and safely penned, families gather around the fire outside the tent. Storytellers are usually the older members of the family; among the Ethiopian Somalis, it is the grandmother who plays the part of narrator.

The tales are told to teach as well as to entertain. Children are taught not only morals and the difference between right and wrong, but useful lessons about the world they live in, and about human nature. The stories teach children to listen, to concentrate and to make judgements based on the dialogue of the characters, as the story unfolds. It encourages them to think and to analyse, and it develops their power of memory.

Tales also serve the adult population. Sometimes they are employed to clarify a situation, to offer advice tactfully to a friend, or to alert someone diplomatically to trouble or to wrongdoing. Like poetry, the tale can express a complex idea or situation economically and simply. The tale has also been used to attack latently corrupt leaders or governments without fear of libel or persecution.

In Ethiopia, there is said to be a tale for every situation (see the boxed text 'Ethiopian Eloquence' earlier in this chapter). Travellers will be surprised how often the locals resort to proverbs, maxims or stories during the course of normal conversation. It is said that the first Ethiopian–Somali proverb of all is: *While a man may tell fibs, he may never tell false proverbs*.

Unlike Western tales, which are often sentimentalised (particularly where animals are involved), these stories are real, objective, often bloody and brutal. There are few Mickey Mouses and Bambis to be found in the tales of the Horn: the stories teach lessons of survival in a hostile, competitive environment where resources are scarce and life is difficult.

Ethiopian theatrical conventions include minimal drama, sparse characterisation (with actors often serving as symbols) and plenty of extended speeches. Verse form is often used still and rhetoric remains a very important element of Ethiopian plays. Audiences tend to be participatory. Modern playwrights include Ayalneh Mulatu.

In more recent years, a new art form has emerged: the circus. A couple have even manage to establish international names for themselves and have gone on tour.

Architecture

Ethiopia boasts some remarkable architecture. Though some monuments – such as the castles of Gonder – show foreign influence, earlier building styles, such as those developed during the Aksumite period, are believed to be wholly indigenous, and are of a high technical standard.

Ethiopia's monumental architecture is almost wholly religious. Since the Ethiopian monarchs had no permanent capital (except during the Lalibela and Gonder periods), few royal palaces were built.

The 'Aksumite style' of stone masonry is Ethiopia's most famous building style. Walls were constructed with field stones set in mortar, along with sometimes finely dressed corner stones. In between came alternating layers of stone and timber, recessed then

Iluminated Manuscripts

Without doubt illuminated manuscripts represent one of Ethiopia's greatest artistic achievements. The best quality manuscripts were created by monks and priests in the 14th and 15th centuries. The kings, the court and the largest and wealthiest churches and monasteries were the main patrons. The manuscripts were characterised by beautifully shaped letters, attention to minute detail, and elaborate ornamentation. Pictures included in the text brought it to life and made it more comprehensible for the uneducated or illiterate.

Bindings consisted of thick wooden boards often covered with tooled leather. The volume was then placed into a case with straps made of rough hides so that it could be slung over a shoulder. Made of goatskin, some demanded the hides of up to 150 animals.

On the blank pages at the beginning or at the end of the volume, look out for the formulae *fatina bere* (literally 'trial of the pen') or *bere' sanay* (literally 'a fine pen'), as the scribes tried out their reeds. Some are also dated and contain a short blessing for the owner as well as the scribe.

Unfortunately, huge numbers of manuscripts have been pillaged from Ethiopia by soldiers, travellers and explorers. Sadly, many manuscripts did not survive the mass destruction of churches by the Muslims and Dervishes in the early 16th and late 19th centuries respectively – few date prior to the 14th century.

Don't miss the chance to see these illuminated manuscripts – the priests of the churches are usually happy to show off their 'treasures'.

projected, and with protruding ends of round timber beams, known as 'monkey heads'. The latter are even symbolically carved into the great obelisks. The Aksumites were undoubtedly master masons.

The Aksumite style is additionally seen in some of the early medieval churches such as Debre Damo, and the motifs continue to inspire modern design today, influencing new hotel and restaurant design. Keep an eye out for it.

Monuments The monolithic granite stelae of the pre-Aksum and Aksumite period are without doubt Ethiopia's most extraordinary architectural achievement. For more information, see the boxed text 'A Quick Guide to Aksum's Stelae' in the Northern Ethiopia chapter.

Traditional Churches Ethiopia has been called a country of churches. Churches are spread all over the landscape and are most often perched upon hills, dominating community life physically and psychologically. Indeed, *debre* (meaning 'mountain' in Ge'ez) often prefixes the names of monasteries.

Churches vary in size and shape, from small and round (most common) to large rectangular and octagonal buildings. Famous rectangular churches include the very beautiful church at Debre Damo and the old church of St Mary of Zion at Aksum.

Ethiopian round churches have several entrances. The eastern entrance leads to the *maqdas*, the Holy of Holies, and is reserved exclusively for the priests. It is here that the sacred *tabot* (the Ark of the Covenant) rests. The southern entrance is reserved for women, the northern one for men. The western entrance can be used by both sexes, but inside, the men go to the left (north) and the women to the right (south).

Rock-Hewn Churches The churches of Lalibela are Ethiopia's most famous rock-hewn churches. Dating from the Zagwe period (around the 12th century) they are considered among the finest early Christian architecture in the world.

The churches are unique in that many stand completely free from the rock – unlike the Coptic churches of Egypt. The buildings show extraordinary technical skill in the use of line, proportion and decoration, and in the remarkable variety of styles. Some of the churches are built in the shape of a cross; others are rectangular.

Lalibela's churches represent the zenith of a rock-hewing tradition that probably predates Christianity, and has resulted in nearly 400 churches across the country. For more information see Lalibela in the Northern Ethiopia chapter.

The rock-hewn churches of the Tigray region (see also the Northern Ethiopia chapter), though less famous and spectacular, are no less remarkable. Many almost certainly pre-date Lalibela and represent the beginning of the rock-hewing tradition.

Castles of Gonder The town of Gonder and its imperial enclosure represent another peak in Ethiopian architectural achievement.

Although Portuguese, Moorish and Indian influences are all evident, the castles are nevertheless a peculiarly Ethiopian synthesis. Some have windows decorated with red volcanic tuff, and barrel- or egg-shaped domes. See Gonder in the Northern Ethiopia chapter.

Painting

Ethiopian painting is largely limited to religious subjects – particularly the life of Christ and the saints. Every church in Ethiopia is decorated with abundant and colourful murals, frescos or paintings (see the boxed text 'Know Your Ethiopian Saints' in the Northern Ethiopia chapter).

Much Ethiopian painting is characterised by a kind of naive realism. Everything is expressed with vigour and directness using bold colour, strong line and stylised proportions and perspective. Like the stained glass windows in European Gothic churches, the paintings served a very important purpose: to instruct, inspire and instil awe in the illiterate and uneducated.

Though some modern artists (particularly painters of religious and some secular work) continue in the old tradition (or incorporate ancient motifs such as that of the Aksumite stelae), many artists have developed their own style. Borrowing freely from the past, but no longer constrained by it, modern Ethiopian painting shows greater originality of expression and, like theatre, is a flourishing medium.

Until recently, the artist was considered a mere craftsmen, but as Western influence has spread the artist has attained a more professional standing, and works of art can be found for sale not only in modern art galleries, and cultural institute exhibitions, but also in hotels and restaurants.

Young artists emerge annually from the Fine Arts School, now part of Addis Ababa University. Among the many to look out for are the painters Behailu Bezabeh, an acute observer of everyday life in the capital; Daniel Taye, who is known for his darker more disturbing images; Geta Makonnen, whose artwork addresses social issues; and the sculptor Bekele Makonnen, with his thought-provoking installations revolving around moral and social values.

Tigist Hailegabreal is a versatile young woman artist who is concerned with women's issues such as prostitution and violence against women.

The vast stained-glass window in Africa Hall in Addis Ababa is the work of one of Africa's best-known painters, Afewerk Tekle. If you're curious as to the identification of the painter of the many poster reproductions stuck up in hotels, restaurants and cafés around the country, it's almost certainly him (see the boxed text 'Afewerk Tekle' in the Addis Ababa chapter).

SOCIETY & CONDUCT

Most Ethiopians live with their families until marriage.

Marriages are usually celebrated with several days of feasting, which can place a huge

The Tabot & The Ark of the Covenant

According to the old Ethiopian tradition, the Ark of the Covenant was carried off from Jerusalem and brought to Ethiopia in the first millennium BC, where it has remained ever since.

Today, every Ethiopian church has a replica of the Ark (or more precisely the Tablets of Law that are housed in the Ark) known as the *tabot*. Kept safe in the inner sanctuary, it is the single most important element of the church, and gives the building its sanctity (rather as the tabernacle does in the Roman Catholic church).

During important religious festivals, the *tabot* is carried in solemn processions, accompanied by singing, dancing, the beating of staffs or prayer sticks, the rattling of the sistrum and the beating of drums. It is a scene that could have come straight out of the Old Testament.

They carried the Ark of God on a new cart...David and all the house of Israel were dancing before the Lord with all their might, with songs and lyres and harps and tambourines and castanets and cymbals.

2 Sam. vi. 3-5

financial burden on the two families (a dowry can range anywhere between Birr3000 and Birr50,000). After marriage, the couple usually join the household of the husband's parents. After a couple of years, they will request a plot of land from the village on which to build their own house. January is a very popular month for weddings, when the harvest is over, the weather is dry, and there are no fasting periods to restrict the wedding feasts.

Divorce is still relatively easy in Ethiopia and marriage can be dissolved at the request of either party – usually adultery is given as justification. In theory, each partner retains the property he or she brought into the marriage, though sometimes allowances are made for the 'wronged' partner.

Legally, women in Ethiopia enjoy a relatively equitable position compared to some African countries.

See also Women Travellers and Social Graces in the Facts for the Visitor chapter.

RELIGION
Faith is an extremely important part of an Ethiopian's life. Christian Ethiopians bring God into everyday conversation just as much as their Muslim counterparts who will say 'thanks be to God', 'God willing', 'God forbid' etc. Some Ethiopians thank God in speeches or include Him in the list of acknowledgments in books.

Pre-Christianity
It is thought that serpents were worshipped in earliest Aksum. Later, such beliefs were replaced by the deification of the sun, moon and stars as practised in southern Arabia. The pantheon also included Astar, an Arabian equivalent of Zeus, the Greek king of the gods. Mahrem, like Ares, was the god of war, and Baher, like Poseidon, the god of the sea. Quite contrary to the Graeco-Roman mythology, the sun was regarded as female, the moon as male.

The pre-Christian symbols of the sun and crescent moon can be seen on the early Aksumite coins and on the famous stele at Metera in Eritrea. The moon remains an important element in Ethiopian folk culture. When Christianity was adopted as the Aksumite state's official religion early in the 4th century, these gods were soon forgotten.

Christianity
Although the Ethiopian population is split fairly evenly between Muslims (35%) and Christians (45%), it is Orthodox Christianity that has traditionally dominated the country's past.

The official religion of the imperial court right up until Emperor Haile Selassie was deposed in 1974, Orthodox Christianity has heavily influenced the political, social and cultural life of the highlands. Today, the church continues to carry great clout among the Ethiopian people and is regarded as the great guardian and repository of the ancient Ethiopian traditions, directly inherited from Aksum.

Ethiopia's connection with Christianity is an ancient and distinguished one. It was the first country (after only Armenia) to adopt Christianity as its state religion.

Christianity in the past also served as Ethiopia's only true unifying factor, although, by the same measure, it has also legitimised the oppression of the people by its rulers.

Ethiopian Orthodox Christianity is thought to have its roots in Judaism – parts of the country were Judaic before conversion to Christianity. This would explain many of the Judaic elements in the church, such as the food restrictions, including the way animals are slaughtered. Even the layout of the traditional round church is considered Hebrew in origin. Ancient Semitic and pagan elements also persist.

The church plays an important part in daily life, regulating many social and even dietary traditions – such as the customary Wednesday and Friday fasts, as well as the fasts during Lent, Advent and *Kweskwam* (40 days preceding the feast of the flight to Egypt). There are also a very large number of feast days, of which 33 days honour the Virgin Mary alone.

Circumcision is generally practised on boys, marriage is celebrated in the presence of a priest, and confession is usually only made during a grave illness. Church services normally take place on Sunday morning at 6 am. If you want to attend an Ethiopian service, you might want to bring a 'prayer stick' as the locals do. With the absence of any pews or stools, it is customary to lean on one or stand. As services last at least two hours, you may need one!

Islam
Ethiopia's connection with Islam is as distinguished as its connection with Christianity (see History earlier in this chapter). It is also one of the very few countries where, in the early

morning, the sound of Christian bells follow hot on the heels of the Muslim call to prayer.

Though bloody wars were fought in the past, Ethiopia's Christian and Muslim inhabitants co-exist in harmony. However, be aware (if with Ethiopian friends) that because of dietary taboos, some Christians can't eat in Muslim restaurants and vice versa.

Fundamentalism is very rare in Ethiopia, and it is uncommon to see women wearing the *hijab* (veil), though the majority wear either headscarves or *shalmas* (a gauze-thin length of fabric draped around the head, shoulders and torso).

Ethiopia's oldest and holiest mosque is that at Negash, north of Wukro in Tigray, believed to date originally from the 8th century. The shrine of Sheikh Hussein in the Bale region is also greatly venerated and attracts national and international pilgrims.

The most famous Muslim city is the walled city of Harar. It is also an important Islamic centre in its own right and is home to an astonishing number of shrines and mosques. In the past, it was renowned as a centre of learning.

Most Muslims inhabit the eastern, southern and western lowlands, but there are also significant populations in the country's predominantly Christian towns, including Addis Ababa.

Lately, there appears to be a fashion for the sponsorship of mosque construction spreading across the country. The patrons are wealthy Saudis, apparently keen to secure their space in heaven. All over Ethiopia, you'll see new mosques carving up the skylines.

The Falashas

Falashas (Ethiopian Jews) have inhabited Ethiopia since pre-Christian times. Despite actively engaging over the years in wars to defend their independence and freedom, few now remain: war, some persecution and emigration in the latter part of the 20th century have greatly reduced their numbers.

Though discriminated against and denied land as craftsmen (as were Christian and Muslim), they were not generally as persecuted in Ethiopia as they were elsewhere. Indeed, many Ethiopians believe they are themselves of Jewish descent.

Tiny populations of *Falashas* remain north of Lake Tana in the northwest; their beliefs combine a fascinating mixture of Judaism, indigenous beliefs and Christianity

Traditional African Beliefs

Traditional African beliefs are still quite commonly found in Ethiopia, particularly among the country's Cushitic peoples, especially in the lowland areas of the west and south (see also the boxed text 'Peoples of Ethiopia' earlier in this chapter). An estimated 11% of the population follows traditional African beliefs.

These range from animism (associated with trees, springs, mountains and stones etc) to totemism (found among the Konso), in which animals are ritually slaughtered and then consumed by the people. Elements of ancestor worship are still found among the Afar. The Oromo traditionally believe in a supreme celestial deity known as Wak, whose eye is the sun.

BIRDS OF ETHIOPIA

The birds of Ethiopia are so numerous, so diverse and so colourful that even the die-hard nonbirder will find it difficult, given time, not to become hooked. To date, 862 species have been recorded (compared with just 250 in the UK), and although South Africa claims more species, Ethiopia boasts the special distinction of possessing a high number of endemics (birds found only in that country). Of these, at least 17 are found only in Ethiopia and at least 13 are semi-endemic, shared only with Eritrea.

Other special bonuses of birding in Ethiopia include the relative ease of spotting many of the species (including at least 20 of the endemics or semi-endemics), the option of birding on foot (due to the scarcity of dangerous animals), and the small number of tourists found at the sites.

The best time to visit Ethiopia for birding is between November and February; July and August are when the heaviest rain falls on the central plateau. The most likely time to spot birds is from dawn to 11am and from 5pm to dusk, although birds can be seen throughout the day.

Habitats

One of the reasons for the number and diversity of Ethiopian birds is the number and diversity of Ethiopian habitats. The Great Rift Valley, with its large freshwater and saline lakes, runs through the central highlands of Ethiopia from north to south. The highlands, which rise to 4620m, support montane forest, juniper woodland, crags and escarpments, and grassland.

Elsewhere, crater lakes and acacia savanna are found, and to the east of the highlands are large areas of semidesert. For more information on birds to look for in particular habitats, see Major Habitats under Flora & Fauna in the Facts about Ethiopia chapter.

Where to See Birds

For more details on the sites and bird species, refer to the relevant sections of this book.

In & Around Addis Ababa Visitors can expect to see at least eight endemics or semi-endemics, such as the black-winged lovebird.

FRANCES LINZEE GORDON

Left: Pelicans at dusk, Abiyata-Shala NP

Northern Ethiopia The seasonally wet highland grassland of the Sululta Plains support a good number of waders including the black-winged lapwing. The Blue Nile gorges around Debre Libanos are home to at least seven endemics or semi-endemics, such as Rueppell's chat and banded barbet. Bahar Dar on the shores of Lake Tana boast good birdlife, as do the Blue Nile Falls (yellow-fronted parrot). The crags and escarpments of the Simien Mountains are home to the lammergeyer and it accidental companion, the thick-billed raven.

Eastern Ethiopia The Akaki wetlands are home to a good variety of waders and ducks; birds seen include the red-chested wheatear and wattled ibis. Debre Zeyit's crater lakes are also good; the white-winged chat is sometimes spotted here. The little village of Ankober is home to the very localised Ankober serin (first recorded in 1976). Awash National Park is one of the best places for birding in Ethiopia. In the Dire Dawa-Harar area, an extra bonus is that much avifauna overlaps with species from the Ogaden area of southeast Ethiopia (unsafe for travellers at the time of writing).

Southern Ethiopia The Rift Valley lakes are home to large numbers of Palaearctic waders and waterfowl and a few semi-endemics such as the brown sawwing. Lake Ziway and Lake Langano are also good. The saline waters of Lake Abiata and Lake Shala are known feeding and nesting grounds of good numbers of greater and lesser flamingos and great white pelicans. Lake Awasa also attracts a good variety including the African pygmy-goose. Lakes Chamo and Abaya are home to a good range of birds including weavers, sunbirds and waxbills. The thickly-forested

FRANCES LINZEE GORDON

hills of Wondo Genet are home to an excellent variety of birds including many semi-endemics such as the Abyssinian slaty flycatcher. The Bale Mountains Park is famous as the home of a large number of endemics and semi-endemics (16 in total) including the Abyssinian longclaw and Abyssinian catbird, and is a must for birders. The areas around Negele, Yabelo and Bale, south of the Bale Mountains, are home to some of Ethiopia's rarest endemics including the elusive and enigmatic Prince Ruspoli's turaco (recently spotted in the Arero forest, east of Yabelo, near the Gewale river).

Right: Yellow-billed stork and sacred ibis on Lake Ziway

Western Ethiopia Woodpeckers, warblers, hoopoes and various birds of prey inhabit the Jimma-Bonga montane forests. The Gefersa Reservoir is good for water fowl and the endemic blue-winged goose.

Bird Species

Of the 10 bird families endemic to the African mainland, eight are represented in Ethiopia; only rockfowl and sugarbirds are absent. Families that are particularly well represented are **falcons**, **francolins**, **bustards** and **larks**.

During the northern winter, some 200 species of Palaearctic migrants cross into Ethiopia from Europe and Asia, via the Sahara Desert, Arabian Peninsula and Red Sea. These migrants add significantly to the already abundant African resident and intra-African migrant populations.

Of the 862 species recorded in Ethiopia, 19 are considered threatened, and five are classified as near-threatened.

If you are interested in tape or CD recordings of Ethiopian birds (UK£8.50), contact **Wildsounds** (☎ *01263-741100*; W *www.wild sounds.com)* in the UK. For books on birds in Ethiopia, see Books in the Facts for the Visitor chapter and Bookshops in the Addis Ababa chapter.

Endemics of Ethiopia Ethiopia boasts more endemic and semi-endemic species in mainland Africa than any other country except South Africa. The following is a list of Ethiopia's endemics (though other may soon join the list). Keep an eye out for them.

• Abyssinian catbird *(Parophasma galinieri)*
• Abyssinian longclaw *(Macronyx flavicollis)*
• Ankober seedeater or serin *(Serinus ankoberensis)*
• Black-headed siskin *(Serinus nigriceps)*
• Degodi lark *(Mirafra degodiensis)*
• Golden-backed or Abyssinian woodpecker *(Dendropicos abyssinicus)*
• Harwood's francolin *(Francolinus hardwoodi)*
• Nechisar nightjar *(Caprimulgus nechisarensis)*
• Prince Ruspoli's Turaco *(Tauraco ruspolii)*
• Salvadori's seedeater or serin *(Serinus xantholaema)*
• Sidamo long-clawed lark *(Heteromirafra sidamoensis)*
• Spot-breasted plover *(Vanellus melanocephalus)*
• Stresemann's or Abyssinian bush crow *(Zavattariornis stresemanni)*
• White-tailed swallow *(Hirundo megaensis)*
• White-throated seedeater *(Serinus xanthopygius)*
• Yellow-fronted parrot *(Poicephalus flavifrons)*
• Yellow-throated seedeater or serin *(Serinus flavigula)*

FRANCES LINZEE GORDON

Left: A pied kingfisher hovering above Lake Chamo.

The Strange Case of the Vanishing Turaco

In a remote patch in the deep south of Ethiopia lives one of the country's rarest, most beautiful and most enigmatic birds – the Prince Ruspoli's turaco, first introduced to the world in the early 1890s. It was 'collected' by an Italian prince (who gave his name to the bird) as he explored the dense juniper forests of southern Ethiopia.

Unfortunately, the intrepid prince failed to make a record of his find, and when he was killed shortly afterwards near Lake Abaya following 'an encounter with an elephant', all hope of locating the species seemed to die with him.

In subsequent years, other explorers searched in vain for the bird. None were successful until the turaco finally reappeared in the 1940s. Just three specimens were obtained, then the turaco disappeared again. It was not until the early 1970s that the bird was rediscovered.

To this day, the turaco is considered Ethiopia's most elusive endemic bird. Almost nothing is known about the species, and its nest and eggs have never been seen, and it is registered in the *Red Book* of 'very endangered species of the world'.

However, recent sightings in the Arero forest, east of Yabelo, around the Gewale river off the Dola-Mena–Negele Borena road, suggest that the bird may not, after all, be as elusive as it would have us believe.

Facts for the Visitor

SUGGESTED ITINERARIES

Ethiopia's attractions are diverse – from fascinating history to challenging trekking and serious birding! In terms of tourism and travel, the country can usefully be divided into four main parts, north, south, west and east, arranged around Addis Ababa, the capital.

In a nutshell, the north is home to the major historic sites; the south is home to some of the best birding and wildlife, as well as some of the more interesting tribal groups; the west makes for good off-the-beaten-track exploration; and the east boasts the old Muslim town of Harar.

Addis Ababa, roughly at the centre of the country, lies at the centre of the air, rail and road transportation network. Well supplied with hotels and restaurants of all categories, it makes a good springboard for travel to the regions surrounding it, which are otherwise as good as separated from one another. Addis Ababa, however, is also worth a couple of days, with several good museums and its famous outdoor market.

Given Ethiopia's size, the state of many roads, and the age of some vehicles, travelling by bus is very slow and time consuming. There are two ways of speeding up road travel: by taking a couple of (very reasonably priced) domestic flights, which can cut out whole days on the road, or (the more expensive option) renting your own vehicle. Note that a 4WD is required for most places outside Addis Ababa.

Historic Sites

Ethiopia's best-known travellers' trail is the so-called **historical route**, which loops through northern Ethiopia. The circuit includes all of the most famous historical and religious sites, including 'the big four': Bahar Dar, Aksum, Gonder and Lalibela. A complete circuit from Addis Ababa covers over 2500km. By road, you're looking at around 10 days' travel before you've even got off the bus. To do it justice you'll need at least 15 days.

Ethiopian Airlines has flights that connect all four towns of the historic route. You could see them all, with time to visit the sites, in a week – at a push. If you have a little longer, the remoter **churches** of Lalibela are worth exploring and make terrific treks by mule or on foot. Another extension that combines

history with trekking is a visit to the **rock-hewn churches** of Tigray. You'll need to add on at least another three or four days to your itinerary. You'll also need to rent a vehicle, unless you have plenty of time. Mekele, one of the closest large towns, can be reached by bus in a day from Aksum and Ethiopian Airlines flies there.

A good compromise that balances cost and time is to use both bus and plane, taking in some scenery but not wasting too many days on the road. Bussing from Addis Ababa as far as Gonder or Aksum, then flying back to Addis Ababa via Lalibela is a good itinerary.

To the east of Addis Ababa lies the colourful and interesting Muslim town of **Harar**, which can be visited in around four days (return trip) from Addis Ababa.

Trekking, Wildlife & Natural Sites

To trek in the spectacular **Simien Mountains**, you'll need a minimum of three days. Six to eight days is better, particularly if you're planning to climb **Ras Dashen**. From Addis Ababa to Debark (which serves as a gateway to the park) by bus takes 2½ to three days. Ethiopian Airlines flies to Gonder, the closest large town.

For a combination of trekking and wildlife, the **Bale Mountains National Park** is one of the best places, particularly for viewing endemic mammals and birds. One day will give you a glimpse of the animals and birds, two will increase your chances of seeing an Ethiopian wolf, and three to four will allow a decent trek. The journey to or from Addis Ababa takes one to 1½ days by bus. Ethiopian Airlines flies to Goba, the nearest large town.

The **Awash** and **Nechisar National Parks** are also good places for wildlife and take a half/full day respectively by bus from Addis Ababa. Ethiopian Airlines flies to Arba Minch (for Nechisar).

If you're keen on birds, the Bale Mountains is a must. The **Rift Valley lakes** in the south are another good spot and are easily accessible from Addis Ababa. A couple of days would give you plenty of time there.

For natural sites, it's hard to beat the **Blue Nile Falls**, which are easily accessible from Bahar Dar in the north and can be included in the historical route. In stark contrast is the

What to Bring

The following list is Ethiopia-specific; these items are additional to the usual items recommended for travel (such as Swiss army knife, alarm clock, plastic bags, toilet paper, concentrated detergent, etc).

Clothing & Footwear

Fleece/cardigan: though warm/hot during the day, it can be cool/cold in the evenings on the high Ethiopian plateau, particularly during the rainy season.

Trousers and long-sleeved tops: shorts or tops with straps are not permitted in churches (Ethiopian women traditionally never expose their shoulder, cleavage or knees).

Flip flops: useful for hotel bathrooms, swimming pools, etc.

Luggage

Day pack: useful for long bus journeys when larger luggage is not accessible, and for short overnight/day excursions.

Electrical & Photographic Equipment

Small torch: useful for villages without electricity or for power cuts, trekking and visiting churches.

Batteries: bring for all items (they can be difficult to get in Ethiopia outside the capital and are often of poor quality).

Film: bring plenty (quality and availability are not always good).

Weather-related Products

Sun protection: hat (for site-seeing or trekking), sun cream (difficult to get outside Addis).

Water bottle: essential for trekking, walking and long bus journeys.

Small folding umbrella: useful for the odd, sudden downpour, particularly in the wet season.

Health-related Products

Mosquito repellent & insecticide: essential for the lowlands.

Personal items: adequate supplies of things like contact lens fluid, women's items, nappies, etc; hardly available in Ethiopia.

Flea powder: for beds in cheapest hotels and for socks when visiting Lalibela's churches.

Food

Sweets/biscuits/high-energy bars: good if you don't take to Ethiopian food, for vegetarians or if weak after stomach problems. Also useful for offering to fellow bus passengers, guides, etc (where sharing is considered a mark of friendship and trust).

Other Items

Pair of binoculars: recommended (even for nonbirders!) to view the stunning birds and wildlife in the parks. Compact ones (7x21) are adequate.

Ear plugs: recommended for light-sleepers or early-nighters. Ethiopian hotels (particularly cheap ones) can be very noisy.

Airline socks: or thick socks for padding about churches (where shoes have to be removed) and to protect against fleas.

Plug: water is scarce in some northern towns and access limited to certain times of the day.

Danakil Depression, one of the hottest areas on earth and home of the Afar people; you'll need your own vehicle (which can be rented from Mekele).

The little-visited **west of Ethiopia** is rich in natural beauty and is great for off-the-beaten-track exploration. To reach **Gambela National Park** in the far West by bus, you'll need around 10 days including the loop back to Addis Ababa.

Cultural Experiences

The tribal groups of the remote **Lower Omo Valley** in the south are the most popular cultural experience and are increasingly attracting tourists. Because of the remoteness of the region, they are most often visited through tours from Addis Ababa, which require a minimum of seven or eight days return.

A cheaper alternative, and one that will also save you time, is to bus or fly to Jinka, then hire a car for two or three days from there.

Public transport runs to some villages, but you'll need a lot of time and a flexible itinerary to travel in this way.

Other worthwhile cultural experiences include attending a major Ethiopian festival, or if you can't do that, visiting one of the larger markets.

PLANNING
When to Go
There's some truth in the old Ethiopian Tourism Commission slogan '13 Months of Sunshine'. Although there's a rainy season from mid-June to the end of September and light rains in March-April, sunshine is practically guaranteed.

Late September, just after the end of the rainy season is a particularly good time to visit. The country is wonderfully green, the wildflowers are stunning and there are fewer visitors at this time.

If you're trekking, camping or planning to explore the west or south, the dry season (October to May) is a better time to travel.

If you're planning a trip to the Omo Valley, you should note that the main rains occur from March to June (and the light rains in November). Many parts of the region become impassable with the rains. Note that with changing global weather patterns, seasons are less and less predictable.

Finally, it's well worth trying to coincide with one of Ethiopia's very colourful festivals (see Public Holidays & Special Events later in this chapter), particularly Timkat or Meskel. Be aware, however, that domestic flights and hotels often fill up far in advance with tour groups. From November to January (over the European and Ethiopian Christmas), airfares usually go up.

Maps
In Ethiopia, the map produced by the ETC (1987; 1:2,000,000) isn't bad, though it's a bit out of date. The map of the capital on the back is more useful. See Maps in the Addis Ababa chapter.

Of the maps currently available outside the country, the best is that produced by International Travel Maps (1998; 1:2,000,000). Though the scale is the same as that of the ETC map, it's much more up to date.

The Cartographia map of Ethiopia, Eritrea and Djibouti (1996; 1:2,500,000) comes second, and isn't a bad choice for the region.

Most major map suppliers stock maps produced outside Ethiopia, including **Stanfords** (☎ 020-7836 1321, fax 7836 0189; **W** www.stanfords.co.uk) in London.

RESPONSIBLE TOURISM
Ecotourism is a concept still little known in Ethiopia. However, some effort on the part of the traveller is a good step in the right direction. Here are a few pointers:

• Water is an extremely precious and scarce resource in some parts of Ethiopia (including the Aksum and Lalibela regions). Try not to waste it in hotels by letting taps and showers run unnecessarily.
• Support local businesses, initiative and skills by shopping at local markets, buying authentic crafts and giving to local charities.
• Resist the temptation to buy any genuinely old artefacts, such as manuscripts, scrolls and Bibles, sold in shops and by hawkers around the country. Ethiopia has already lost a vast amount of its heritage.
• Be sensitive to wildlife.
• Litter, campfires and off-road driving can harm or disturb animals and nesting birds.

See also Social Graces and Tipping later in this chapter.

An excellent organisation in the UK which can provide more information for concerned travellers is London-based **Tourism Concern** (☎ 020-7753 3330; **W** www.tourismconcern.org.uk).

Church Etiquette
Churches in Ethiopia are considered very hallowed places. The following are a few pointers when visiting a church:

• Always remove shoes before entering a church.
• Try and wear clothing that covers all parts of the body.
• Never try to enter the inner Holy of Holies, which is reserved strictly for the priests.
• Avoid smoking, eating or drinking in a church, or talking or laughing loudly.
• Be sensitive when taking photos.
• Resist the temptation to photograph old manuscripts in sunlight, even if the priests offer to move the manuscripts into the sun for you. Sunlight can cause great damage.
• During prayer time, try not to stray into the areas reserved for the opposite sex.
• A contribution to the upkeep of the church is greatly appreciated after a visit.

TOURIST OFFICES
Local Tourist Offices
The **Ethiopian Tourism Commission** *(ETC;* W *www.ethiopiatourism.com)* has a tourism office open to travellers (see the Addis Ababa chapter). Independent tourist offices can be found in the regional capitals.

Staff in all of these offices do their best to help, but often have limited experience in dealing with tourists directly (independent travel is still quite a recent thing). With a few exceptions, a special visit is not often worthwhile, and you'll leave with little more than a fistful of brochures. The best source of information is the Addis-based travel companies (though naturally they will expect to sell you something) or outside Addis, the manager of your hotel!

Tourist Offices Abroad
No national tourist office exists abroad. The Ethiopian embassies and consulates try to fill the gap, but generally just hand out the usual tourist brochures.

An active, nonpolitical organisation in the UK is the **Anglo-Ethiopian Society** *(W www .anglo-ethiopian.org; c/o 4 Gloucester Rd, London SW7 4RB)*, which aims 'to foster a knowledge and understanding of Ethiopia and its people'. Membership costs £8 annually. The society holds regular gatherings, including talks on Ethiopia. A well-stocked library on Ethiopia and Eritrea is open to members. There's a tri-annual Newsfile.

VISAS & DOCUMENTS
Passport
Carry your passport with you at all times. Ensure that it will be valid for the entire period you intend to remain overseas. If your passport is lost or stolen, immediately contact your country's representative (see Embassies & Consulates later in this chapter).

Visas
Be aware that visa regulations can change. The Ethiopian embassy in your home country is the best source of up to date information.

Currently, all visitors except Kenyan and Djiboutian nationals need visas to visit Ethiopia.

Nationals of 33 countries can obtain tourist visas on arrival at Bole International airport. These include most of Europe, the USA, Canada, Australia and New Zealand. Tour operators are also permitted to organise visas on arrival for their groups.

Some travellers may still prefer to get visas in advance from the Ethiopian embassy in their home country (see Embassies & Consulates later in this chapter), as the process upon arrival is not swift and after a night flight, can be tiresome. It also includes a trip to the bank to change money first, as visas can currently only be paid for in birr. Visas are valid from the day of arrival, not the day of issue.

Some Ethiopian embassies may require some or all of the following to accompany visa applications: an onward air ticket (or airline itinerary), a visa for the next country you're planning to visit, and proof of sufficient funds (officially a minimum of US$50 per day).

Presently, Ethiopian law allows multiple-entry visas to be issued only to those on business, those working for NGOs or those working for the government. The exception to the rule is US citizens, who benefit from a reciprocity agreement: a multiple-entry tourist or business visa is available and is valid for a period of up to 24 months.

If your country is not among those covered by the new regulation and there is no diplomatic representation, you can ask the airlines or tour operator to order you a visa upon arrival. Visas cannot be obtained on arrival without prior arrangement at immigration.

Tourist visas cost Birr315 for EU nationals, US citizens and Australians (Birr325 for business visas) and Birr140 for African nationals (Birr150 for business visas). These are valid for between one and three months, depending on the application and special requests.

Transit Visas Travellers of all nationalities can also obtain transit visas on arrival or at the embassy in your home country and are valid for a minimum of three days and maximum of seven days.

Business Visas These can be obtained in two ways: from your embassy in advance (a cover letter from your company must accompany your application), or if the business is based in Ethiopia, then an application can be lodged by the company directly with the Department of Immigration in Addis Ababa (see later). You will then be faxed a Visa Order sheet to present at immigration.

Multi-entry business visas can be obtained for up to a maximum period of six months, if you can demonstrate that your business will take you in and out of Ethiopia several times.

Visa Extensions To extend all tourist and business visas, go to the **Immigration Office** (☎ *55 38 99; PO Box 5741, Addis Ababa; open 8.30am-12.30pm & 1.30pm-5.30pm Mon-Fri)*. Visa extensions normally take 24 hours to process, though if it's urgent you can obtain an extension the same day, or even within one hour (but you'll need to show proof of 'urgency' such as air tickets, etc).

Make sure you plan your itinerary so that you're back in Addis Ababa in time to renew your visa if you need to. If this is difficult, you should come to a special agreement with immigration in advance.

In theory, visas can be extended up to a maximum of nine months, but there must be a very valid reason (such as a renewed business contract) for doing so. Note that just citing tourism is not considered a good enough excuse for extending visas by more than a couple of months in total.

If you're extending your business visa, you'll need to bring a letter from your company explaining your business and need for an extension.

If necessary, your visa can be extended up to 10 days, but do this before the expiry date of your current visa. Note that visas should not be allowed to expire before applying for a visa extension. Although you may be granted a grace period of up to 10 days, it's best not to count on it (there is a fine of over Birr200 for every month in excess of your visa).

If you're stuck somewhere or are ill, you can send a friend or colleague, or, in theory, send your application through your embassy, which should extend it on your behalf (if you have good enough reasons to persuade them).

Cautious Copies

All important documents (passport data page and visa page, credit cards, travel insurance policy, air/bus/train tickets, driving licence, etc) should be photocopied before you leave home. Leave one copy with someone at home and keep another with you, separate from the originals.

You can also store details on Lonely Planet's free online Travel Vault. Your own password-protected Travel Vault is accessible online anywhere in the world – create it at W www.ekno.lonelyplanet.com.

Travel Insurance

A travel insurance policy to cover theft, loss and above all medical problems is essential for travel in Ethiopia. A variety of policies is available. Check that the policy includes all the activities you want to do. Some specifically exclude 'dangerous activities' such as white-water rafting, rock climbing, motorcycling and diving. Sometimes even trekking is excluded.

Above all, check that the policy covers an emergency flight home, and one that pays doctors or hospitals directly, rather than you having to fork out on the spot and claim later. Doctors in Ethiopia normally expect immediate cash payment.

If you have to claim later (often within a month of your return), it's essential to keep all documentation of medical treatment.

Other Documents

A vaccination against cholera is required for anyone who has visited or transited a cholera-infected area within six days prior to arrival in Ethiopia.

If you're bringing your own car, you'll need all the appropriate documentation (see under Land in the Getting There & Away chapter). An international driving licence is required in Ethiopia.

EMBASSIES & CONSULATES
Ethiopian Embassies & Consulates Abroad

Ethiopia has diplomatic representation in the following countries:

Australia (☎ 03-9417 3419) 38 Johnston Street, Fitzroy, Victoria 3065; W www.consul.com.au /index.html
Canada (☎ 613-235 6637) Suite 208, 112 Kent St, Tower 8, Ottawa
France (☎ 01 47 83 83 95) 35 Ave Charles Floquet, 75007, Paris
Germany (☎ 30-772 060) Boothstr. 20a, 12207, Berlin
UK (☎ 020-7589 7212) 17 Prince's Gate, London, SW7 IPZ
USA (☎ 202-364 1200) 3506 International Drive, NW Washington DC 20008

Embassies & Consulates in Ethiopia

The following embassies and consulates are located in Addis Ababa. Street names are not given here, as few are used by the locals and many streets have several names. Check the main Addis Ababa map for locations of the embassies.

Australia (see Canada)
Belgium (☎ 61 18 13)
Canada (☎ 71 30 22) (also represents Australia)
Djibouti (☎ 61 30 06)
Eritrea (☎ 51 29 41) Currently closed
France (☎ 55 00 66; ⓔ amba.france@telecom .net.et)
Germany (☎ 55 04 33; ⓔ german.emb.addis@ telecom.net.et)
Italy (☎ 55 30 42; ⓔ italembadd@telecom.net.et)
Kenya (☎ 61 00 33)
Netherlands (☎ 71 11 00; ⓔ netherlands.emb@ telecom.net.et)
Somalia (☎ 71 22 11)
Somaliland (☎/fax 63 59 21, fax 62 78 47)
Spain (☎ 55 02 22; ⓔ embaespet@mail.mae.es)
Sudan (☎ 51 64 77)
UK (☎ 61 23 54; ⓔ b.emb4@telecom.net.et)
USA (☎ 55 06 66; ⓔ usembassy@telecom.net.et)

CUSTOMS
If you're bringing with you anything of value such as a video camera or laptop computer, you may be required to register it on your passport as you enter Ethiopia at immigration (to deter black market trading).

You may import two litres of spirits and 200 cigarettes or 100 cigars duty free.

Permits
Note that if you buy any souvenir that either is or looks antique, you'll need a clearance permit from the **Department of Inventory and Inspection** (☎ *11 36 84; open 8.30am-12.30pm & 1.30pm-5.30pm Mon & Wed, 8.30am-11.30am & 1.30pm-5.30pm Fri)* at the Centre for Research and Conservation of Cultural Heritage (CRCCH) of the National Museum in Addis Ababa. It's found to the left of the National Museum (see National Museum in the Addis Ababa chapter).

There is no limit to the value of souvenirs that can be exported, but see the boxed text 'List of Banned Souvenirs'. If you don't get a permit, and undeclared souvenirs are found at the airport (by x-ray or search), you risk having them confiscated.

If you're sending objects by post, cargo or freight you'll also need a permit. Don't rely on the assurances, 'permits' or other slips of paper issued by the souvenir-shop keepers. If in doubt, get a receipt and an assurance from the shopkeeper that an item can be exchanged for something else if an export

---

In Search of Souvenirs

During the last several hundred years, thousands of manuscripts and other national treasures, including gold and silver crosses and even a giant stele (!), have left Ethiopia as 'souvenirs'. Most will probably never be recovered.

Today, tourists, antique dealers, professional thieves and even diplomats are responsible for the disappearance of works of art. In 1996, a German tourist removed several items from the National Museum at Aksum, and in March 1997, a Belgian tourist almost succeeded in removing Lalibela's famous 7kg gold cross. Things have become so critical that a new World Bank–funded, four-year project will soon attempt a nationwide, computerised inventory of Ethiopia's treasures.

In the meantime, basic controls are imposed. Though they can seem irksome for the traveller, without them, and at the current rate of 'souvenir' removal, it is thought that Ethiopia would be bereft of most of her treasures by 2020.

---

permit is denied. If it is, you can take it back. Note that items are never confiscated by the department (only at the airport). If something is of outstanding interest, it will be bought back from you by the museum.

A permit costs Birr1 per three items; you'll need to list among other things where and when you bought your souvenir, and give a telephone number – use your hotel's. Once the object has been inspected, it's wrapped, sealed and stamped. Bring your own wrapping paper, masking tape or cardboard boxes. The permits will need to be shown at the airport – hang onto them.

Endangered Species
Ethiopia is a party to the Convention on International Trade in Endangered Species of Wild Fauna and Flora (Cites). It's therefore illegal to export any endangered species or their products, such as ivory, tortoiseshell or leopard skins – all found in Ethiopian shops.

Currency
Upon arrival in Ethiopia, visitors must declare foreign currency. There is no limit to the amount of currency that can be brought in, but no more than Birr100 can be exported and imported.

List of Banned Souvenirs

The following list is adapted from the official catalogue of objects that are now denied export permits. Be warned that currently much parchment is being denied permission.

• Animal and plant fossils and any prehistoric items such as stone tools, bones or pottery
• Anything of outstanding anthropological or ethnographical interest
• Anything with an ancient inscription on it
• Old processional or hand crosses that bear the names of kings or religious leaders; or any currently in use at churches or monasteries
• Any items (including manuscripts, books, documents or religious objects such as chalices, crosses and incense burners) currently serving in churches
• Any old wooden items
• Coins and paper money not currently in circulation
• Wildlife products including all ivory
• Any items of exceptional artistic interest whether old or modern
• Art with outstanding historical value, such as engravings with historical figures
• Any items formerly belonging to the emperor, his family or to Ethiopian nobles

MONEY
Currency

Ethiopia's currency is the birr. It is divided into 100 cents in 1, 5, 10, 25 and 50 cent coins, and there are 1, 5, 10, 50 and 100 birr notes. A weekly auction determines the exchange rate.

Exchange Rate

Since January 2002, the exchange rate has averaged around Birr8.56 to the US$1.

For up-to-the-minute exchange rates, go to the subwwway section of LP's website (W www.lonelyplanet.com/subwwway/). It provides links to currency converters. At the time of going to press, the exchange rates were as follows:

country	unit		Birr
Australia	A$1	=	5.66
Canada	C$1	=	6.22
Euro zone	€1	=	9.86
Japan	¥100	=	7.38
Kenya	KSh100	=	11.76
UK	UK£1	=	13.93
USA	US$1	=	8.75

Exchanging Money

US dollars are still the best currency to carry both in cash and in travellers cheques. Note also that a few things (such as airport departure tax) must be paid in US dollars only; bring a wad of US$10 notes. Note that bank exchange receipts must be shown when changing birr back into dollars.

Cash Outside the capital, very few places (except banks in the larger towns) accept travellers cheques or credit cards. You'll have to rely on cash.

Banks The state-owned Commercial Bank of Ethiopia offers foreign exchange facilities, and has branches in the major towns and tourist sites throughout the country (with the notable exception of Lalibela).

Opening hours vary from region to region but banks are usually open from at least 9am to noon Monday to Saturday, and often for a couple of hours in the afternoon too (but not on Saturday).

Take your passport, which is sometimes needed even for exchanging cash.

More and more private banks are opening in the capital and elsewhere; these normally keep longer hours than the Commercial Bank, and are quicker with money exchanges.

Travellers Cheques All banks in the capital and the larger towns (but not smaller ones) exchange travellers cheques. In the capital, a few major hotels and travel agencies also accept them. Like cash, travellers cheques are best carried in US dollars.

The Commercial Bank of Ethiopia levies a 0.5% charge (0.2% for cash), a 'postage' charge of Birr7.10 per five cheques cashed, and a 'revenue stamp' of 20¢ per cheque. Private banks charge around the same. Sometimes, in smaller towns without computers, a 'cable charge' of up to Birr50 is made by the Commercial Bank for calling Addis Ababa to establish the day's exchange rate. Check in advance.

Credit Cards Some of the larger hotels, some airlines (including Ethiopian Airlines) and a few travel agents now accept credit cards. A commission of up to 5% is sometimes charged; check in advance.

Some private banks (such as the Dashen Bank) can give cash advances with a credit card (usually Visa and Mastercard); there's a 5% commission charge. Outside the capital, credit cards are as good as useless.

At the time of writing, the Commercial Bank had just finished installing ATMs in several locations in Addis Ababa. The machines were undergoing a trial run.

International Transfers In theory, transfers by telex should take no more than four days, though in practice it's often much longer. Some travellers have reported delays of between four and six weeks.

Transfers can be made in all the major currencies and there's no limit to the amount. The Commercial Bank charges a service fee of 25¢ per Birr100 transferred for up to Birr150,000.

If you need a transfer urgently, Western Union (see Money in the Addis Ababa chapter) is the best bet, though it's not cheap and takes a bit of organising.

Black Market The black market is in decline as the official and free rates for the Ethiopian birr converge. It's rare to be offered a rate much above 10% more than that offered by the banks.

Remember that the black market is still illegal, and penalties range from hefty fines to imprisonment. If you do indulge, stick to the shops, and be very wary of other places – particularly Merkato and the Piazza in Addis Ababa, where's there's a good chance of being swindled or even robbed.

Security
The risk of theft is low in Ethiopia and diminishes even further outside the capital (though you'll still need to be vigilant). Ethiopian hotels have a reputation for being fairly safe too.

A money belt, ideally concealed under clothing, is still the best way of carrying around cash and documents. It's not a bad idea to keep an emergency stash of, say, US$100 hidden somewhere. This can prove a life-saver after a theft.

The great majority of travellers experience no problems in Ethiopia; those who do sometimes invite thieves (such as by leaving belongings unattended). Be aware that professional thieves sometimes operate at major festivals and markets (such as Bati), targeting Ethiopians as well as foreigners.

Costs
For most day-to-day costs, Ethiopia is a very inexpensive country in which to travel. Budget travellers can get by very adequately

on US$10 per day (particularly outside the capital). The cheapest hotels cost from US$2 to US$2.50.

However, don't forget to allow for extra costs such as guides, or national park or historic site entrance fees. Entrance fees vary from Birr10 to Birr100 (for Lalibela). Additionally, prices of some hotels go up during the peak season.

If your time is restricted, you may want to consider some internal flights. For the historical route, you're looking to pay a very reasonable US$75 to US$130 per leg.

If you're staying in mid-range hotels, you should budget around US$20 per day.

Car hire and organised tours are expensive in Ethiopia. As tourism is still relatively undeveloped, most tours are custom-made and accordingly are expensive.

If you're keen to visit a remote area that is only really accessible in a private 4WD, you could keep costs down by trying to organise your own group before approaching an agency or by tagging along with a pre-organised group (see Organised Tours in the Getting Around chapter).

There are very few discounts offered to students and none to senior citizens.

Tipping
Tips (*gursha* in Amharic) are considered a part of everyday life in Ethiopia, and help supplement often very low wages. If someone acts as an informal guide or porter, it is usual to offer them 'tea money' – a nominal amount to show appreciation for their services.

It's worth bearing in mind too that tipping is a vital source of revenue for the nation's poor in those countries where there is no social welfare system. The maxim 'little but often' is a good one, and even very small tips are greatly appreciated.

By the same measure, it is a great mistake to overtip. Grossly distorted tips unfairly raise the expectations of the locals, undermine the social traditions of the country and may spoil the trips of future travellers. Local guides can start to select only those tourists who look lucrative, and can react very aggressively if their expectations are not met.

If a professional person helps you (or someone drawing a regular wage), it's probably better to show your appreciation in other ways: shaking hands, exchanging names, or an invitation to have a coffee and pastry are all local ways of expressing gratitude.

Tips for Tipping

Tipping can be a constant source of worry, hassle or stress for travellers. This guide has been compiled with the help of Ethiopians.

- In the smaller restaurants in the towns, service is included, and Ethiopians don't tip unless the service has been exceptional (Birr2 to Birr5).
- In bars and cafés, sometimes loose coins are left. However, in the larger restaurants accustomed to tourists, around 10% will be expected.
- In the large hotels, staff will expect a minimum of Birr10 per service.
- Outside the large hotels, luggage handlers will expect a tip from around Birr2 to Birr5 per bag, and people acting as impromptu guides around Birr10.
- For the assistance of a child, Birr1 or Birr2 is enough.
- Taxi drivers in Addis Ababa expect around Birr2 added to the fare; car 'guards' (often self-appointed) expect the same.
- At traditional music and dance shows in bars, restaurants and hotels, an audience shows its appreciation by placing money (around Birr10) on the dancers' foreheads or in their belts.

Furnishing yourself with a good wad of small notes – Birr1 and Birr10 – in particular is a very good idea. You'll need these for tips, taking photographs, etc. You should budget around Birr50 for tips per week.

Bargaining

Prices are usually fixed in Ethiopia. Haggling over prices can sometimes greatly offend Ethiopians. However, all the usual discounts apply for long stays in hotels, seasonal discounts, extended car hire, etc, and you shouldn't hesitate to ask for them in these instances.

The few exceptions, where haggling is almost expected, are at the local markets and with the local taxi and *gari* (horse-drawn cart) drivers. Don't forget that haggling is meant to be an enjoyable experience. If you're light-hearted and polite about it, you'll end up with a much better price!

POST & COMMUNICATIONS
Post

Ethiopia has quite an efficient and reliable postal service. All mail in Ethiopia is delivered to PO boxes only.

There's a free poste restante service in Addis Ababa (address mail to 'Poste Restante, Addis Ababa, Ethiopia') and in many of the larger towns. When you collect it, make sure you check under your first name as well as your surname, as Ethiopians go by their first name.

The post office opening hours across the country are usually from 8am to noon and from 1pm to 4pm weekdays, and on Saturday morning. In Addis Ababa the post office hours are longer.

Postal Rates

Airmail costs Birr1.90 for postcards, Birr1.95/2.45/3.45 for a letter up to 20g to Africa/Europe and the Middle East/Americas, Australia and the Far East. Letters should take between five and eight days to arrive in Europe; eight to 15 days for the USA or Australia.

Parcel Post & Courier Services Surface mail from the main post office in Addis Ababa takes between five and seven months to reach Europe. A small parcel of between 1kg and 2kg costs Birr13.90 worldwide.

An airmail parcel between 1kg and 2kg costs Birr63.90/113.95/213.90 to reach Africa/Europe/Americas. Airmail parcels take eight to 10 days to Europe and 10 to 12 days to Asia, Australia and the USA. Various additional charges (up to Birr5) may be applied. Insurance (to a maximum value of Birr800) is available for Birr165 per parcel.

Express Mail Service (*EMS;* ☎ 15 20 72), based in Addis Ababa, delivers packages weighing 0.5kg to 20kg worldwide in three to five days. Depending on the country you're sending to, the first 0.5kg costs from Birr142 to Birr220, plus from Birr45 to Birr85 for each additional 0.5kg.

All parcels are subject to a customs inspection, so leave them open. Don't forget the souvenir clearance permit (see Customs earlier in this chapter).

Various other courier services have offices in Addis Ababa including DHL.

Telephone & Fax

Telecommunication networks are fairly basic in Ethiopia (around three main lines per 1000 people), but phoning home is not usually a problem.

When calling Ethiopia from abroad, use the Ethiopian country code (☎ 251). When calling abroad from Ethiopia, use ☎ 00 followed by the appropriate country code.

In most of the larger towns there are public telephone boxes that accept both coins and cards, but international calls and faxes are best made from the telecommunications offices found in most towns.

To telephone here, you'll be asked if the call is for up to three minutes or 'open'. A deposit must then be paid for a three-minute/open call, then you must wait to be assigned a cabin. Just one call at a time can be made. You can wait up to an hour.

International rates are calculated per minute: Birr10 worldwide. Calls through the operator cost Birr33 for the first three minutes, then Birr10 per minute. Collect calls can be made to the UK, USA and Canada only, but you still have to pay a 'report charge' of from around Birr5-8, plus a Birr10 (refundable) deposit. Fax rates are Birr10 per minute worldwide (plus 15% tax).

Domestic calls cost from up to Birr2 per minute depending on the distance for the standard rate, and up to Birr1.34 for the off-peak rate (from 8pm to 8am and on Sunday and public holidays). You must leave a Birr10 deposit. Within Addis Ababa and in nearby towns, the rate is Birr0.20 per six minutes.

After hours, it's possible to make calls and send or receive faxes from the larger hotels, but rates are expensive (up to 20% more). When calling, contact the following services:

Directory assistance	☎ 97
International operator	☎ 98
Domestic operator	☎ 99

Phone Cards Telephone cards are available in denominations of Birr25, Birr50 and Birr100.

Mobile & Satellite Phones In 1999, Sweden's Eriksson in partnership with the Ethiopian Telecommunications Corporation (ETC) set up a mobile phone service for Addis Ababa and its immediate surrounds.

If a mobile phone is essential for you when in Addis Ababa, you could always bring your SIM card and hire a phone locally. International calling rates using the Ethiopian Telecommunication mobile telephone network currently costs Birr10.72 per minute.

Email & Internet Access
Ethiopian Telecommunication retains a monopoly over Internet provision and currently there is just one server (W www.telecom.net.et) in operation in Ethiopia. Internet access is still underdeveloped and expensive, but is slowly on the increase.

In the capital and the larger towns, you can normally find one or two Internet cafés. Machines are often slow and power cuts and maintenance problems cause difficulties. Rates vary from Birr1 and Birr3 per minute.

For Internet cafés, remember that you'll need three pieces of information to access your Internet account: your incoming (POP or IMAP) mail server name, your account name and your password.

Opening a free ekno web-based email account online at W www.ekno.lonelyplanet.com is an option for collecting email through Internet cafés.

See W www.teleadapt.com or W www.warrior.com for information on travelling with a portable computer.

DIGITAL RESOURCES
More and more websites on Ethiopia are cropping up. The following are among the most useful:

Addis Tribune This site is good for the latest news on current affairs, culture, the economy, sport and other goings-on, particularly within the capital. (W www.addistribune.com)

CyberEthiopia Like an Ethiopian *Yahoo!*, CyberEthiopia has quite useful information categorised into different sections. (W www.cyberethiopia.com)

Ethiopian Airlines This site includes the latest news on domestic and international flights, reservation options and schedules. (W www.flyethiopian.com)

Ethiopian News A comprehensive web guide to Ethiopia, this site gives updated daily news as well as business links and cultural information. There's also a chat service and a very useful calendar of upcoming events and public holidays. (W www.ethio.com)

Ethiopian Tourism Net This is probably the best place to start for a concise overview of the country's main attractions. It also offers a lot of practical tips. (W www.tourethio.com)

Travel Health Online This is an excellent way to quickly evaluate your 'disease risk summary' in the region. (W www.tripprep.com)

Ethio Market Providing a directory of service providers, private industry and commerce, Ethio Market may be useful to business travellers. (W www.ethiomarket.com)

For a wide selection of other websites on Ethiopia go to W www.waltainfo.com and go to Links.

BOOKS

In the UK, the **Africa Book Centre** (☎ 020-7240 6649, fax 7497 0309; **w** www.africa bookcentre.com) is a great place to browse for books on Ethiopia. Staff can order any not held in stock.

L'Harmattan (☎ 01 40 46 79 11; **w** www .editions-harmattan.fr) in Paris is a French equivalent.

For local books and older books, there are various bookshops and second-hand book-stalls in Addis Ababa (see that chapter for more information).

There are innumerable books on Ethiopia; what follows is just a very small, but reasonably eclectic selection of books that are also among the more widely available.

For a selection of health guides, see Health later in this chapter.

Guidebooks

The government-sponsored *Spectrum Guide to Ethiopia*, though a bit out of date, is still informative and is lavishly illustrated with first-class photos.

Travel

Dervla Murphy's *In Ethiopia with a Mule* is quite an entertaining read (if you like the how-to-travel-in-the-most-difficult-and-un-comfortable-manner-possible genre), though it doesn't offer much insight into Ethiopia.

Wilfred Thesiger's *Life of My Choice* includes reminiscences of the author's child-hood and early adult years in Ethiopia (including the coronation of Haile Selassie). *The Danakil Diary* records Thesiger's epic journey in the 1930s across uncharted Afar territory in search of the end of the Awash river.

Philip Marsden-Smedley's *A Far Country* is another travelogue, but is better researched and more insightful than most.

Evelyn Waugh's *Remote People*, though rather dated now, includes some wry impres-sions of Ethiopia in the 1930s. *Waugh in Abyssinia* is based on the author's time as a correspondent to cover the Italian-Ethiopian conflict in the 1930s.

The charming *A Cure for Serpents* by the Duke of Pirajno recounts the duke's time as a doctor in the Horn and is beautifully and engagingly written. Episodes include encoun-ters with famous courtesans, noble chieftains and giant elephants.

The newly reprinted (locally) *Ethiopian Journeys* by the well-respected American writer, Paul Henze, charts travels during the emperor's time. Recently published locally is *Off the Beaten Trail*, by John Graham, which is based on travels around the country during the author's time as an aid worker.

Recently published titles are *In Search of King Solomon's Mines* by Tahir Shah; and Nicholas Clapp's *Sheba: Through the Desert in Search of the Legendary Queen*.

History & Politics

A second edition of Bahru Zewde's widely acclaimed *A History of Modern Ethiopia 1855-1991* was recently published. Two particularly readable histories are Harold G Marcus' *Ethiopia*, and Richard Pankhurst's *The Ethiopians*. Paul Henze's *Layers of Time* offers another excellent overview of Ethiop-ian history. If you read French, *Histoire de l'Ethiopie* by Berhanou Abebe is also good.

For those intrigued by the fascinating an-cient civilisation of Aksum, *Ancient Ethiopia* by Professor David W Phillipson (now in paperback) is a must and is an easy read. The author directed archaeological research at Aksum during most of the 1990s. Though older, and now a little out of date, Stuart Munro-Hay's *Aksum: An African Civilisation of Late Antiquity* is well regarded.

Another well-regarded, more academic book is Edward Ullendorff's *The Ethiopian*. For a history of Islam, *Islam in Ethiopia* by J Spencer Trimingham is considered good. Outstanding for its insight into Amharic cul-ture (with the possible exception of a rather far-fetched Chapter 6!) is Donald N Levine's imaginative *Wax & Gold. Greater Ethiopia* by the same author is one of a number of other anthropologically orientated works on the country. David Buxton's *The Abyssinians* is also good for cultural insights.

The Emperor by Ryszard Kapuscinski consists of a series of interviews with the servants and closest associates of the de-posed Emperor Haile Selassie. The bizarre episodes recounted offer insights into the im-perial court, though some historians question its authenticity. Richard Pankhurst's *A Social History of Ethiopia* is also interesting.

Bahru Zewde's *Pioneers of Change in Ethiopia – The Reformist Intellectuals of the Early Twentieth Century* is more interesting than it sounds, dealing with the beginnings of modernisation in Ethiopia. The new *Remap-ping Ethiopia – Socialism & After* is a collec-tion of political essays.

A modern classic of historical travel writ-ing is Alan Moorehead's *The Blue Nile*, which is the story of the river, its people and its 'discovery'. It's as much an adventure story as a history.

For different accounts of the Ethiopian–Eritrean war in the 1980s, Thomas Keneally's *Towards Asmara* is recommended. Paul Henze's *Eritrea's War* (published locally) deals with the Eritrean-Ethiopian war of the late 1990s.

Amedeo by Sebastian O'Kelly is a nonfiction account of a love affair between a Harari woman and an Italian cavalry officer.

Language
Lonely Planet's *Ethiopian Amharic Phrasebook* is highly recommended for those spending more than a few days in Ethiopia. It's also informative and entertaining on Ethiopian culture and etiquette.

Colloquial Amharic by David Appleyard is a comprehensive teach-yourself course, complete with cassettes.

Cheap and widely available in the capital is *Amharic for Foreigners* by Semere Woldegabir, with a basic introduction to grammar and vocabulary. For those who've got to grips with the Amharic *fidal* (alphabet), useful conversation books are available in Addis Ababa. They're written for Ethiopians learning English or French, but work just as well in reverse!

Art
African Zion: The Sacred Art of Ethiopia contains a series of interesting and well-illustrated essays on Ethiopian Christian art.

Art that Heals by Jacques Mercier is an intriguing and well-illustrated exploration of the ancient Ethiopian traditional belief that art and healing are connected. The French illustrated *Æthiopia* contains a series of essays by many leading authorities on all things cultural.

Wildlife
The *Collins Guide to Wildflowers of East Africa* is a useful and well-illustrated guide. For bird books, see the special section 'Birds in Ethiopia'. For mammals, the Collins Field guide *Larger Mammals of Africa* is not bad. Jonathan Kingdon's well-respected *The Kingdon Field Guide to African Mammals* is better for the more serious wildlife spotter.

There is still no comprehensive field guide to the birds of Ethiopia. The Princeton Illustrated Checklist *Birds of Eastern Africa* by Ber van Perlo isn't bad and will do for most. The new *Endemic Birds of Ethiopia & Eritrea*

by Jose Vivero (published locally) makes an excellent addition.

For the more serious birder, the **Ethiopian Wildlife and Natural History Society** *(PO Box 60074, Addis Ababa)* publishes the *Important Bird Areas of Ethiopia*, a very useful 300-page inventory covering the entire country.

Excellent bird-watching reports on Ethiopia are available in English from Steve Whitehouse (☎ *0190 545 4541;* W *www.fbris.co .uk)*, who runs an information service on bird-watching abroad.

Photographic
Of the coffee-table books Carol Beckworth and Angela Fisher's *African Ark* contains stunning photographs of the peoples of the Horn. *The Mountains of Rasselas* by Thomas Pakenham (author of the excellent *Scramble for Africa*) is a well written, well illustrated account of Pakenham's two journeys through Ethiopia.

Mohamed Amin's *Journey Through Ethiopia* makes a good souvenir. A more idiosyncratic view of Ethiopia is *Bless Ethiopia* by the Japanese photographer, Kazyoshi Nomachi.

General
One of the best-known books about Ethiopia is Graham Hancock's *The Sign and the Seal*. The author spent ten years trying to solve one of the greatest mysteries of all time: the bizarre 'disappearance' of the Ark of the Covenant. The book has been likened to a great detective story and though the research and conclusions raised an eyebrow or two among historians, it is very readable and gives a good overview of Ethiopia's history and culture, however tenuous the facts!

If you're trying to interest children in Ethiopia, try *Ethiopia: The Roof of Africa* by Jane Kurtz. *When the World Began* by Elizabeth Laird is a collection of some of the delightful traditional tales of Ethiopia (see the boxed text 'Oral Literature - Tales Tall & True' in the Facts About Ethiopia chapter).

If you fancy preparing a deft *doro wat* for your friends when you get back home, *Exotic Ethiopian Cooking* by DJ Mesfin is a great easy-to-follow cookbook, including even a recipe for *tej* (Ethiopian honey wine)!

Charles Nicholl's *Somebody Else* is an account of the French poet Rimbaud's travels in Africa, including Ethiopia.

Evelyn Waugh's amusing novel *Black Mischief* is said to be partly drawn from the Abyssinia of the 1930s.

ETHIOPIA

David Turton has written various papers and publications on the fascinating tribes of the Lower Omo Valley.

Francis Falceto's *Ethiopiques* is actually a CD, but is accompanied by informative and comprehensive text on Ethiopia's music – from ancient to more modern.

The Ethiopian Orthodox Church, published by the Ethiopian Church Mission in Addis Ababa, is good for those keen to find out more about this ancient institution. Steven Kaplan's *The Holy Men and Christianisation of Early Solomonic Ethiopia* is also interesting.

FILMS

Ethiopia, which was never colonised, missed out on the 'benefit' of colonial support for setting up a film industry enjoyed by other African countries in the mid-1950s and '60s.

Solomon Bekele was one of the pioneers of Ethiopian cinema and is best known for his Amharic feature film *Aster*. Ethiopia's most famous English-speaking film-maker is Haile Gerima, whose latest film *Adwa* (released in early 2000) deals with a recurring theme, the Ethiopian defeat of the Italians at Adwa (see the boxed text 'The Battle of Adwa' in the Northern Ethiopia chapter).

Among the best known documentaries about Ethiopia is Jonathan Dimbleby's *Ethiopia: The Unknown Famine*. Other subjects for documentaries have included the poet Rimbaud, the struggle for freedom against the Derg and ethnographic studies (such as *Tsemaco* directed by Zekarias Hailemariam).

The Hollywood-produced *Endurance*, a biography of the famous athlete Haile Gebreselassie, was released in 1998. It was well received internationally. (See also the boxed text 'An Interview with Africa's Giant – Haile Gebreselassie' later in this chapter.) More recent is Tariq Shah's film *In Search of King Solomon's Mines* (released in 2003) – see Books earlier.

NEWSPAPERS & MAGAZINES

The best-known English language newspapers are the government-owned *Ethiopian Herald* (published Monday to Saturday), the privately owned *Monitor* and the weekly, privately owned *Addis Tribune*.

Other weekly private newspapers include the *Fortune*, the *Reporter* and the *Sun*. The *Berissa* is a weekly Oromo paper and *Al Ahem* is Arabic. Other weeklies include the new *Sub-Saharan Informer*, *Capital* and *The Scope*.

All are published in Addis Ababa and, apart from the *Ethiopian Herald*, are only available in the capital. The *Ethiopian Herald* can usually be found in the Mega Enterprise bookshops in the towns, though sometimes it's a few days old.

The well-respected *Addis Tribune* is a good source of information on forthcoming entertainment and cultural events in Addis Ababa. Of all the papers, it is probably the one of most interest to travellers.

The weekly *Press Digest* and *Days Update* (both Birr15) give useful summaries of the most important stories from the week's Amharic and English press. International newspapers are available in the larger hotels in the capital. There are newspaper reading rooms in the international cultural centres in Addis Ababa (see Information in that chapter).

RADIO & TV

The government retains control of television and radio, but is encouraging the founding of regional radio stations in local languages. The first private radio station should be operational soon.

Radio Ethiopia broadcasts in six local languages, plus English, French and Arabic for around 1½ hours each per day. English-language radio can be heard from 1.30pm to 2pm and 7pm to 8pm weekdays. The BBC World Service can be received on radios with shortwave reception, though frequencies vary according to the time of day (try 9630, 11940 and 17640 MHz)

Ethiopia's single television channel broadcasts every weekday evening from around 6pm to midnight (from noon on the weekends). From 10.30pm to midnight there is a broadcast in English. A new, pan-African channel called TV Africa broadcasts daily

Woman walking past a modern house, Addis Ababa

Girl in traditional dress, Harar

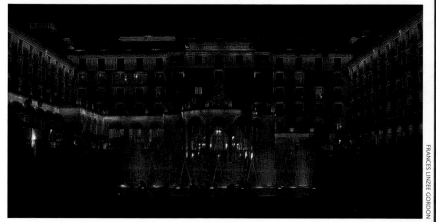
The Sheraton's 'dancing fountain', Addis Ababa

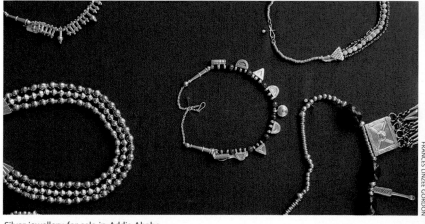
Silver jewellery for sale in Addis Ababa

Man dressed as an Abyssinian warrior at the Timkat festival

Berbere, a special Ethiopian blend of spices

between 4pm and 8pm (GMT). Some of the larger hotels, bars and restaurants have satellite dishes that receive CNN among other channels.

PHOTOGRAPHY & VIDEO
Film & Equipment
Decent print film is quite widely available in the capital and costs around Birr30 for a 36-exposure Kodak film. Some slide film is also available. Outside Addis Ababa, it's difficult to find film except in the larger towns, and products may not always be fresh.

Photographic equipment is pretty limited in Addis Ababa; the best place to head to is the Piazza. In the larger hotels, such as the Hilton, a limited selection of compact cameras is on sale, but the prices are quite high.

Photo development in the capital is of a good quality, can be done in around 45 minutes, and represents quite good value: from Birr50 for 36 exposures.

Nowadays most airport x-ray machines do not interfere with film. If you want to be on the safe side, carry film in hand luggage and ask for it to be hand checked.

See also Taking Photographs under Social Graces later in this chapter.

For advice on how to get good holiday snaps, see Lonely Planet's *Travel Photography*.

TIME
Ethiopia is three hours ahead of GMT/UTC.

For many travellers, one of the most curious idiosyncrasies of the country is the way time is expressed. Time is measured – in fact perfectly logically – using the 12-hour day. In other words, the Ethiopian clock begins just after daybreak, at 1 o'clock (7am our time), and ends when dusk starts to fall, at 12 o'clock (6pm our time). Instead of using 'am' or 'pm', Ethiopians use 'in the morning', 'in the evening' and 'at night' to indicate the time of day.

The system is used widely, though the 24-hour clock is used occasionally in business. Be careful to ask if a time quoted is according to the Ethiopian or 'European' clock (*Be habesha/faranji akotater no?* – Is that Ethiopian/foreigner's time?). For the purposes of this book, all times quoted are by the European clock.

Until you get used to the system, the easiest way to translate local time into Western time is by adding six hours to it.

ELECTRICITY
Ethiopia's electricity supply is 220V, 50 cycles AC. Power cuts are common during the rainy season and in smaller towns with erratic or oversubscribed supplies.

If you're planning to take a laptop with you, make sure you have something to protect

Tips for Photographers in the Horn

- Be aware that it is strictly forbidden to photograph 'sensitive areas', including military and police installations and personnel, industrial buildings, government buildings, residences and royal palaces; and major 'infrastructure' such as bridges, dams, airports. Penalties for contravening this law range from confiscation of film and camera, to between three months' and one year's imprisonment!
- Never leave equipment or film in a car or in the hot Ethiopian sun, and try to get film processed as soon after exposure as possible. High temperatures can wreck equipment and play havoc with film colour.
- The morning and late afternoon are the best times to take photos in Ethiopia – before 8am and after 4pm ideally. The light is gentler and there's less contrast between light and shade.
- Spot-metering – if you have it – is great for photographing faces, particularly dark ones in difficult conditions.
- Ethiopia's many hours of sun each day permit the use of slow film (such as ISO50 for slide film or ISO100 for print film), which can yield clear, fine-grained and colour-saturated pictures.
- A flash is useful for indoor scenes such as the *azmaris* or dance spectacles in Addis Ababa.
- A small zoom lens of some sort is great, both for wildlife and for photographing Ethiopia's colourful people (but don't forget to show sensitivity and tact).
- Bring plenty of batteries with you. Outside the capitals, batteries are often old, and of very poor quality.
- Beware dust which can wreak havoc with the electronics. A UV filter on each lens is essential as a protector as well as a filter. A dust blower (either compressed air or manual) is a must, as is a decent lens cloth.

it against the variations in current, as power surges occur frequently.

A variety of sockets are found around the country. A relic from the brief Italian period, a good many take the continental, two-pin, earth prong (two round prongs), rated at 600 W.

It's a good idea to bring an adaptor. Visitors from the USA and Canada (with 120V at 60Hz) should be careful to choose one appropriate for their equipment.

LAUNDRY

A good laundry service is offered by all hotels, from the very cheapest to the most expensive. Prices correspond with the room rates: budget hotels will charge little, smart hotels will charge a great deal. The local washing powder, Omo, is widely available in the shops.

Dry cleaning can be found in Addis Ababa and some of the largest towns; they'll do sleeping bags.

TOILETS

Both sit-down and squat toilets are found in Ethiopia, reflecting European and Arab influences respectively.

Public toilets are found in almost all hotels and restaurants, but they may not form your fondest memories of Ethiopia. In small towns and rural areas, the most common arrangement is a smelly old shack, with two planks, a hole in the ground, and all the flies you can fit in between. You may suddenly find that you can survive the next 1000km after all.

Toilet paper is very rare in any toilet; you're best advised to carry your own.

Be Seven Years Younger

Another great Ethiopian idiosyncrasy that confounds many travellers is the calendar. Based on the Julian system, it is roughly 7½ years 'behind' the Western Gregorian calendar. The year 2003–04 is thus '1996' in the Ethiopian calendar, while '1997' begins in September 2004. Just to confuse you thoroughly, the Ethiopian fiscal year begins on 8 July, and the Ethiopian New Year is rung in on 11 September.

The Julian calendar is named after Julius Caesar, and developed as a result of a dispute over the exact date of Christ's birth. It is made up of 12 months of 30 days each and a 13th month of five or six days. Hence the ETC's challenge to 'Visit Ethiopia and be seven years younger'!

HEALTH

One who hides his illness has no medicine; one who hides his problem has no remedy.
Ethiopian proverb

Travel health depends on three things: your predeparture preparations, your daily health care while travelling, and how you handle any medical problem that may arise.

While the Horn boasts a fabulous selection of tropical diseases, and the potential dangers can seem quite worrying, in reality few travellers experience anything more than a few undignified trots to the toilet. Don't let the following pages put you off.

Predeparture Planning

Medical facilities are limited in Addis Ababa and decidedly lacking outside the capital. Although doctors are quite well trained, supplies and modern equipment are in short supply. Emergency assistance is also severely limited outside the capital. While there's no undue cause for alarm, travellers are best advised to travel well-prepared: adequately immunised, with sufficient supplies of prescription drugs and with a reasonable medical kit (see the boxed text).

Immunisations Planning ahead (at least six weeks before travel) with a doctor is absolutely essential. Some vaccinations require more than one injection; others should not be given together or may not suit some people. If you're pregnant or suffer from allergies, inform your doctor when discussing immunisations.

Malaria Medication Antimalarial drugs do not prevent you from being infected but kill the malaria parasites during a stage in their development and significantly reduce the risk of becoming very ill or dying.

You should seek expert advice on antimalarial medication. There are many factors to consider, including the area you plan to visit, the side effects of medication, your medical history and whether you are a child or adult or are pregnant. Travellers going to isolated areas in high-risk countries may like to carry a treatment dose of medication for use if symptoms occur.

Health Insurance Adequate health insurance in essential in Ethiopia. See Travel Insurance under Visas & Documents earlier in this chapter.

Travel Health Guides For advice on travel health for younger children, try Lonely Planet's *Travel with Children* by Cathy Lanigan.

There are some excellent travel-health websites on the Internet. Go to the Lonely Planet home page (W *www.lonelyplanet.com /weblinks/wlheal.htm*) to find links to the websites of the World Health Organization and the US Centers for Disease Control & Prevention.

Other Preparations If you're going on a long trip, a dental check up is a very good idea before you leave. If you wear glasses take a spare pair and your prescription.

If you require a particular medication take an adequate supply, as it may not be available locally. A note of the generic name rather than the brand name will make getting replacements easier.

Basic Rules

Food There is an old colonial adage that says: 'If you can cook it, boil it or peel it you can eat it ...otherwise forget it'. Vegetables and fruit can also be washed with purified water. Beware of ice cream that is sold in the street or anywhere it might have melted and refrozen. If there's any doubt (such as from recent power cuts), steer well clear.

Though raw or undercooked meat (particularly in the form of mince) is a national delicacy in Ethiopia, it can be risky.

Busy, local places are often safer than 'smart' places, since food is cooked and eaten quickly and is usually not reheated. Standards of hygiene in Ethiopia vary. The best rule of thumb is to head for the places popular with the locals.

Water The number one rule is *be careful of the water* and especially ice. Though some travellers drink tap water in Ethiopia and suffer no ill consequences, it's probably best to err on the side of caution, and it is strongly advised in rural areas. Bottled water or soft drinks should be fine.

Take care with fruit juice; water may have been added. Milk is sometimes dodgy if it's unpasteurised, though boiled milk is fine if it is kept hygienically. Tea or coffee should also be OK, since the water should have been boiled.

Water Purification The simplest way of purifying water is to boil it thoroughly. Note that at high altitude water boils at a lower tem-

perature, so in order to kill germs, it needs to be boiled for longer.

A water filter is a good idea for long trips, or for trekking. There are two main kinds. Total filters remove all parasites, bacteria and viruses. Though more expensive than simple filters, they can save on buying bottled water.

Simple filters (which can even be a nylon mesh bag) remove dirt and larger foreign bodies so that they can work in combination with chemical solutions. It's essential to understand how the filter you buy works (if water is dirty, for example, chemical solutions may not work). Note that filtering will not remove all dangerous organisms. If you cannot boil water, it should be treated chemically.

Chlorine tablets will kill many pathogens, but not some parasites like giardia and amoebic cysts. Iodine is more effective and is available in tablet form. Follow the directions carefully and remember that too much iodine can be harmful.

Medical Problems & Treatment

Self-diagnosis and treatment can be risky, so you should always seek medical help. If you do require help, you can visit one of the quite numerous private clinics in Ethiopia. Appointments are not usually necessary; you just walk in.

For a lab test (a very good idea if you suspect malaria, giardia or other illnesses that demand immediate attention), it costs around Birr30 for a 'consultation', and Birr25 to Birr30 for the test itself (note that you may need more than one). The test takes around two hours. You will then be given a prescription.

Many drugs are freely available over the counter. Pharmacists usually speak good English, are helpful and above all, are very familiar with the symptoms of the most common local diseases. Clinics and pharmacies are marked on the maps of all the towns.

Although drug dosages are given in this section, they are for emergency use only. Correct diagnosis is vital. Generic names for medications are used – check with a pharmacist for brands available locally.

Note that antibiotics should ideally be administered only under medical supervision. Take only the recommended dose at the prescribed intervals and use the whole course, even if the illness seems to be cured earlier. Stop immediately if there are any serious reactions. Some people are allergic to commonly prescribed antibiotics such as penicillin; if this is the case, carry this information (eg on a bracelet) when travelling.

Environmental Hazards

Altitude Sickness Travellers trekking in the Bale or Simien Mountains are most likely to suffer from altitude sickness, although new arrivals in Addis Ababa (at between 2300–2500m) sometimes experience mild symptoms for the first 48 hours or so.

Symptoms of Acute Mountain Sickness (AMS) usually develop during the first 24 hours at altitude but may be delayed up to three weeks. Mild symptoms include headache, lethargy, dizziness, difficulty sleeping and loss of appetite.

Severe symptoms – which can develop without warning – include breathlessness, a dry, irritative cough, severe headache, lack of coordination and balance, confusion, irrational behaviour, vomiting, drowsiness and unconsciousness. AMS can be fatal.

Treat mild symptoms by resting at the same altitude until recovery, usually a day or two. Paracetamol or aspirin can be taken for headaches. If symptoms persist or become worse, however, *immediate descent is necessary*; even descending 500m can help. To prevent acute mountain sickness:

- Ascend slowly: have rest days and spend a couple of nights at each rise of 1000m.
- Sleep at a lower altitude than the greatest height reached during the day if possible. Once above 3000m, avoid increasing the sleeping altitude by more than 300m per day.
- Drink extra fluids. Extra moisture is lost as you breathe in the dry mountain air.
- Eat light, high-carbohydrate meals for more energy.
- Avoid alcohol (which increases dehydration), sedatives and sleeping pills.

Heat Exhaustion Dehydration and salt deficiency can cause heat exhaustion. Drink sufficient liquids and avoid activities that are too physically demanding.

Salt deficiency is characterised by fatigue, lethargy, headaches, giddiness and muscle cramps; salt tablets may help, but adding extra salt to your food is better.

Heatstroke Long, continuous periods of exposure to high temperatures and insufficient fluids can leave you vulnerable to heatstroke. It can be fatal, and is a real risk in areas such as the Danakil desert.

Symptoms include reduced sweating (or not at all) and a high body temperature (39° to 41°C or 102° to 106°F). Where sweating has ceased, the skin becomes flushed and red. Severe, throbbing headaches and lack of coordination will also occur, and the sufferer may be confused or aggressive. Eventually the victim will become delirious or start to convulse.

Hospitalisation is essential, but in the interim get victims out of the sun, remove their clothing, cover them with a wet sheet or towel and then fan them continually. Give fluids if they are conscious.

Everyday Health

Normal body temperature is up to 37°C (98.6°F); more than 2°C (4°F) higher than this indicates a high fever. The normal adult pulse rate is 60 to 100 per minute (children 80 to 100, babies 100 to 140). As a general rule the pulse increases about 20 beats per minute for each 1°C (2°F) rise in temperature.

Infectious Diseases

Diarrhoea Simple things like a change of water, food or climate can all cause a mild bout of diarrhoea, but a few rushed toilet trips are not necessarily indicative of a major problem.

Dehydration is the main danger with any diarrhoea particularly with children or the elderly. Fluid replacement is essential. Weak black tea with a little sugar or soft drinks allowed to go flat and diluted 50% with clean water are all good.

With severe diarrhoea a rehydrating solution is advised in order to replace lost minerals and salts. Commercially available oral rehydration salts (ORS) are useful; just add them to boiled or bottled water. You can also make up your own: six teaspoons of sugar and a half teaspoon of salt added to a litre of boiled or bottled water.

You need to drink at least the same volume of fluid that you are losing in bowel movements and vomiting. Urine is the best guide to the replacement required – if you have small amounts of concentrated urine, you need to drink more. Keep drinking small amounts often and stick to a bland diet as you recover.

Gut-paralysing drugs such as loperamide or diphenoxylate bring relief from the symptoms, but do not actually cure the problem. Only use these drugs if you do not have access to toilets such as on a bus journey.

In certain situations antibiotics may be required: diarrhoea with blood or mucus (dysentery), any diarrhoea with fever, profuse watery diarrhoea, or persistent diarrhoea not improving after 48 hours. In these instances gut-paralysing drugs should be avoided.

A stool test may be necessary to diagnose the bug causing your diarrhoea. Where this is not possible the recommended drugs for bacterial diarrhoea (the most likely cause of severe diarrhoea in travellers) are norfloxacin 400mg twice daily for three days or ciprofloxacin 500mg twice daily for five days. These are not recommended for children

(who should be given co-trimoxazole with dosage dependent on weight). Pregnant women should use Ampicillin or amoxycillin, but medical advise should be sought.

Two other causes of persistent diarrhoea in travellers are giardiasis and amoebic dysentery. **Giardiasis**, quite common in Ethiopia and Eritrea, is caused by a common parasite, *Giardia lamblia*. Symptoms include stomach cramps, nausea, a bloated stomach, watery, foul-smelling diarrhoea and frequent gas. Giardiasis can appear several weeks after you have been exposed to the parasite. The symptoms may disappear for a few days and then return; this can go on for several weeks.

Amoebic dysentery, caused by the protozoan *Entamoeba histolytica*, is characterised by a gradual onset of low-grade diarrhoea, often with blood and mucus. Cramping abdominal pain and vomiting are less likely than in other types of diarrhoea, and fever may not be present. It will persist until treated and can recur and cause other health problems.

You should seek medical advice if you think you have giardiasis or amoebic dysentery, but where this is not possible, tinidazole or metronidazole are the recommended drugs. Treatment is a 2g single dose of tinidazole or 250mg of metronidazole three times daily for five to 10 days.

Hepatitis This is a general term for inflammation of the liver. It is a common disease in Ethiopia and the Horn, caused by several different viruses.

Symptoms include fever, chills, headache, fatigue, feelings of weakness and aches and pains, followed by loss of appetite, nausea, vomiting, abdominal pain, dark urine, lightcoloured faeces, jaundiced (yellow) skin and yellowing of the whites of the eyes.

Hepatitis A and E are transmitted by contaminated food and drinking water. If infected, seek medical advice then rest, drink lots of fluids, eat lightly and avoid fatty foods.

Hepatitis B is spread through contact with infected blood, blood products or body fluids, such as through sexual contact, unsterilised needles and blood transfusions, or contact with blood via small breaks in the skin. Other potential infections occur from having a shave, tattoo or body piercing with contaminated equipment.

The symptoms of hepatitis B may be more severe than type A and the disease can lead to long-term problems such as chronic liver damage, liver cancer or a long term carrier state. Hepatitis C and D are spread in the same way as hepatitis B and can also lead to long-term complications.

There are vaccines against hepatitis A and B, but there are currently no vaccines against the other types of hepatitis. Following the basic rules about food and water (hepatitis A and E) and avoiding risk situations (hepatitis B, C and D) are important preventative measures.

HIV & AIDS Infection with the human immunodeficiency virus (HIV) may lead to acquired immune deficiency syndrome (AIDS), which is a fatal disease. HIV is spread in exactly the same way as hepatitis B (see earlier). If you do need an injection, ask to see the syringe unwrapped in front of you, or take a needle and syringe pack with you.

Ethiopia has a large number of prostitutes among whom the incidence of HIV infection is high (as it is among the population in general). Good quality condoms are widely available and (subsidised by the government) are cheap.

Fear of HIV infection should never preclude treatment for serious medical conditions.

Worms These parasites are relatively common in Ethiopia and the Horn. Worms may be ingested through food such as undercooked meat. The Ethiopian tradition of eating raw meat as well as the delicacy *kitfo* (undercooked or raw mince) is the cause of tapeworm infestation, particularly outside the capital.

Worms such as hookworms can enter through your skin. Infestations may not show up for some time. Although they are generally not serious, they can cause severe health problems later if untreated.

Consider having a stool test when you return home if you suspect you have worms.

Meningococcal Meningitis This serious disease can be fatal and recurring epidemics are reported in sub-Saharan Africa.

A fever, severe headache, sensitivity to light and neck stiffness, which prevents forward bending of the head, are the first symptoms. There may also be purple patches on the skin. Death can occur within a few hours, so urgent medical treatment is required.

Schistosomiasis Also known as bilharzia, this disease is transmitted by minute worms that infect certain varieties of freshwater snails found in rivers, streams, lakes and particularly behind dams. There is a high risk of bilharzia in much of Ethiopia's fresh water.

The infection often causes no symptoms until the disease is well established. Symptoms (which may appear several weeks or even years later) include a high fever, abdominal pain, and blood in the urine. Damage to internal organs is irreversible. A blood test is the best diagnosis, but should not be taken until a number of weeks after exposure.

Avoiding swimming or bathing in fresh water. If you do get wet, dry off quickly and dry your clothes as well.

Sexually Transmitted Infections HIV/AIDS and hepatitis B can be transmitted through sexual contact – see the relevant sections earlier for more details.

Other STIs include gonorrhoea, herpes and syphilis; sores, blisters or rashes around the genitals and discharges or pain when urinating are common symptoms.

Chlamydia infection can cause infertility in men and women before any symptoms have been noticed. Syphilis symptoms eventually disappear completely but the disease continues and can cause severe problems in later years.

While abstinence from sexual contact is the only 100% effective prevention, using condoms is also effective. STIs are treated with antibiotics, though there is no known cure for herpes or HIV.

Typhoid Typhoid fever is a dangerous gut infection caused by contaminated water and food. It requires immediate medical attention.

Early symptoms include headaches, body aches and a fever, which rises to around 40°C (104°F) or more. The victim's pulse is often slow. There may also be vomiting, abdominal pain, diarrhoea or constipation.

In the second week, a few pink spots may appear on the body; trembling, delirium, weakness, weight loss and dehydration may occur. Unless treated, serious complications may occur.

Insect-Borne Diseases

Chagas' disease, filariasis, leishmaniasis, Lyme disease, sleeping sickness, typhus and yellow fever are all insect-borne diseases, but they do not pose a great risk to travellers. For more information on them see Less Common Diseases later.

Malaria This potentially fatal disease is spread by the *Anopheles* mosquito which breeds in permanent or temporary pools of still water. Prophylaxis is essential in Eritrea and in many parts of Ethiopia.

Malaria is a major public health problem in Ethiopia, with between one and two million clinical cases reported each year. One of the most dangerous strains of malaria, and most resistant to chloroquine, *Plasmodium falciparum*, is responsible for up to 70% of malaria cases in Ethiopia (and Eritrea).

Though malaria is generally absent in Ethiopia at altitudes above 1800m, epidemics have occurred in areas above 2000m. The central plateau, Addis Ababa, the Bale and Simien Mountains, and most of the northern historical route areas are traditionally considered safe areas, but are not wholly risk free.

For short-term visitors, it's probably wise to err on the side of caution. If you're thinking of travelling outside these areas, you should definitely take prophylactics. Most transmission takes place after the rainy season, from August or September to November, and after the light rains from March to April or May.

Malaria symptoms range from fever, chills and sweating, headache, diarrhoea and abdominal pains to a vague feeling of ill-health.

Seek medical help immediately if malaria is suspected. Without treatment malaria can rapidly become more serious and can be fatal. Note that malaria usually takes between one week and three months to develop (though it can take up to a year). Be vigilant for possible symptoms when you return home and finish your course of tablets.

There is a variety of medications such as mefloquine, Fansidar and Malarone. You should seek medical advice before you travel, on the appropriate medication and dosage for you. If medical care is not available, malaria tablets can be used for treatment. Note that you need to use a different malaria tablet than you were taking when you contracted malaria.

The best way to avoid malaria is to avoid mosquito bites. The following tips will also reduce your risk of being bitten:

- Wear light-coloured clothing, long trousers and long-sleeved shirts.
- Use mosquito repellents containing the compound DEET on exposed areas.
- Avoid perfumes or aftershave.
- Use a mosquito net impregnated with mosquito repellent (permethrin).
- Use the insecticide sprays which are quite widely available in Ethiopia (Birr17 to Birr23) for a raid on your room before turning in.

Dengue Fever This viral disease is transmitted by mosquitoes and is fast becoming a major public health problem in the region. Unlike the malaria mosquito, the *Aedes aegypti* mosquito (which transmits the dengue virus) is most active during the day, and is found mainly in urban areas, in and around human dwellings.

Symptoms of dengue fever include a sudden onset of high fever, headache, joint and muscle pains (hence its old name, 'breakbone fever') and nausea and vomiting. A rash of small red spots sometimes appears three to four days after the onset of fever. In the early phase of illness, dengue may be mistaken for other infectious diseases, including malaria and influenza.

Of the four strains, the haemorrhagic fever (DHF) is the most serious and can be fatal. It usually affects residents of the country rather than travellers and is characterised by heavy bleeding.

If you suspect an infection, seek immediate medical attention. Aspirin should be avoided, as it increases the risk of haemorrhaging. There is no specific treatment and no vaccine for dengue fever. Like malaria, the best prevention is to avoid mosquito bites.

Cuts, Bites & Stings

Wash cuts well and treat with an antiseptic such as povidone-iodine. Where possible avoid bandages and Band-Aids, which can keep wounds wet.

Unless you receive multiple stings or are allergic to them, bee, wasp or hornet stings are usually only painful rather than dangerous. Travellers with an allergy should bring with them antihistamine tablets. Calamine lotion or a sting relief spray will give relief and ice packs will reduce the pain and swelling.

In the heat of the lowlands of Ethiopia, infection takes hold quickly. Look after cuts and resist scratching mosquito bites.

Bedbugs, Fleas & Lice Bedbugs and fleas are quite common in some of the cheapest hotels or in rural areas. Dirty mattresses and bedding – evidenced by spots of blood on bedclothes or on the wall – are favourite haunts. Bedbugs leave itchy bites in neat rows. Calamine lotion or a sting relief spray may help.

Lice also cause itching, and can infest your hair (head lice), your clothing (body lice) or your pubic hair (crabs). Lice are caught through direct contact with infected people or by sharing combs, clothing and the like.

Powder or shampoo treatment will kill the lice and infected clothing should then be washed in very hot, soapy water and left in the sun to dry.

Ticks These can cause skin infections and other more serious diseases including typhus. If you've been walking through bush, give your body a brush down; ticks are quite common in Ethiopia and Eritrea.

If you find a tick attached, press down around the tick's head with tweezers, grab the head and gently pull upwards. Avoid pulling the rear of the body as this may squeeze the tick's gut contents through the attached mouthparts into the skin, increasing the risk of infection and disease. Smearing chemicals or applying lighted cigarettes on the tick will not make it let go and is not recommended.

Snakes Apart from the occasional python, snakes are not often seen in Ethiopia and Eritrea. But wearing boots, socks and long trousers will minimise the risk of being bitten when trekking in undergrowth where snakes may be present.

Be particularly careful when collecting firewood, or when climbing (and putting your hands into holes and crevices). Rocky crevices are the preferred habitat of Africa's most dangerous snake, the puff adder.

Snake bites do not cause instantaneous death and antivenins are usually available. If you are bitten, immediately wrap the bitten limb tightly, and then attach a splint to immobilise it. Keep the victim still and the bitten area below heart level until medical help arrives. Avoid aspirin or alcohol, though paracetamol is OK. Tourniquets and sucking out the poison are now comprehensively discredited.

Women's Health

Gynaecological Problems Antibiotic use, synthetic underwear, sweating and contraceptive pills can lead to fungal vaginal infections, especially when travelling in hot climates. Thrush or vaginal candidiasis is characterised by a rash, itch and discharge. Nystatin, miconazole or clotrimazole pessaries are the usual treatment.

Pregnancy Travel to Ethiopia and Eritrea during pregnancy is not really advisable, as some vaccinations (such as yellow fever) used to prevent serious diseases are not advised during pregnancy.

Less Common Diseases

The following diseases pose a small risk to travellers, and so are only mentioned in passing. Seek medical advice if you suspect symptoms.

Cholera Outbreaks of cholera are generally widely reported, so you can usually avoid problem areas. Cholera is the worst of the watery diarrhoeas, medical help should be sought. Fluid replacement is the most vital treatment – the risk of dehydration is severe as you may lose up to 20L a day.

If there is a delay in getting to hospital, then begin taking tetracycline. The adult dose is 250mg four times daily. It is not recommended for children under nine years nor for pregnant women. Tetracycline may help slow down the illness, but fluid rehydration is essential to avoid death.

Filariasis This is a mosquito-transmitted parasitic infection found in Ethiopia. Possible symptoms include fever, pain and swelling of the lymph glands; inflammation of lymph drainage areas; swelling of a limb or the scrotum; skin rashes; and blindness. Medical advice should be obtained promptly if an infection is suspected.

Leishmaniasis This is a group of parasitic diseases transmitted by sandflies. Cutaneous leishmaniasis affects the skin tissue causing ulceration and disfigurement, and visceral leishmaniasis affects the internal organs. A sudden rise in the number of cases of leishmaniasis was reported in the Horn of Africa in 1998. If you suspect it, seek medical advice immediately. Avoiding sandfly bites is the best precaution.

Rabies Many animals can be infected by this fatal virus, including dogs, cats, bats, monkeys and other wild animals.

The disease is transmitted through the animal's saliva. Any bite, scratch or even lick from an animal should be immediately scrubbed with soap and running water, and alcohol or iodine solution applied. Immediate medical help is required to prevent the onset of symptoms and death.

Sleeping Sickness Trypanosomiasis, or sleeping sickness, is found in some parts of lowland Ethiopia. The disease is borne by the tsetse fly, though only a small percentage of the insects actually carry it.

The flies are attracted to large moving objects such as vehicles, to perfume and aftershave and to colours such as dark blue. There is no deterrent except avoiding the bites. Swelling at the site of the bite, five or more days later, is the first sign of infection; two to three weeks later, fever follows. The disease can be fatal unless treated.

Tetanus The tetanus germ is found in the soil and in animal faeces. The first symptom may be discomfort in swallowing, or stiffening of the jaw and neck; this is followed by painful convulsions of the jaw and whole body. The disease can be fatal, but can be prevented by vaccination.

Tuberculosis A bacterial infection, tuberculosis (TB) is usually transmitted from person to person by coughing. Occasionally, it is transmitted through consumption of unpasteurised milk (boiled milk, yoghurt and cheese are usually safe). Infection is usually only through close household contact with infected people.

Typhus This disease is spread by ticks, mites or lice. Symptoms include fever, chills, headache and muscle pains. Often a large painful sore appears at the site of the bite. Nearby lymph nodes are also swollen and painful. Though serious, typhus can be treated.

Yellow Fever This viral disease is endemic in many African countries and is transmitted by mosquitoes. The initial symptoms are fever, headache, abdominal pain and vomiting. Seek medical care urgently and drink lots of fluids.

SOCIAL GRACES

Greetings The Ethiopian highlanders attach great importance to etiquette. Greetings are characterised by a very lengthy exchange of inquiries; the longer the exchange, the greater the friendship. Questions turn on the health of the family, the crops, weather, even the animals.

It is also common to send greetings to relatives even if you've never met them. Once you've made an Ethiopian acquaintance, you'll be expected to follow this ritual, too. Neglecting to do so is considered impolite. It's also customary to do this before getting down to any business matter.

A nod or head bow accompanying greetings shows special respect, thanks or appreciation.

Deference is also shown by supporting the right arm (near the elbow) with the left hand during shaking. Among close friends, hands can remain joined for the duration of the conversation.

Handshaking in Ethiopia is important. If you enter a room full of people, you should try and shake hands with everyone (including children). If hands are dirty or wet, you will be offered a wrist, with the hand hanging down rather limply. It is polite also to kiss babies or young children, even if you've just met them.

Kissing on the cheek is very common among friends and relatives of either sex, but in Ethiopia, three kisses are given (right, left, right), and they are interspersed with the greeting formulae. The cheek is touched rather than kissed, though kissing noises are made. 'Long-lost' friends may kiss up to five times.

Dress Ethiopians are conservative in their dress and it is appreciated if visitors follow suit. Ethiopian women traditionally never expose their shoulders, knees, cleavage or waist in public. See also Church Etiquette under Responsible Tourism earlier.

An effort to look smart is seen as showing respect to those you are meeting. If visiting government offices or on business, wearing a tie and decent shirt for a man is a minimum.

Names Names are important in Ethiopia, and the exchange of names – rather like the exchange of addresses in the West – is the first important stage in forming a friendship. If someone has helped you with something, ask his/her name.

Ethiopians take their father's first name as their second name. If you ask an Ethiopian their name, they will give you their first name only. When introducing yourself, do the same. Surnames are not really used in Ethiopia. A woman's name does not change on marriage.

Ethiopians are always addressed, formally and informally, by their first names. To formalise a first name you just add *Ato* (Mr) for a man, *Weizero* (Mrs) for a married woman and *Weizerit* (Miss) for an unmarried woman.

Taking Photographs Many Ethiopians – particularly outside the capital are unused to tourists pointing cameras at them. Many may feel seriously threatened or compromised, particularly the women. Be sensitive. Try and ask permission first – even with basic

What's in a Name?

Ethiopian Christian names usually combine a religious name with a secular name.

Common male secular names include *Hagos* (Joy), *Mebratu* (The Light), and *Desta* (literally 'Pleasure'; it's also a woman's name). For women, names include *Ababa* (Flower), *Zawditu* (The Crown), and *Terunesh* (You're Wonderful).

Some Ethiopian names have particular meanings. Names like *Mitiku* or *Mitke* (Substitute) and *Kassa* (Compensation) are given to children after the death of a brother or sister. *Masresha*, roughly meaning Distraction, is given after a family misfortune. *Bayable* means 'If he Hadn't Denied It', and is given to a bastard-child whose father refuses to acknowledge it. *Tesfaye* (meaning My Hope) is often given to a child by a poor or single mother who looks forward to her child's future success in life. Other names can mean 'That's the Last!' or 'No More!' after a long string of children.

Many Christian names are compounds made up of two names. *Wolde* means 'Son of', *Gebre* 'Servant of', *Haile* 'Power of', *Tekle* 'Plant of', *Habte* 'Gift of'; so that *Gebre-Yesus* means 'Son of Jesus', *Habte-Mikael* 'Gift of Michael', etc.

The *Yedabo sim* (literally 'Name of the Bread') is the tradition of giving a bride a new second name on her wedding day.

sign language. Best of all, use a local as an interpreter or go-between. Never take a photo if permission is denied.

In other areas, where people are starting to depend on tourists for income, the opposite is true. In the Lower Omo Valley, money is often demanded. However, be sure to agree the fee first.

Be sensitive in areas such as *tej beats* (local pubs) or even restaurants; eating and particularly drinking is rather a private affair in Ethiopia (drinking is still considered rather shameful).

Other Etiquette When receiving a gift, both hands should be extended. Using only one is seen as showing reluctance or ingratitude.

Friends of the same sex can often be seen holding hands in the street, or with arms wrapped around one another. But opposite-sex couples – even married ones – never display affection in public.

When attracting someone's attention, such as a waiter or porter, it is polite to call *yikerta* (excuse me). In restaurants, waiters aren't ignoring you (though it may seem like it); simply clap your hands to call them when you need them. Whistling or snapping your fingers, by contrast, is considered rude. Don't be offended if waiters snatch away your plates the moment you've finished; it's considered impolite to leave dirty dishes in front of customers. See also the boxed text 'Eating Etiquette' under Food later in this chapter.

If you're sitting in a café and someone joins your table, it's customary to pay for their coffee or drink when you come to pay for yours. If someone else leaves the table first, the same will be done for you. It's also customary to invite those rendering services to you, such as guides or drivers, to coffee or meals.

Punctuality is important as tardiness is seen as a sign of disrespect. Conversely, you may be kept waiting, which is sometimes a demonstration of the other person's prestige or status. Remember that some Africans see Westerners as arrogant and proud; a smile works wonders. See also Bribery & Bureaucracy later in this chapter.

Making rude noises of any sort is considered the height of bad manners by most Ethiopians. If you do breach this strict rule of social conduct, a quick *yikerta* (excuse me) is probably the best way out!

WOMEN TRAVELLERS

Compared with many African countries, Ethiopia is pretty easy-going for women travellers, so long as you're aware of a few unspoken codes of etiquette.

Female Phobia

In some of the monasteries and holy sites of Ethiopia and Eritrea, an ancient prohibition forbids women from setting foot in the holy confines. But the holy fathers believe in going strictly by the book: the prohibition extends not just to women but to all female creatures, even she donkeys, hens and nanny goats.

Attitudes Towards Local & Foreign Women

Because of Hollywood cinematic 'glamour', foreign women (in particular white women) are sometimes seen in some countries as 'easier' than local women. Conversely, with Ethiopia's relatively permissive society, foreign women are sometimes seen as an exotic alternative to local fun.

Drinking alcohol, smoking, and wearing excessive make-up and 'inappropriate' clothes are indications to the male population of 'availability' – as this is also the way local prostitutes behave. Apart from the young of the wealthier classes in Addis, no 'proper' woman would be seen in a bar.

Be aware also that 'respectable' Ethiopian women – even if they're willing – are expected to put up a show of coyness and modesty. Traditionally, this formed part of the wedding night ritual of every Amhara bride: a fierce struggle with the groom was expected of them. Consequently, some Ethiopian men may mistake your rebuttals for encouragement. The concept even has a name in Amharic: *maqderder* (and applies equally to feigned reluctance for other things such as food). If you mean no, make it very clear from the start.

Beware of accepting an invitation to an unmarried man's house, under any pretext. It is considered a latent acceptance of things to come. Dinner invitations often amount to 'foreplay' before you're expected to head off to some seedy hotel. Even a seemingly innocent invitation to the cinema can turn out to be little more than an invitation to a good snog in the back row!

Adultery is quite common among many of Ethiopia's urban population, for men as well as women. For this reason, a wedding ring on a woman traveller – bogus or not – has absolutely no deterrent value in the Horn. In fact, quite the reverse! Married women even seem to be considered easier prey.

Women travellers in the company of a male traveller are sometimes ignored in conversation, or when ordering at a restaurant, or asking directions, etc. This is considered a sign of respect for the woman, not a slight; conversation is seen to be properly directed through the men.

If you want to learn more about women in Ethiopia or get in touch with them, contact the excellent Addis Ababa–based **Ethiopian Women Lawyers Association** (EWLA; ☎ 61 25 11; e ewla@telecom.net.et.), which campaigns for women and their rights (and represents them in court).

Safety Precautions

The best advice always is: 'When in Rome...'. Be aware of the signals your clothing or behaviour are giving off and keep in mind local attitudes to foreign women.

Many cheap hotels in Ethiopia double as brothels. Ethiopian men may naturally wonder

Prostitution in Ethiopia

The social stigma attached to prostitution in the West is lacking in Ethiopia. Many prostitutes are students trying to make ends meet. Others are widows, divorcees or refugees – all with little or no hope of finding other forms of employment. With no social security system either, it is often their only means of survival. Though not exactly a respected profession, prostitution is considered a perfectly viable means of making a living for such women. Some very beautiful or accomplished prostitutes even become well-known figures in society.

Visiting a prostitute is considered a fairly normal part of a young boy's adolescence and bachelor life at least in the cities. Once married, it is considered shameful, however, and married men who can afford it often keep permanent mistresses or girlfriends instead.

Male travellers should be aware that almost 100% of the women encountered in smaller bars, restaurants and nightclubs are prostitutes (in Addis Ababa, where women are more liberated, the percentage is lower). Often, it's very hard to distinguish them from 'ordinary' women: they're usually young, attractive and quite soberly dressed.

In the bars, their mission is to extract from you as many drinks (for the bar or hotel) and as much money (for themselves) as possible. In exchange for your custom, they get a room at the bar/hotel.

Be careful not to be talked into buying a prostitute a drink. One it is considered a sign of interest; two and you're as good as booking the girl's services. Be aware that the HIV infection rate is very high among prostitutes in Ethiopia (some estimate up to 50%), and is ever on the increase. See also the boxed text 'AIDS in Africa' under Population & People in the Facts about Ethiopia chapter.

about your motives for staying here, particularly if you're alone. While there's no cause for alarm, it's best to keep a low profile and behave very conservatively – keep out of the hotel bar for example, and try and hook up with other travellers if you want to go out.

If there aren't any other travellers around, here's a quick trick: pick a male Ethiopian companion, bemoan the problems you've been having with his compatriots and appeal to his sense of pride, patriotism and gallantry. Usually any ulterior plans he might have been harbouring himself are soon converted into sympathy or shame and a personal crusade to protect you!

GAY & LESBIAN TRAVELLERS

Homosexuality has long been denounced in Africa as 'un-African'. At the end of 1999, leaders in Zimbabwe, Uganda and Kenya famously condemned the practice, culminating in President Mugabe's description of homosexuals as 'lower than pigs and dogs'.

In Ethiopia and Eritrea, homosexuality is severely condemned – traditionally, religiously and legally – and remains a topic of absolute taboo. Don't underestimate the strength of feeling. Reports of gays being beaten up are not uncommon. In Amharic, the word *bushti* (homosexual) is a very offensive insult, implying immorality and depravity. One traveller wrote to us to report expulsion from a hotel and serious threats just for coming under suspicion. If a hotel only offers double beds, rather than twins, you and your companion may even be refused occupancy.

Women may have an easier time: even the idea of a lesbian relationship is beyond the permitted imaginings of many Ethiopians! Behave discreetly, and you will be assumed to be just friends.

Note that the Ethiopian penal code officially prohibits homosexual acts, with penalties of between 10 days' and 10 years' imprisonment for various 'crimes'. Although gay locals obviously exist, they behave with extreme discretion and caution. Gay travellers are advised to do likewise.

Information on homosexuality in the Horn is hard to come by, even in the well-known gay publications. Try the **International Lesbian and Gay Association** *(ILGA;* W *www .ilga.org)* for more information.

DISABLED TRAVELLERS

There is no reason why intrepid disabled travellers shouldn't visit Ethiopia. The recent civil war in the country left many soldiers disabled, so you should expect to find at least some degree of empathy and understanding.

For those with restricted mobility, all the sites on the historical route are easily reached by internal flights. Passengers in wheelchairs can be accommodated. Car rental with a driver is easily organised (though it's expensive). Be aware that some roads can be rough, and hard on the back.

Taxis are widely available in the large towns and are good for getting around. None have wheelchair access. In Addis Ababa a few hotels have lifts; at least two (the Sheraton and Hilton hotels) have facilities for wheelchair-users. Kerb ramps on streets are nonexistent, and potholes and uneven streets are a hazard.

Outside the capital, facilities are lacking, but many hotels are bungalow affairs, so at least steps or climbs are avoided.

For those restricted in other ways, such as visually or aurally, you'll get plenty of offers to help. Unlike in many Western countries, Ethiopians are not shy about coming forward to offer assistance.

A valuable source of general information is the **Access-Able Travel Source** *(*W *www .access-able.com).* This site has useful links.

Before leaving home, visitors can get in touch with their national support organisation. Ask for the 'travel officer', who may have a list of travel agents that specialise in tours for the disabled.

SENIOR TRAVELLERS

Traditionally, older citizens are accorded great respect in Ethiopia and the Horn, and in many tribal groups, older men constitute the village council, acting as judges, mediators and negotiators in daily affairs. Accordingly senior travellers will be offered a genuine welcome.

Older travellers interested in Ethiopia's culture have long formed the bulk of its tourism. As a result, at least in the capital and along the historical route, Ethiopia is reasonably geared up to meet the requirements of this age group with quite comfortable hotels and restaurants.

Taxis are readily available in Addis Ababa, and comfortable and air-conditioned cars can be hired for trips outside the capital. Travel by road can be hard-going, particularly for those with bad backs, so it might be an idea to opt for some internal flights where possible.

TRAVEL WITH CHILDREN

Ethiopians are very welcoming and open towards children, and there are no particular reasons for not taking the kids with you. However, many useful facilities for babies – such as cots in hotels, safety seats in hired cars, highchairs in restaurants and nappy-changing facilities – are almost totally lacking outside the smarter hotels in Addis Ababa. There are no childcare agencies either.

Items such as disposable nappies, baby food, milk powder and toys are available in some of the expat supermarkets of Addis Ababa, but bring adequate supplies of high-protection sunscreen.

Medical facilities are not bad in Addis Ababa (where there's a special 24-hour children's clinic with fully qualified paediatricians) and the larger towns, but in the smaller ones facilities and expertise can be severely limited.

Lonely Planet's *Travel with Children* by Cathy Lanigan contains detailed information about planning 'happy' family holidays.

DANGERS & ANNOYANCES

Compared with many African countries, Ethiopia – and even its capital, Addis Ababa – is a remarkably safe place. Serious or violent crime is rare; against travellers it's extremely rare. Outside the capital, the risk of petty crime drops still further.

A simple traveller's tip? Always look as if you know where you're going. Thieves and con artists get wind of an uncertain newcomer in a minute.

Though the following list may be off-putting and alarming, it's very unlikely you'll encounter any difficulties – and even less likely if you're prepared for them.

Theft

Pickpocketing is the biggest concern, but is a problem mainly in Addis Ababa and other large towns, in particular Shashemene, Nazret and Dessie. Often pickpockets work in teams or two or more. Whilst one distracts you, the other will target your pockets. Distraction techniques range from bumping into you to offering to brush off a deposit left on your shoulder by a bird!

Keep an eye on your belongings at bus stations. Be wary also of people offering to put your bags on the roof of the bus. See also Security under Money earlier in this chapter, and Dangers & Annoyances in the Addis Ababa chapter.

Shiftas & Civil Disturbances

In some of the remoter areas, such as the Ogaden Desert in the southeast, near the Kenyan border, along the Awash–Mille road at night, and in the far west, *shiftas* (bandits) are sometimes reported. These are usually ex-soldiers reluctant to forego their weapons and mercenary lifestyle. However, most of these places lie far from the main tourist trails. In fact, tourists are very rarely targeted; indeed they are positively avoided for fear of government repercussions.

During the past five years, around three terrorist bombs have been planted in public places. However, such incidents seem to be isolated and are extremely rare; much rarer than say in either Britain or Spain!

If you're concerned, check your government's latest security reports on countries (such as those published by the British Foreign Office reports).

Scams & Rip-Offs

Compared to other African countries, Ethiopia has few scams and rip offs to boast of, though incidences of the old chestnuts (see the boxed text 'Siren Scam' under Dangers & Annoyances in the Addis Ababa chapter) do seem to be on the increase.

The majority involve pretty harmless and – for most travellers – pretty transparent confidence tricks, but you should be aware of them. Apart from the Siren Scam, other common methods are 'hard luck' stories, or those soliciting sponsorship for travel or education in Ethiopia or abroad – though some of these cases may be genuine.

Also look out for fake antiques in the shops.

At the Airport

Taxi touts and guides can be a problem at airports, both at Addis Ababa and on the historical route (particularly Bahar Dar and Lalibela). Their mission is to steer you to cars or hotels and in doing so, earn a commission for themselves and a higher rate for you. Before arrival, decide on the hotel you wish to stay at and check hotel and taxi prices from the book (though be aware that these will increase with time). Then negotiate the taxi rate *before* you get in and insist on your destination.

The majority of Ethiopian taxi drivers are helpful, charming and honest.

Bribery & Bureaucracy

Bribes are very rarely extracted from foreigners. Bureaucracy is lessening, though any state-related activity such as procuring visa extensions, money exchange in government banks, or telephone calls from telecommunications do require a degree of patience.

One tip: deference to figures of authority is an important part of Ethiopian (and particularly Amhara) cultural etiquette. If you're polite and deferential to policemen and officials in general, you'll be amazed how much more forthcoming passage or permission is. If you're a woman, a smile works wonders!

Begging & Giving

Many travellers find that the begging they counter is one of the most distressing aspects of travel in Third World Countries.

After the recent war with Eritrea, the threats of famine, population displacement and the general drift towards cities, Ethiopia has its fair share of beggars. Some travellers resent being 'targeted' by beggars because they are foreign. However, the work of high-profile aid efforts has made this inevitable. Foreigners are often seen as dispensers of charity. The old Ethiopian pride and self-reliance has been undermined – albeit unintentionally.

It's difficult to know when to give, to whom and how much. Not a bad rule of thumb is to give to those who can't earn a living – such as the disabled, the ill, the elderly and the blind.

Ethiopians give small coins to beggars – doing so is thought to bestow a blessing on the giver. If you don't want to donate money, say instead *igzabier yisteh/yistesh* (m/f) (God bless you) with a slight bow of the head; this is a polite and acceptable way of declining to give.

Try to avoid the temptation to hand out pens or sweets to children. It unfairly raises their expectations, teaches them to beg and to miss school and can spoil the visits of travellers after you.

If feelings of guilt are getting the better of you (and they may well), a much better idea is to donate to a local charity, or patronise charitable gift shops (listed in some of the towns, particularly Addis Ababa).

Your embassy (and the Anglo-Ethiopian Society – see under Tourist Offices earlier) has lists of charities operating in Ethiopia. If you want to make a longer-term contribution, consider sponsoring an Ethiopian child through an organisation such as Plan International UK (W www.plan-international.org .uk). It costs just around UK£12 per month.

Guidelines for Guides

Few official guides exist in Ethiopia, and even fewer are subject to regulation. As everywhere, the profession can attract mercenary types in for an easy buck.

Some guides resort to aggression, hysterics or sulking to extract money from tourists; others to hard luck stories or appeals for 'sponsorship'. Others claim special expertise and that this and other guidebooks are wholly or partly 'wrong'. Some travellers have claimed their trips were ruined by guides.

To avoid a similar experience, here are a few tips:

• Choose a guide you're comfortable with. Test their knowledge of English and of the sites in advance, perhaps over a coffee.
• Ensure that your expectations are clearly understood before starting – such as what you want to see and how much time you have.
• Negotiate a fee in advance. Be aware that some may ask initially up to five times the going rate or more. Check this book for quotes.
• If the service has been good, it's fair and polite to tip a bit extra at the end, but don't be pressured into it, particularly if the tour was poor.

Self-Appointed Guides

High unemployment has spawned many self-appointed and unofficial guides. You will be approached, accompanied for a while, given unasked for information and then charged. Be wary of anyone who approaches you unasked, particularly at the exit of bus stations, etc. Unfortunately, there is almost always an ulterior motive. Be polite but firm – but also not paranoid!

Mobbing & Faranji Frenzy

The most common – and unfortunately the most wearisome – annoyance in Ethiopia is the famous '*faranji* frenzy'. It can take the form of screaming, giggling, shouting or sniggering children and greets the traveller at almost every turn in Ethiopia. For the new arrival as much as for the old-timer, the phenomenon is in turn distressing, exhausting, infuriating and demoralising. Unfortunately you're never likely to get used to it.

Like begging, there is no clear response. Ignoring it or, even better, treating it with humour is probably the best answer. Anger only provokes children more (there can be few things more tempting than a grumpy *faranji*!). An Amharic *hid!* (clear off!) for a boy, *hiji!* for a girl or *hidu!* for a group is the Ethiopian response, and sends children scuttling, but it can have the reverse effect, and is considered rather harsh from a foreigner. By contrast, a smile quickly dissipates tension and always gets a positive reaction.

If you're a 'captive spectacle' – such as when you're waiting for a bus – the best response is to break the animal in a zoo feeling. Try and communicate with the children by asking their name: *semesh/semeh man no?* for a boy/girl, or with sign language. You'll soon transform the howling mob into delightful and charming individuals.

The shouts of 'You, you!' is what most raises the hackles of travellers. Bear in mind, however, that the Amharic equivalent *(Ante!/Anchee!)* is the colloquial way of catching someone's attention. In other words, it's not as rude and aggressive as it sounds in English.

It's worth bearing in mind too that tourism is still undeveloped in Ethiopia. Much attention stems from the natural curiosity of children. Above all, it is almost *never* aggressive or hostile.

Most importantly, it may give you a very useful insight into what it may be like for minority groups with different skin colours in your home country. The only difference is that in Ethiopia, you may be sure the undue attention is motivated by curiosity, not, as in the West, by hostility and suspicion born from racism. It's a lesson you may never forget.

Land Mines

Years of war are responsible for a major problem in Ethiopia and Eritrea: land mines. Despite the government's best efforts – defusing more than 5000 mines to date – many still litter the countryside, and continue sporadically to kill and maim the population.

Most travellers have nothing to fear from mines. Trekkers and drivers in remote areas should take care. Anywhere fighting has occurred, such as the Ogaden and parts of Tigray, are known mined areas. Check with local village officials before setting out. Keep to paved routes, or if you are trekking never stray off track. A useful phrase might be *Fenjy alle?* (Are there mines here?) Popular trekking areas such as the Simien and Bale Mountains National Parks are perfectly safe.

Dangerous Animals

Traditionally dangerous animals such as the elephant and buffalo are confined to very restricted areas in Ethiopia – you'd be very lucky to see one at all!

If you're rafting or fishing, beware the hippo, responsible for more deaths in Africa than any other animal. The rules are simple: stay away from any densely vegetated shore area. Though not aggressive per se, hippos will trample anything that gets between them and the water. If in a boat, steer well clear of mothers with young, who will attack if they feel threatened.

The crocodile poses a considerable danger on rivers and on riverbanks. Stay away from both if crocodiles frequent the area, and don't dangle limbs from boats.

The spotted hyena is common in rural areas in the Horn and is a notorious scavenger. If camping, sleep inside a tent, or at least close to a campfire.

LEGAL MATTERS

Remember that when in Ethiopia, you're subject to Ethiopian laws. If you're arrested, you must in theory be brought to court within 48 hours. You have the right to talk to someone from your embassy as well as a lawyer.

Drugs

Penalties for possession, use or trafficking of illegal drugs (including hashish) are strictly enforced in Ethiopia. Convicted offenders can expect both fines and long jail sentences.

Consumption of the mildly stimulating leaf chat is permitted in Ethiopia (see the boxed texts 'Chat Among the Pigeons' in the Eastern Ethiopia chapter), but not in Eritrea.

Alcohol

Alcohol cannot be served to anyone under 18 years of age in Ethiopia. Disturbance caused by those under the influence of alcohol is punishable by three months' to one year's imprisonment. Driving while under the influence attracts a fine of around Birr150.

BUSINESS HOURS

Business hours vary from region to region and usually correspond to the climate. In the hot lowlands, such as in Gambela, there is sometimes a siesta during the hottest hours of the day, but offices open earlier.

Government offices in the highlands open from around 8.30am to 12.30pm (to 11.30am

Friday) and 1.30pm to 5.30pm Monday to Friday. Most private organisations and NGOs open from 8am to 1pm and 2pm to 5pm weekdays. Shops usually operate half an hour later, restaurants from noon to around 2pm and from 6.30pm to around 10.30pm daily except Sunday. In the smaller towns and rural areas, restaurants may stop serving – or run out of food – as early as 8.30pm.

For bank and post office hours, see Banks and Post & Communications earlier in this chapter.

PUBLIC HOLIDAYS & SPECIAL EVENTS

Religious and secular festivals in Ethiopia are often colourful events with pageantry, music and dancing. If you can coincide with one, don't miss it.

Ethiopia's public holidays can be divided into three categories: national secular holidays, Christian Orthodox festivals and Islamic holidays.

Because the country follows the Julian calendar of 13 months (see the boxed text 'Be Seven Years Younger' earlier in this chapter), some events trail those of the Western Gregorian calendar by around one week. The following dates are correct by the Gregorian calendar.

National Holidays

National holidays include the following:

Victory of Adwa Commemoration Day 2 March
Ethiopian Patriots' Victory Day (also known as Liberation Day) 5 May
International Labour Day 1 May
Downfall of the Derg 28 May

Christian Orthodox Festivals

Major Ethiopian Orthodox festivals include:

Leddet (also known as Genna or Christmas) 6-7 January. Less important than Timkat and Meskel, Leddet is still significant. The faithful attend all-night church services, often moving from one church to another. On Christmas day, the traditional games of *genna* (a kind of hockey) and sometimes *gugs* (a kind of polo) are played, along with horse racing. Priests don their full regalia. Lalibela is one of the best places to experience Leddet; Addis Ababa is also good.

Timkat (Epiphany, celebrating Christ's baptism) 19 January. This three-day festival is the most colourful of the year. The church *tabots* (replicas of the Ark of the Covenant) are taken to a nearby body of water on the afternoon of the

eve of Timkat. During the night, the priests and faithful participate in a vigil around the *tabots*. The following morning, the crowds gather around the water, which is blessed, then splashed onto them; religious vows are renewed. The *tabot* is then paraded back to the church accompanied by much singing and dancing. Gonder is considered the best place to be for Timkat; Addis Ababa is also good (head for Jan Meda).

Good Friday March/April. From Thursday evening before Good Friday, the faithful fast until the Easter service, which ends at 3am on Easter Sunday.

Fasika (Orthodox Easter) March/April. Fasika marks the end of a vegetarian fast of 55 days, in which no animal product is eaten. Officially, nothing should be consumed until the daily church service finishes at around 3pm. In the past, many of Ethiopia's enemies took advantage of the fasting period to inflict heavy casualties on its weakened armies.

Kiddus Yohannes (New Year's Day) 11 September. Ethiopian New Year (also known as Enkutatash) is an important family and social event. Traditionally, new clothes are bought for the occasion, particularly for the children, and relatives and friends are visited. Special feasts are prepared. The traditional game of *gugs* can sometimes be seen.

Meskel (Finding of the True Cross) 27 September. This two-day festival is the most colourful festival after Timkat. Bonfires are built topped by a cross to which flowers are tied – most commonly the Meskel daisy. After the bonfires are blessed, they are lit, and dancing and singing begins around them. Priests don their full regalia. Addis Ababa, Gonder and Aksum are good places to experience Meskel.

Festival of Maryam Zion 30 November. This festival is exclusive to Aksum, celebrating the namesake of the famous church of St Maryam of Zion (believed by Ethiopians to house the original Ark of the Covenant). There is much singing and dancing (see Aksum in the Northern Ethiopia chapter).

Kulubi Gabriel 28 December. Although not on the official religious holiday list, large numbers of Ethiopians make a pilgrimage to the venerated Kulubi Gabriel church near Dire Dawa in the east (see the boxed text 'Kulubi Gabriel' under Asaita in the Eastern Ethiopia chapter). If you're in the area, don't miss it.

Islamic Holidays

Islamic holidays are not particularly conspicuous in Ethiopia but they are important events for the Muslim population. Festivals include Ras as-Sana (the Muslim New Year), Mawlid an-Nabi (the Prophet's birthday),

Lailat al-Mira'ji (Ascension of the Prophet Mohammed), Eid al-Fitr, Eid al-Adha and Al-Ashura. Exact dates move forward from year to year, as they depend on the Islamic calendar (which is 10 or 11 days shorter than the Julian calendar).

ACTIVITIES
Trekking & Rock Climbing
Trekking is the most developed activity in Ethiopia. Both the Simien and Bale Mountains offer good trekking and good wildlife. See the relevant sections, as well as under Flora & Fauna – National Parks in the Facts about Ethiopia chapter.

There is untapped potential for rock climbing, particularly around Mekele in the region of Tigray, which offers sandstone climbs in the HVS – E2 (4c-5c) range, though you'll have to come out fully equipped and self-sufficient and prepared to locate your own routes. Contact Village Ethiopia (see under Organised Tours in the Getting Around chapter), which has catered to climbers in the past.

Bird Watching
Various tour agencies both inside and outside Ethiopia offer excellent bird-watching tours. See Organised Tours in the Getting Around chapter.

White-Water Rafting & Kayaking
Rafting began in Ethiopia in the 1970s, when an American team rafted the Omo River in the southwest. Travel agencies now regularly run trips (See Organised Tours in the Getting Around chapter).

The Omo River rafting season is from September to October (after the heavy rains). Tours usually last from one to three weeks. The white water (classed as a comparatively tame three or four on the US scale) is not the main attraction, rather the exposure to wildlife (particularly birds) and tribal groups (such as those along the Omo River).

In theory, excellent kayaking could be had on many of Ethiopia's rivers, including the Blue Nile, Omo and Awash Rivers, but it's not for the inexperienced. Trips need to be well planned, well equipped and well backed up. In the past, some badly planned trips have gone tragically wrong. Get in touch with the Addis Ababa–based tour agencies who will put you in touch with experienced kayakers in Ethiopia.

Fishing
Ethiopia's lakes and rivers are home to over 200 species of freshwater fish including very large catfish (up to 18kg), tilapia, large barbus, tigerfish, the brown and rainbow trout and the famously feisty Nile perch.

Fly-fishing, bait fishing with float and leger, freelining, threadline spinning and trolling are all permitted fishing practices, but you'll need to be totally self-sufficient as far as equipment is concerned.

Popular fishing spots include Lake Tana and around the Blue Nile Falls in the north, the Rift Valley lakes in the south, and the Baro River in the west. Fishing is permitted everywhere in Ethiopia (bar the usual sensitive areas), with the exception of rivers in the Bale Mountains National Park, where endemic species are found.

COURSES
Amharic language and dance classes are available in the capital. Unless you're spending long periods there, classes will need to be scheduled with a private tutor, which can be expensive (see Courses in the Addis Ababa chapter).

WORK
Travellers in Ethiopia on tourist visas are not allowed to take up employment. If you're planning to work, you will have to apply to the Ministry of Labour and Social Affairs for a work permit, and to the Department of Immigration in the Ministry of the Interior for a residence permit. Both ministries are found in Addis Ababa.

ACCOMMODATION
Tourism is still relatively undeveloped in Ethiopia. Outside Addis Ababa and the main towns, accommodation can be limited in range. Even in the capital, there are no hostels, homestays, or university or rental accommodation available to travellers.

Camping
Tents are useful in Ethiopia for trekking, the exploration of remote regions and to save money on extended stays. If you're just planning a short trek, tents can be hired in the capital. Otherwise, cheap hotels are found almost everywhere.

In theory, you can camp anywhere, bar the obvious off-limits sites, such as military installations. 'Established' camping grounds have been set up in some parts of the country such as in the national parks, but most lack any kind of facilities and consist of little more than a clearing beside a river. It is essential to treat drinking water at the sites.

In the last couple of years, a few privately owned, upmarket camping grounds have sprung up around the country, including near Lake Langano, in the Omo Valley and Arba Minch and in the Afar region. Tents can be pitched here (or hired); some camping grounds offer bungalow accommodation too. Though they're comparatively expensive, they're well designed, eco-friendly and offer great outdoor experiences if you can afford a night or two. See Organised Tours in the Getting Around chapter. Some of the tour agencies also offer fully equipped camping trips (including guide, cook, vehicle and driver).

Hotels

Hotels are cheap and plentiful. Outside the larger towns, however, facilities are distinctly lacking. Nor is maintenance a high priority; the best budget hotels are often those that have just opened. If you hear of a new hotel in town, it may be the best place to head.

Faranjis are usually charged a different rate to Ethiopians. This isn't as unfair as it sounds: prices are still dirt cheap, and you'll always be given priority as well as the best rooms, facilities and service. Ethiopians could never afford to pay similar prices. Some hotels (particularly government-owned ones) charge tax (up to 20%) on top of room prices; check in advance.

Note that in Ethiopia, a room with a double bed is confusingly called a 'single', and a room with twin beds a 'double'. In our reviews we have used the usual interpretation of singles, doubles and twins. Prices for one or for two people are often the same – in other words, there are rarely single rates. Single sex couples are often charged more than mixed couples.

In the budget hotels, always take a peek at the room (and bathroom) before accepting it. Few owners of budget hotels speak much English; the Lonely Planet Ethiopian Amharic Phrasebook really is a good investment here. See also the language chapter at the back of this book.

During the high season (October to January) and particularly over the major festivals some of the mid-range to top-end hotels quickly fill up with tour groups in towns such as Lalibela and Aksum. Reservations should be made as far in advance as possible – even

six months is not too long. Try and get the reservation in writing; occasionally independent travellers are bumped off reservations by tour group mass bookings.

There are no left-luggage facilities in Addis Ababa. However, most of the hotels catering to foreign travellers provide a pretty safe service for no extra charge.

Budget Cheap hotels make up around 90% of hotels in Ethiopia (they cater to local demand) and usually consist of pretty spartan rooms with access to a shared (usually cold) shower and toilet. Many double as drinking dens and brothels. However, given Ethiopia's permissive society (see the boxed text 'Prostitution' earlier in this chapter), these are less seedy and surreptitious than they sound. However, they can be noisy. Bring earplugs if you sleep lightly. Resist the water provided in the White Horse whisky bottles by the bed. It's for washing after the night's energetic activities (as is the ubiquitous plastic potty)!

In rural areas, 'hotels' sometimes consist of a bed in a hut on a dirt floor without either running water or electricity.

Most budget hotels cost from Birr17 to Birr22; sometimes Birr1to Birr2 is charged for the use of a shared shower.

Mid-Range Many of the original 'tourist class' hotels were nationalised in the 1970s and '80s under the socialist Derg. Today, they continue to be run by state-owned chains, though the government is currently trying to sell them off to the private sector. Most of the government hotels quote rates in US dollars. You can pay in birr but the rate will be pegged to the daily dollar equivalent.

Prices range from US$20 to US$50, and facilities usually include a room with private shower, as well as an adequate restaurant, parking and a garden. Though usually clean and quiet, the majority are looking tired and run-down, and very rarely offer good value for money.

Worth singling out, however, is the Ghion Hotel Group. Its chain of hotels – on the historical route – boasts exceptional settings and an attractive, traditional design. Though not bargains (singles/doubles US$37.50/50), they're well worth considering. In many places, they represent the top range.

The other government chains include the Ras Hotel Group, the Wabe Shebele Group and the Ethiopia Hotel Group. The Bekele Mola Hotel Group is a private chain that offers a similar standard and style of accommodation, though it usually offers better value.

Most of the larger towns also have private hotels, which offer clean rooms with private bathrooms; many are much better value that the state-owned hotels, costing US$4 to US$6 per night.

Top End The new, five-star 'Luxury Collection' Sheraton Hotel is Addis Ababa's pride and joy, and rivals anything on the continent for facilities and comfort. In many of the larger towns, and along the historical route, private top-end hotels are mushrooming.

FOOD
Like its wildlife, many of Ethiopia's dishes are 'endemic', and take a bit of getting used to! Ethiopia's food provokes strong reaction. Short-term visitors on the whole loathe it, longer-term visitors usually loathe it – then come to love it. Some loathe it – and go on loathing it. In the author's opinion, you need to be very hungry five times running.

For those who never quite come round, there is a wide selection of international food available in Addis Ababa: from Indian and Chinese to Italian and Armenian (see Places to Eat in the Addis Ababa chapter). These places cater to a large expat community from a large number of countries, and the standard is often high.

Prices are reasonable by Western standards. Mains cost around Birr30 to Birr60 even in the most expensive restaurants. Note, however, that a 15% tax may be added to the bill – check in advance if you're on a budget.

Wine normally costs from Birr50 to Birr60 for local varieties and around Birr150 for imported varieties.

Outside Addis Ababa, you'll find little more than local fare. If you don't take to it – and short-stay visitors often don't – you can usually find an Italian-style dish somewhere on the menu (complete with usually overcooked pasta) such as spaghetti bolognese or lasagne. Prices are cheap: a meal for two rarely costs more than about Birr15 to Birr25.

In the larger towns, the tourist-class hotels have a greater selection of *faranji* food (particularly the government-owned hotels which have been serving up the same old nosh for years). However, the cuisine is not known for either diversity or imagination. It's normally fish or meat cutlet with salad and veg. Standards are improving.

In many of the towns, you will find a *keak beat* (cake shop), which serves various pastries and fresh fruit juices. They're good places for breakfast. Many open pretty early (from around 6am). For standard restaurant hours, see Business Hours earlier in this chapter.

Traditional Food
Contrary to the impressions of most travellers, Ethiopian cooking is quite varied and complex. Though all restaurants seem to offer exactly the same fare, other dishes are often available. It's worth experimenting too – prices are so cheap, you can afford to make the odd mistake.

Edible Cutlery

However rude you are about *injera* (the famous Ethiopian 'pancake'), it does its job. Slightly bitter, it goes well with spicy food. Like bread, it's filling; and like a pancake, it's good for wrapping around small pieces of food and mopping up juices. It's also easier to manipulate than rice and doesn't fall apart like bread – quite a clever invention, really. And no need for plates or cutlery either (or napkins or tablecloths).

Although to you all *injera* may look like old grey kitchen flannel, grades and nuances do exist. With a bit of time and perseverance, you may even become a bit of an *injera* connoisseur.

Low-quality *injera* is traditionally dark, coarse and sometimes very thick and is made from millet or even sorghum. Good-quality *injera* is pale (the paler the better), regular in thickness, smooth (free of husks, etc) and *always* made with the indigenous Ethiopian cereal *tef*. Because *tef* grows only in the highlands, the best *injera* is traditionally found there, and highlanders tend to be rather snooty about lesser lowland versions.

In some of the smaller restaurants, menus are only available in Amharic. If you want to ask if something's on the menu, just add an *alle*? For example, *Doro wat alle?* – Is there *doro wat*?

Vegetarian Apart from on fasting days (see later), Ethiopians are rapacious carnivores and vegetables are often conspicuous by their complete absence. Meat is considered a luxury; vegetables are for poor households only.

If you're vegetarian, the best plan is to order alternative dishes in advance. If not, some dishes such as shiro (chick pea puree) are quite quickly prepared.

On Wednesday and Friday, vegetarians can breathe easy. These are the traditional fasting days, when no animal products should be eaten. Ethiopian fasting food most commonly includes lentils, potatoes, cabbage, spinach and beetroot. Useful phrases include *sega albellam* (I don't eat meat) and *atkilt-b-dabbo* (vegetables with bread).

If you're concerned about available vegetarian food, you may even want to consider travelling during a fasting period, such as the one before Fasika (see Public Holidays earlier in this chapter). By the same token, nonvegetarians may want to avoid this period (though the fancier hotels always cater for both options all the time).

Injera You're never likely to forget your first experience of *injera*. It's a constant source of fascination among travellers and a favourite talking point.

Injera is the national staple, serving as the base of every meal. Spread out like a large, thin pancake, food is simply heaped on top of it. An American tourist once famously mistook it for the tablecloth. Occasionally, *injera* is served rolled up beside the food or on a separate plate.

Traditionally, *injera* is served on a communal tray on a *mesob* (a colourful, mushroom-shaped table, woven like a basket). You simply tear off a piece of injera with your right hand (see the boxed text 'Eating Etiquette'), and wrap it around the food served with it. You can ask for as much injera as you want with a meal (there's no extra charge).

Wat The favourite companion of injera, *wat* resembles a meat stew minus the vegetables.

In the highlands, lamb is the most common constituent of wat. Beef wat is encountered in the large towns, and goat wat most often in the arid lowlands. Ethiopian Christians as well as Muslims avoid pork.

Ethiopian food is spicy rather than hot (as tourist literature describes it). It's nothing compared to a good *vindaloo* or similar Indian dish, but it has a kick, and it may provoke a dab or two at your nostrils with a handkerchief.

Most travellers take it in their stride. *Kai wat* tends to be spicier than other dishes. If you don't care for spicy food, ask for *alicha* (mild) food, which is almost always available. Many tourist-class hotels deliberately serve travellers toned-down versions of the traditional Ethiopian dishes. If you like your food spicy, make sure you ask for it (it can verge on the insipid side otherwise).

Tere Sega Considered something of a luxury in Ethiopia – and akin perhaps to smoked salmon in the West – is *tere sega* (raw meat). It is traditionally served by the wealthy at weddings and other special celebrations.

Some restaurants also specialise in it. Not unlike butcher shops in appearance, these places feature carcasses hanging near the entrance and men in bloodied overalls brandishing carving knives. The restaurants are not as gruesome as they sound: the carcass is to demonstrate that the meat is fresh, and the men in overalls to guarantee you get the piece you fancy – two assurances you don't always get in the West.

A plate and a sharp knife serve as utensils, and *awazi* and *berbere* as accompaniments. Served with some local red wine, and enjoyed with Ethiopian friends, it's a ritual not to be missed – at least not for red-blooded meat eaters.

Contrary to popular belief, Ethiopians do not carve meat from living animals. James Bruce, the famous 18th-century Scottish explorer, was responsible for perpetuating this myth. Whether it ever occurred in the past, remains uncertain. Most historians discredit many of Bruce's tales including this one.

Kitfo The next big treat for the ordinary Ethiopian – akin perhaps to fillet steak in the West – is *kitfo*. The leanest meat is reserved for this dish, which is then minced and warmed in a pan with a little butter, berbere and sometimes *tosin* (thyme). Like the French steak tartare, which it greatly resembles, it can be bland and disgusting, or tasty and divine. If you're ravenous after a hard day's travelling, it's just the ticket, as it's very filling.

Traditionally, it's served just *leb leb* (warmed not cooked), though you can ask for it to be *betam leb leb* (literally 'very warmed', ie, cooked!). A *kitfo special* is served with *aib* (like a kind of dry cottage cheese) and *gomen* (minced spinach).

In the Gurage region (where it's something of a speciality) it's often served with *kotcho* or *enset*. *Kitfo beats* (restaurants specialising in *kitfo*) are found in the larger towns.

Other Dishes Other meat dishes to look out for include the delicious *kwalima* (beef sausage), a speciality of the city of Harar. It resembles a Spanish *chorizo*, but is usually served on special occasions only.

Ethiopians are not great fish eaters, despite the number of lakes and rivers. You won't come across it very often, except in towns or resorts on the very edge of lakes. Some of the nomadic tribes (such as in the Ogaden) positively revile it. If you do encounter it, it's well worth opting for. The fish is usually exceptionally fresh and simply but well cooked (usually grilled or fried in batter) and served with lemon.

Desserts aren't commonly encountered either: usually just a bit of fruit is offered, or a creme caramel that once lived in a packet.

Fast Food & Snacks
Fast food is a welcome option for travellers who don't take to local fare. In Addis Ababa,

---

Eating Etiquette

Eating from individual plates with individual meat and individual vegetables, strikes most Ethiopians as hilarious, as well as rather bizarre and wasteful. In Ethiopia, food is always shared from a single plate without the use of cutlery.

Sharing a meal with an Ethiopian is a wonderful way of cementing new friendships. But Ethiopian etiquette can be refined and complex:

• If you're invited for a meal at an Ethiopian's house, it's customary to bring a small gift such as pastries or flowers in the town; sugar, coffee and fruit in the country.

• In households and many of the restaurants, a jug of water and a basin are brought out to wash the guests' outstretched hands before the meal. You remain seated throughout (though it's polite to make a gesture of getting up if the person serving you is older). You will be handed a towel afterwards.

• In a restaurant, it's usual to invite those around you, even strangers, to join you, with an *Enebla!* (Please join us!) If you in turn are invited, it's polite to accept a morsel of the food to show appreciation. Or if this is difficult, pat your stomach contentedly to show that you've had your fill.

• Use just your right hand for eating. The left – as in Muslim countries – is reserved for personal hygiene only; keep it firmly tucked under the table.

• Avoid touching your mouth or licking your fingers.

• Don't put food back onto the food plate – even by the side. It's better to discard it onto the table or floor, or keep it in your napkin.

• Take from your side of the tray only; reaching is considered impolite.

• However hungry you are, try not to guzzle. Greed is considered rather uncivilised.

• Filling your mouth too full, or on both sides of your cheeks, is also considered impolite.

• The tastiest morsels will often be laid in front of you; it is polite to accept them or, equally, to divide them among your fellow diners.

• The meat in dishes such as *doro wat* is usually saved until last, so don't hone in on it immediately!

• Don't be embarrassed or alarmed at the tradition of *gursha*, when someone – usually the host – picks the tastiest morsel and feeds it directly into your mouth. The trick is to take it without letting your mouth come into contact with the person's fingers, or allowing the food to fall. It is a mark of great friendship or affection, and is usually given at least twice (once is considered unlucky). Refusing to take *gursha* is a terrible slight to the person offering it!

• It is considered good manners – and essential in the rural areas – to leave some leftovers on the plate after a meal. Failing to do so is sometimes seen as inviting famine, and may seriously upset the household.

• It is considered perfectly proper to pick your teeth after a meal with a toothpick (usually supplied in restaurants).

there are a number of fast food places which are not bad, but prices are usually higher than local restaurants. Outside town, fast food is rarely found, though local snacks such as *kolo* (roasted barley) and *bekolo* (popcorn) make great in-between-meal fillers, or novelties with which to while away long bus journeys.

Self-Catering

Supermarkets in the capital are reasonably well supplied, and campers and trekkers should have no problems stocking up. For variety and choice, Addis Ababa is the place to do it.

Outside the capital, provisions are limited. Most grocers stock little more than sugar, coffee, packets of pasta, tomato puree and pretty bland biscuits.

However, good markets are found throughout the country, selling a wide and wonderful selection of fresh fruit and vegetables. Saturday is the main market day throughout Ethiopia.

DRINKS
Coffee

Ethiopia has a well-founded claim to be the original home of coffee, and the famous 'coffee ceremony' is an integral part of Ethiopian culture and etiquette. As a result of Italian influence, macchiato, cappuccino and a kind of caffe latte known as a *buna beweta* (coffee with milk) are also available in many of the towns. Sometimes the herb rhu (known locally as *t'ena adam*, or health of Adam) is served with coffee, as is butter.

Ethiopians seem to have sweet tooths. Large quantities of sugar are automatically added to hot drinks as well as to fruit juices. If you don't want sugar, make it clear when you order. Ask for the drink *yale sukkar* (without sugar). If you want milk with your tea or coffee, ask for *betinnish wetet* (with a little milk). Soft drinks are widely available.

Tea

In lowland Muslim areas, *shai* (tea) is often preferred, and is offered black, sometimes spiced with cloves or ginger.

Water

The water in Addis Ababa is considered safe to drink, but as in many places, new arrivals may experience problems. Ambo is the most famous brand of mineral water – Ambo is now used as a generic name for sparkling mineral water. It's so fizzy that it keeps its sparkle even in a glass left overnight! It costs Birr3 to Birr4 for a 750ml bottle and is widely available. *Highland* is a new, still mineral water, sold in plastic bottles.

Fruit Juice & Soft Drinks

In most towns, you'll find a *jus beat* (juice bar), which serves delicious, freshly squeezed

---

The Coffee Ceremony

The coffee ceremony typifies Ethiopian hospitality. An invitation to attend a ceremony is a mark of friendship or respect – though it's not an event for those in a hurry.

When you're replete after a meal, the ceremony begins. Freshly cut grass is scattered on the ground 'to bring in the freshness and fragrance of nature'. Nearby, there's an incense burner smoking with *etan* (gum). The 'host' sits on a stool before a tiny charcoal stove.

First of all coffee beans are roasted in a pan. As the smoke rises, it is considered polite to draw it towards you, inhale it deeply and express great pleasure at the delicious aroma by saying *betam tiru no* ('lovely!'). Next the beans are ground up with a pestle and mortar; the beans are then brewed up with water in a pan.

When it's finally ready, the coffee is served in tiny china cups with at least three spoonfuls of sugar. At least three cups must be accepted. The third in particular is considered to bestow a blessing – it is the *berekha* (blessing) cup. Sometimes popcorn is passed around. It should be accepted with two hands extended and cupped together.

In offices, where time is more pressing, a cup of ready-prepared coffee is offered instead, but the gesture of welcome or respect is the same. Cups should always be accepted, even if you only have a sip.

juices. The local favourite is *spris*, a mixture usually consisting of avocado, mango and papaya; it's surprisingly delicious.

Alcoholic Drinks

In the larger towns, all the usual spirits are found – imports as well as dirt-cheap local versions. An Addis Ababa Piazza speciality is a *gin fir fir* – gin and beer! If you want to raise an eyebrow or two in smart Addis Ababa society, try ordering it.

Drunkenness is considered rather uncivilised in Ethiopia; if you've had one too many, try at least to pretend that you haven't.

Beer Ethiopian beer is generally mild, quite smooth and drinkable. It's also cheap at Birr4 to Birr5. There are a number of varieties. Top of the pops among the locals currently is Harar. Bati is also popular; Meta is lighter. Bedele 'gives headache in morning' as a local connoisseur put it – it's a little stronger! It's also the only Ethiopian beer currently exported. Castel is probably the strongest. Dashen is the newest brand.

Home-brews include *tella*, made from finger millet, maize or barley. Every village and monastery brews it. Slightly bitter, often unfiltered, it's nevertheless amazingly refreshing if you're thirsty (though note that the water used for brewing may be unsafe).

Nonalcoholic beer is also available including a brand made in the Muslim town of Harar.

Wine Though no cause for huge celebration, local wine isn't at all bad, particularly the red Guder and – perhaps second-best – Dukam. Of the whites, the dry Awash Crystal is about the best bet. Unless you're an aficionado of sweet red, avoid Axumite. Wine is very reasonably priced in restaurants. In the Addis Ababa supermarkets, there's a selection of European and South African wines.

Guder is also sold in a type of beer bottle, complete with metal cap, and chilled contents. If you don't want it chilled (and it tastes far better at room temperature) make it clear when you place your order.

Araki If you're not catching an early bus the next morning, try the local *araki*, a grain spirit not unlike Greek *ouzo*, which will make you positively gasp. The Ethiopians believe it's good for high blood pressure! *Dagem araki* is twice-filtered and is finer. A 1.5L bottle costs just Birr15 (less than US$2).

Tej One drink not to be missed is *tej*, a delicious – and sometimes pretty powerful – local 'wine' made from honey, and fermented using a local shrub known as *gesho*.

Tej used to be the drink of the Ethiopian kings. Today some of the better restaurants or *tej beat* brew their own. Towns famous for their *tej* are Addis Ababa, Debre Markos, Arba Minch and Jimma and Bonga. It is served in little flasks known as *birille* (Birr2 to Birr5).

Tej can be flavoured with coffee and even chat, and comes in varying degrees of sweetness – the dryer it is, the more alcoholic. *Derek* is dry, *mahakalenya* is medium sweet, and *laslasa* or *bers* is sweet and pretty mild.

ENTERTAINMENT

Addis Ababa boasts the usual city entertainments including quite decent cinemas (showing films in English), nightclubs and a number of theatres (though plays are almost all in Amharic). A few of the larger hotels in the capital stage traditional dance and music shows.

Ethiopians love to dance, and in the smaller bars such as in the Piazza in Addis Ababa, you'll get plenty of chances to see dancing. Traditional dancing is quite unique in style, with various variations on shaking body parts. If you give it a go, you'll win lots of friends.

Music in the town bars is for the most part Amharic pop, which, like the food, takes a bit of getting used to. Western pop, jazz, reggae and various other types of music are also heard in Addis Ababa. Most bars close around 10pm or 11pm on weeknights, but open until at least 2am on Friday and Saturday.

Nightclubs in Addis Ababa tend to be more 'westernised' in ambience and music. They are expensive by Ethiopian standards (from Birr10 to Birr20 for entrance and per drink) and attract a wealthier crowd, many of them 'returnees'. They don't really get going until the weekend; then some don't close until 5am or later.

Outside the capital, entertainment is limited to a few bars and cafés, *biliardo* (Italian billiards) and (the latest craze) table tennis.

For more information, see Entertainment in the Addis Ababa chapter; see also Arts in the Facts about Ethiopia chapter.

SPECTATOR SPORTS

See also Spectator Sports in the Addis Ababa chapter.

Running

Ethiopia is known for its extraordinary pantheon of long-distance runners. Haile

An Interview with Africa's Giant – Haile Gebreselassie

Is there a race left, or a record in the world, that you dream of now?

The marathon. The marathon is very important to us Ethiopians. We won it in '60, in '64, and in '68...want to win an Olympic marathon.

Why do you think so many Ethiopians have made great long-distance runners?

We are poor, we don't have cars and we are a big country. In my village if you are rich, you have a donkey, if you don't, you walk. I was poor, I must walk many, many kilometres every day to school. Maybe also the height; the Ethiopian highlands, they are nearly 3000m...we know how to breathe.

You mentioned God. Are you a religious man?

I am Orthodox...In Ethiopia, our religion is very old and very important to us. Before a race I say: 'Please God, give me a nice little day'.

What are your ambitions in the long-term?

I want to help my people. We have a beautiful country – we are rich, but we have nothing in our stomachs. I am afraid for the future. ...Education. We must educate the people: two babies not ten.

And what about Ethiopia's image abroad?

Everyone they think Ethiopia is desert. Some American athletes they come here, and you know what? They bring everything with them: food, bread – even water!

I have made a big mistake 'til now. I know only Addis Ababa and Asela! I know Europe, America...I am ashamed. I have seen Aksum only on television! But in Ethiopia we say 'Seeing is better than hearing'.

Then we'll have to send you a copy of this Lonely Planet guidebook, Haile...

Gebreselassie, one of the most famous, and still breaking records today, is arguably the greatest long-distance runner in the world, and one of the best of all time. Many people know Ethiopia only through this man.

At just 1.6m (5 feet 3 inches) tall, Africa's 'giant' has won two Olympic and four World 10,000m gold medals, and has set no fewer than 15 world records over distances between 3000m and 10,000m; three of these remain unbeaten – the 3000m, 5000m and 10,000m. In February 2003, he broke a new world record in the two-mile race in Birmingham.

Other great athletes include Abebe Bikila, the marathon runner of the 1960s, who took gold medals at both the Tokyo and Rome Olympics (famously running barefoot at the latter). The legendary Belayneh Densamo held the world record for the marathon for close to a decade (1989–98), with a time of 2:06:50. Dubbed by some the 'new Haile Gebreselassie' is 20-year-old Kenenisa Bekele, who has recently dominated World Cross Country Championships. Another rising star to look out for is the 2000 Olympic Marathon champion, Gezahegne Abera, who won the London Marathon men's title in April 2003.

Ethiopian women in recent years have been causing no less of a sensation. At the Barcelona Olympics, Derartu Tulu became Ethiopia's first woman gold medallist in the 10,000m event. Other remarkable runners are Fatuma Roba, who won the 1996 Olympic Marathon, and Gete Wami, who took a bronze in the 10,000m at the Atlanta Olympics. In Stuttgart, Germany, Birhanie Aderie broke a world record when she won the 3000m at the 2002 indoor championships. Other women winning races in Europe throughout 2003 include Worknesh Kidane.

Other Sports

By far the most popular national sport is football (soccer). There are 15 football teams in Addis Ababa alone, and another 29 across the country. Other popular sports include volleyball, tennis, basketball, table tennis and *carambula*, a kind of pool without the cues. Introduced by the Italians, it's particularly popular in Tigray.

Ethiopia also boast its own indigenous sports. *Genna* is a variety of hockey without boundaries, traditionally played at Christmas.

Gugs is also most commonly seen at festivals, including New Year (September 11) or Meskel (September 27), and is a physical – and sometimes fairly violent – game of tag on horseback. In the past, the games prepared young warriors for war. If you're in Addis Ababa during one of the festivals, don't miss them. The Jan Meda Race Ground normally hosts the event.

SHOPPING

Ethiopia has a good selection of souvenirs. To get a good idea of the range and quality of potential purchases, a trip to the excellent Ethnological Museum in Addis Ababa is useful (see the Addis Ababa chapter). See also the boxed text 'Arts & Crafts' in the Western Ethiopia chapter.

Good souvenir shops are found in the capital as well as in some of the towns on the historical route. Quality and artistry ranges from poor to very high, so it's worth comparing shops and wares. Prices in some places largely depend on your skills of negotiation. Don't forget the export regulations (see under Customs earlier in this chapter).

The *gabi*, the white, cotton toga worn by the highlanders, makes a great – though rather bulky – travelling companion. It serves as a blanket, pillow, mattress, cushion (on long bus journeys) and wraps against the cold.

Shipping items home is reasonably priced (see Post & Communications earlier in this chapter).

Getting There & Away

AIR
Airports
Bole international airport at Addis Ababa is the principal international airport in Ethiopia. The new airport building (which opened in January 2003 at a cost of US$135 million) contains banks (open 24 hours), a post office, souvenir and duty-free shops, a café and restaurants (accepting both US dollars and birr), a business centre (with Internet and fax access) and free trolleys. Porters expect to be tipped at least Birr2 per bag.

An Ethiopian Tourism Commission office at the airport can make reservations at hotels free of charge. Regional airports are currently being upgraded.

Because of recent increased security concerns, most airlines recommend checking in at least 2½ hours prior to departure.

In Ethiopia, check-in closes one hour before departure.

Tickets
Many travel agencies now have websites – some agents operate only online – and using the Internet is an easy way to compare prices.

Online ticket sales work well for one-way or return trips on specified dates and travel agents can provide information on special deals, strategies for avoiding layovers, and advice on travel insurance.

Beware of cheap flights advertised by obscure agencies. Try to chose a bonded agent, such as one covered by the Air Travel Organiser's Licence (ATOL) scheme in the UK (Ⓦ www.atol.org.uk), or pay by credit card. Sending money (even cheques) is generally not advisable – some travellers have reported being ripped off by fly-by-night mail-order ticket agents.

Note that if, after purchasing a ticket, you want to make changes to your route, you need to contact the original travel agent, not the airline. Tickets can be difficult or impossible to change; think carefully about itineraries before buying one.

For Ethiopia, travel during the month of August and over Easter, Christmas and New Year, should be booked well in advance. Ethiopians living abroad tend to visit their families during this time, and tour groups often try to coincide with the major festivals.

Prices of flights go up during this period too. For most airlines the high season is from

Warning

The information in this chapter is particularly vulnerable to change: Prices for international travel are volatile, routes are introduced and cancelled, schedules change, special deals come and go, and rules and visa requirements are amended. You should check directly with the airline or a travel agent to make sure you understand how a fare (and ticket you may buy) works and be aware of the security requirements for international travel.

The upshot of this is that you should get opinions, quotes and advice from as many airlines and travel agents as possible before you part with your hard-earned cash. The details given in this chapter should be regarded as pointers and are not a substitute for your own careful, up-to-date research.

---

1 July to 31 August, and from 16 December to 7 January. Tickets are valid for a period of between one month and one year. Note that prices quoted here do not include tax which is generally from US$65 to US$75 for return flights. The departure tax for Ethiopia (US$20 one way) must be paid before leaving Bole international airport.

Airlines
Ethiopia's only international and national carrier, **Ethiopian Airlines** (Ⓦ www.flyethiopian .com), is rated as one of the best airlines in Africa and has a good record (the US Federal Aviation Authority gave it a No 1 rating for compliance with international aviation safety standards). It is also one of the largest African carriers, with a modern fleet of 737s, 757s and 767s. There are 50 or so offices worldwide, which sell both international and domestic tickets directly. Reconfirmation of bookings is essential.

Other major airlines currently serving Ethiopia include Kenya Airways (in conjunction with KLM), EgyptAir, Lufthansa, Saudi Arabian Airlines, British Airways (with British Mediterranean) and Djibouti Airlines.

Choosing the national carrier, Ethiopian Airlines, brings with it three major perks: a remarkably generous 40kg baggage allowance (as compared to the standard 20kg), the option of changing your return date as many times as you wish with no extra charge, and generous discounted fares on domestic flights, if applicable (see Discounts under Air in the Getting Around chapter).

Note that Ethiopian Airlines' free baggage allowance across the Atlantic is restricted to two pieces only (not exceeding 32kg each), and with a combined height, width and length dimension of 158cm. Excess baggage for the US and Canada costs US$135 per piece (oversized US$270 per piece), and for the rest of the world 1.5% of a one-way economy-class fare per kg. One piece of hand luggage officially is allowed not exceeding 7kg.

Travellers with Special Needs
With sufficient advance warning, airlines can usually cater to travellers with special needs including young children and people disabilities (see the useful disability-friendly website W www.everybody.co.uk).

Ethiopian Airlines accommodates various needs including special meals for Muslims, Jews (kosher), Hindus, vegetarians, diabetics and the blind. Special meals for babies and children are also offered, and there is an escort service for children over two years of age. A wheelchair service is available.

Departure Tax
The international departure tax is US$20, which must be paid at the airport. Note that all foreign nationals (except those with residence permits) are charged in US dollars, keep some set aside for this (it can be a hassle to change birr back into dollars). Have the exact amount; change is not always available. Travellers cheques in US dollars are accepted, but a commission is charged.

USA & Canada
San Francisco is the capital of discount travel agents (consolidators) in America, although some good deals can be found in Los Angeles and New York.

STA Travel (☎ 1-800-329-9537; W www.sta travel.com) has offices in many major US cities.

Canadian discount air ticket sellers (also known as consolidators) tend to have fares around 10% higher than those sold in the USA. **Travel CUTS** (☎ 800-667-2887; W www .travelcuts.com) is Canada's student travel agency with offices in all major cities.

Ethiopian Airlines flies direct to both Washington and New York, and has 'special fare agreements' with US airlines to around 20 other US cities. There are plans to open a new flight to Toronto, Canada, by 2007.

Examples of fares include the direct flight from New York (Newark) to Addis Ababa for US$1670/1365 for high/low season return. For the west coast, Ethiopian Airlines has flights from San Francisco to Addis Ababa from US$2000/1700 for high/low season return. United Airlines also flies to Addis Ababa for similar prices.

UK
Catering particularly to students or travellers under 26 years is **STA Travel** (☎ 0870 160 0599; W www.statravel.co.uk), which has branches across the country.

From the UK, Kenya Airlines has return flights via Nairobi for UK£739/486 for the high/low season, valid for three months (tickets valid for six months are also available). Lufthansa offers return flights for UK£561/ 462 for the high/low season, valid for three months. Ethiopian Airlines has return flights for UK£554/524 for the high/low season, valid for one month. British Airways/Mediterranean has return flights for UK£549/512 for the high/ low season, valid for three months. EgyptAir has return flights for UK£446 throughout the year, valid for six months. Saudi Arabian Airlines offers similar prices to EgyptAir.

Continental Europe
In France, **OTU Voyages** (☎ 0820 817 817; W www.otu.fr) and **Voyageurs du Monde** (☎ 01 40 15 11 15; W www.vdm.com) offer some of the best services and deals and have branches countrywide. **Nouvelles Frontières** (W www.nouvelles-frontieres.com) even has branches worldwide.

In Italy, **CTS Viaggi** (☎ 840 501 150; W www .cts.it) is a student and youth specialist with branches in major cities. In Spain, recommended agencies include **Barcelo Viajes** (☎ 902 116 226; W www.barcelo-viajes.es), with branches in major cities.

Ethiopian Airlines connects Ethiopia to many European cities including Amsterdam, Copenhagen, Frankfurt and Rome directly, with onward flights to another 21 cities including Paris, London, Berlin, Madrid and Milan. By 2004, a new direct flight to Paris should have commenced.

Australia & New Zealand
There are no direct flights from Australia or New Zealand to Ethiopia. **Qantas** (W www .qantas.com.au), from Sydney and Perth,

and **South African Airways**, from Perth, have several flights weekly to Johannesburg, from where you can connect to Nairobi. Expect to pay around A$2450 for a low-season return fare.

Via the Middle East, one route to try is **Emirates Airlines** (W *www.emirates.com*) via Dubai to Nairobi for around A$2260. Other routes include via Mumbai (Bombay) on Qantas and **Air India** (W *www.airindia.com*), or via Mauritius on **Air Mauritius** (W *www.airmauritius.com*).

A round-the-world (RTW) ticket is another possibility. However, East African destinations are often not part of standard RTW packages, so you'll probably need to pay a bit more to include them – usually from about A$2600.

From New Zealand, a return flight on Qantas and South African Airways via Sydney and Johannesburg usually costs from about NZ$2900. RTW tickets from New Zealand are similarly priced to those from Australia, with fares from about NZ$3000.

In Australia, agents for cheap fares include **STA Travel** (*Australia-wide* ☎ *131 776;* W *www.statravel.com.au*), with offices in major cities and on many university campuses; and **Flight Centre** (*Australia-wide* ☎ *131 600;* W *www.flightcentre.com.au*), with branches throughout Australia.

In New Zealand, **Flight Centre** (☎ *09-309 6171;* W *www.flightcentre.co.nz*) has branches throughout the country, as does **STA Travel** (☎ *09-309 0458;* W *www.statravel.co.nz*).

The Middle East

Ethiopian Airlines currently flies to Lebanon, Israel, Saudi Arabia (Jeddah and Riyadh), the United Arab Emirates and Yemen.

Standard fares include: Jeddah for US$445/547 one way/return; Riyadh for US$608/645; and Sana'a for US$318/339. Other airlines offering similar prices include Yemenia, and Saudi Arabian Airlines.

Africa

Nairobi and Johannesburg are probably the best places in East and South Africa to buy tickets. Get several quotes from different airlines and agencies, as prices vary. In Nairobi both **Flight Centres** (☎ *02-210024*) and **Let's Go Travel** (☎ *02-340331;* W *www.letsgosafari.com*) are recommended.

In South Africa both **Rennies Travel** (☎ *011-833 1441;* W *www.renniestravel.co.za*) – the agent for Thomas Cook – and **STA Travel**

(☎ *021-418 4689*) are recommended and have offices throughout the country.

Ethiopian Airlines flies either directly or in conjunction with other carriers to around 35 African countries including Djibouti, Egypt, Sudan, Kenya and South Africa. It offers daily flights to West Africa – still the only airline to do so. A new route to Cameroon may open before 2007.

Until 1998 Ethiopian Airlines flew twice daily to Asmara, Eritrea, for US$118/236 one way/return. However, services will remain suspended until better relations are re-established between the two countries. The simplest and cheapest way currently of reaching Eritrea from Ethiopia is via Djibouti.

A number of other airlines also connect Djibouti and Addis Ababa with Asmara on their way elsewhere (such as to Cairo, Khartoum or Nairobi). See Getting There & Away in the Eritrea chapter for details and prices of airlines flying in and out of Asmara.

Ethiopian Airlines currently flies four times a week to Djibouti from Addis Ababa (sometimes via Dire Dawa) for US$181/330 one way/return. Djibouti Airlines departs Djibouti town three times a week to Addis Ababa for US$212 return.

Other standard fares offered by Ethiopian Airlines include: Egypt from US$738/783 one way/return; Kenya from US$384/542; and (if operating) Sudan from US$388/415 (all departing from Addis Ababa).

At the time of writing, Kenyan Airlines was promising to schedule a new, thrice-weekly service between Nairobi and Moyale (via Wajir and Mandera in Kenya). If it does, prices should drop dramatically. Currently a small private company, Aban Agencies, sells one-way tickets to Nairobi from KSh8000 to KSh10,000 depending on the season (KSh6000 from Nairobi). See under Moyale in the Southern Ethiopia chapter.

EgyptAir flies between Addis Ababa and Cairo for around US$619/768 one way/return.

LAND
Border Crossings

There are six official points of entry by land into Ethiopia from neighbouring countries: at Rama and Zela Anbessa coming from Eritrea (currently closed following the border dispute); at Galafi and, by train, at Doualé coming from Djibouti; at Moyale from Kenya; and at Humera (closed at the time of writing) and Metema from Sudan. All have full customs and immigration checks.

Your Own Vehicle

If you're taking your own car or motorcycle into Ethiopia, you should always carry with you and be ready to show:

• your passport
• a permit for your vehicle (available from the Transport and Communications Bureau; see following)
• the vehicle's registration papers
• proof of insurance (third-party is mandatory) covering all the countries you are visiting

A carnet de passage is a good idea. It acts as a passport for the vehicle and as a temporary waiver of import duty (cars can be imported into Ethiopia for a period of four months duty free). The carnet should list any expensive spare parts that you're planning to carry with you, such as a gearbox. Contact your local automobile association for details about documentation. Also check which spare parts and fuel are likely to be available for the make of your vehicle.

Liability insurance is not often available in advance for Ethiopia and Eritrea but has to be bought when crossing the border. The cost and quality of such local insurance vary widely. Check details carefully, or you may find that you are effectively travelling uninsured.

Ethiopian law currently recognises international driving licences for a period of seven days only. To get an Ethiopian-endorsed licence, you'll need to do the following:

• Take your domestic licence to your embassy. If it's in English, get a photocopy certified; if it's in any other language, get a full translation certified (by your embassy).
• Take this copy of your licence to the **Ministry of Foreign Affairs** (☎ 51 73 45) Office No 1, opposite the Hilton Hotel, Addis Ababa, and pay Birr320 for an official stamp.
• Take the copy and stamp, along with two passport photos, to the Driving Licence & Issuing Department of the **Transport and Communications Bureau** (☎ 61 46 90, ext 503) on the Asmara road, where you fill out further forms, pay Birr30 and wait around two hours until the licence is ready. It's then valid for two years.

The overland route from South Africa to Ethiopia via Zimbabwe, Zambia, Tanzania and Kenya is quite well trodden, and should present few problems.

Djibouti

Bus There are no direct buses between Addis Ababa and Djibouti town. However, since the outbreak of the conflict with Eritrea, Ethiopia has diverted its commerce through Djibouti's port. Every day, countless trucks rattle along the roads connecting the two countries. A new highway now links the two countries, which has speeded up travel between them.

You can normally find a seat with one of these trucks from Addis Ababa (from Birr160 to Birr200; three days via Awash, Logia and Dikhil). Otherwise, you can take buses or trucks in short hops. The Awash to Asaita, Mille, and Asaita sections in the Eastern Ethiopia chapter give details. Flying or, if you have the time, taking the train are simpler options.

Train The Addis Ababa–Djibouti Town train still trundles along the old, nineteenth-century tracks. It's in urgent need of rehabilitation in order to improve reliability, capacity and safety, and although EU and French funding has recently been promised, it's unlikely that any changes will be seen any time soon.

The train stops at various small towns in Ethiopia before finishing the first leg at Dire Dawa, 453km east of Addis Ababa. There, travellers rest overnight and take the next leg to Djibouti town the following morning.

There's not much to be said in favour of taking the first leg from Addis Ababa to Dire Dawa. It's an overnight journey and sleepers are no longer available. The best bet is to do the first leg by bus.

The second leg of the journey between Dire Dawa and Djibouti town is worthwhile, to enjoy a transport relic as well as the changing landscape. When Evelyn Waugh made the journey in the 1930s he described the landscape as 'that intolerable desolation of French Somaliland'.

See also the boxed text 'A Dream Come True' in the Eastern Ethiopia chapter for the railway's story.

Classes & Reservations There are three classes: 1st, 2nd and 3rd. However, not all classes are available on all trains (see Costs following).

Third class is furnished with little more than benches. Second class has reasonably comfortable padded seats. The 1st-class carriage is limited to just 14 people. The seats in the 1st- and 2nd-class carriages are numbered, so you're guaranteed a place. There are plans to number seats in third class also.

Tickets for Dire Dawa and Djibouti can be bought from the ticket counter at the train station in Addis Ababa up to a maximum of one hour in advance. With recent government clamp downs on contraband smugglers, seats are at less of a premium than they used to be. It's not normally a problem finding one. Queuing for up to an hour before the ticket counter opens should ensure you a seat. Porters will expect to be tipped from Birr2 to Birr5 per piece of luggage.

From Dire Dawa to Addis Ababa, tickets can be bought at the Dire Dawa train station up to two hours in advance.

Soft drinks and small snacks – as well as *chat* (known as *qat* in Djibouti), a mildly intoxicating leaf – are available on the train but it's a good idea to bring your own food and drinks, particularly water. There are (usually nonflushing) flushing toilets aboard.

Get a seat on the left-hand side of the train for views when travelling from Ethiopia to Djibouti (and vice versa from Djibouti). On the right, the blinds are drawn against the sun.

Costs Train travel is pretty cheap. Tickets from Addis Ababa to Dire Dawa (or vice versa) cost Birr75/55/41 in 1st/2nd/3rd class; trains leave three times a week, or every two days – in other words, the days change. Currently, only 2nd- and 3rd-class carriages are available on this leg. The trains depart at 2pm from Addis Ababa, and at 2.30pm from Dire Dawa and take around 13½ hours (though up to 24 hours is possible).

At the time of writing, the passenger service from Dire Dawa to Djibouti had been stopped due to terrorist sabotage on the engines of passenger trains, and derailment. However, cargo trains which were converted to passenger travel, were running instead.

Currently, the cargo trains leave daily for Djibouti at 3.30pm. Tickets, which cost Birr58/30 for 1st/2nd class, can be bought from 1.30pm onwards, and boarding starts at 2pm. In theory the journey takes from 12 to 13 hours, although 24 hours or more has been reported!

Normal passenger services should resume soon. Enquire when you get there. From Dire Dawa to Djibouti it used to cost Birr43/32 for 2nd/3rd class (1st class was unavailable) and trains left on fixed days: Tuesday, Thursday and Saturday at 6am. The journey took around 10 hours (arriving at around 4pm).

Note that journey times on the train vary hugely.

Car & Motorcycle The quickest road to Djibouti Town is via Awash, Mille, Logia and Galafi in Ethiopia, and Yoboki and Dikhil in Djibouti. The border at Galafi still sees pretty few tourists. It's a good idea to visit the immigration office in Addis Ababa (as well as the Djibouti embassy for the obligatory visa) – see Visas in the Facts for the Visitor chapter.

If coming from Djibouti, it's a good idea to get a letter from the Ethiopian embassy in Djibouti explaining your route, then go and see immigration in Addis Ababa after your arrival. Without entry/exit stamps on your passport, you could face real problems when you try to leave or re-enter Ethiopia: some travellers have been detained for several days or even weeks.

Fuel (diesel particularly) is quite widely available in Ethiopia, though you'll need to be more self-sufficient for more remote regions such as the Omo Valley (see the South Ethiopia chapter). Garages (mechanics) are also found widely and are cheap and quite good.

See Road Rules & Advice in the Getting Around chapter.

Eritrea

Since the conflict with Eritrea in the late 1990s, all border crossings between the two countries have been closed. Until good relations are re-established between the two countries (sadly believed unlikely for some time), they will continue to be closed.

Security

Keep a sharp eye on your possessions at all times. Thieves and pickpockets are known to operate on the trains. If you leave your seat (to go to the toilet etc), ask a fellow passenger to keep an eye on your things.

Sudan

Formerly, it was possible to take a bus from Gambela into Sudan. However, because of the current ethnic tensions in the area, the border is closed to foreigners. Check the current situation when you get there.

The route into Sudan via Humera and Eritrea, is also currently closed. The other official border crossing is at Metema (180km from Gonder). There are no direct buses from Addis Ababa. The best option is to go to Gonder first and catch a bus and then a pick-up truck to Metema (see under Gonder in the Northern Ethiopia chapter).

The road on the Ethiopian side of the border has recently been upgraded. However, for the Sudanese side (from Gallabat to Gedaref), a 4WD is essential. In the wet season, even trucks can get stuck. The road should eventually be improved.

Be aware that Ethiopian tour companies do not usually allow their vehicles into Sudan, because of the difficulty of obtaining insurance cover when there.

Kenya

There are usually few problems travelling between Ethiopia and Kenya. Twin-towned Moyale serves as both the Ethiopian and Kenyan frontier town.

From Moyale to Nairobi there are currently two routes: via the towns of Wajir or Isiolo in Kenya.

The road via Wajir is faster and safer, but, because it's a dirt road, it's difficult or impassable during the rains (April to June and November to December).

The road to Isiolo is all-weather, but slower, and the last 10km are still prone to banditry (though the authorities hope to have the problem resolved soon). Trucks travel in convoy for safety.

At the time of writing, there were no buses from Moyale to either town (due to the condition of the roads) though by the end of 2004 an asphalted road should connect Moyale with Isiolo. Check when you get there. Trucks do make the journey. For further details, see Moyale in the Southern Ethiopia chapter.

The Ethiopian and Kenyan borders are open daily from 6.30am to 6pm. To avoid missing the early morning trucks from the Kenyan side, it's a good idea to clear Ethiopian customs and immigration the night before you intend to travel. Note that **Ethiopian immigration** (☎ 44 00 82; open 8am-noon & 2pm-6pm Mon-Fri, 9am-11am & 3pm-5pm Sat & Sun) cannot issue Ethiopian visas; these must be obtained at the Ethiopian embassy in Nairobi.

At **Kenyan immigration** (☎ 185-2074) tourist visas cost US$50 (valid for three months) unless your home country has a visa abolition agreement. It's payable in US dollars or euros, but not birr. Transit visas cost US$20 (valid for seven days).

Remember to get rid of all Kenyan shillings and birr before leaving the respective countries.

Somalia

The area between Ethiopia and Somalia is still officially declared unsafe. Check the current situation before you travel. At the time of writing, there were no direct buses from Addis Ababa to Somalia but you can travel by truck to Somalia from Jijiga (see the Eastern Ethiopia chapter). Access to Somalia is much easier – and safer – overland from Djibouti.

Europe

The overland route from southern Europe to Ethiopia is known as the 'Nile Route', and passes through Egypt, Sudan and Eritrea. Because the Eritrea–Ethiopia border is closed, the last leg is impossible, and travellers are presently obliged to travel between Ethiopia and Eritrea via Sudan. Check out the security situation here too.

RIVER

In the past, it was possible to take a passenger boat from Gambela in southern Ethiopia to Sudan via the Baro River. Services were not operating at the time of writing, but there were plans to re-establish them. See the Gambela section in the Western Ethiopia chapter.

Getting Around

AIR
Domestic Air Services

Ethiopian Airlines (**W** *www.flyethiopian.com*), the national carrier, provides the only regular domestic air service (see the Getting There & Away chapter for more details).

It's well worth considering a domestic flight or two, even if you're travelling on a budget. Most flights are very reasonably priced (they are subsidised by revenues raised from international flights) and cut out days spent on the road. Special discounted fares are available (see Discounts later). A good compromise between cost and time over long distances is to take the bus one way, and the plane the other.

Most flights leave from Addis Ababa, but a few connect other towns to one another. The north is particularly well served; for the more popular routes, there are departures at least three times a week, if not daily.

With the lower-altitude flying of the domestic planes, and the usually clear Ethiopian skies, you'll still see some landscape, too. The views – such those you see when flying over the Simien Mountains – are stunning. If you want a window seat, check in early.

A pretty thorough body and luggage search now forms a routine part of Ethiopian air travel. Carrying as little hand luggage as possible cuts down on the latter. Electrical and photographic equipment in particular come under scrutiny. Items such as cigarette lighters, matches, cables and pocket knives are prohibited in hand luggage. When buying souvenirs, don't forget the restrictions on antiquities (see Customs in the Facts for the Visitor chapter).

The baggage limit is 20kg on domestic flights. Don't bring bulky hand luggage: many of the planes are small.

Note that because the Dire Dawa flight goes on to Hargeisa in Somalia, it leaves from the international terminal.

Domestic Departure Tax

A charge of Birr10 (payable in birr only) is made for domestic departure tax. The tax is payable for each departure from Addis Ababa only (in other words, just once for the historical route).

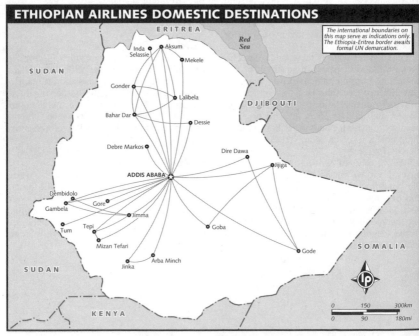

ETHIOPIAN AIRLINES DOMESTIC DESTINATIONS

The international boundaries on this map serve as indications only. The Ethiopia-Eritrea border awaits formal UN demarcation.

Shepherd boys in Simien Mountains National Park

Christian priest with Ethiopian crosses outside a rock-hewn church, Lalibela

Priest studying the holy scriptures

Children of Lalibela

Tigrayan girls with *shoruba* hairstyle

Reservations

In theory you can buy a ticket and fly on the same day, but in practice flights should be booked well in advance. With the recent upgrading of many runways to an all-weather status, the popularity of flights has increased. Booking one month in advance is advised; six months to be sure of dates, particularly on the historical route and during major festivals (see Suggested Itineraries and Public Holidays & Special Events in the Facts for the Visitor chapter).

Domestic flights can be booked at Ethiopian Airlines offices in your own country. Don't worry if you're still uncertain of your itinerary; dates can be altered as many times as you like for no extra charge at Ethiopian Airlines offices in Ethiopia.

It is *essential* to reconfirm all flights, domestic as well as international. Officially, this should be done 72 hours in advance. In practice, you can normally get away with 48 hours in advance, but never leave it less than 24 hours – and even then it is a risk. If you are visiting the historical route and are not spending more than 72 hours in any one place, you do not need to reconfirm each leg; only when the 72-hour period is broken.

Note that schedules do occasionally change. Flights are sometimes cancelled at the last minute because of mechanical faults or weather conditions (particularly on the smaller planes or when landing on airstrips that are not all-weather such as that at Jinka). Because many planes are small they can be oversubscribed; if you don't bother reconfirming, your place will soon be allocated to someone else.

Beware of planning an itinerary that's so tight that it doesn't make allowances for these changes.

Costs

Though not quite the bargain they once were, domestic flights still represent very good value.

Currently only the Ethiopian Airlines offices in Addis Ababa and Gonder accept credit cards, though other offices should accept them soon. Offices should, in theory, also accept Ethiopian birr (with foreign exchange slips from a bank) for payment as well as other currencies. A few only accept US dollars. Travellers cheques are not currently accepted in any office.

Ethiopian domestic-flight tickets are also available for purchase (at the standard rate) on **Travelocity** (W *www.travelocity.com)* and **Expedia** (W *www.expedia.com)*.

The following gives examples of standard one-way economy fares. Domestic fares do not vary seasonally.

Flights leaving from Addis Ababa:

destination	cost (Birr)
Aksum	1047
Arba Minch	617
Bahar Dar	593
Dessie	445
Dire Dawa	770
Gambela	785
Gonder	795
Jijiga	1164
Jinka	731
Lalibela	795
Mekele	1001

Flights between the different legs on the historical route in the north can save you many days on buses.

journey	cost (Birr)
Aksum to Mekele	262
Aksum to Lalibela	535
Aksum to Gonder	559
Aksum to Bahar Dar	661
Bahar Dar to Gonder	238
Bahar Dar to Dessie	425
Bahar Dar to Lalibela	445
Bahar Dar to Mekele	608
Gonder to Lalibela	335

See the Getting There & Away section in the Addis Ababa chapter for more information.

Discounts

There are no discounts available for students or senior citizens, and air passes are not yet offered. However, one good-value discount, the 'Group Fair Discount', is currently available, which offers 50% to 60% off the standard domestic fares.

Note the following conditions: there must be three or more of you travelling together; your incoming international flights must have been with Ethiopian Airlines; and your domestic flights must be booked *before* leaving home, at the same time as your international flights. You are then eligible for a 50% to 60% discount on all flights around the historical route, plus any add-ons to any other domestic destination served by Ethiopian Airlines.

LAND

In the 1990s, as part of a general effort to revive the economy, road building became a top governmental priority, with more than 20% of the capital budget allocated to it. In 1997 a huge investment project was launched, the 'Road Sector Development Program', in partnership with 13 international developers and donors. It's currently in progress, with an overall target implementation date of June 2007.

As a result, roads are appearing at a tremendous pace all around the country. Since 1997 nearly 3000km of trunk roads have been constructed, rehabilitated or upgraded at a cost of half a billion US dollars.

For the traveller, the project means three things: journey times are being slashed dramatically, previously inaccessible areas are now opening up (particularly to public transport), and travel is becoming much more comfortable. In the next two to three years, good surfaced roads should extend from Addis Ababa all the way to Adigrat in the far north, Gonder in the northwest and to Jijiga in the far east.

The project has not gone without hitches: problems with road design and construction, among others, dog the work. Additionally, as roads have improved, speed has increased and the number of accidents in Ethiopia has risen significantly (though the rate is still low by African standards).

Ethiopia's road system is still far from extensive. By 2002 road density was still just 27km per 1000 sq km (still one of the lowest in the world, even by African standards). The national network covers just 35% of the country.

Bus

A good network of buses connects all the major towns of Ethiopia. For the smaller towns and villages, light transport services operate (see the Light Vehicles section following).

Buses are cheap but slow. On sealed roads you can expect to cover around 50km an hour, but on dirt roads, 30km or less. In the rainy season, journeys can be severely disrupted. Some buses would be vintage pieces in other countries – look out for the Italian Fiat models that are over 50 years old.

Unlike most African countries, standing in the aisles on buses is illegal in Ethiopia (bar the city buses in Addis Ababa), making them both safer and more comfortable. On the longer journeys, there are usually scheduled breakfast and lunch stops for between 20 and 30 minutes. There are no toilets on board.

The major drawback with bus travel is the size of the country. For the historical route alone, you're looking to cover over 2500km – about ten days spent just sitting on a bus.

Most long-distance buses set off early. Although scheduled to 'leave' at 6.30am or earlier, they don't actually get going till at least another hour after that. But don't think you can roll up late. Even if you already have your ticket, you still have to put in an appearance at this time. Remember that the Ethiopian clock is used locally (see Time in the Facts for the Visitor chapter), though Western time is used when quoting bus times in this book.

Most buses are demand driven. In other words, they leave when they are full. If they are not full, they may not leave at all. Long

---

The Joys of Bus Travel

In the rural areas, you may discover that your ticket actually counts for two places: your seat and the seat on your lap. So apart from sitting next to someone, and someone else's shopping, chicken or baby, you may find yourself holding someone else's shopping, chicken or baby.

All those extra lungs can make the bus seem a bit steamy. But never ever try to open a window. A riot is likely to erupt at the slightest crack, and the window will be slammed shut. Ethiopians are convinced that an airflow of any sort will prove almost certainly fatal to them.

Windows are reserved for 'emergencies' only. According to one Ethiopian, you can tell where a bus has come from by the amount of vomit down its sides. Some Ethiopians may not be so well travelled as you, and find the narrow, winding roads of the Highlands just a little unsettling.

Serious accidents tend to be fairly rare. For extra safety, many drivers dangle garish plastic virgins or one of an array of Ethiopian saints from mirrors, dashboards or windscreens. Protection is the important thing, rather like the Muslim belief in fate, no matter how reckless the driving.

Additionally, some drivers may rely on *chat* (the mild narcotic) to keep them vigilant, or, more commonly, Amharic music – played at full blast. Not much chance of the driver falling asleep at the wheel – or of the passenger getting a nap.

waits are often experienced in remote areas. In general, the earlier you get to the bus station, the better chance you have of catching one of the first buses out of town.

On the longer journeys quoted in this book, there may be one or even two overnight stops at cheap hotels en route (check in advance). Often you will not be allowed to remove your luggage from the roof rack; keep toiletries and other overnight items with you in a small bag on the bus. There are no night buses; Ethiopian law stipulates that all long-distances buses must be off the road by 6pm.

Reservations & Costs One government bus association and around a dozen private ones operate in Ethiopia. The private-bus procedure is less afflicted by bureaucracy, but is less ordered. Seats are not assigned; hence the scrum that can ensue when the doors open. You buy your ticket on the bus from the conductor and the bus leaves when it's full.

For government buses (Walia buses), you must buy your ticket in advance then wait outside the bus until it's ready to depart. Once the bus is loaded with luggage, passengers board, tickets are again checked and the bus eventually sets off.

Prices are competitive among private companies; government buses are a few birr cheaper, but tend to be older, sometimes slower, and less comfortable.

Tickets for most long-distance journeys (over 250km) can usually be bought in advance (and sometime must be). If you can, do: it guarantees a seat and cuts out the touts who sometimes snap up the remaining tickets to resell for double the price to latecomers. Most ticket offices are open daily from 5.30am to 5.30pm. For short distances (less than 250km), tickets can usually only be bought on the day.

Buses are very cheap in Ethiopia, and work out at around US$1.50 per 100km. There is just one class of travel.

Light Vehicles
Between Towns Light vehicles such as minibuses, 4WDs and pick-up trucks often connect neighbouring towns. Where there is no bus service, they also serve the smaller towns and villages, particularly on market days (usually Saturday, and sometimes a weekday too).

The vehicles are privately owned and slightly more expensive than the buses, but are faster. In the more remote regions services can be infrequent and erratic, so if you're relying

---

Taxi Terminology

In the towns, villages and countryside of Ethiopia and Eritrea, taxis offer two kinds of service: 'contract taxis' and 'share-taxis'. Share-taxis ply fixed routes, stop and pick people up when hailed and work to all intents like little buses. They become 'contract taxis' when flagged down (or 'contracted') for a private journey. The fare is then split between all passengers.

Though not really 'taxis' at all, minibuses, trucks, 4WDs and various other kinds of cars can all be contracted in this way. Contracting a large minibus for yourself is seen as perfectly normal if you should want to. Before hiring a contract taxi, always negotiate the fare before you get in, or you may be asked far above the going rate at the end of the journey.

---

on this form of transport, you'll need time and flexibility on your side.

Petrol stations or market areas are commonly the collection points. Taxis are not marked and the type of vehicle usually matches the terrain they have to travel on. Ask the locals.

Within Towns In many of the larger towns, a minibus service provides a quick, convenient and cheap way of hopping about town (from around 75¢ for short journeys). 'Conductors' generally shout out the destination of the bus; if in doubt, ask.

Taxis operate in many of the larger towns including Addis Ababa. Prices are reasonable, but foreigners as well as well-heeled Ethiopians are always charged more for 'contract services' (see the boxed text 'Taxi Terminology'). Fares are usually between Birr10 and Birr15 depending on the distance. If in doubt, ask your hotel for an estimate.

Travellers Lore

Once there was a dog, a goat and a donkey. They wanted to go on a journey together, and decided to take a taxi. The donkey paid and got out, the dog paid, got out but never got his change, and the goat got out but never paid.

To this day, and whenever a vehicle passes, the dog still chases his change, the goat still scatters at the first approach, and the donkey just plods tranquilly on.

Ethiopian folk tale

Garis (horse-drawn carts) are a popular local means of getting about town. They're cheap (usually no more than Birr1 to Birr2) and are useful to travellers in two ways particularly: as cheap transportation to hotels from bus stations, and for city tours. Be aware that in many towns now they are banned from operating on the principle roads and must stick to the back ones. Most drivers speak little or no English; you may have to enlist a local to act as interpreter.

Car & Motorcycle

For information on the documentation required to take your own car or motorcycle into Ethiopia, see the boxed text 'Your Own Vehicle' in the Getting There & Away chapter.

Road Rules & Advice Driving is on the right-hand side of the road. The speed limit for cars and motorcycles is 60km/h in the towns and villages and 100km/h outside the towns. The standard of driving is generally not high; devices such as mirrors or indicators are usually disregarded. On highland roads, drive defensively and beware of trucks coming fast the other way. Also keep a sharp eye out for a row of stones or pebbles across the road; it marks roadworks or an accident.

In the outskirts of the towns or villages, look out for people, particularly children playing on the road or kerbside. Night driving is not recommended. *Shiftas* (bandits) still operate in the more remote areas (see Dangers & Annoyances in the Facts for the Visitor chapter). Additionally, some trucks park overnight in the middle of the road – without lights.

In the country, livestock is the main hazard; camels wandering onto the road can cause major accidents in the lowlands. Many animals, including donkeys, are unaccustomed to vehicles and are very car-shy, so always approach slowly and with caution.

Land mines still pose a threat throughout the country; drivers should always stay on sealed roads or existing dirt tracks. During the rainy season, some roads, particularly in the west and southwest, become impassable. Check road conditions with the local authorities before setting out.

Fuel (both petrol and diesel) is quite widely available, apart from the more remote regions such as the southwest. Unleaded petrol is not available. Diesel is cheap and costs from around Birr2.25 to Birr2.90 per litre. Petrol costs around Birr4.50 per litre.

Rental Cars and 4WDs are easily hired from agencies in Addis Ababa (see Organised Tours later in this chapter), though they're not cheap, even by Western standards. Outside the capital, a 4WD is necessary for most places (though roads are improving daily). Motorcycles cannot currently be rented.

Outside the capital, few vehicles are available for rent. Some Addis Ababa–based agencies have branch offices in towns on the historical route and can rent cars, but only by prearrangement. Increasingly, private individuals rent to tourists. Be aware of the risks, particularly regarding insurance and the condition of the car.

Though expensive, the chief advantage of vehicle rental is the time that can be saved, especially in the more remote regions (where much time can be lost waiting for infrequent, erratic and slow buses). Note also that some national parks can only be entered with a vehicle.

If you're travelling solo, or as a couple, you can reduce the cost of vehicle rental by joining up with other travellers. Most vehicles accommodate around five passengers, though some take up to ten (with benches in the back).

To hire a car, you must have a valid international driver's licence and be between 25 and 70 years old. Vehicles can't be taken outside Ethiopia. Rental prices vary and are usually open to quite a bit of negotiation, so shop around. If hiring for over a week, discounts are usually available. A deposit of at least Birr1000 is required for a car; Birr2000 for a 4WD.

Drivers are included in the hire cost with 4WDs (and are usually obligatory). They can be very useful as guides-cum-interpreters-cum-mechanics. Sometimes there's an additional charge if the driver clocks up more than eight hours in a day; check in advance. Also check if the driver gets a daily allowance to pay for food and accommodation. Usually it's pretty paltry. A nice gesture is to at least share food together (which costs very little). Tips are expected afterwards.

Note that many drivers are reluctant to drive at night. This is in part a leftover from the curfews imposed by the Derg (Socialist military junta that governed Ethiopia from 1974 to 1991), but is also a sensible precaution against *shiftas* (bandits; see Road Rules & Advice earlier). If you're expecting to travel at night, be sure to discuss this with the agency in advance.

Cars cost from US$50 per day. The first 50km are usually free, then it's from US$0.20 per kilometre. A 4WD costs from around US$100 per day including unlimited kilometres, a driver, fuel, third-party insurance and a collision damage waiver. Prices vary greatly depending on the period of rental, the season and negotiation. Ensure that you check that all government taxes and service charges are included, particularly with the National Tour Operation (NTO), or you may end up paying up to 25% more.

Given Ethiopia's size, a deal with unlimited kilometres is the best bet. Car hire is a lot cheaper if you organise it yourself in Ethiopia rather than through an agency outside the country.

Purchase If you're looking to buy a second-hand vehicle, expect to pay a minimum of US$15,000 to US$20,000. With the large expat community that is resident in Addis Ababa, vehicles are usually easy to find; one of the local English-language newspapers is the best place to start.

Bicycle
Ethiopia's irregular terrain and, in many areas, rough roads are not ideally suited to cycling. However, if you're totally self-sufficient with plenty of spare parts, a good repair kit and the capacity to carry sufficient amounts of water, there's nothing to stop you. Road conditions are also greatly improving.

Quite decent cycles can be hired in some of the larger towns and are very cheap (Birr3 to Birr4 per hour). Though normally rented by the hour or day and for use inside town, you can usually persuade someone to rent you one for a longer period, as well as for use outside the town.

Punctures are easily repaired – just head for any *gommista* (tyre repairer) or garage. Many mechanics are also more than happy to help with cycle problems, and often turn out to be ingenious improvisers.

Cyclists should show the usual caution when travelling around the country: never travel after dark, be wary of thieves and keep the bicycle well maintained. Brakes need to be in good working order for the mountainous highland roads.

Be particularly wary of dogs (and the risk of rabies); sometimes it's best to dismount and walk slowly away. Cycling in the rainy season can be very hard going.

Note the customs regulation regarding the importation of a bicycle. A deposit must usually be left (amounting to the cycle's worth) at customs at the port of entry on arrival. When you leave, this will be returned. This is to deter black market trading.

Cycles are accepted aboard Ethiopian Airlines international flights. On domestic flights you'll need to check first whether bicycles are accepted (some planes are pretty tiny).

Cycles new and second-hand can be bought in Addis Ababa, but prices are rarely much cheaper than elsewhere.

Finally, a few tips from a seasoned African cyclist: check and tighten screws and nuts regularly, take a spare chain, take a front as well as rear pannier rack, and pack a water filter in case you get stuck somewhere remote.

Hitching
In the past, if someone asked for a ride in Ethiopia, it was usually assumed that it was because they couldn't afford a bus fare and little sympathy was spared for them. Many Ethiopians also suspected hitchers of hidden motives such as robbery.

However, for some towns not readily served by buses or light vehicles (see earlier), hitching is quite normal, and you will be expected to pay a 'fare'. Negotiate this in advance. The best place to look for lifts is at the hotels, bars and cafés in the centre of town.

Be aware that the density of vehicles on many roads is still very low in Ethiopia; on the remote roads, you'll be lucky to see any. NGO vehicles sometimes oblige, but you'll be expected to contribute towards fuel.

Train
The Addis Ababa–Djibouti train stops at various small towns in Ethiopia on its way to Dire Dawa and the end of the first leg. It's dilapidated, hot and slow, but if you've got time, you may want to give it a go. For more information, see the Getting There & Away chapter.

> ### Hitching
> Hitching is never entirely safe, and it's not recommended. Travellers who decide to hitch should understand that they are taking a small but potentially serious risk. Hitching is safer in pairs. Additionally, try and let someone know where you're planning to go. Women should never hitch alone.

ETHIOPIA

BOAT
The only domestic boat service currently available is that on Lake Tana, where a limited ferry service operates (see the Northern Ethiopia chapter).

ORGANISED TOURS
For the independent traveller, incorporating an organised tour into your travels in Ethiopia is useful for four things: specialised activities such as white-water rafting; access to remote regions with limited public transport such as the Lower Omo Valley or the Danakil Depression; 'themed trips' (such as bird-watching) with expert guides; and to help those with limited time who are keen to see as much as possible.

If you're interested in taking a tour, contact the agencies in advance and compare itineraries and prices. Most now have websites that you can visit first (see the list following).

To reduce the cost of tours (few are cheap), hook up with a group of other travellers, or contact the agency far in advance to see if there are pre-arranged tours that you can tag onto. You'll need to be flexible with your dates

NTO, the government-owned travel agency, once had a monopoly. Its drivers and guides have excellent reputations, but its prices remain uncompetitively high. A cluster of much more competitive private operators has sprung up in the past ten years, all based in Addis Ababa.

Agencies offer all or some of the following: guides, car hire, camping equipment hire, historical route tours, bird-watching and wildlife-viewing, white-water rafting, fishing, Omo Valley tours, photo safaris, Simien and Bale Mountain trekking, Rift Valley lake trips, and Danakil and Afar excursions. Some have branches in towns outside Addis Ababa, from where (if prebooked) you can hire a car or guide or take a tour.

Some agencies also have very attractive, 'eco-friendly' lodges and campsites, including Ethiopian Rift Valley Safaris (in the Omo Valley); Green Land Tours (at Arba Minch and Turmi, with lodges planned on Lake Langano, Bale Mountains and Lalibela); and Village Ethiopia (in Bilen, near Awash).

Though prices are officially fixed, most are very open to negotiation, particularly during the low season. Many agencies now accept credit cards. The following list is not exhaustive, but includes agencies recommended by the Tourism Commission, Ethiopians in the travel industry, and travellers themselves. See the Addis Ababa maps for all agency locations.

Bahir Dar Tour & Travel Agency (☎ 12 38 02, e bahardar.tour@telecom.net.et)
Ethiopian Rift Valley Safaris (☎ 55 21 28, e ervs@telecom.net.et)
Ethio-Fauna Safaris (☎ 50 53 01, e ethfauna@hotmail.com)
Ethio Travel & Tours (☎ 56 71 50, 56 71 51, w www.ethiotravelandtours.com)
Experience Ethiopia (☎ 15 23 36, w www.telecom.net.et~eet)
Four Seasons Travel & Tours (☎ 62 53 10, e fsta@telecom.net.et)
Galaxy Express Services (☎ 51 03 55, e galaxyexpress@telecom.net.et)
Green Land Tours (☎ 63 25 97, w www.greenlandtours.net)
Hess Travel Ethiopia (☎ 51 58 20, w www.hesstravelethiopia.com)
National Tour Operation (NTO; ☎ 51 48 38, e nto@telecom.net.et)
Red Jackal Tour (☎ 55 99 15, e redjackal@telecom.net.et)
Rocky Valley Safaris (☎ 15 24 62, e rockyvalley@telecom.net.et)
Travel Ethiopia (☎ 51 01 68, w travelethiopia.tripod.com)
T-Tam Travel & Tours (☎ 51 40 55, w www.ttamtour.com)
Village Ethiopia (☎ 55 22 69, w www.village-ethiopia.com)
Wonz-Dar Expeditions (☎ 75 76 04, e wonzdar@telecom.net.et)
Yumo Tours (☎ 51 88 78, w www.yumo.net)

Addis Ababa አዲስ አበባ

☎ 01 • pop 5,000,000

Founded little more than a century ago, Addis Ababa, which in Amharic means 'New Flower', is a relatively new capital city. However, the flower aspect of its nomenclature is more open to debate. Addis Ababa, at first sight, is noisy, dusty, sprawling and shambolic. But it's also a colourful and vibrant city that grows on you surprisingly quickly, helped undoubtedly by its gorgeous climate of seemingly perpetual blue skies and cool highland air.

Despite its huge size – it is the third largest city in Africa, with an estimated population of five million – it retains a small-town feel. The donkeys trotting intrepidly through the red lights and snarling traffic of Meskel Square, and the goats grazing on the neat verges of the high-rise buildings, are a reminder that Ethiopia is still a firmly rural, agricultural society.

Addis Ababa is a strange mix of the past and the present: the old imperial statues and emblems coexist alongside the hammer and sickle placards of the former Marxist regime, as well as the slick advertisements of the new private-sector banks. Wattle-and-daub huts stand not far from austere Fascist buildings and luxurious high-rise hotels. On the streets, priests in medieval-looking robes mix with African bureaucrats, Western aid workers and young Ethiopian women with cell phones.

Though most travellers can't wait to hurry out of the capital the moment they hurry in, it's worth giving the city at least a couple of days. The Merkato is one of the largest outdoor markets on the continent, and some of the museums are among the most important in sub-Saharan Africa.

There are plenty of 'cultural experiences' worth investigating too, such as Ethiopian folk dancing and singing, the age-old entertainment provided by the *azmaris* (wandering minstrels), and even a trip to a *tej beat* (a kind of Ethiopian pub). Also in the capital, you'll find some of the best Ethiopian cooking in the country.

Addis Ababa, though capital of one of the ten poorest countries in the world, is hardly lacking in facilities, with high-standard hotels, international restaurants and innumerable little pastry shops, cafés and bars – not to mention a fair range of hip nightclubs. It is also centrally placed, standing at the

Highlights

- Meander through Merkato, the largest market in East Africa, where you can buy anything from a camel to a Kalashnikov
- Visit the National Museum, one of the most important in sub-Saharan Africa and home to the fossilised hominid Lucy
- Venture into a *tej beat*, the Ethiopian equivalent of a pub, to drink with the locals

The international boundaries on this map serve as indications only. The Ethiopia–Eritrea border awaits formal UN demarcation.

SUDAN · ERITREA · DJIBOUTI

ETHIOPIA

⊙ Addis Ababa pp104-5
Central Addis Ababa & the Bole Road Area pp108-9
Piazza p110

KENYA · SOMALIA

crossroads of the country's air, rail and road transportation network.

Ever the small town, it is also friendly, laid-back and amazingly safe compared with many African – and Western – capitals. Colourful, cheap and cheerful, it's a pretty easy city in which to settle.

HISTORY

Throughout Ethiopia's history her capitals have been transient – shifting like giant camps according to the political, economic and strategic demands of her rulers. Addis Ababa was no exception.

At the end of the 19th century Menelik II moved his capital first from Ankober in the region of Shoa to a site on Wuchacha Mountain, and finally to Entoto, to the north of the present-day city. There, the capital could easily be defended against rebellion from within and attacks from without. Later, as Menelik tightened his grip on the country,

ETHIOPIA

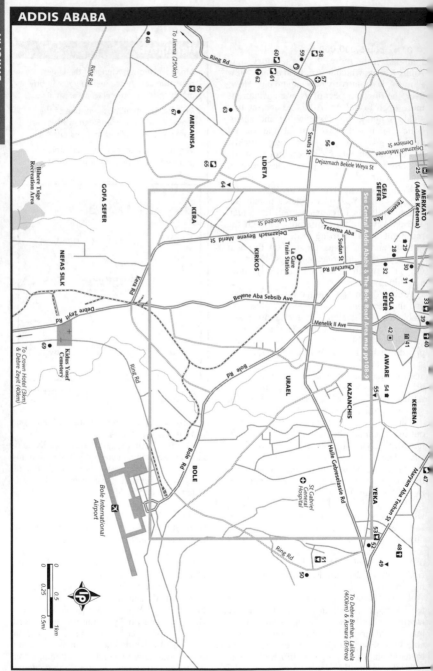

ADDIS ABABA

ADDIS ABABA

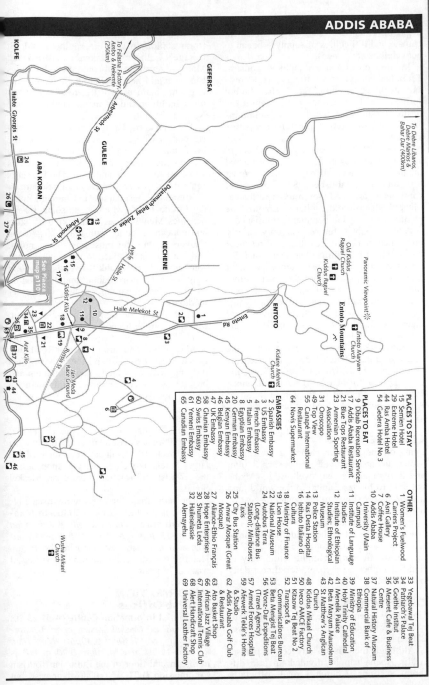

KOLFE

GEFERSA

GUELE

To Debre Libanos,
Debre Markos &
Bahar Dar (400km)

To Falasha Factory,
Ambo & Nekemte
(250km)

ABA KORAN

KECHENE

Old Kiddus
Raguel Church

Kiddus Raguel
Church

Panoramic Viewpoint

See Piazza
map p110

Haile Melekot St

ENTOTO

Entoto Rd

Entoto
Mariam
Church

Entoto Mountains

Kidane Mehret
Church

Jan Meda
Race Ground

Arat Kilo

Wusha Mikael
Church

PLACES TO STAY
15 Semien Hotel
29 Extreme Hotel
44 Ras Amba Hotel
54 Gedera Hotel No 3

PLACES TO EAT
9 Dibab Recreation Services
17 Addis Ababa Restaurant
21 Blue Tops Restaurant
23 Armenian Sporting
   Association
31 Oroscopo
49 Top View
55 Canapé International
   Restaurant
64 Novis Supermarket

EMBASSIES
2 Spanish Embassy
3 US Embassy
4 French Embassy
5 Egyptian Embassy
8 Italian Embassy
20 German Embassy
45 Kenyan Embassy
46 Belgian Embassy
47 UK Embassy
58 Ghanian Embassy
60 Swiss Embassy
61 Yemeni Embassy
65 Canadian Embassy

OTHER
1 Women's Fuelwood
   Carriers Project
6 Asni Gallery
7 Coffee House
10 Addis Ababa
   University (Main
   Campus)
11 Institute of Language
   Studies
12 Institute of Ethiopian
   Studies; Ethnological
   Museum
13 Police Station
14 Ras Desta Hospital
16 Istituto Italiano di
   Cultura
18 Ministry of Finance
19 Lion House
22 National Museum
24 Autobus Terra
   (Long-distance Bus
   Station); Minibuses;
   Taxis
25 City Bus Station
26 Anwar Mosque (Great
   Mosque)
27 Alliance-Ethio Français
28 Hope Enterprises
30 Shumeta Leda
32 Hailesalassie
   Alemayehu
33 Yegebawal Tej Beat
34 Patriarch's Palace
35 Ministry of Education
36 Meseret Cafe & Business
   Centre
37 Natural History Museum
38 Commercial Bank of
   Ethiopia
39 Ministry of Education
40 Holy Trinity Cathedral
41 Menelik Palace
42 Beta Maryam Mausoleum
43 St Matthew's Anglican
   Church
48 Kiddus Mikael Church
50 Iveco AMCE Factory
51 Kitaw Tej Beat No 2
52 Transport &
   Communication Bureau
53 Beta Mengist Tej Beat
56 Wonz-Dar Expeditions
   (Travel Agency)
57 Armed Forces Hospital
59 Atewerk Tekle's Home
   & Studio
62 Addis Ababa Golf Club
63 Ato Basket Shop
66 African Jazz Village
67 International Tennis Club
68 Alert Handicraft Shop
69 Universal Leather Factory

Entoto began to lose its strategic value, and its inconveniences – such as an inclement climate and difficulties of supply – began to outweigh its advantages.

In the meantime, Menelik's consort, Taitu, had her eye on a different site. Known as Filwoha or 'Boiling Water', after the hot springs found there, the spot lay amid the fertile foothills of the Entoto Mountains and benefited from a pleasant temperate climate.

In 1886, Menelik granted some land to Taitu on which to build. The queen named the new site Addis Ababa, and a settlement was quickly established. Soon the royal court began to spend more time here than at Menelik's sterile old capital at Entoto. The population grew and commerce flourished.

Addis Ababa's future was only briefly threatened in 1900, when the usual resource crisis (which had afflicted so many of Ethiopia's capitals in the past) arose. Menelik briefly contemplated establishing yet another capital at Addis Alem. However, the city was saved by the introduction of the eucalyptus tree. With its rapid growth, the tree could meet the demand for wood of the ever-increasing population.

Today Addis Ababa is very much at the centre of things. Since 1958, it has been the headquarters of the United Nations Economic Commission for Africa (ECA) and, since 1963, the secretariat of the Organisation of African Unity (OAU). Many regard the city as 'Africa's diplomatic capital'.

CLIMATE

Lying on the southern slopes of the Entoto Mountains at an altitude of between 2300m and 2500m above sea level, Addis Ababa is the third highest capital in the world, and despite its proximity to the equator – just 8° north – enjoys a temperate climate with an average temperature of just 16°C.

Between late October and mid-January, the temperature can drop by almost 20°C to just above freezing at night. From July to mid-September, be prepared for almost daily rainstorms.

ORIENTATION

Until very recently there was no urban planning in the capital; Addis Ababa sprawls over 250 sq km.

Although there is no city centre per se, Addis Ababa can be divided up into different sections. Churchill road (officially known as Churchill Ave) marks the central part of town and runs north to south. La Gare (train station) marks the southern end; St George's Cathedral, marks the northern end. Many government and commercial buildings can be found here including Ethiopian Airlines, the main post office, telecommunications building and (a major landmark) the National Theatre.

The area known as the Piazza at the northern end of Churchill road is a legacy of the brief Italian occupation. It's here that many of the budget hotels can be found, as well as a rash of little cafés and bars. The Piazza is centred roughly around De Gaulle Square.

Running almost parallel to Churchill Road, the Entoto Road, which at its southern end becomes Menelik II Ave, is a kind of 'state and education' zone, with the Addis Ababa University and the museums in the north, and the National Palace in the south. At the southern end of Menelik II Ave, the huge and ugly Meskel Square, rebuilt and enlarged by the Derg as a parade ground, is another landmark.

To the west, the famous open-air market, Merkato, can be found.

The new area of expansion is to the southeast, on and around Bole Road, between Meskel Square and the airport. It's a thriving area with many new buildings and businesses, which contrasts sharply with the rest of the city.

Maps

The ETC map of the country (1987, 1:2,000,000) has a useful map of Addis Ababa on the back. It's available from some of the larger hotels as well as the **gift shop** beside the Tourist Information Centre on Meskel Square.

The same map, but at its normal scale (1: 15,000), is produced by the **Ethiopian Mapping Authority** (EMA; Menelik II Ave; open 8.30am-12.30pm & 1.30pm-5.30pm Mon-Fri), which is situated opposite the Hilton Hotel in the centre. At the time of writing, it was out of print.

INFORMATION
Tourist Offices

The **Tourist Information Centre** (☎ 51 23 10, fax 51-38-99; Meskel Square; open 8.30am-12.30pm & 1.30pm-5.30pm Mon-Thur, 8.30am-11.30am & 1.30pm-5.30pm Fri) is in the ground floor of the Ethiopian Tourism Commission (ETC). Staff do their best, but don't expect much more than the usual brochures (some of which are useful).

If you're looking for advice on itineraries, your best bet is the **National Tour Operation** (NTO; ☎ 51 48 38; e nto@telecom.net.et; Ras Desta Damtew St) or one of the private travel agencies (see also under Organised Tours in the Getting Around chapter), whose staff have a much greater knowledge and experience of travel in Ethiopia.

Several English-language publications can be of use to travellers, especially the weekly *Time Out Addis* and the monthly *What's Up*. These list restaurants, shopping venues, nightclubs and events. They are available (haphazardly) at the larger hotels, smarter restaurants and art galleries. Ask also for the *Addis Guide* at the tourist office.

Money
Both government and private banks operate in Addis Ababa. Exchange rates are very similar at both. However, private banks usually have shorter queues. Ethiopian law does not currently allow foreign banks to operate in Ethiopia, though this is likely to change.

The branch of the **Commercial Bank of Ethiopia** (Menelik II Ave; open 6am-10.30pm daily) at the Hilton Hotel in the centre, keeps longer hours than normal. The Hilton also hosts a branch of the **United Bank** (open 6.30am-10.30pm). Even more central is the branch of the **Commercial Bank of Ethiopia** (open 7am-9.30pm daily) at the Ghion Hotel.

Private banks include **Wegagen Bank**, **Bank of Abyssinia**, **Nib International Bank** and **Dashen Bank**. They have several branches in town and are easy to find. At the time of writing, the Commercial Bank had just finished installing ATMs in several locations in Addis Ababa. The machines were undergoing a trial run. Inquire at the bank when you get there.

For cash advances on credit cards, you can try the branch of **Dashen Bank** (open 8am-noon & 1pm-5pm Mon-Fri, 8am-noon Sat) off the Bole road, near Dembel Building; there's a commission of 5% for cash advances.

If you need a money transfer, you can go to **Western Union** (☎ 53 38 01, fax 53 32 29; Ras Makonnen Ave; open 8am-noon & 1pm-4.30pm Mon-Fri, 8am-1pm Sat). It has several branches in the city.

See also Money in the Facts for the Visitor chapter.

Post & Courier Services
The **main post office** (Churchill Road; open 8am-6pm Mon-Fri, 8am-4pm Sat, 10am-noon Sun) is very central. It has a courier service, called **EMS** (☎ 15 32 72; open 8am-6pm Mon-Sat, 10am-noon Sun). The courier service **DHL** (☎ 61 49 85) has several offices about town; in the centre there's one on Ras Makonnen Ave near Western Union. For more information see Post & Communications in the Facts for the Visitor chapter.

Telephone & Fax
The **telecommunications office** (open 8am-10pm daily), at the southern end of Churchill Road, offers both phone and fax services.

The yellow public phone boxes around town take two 10¢ coins; some accept phonecards.

Email & Internet Access
Internet access and email facilities are now relatively widely available in Addis Ababa, especially in the centre and along Bole Road. Among the more convenient outlets are **Meseret Cafe & Business Centre** (open 8am-8pm daily) in Arat Kilo, near the Natural History museum, and **Business Centre** (Bole Rd; open 9am-8.30pm) on the 4th floor of the Dembel building, a few paces from the intersection with Meskel Flower road. The former charges 40¢ per minute, the latter charges 50¢ per minute. The **main telecommunications building** (Churchill Road; open 8am-6pm Mon-Fri, 8am-4pm Sat, 10am-noon Sun) also has Internet access and charges 35¢ per minute.

Other Internet centres are dotted in the Piazza, in the vicinity of Baro and Wutma Hotels, and along Bole road. Most of the mid-range and top-end hotels, including the Hilton and Sheraton, provide Internet access but are much more expensive. You don't need to be a guest.

Connections are still pretty slow, so be patient.

Travel Agencies
For information on travel agencies, see Organised Tours in the Getting Around chapter. For day tours of Addis Ababa see Organised Tours later in this chapter.

Bookshops
Mega Bookshop (☎ 51 88 96), next to the Shell station off Meskel Square, has a good selection of books and has various branches around town.

CENTRAL ADDIS ABABA & THE BOLE ROAD AREA

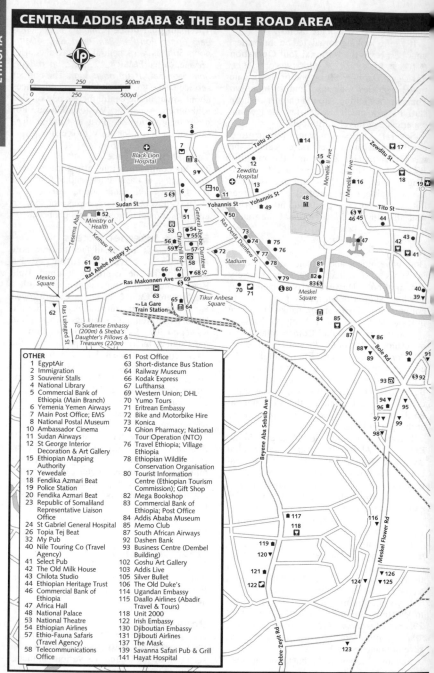

OTHER
1 EgyptAir
2 Immigration
3 Souvenir Stalls
4 National Library
5 Commercial Bank of Ethiopia (Main Branch)
6 Yemenia Yemen Airways
7 Main Post Office; EMS
8 National Postal Museum
10 Ambassador Cinema
11 Sudan Airways
12 St George Interior Decoration & Art Gallery
15 Ethiopian Mapping Authority
17 Yewedale
18 Fendika Azmari Beat
19 Police Station
20 Fendika Azmari Beat
23 Republic of Somaliland Representative Liaison Office
24 St Gabriel General Hospital
26 Topia Tej Beat
32 My Pub
40 Nile Touring Co (Travel Agency)
41 Select Pub
42 The Old Milk House
43 Chilota Studio
44 Ethiopian Heritage Trust
46 Commercial Bank of Ethiopia
47 Africa Hall
48 National Palace
53 National Theatre
54 Ethiopian Airlines
57 Ethio-Fauna Safaris (Travel Agency)
58 Telecommunications Office

61 Post Office
63 Short-distance Bus Station
64 Railway Museum
66 Kodak Express
67 Lufthansa
69 Western Union; DHL
70 Yumo Tours
71 Eritrean Embassy
72 Bike and Motorbike Hire
73 Konica
74 Ghion Pharmacy; National Tour Operation (NTO)
76 Travel Ethiopia; Village Ethiopia
78 Ethiopian Wildlife Conservation Organisation
80 Tourist Information Centre (Ethiopian Tourism Commission); Gift Shop
82 Mega Bookshop
83 Commercial Bank of Ethiopia; Post Office
84 Addis Ababa Museum
85 Memo Club
87 South African Airways
92 Dashen Bank
93 Business Centre (Dembel Building)
102 Goshu Art Gallery
103 Addis Live
105 Silver Bullet
106 The Old Duke's
114 Ugandan Embassy
115 Daallo Airlines (Abadir Travel & Tours)
118 Unit 2000
122 Irish Embassy
130 Djiboutian Embassy
131 Djibouti Airlines
137 The Mask
139 Savanna Safari Pub & Grill
141 Hayat Hospital

CENTRAL ADDIS ABABA & THE BOLE ROAD AREA

PLACES TO STAY
13 Addisu Filwoha Hotel & Hot Springs
14 Sheraton Hotel
16 Hilton Hotel; United Bank
21 Central Shoa Hotel
28 Classic Hotel
29 Debre Damo Hotel
30 Axum Hotel
31 Holiday Hotel
33 Queen of Sheba Hotel
34 Plaza Hotel
38 Yordanos Hotel
49 Finfine Adarash Hotel & Restaurant
52 Lido Hotel
56 Ras Hotel; Galaxy Express; Rocky Valley Safari
60 Wabe Shebelle

65 Buffet de la Gare
75 Ghion Hotel; Commercial Bank of Ethiopia
81 National Hotel
90 Wanza Hotel
96 Empire Hotel
101 Atlas Hotel
107 Desalegn Hotel
117 Global Hotel
119 Hawi Hotel
121 Hotel Concord; Dome Nightclub
127 Ibex Hotel
133 Meridian Hotel; La Gazelle Piano Bar; Four Seasons Travel & Tours
140 Bole International Hotel
142 GG Royal Hotel
143 Imperial Hotel

PLACES TO EAT
9 Dashen Traditional Restaurant
22 Zebra Grill
25 Yohannis Gurage Kitfo Beat
27 Bekelech Kitfo Beat
35 Tsige Bayu (Nat Gwada Restaurant)
36 Medera Jamaican Restaurant & Bar
37 Girma Kitfo Beat
39 Tiru Restaurant
45 Le Notre
50 Cottage Restaurant and Pub
51 Shi Solomon Supermarket
55 Addisu Pastry
59 Cafe Miru
62 Ras Restaurant

68 La Brasserie
77 China Bar & Restaurant
79 Connection Pastry; Wegagen Bank
86 Rainbow Seoul Restaurant
88 Fasika Restaurant
89 Pizza Deli Roma
91 Al Mendi Restaurant
94 Mmmm My Flavour
95 Purple Café
97 Jewel of India
98 Gazebo Pizza Bar & Restaurant
99 La Parisienne Café & Bakery
100 Roby Pastry; Hess Travel Ethiopia
104 Gursha
108 Shangri-la Restaurant & Bar
109 Peacock Bar & Restaurant; T-Tam Travel & Tours
110 Makush Art Gallery & Restaurant; Ethio Supermarket; City Café & Pastry
111 Sangam Restaurant
112 Habesha Restaurant
113 Likie Bar & Restaurant
116 Shaibani Restaurant
120 Pizzeria Don Vito
123 Agelgil – Villa Verde
124 Leo's Restaurant
125 Le Jardin
126 Abyssinia Restaurant
128 Betel Pastry
129 Karamara Restaurant
132 Bombay Brasserie
134 Saay Pastry
135 Aladdin
136 Olympic Cafe
138 Satellite Restaurant & London Cafe; Palace Pastry
144 Hill Belt

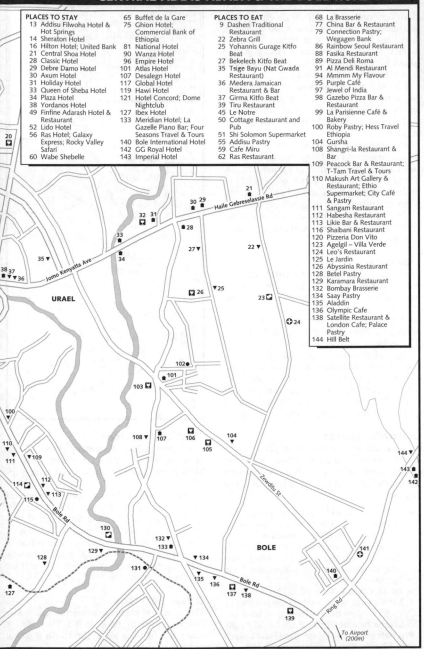

Bookworld (☎ 55 90 10; Wavel St; open 9am-8pm Mon-Sat) in the Piazza, is the best place for books in English (as well as some in French), but because books are imported, prices are a bit higher than at home. There's a small section on Ethiopia. The shop also stocks European and US magazines and has a good selection of postcards.

The **African's Bookshop**, diagonally opposite the British Council in the Piazza, is one of the best places for second-hand books on Ethiopia, particularly those currently out of print.

The **university bookshop** (☎ 51 88 96) stocks, among other things, the comprehensive Checklist of the Birds of Ethiopia by EK Urban and LH Brown. The book lists 827 of Ethiopia's bird species, as well as their range, status, abundance and time of breeding.

The big hotels such as the Ghion and the Hilton sell a good selection of magazines and newspapers.

Libraries

The library of the excellent **Institute of Ethiopian Studies** (IES; ☎ 11 57 72; W www.ies -ethiopia.org; open 8am-noon & 1pm-5pm Mon-Thur, 8am-11.30am & 1pm-5pm Fri), north of the Piazza, boasts the best collection of books in English on Ethiopia in the world. It's free for a half-day's casual use.

The collection of 20,000 books on Ethiopia housed in the **National Library** (☎ 51 62 47; open 9am-5pm Mon-Fri except Mon morning, 8.30am-4pm Sat, 8.30am-noon Sun), west of Churchill Road in the centre, includes quite a good English-language section.

Cultural Centres

National cultural centres are a good source of information and offer various forms of entertainment, including films, performances and exhibitions, and they have libraries. They include:

Alliance-Ethio Français (☎ 55 02 13, fax 55 36 81) West of the Piazza. Open from 10am to 12.30pm and from 1.30pm to 6.30pm weekdays.

Istituto Italiano di Cultura (☎ 11 36 55, fax 55 22 86) North of the Piazza. Open from 8am to 2pm Monday to Friday and from 3.30pm to 6.30pm on Tuesday and Thursday.

The British Council (☎ 55 00 22, fax 55 25 44, e britcoun.di@telecom.net.et) On the Piazza. Open from 10am to 6pm Tuesday to Saturday.

The Goethe Institut (☎ 55 28 88, fax 55 12 99, e gci@telecom.net.et) East of the Piazza. Open from 10am to 6pm weekdays.

PIAZZA

PLACES TO STAY	OTHER
20 Wutma Hotel	1 Hager Fikir Theatre
21 Baro Hotel	2 Gold & Silversmiths
22 Taitu Hotel; Red Jackal Tour	3 British Council
	4 African's Bookshop
PLACES TO EAT	6 City Hall Theatre & Cultural
5 Soul Kid Patisserie	Centre
8 Herman Cafe & Restaurant	7 St George Cathedral
14 Tomoca	9 Ethiopian Airlines
17 Ristorante Castelli	10 Ethio Travel & Tours
18 Cafe Chaud	11 Post Office
19 Omar Khayyam	12 Ethiopian Rift Valley Safaris
	13 Bookworld
	15 Bahir Dar Tour & Travel
	Agency
	16 Commercial Bank of
	Ethiopia

Medical Services

The central **Ghion Pharmacy** (☎ 51 86 06; open 8am-9pm Mon-Sat), northwest of Meskel Square, is well stocked with supplies.

The private **St Gabriel General Hospital** (☎ 61 36 22; open 24hr) east of the centre off the Asmara road, has good X-ray, dental, surgery and laboratory facilities. A consultation only costs Birr50. Another reliable option is **Hayat Hospital** (☎ 62 44 88) just off the ring road near the airport. A consultation will set you back Birr75.

Other Services

There are numerous laundries in Addis Ababa, especially on Bole Rd. They charge about Birr10 for a shirt, Birr15 for a jacket and Birr10 for trousers.

You'll find several photo shops in central Addis Ababa, including **Kodak Express** west of Meskel Square on Ras Makonnen Ave, and **Konica** near Ghion Hotel. As an indication o f price, 36 exposure colour print film costs Birr20. Developing can be done in 45 minutes and costs Birr53.

Emergency

Emergency 24-hour numbers include:

police	☎ 91
fire brigade	☎ 93
Red Cross Ambulance service	☎ 92
	☎ 11 18 82

Dangers & Annoyances

Violent crime in Addis Ababa is fortunately rare, particularly where the visitor is concerned. However, petty theft and confidence tricks are a problem and though there's no cause for alarm, travellers should always be vigilant.

The Merkato has the worst reputation for petty theft and pickpockets abound – targeting not just *faranjis* (foreigners) but Ethiopians, too. A new ploy seems to be to grab you by the arm, to wrestle you or even lightly kick or punch you while a companion cleans out your pocket. Sometimes you are distracted from the frisking by oral abuse too: the shouting of apparently anti-*faranji* comments or whatever. In such areas, travellers are advised to leave all hand luggage and jewellery in their hotel. Beware also the souvenir shops on Churchill Road. See also the Dangers & Annoyances and Money sections in the Facts for the Visitor chapter.

Other spots where you should be vigilant include the theatre area of downtown, outside some of the larger hotels (most snatch-thieving occurs in a circle between the Ethiopia Hotel, Stadium, Ghion Hotel, Ethiopian Tourism Commission and Ras Hotels at the southern end of Churchill road), the Piazza and at the minibus stands. In the city, particularly around the National Theatre, adult gangs sometimes operate. Common ploys are to feign a fight or argument and, when one man appeals to you for help, the other frisks your pockets.

Siren Scam

One scam that seems to be on the increase in Addis Ababa is the 'siren scam'. It takes various forms, from offering you to take you to a 'cultural show' venue (often by the name of Abyssinia or Jamaica) or to enjoy a traditional coffee ceremony.

The venue turns out to be a small room in a private house where a hostess will promptly dish copious quantities of *tej* (honey wine) and, perhaps, traditional dancers and musicians will perform.

Suddenly the 'entertainment' comes to an end and between Birr700 and Birr1000 is demanded. Approaches are made to couples or groups as well as to single males. Most commonly, the person approaching you is a young, well-dressed Ethiopian male, often claiming to be a student.

If you end up in a situation like this, offer to pay for anything you've consumed, and if it's not accepted, threaten to call the police. The area around the hotels in the Piazza, along Churchill Road and around the telecommunications office in the centre seem to be the most common hunting ground for potential victims.

NATIONAL MUSEUM
ብሔራዊ መ-ዝየም

The National Museum (☎ 11 71 50; admission Birr10; open 8.30am-5.30pm Mon-Fri, 9am-5.30pm Sat & Sun), east of the Piazza off the Entoto road, must rank among the most important sub-Saharan museums in Africa. Its collection was gathered in the 20th century, mainly by French archaeologists working in the north (and Eritrea).

The basement level contains **Lucy**, the fossilised hominid discovered in 1974 (see the boxed text 'Lucy in the Sky' in the Facts about Ethiopia chapter), who is the star of the exhibition. The exhibit is in fact a plaster cast (albeit a good one); the real bones are preserved in the archives of the museum.

The ground floor focuses on the pre-Aksumite, Aksumite, Solomonic and Gonder periods, with a wide array of artefacts, including pots, earthenware, statues and bowls. Look out for the beautiful, pre–1st century AD bronze oil lamp showing a dog chasing an ibex. The middle of the room hosts a collection of lavish royal paraphernalia, including the enormous and rather hideous carved wooden throne of Emperor Haile Selassie.

On the 1st floor, there's a good display of Ethiopian art ranging from early (possibly 14th-century) parchment, to 20th-century canvas oil paintings by leading modern artists such as Afewerk Tekle (see the boxed text 'Afewerk Tekle' later in this chapter). The

2nd floor contains a collection of secular arts and crafts including traditional weapons, jewellery, utensils, clothing and musical instruments. English-speaking guides are available. All photography is forbidden.

The little *tukul* (traditional cone-shaped hut) set in the gardens outside is a good place for a drink or a cheap lunch.

The Department of Inventory and Inspection of the Centre for Research and Conservation of Cultural Heritage (CRCCH) is next door to the museum. This is where you bring souvenirs for inspection in order to obtain an export permit (see Customs in the Facts for the Visitor chapter).

ETHNOLOGICAL MUSEUM

Haile Selassie's former palace is now home to Addis Ababa University's main campus north of the centre off the Entoto road.

The palace building itself now houses the library of the Institute of Ethiopian Studies (see Libraries earlier in this chapter) and, on the first and 2nd floors, the Ethnological Museum *(student/adult Birr1/20; open 8am-noon & 1.30pm-5pm Tues-Thur, 8am-11.30am & 1.30pm-5pm Fri, 10am-6pm Sat & Sun)*. The museum, undoubtedly the best in Ethiopia, has been completely refurbished and now boasts an attractive, modern and imaginative layout.

On the ground floor, there's an exhibition dedicated to the history of the palace.

The 1st floor contains superb artefacts and handicrafts from the peoples of Ethiopia, displayed in a very original way. What makes this section outstanding is its thematic approach and layout based upon the life cycle. The rationale behind it is to avoid the conventional and more static approach which follows a geographical distribution. The visit begins with the foundation myths, including Queen of Sheba, coffee and *chat*. Then comes Childhood, with birth, games, rites of passage and traditional tales. Adulthood deals with beliefs, nomadism, traditional medicine, war, pilgrimages, hunting, body culture and handicrafts. The last topic is Death and Beyond, with burial structures, stelae and tombs. Each theme and sub-theme is backed up by informative panels in English. Within these stages, different topics are addressed through different ethnic groups. The exhibition gives a great insight into the many rich cultures of the peoples of Ethiopia.

Other rooms on this floor show the preserved bedroom and bathroom of Emperor Haile Selassie, and an excellent selection of Ethiopian coins.

The 2nd floor, devoted to the traditional Ethiopian instruments, is another highlight. Drums, flutes, finger pianos, rattles, trumpets and lyres are delightfully displayed. The adjacent main room focuses on religious art, with an exceptional series of diptychs, triptychs, icons, crosses and magic scrolls. Magic scrolls, like the Roman lead scrolls, were used to cast curses on people or to appeal to the gods for divine assistance. The collection of icons is the largest and most representative in the world. Panels in English explain the evolution of styles and representations.

ADDIS ABABA MUSEUM
አዲስ አበባ ሙዝየም

The Addis Ababa Museum *(☎ 15 31 80; admission Birr2; open 8.30am-12.30pm & 1.30pm-5.30pm Mon-Fri, 8.30am-noon Sat & Sun)*, founded in 1986 on the centenary of the city as the capital, is housed in one of the oldest residential buildings in town on the southern edge of Meskel Square. It once belonged to one of Menelik's warlords.

The museum deals with the 'political, cultural and architectural history of the city'. The most interesting exhibition is the excellent collection of paintings and old photos, including candid portraits of the redoubtable Empress Taitu, rakish Lej Iyassu, and the very beautiful Empress Zewditu as a young woman. The photo of Menelik's old capital at Entoto shows just a hill dotted with little, round huts.

The museum also has a 'first-in-Ethiopia room', which includes a picture of the first telephone in Ethiopia and another of the first motor car in Addis Ababa (1907).

Upstairs, look out for the photos of the Ethiopian 'warlords' in their magnificent traditional warrior garb, and for royal paraphernalia, including swords and ceremonial robes.

NATURAL HISTORY MUSEUM
የተፈጥሮ ታሪክ ሙዝየም

The Natural History Museum *(☎ 57 16 77; admission Birr10; open 9am-5pm Tues-Sun & holidays)*, east of the Piazza, dates from the 1930s, when an Italian collected examples of Ethiopian mammals and birds. The collection has been greatly increased in the last eight years (with international assistance) and now includes bats, rodents, insects, reptiles (including snakes) and amphibians.

The museum is probably of most interest to birders, with 10 good bird cabinets showing 450 species, including the country's endemics, displayed against painted dioramas.

RAILWAY MUSEUM
የምድር ባቡር ሙ-ዝየም

The railway 'museum' *(Musée du Chemin de Fer; ☎ 51 72 50, ext 334; admission Birr30; open by appointment)* near La Gare consists of four decrepit carriages that once belonged to Emperor Haile Selassie (two apparently came from Queen Elizabeth of England). The museum is probably only of interest to train buffs.

NATIONAL POSTAL MUSEUM
ብሔራዊ የፖስታ ሙ-ዝየም

The postal museum *(admission Birr1; open 9am-12.30pm & 1.30pm-5.30pm Mon-Thur, 9am-11.30am & 1.30pm-5.30pm Fri)*, next to the main post office, houses a complete collection of Ethiopian stamps, ranging from the very first ones minted by Menelik in 1894 to present-day examples. Subjects range from Ethiopian trees to beetles, medicinal plants and lakes Many stamps have won international awards. You can also see original drawings and designs.

Stamps can't be bought here; if you're interested in buying collectables, try the main post office, which sometimes sells old stamps to travellers, as well as first-day covers.

ST GEORGE CATHEDRAL & MUSEUM
ቅዱስ ጊዮርጊስ ቤተ ክርስቲያንና ሙ-ዝየም

The cathedral, in the Piazza, was built by Emperor Menelik in 1896 following the victory at Adwa (see the boxed text 'The Battle of Adwa' in the Northern Ethiopia chapter) and in thanks to St George (Ethiopia's patron saint), whose icon was carried into battle. Greek, Armenian and Indian artists worked on the church. The Empress Zewditu (in 1916) and Emperor Haile Selassie (in 1930) were both crowned here and their coronation garb can be seen in the museum.

The cathedral is traditional in form: octagonal, but Neoclassical and rather severe in style. It's not outstandingly beautiful, but the guided tour provides an interesting and useful explanation of the Orthodox church layout and peculiarities.

Also of interest are some of the interior paintings, particularly those by Afewerk Tekle (see the boxed text 'Afewerk Tekle' later in this chapter) commissioned by the emperor when the artist was still a very young man. On the eastern side is a depiction of Emperor Haile Selassie's coronation, the well-known Queen of Sheba and King Solomon painting

and the depiction of the Last Judgment. High up is quite a striking mosaic of Christ, with his arms held wide open.

The **museum** *(admission Birr10; open 9am-noon & 2pm-5pm Tues-Sun)* is well presented and contains probably the best collection of ecclesiastical paraphernalia in the country outside St Mary of Zion in Aksum. Items include beautiful hand crosses, prayer sticks, holy scrolls and ceremonial umbrellas. It's also a very good introduction to the Ethiopian Orthodox church, explaining its traditions and ceremonies.

Admission includes a good guided tour of the church and museum (but an additional tip is expected). Flash photography is not permitted.

HOLY TRINITY CATHEDRAL
ቅዱስ ስላሴ ቤተ ክርስቲያን

Holy Trinity Cathedral *(admission Birr25; open 7am-6pm daily)*, off the Entoto Road north of the centre, is the biggest Orthodox church in the country. With its large dome and spindly pinnacles, it's one of the landmarks of the city and is a strange mishmash of international styles. It provides an interesting and sometimes poignant glimpse into many historical episodes of Ethiopia's history.

Inside, the most notable features are the two beautifully carved thrones for the emperor and empress, made of white ebony, ivory and marble. Perpendicular are the four smaller thrones for the princes and princesses.

To the north of the Holy of Holies are the tombs of the emperor and empress, which display Aksumite elements in their design. The remains of the emperor were transferred here from Beta Maryam Mausoleum in 2001.

Look out for the murals on the south wall depicting the emperor making his famous speech to the League of Nations (see Italian Occupation under History in the Facts about Ethiopia chapter). Some of the emperor's children (including the crown prince, who died in the USA in 1997) are buried in the underground crypts.

The churchyard outside is the burial place of many patriots who lost their lives during the Italian occupation, including Ras Imru, one of the great resistance fighters. In front of the cathedral is the tomb of British suffragette Sylvia Pankhurst, daughter of the famous Emmeline Pankhurst. Sylvia was one of the very few people outside Ethiopia who protested against the Italian occupation; she later lived in Ethiopia.

To the south of the cathedral is a memorial to the ministers and officials killed by the Derg in 1974 and buried in a common grave (see History in the Facts about Ethiopia chapter).

MENELIK PALACE
የሚኒሊክ ቤተ መንግስት

North of the centre off the Entoto road, surrounded by a stone wall, the old Menelik Palace (also known as 'the Gibbi') is now the government's main headquarters and is not open to the public.

BETA MARYAM MAUSOLEUM
ቤተ ማርያም መቃብር

Lying to the south of the old Menelik Palace is the Beta Maryam Mausoleum, also known as Menelik's Mausoleum (admission Birr30; open 9am-noon & 3pm-6pm daily), where Empresses Taitu and Zewditu and Emperor Menelik lie buried. Built in 1911, the grey stone mausoleum is surmounted by a large gilt crown with four small cupolas on each corner. It's not outstandingly interesting either inside or out. For a guided tour, you'll be charged about Birr30.

NATIONAL PALACE
ብሔራዊ ቤተ መንግስት

Formerly known as the Jubilee Palace, the National Palace (Menelik II Ave), in the city centre, was built in 1955 to commemorate the first 25 years of Emperor Haile Selassie's reign. Currently the palace is the state residence of the president and is not open to the public.

AFRICA HALL
አፍሪካ አዳራሽ

Built in 1961 by Emperor Haile Selassie, Africa Hall, near Meskel Square, is the seat of the UN's Economic Commission for Africa (ECA). The Italian-designed building is not very interesting, apart from the frieze-like motifs that represent traditional Ethiopian *shamma* (shawl) borders.

Far more interesting is the monumental stained-glass window inside, by the artist Afewerk Tekle, entitled 'Africa: Past, Present and Future'. Measuring 150 sq m, it fills one entire wall and is one of the biggest stained-glass windows in the world. It's well worth a visit; during some hours of the day, the white marble floor of the foyer is flooded with colour.

To visit, you need to make an appointment through the ECA (☎ 51 72 00, fax 51 03 65).

LION HOUSE
የአንበሳ ቤት

If you're not keen on zoos, avoid this one (admission 50¢; open 8.30am-5.30pm Mon-Fri, 9am-6pm Sat & Sun). Opposite the ministry of finance, north of the centre off the Entoto road, the Lion House is home to 20 or so resident

---

A Key to 'Africa: Past, Present and Future'

Inside Africa Hall is a monumental stained-glass window by the artist Afewerk Tekle. The following interpretation of the work comes from an interview with the artist.

The first panel represents 'Africa: Past'. Red is the predominant colour, symbolic of Africa's struggle against both ignorance (symbolised by the heavy shadow) and colonialism (the smug-looking dragon). The disintegrating state of Africa is represented by the disunited family and the lost child in the middle foreground. The skeleton with the whip shows evil driving the African continent – carried by a group of Africans – further and further into backwardness. The black chain framing the picture symbolises slavery.

The panel on the left represents 'Africa: Present'. The predominant colour is green, and Africa, symbolised by the man wielding a heavy double-handed sword, is struggling to slay the dragon of colonialism. In the background, a new sun rises; from it emerges all the peoples, religions and races of Africa. Above, the powers of evil, represented again by the skeleton, is taking flight, banished at last.

The middle panel shows 'Africa: Future'. Yellow is the predominant colour. In the foreground a family advances bearing torches, symbolic of a reawakening and the illumination brought by knowledge. Rallying behind are the other African countries, united and resolute in their aim for advancement. On the right, the knight in armour represents the United Nations holding out the scale of justice. In the background, a more serene landscape depicts an African arcadia, in which peace and harmony reign on the continent at last.

Abyssinian lions, the descendants of those belonging to Emperor Haile Selassie. He used them as a royal entourage, often travelling with them and making gifts of them. Feeding time is at noon.

MERKATO
መርካቶ

Merkato (*Addis Ketema or New Town; open 8.30am-7pm Mon-Sat*) is the largest market in East Africa. At first sight it appears to be an impenetrable mass of stalls, produce and people; on closer inspection the market reveals a careful organisation with different sections for different products – rather like the layout of a traditional Muslim market.

It's said that you can buy anything here, from a Kalashnikov or camel to the most precious incense. Some of the most interesting sections include the spice market (which is so pungent it may make you sneeze), and the 'recycling market', where locals in open-air workshops turn old tyres into sandals, decrepit corrugated iron into metal buckets and olive oil tins from Italy into coffee pots and tiny scoops.

The two large covered buildings next to the city bus station are known as the Addis Gebeya (New Market). Here you'll find the cloth shops, tailors and curio stalls. Don't forget that bargaining is the order of the day; some dealers are master salesmen and have been known to fleece gullible tourists. The best thing is to come with a guide, who can also act as interpreter; ask your hotel to provide one.

The market has a reputation for thieves and pickpockets but as long as you're vigilant and sensible (a money belt is a great idea), there's no cause for alarm. Beware also of the *delalla* (commission agents), who will want to 'show you a shop'. Overall, a stroll in the Merkato in a fantastic experience not to be missed.

Merkato is at its liveliest on Saturday, when people from all over the country come in. See also Shopping in the Facts for the Visitor chapter.

THE ASNI GALLERY
አስኒ ጋለሪ (የቢኤል አዳራሽ)

About 4km northeast of the centre, past the French embassy, you'll find the excellent Asni Gallery (☎ 11 73 60 ; *admission Birr10; open 2.30pm-5.30pm Tues, Wed & Fri, 10am-5.30pm Thur & Sat, closed Aug*). Housed in the 1912 villa of Lej Iyassu's minister of justice, Afe Negus Tilahun, the gallery annually

hosts five or six contemporary art exhibitions of emerging and established Ethiopian artists. Other events include workshops and lectures and are usually advertised in the *Addis Tribune*. There is also a shop selling art and craft-style souvenirs.

For details of its vegetarian buffet lunches on Thursday and Saturday, see Places to Eat later in this chapter.

To get there, take a taxi from Arat Kilo or a minibus.

AFEWERK TEKLE'S HOME & STUDIO
የአፈወርቅ ተክሌ ቤት ና ስቱዲዮ

A member of several international academies (including the French one) and with a drawer full of international decorations – 91 at last count, including the British Order of Merit – Afewerk Tekle is considered among Africa's greatest artists.

A tour of Afewerk's home and studio (☎/fax 71 59 41; **W** *www.afewerktekle.org; closed July 1-Sept 15*), southwest of the centre, is offered by the artist himself (by appointment only). The tour takes one hour and includes the artist's most famous paintings

Afewerk Tekle

Born in 1932, Afewerk Tekle is one of Ethiopia's most distinguished and colourful artistic figures. Educated at the Slade School of Art in London, he later toured and studied in continental Europe, before returning to work under the patronage of Emperor Haile Selassie. A painter as well as a sculptor and designer, he is also a master fencer, dancer and toastmaster.

Proud to have 'survived three regimes' (when friends and peers did not), his life has hardly been without incident. In almost cinematic style, a 'friendly' fencing match turned into an attempt on his life, and a tussle over a woman led to his challenging his rival to a duel at dawn. In the royal court of the emperor, he once only just survived an assassination attempt by poisoned cocktail.

The artist famously makes his own terms and conditions: if he doesn't like the purchaser he won't sell, and his best-known paintings must be returned to Ethiopia within a lifetime. In 1998, he was apparently offered no less than US$10 million for the work considered his masterpiece, *The Meskel Flower*.

such as *The Meskel Flower*, *Mother Ethiopia* and *The Simien Mountains*. The tour costs US$50 (free for students), payable in dollars or birr, as a donation for upkeep of the studio. Photography is permitted in the compound, but not in the house.

If you're thinking of souvenirs, signed and numbered reproductions on canvas are a snip at US$200 to US$350. The artist is particular about being addressed by his formal title 'Maître Artiste World Laureat', though 'Maître' will do for short!

The house and studio is west of the centre in a side street off the Ring Road, 200m from the Ghanian embassy.

WATER ACTIVITIES & MASSAGE

If you're grubby, tired and stiff, you might fancy a trip to the **Addisu Filwoha Hotel and Hot Springs** (*Filwoha Hotel*; ☎ *51 09 02; open 6am-12.30pm and 2pm-7.30pm daily*), east of Churchill Rd, where Addis Ababa's original *raison d'être*, its natural hot mineral water, is piped into the complex. A full massage with oil costs Birr60. A sauna bath costs Birr20/24 for second/first class.

A sauna or massage is also possible at the Hilton or Sheraton Hotels (see Places to Stay later in this section) but it's much more expensive (about Birr100 to Birr120).

If you fancy a dip in the thermal waters of a swimming pool in the centre of town, the Hilton charges Birr80. The Sheraton has the best pool in town (Mon-Fri/Sat & Sun Birr75/100). The swimming pool at the Ghion Hotel is way cheaper for a swim (children/adults Birr8/14) but it gets very crowded on Saturday and Sunday.

SPORTS

The Hilton has a gym (*Birr62 per day*), table tennis, minigolf, ground tennis and squash costing between Birr16 and Birr60 per hour or game.

Tennis is cheaper at the **International Tennis Club** (☎ *20 01 45; Birr10 per hour; open 6am-midnight Tues-Sun*) southwest of the centre.

You can play golf at the restored nine-hole **Addis Ababa Golf Club & Restaurant** (☎ *71 30 62*) off Ring Road in the southwest. Daily green fees are Birr100 Monday to Friday and Birr150 on Saturday and Sunday. A thwack on the driving range costs Birr20 plus Birr20/35 for 50/100 balls. It's also got a good restaurant; every Sunday there's a barbecue lunch for Birr70.

LANGUAGE COURSES

The **Institute of Language Studies** (☎ *11 90 43*) at Addis Ababa University, northeast of the Piazza off the Entoto Road, teaches three Ethiopian languages (Amharic, Tigrinya and Orominya) and charges Birr100 per hour for scheduled classes. The building is immediately to the left of the main university gates. Head for room 210 on the 2nd floor. See also the Language chapter.

ORGANISED TOURS

Some agencies, including **T-Tam Travel & Tours** (☎ *51 40 55*; W *www.ttamtour.com*) and **Nile Touring Co** (☎ *51 38 60, fax 51 35 53*; W *www.ethiomarket.com/niletour*), east of Meskel Square, can organise walking tours of Addis Ababa.

For contact details of travel agents in Addis Ababa, see Organised Tours in the Getting Around chapter.

For day excursions out of the capital see Around Addis Ababa later in this chapter.

PLACES TO STAY

Accommodation in Addis Ababa runs the gamut from cheapies to a couple of four- and five-star premises, but the choice is wider in the middle price range, with good value options – especially the newer ones – dotted around various parts of the city. Don't expect a personal atmosphere or a degree of sophistication, though. Hotels are typically concrete buildings with no particular charm, but they usually have good facilities.

PLACES TO STAY – BUDGET

Many of the cheapest hotels are found in the Piazza. They tend to be small and lugubrious. Inevitably some may double as brothels. Many rooms cost the same for one or two people. If you want a modicum of comfort, pick one of the following reliable ports of call.

Baro Hotel (☎ *55 98 46*, ☎/*fax 55 14 47*; e *barohotel@telecom.net.et; singles with shower Birr50-60, doubles with shower Birr70*) in the Piazza has long been a favourite with budget travellers. It is set in an attractive and leafy compound (with car parking), and it's clean on the whole. Ask to see a few rooms; some are better than others. There's a café serving snacks. Staff are friendly and can organise 4WD trips within Ethiopia. Facilities include free left-luggage, satellite TV on the premises, Internet access and fax service.

Wutma Hotel (☎ 56 28 78; e wutma@ yahoo.com; singles or doubles with shower Birr53-70) opposite the Baro has 15 small but clean rooms. It is another hang-out for shoestringers, though it lacks the attractive setting of the Baro. Luggage can be stored in lockers for Birr3 per day. The people who run the place can help you organise 4WD rental. Breakfast can be served on request.

Taitu Hotel (☎ 55 32 44, 56 07 87, fax 55 34 67; singles or doubles with shared shower Birr46-138, with private shower Birr115-167) also in the Piazza was built by Menelik's wife, Empress Taitu, in 1907, and was the country's first government hotel. There are several buildings in the compound. It used to be a wonderful old place with period furniture, high ceilings and creaking floors but now it has lost much its character and is in need of a facelift. Still, it is good value, especially if you manage to get a discount. The more expensive rooms, in the main building, are very spacious. There's also a garden, parking and a restaurant.

Finfine Adarash Hotel & Restaurant (☎ 51 47 11; singles or doubles with shower US$20), just east of Churchill Rd, is better known for its traditional restaurant (see Places to Eat & Drink later in this chapter) but has decent, though rather worn rooms. Around the back are 12 clean rooms (with bathrooms shared between two rooms). Rates are open to negotiation. The leafy garden at the back makes a peaceful escape from the city.

Debre Damo Hotel (☎ 61 26 30, 61 29 21, fax 62 29 20; singles or doubles with shared shower Birr50, singles/doubles with shower Birr75/180, suites Birr250). This two-storey hotel occupies an unsightly brick building tucked off Haile Gebreselassie Rd, near the Axum Hotel. This place is more inviting than it looks from the outside. It offers small but clean and tidy rooms set around a peaceful courtyard, and staff are friendly. Facilities include a restaurant, bar and email service. All in all, it's one of the best-value places in this price range.

Wanza Hotel (☎ 50 48 93, 15 61 77; singles/ doubles with shower Birr50/70) is one of Addis Ababa's best-kept secrets. It is a low-key and friendly family-run place conveniently just off Bole Rd, close to the city centre. It offers compact but clean rooms with good facilities (private shower, soap, towel etc).

GG Royal Hotel (☎ 29 23 29/30, fax 29 31 23; singles/doubles US$17/34). Close to Imperial Hotel on the Ring Rd, and about to

2km from the airport, this rather styleless but modern establishment features spacious good-value rooms (especially the singles), with satellite TV, telephone and balcony. It has a bar, restaurant and pastry shop. The main drawback is the out-of-the-way location.

PLACES TO STAY – MID-RANGE

Most of the old government-run hotels in this category are overpriced, run-down and depressing. By far the best value is that offered by the mass of new private hotels that have sprung up outside the city centre. Most lie along major roads and are well connected by the city's minibus service. Most hotels have private parking.

Centre

Ghion Hotel (☎ 51 32 22, fax 51 02 78, 50 51 50; Ras Desta Damtew St; e ghion@telecom .net.et; singles/doubles US$55/68, bungalows from US$68, apartments from US$81) is something of an institution. Though it has the advantage of an unbeatable central location near Meskel Square, it now seems a bit overpriced compared with some of the private hotels. It provides far from dazzling accommodation in three types of rooms, including bungalows. The real drawcard here is the large and lush gardens in the middle of the city. It's a popular place with tour groups and is often booked up from October to January; reservations are advised. It has several restaurants, including a traditional one (see Places to Eat later). Facilities include banking and Internet access. Credit cards are accepted.

Buffet de la Gare (☎ 51 78 88, fax 51 59 59; singles/doubles Birr90/120), near the railway station, is one of the best-value hotels in town. It's an atmospheric place with quite well-furnished and clean rooms. In addition, there's a good restaurant, a lively bar, parking and an attractive, peaceful garden.

Ras Hotel (☎ 51 70 60, fax 51 73 27; singles Birr120-210, doubles Birr135-225), right in the centre, is a government-run place. As in most government-run hotels, you'll have to do with well-worn and uninspiring rooms. Some have wooden floors. Facilities include a restaurant, bar and terrace café.

National Hotel (☎ 51 51 66, 51 37 68, fax 51 34 17; singles US$17-27, doubles US$27, twins US$23-32). This greyish Soviet-style building lacks any trace of charm but it's conveniently near Meskel Square and has adequate rooms with satellite TV. There's also a restaurant and Internet access is available.

Lido Hotel (☎ 51 44 88, 53 32 47, fax 51 63 66; ℯ lido@telecom.net.et; singles or doubles Birr125-185), near the ministry of health, is good value, with smallish but adequate rooms around a pleasant courtyard. Rates include breakfast for one person. There was a major extension project at the time of writing and the Lido is set to be turned into a smart and modern five-storey building.

Yordanos Hotel (☎ 51 57 11, fax 51 66 55; singles/doubles US$25/35, semi-suites US$40, suites US$42) is popular with tour groups. It is well positioned, east of Meskel Square. Besides that, it has 36 ordinary and slightly overpriced rooms. The cheapest are fairly cramped. It has a small bar and restaurant. Credit cards are accepted but a 6% commission is added to the bill.

North of the Centre

Extreme Hotel (☎ 55 37 77, fax 55 10 77; doubles/twins US$17/25) is just south of the Piazza. Its name is somewhat off-putting, but it is a fine place to rest, with good facilities, including a restaurant, bar, sauna, gym and a welcoming touch of greenery in the courtyard. Rooms are smallish but perfectly adequate, with satellite TV, telephone and towels.

Semien Hotel (☎ 55 00 67, fax 55 14 10; ℯ semienhotel@telecom.net.et; Dejazmach Belay Zeleke St; singles/doubles/twins Birr193/234/248) north of the Piazza is a rather nondescript multistorey building but it offers good-value and clean rooms with well-kept bathrooms, satellite TV, telephone and balcony. There's also a gym and sauna. The snack bar on the 7th floor affords terrific views.

Ras Amba Hotel (☎ 55 66 34, 51 32 60, fax 55 15 87; ℯ rahot@telecom.net.et; singles/doubles US$36/48), east of the Piazza, can be recommended. It's in a quiet, tucked-away location and is relatively modern and comfortable. Singles are on the small side. There's a restaurant and a bar on the top floor, with superb views. Internet facilities are available. Prices include breakfast.

Bole Road Area

Empire Hotel (☎ 50 98 25, 50 98 24; Meskel Flower Rd; singles or doubles US$30-40) is very convenient, just off the main road, near the intersection with Bole Road. It's not the fanciest place, situated in a white, modern concrete building, but it features clean rooms with satellite TV. The cheapest ones are fairly small; the more expensive ones are bigger. There are numerous restaurants in the vicinity.

Ibex Hotel (☎ 65 44 00, fax 65 37 37; ℯ ibex@ telecom.net.et; singles/doubles US$34/44), five minutes from the airport, southeast of the centre, has good facilities including sauna, steam bath, restaurant, bar, lounge and Internet services. Rooms are no-frills but are kept tidy and have satellite TV. There is live music on some evenings. Prices include breakfast. Credit cards are accepted but there is a commission.

Atlas Hotel (☎ 61 16 10, 18 48 62, fax 61 36 61; singles/doubles Birr208/224). Rooms are on the smallish side but this hotel in Urael, southeast of the centre, is excellent value. It's well kept and has good facilities, including restaurant, TV and balcony for those facing the road.

Desalegn Hotel (☎ 62 45 24, fax 62 38 84; ℯ desalegne@telecom.net.et; singles or doubles US$45, twins US$50, suites US$62) is an excellent choice in this price range. This friendly, modern place midway between Haile Gebreselassie Road and Bole Road offers cosy, well-furnished and sizable rooms with satellite TV, fridge and balcony. The hotel facilities are also good and include a restaurant, a terrace bar with panoramic views, pastry shop, sauna, gym and Internet access. Prices include breakfast.

Bole International Hotel (☎ 63 30 00, 63 38 40, fax 62 78 80; singles/doubles/twins US$37.50/44/50) is a very convenient place for those who want to be close to the airport. This white, modern concrete building offers ordinary but well-appointed rooms and boasts good facilities in tranquil surroundings. Rates include breakfast. It's quite far from most of the city's action, but there is a bar and restaurant on the premises.

Meridian Hotel (☎ 61 50 50, 61 45 38, fax 61 50 92; ℯ meridian-hotel@telecom.net.et; Bole Rd; singles or doubles US$72, twins US$80, suites US$84-96). Sure, this place is well located and it has bright, comfortable and spacious rooms, but the posted rates are outrageous in comparison with other establishments of the same category. Fortunately, discounts of up to 40% are offered and make this mid-range hotel a valuable option. It has Internet facilities, a bar, restaurant, laundry facilities and a gym. Good news: rates include breakfast.

Debre Zeyit Road Area

The low-key **Hawi Hotel** (☎ 65 44 99, 16 47 13; Debre Zeyit Rd; singles/doubles with telephone Birr90/120), south of the centre, is a good-value option, with small but well-maintained rooms at unbeatable prices. It has a restaurant and bar.

Hotel Concorde (☎ 65 49 59, fax 65 31 93; e hotelconcorde@telecom.net.et; Debre Zeyit Rd; singles or doubles US$21-27). This popular place offers clean and cosy rooms with balcony, but the real drawcard here are the facilities, with a good Chinese restaurant, a famous nightclub and a piano bar.

Haile Gebreselassie Road Area

Plaza Hotel (☎ 61 22 00, fax 61 30 44; Haile Gebreselassie Rd; singles/doubles US$22/26) is not an architectural gem but it's clean and well run and has comfortable rooms with satellite TV and telephone.

Holiday Hotel (☎ 61 20 81, fax 61 26 27; Haile Gebreselassie Rd; singles/doubles/twins Birr136/149/174) is good value. It has simple but tidy rooms with satellite TV, telephone, a small bar/lounge and private bathroom. There's a decent restaurant decorated with a wooden ceiling. Prices include breakfast for one person.

Classic Hotel (☎ 61 35 98, fax 61 09 46; Haile Gebreselassie Rd; singles/doubles Birr155/185) opposite Holiday Hotel has fairly unexciting and dark rooms but it's clean and quiet despite the location. Ask for a room upstairs; those on the ground floor are less bright because of a thick curtain of flowers and leaves. Prices include breakfast.

Axum Hotel (☎ 61 39 16, fax 61 42 65; Haile Gebreselassie Rd; singles/doubles/twins US$32/36/40) has tidy rooms with telephone and satellite TV. Its restaurant features a tastefully woodcarved ceiling and armchairs. Prices include breakfast. Credit cards are accepted for a 6% commission.

Central Shoa Hotel (☎ 61 14 54, fax 61 00 63; Haile Gebreselassie Rd; singles/twins Birr165/197) is a well-run place offering small but clean and comfortable rooms with satellite TV, fridge and telephone. There's a cosy lounge and a restaurant.

Though a bit out of the way, **Gedera Hotel No 3** (☎ 53 19 00, fax 53 38 93; singles/doubles Birr127/178, suites Birr263), northeast of the centre, is a reliable option, with acceptable rooms equipped with satellite TV. The rooms are a bit tired looking, but the design of the compound does not lack charm, with a mixture of bricks and large windows. Prices include breakfast. There's a restaurant and bar on the premises.

PLACES TO STAY – TOP END

Queen of Sheba Hotel (☎ 18 00 00, 61 54 00, fax 61 31 74; e queenshebahotel@telecom.net.et; Haile Gebreselassie Rd; singles & doubles US$59-109), opposite Plaza Hotel, is a modern and rather impersonal establishment, with clean, airy and well-furnished rooms. There's no particular drawback about this place, except the slightly high prices. Credit cards are accepted.

Wabe Shebelle (☎ 51 71 87, fax 51 84 77; Ras Abebe Aregay St; singles/doubles US$39/46, suites US$66/70) is a towering building west of the centre. It's rather overpriced but the rooms are well-furnished and clean, with satellite TV, fridge and telephone. There's a rooftop restaurant and Internet facilities.

Global Hotel (☎ 66 47 66, fax 66 47 23; W globalhotel.com.et; Debre Zeyit Rd; singles/doubles US$51/61, twins US$75, studios from US$71, suites US$115) is a relatively plush outfit, south of the centre, in a white, massive building. It has good facilities, including a restaurant, bar, piano bar, sauna, massage service and Internet access. The rooms are bright, spacious and comfortable, with TV, telephone and balcony. Prices include breakfast.

Imperial Hotel (☎ 29 33 29, fax 29 33 32; e imperialhotel@telecom.net.et; singles/double/suites US$66/84/114), 2km from Bole airport, is the closest thing Addis Ababa has to a modern business hotel. Though there's nothing fancy about the neighbourhood, this establishment features good facilities, including a sauna and steam room, good restaurant, conference room, gym, nightclub, travel agency and a small business centre with Internet access. It also has Jacuzzis in the suites. The smallish but comfortable and modern rooms have satellite TV and video, phone and balcony. Credit cards are accepted for a commission of 6%. Rates include breakfast and are negotiable during slack times.

Hilton Hotel (☎ 51 84 00, fax 51 00 64; e hilton.addis@telecom.net.et; singles/doubles from US$219/258) in the centre wouldn't win a beauty contest. Nevertheless, its 402 rooms are comfortable, with satellite TV, air-con, a minibar and balcony. It was built in 1969 and is 12 storeys high. There are facilities for visitors in wheelchairs. It has a swimming pool, a health club, sauna and massage service, tennis courts, banking facilities, squash court and minigolf. It also hosts travel agencies, an Ethiopian Airlines office and an NTO office.

Sheraton Hotel (☎ 17 17 17, fax 17 27 27; W www.sheraton.com; singles or doubles from US$200, deluxe suite US$2500, villa US$4200), in the centre, is the top of the heap. In 1998 it became the first 'luxury collection' hotel in Africa. Though it rises like a lotus flower rather incongruously from the shacks around, it looks beautifully designed and is the epitome of class. Neoclassical in style, it also incorporates lots of Ethiopian traditional designs, architectural features and building materials (90% of its marble is Ethiopian). No expense has been spared: from Persian carpets and original Ethiopian paintings, to furnishings plated with 24-carat Ethiopian gold. It has 392 rooms, including suites and villas. Four rooms are specially designed for people in wheelchairs.

PLACES TO EAT

Most restaurants in Addis Ababa open from around noon to 3pm and from 7pm to 10pm.

Many restaurants – particularly the smarter ones – add a tax of up to 15% to bills; check in advance.

See the Language chapter for a Food Glossary.

Ethiopian

For those who want a genuine culinary experience, there's no shortage of excellent Ethiopian restaurants in Addis Ababa. They offer a 'traditional experience': traditional food (called 'national food') in traditional surrounding with traditional music in the evening. Food is usually served by costumed staff. You sit in the short traditional Ethiopian chairs, eating from a communal plate, on a *mesob* (Ethiopian table). Prices tend to go up at night to subsidise the entertainment. Beverages cost Birr10 to Birr15.

If you feel more adventurous, try the *kitfo beats*, lesser known than the traditional Ethiopian restaurants and usually ignored by tourists. These restaurants specialise in *kitfo* (minced beef mixed with warm *berbere* and butter).

Centre and Piazza If you've never tried Ethiopian food, you can start at **Dashen Traditional Restaurant** (☎ 52 97 46; mains Birr11-23). This welcoming Addis Ababa landmark, popular with officials and expats, is on a side street behind the main post office. Try the delicious 'fasting' food (vegetarian dishes usually eaten during the traditional fasting days Wednesdays and Fridays) with fish (Birr23), which includes up to eight dishes on fresh *injera*. The setting is an added bonus, with a traditional, cosy interior enlivened with paintings, wooden floor and candlelight at night. The closed courtyard is also enjoyable, as is the adjoining bar. Imported wines (about

Birr100) are available, as is *tej* (Birr6). There's live music Thursday to Sunday at dinner.

Tiru Restaurant (☎ 15 95 51; mains Birr15-20), east of Meskel Square, opposite Yordanos hotel, does reliable Ethiopian fare at reasonable prices, including fasting food on Wednesday and Friday. There's a simple outdoor seating area and an intimate, traditionally decorated interior.

Fasika Restaurant (☎ 51 41 93; mains Birr30-35; open Mon-Sat), off the northern tip of Bole Road, close to the Addis Ababa Museum, is renowned for its delightful exotic decor and atmosphere. It's also a reliable place to get an initiation to Ethiopian specialities, such as *doro wat* (chicken drumstick or wing in a hot sauce). There's music from 9pm from Monday to Saturday.

Addis Ababa Restaurant (☎ 11 35 13, 56 61 57; mains Birr12-25) is a long-standing favourite. It is housed in a former aristocrat's residence just north of the Piazza. It has nine rooms varying in size and specialises in Ethiopian food. This is the perfect place to taste *kitfo*, *tibs* (sliced lamb) or *doro wat*, along with quality *tej* (it has its own brewery) or *buna* (coffee).

Finfine Adarash Hotel & Restaurant (☎ 51 47 11; mains Birr12-25) is also well known for its food and has a special vegetarian or 'fasting' menu on Wednesday and Friday. The restaurant is central and housed in the former home of a nobleman; there are also tables in little niches outside in the garden. There's traditional music and dancing in the garden every Sunday afternoon.

Ghion Hotel (Ras Desta Damtew St; mains Birr20-60) has a traditional restaurant which is a good place to see Ethiopian dancing in a pleasant atmosphere. Dancing takes place on Tuesday, Thursday and Saturday from 7pm until around 11pm. Reservations are a good idea.

The simpler **Tsige Bayu** (Nat Gwada Restaurant; dishes Birr 30), in a private house just east of the centre, is known for its excellent fish dishes served on fasting days. The menu is in Amharic only.

Girma Kitfo Beat (mains Birr25), east of Meskel Square, a few doors to Yordanos Hotel, is a simple but decent *kitfo beat*.

Bole Road Area Southeast of the centre on the Bole road are two reputable 'traditional experience' restaurants. The fashionable **Habesha Restaurant** (☎ 51 83 58; mains Birr20-25) has live music (and dancing on some nights)

from 8pm. For newcomers to Ethiopian fare, this is the perfect place to taste *zilzil tibs* (marinated beef cooked on clay) or *alicha firfir* (cubes of lamb meat in a mild sauce of ginger). The **Karamara Restaurant** (☎ *15 80 53; mains Birr15-25)*, further south, set in a *tukul* house, is also recommended, though it's a bit more touristy than its siblings. There's traditional music from 8.30pm to midnight nightly. You'll appreciate the appetizing Ethiopian specialities served here, such as *kitfo*, *tibs* or *zilzil*. For a full Ethiopian experience, order a flask of *tej* (honey wine).

Cognoscenti also praise **Gursha** (☎ *63 25 45; mains Birr18-35; open Mon-Sat)*, a more discrete place in the main avenue running parallel to the east of Bole Road, south of Atlas Hotel. You'll enjoy the traditional setting and, weather permitting, the congenial outdoor dining area. The menu offers a wide selection of veggie dishes. The vegetable combo (Birr25) is a favourite. As in other Ethiopian restaurants, there's live music in the evening.

Shangri-la Restaurant & Bar (☎ *63 24 24; mains Birr17-34)*, opposite Desalegn Hotel, is the one of the newest on the culinary scene in Addis Ababa. It boasts a traditional interior with wood panelling and works of famous Ethiopian painter Afewerk Tekle. Well-heeled Ethiopians and expats come here to enjoy the cosy atmosphere. It specialises in *kitfo* – there's a small butcher's shop on the premises – but also offers *beyainatu* (vegetarian dishes) on Wednesday and Friday, and even pasta if you're not game to try raw meat. There's a cosy bar and an outdoor dining area.

Abyssinia Restaurant (☎ *16 77 69; Meskel Flower Rd; mains Birr12-20)* is a more recent option a few doors away from Le Jardin. The menu comprises such common standards as *tibs*, *bozena shiro* (chickpeas with minced beef), *doro wat*, *kwanta firfir* (spicy beef) and vegetable options, all prepared with care. The decor is a subtle mix of traditional and modern. A small garden adds a touch of greenery.

Likie Bar & Restaurant (☎ *51 78 33; Bole Rd; mains Birr7-16)*, about 150m from Habesha Restaurant, in the basement of a modern building (there's no sign, but look for the orange canvas), is one of Addis Ababa's best-kept secrets. It's not a traditional Ethiopian restaurant per se, but a casual little place very popular at lunchtime. It has superb fasting food on Wednesday and Friday, as well as meat dishes the other days, such as boiled mutton or mince meat, at unbeatable prices. An added bonus is the terrace.

Agelgil – Villa Verde (☎ *65 32 99; mains Birr20-40; closed Wed)*. This is a new player on the traditional cuisine and entertainment scene. It's in a rather odd location, off Meskel Flower Rd, near the railway tracks. It serves the usual specialities and offers a show in the evening. There's a relaxing outdoor seating area.

East of the Centre Off Haile Gebreselassie Rd, close to Classic Hotel, **Bekelech Kitfo Beat** (☎ *18 12 83; normal/special kitfo Birr25/27)* is one of the smartest *kitfo beats* in Addis Ababa. It's a bright, clean place very popular with locals at lunchtime. Each order of *kitfo* is accompanied by small servings of *ibe* (dry-curd cottage cheese) and *kocho* (flat bread made from the roots of banana tree).

Yohannis Gurage Kitfo Beat *(normal/special kitfo Birr14/17, buffet kitfo Birr25)*, 300m from Bekelech Kitfo Beat, is another reputable place with a menu in English, but no sign outside. It's a large but unpretentious place with seating indoors and outdoors, but sometimes it's hard to find a free table. If you haven't tried raw meat, this is a good opportunity.

Italian

For those who don't take to local food, there's no shortage of Western fare, reflecting the influence of the city's immigrant populations. Much of it is excellent. The largest influence is the Italian one.

Blue Tops Restaurant (☎ *55 09 34; mains Birr20-72)*, a well-known place north of the centre on Entoto Road, is a favourite haunt of expats and has two restaurants, one for lunch and snacks (open all day) and a more formal Italian restaurant (roughly the same menu but twice the price). Ice cream, milkshakes, pizza and toasted sandwiches are available. There's also a decent wine list.

Ristorante Castelli (☎ *56 35 80, 57 17 57; mains Birr35-80; open Mon-Sat)*, usually known just as 'Castellis', is an Italian-run place in the Piazza. Long considered the best restaurant in Addis Ababa, it has prices to match. The four rooms are pretty stylish, with wood panelling. All dishes are homemade. Be sure to try one of the excellent pasta dishes. Reservations are advised in the evening and at weekends. There's a good selection of imported Italian wines from Birr150.

If you want to eat on the cheap, head just south of the Piazza **Oroscopo** *(mains Birr10-20)*, an unassuming place serving pizzas and pasta.

Pizza Deli Roma (☎ 51 12 04; Bole Rd; pizzas Birr10-34) is a rather impersonal place near the northern end of Bole Road, but it offers a selection of about 40 good pizzas, including some with vegetarian toppings.

Canapé International Restaurant (☎ 51 93 14; mains Birr15-40; closed Sun lunchtime), northeast of the centre, in a brick house about 100m from the Gedera No3 Hotel, is a popular place for quite good Italian food. The interior has a cosy, intimate feel. The standards include a long list of antipasti, pasta, risotto, meat dishes and fish.

Le Jardin (☎ 16 69 56; Meskel Flower Rd; mains Birr25-45) is a great place, not only for its attractive setting (there's a garden), but also for its quality pizzas and pasta. If you're after something a bit more unusual, try the penirli (Greek pizza).

Gazebo Pizza Bar & Restaurant (☎ 15 07 66; Meskel Flower Rd; mains Birr20-25) specialises in pizza cooked in traditional Italian ovens. You can eat in the attractive garden.

Pizzeria Don Vito (☎ 65 38 09; Debre Zeyit Rd; mains Birr20-64; open Wed-Mon), an Italian-run place south of the centre, lacks any atmosphere, but does excellent authentic, thin-crust pizzas (as well as home-made pasta and meat dishes).

Other European

Mmmm My Flavour (☎ 15 04 14; Meskel Flower Rd; mains Birr30-40; closed Sun lunchtime) south of the centre off Bole Road is known as the place for a romantic evening, but also as 'Mmmm My Wallet' for its prices. It's definitely plush, and the food is consistently good (a mixture of European cuisines) and more imaginative than some places, and includes some veggie dishes. There's an adjoining bar with live music in the evening.

Cottage Restaurant and Pub (☎ 51 63 59; mains Birr25-60), a cosy place in the centre, is designed like a Swiss chalet and has a good and varied menu and an excellent (imported) wine list. It has prices to match but is worth it. Meat dishes and fondue (Birr105 for two) are something of a speciality. The veal medallions with morille sauce or the veal escalope cordon bleu are excellent. The menu includes pizzas (Birr20 to Birr35).

La Brasserie (☎ 51 48 85; Ras Makonnen Ave; mains Birr22-160), midway between the stadium and the train station, is famed for its seafood. If you fancy prawns, Nile perch, tilapia or a seafood platter, this is the place to go. The interior is a blend of chic and rustic, with wooden floors and a chimney. The menu also offers several meat dishes and pasta. There's a pleasant outdoor seating area, but it's quite afflicted by the noise of the avenue nearby.

Peacock Bar & Restaurant (☎ 44 55 32; Bole Rd; mains Birr15-20) near Habesha Restaurant on the Bole road, is simple but ever popular. It's among the cheaper restaurants serving 'faranji food'. It's also famed for its macchiato, which can be sipped on the terrace.

Makush Art Gallery & Restaurant (☎ 52 68 48; Bole Rd; mains Birr25-50). On the first floor of a modern building, this is a new player on the cuisine scene in Addis Ababa. Choice is pretty limited, with rather expensive pizzas, pasta and sandwiches, but the best feature is the artistic decor – it's in an excellent art gallery, with paintings and woodcarvings.

Hill Belt (☎ 61 21 60; mains Birr15-30) is quite a swish restaurant that has won various local awards. It serves good and varied food (such as Singapore noodles, beef stroganoff or shish kebab) in an attractive setting. The only drawback is the location, quite out of the way, just off the Ring Road 4km southeast of the centre, in the vicinity of Imperial Hotel.

Zebra Grill (☎ 62 36 30; Birr15-30), in Haya Hulet district near St Gabriel Hospital, is an atmospheric place, with a thatched roof and soft lighting. The menu focuses on grilled food, with imaginative and well-prepared dishes such as chicken Montego Bay or Jamaican-style chicken. Or you could try their nibbles or sandwiches. There's music on some evenings.

Ras Restaurant (mains Birr12-20) is an old-fashioned restaurant just southeast of the centre, near Mexico Square, at the side of the Chamber of Commerce. The food – meat and pasta – is not overwhelming but prices are unbeatable. There's a peaceful outdoor area, shielded from the noisy street by a hedge of plants and flowers.

Top View (☎ 63 73 40; mains Birr20-60). This immaculate, Western-style eatery boasts an unbeatable position, perched on a hill slope near Kiddus Mikael Church, east of the centre. It offers a wide selection of snacks and more filling dishes, including pasta, soups and meat. The outstanding view comes at a cost – it's relatively pricey.

Café Miru (mains Birr8-15) near Ras Hotel is very busy at lunchtime. The ground floor is a pastry shop serving tantalizing cakes, coffee and fruit juices; upstairs there's a small and lively restaurant offering simple and hearty dishes, including pasta, meat and sandwiches at very reasonable prices.

Satellite Restaurant & London Cafe (☎ 62 12 93; Bole Rd; mains Birr30-95). You can't miss this restaurant, towards the southern end of Bole Road, near the airport. It's housed rather incongruously in a plane fuselage jutting from the front of a building. Waitresses are dressed like air hostesses. It's quite an upmarket joint offering international food. The fillet of fish in white wine or the ravioli Genoa style are worth a try.

Leo's Restaurant (☎ 66 86 97; Meskel Flower Rd; mains Birr12-25) is a civilised place opposite Le Jardin. You can enjoy imaginative cooking, such as roasted farm chicken with teriyaki sauce or sautéed fish a la mexican, or munch a snack on the shady terrace.

Asni Gallery (☎ 11 73 60), an excellent spot, has a simple but tasty vegetarian buffet lunch of around eight dishes (Birr40, including one drink) served at 1pm on Thursday and Saturday. The surroundings and the peaceful veranda make it a worthwhile option. (See Asni Gallery section earlier in this chapter)

The Sheraton (see Places to Stay earlier in this chapter) hosts several restaurants, including **Summerfields**, renowned for its sumptuous daily lunch/dinner buffet (Birr140).

Gazebo at the Hilton (see Places to Stay earlier in this chapter) has a popular poolside brunch (Birr135, including wine) from noon to 3pm every Sunday. The **Kaffa House** (mains Birr56-68), also at the Hilton, is probably the best place in town to devour a filling burger.

Asian
China Bar & Restaurant (☎ 51 37 72; mains Birr20-80) near Meskel Square gets mixed reports from expats. The decor is quite attractive, with a remarkable carved ceiling. It has a good range of Chinese dishes, including dumplings, seafood, meat and vegetables.

Rainbow Seoul Restaurant (☎ 51 23 11; Bole Rd; mains Birr33-180) serves Korean, Japanese and Chinese food. Unimpressive decor is compensated for by an extensive and imaginative menu, including veggie options.

Indian
If you've got a craving for a curry, try **Sangam Restaurant** (☎ 51 89 76; Bole Rd; mains Birr25-40), near City Café & Pastry. Expats in the know and those who just want a good Indian meal eat here. The menu offers tandoori dishes, curries and great vegetarian choices.

The sophisticated **Shaheen Restaurant** (☎ 17 17 17; mains Birr40-110) in the Sheraton (see Places to Stay earlier in this chapter) offers a feast of Indian specialities but is dauntingly expensive – at least by Ethiopian standards. The express lunch at Birr91 is more affordable.

Bombay Brasserie (☎ 18 23 43; mains Birr10-40). About 100m from Bole road, just behind Saay Pastry, this place is renowned for its wide choice of Indian specialities, including delicious tandoor and vegetable dishes. Try the chicken mugblai (chicken cooked in a mild sauce with egg, Birr28).

The Jewel of India (☎ 51 31 54; Meskel Flower Road; mains Birr20-75) is above-average, with a menu featuring more than 150 dishes. It focuses on traditional Indian specialities, including vegetarian snacks. There's a good-value express set menu at lunchtime from Monday to Friday (Birr45).

Middle Eastern
Aladdin (☎ 61 52 56; mains Birr15-35). About 100m from Bole road, Aladdin is an upmarket Armenian restaurant serving mouth-watering and imaginative dishes, including vegetable dishes. The mezzes are superb, but the kebabs are just as delicious. An added bonus is the smooth, intimate and exotic decor. Service is excellent, and a good wine list encourages a long, relaxed dinner.

Omar Khayyam Restaurant (☎ 11 22 59; mains Birr6-12) in the Piazza is excellent and does great-value and tasty Middle Eastern food in simple but attractive surroundings, including a terrace. It offers a welcoming and quiet escape from the hurly-burly of the Piazza. The shish kebab is recommended.

Al Mendi Restaurant (☎ 51 21 43; mains Birr15-60) southeast of the centre, off Bole Road, is an excellent Arabian-style eatery with a good selection of tasty dishes, including mendi (sheep), shish kebab, lamb and chicken. The fetira (bread with honey) makes a great accompaniment. You can also come here to chew chat!

The **Armenian Sporting Association** (☎ 11 35 72; mains Birr15-30; open Mon-Sat for dinner), just northeast of the Piazza, is worth a try. It offers a good selection of savoury Armenian dishes, such as mint soup, basturma (pressed beef, preserved in spices), dolma (stuffed vine leaves), shish kebab and delicious home-made yoghurt at reasonable prices.

The family-run **Shaibani Restaurant** (Meskel Flower Rd; mains Birr10-70) is another modest

ETHIOPIA

but worthy option, with a wide assortment of Middle Eastern dishes at honest prices. The hearty 'shaibani special', with rice, chicken, meat, fish and *injera* (Birr50), is a favourite.

Jamaican

Medera Jamaican Restaurant & Bar *(mains Birr10-15)*. Next to Yordanos Hotel, this place is little more than a few tables but is quite atmospheric. There's a limited choice of dishes, but prices are hard to beat. Guess what? There's a reggae feel here. It gets lively on Friday and Saturday nights (see Entertainment later in this chapter).

Cafés & Pastry Shops

Most cafés are open from around 7am to 6pm daily, and are great for breakfast. Most pastries cost from Birr1 to Birr5; fruit juices cost from Birr5 to Birr15.

Centre and the Piazza In the Piazza, **Tomoca** is a great old Italian café, which serves delicious coffee. You'll enjoy the old-fashioned atmosphere, though it's somewhat marred by a loud satellite TV broadcasting CNN. It also sells five types of coffee (ground or beans) for Birr34 for a kilo, as well as traditional coffee pots for Birr20.

Soul Kid Patisserie *(Adwa Ave)*, very close to the British Council, is resoundingly popular with locals. It has good coffee and savoury pastries.

Herman Cafe & Restaurant *(Adwa Ave)* is at the top of a building situated at the intersection of Adwa Ave and De Gaulle Square. It affords superb views on the Piazza area and provides a pleasant escape from the hustle and bustle of De Gaulle Square. There's an adjoining restaurant, and a busy pastry shop on the ground floor.

Sweet-tooths will also be satisfied at **Cafe Chaud**, just off De Gaulle Square. It doesn't necessarily impress from the outside, but you'll be surprised to discover the clean, tidy and trendy interior. There's a large seating area downstairs with marble-topped tables and metal chairs. It has pizzas, fruit juices and cakes.

Addisu Pastry *(Churchill Rd)* opposite Ras Hotel is a pleasant spot to sip a fruit juice or a coffee. There are some savoury pastries too. It's standing room only and can get very busy.

Connection Pastry, near the Ghion Hotel in the centre, has a good selection of pastries, fruit juices and milkshakes. Try the 'fruit punch', in fact a fruit salad (Birr3.50). Black

and white tiling and mirrors on the walls add to the ambience.

Le Notre *(Tito St)*, next to Commercial Bank of Ethiopia, is a large and trendily furnished French pastry shop which serves irresistible delicacies, including cakes, croissants, pies and snacks, in a civilised atmosphere. Prices range from Birr3 to Birr30. You can order a *macchiato* or a fruit juice.

Sunrise Cafe next door to Goethe Institute, boasts a central location. A perfect spot with a large, open terrace from which to watch the world go by, it is inevitably packed throughout the day. Here you can sip a fruit juice or a *macchiato* or munch a snack any time of the day. Cakes and pastries are also on offer.

Need a rest after the visit of the Ethnological Museum? Head for **Dibab Recreation Services**, a quaint little café in the middle of a little square, just across the university entrance. It's an ideal place to unwind in the sun over a pastry and a cup of coffee. Students make up most of the clientele.

Bole Road Area A good place to start the day is **Palace Pastry** *(Bole Rd)*, a few paces from the unmissable Satellite Restaurant & London Café (see Other European earlier in this section). It serves breakfast for about Birr7, fruit juices, pastries, snacks and sandwiches. There's a front terrace.

Betel Pastry off Bole Rd, on the road leading to Ibex Hotel, concocts good pastries and boasts an attractive interior, with metal chair, blue walls and embedded stones. The *macchiato* is excellent.

City Café & Pastry *(Bole Rd)*, near the Makush Art Gallery & Restaurant, is one of the best pastry shops in town. It's owned by a returnee from America who brought with him many of his recipes. Try the tantalizing apple strudel. Ice creams are also available.

Purple Café *(Bole Rd)*, near the corner of Meskel Flower Rd, is unmistakably purple and is also good; the delicious *mille feuilles* are a speciality. Hot chocolate, juices and ice cream are also available. It's popular with a younger local crowd and is pretty lively.

Roby Pastry *(Bole Rd)* is a good place with a shady terrace where you can enjoy a cup of coffee or a fruit juice. Mouth-watering cakes and pastries are also available.

Further south, **Saay Pastry** *(Bole Rd)*, near Meridian Hotel, also has a tempting selection of treats, including freshly baked croissants and doughnuts, as well as ice creams and fruit juices. It also does a wonderful *macchiato*.

As its name suggests, **La Parisienne Cafe & Bakery** *(Meskel Flower Rd)*, off Bole road, is designed like a French café. It is quite a hip hangout, especially at lunchtime, and a great place for breakfast or for a treat any time of the day. It specialises in tantalizing croissants (chocolate, cheese, cream etc) fresh from the oven. It also sells a good variety of wholemeal bread, as well as teas (Birr3) and more unusual fruit juices (including ginger, hibiscus and avocado). The shady terrace is good for people-watching.

Olympic Café *(Bole Rd)* belongs to famous marathon-runner Haile Gebreselassie. The place is quite sterile, but it serves an excellent coffee as well as fruit juices, milk shakes, pastries and snacks.

Self-Catering
Shi Solomon Hailu Supermarket *(Churchill Rd; open 8am-8pm daily)* near the National Theatre in the centre is quite well stocked with Western faves, from cereals and biscuits to mineral water and tomato ketchup.

Novis Supermarket *(open 8.30am-7.30pm Mon-Sat, 9am-1pm Sun)*, southwest of the centre, is a favourite with the expat community and stocks everything from smoked salmon to Italian chocolates and cheeses.

Ethio Supermarket *(Bole Rd; open 24hr; Bole Rd)*, conveniently, is in the same building as Makush Art Gallery & Restaurant.

ENTERTAINMENT
Pubs & Bars
Most places charge around Birr5/15 for local/imported beer, and are open until 2am during the week, and 5am on the weekend.

The cluster of **bars** in the Piazza around the National and Taitu Hotels are simple and cheap but very atmospheric places, where locals come for a beer and to dance to their favourite Amharic tunes. It's a great area for bar-hopping and is safe for women: follow the music. Another area worth exploring is Kazanchis, east of the centre, with down-to-earth but authentic bars often turning to impromptu dance floors late in the evening. You'll also find a host of typical, unpretentious but lively Ethiopian joints in Haya Hulet – follow the street leading from Bole Road to St Gabriel Hospital and you'll come across one of them.

Street names are given in the following reviews when useful and appropriate.

The Old Duke's is the closest thing Addis Ababa has to a pub, and it wouldn't look out of place in Dublin or Melbourne. Happy hour is from 5.30pm to 7pm. It's about 500m from the Atlas Hotel, southeast of the centre.

Buffet de la Gare, the bar at the Hotel de la Gare near the railway station, is also an atmospheric place to knock back a St George in the evening.

My Pub *(Haile Gebreselassie Rd)*, east of the centre, is like an American bar and English pub rolled into one, with pool table, darts and juke box. It's a bit garish and expensive, but it is a convenient meeting place and remains open late. It has a very good selection of spirits and liquors and also serves snacks.

The Old Milk House, near Africa Hall in the centre, is a Dutch-owned bar in a welcoming shady courtyard. It was a resoundingly popular place at the time of writing, with a mixed crowd of expats and locals. It has a pool room and serves various snacks and pizzas and has a barbecue on Friday evenings.

The Mask *(Bole Rd)* at the southern end of Bole Road, off the main avenue, is a trendy though somewhat gaudy bar, popular with expats and well-heeled locals. It's named after the series of masks that adorn the walls. It's a good spot to whet your palate with a cocktail (Birr12 to Birr50). The bar at **Makush Art Gallery & Restaurant** *(☎ 52 68 48; Bole Rd)* is a civilised and sophisticated venue overlooking Bole Road and is a good place for a predinner drink.

Ras Amba Hotel, east of the Piazza, has an outdoor terrace which is a great place for a drink at sunset.

Ghion Hotel is in the centre of town. For a 'sundowner', the veranda of the traditional restaurant here looks on to the garden; it's another early-evening place.

Wabe Shebelle hotel has a balcony on the top-floor restaurant which affords a terrific 360-degree panoramic view of the city. If you're after something more formal, try the bars at the **Hilton Hotel** and the **Sheraton Hotel**. They are unsurprisingly much more expensive and more sterile than any other places.

Tej Beats
A *tej beat* (pronounced 'tedj bet') is a kind of Ethiopian pub, serving *tej* instead of beer. If you're in search of an authentic experience, a drink in a *tej beat* is a must. A flask of *tej* costs around Birr1.50. Most are open to around 10pm, but are busiest in the evening. Women should be aware that these places are the traditional haunt of men and should keep a low profile. Ask for directions, there's no sign.

Though a bit out of the way, **Kitaow Tej Beat No 2** is one of the most authentic *tej beats* in Addis Ababa. Punters sit on long benches in a courtyard, though there's also seating inside. It lies 100m off the Ring Road opposite the Iveco AMCE building, east of the centre. Follow the side street off the Ring Road – it's through the green gates on your right.

Beta Mengist Tej Beat, north of Kitaow Tej Beat No 2, off Haile Gebreselassie Road, is like a huge beer hall. It's not signposted (look for Wubet House, it's in a side street close to this building), but you can't miss it for the noise. It's a pretty rowdy place, so come prepared. Note that it's for men only.

Topia Tej Beat is known for its high-quality *tej*. It's tucked off Haile Gebreselassie Road, in a side street about 300m south of Classic Hotel.

If you want something more central, head for **Yegebawal Tej Beat** east of the Piazza, very close to the Mobil Petrol Station, in the vicinity of the Ministry of Education. It boasts a lively and congenial atmosphere but gets a bit rougher in the evening.

Note that most traditional restaurants also serve the precious liquid and are good places to get an initiation in more genteel surroundings. We particularly recommend the less touristy **Addis Ababa Restaurant** (see Ethiopian under Places to Eat & Drink earlier in this chapter), which serves excellent, home-made *tej*.

Jazz Clubs
Coffee House opposite the Egyptian embassy in the centre features good jazz nightly from Thursday to Sunday. You can nibble on some snacks or order grilled food while listening to the band.

African Jazz Village is a quite civilised jazz club southwest of the centre, in Mekanisa. Though out of the hub of things, it's well worth the trip. The clientele are mainly middle-class Ethiopians and expats looking for a relaxed time in a cosy atmosphere. Another draw is the setting; it's housed in a *tukul*. A beverage will set you back Birr10 to Birr20. It's open on Friday and Saturday from 9pm.

Imperial Hotel (see Places to Stay earlier) has a jazz night in its diminutive but civilised top-floor bar on Thursday night.

La Gazelle Piano Bar (Bole Rd) is also worth a look. There's a band playing traditional music until 10pm, from when the stage is devoted to jazz. It also houses a restaurant.

Nightclubs
Most clubs get going about 11pm, and stay open until around 2am during the week and 5am on the weekend. Cover charges vary widely depending on the venue or the day of the week. Admission generally costs Birr20 Monday to Friday and Birr30 on Saturday and Sunday (but is sometimes free). Beer costs Birr10 to Birr15, spirits from Birr12 to Birr25. If you fancy a big night out, it's not a bad idea to hire a taxi for the night (around Birr40 per hour).

If you want a genuinely Ethiopian experience, head for the row of **bars/clubs** in the street that leads to Merkato from the Semien Hotel north of the Piazza – this area is known as 'Datsun Sefer'. With their twinkling lights at the front, they are unmissable. These tiny places attract a colourful crew and play a good mix of African music.

Male travellers should be aware that most single Ethiopian women encountered in the nightclubs are prostitutes.

Memo Club south of Meskel Square was one of Addis Ababa's hot spots at the time of writing. It's a fairly large place with the usual silver mirror balls and full-length mirrors for the more narcissistic movers. It plays a mixture of African and Western music and is a favourite with male expats. Sometimes there's a bar and grill outside.

Silver Bullet, not far from Atlas Hotel, is favoured by young foreigners, who seem to enjoy the rather garish Tex-Mex decor and unashamedly Western music. It also serves good cocktails and acceptable Tex-Mex nosh.

Dome Nightclub (*Debre Zeyit Rd*) better known as the Concorde after the hotel that houses it, is one of Addis Ababa's best-known and long-standing clubs. The evening usually starts with a band playing Ethiopian music (sometimes modern) until 11.30pm nightly except Monday, then it turns to a regular dance club. Male foreigners seem to cherish the place – less for the music than for the great number of local girls waiting for them. The music is predominantly Western but with some African hits.

Unit 2000 is the place to head for if you're after West African beats. It's tucked away in a side street off Debre Zeyit Rd near Global Hotel, and feels more like a private party in a house. There's a congenial and cosy atmosphere.

Select Pub, in a side street near ECA and the Old Milk House, is worth checking out. Though relatively elegant, it oozes ambience.

There's Ethiopian live music every night but it also plays various hits.

Gaslight in the Sheraton (see Places to Stay earlier) is hip and appeals to a wealthier crowd. It features a plush decor with a large dance floor, and generally plays Western music. Despite all this, the atmosphere is sometimes lacking. You do, of course, need to be reasonably smartly dressed to get in here.

Savanna Safari Pub & Grill (Bole Rd), at the southern tip of the Bole road, close to the airport, is more an entertainment complex with several dance areas, bars and music. The crowd is mixed although you can expect a predominance of young foreigners.

Addis Live, a stone's throw from Atlas Hotel, southeast of the centre, attracts a younger crowd (mainly Ethiopian) and plays a good mix of music. It also has a bar and grill outside.

Medera Jamaican Bar & Restaurant (Haile Gebreselassie Rd), next door to Yordanos Hotel east of Meskel Square, is little more than a room but gets lively on Friday and Saturday evenings when there's a party with a DJ. As you may imagine, the music is essentially reggae.

Azmari Beats

The *azmari* is an Ethiopian equivalent to a stand-up comedian; the *azmari* tradition is very ancient. Though performances are always in Amharic, it's still a fun thing to watch. Admission to the *azmari beats* is free; drinks cost about Birr10 (even for mineral water). Most *azmari beats* are dotted along the northern end of Zewditu St. They usually don't have a sign, but look out for the thatched twin-peaked roofs above the entrance.

Yewedale ('He Likes It'; Zewditu St) is one of the best *azmari beats* in town, and is resoundingly popular; it's often hard to find a seat. Some of the best Addis Ababa *azmaris* perform here.

Fendika Azmari Beat (Zewditu St) has two venues, and is a recommended cultural experience for newcomers.

Traditional Music, Dance & Theatre

For general information on Ethiopian music and dance see Arts in the Facts about Ethiopia chapter. Many of the hotels and restaurants put on traditional shows (see Ethiopian under Places to Eat & Drink earlier in this chapter).

Crown Hotel (☎ 34 14 44), though lying 12km south of the centre on the Debre Zeyit road, puts on excellent traditional dancing show in town in its giant *tukul*, and is popular among Ethiopians as well as with foreigners. The dancing (of about 13 different ethnic groups) takes place every evening from 7pm to around midnight. Friday, Saturday and Sunday are the best nights, but don't leave it too late as some of the best dancing takes

---

Mincing Minstrels

An ancient entertainment that continues to this day is that provided by the *azmari*, or wandering minstrel, and his *masenko* (single-stringed fiddle). In the past, the *azmari* accompanied caravans of highland traders to make the journey more amusing.

At court, resident *azmaris*, like the European jesters, were permitted great freedom of expression – so long as their verses were witty, eloquent and clever.

During the Italian occupation, the *azmaris* kept up morale with their stirring renditions of Ethiopian victories and resistance. So successfully, in fact, that many were executed by the Italians.

Today, *azmaris* can be found at weddings and special occasions furnishing eulogies or poetic ballads in honour of their hosts.

In certain bars (azmari beats) of the larger towns, some *azmaris* have become celebrities in their own right and, like stand-up comics, attract a loyal following. The cleverest can compose their rhyming verses spontaneously, and may even use the audience as the butt of their jokes. Sometimes the humour is light and whimsical, sometimes bitingly satirical, and more often than not extremely vulgar. It revolves on clever puns, complex double meaning and learned allusion. Don't miss the chance to see them.

place early evening. Food (Birr15) and drink (from Birr5) is served, and photos and videos can be taken.

Currently almost all theatrical productions are staged in Amharic (see Theatre under Arts in the Facts about Ethiopia chapter).

National Theatre (☎ 15 82 25; tickets Birr6₋10) is in the centre. There are shows on Tuesday, Wednesday, Thursday and Friday, starting at 3pm. On the weekend, shows start at 1pm.

City Hall Theatre & Cultural Centre, a plush 1000-seat place in the Piazza, shows productions Tuesday to Sunday for Birr10. Sometimes there is traditional Ethiopian music during public holidays.

Hager Fikir Theatre (☎ 12 27 48), near City Hall Theatre, also stages theatre, musicals and dancing.

Cinema

Ambassador Cinema (tickets Birr5) in the centre puts on the usual diet of action-packed and slightly dépassé Hollywood movies (in English). Films are shown daily in three sessions.

SPECTATOR SPORTS

At **Jan Meda Race Ground** northeast of the Piazza, there's horse racing from mid-November to mid-June on Saturday and Sunday mornings. If you're in Addis Ababa for Ethiopian Christmas (January 7th), don't miss the festivities here (including the traditional game of *genna* – see Public Holidays & Special Events in the Facts for the Visitor chapter).

If you fancy watching a bit of the nation's favourite sport, there's the 27,000-seat **football stadium** (tickets Birr7-20). The National League games begin at 4pm every Sunday and attract big crowds. Sometimes athletics, cycling and boxing events are held here, as well as pop concerts. Events are advertised in the *Ethiopian Herald*.

SHOPPING

Addis Ababa is a great place for souvenir shopping. Along Churchill Road there's a string of souvenir stalls where you can haggle over prices. Take a good look around as quality and prices vary hugely. The Piazza area is also worth investigating. Top-end hotels also house well-stocked curio shops and are good for last-minute pressies for the family back home. Most shops are closed on Sunday.

Hope Springs Eternal

For the street children of Addis Ababa, meal tickets aren't a bad idea; these can be bought in Addis Ababa from **Hope Enterprises** (☎ 56 03 45). Booklets of eight meal tickets cost just Birr4; the recipient can exchange the ticket for a 'simple but nourishing meal' at the centre. The office is open Monday to Friday from 8am to 6pm.

Shumeta Leda (☎ 12 65 41; Churchill Rd) just south of the Piazza is good, with Harari baskets from Birr5 and Birr15, wall rugs from Birr6 per 'panel', head rests from Birr30, beads, and Afar knives from Birr120. It's also got a good selection of jewellery and woodcarvings.

Haileselassie Alemayehu (☎ 12 95 03; Churchill Rd), just north of the centre, is also good, with a popular mix-and-match bead counter, jewellery, paintings, baskets, icons, woodcarvings and traditional clothing.

Gift Shop (Meskel Square), beside the ETC, is particularly good for books on Ethiopia, including the ETC pamphlets, such as *Endemic Birds*. It also sells postcards (Birr1.25).

St George Interior Decoration & Art Gallery (☎ 51 09 83; Taitu St) in the centre has exquisite (but very pricey) traditionally inspired modern furniture. Other items include well-designed jewellery, crosses and cushions.

Goshu Art Gallery (☎ 61 47 47), southeast of the centre between the Bole road and the Haile Gebreselassie road, has some more unusual items including *washint* (traditional flutes) for Birr75, as well as skin and canvas paintings (from Birr3000).

Sheba's Daughter's Pillows & Treasures (☎ 51 24 30), south of the centre 100m across from the Sudanese Embassy, has a good selection of high-quality souvenirs. It stocks cushion covers in traditional fabric, Jimma wooden stools, a beautiful selection of silver jewellery and old shields. But it's not for the impecunious.

Chilota Studio (☎ 53 33 29), an excellent place in the centre close to Africa Hall, sells good souvenirs such as baskets, pots, headrests, paintings and cushion covers; many items are attractively framed.

Makush Art Gallery & Restaurant (☎ 52 68 48; Bole Rd) has an excellent, carefully selected collection of high-quality furniture

Shepherd boys, Simien Mountains

Granite stele, Aksum

Looking out over the Geech Abyss, Simien Mountains National Park

Emperor Fasiladas' palace in the Royal Enclosure, Gonder

Shepherd boy, Simien Mountains

The Blue Nile Falls, near Bahar Dar

Watching the mist rise above the valley, Tigray

and paintings from various Ethiopian artists. It also serves as a bar and restaurant (see Places to Eat earlier in this chapter).

Lulseged Retta (☎ 55 23 02), the talented artist known for his wide-eyed people, has a studio which can be visited by appointment. Paintings cost from Birr3500; posters from Birr50.

Ato Worku Saboka shop (*'Falasha Factory'; Ambo Rd*) is probably the best place in the country for traditional (but fired in modern kilns) Falasha red pottery, sold at very reasonable prices. Items range from little hen vases (Birr6) and *doro wat* plates (Birr20), to large sculptures or pots (Birr80). It's 9km northwest of Addis Ababa (around 500m after the Gullele soap factory).

Ato Basket shop (☎ 20 10 49) southwest of the centre, just on the side of the road, is the best place in town for baskets. It sells everything from hats and pots to *mesob*, chairs and huge laundry baskets (great for getting excess luggage home). Prices are negotiable.

Universal Leather Articles Factory (☎ 42 41 22; Debre Zeyit Rd) this outlet, as the name suggests, turns out good-quality leather articles, such as bags and jackets. The stock is fairly limited though.

In the Piazza, most of the city's goldsmiths and silversmiths are found. Gold goes for Birr95 to Birr105 per gram depending on the carat; silver costs Birr13 per gram.

Charity Shopping

Many first-timers in Addis Ababa are disturbed by the sight of the city's poor. Shopping at these excellent shops is a great way to improve their lot.

Women's Fuelwood Carriers Project, tucked in a back street north of the centre off Entoto Road, just beyond the Spanish

---

The Firewood Carriers

An all-too-familiar sight in and around Addis Ababa is the firewood carrier. Many of these women walk up to 30km to gather bundles that weigh an average of 35kg – often more than their total body weight. Bent like question marks under their loads, the majority of these women earn less than US$12 a month. Yet their work is their only means of survival; usually they are the only income-earners in the family.

---

embassy (look out for the signposts 'WFC project'), is a modest charity shop selling a small selection of well-made souvenirs including hand-woven shawls (Birr40), straw hats, robes, and poufs (Birr75). You can also see traditional spinners and weavers at work.

Alert Handicraft Shop (☎ 71 31 19), in the compound of the Alert Hospital, southwest of the centre off the Ring Road, sells a good range of crafts including wall hangings, tea cosies, embroidered cushion covers, table cloths and matching napkins; many are made by people who once had leprosy.

GETTING THERE & AWAY
Air

Most airlines accept credit cards. The most useful for travellers include:

British Airways (☎ 51 59 13, fax 51 06 55) Office at the Hilton Hotel

Daallo Airlines (☎ 15 76 08, 53 46 87, fax 53 46 88) Represented by Abadir Travel & Tours, Bole Rd

Djibouti Airlines (☎ 63 37 02, fax 61 47 69) Off Bole Rd

EgyptAir (☎ 56 44 93, fax 55 22 03), Churchill Road

Kenya Airways (☎ 51 30 18, fax 51 15 48) Office at the Hilton Hotel

Lufthansa (☎ 51 56 66, fax 51 29 88) Office on the corner of Churchill Rd and Ras Makonnen Ave

Saudi Arabian Airlines (☎ 51 26 37, fax 51 43 99) Office next to Ambassador Cinema

South African Airways (☎ 51 16 00, 53 78 80) Flamingo Rd

Sudan Airways (☎ 50 47 24, fax 50 47 25) Office next to Harambee Hotel

Yemenia Yemen Airways (☎ 52 64 41, fax 51 44 04) Ras Desta Damtew St

Ethiopian Airlines There are about a dozen Ethiopian Airlines offices dotted around Addis Ababa, including branches at the Hilton Hotel and near the National Theatre in the centre and on De Gaulle Square in the Piazza. The **branch** (☎ 51 15 40; open 6am-9pm Mon-Sat) at the Hilton generally has far shorter queues than the other offices. Schedules change quite frequently and flight durations depend on the type of plane used, so it is important to check these details carefully in advance. Flight duration includes any stopover ground time. For prices on some of the following domestic routes see also the Getting Around chapter earlier. The following flights all leave from Addis Ababa.

destination	duration	frequency
Aksum via Mekele or Bahar Dar	2h	daily
Arba Minch	1½h	2 weekly
Bahar Dar (Lake Tana)	35min	3 daily
Debre Markos	-	1 weekly
Dessie	1h	daily
Dire Dawa	1h	2 daily
Gambela via Jimma	2h	4 weekly
Goba	1h	1 weekly
Gonder via Bahar Dar	1h	2 daily
Jijiga via Dire Dawa	3h	5 weekly
Jimma	1h	5 weekly
Jinka via Arba Minch	2¼h	2 weekly
Lalibela (direct)	1h	2 weekly
Lalibela via Bahar Dar	1¾h	3 weekly
Mekele	1½h	2 daily
Mizan Tefari via Jimma	1¾h	1 weekly
Shire	2½h	2 weekly

Bus
There are two bus stations (for long- and short-distance buses) in Addis Ababa. Autobus Terra, the long-distance station (for any journey over 250km), is found at Merkato, west of the Piazza. The short-distance station is found near La Gare on Ras Makonnen Ave in the centre. (See also Bus in the Getting Around chapter earlier). Note that buses for Shashemene depart from the short-distance station.

Long-Distance Station For information on departures call ☎ 13 59 03. Buses for the following destinations leave officially at 6.30am:

Aksum (Birr105.50, 2½ days) via Shire, Dessie and Mekele
Arba Minch (Birr46.45, 12 hours)
Awash (Birr20.85, six hours)
Bahar Dar (Birr57.70, 1½ days) via Debre Markos or Dangala
Dessie (Birr36.80, nine hours)
Dire Dawa (Birr52.65, 11 hours)
Gambela (Birr77.25, two days) via Jimma
Goba (Birr45, 12 hours)
Gonder (Birr77.75, two days) via Debre Markos or Dangala
Jijiga (Birr65.30, two days) via Hirna Jimma
Nekemte (Birr30.15, 8½ hours)

Short-Distance Station For information on departures call ☎ 15 36 06. Buses leave

regularly for the following destinations from 5.45am to around 6pm:

Debre Zeyit (Birr3, 45 minutes)
Lake Langano (Birr20, five hours) take the Shashemene bus and ask to be dropped off en route
Nazret (Birr9, two hours)
Shashemene (Birr20, five hours)

Train
Addis Ababa's train station (La Gare) is officially known as Chemin de Fer Djibouto–Ethiopien. The only railway line in Ethiopia runs between Addis Ababa and Djibouti town.

For information on trains to Djibouti call (☎ 51 72 50, ext 321). See also Train in the Getting There & Away and Getting Around chapters earlier.

The ticket office is open when the train is in, until 1pm. In principle the train leaves at 2pm.

Car & Motorcycle
Cars are best hired from travel agencies in Addis Ababa. See Organised Tours in the Getting Around chapter for details of car rental.

GETTING AROUND
Good news: though Addis Ababa is a sprawling city, it's fairly easy to get around, with several options to choose from. The most useful option for travellers is the cheap and efficient minibuses that take little time to get used to. Taxis abound and are another possibility, especially in the evening.

To/From the Airport
Bole International Airport lies just 5km southeast of the city; both international and domestic flights depart from here.

Minibuses serve the airport daily from 6am to 8pm. To the airport from the Piazza, Mexico Square or Meskel Square costs up to Birr1.20. Some charge an additional Birr2 or Birr3 for luggage (see also Minibus).

Taxis to the airport should cost between Birr35 and Birr50, but cost slightly more at night or early in the morning. From the airport, it costs around Birr35 with a blue taxi, though you'll be asked for at least double or triple this (see Dangers & Annoyances in the Facts for the Visitor chapter). A taxi association has set up a little office at the exit of the airport and charges a 'fixed rate' (negotiable) of Birr45 (Birr50 at night), which at least cuts

ETHIOPIA

out the touts. Taxi drivers belonging to this association have yellow taxis.

You can make the airport dash in a Mercedes-Benz NTO taxi (see also Taxi) from the Hilton for Birr45 to Birr50 during the day (Birr85 to Birr100 after midnight).

Bus
Buses in Addis Ababa are considered the poor man's transport. They are cheap but slow, run less regularly than the minibuses and are notoriously targeted by pickpockets – the minibuses are a much better bet.

Minibus
Addis Ababa is served by an extensive network of little blue and white minibuses, which are fast, efficient, cheap and a great way of getting around.

Minibuses operate from around 5.30am to 8.30pm every day. Journeys cost from 55¢ to Birr1.25 depending on distance.

Minibus stops can be found around town. Major ones include those on Ras Makonnen Ave; in front of La Gare; at Merkato; on De Gaulle Square in the Piazza; and in front of the main post office on Churchill Road in the centre. If in doubt, ask at the stop as people are always willing to help.

There are two principal minibus stations: Meskel Square in the centre and Arat Kilo northeast of the Piazza. Roads around these intersections branch out spider-like, and minibuses ply the routes back and forth. To catch a minibus, check out the road on which your destination lies, and hop on at the start of the road that leads there. The conductors shout out the names of the main destination of the bus.

Car & Motorcycle
Parking is not usually too much of a problem in Addis Ababa. Most of the larger hotels and restaurants have parking spaces – often guarded – and don't usually mind you leaving your car there. In other places, it's worth paying for a guard; thieves work incredibly quickly.

Taxi
Most taxis operate from 6am to 11pm. Short journeys (up to 3km) usually cost foreigners Birr20 (more at night). Medium/long journeys cost Birr30/50. If you share a taxi, the normal fare is split between each person.

If you want to visit a lot of places in Addis Ababa, it's a good idea to hire a taxi for a half or full day; negotiate the rate (Birr250 for a full day is pretty reasonable). A 'city tour' lasting a couple of hours should cost around Birr100.

Taxis can be found outside many of the larger hotels in the centre, as well as the National Theatre, stadium, and on De Gaulle Square in the Piazza. At night, many line up outside the nightclubs.

The **NTO** (☎ 15 17 22) at the Hilton Hotel has a fleet of yellow Mercedes-Benz, but prices are about thrice that of local taxis (and six times at night). They're only useful for trips to the airport (prices are about the same as local taxis) or, as a last resort, at night – the service is 24 hours. During the day journeys cost around Birr40 to Birr50 (Birr85 to Birr100 after midnight).

Bicycle & Motorcycle
Bicycles can be hired from beside the stadium in the centre for Birr10 per hour or Birr30/50 per half/full day. They are available from 7am to 6pm Monday to Friday (until 5.30pm on the weekends). Make sure you get one with a lock. You can also hire motorcycles for Birr30 per hour or Birr200 per day.

Around Addis Ababa

There are many interesting and pleasant places within a day's trip of Addis Ababa. Places include Mt Yerer, Mt Zuqualla, the crater lakes of Debre Zeyit, the hot-spring resorts of Sodore (see the Eastern Ethiopia chapter for all of these) or Ambo (Western Ethiopia chapter) and the stelae field at Tiya (Addis Ababa to Ziway in the Southern Ethiopia chapter). The Akaki wetlands (Eastern Ethiopia chapter) is a very good place for birders.

For those spending any time in the city, the booklets *Twenty One Day Trips from Addis Ababa*, available from the **Ethiopian Heritage Trust** (☎ 15 88 02) in the centre, or *Ethiopia: One to Two Days from Addis Ababa* published by the ETC, are recommended.

ENTOTO MOUNTAINS
የእንጦጦ ተራሮች
The Entoto road leads north past the university and the US embassy, to the top of the Entoto Mountains, the site of Menelik's former capital. There's a terrific but windy panoramic view of Addis Ababa below. Near

the summit is the octagonal **Entoto Maryam Church** *(open Sun only)*, which contains mural paintings.

Next to the church is a **museum** *(admission Birr10; open Tues-Sun)*, which contains a large collection of religious garb mostly dating from Emperor Menelik's time.

About 1km west of Entoto Maryam is **Kiddus Raguel Church** *(admission Birr20)*. Nearby is the old rock-hewn **Kiddus Raguel Church** *(admission Birr20)*. In theory, these sites are open every day. You'll certainly be approached by so-called guides, whose competencies are dubious. They charge about Birr30.

A 'natural park' measuring 13 sq km is being established by the Ethiopian Heritage Trust above the Kidane Mehret Church. It's currently a pleasant place to ramble and a good spot for birdwatchers.

To get to Entoto, take a taxi or minibus to its terminus from Arat Kilo, from where another minibus will take you to Entoto Maryam Church.

WUSHA MIKAEL CHURCH
ኡሻ ሚካኤል ቤተ ክርስቲያን
Wusha Mikael Church *(admission Birr30)* is a 30-minute walk up a hill behind the Kiddus Mikael's church (both east of the British embassy). Though local priests date it back to the 3rd century AD, it most probably dates back to the 12th century. If you're not planning to visit the churches at Lalibela or Tigray in the north, it's definitely worth a peek as an example of this extraordinary building tradition. Unfortunately, for four months of the year (July to October), the church is likely to be flooded with rainwater.

BIHERE TSIGE RECREATION CENTRE
የእንጦጦ ተራሮች
The large and wooded Bihere Tsige Recreation Centre *(admission Birr1; open 8.30am-5.30pm daily)* is the closest thing Addis Ababa has to a park. Covering a large area of over 400 sq km, the gardens contain more than 6000 varieties of flowers, shrubs and trees. It's a very pleasant place for a nice walk in the late afternoon, or for a lovely picnic. The park lies 5km southwest of the centre off the Debre Zeyit road. A minibus from Meskel Square will drop you off around a 20-minute walk from the edge of the park.

Northern Ethiopia

I weary of writing more about these buildings, because it seems to me that I shall not be believed if I write more ... but swear I by God in Whose power I am, that all that is written is the truth, and there is much more than what I have written, and I have left it that they may not tax me with its being falsehood.

Francisco Alvares
(early-16th-century Portuguese writer)
From *Ho Preste Joam das Indias: Verdadera informacam das terras do Preste Joam*
(Lisbon 1540; Lisbon 1889)

Since the 16th century, European travellers have returned from northern Ethiopia with incredible stories of ancient civilisations, extravagant courts and marvellous buildings. Today's travellers are no less amazed at the sites they find here.

Known as the historical route, a trip north of Addis Ababa takes in all of Ethiopia's most famous monuments, including the ancient stelae of Aksum, the medieval rock-hewn churches of Tigray and Lalibela, and the 16th-century castles of Gonder.

The region is also exceptional for its landscape. Once the centre of tremendous volcanic activity, the landscape is riven by great canyons and chasms and gorges. At the highest point sits Ras Dashen (4543m), the fourth-highest mountain in Africa, forming part of the very beautiful Simien Mountains. At the lowest point lies the Danakil Depression, 100m below sea level, and one of the lowest, hottest and most inhospitable places on Earth.

In between these elevations, and in complete contrast again, are the famous Blue Nile Falls and Blue Nile Gorge. Lake Tana, Ethiopia's largest lake, is home to a group of remote island monasteries, sanctuaries for centuries of Ethiopian ecclesiastical tradition; the Ark of the Covenant itself was supposed to have resided here for a time. Nearby is the source of the Blue Nile, the location of which puzzled and preoccupied humans for millennia.

Warning

Note that all bus journey duration times in this chapter are indications only. Times vary greatly according to individual vehicle, weather and road conditions.

Highlights

- Roam the rock-hewn churches of Lalibela, rated among the Christian world's greatest historical sites

- Take a tour of the tombs, ruined palaces and stelae of Aksum, the 'last of the great civilisations of Antiquity to be revealed to modern knowledge'

- Stroll among the spectacular scenery of the Simien Mountains and spot the gelada baboon

- Take a step back into Ethiopia's Renaissance and wander the castles and palaces of the legendary court of Gonder

- Marvel at the Blue Nile Falls, or take a boatride to the remote island monasteries of Lake Tana

- Combine climbing with culture and seek out the rock-hewn churches of Tigray, hidden like jewels in the arid Tigrayan mountains

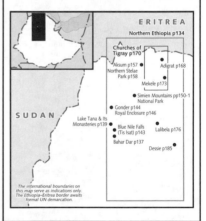

ERITREA

Northern Ethiopia p134

Churches of Tigray p170

Aksum p157
Northern Stelae Park p158

Adigrat p168

Mekele p173

Simien Mountains pp150-1 National Park

SUDAN

Gonder p144
Royal Enclosure p146

Lake Tana & Its Monasteries p139

Blue Nile Falls (Tis Isat) p143

Lalibela p176

Bahar Dar p137

Dessie p185

The international boundaries on this map serve as indications only. The Ethiopia–Eritrea border awaits formal UN demarcation.

Providing a tremendous insight into Ethiopian history, religion, geography and culture, a trip north of the capital is an absolute must for every traveller to Ethiopia. Well served by both the national airline and the bus companies, the area has the added advantage of ease of access. Most travellers work northwards from Addis Ababa, then northwest to Bahar Dar, Gonder and Aksum, before turning eastwards and beginning the loop southwards. A brief deviation

ETHIOPIA

west to Lalibela completes the historical route. A trip to the Simien Mountains makes a terrific break to the culture-bashing in between.

To get the most out of the sites, it's well worth having another quick flick through the History section of the Facts about Ethiopia chapter. The historical route covers a distance of around 2700km – you should have plenty of time to do so!

ADDIS ABABA TO DEBRE MARKOS

Debre Markos, a day's drive from Addis Ababa, serves simply as a convenient staging point on the way north. There are, however, a few places en route that might be worth a detour if you have the time.

On the way north, look out for the roadside vendors selling various regional specialities

The Deadly Dula

The *dula* is the chosen travelling companion of almost every Amhara man. A kind of hardwood staff, measuring about 1m long, it serves a variety of purposes: to carry loads to and from market, to brace the shoulders on long treks, to lean on during never-ending church services, and to defend oneself in times of need.

In the past, every Amhara was skilled in its use. The *gabi* (toga) was spun around the left arm to make a quick shield, and the right arm brought the stick crashing down on the adversary's cranium – sometimes with devastating consequences. Today its most common use is for fending off unfriendly dogs.

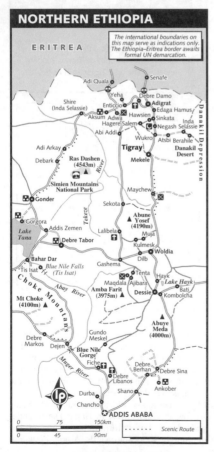

NORTHERN ETHIOPIA

The international boundaries on this map serve as indications only. The Ethiopia–Eritrea border awaits formal UN demarcation.

ERITREA

Adi Quala
Senafe
Yeha
Shire (Inda Selassie)
Enticcio
Debre Damo
Adigrat
Edaga Hamus
Aksum
Adwa
Hawsien
Sinkata
Inda
Hagere Salem
Negash Selassie
Abi Addi
Wukro
Atsbi Berahile
Adi Arkay
Tigray
Danakil Desert
Debark
Ras Dashen (4543m)
Mekele
Simien Mountains National Park
Gonder
Maychew
Gorgora
Sekota
Abune Yosef (4190m)
Lake Tana
Addis Zemen
Lalibela
Muja
Debre Tabor
Kulmesk
Bahar Dar
Gashema
Dilb
Woldia
Blue Nile Falls (Tis Isat)
Tis Isat
Tenta
Hayk
Lake Hayk
Maqdala
Ajibara
Bati
Amba Farit (3975m)
Dessie
Kombolcha
Mt Choke (4100m)
Abuye Meda (4000m)
Gundo Meskel
Debre Markos
Dejen
Blue Nile Gorge
Fiche
Debre Berhan
Debre Sina
Debre Libanos
Ankober
Durba
Shano
Chancho
ADDIS ABABA

Danakil Depression
Tekeze River
Abay River
Choke Mountains
Muger River

0   75   150km
0   45   90mi

· · · · · · · Scenic Route

such as well-made and very cheap basketware, and the *araki* (local liquor) sold in White Horse whisky bottles.

Keep an eye out also for the shepherds or goatherds in their delightful reed 'raincoats', the Amhara women in their pleated highland skirts, and the men carrying their indispensable *dula* (see the boxed text 'The Deadly Dula').

Muger River Gorge
የሙ-ገር ወንዝ ሸለቆ

The Muger River Gorge, accessible from the village of Durba, 17km from Chancho, is a good spot for a bit of rambling and wildlife-watching. The endemic gelada baboon (see the boxed text 'Monkey Trouble' later in this chapter) is often seen here, as are a good variety of birds.

From Chancho (42km north of Addis Ababa), one or two Ford share-taxis run to Durba every morning, five or six on market day on Saturday (Birr5, 45 to 60 minutes). To continue on to Debre Markos (Birr27.50, nine hours) or back to Addis Ababa (Birr5, one hour), buses stop en route between the two towns. Minibuses also run to Addis Ababa.

Debre Libanos & Fiche
ደብረ ሊባኖስና ፍንጨው

Lying 110km north of Addis Ababa, 4.2km off the main Addis Ababa–Debre Markos road, is one of Ethiopia's most holy sites. The monastery of **Debre Libanos** (admission Birr20, video cameras Birr50) was founded in the 13th century by a priest credited not only with the spread of Christianity throughout the highlands, but also with the restoration of the

Solomonic line of kings. The priest was Tekla Haimanot, today one of Ethiopia's most revered saints (see the boxed text 'Know Your Ethiopian Saints' later in this chapter).

Although no trace of the ancient monastery remains – it was a casualty of the Muslim–Christian wars – the site is impressively set beneath a cliff on the edge of a gorge and is a peaceful place to wander.

Debre Libanos has great significance for Ethiopians. Since the saint's time, it has served as the principal monastery of the old Shoa region, and it remains one of the largest and most important in the country. Five religious schools are found in the premises; watch for the little novices in white *gabis*.

Today many Ethiopians continue to make pilgrimages to the monastery and some still seek the curative holy waters – said to be particularly good for evil spirits and stomach disorders! Badly crippled children wait in hope of cures – and alms. On the roadside, vendors sell holy trinkets to pilgrims.

The present **church**, the latest in a succession of structures, was built in 1961 by Haile Selassie. A priest apparently prophesied that the construction of a new church would ensure a long reign. The old church was replaced with one in the emperor's peculiar style: monumental, hybrid and pretty hideous.

The church interior doesn't contain a great deal of interest, beyond what is believed to be the tomb of the saint. The stained-glass windows and mural paintings are not in fact by Afewerk Tekle, as church literature likes to make out.

Five minutes up the hill from the monastery is Tekla Haimanot's **cave**, where the saint is said to have done all his praying. It's also the source of the monastery's holy water.

If you continue up the hill from the cave, there's a marvellous **view** of the monastery in its dramatic setting. The cross-shaped tomb next to the car park is dedicated to those executed by the Fascists (see the boxed text 'Death at Debre Libanos' following).

Near the turn-off to the monastery is the so-called **16th-century Portuguese Bridge**, in fact built at the end of the 19th century by the Emperor Menelik's uncle, Ras Darge. However, like all of Debre Libanos, the scenery and atmosphere make up for the lack of tangible historical remains. Look out for the gelada baboons, which are often seen here, as are the huge and soaring lammergeyer birds.

Tickets are bought from the little office inside the (walled) church compound on the

Death at Debre Libanos

During the Italian occupation, Debre Libanos was the scene of some of the worst excesses of Fascist brutality. Following the attempt on the life of the infamous viceroy Graziani, the monastery, long suspected as a hotbed of rebel activity, was singled out for reprisal.

On 20 May 1937, 267 monks – 'all without distinction' – were executed; a week later, Graziani ordered the execution of all of the 129 young deacons as well. Satisfied at last, he wrote to Mussolini, 'The monastery is closed – definitively'.

right as you enter, and include a guided tour. Ask for the deacon, Belete Negash – himself cured from stomach ailments!

From Addis Ababa to Debre Libanos two buses run daily (Birr10, 2½ to three hours). If you miss them, you can take a bus to the nearby 'junction town' (as opposed to the main town) of Fiche (Birr10, three hours, five buses per day). From there you can take a minibus to the monastery, 16.5km to the north (Birr3, around 30 minutes, three or four minibuses daily).

If you get stuck in Fiche, the **Alem Hotel** *(rooms with shower Birr30-35)*, on the main Addis Ababa–Debre Markos road, is the best bet. From Fiche, you can usually find a seat on one of the buses plying the Addis Ababa–Debre Markos route.

Blue Nile Gorge
አባይ ሽለቆ

North of Fiche, around 100km from Addis Ababa, begins one of the most dramatic stretches of road in Ethiopia. Dropping more than 1000m, the road gradually winds down to the bottom of the Blue Nile Gorge.

For centuries the Blue Nile River separated the old provinces of Shoa and Gojam, running south of Lake Tana all the way to Sudan. The present road and bridge were built by the Italians, who demonstrated their usual flair for civil engineering with some beautiful construction. Keep an eye out for the lammergeyer birds soaring in the thermals above.

If you need a place to stay and eat, the **Alem Hotel** *(☎ 71 00 10; rooms from Birr30, with private shower Birr50)* in Dejen, 118km from Fiche at the bottom of the gorge, is the best bet, with simple but clean rooms. It lies just behind the Agip petrol station.

Debre Markos
ደብረ ማርቆስ

Halfway between Addis Ababa and Bahar Dar (around 310km north of Addis), Debre Markos makes a good staging post, and many buses from Addis Ababa stop overnight here. Although there is not much of interest in Debre Markos, it's well furnished with hotels and restaurants. If you're filling time, the 19th-century Church of Markos with its well-executed paintings is worth a peek, as is the market, which has a good selection of basketware.

Adequate hotels include the **Tourist Hotel** (☎ 71 24 58; rooms Birr20, with private shower Birr30-50). Despite its unpromising appearance, it's good value. It lies in the middle of town, off the main Addis Ababa–Bahar Dar road. Up a notch is the **Shebel Hotel** (☎ 71 14 10; rooms with shower Birr50-70), on the main street, near the entrance to the town if coming from Addis Ababa.

One bus leaves daily for Addis Ababa (Birr27.50, nine to 10 hours) and Bahar Dar (Birr27, 7½ to eight hours). The roadside north is often littered with *araki* hawkers. Their liquor is distilled from locally produced wheat or sorghum.

BAHAR DAR
ባህርዳር

☎ 08 • pop 96,140 • elevation 1880m

With its wide avenues lined with palms and flamboyant trees, and its scenic location on the southern shore of Lake Tana, Bahar Dar is one of Ethiopia's most attractive towns. It makes a pleasant base from which to explore the area's main sites: the Blue Nile Falls and the island monasteries of Lake Tana.

Though more geared up to tourism than most other towns in Ethiopia, Bahar Dar still retains an identity of its own. For centuries right up to the present day, Bahar Dar has been an important commercial centre, symbolised by its famous *tankwa*, the open-ended papyrus canoe that continues to be used on Lake Tana for trade today.

In the 16th and 17th centuries, various temporary Ethiopian capitals were established in the vicinity of Lake Tana. It was also here that the Jesuits attempted – with disastrous consequences – to impose Catholicism on the Ethiopian people. One Jesuit building, which was built by the well-known Spanish missionary, Pero Pais, can still be seen today in the compound of St George's church.

In the 1960s Haile Selassie toyed with the idea of moving his capital to Bahar Dar.

Information
A little **Tourist Information Center** (☎ 20 11 12) can be found in the centre of town, but frankly it's not worth a special visit. **Internet access** (Birr1-1.50 per minute) can be had at the Ghion and Papyrus Hotels.

Dangers & Annoyances Malaria is endemic in Bahar Dar, particularly during May and from mid-September to mid-October; make sure you take adequate preventive measures.

Unfortunately, tourist hustling has increased in recent years (partly due to high unemployment). Concerned, the local administration has plans to introduce official guides (with ID and perhaps uniform) by the end of 2003. The worst-affected area is around the bus station (where you should also watch your belongings). Hustlers will attempt to lead travellers to hotels, boats or even buses where you will be charged more in order to accommodate their commission.

Many travellers have also complained of hassle from children, particularly around the market and on the Zege Peninsula. The best deterrent is an official guide. Ask for one at your hotel.

Things to See
The bustling **markets** of the town are well worth exploring, particularly on Saturday, the main market day. Look out for the colourful, striped, woven cloth (scarves go for about Birr20) and the delightful *agelgil*, a kind of leather-bound lunch box, still used by local travellers for transporting their *injera* and *wat* (stew). The Bahar Dar version of the *agelgil* is furry, since it's made from goatskin. Good coffee can also be bought here.

The famous **outlet of the Blue Nile** lies some 5km outside the town, around 1km from the Blue Nile bridge. Along the river, keep an eye out for hippos and crocodiles.

The former **Palace of Haile Selassie** lies on a hill 5km northeast of town. It's approached via a long avenue of jacaranda trees. It's not currently open to visitors but there's a good, panoramic view from in front of the entrance gates (over the Blue Nile River, Lake Tana and the town). On the way up to the palace, you'll pass a new monument erected in memory of the martyrs of the Derg.

Around 2km west of town, beyond the Ghion Hotel, is **Weyto village**. The Weyto people are known for their production of *tankwa* boats; you can watch the skilled artists

ETHIOPIA

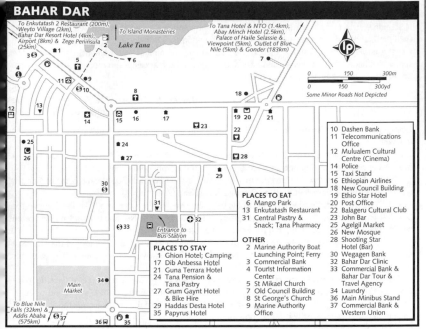

BAHAR DAR

To Enkutatash 2 Restaurant (200m),
Weyto Village (2km),
Bahar Dar Resort Hotel (4km),
Airport (8km) & Zege Peninsula
(25km)

To Island Monasteries

Lake Tana

To Tana Hotel & NTO (1.4km),
Abay Minch Hotel (2.5km),
Palace of Haile Selassie &
Viewpoint (5km), Outlet of Blue
Nile (5km) & Gonder (183km)

0   150   300m
0   150   300yd
Some Minor Roads Not Depicted

Main Tana

Entrance to
Bus Station

Main
Market

To Blue Nile
Falls (32km) &
Addis Ababa
(575km)

PLACES TO EAT
6 Mango Park
13 Enkutatash Restaurant
31 Central Pastry &
   Snack; Tana Pharmacy

OTHER
2 Marine Authority Boat
   Launching Point; Ferry
3 Commercial Bank
4 Tourist Information
   Center
5 St Mikael Church
7 Old Council Building
8 St George's Church
9 Marine Authority
   Office
10 Dashen Bank
11 Telecommunications
   Office
12 Mulualem Cultural
   Centre (Cinema)
14 Police
15 Taxi Stand
16 Ethiopian Airlines
18 New Council Building
19 Ethio Star Hotel
20 Post Office
22 Balageru Cultural Club
23 John Bar
25 Agelgil Market
26 New Mosque
28 Shooting Star
   Hotel (Bar)
30 Wegagen Bank
32 Bahar Dar Hotel
33 Commercial Bank &
   Bahar Dar Tour &
   Travel Agency
34 Laundry
36 Main Minibus Stand
37 Commercial Bank &
   Western Union

PLACES TO STAY
1 Ghion Hotel; Camping
17 Dib Anbessa Hotel
21 Guna Terrara Hotel
24 Tana Pension &
   Tana Pastry
27 Grum Gaynt Hotel
   & Bike Hire
29 Haddas Desta Hotel
35 Papyrus Hotel

at work. Though the *tankwas* look as flimsy as paper – in fact they are paper: papyrus – they can take huge loads, including firewood and even oxen.

Places to Stay

The Ghion Hotel offers **camping** *(Birr25 per tent)* in its lovely gardens. Tents and mattresses can also be hired (Birr40 per person, per night), and there is access to a hot shower. Camping is also permitted on the islands of Lake Tana (see later).

Tana Pension *(☎ 20 13 02; rooms with shared shower Birr20)* stands head and shoulders above the other budget options with simple but clean rooms.

Haddas Desta Hotel *(☎ 20 03 09; rooms without/with shower from Birr20/40)* is another good-value place.

Guna Terrara Hotel *(☎ 20 09 76; rooms with shared shower Birr30)* makes a third choice in the budget range.

Grum Gaynt Hotel *(☎ 20 08 32; doubles/ twins with cold shower and balcony Birr45/ 60)* is reasonably good value.

Abay Minch Hotel *(☎ 20 00 38; rooms Birr50)*, clean and peaceful, beyond the Tana Hotel, promises to reopen at the end of 2003.

Ghion Hotel *(☎ 20 07 40; e ghionbd@ telecom.net.et; single/doubles with shower Birr50/75, lakeside family bungalows with verandas Birr200)* offers good value in a beautiful lakeside setting. It's also well-managed and friendly. Sailboards for windsurfing can also be hired (Birr50 per two hours).

Papyrus Hotel *(☎ 20 51 00, fax 20 50 47; singles/doubles/twins with balcony and TV Birr100/150/200)* is new, large and comfortable and has a pool. It offers the best value in the mid-upper range.

Dib Anbessa Hotel *(☎ 20 14 36; e getbig@ telecom.net.et; singles/doubles with balcony Birr110/135.20)* is modern and comfortable and has a garden.

Tana Hotel *(☎ 20 05 54, fax 20 20 42; singles/doubles/suites US$37.50/50/75)* forms part of the state-owned Ghion Hotel chain (see Accommodation in the Facts for the Visitor chapter). It lies a couple of kilometres north of town on the Gonder road, and its rooms are attractive, but not special. The chief advantage is the location on the lake; come here for breakfast or a drink at dusk. The gardens are considered one of the best spots for bird-goggling.

Bahar Dar Resort Hotel, on the lake front around 4km from town, is still waiting to

ETHIOPIA

James Bruce: In Search of the Source

Half undressed as I was by the loss of my sash, and throwing my shoes off, I ran down the hill towards the little island of green sods, which was about two hundred yards distant.

...It is easier to guess than to describe the situation of my mind at that moment – standing in the spot which had baffled the genius, industry and enquiry of both ancients and moderns, for the course of near three thousand years.

James Bruce
Travels to Discover the Source of the Nile
(1790; Gregg, Godstone, 1971)

One of the first European explorers in Africa was a Scot, James Bruce, who had a passionate interest in unknown lands.

After serving as consul general in Algiers, he set off in 1768 in search of the source of the Nile – a puzzle that had preoccupied people since the time of the Egyptian Pharaohs.

After landing in Massawa, Eritrea, he made his way to the powerful and splendid court of Gonder, where he became a close friend of the Empress Mentewab.

In 1770 he reached the source of the Abay, the main river that empties into Lake Tana, above the Blue Nile Falls. There he declared that the mystery of the source of the Nile had been solved, dedicated his discovery to King George III, and returned home to national acclaim.

In fact, Bruce had traced only the source of the Blue Nile River, the main tributary of the Nile. Not only that, but he had been beaten to his 'discovery' – as he very well knew – over 150 years earlier by a Spanish Jesuit, Pero Pais.

Of greater interest was the account of his journey, *Travels to Discover the Source of the Nile*, published in 1790. It remains a very useful source of information on the history of Ethiopia and customs of the people. At the time, his contemporaries considered much of it as gross exaggeration, or even as pure fiction. Given his earlier claims, no wonder.

---

open. Rooms with fridge and TV should cost around US$50.

Places to Eat

Enkutatash Restaurant, very popular locally, offers good fresh fish for Birr5 to Birr12.

Enkutatash 2, spawned by the success of No 1, is a little more upmarket and also good.

Tana Hotel has a restaurant with a good reputation for *faranji* (Western) food, as does **Dib Anbessa Hotel**, though they're not the cheapest options (mains around Birr8 to Birr16).

Tana Pastry is a good place for a pastry, fruit juice or breakfast. If you're waiting for a bus, **Central Pastry & Snack**, opposite the station, is also good.

Mango Park boasts a tiered terrace overlooking the lake. It's a cool and pleasant place for a drink at dusk (and cheaper than the Tana Hotel). It's popular with local students, families and pelicans.

Entertainment

Bahar Dar's music scene is not quiet as it once was. Try the bars down from the Ethio Star Hotel such as **John Bar** and **Shooting Star Hotel**. The **Balageru Cultural Club** usually hosts live, traditional Amhara dancing.

Getting There & Away

Ethiopian Airlines (☎ 20 00 20) has two or three flights daily to Addis Ababa, and one or two to Gonder, Lalibela and Aksum.

Two buses leave daily for Addis Ababa (Birr57.70 via Debre Markos, Birr51.30 via Mota, 1½ days) and for Debre Tabor (Birr12.70, three hours). One bus leaves daily for Debre Markos (Birr30.20, nine hours) and another leaves for Gonder (Birr20, four to five hours). For Debark (and the Simien Mountains), first go to Gonder.

Getting Around

Taxis cost Birr5 to Birr10 for short hops and Birr20 for rental by the hour (negotiate hard), but aren't allowed outside the town. Minibuses are good for getting around town (see the Getting Around chapter). For the airport (8km), taxis ask Birr40 to Birr50 (one to four people) and contract minibuses cost Birr80 to Birr90.

Various tour companies, including the government-owned **NTO** (*National Tour*

ETHIOPIA

Organisation; ☎ *20 05 37),* based at the Tana Hotel, hire out cars and offer trips to the main attractions in and around Bahar Dar. The Ghion Hotel also offers tours. Compare prices as they vary hugely. For car hire, **Bahir Dar Tour & Travel Agency** *(*☎ *20 01 75)* offers competitive rates, but note that this must be prearranged (see Organised Tours in the Getting Around chapter).

Bicycles can be hired at the Ghion Hotel for Birr20 per day, or on the corner of the Grum Gaynt Hotel for Birr3 per hour.

AROUND BAHAR DAR
Lake Tana & its Monasteries

Covering over 3500 sq km, Lake Tana is Ethiopia's largest lake and has long been known to the outside world – the Egyptians called it Choloe Palus, the Greeks knew it as Pseboe. Today, the lake is most famous as the home of the monasteries established on some 20 of its 37 islands.

Many of the monasteries date from the late 16th or early 17th century, though most were founded much earlier and may even have been the site of pre-Christian shrines. Many have long provided safe sanctuaries for royal treasures and tombs, and are still tremendous havens of peace.

Information Boat excursions are worthwhile; the arrival by boat is certainly part of the charm of a visit to the remote and beautiful islands. Women can visit only certain monasteries, but fortunately these number among the most interesting.

To reduce the cost, it's a good idea to try and hook up with other travellers and form a small group. The manager of the Ghion Hotel (a popular travellers' choice) may be able to help.

To visit some of the more remote islands (via a few closer to home), you're looking at a full day's excursion. Bring lots of Birr1 and Birr10 notes for tips and admission fees; the priests never have change. A fee of between Birr50 and Birr100 is charged for video cameras.

Also allow enough time for the keeper priests to be located; sometimes you can wait up to 20 minutes. For information on Church Etiquette, see under Responsible Tourism in the Facts for the Visitor chapter.

If you're short of time, a 'monastery short list' might consist of Narga Selassie, Ura Kidane Meret, Kebran Gabriel, Tana Cherkos and Daga Estefanos. If you're keen on birds, you may want to head for Mitsel Fasiladas Island, a breeding ground for wetland birds. Other places known for birdlife include the area around Debre Maryam and the outlet of the Blue Nile; the eastern shore of Lake Tana; and the southwestern end of Narga Selassie.

To visit all the islands, you'll need two days.

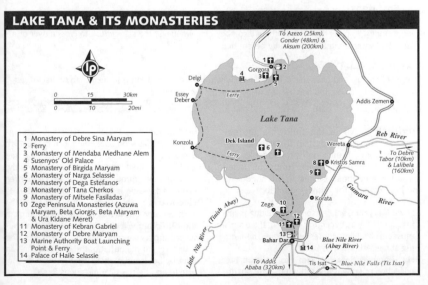

LAKE TANA & ITS MONASTERIES

To Azezo (25km),
Gonder (48km) &
Aksum (200km)

Delgi

Gorgora

Essey Deber

Ferry

Lake Tana

Addis Zemen

Reb River

Konzola

Dek Island

Ferry

Wereta

To Debre Tabor (10km) & Lalibela (160km)

Kristos Samra

0   15   30km
0   10   20mi

Kirstos Samra

Gumara River

Zege

Korata

1 Monastery of Debre Sina Maryam
2 Ferry
3 Monastery of Mendaba Medhane Alem
4 Susenyos' Old Palace
5 Monastery of Birgida Maryam
6 Monastery of Narga Selassie
7 Monastery of Dega Estefanos
8 Monastery of Tana Cherkos
9 Monastery of Mitsele Fasiladas
10 Zege Peninsula Monasteries (Azuwa Maryam, Beta Giorgis, Beta Maryam & Ura Kidane Meret)
11 Monastery of Kebran Gabriel
12 Monastery of Debre Maryam
13 Marine Authority Boat Launching Point & Ferry
14 Palace of Haile Selassie

Bahar Dar

Little Nile River (Tinish Abay)

Blue Nile River (Abay River)

To Addis Ababa (320km)

Tis Isat

Blue Nile Falls (Tis Isat)

ETHIOPIA

Know Your Ethiopian Saints

There's hardly a church in Ethiopia not adorned with colourful, vibrant and sometimes very beautiful wall paintings. At first sight, the subjects depicted look more like mythological characters than biblical ones; for the non-Orthodox onlooker, they can be difficult to interpret. In fact, the paintings usually follow a set pattern, depicting again and again the key personalities of Ethiopia's peculiar pantheon of saints. Here's a quick key:

St George

The patron saint of Ethiopia features in almost every church. He is depicted either as the king of saints, with St Bula – who at first refused to recognise his kingship – looking on petulantly in the background, or as the great dragon slayer on his horse. In Ethiopia, the archetypal damsel in distress has a name: she's known as Brutawit, the girl from Beirut.

St Tekla Haimanot

The saint prayed for seven years standing on just one leg, until the other finally withered and fell off! Throughout, a bird brought him just one seed a year for sustenance. For his devotion, God awarded him no fewer than three sets of wings. The saint is normally depicted in his bishop's attire, surrounded by bells; sometimes the detached leg is shown flapping off to heaven, or else brandished by an angel.

Abuna Aregawi

One day, while wandering at the foot of a cliff, Abuna Aregawi spotted a large plateau high above him. Deciding it was the ideal spot for a nice, quiet hermit's life, he prayed to God for assistance. Immediately, a large python stretched down from above and lifted him onto the plateau. The famous monastery of Debre Damo was founded then. The saint is usually depicted riding up the snake – like a kind of snakes and ladders game in reverse.

St Gebre Manfus Kiddus

One day, while preaching peace to the wild animals in the desert, this Ethiopian St Francis of Assisi came across a bird dying of thirst. Lifting it up, he allowed the bird to drink the water from his eye. The saint is usually depicted clad in furs and girded with a hempen rope. Leopards and lions lie at his feet, and the bird flaps near his head.

St Eostateos

St Eostateos (or St Thaddeus) is said to have arrived in Ethiopia borne up the Nile from Egypt on three large stones. Apparently water continued to obey him: whenever the saint chose to cross a river or a lake, the waters parted conveniently before him.

Abuna Samuel

Abuna Samuel lived near the Takezze River, where he preached and performed many miracles, accompanied by a devoted lion. He is usually depicted astride his lion.

Highlights All of the following journey times are for a one-way trip from Bahar Dar (though note that times will vary considerably with the power of the boat). Times calculated are for a speedboat. Check in advance with the boat captain for journey durations.

Azuwa Maryam Contains some interesting paintings (probably 19th century or later) and a small museum. It's five minutes' walk from the landing stage. Admission is Birr20.

Beta Giorgis & Beta Maryam Has an important collection of crowns in a little 'museum' (attrib-uted to Yohannes IV) and interesting paintings in monasteries – probably dating from the 19th century or later. It's on the Zege Peninsula, half an hour by boat and a short walk from the landing stage through lemon trees and coffee plants. Admission is Birr20 for both churches.

Debre Maryam The original church is from the 14th century, but it was rebuilt by Tewodros in the 19th century. It contains beautiful old manuscripts and a collection of church treasures. The church is near the outlet of the Blue Nile, half an hour by boat and a short walk through coffee, mango and fig trees. Admission is Birr20.

Know Your Ethiopian Saints

St Yared
Ethiopia's patron saint of music is sometimes shown standing before his king with an orchestra of monks along with their sistra, drums and prayer sticks. In the background, little birds in trees learn the magic of music.

St Mikael
The judge of souls and the leader of the celestial army, St Mikael evicted Lucifer from heaven. In most churches, the portals to the Holy of Holies are guarded by a glowering Mikael, accompanied by Gabriel and Raphael, fiercely brandishing their swords.

Belai the Cannibal
Belai the Cannibal is a favourite theme in religious art. Devouring anyone who approached him including his own family, Belai yet took pity one day on a leper begging for water in the Virgin's name. After Belai died – some 72 human meals later – Satan claimed his soul. St Mikael, the judge, balanced Belai's victims on one side, the water on the other. However, the Virgin cast her shadow on the side of the scales containing the water, and caused them to tip. Belai's soul was saved.

St Gabriel
God's messenger is usually represented cooling the flames of a fiery furnace or cauldron containing three youths condemned by Nebuchadnezzar: Meshach, Shadrach and Abednego.

St Raphael
Raphael apparently once rescued an Egyptian church from the tail of a thrashing whale beached on the land. He's usually depicted killing the hapless whale with his spear.

St Gebre Kristos
This Ethiopian prince sacrificed all his belongings to lead a life of chastity, and ended up a leprous beggar. He's usually depicted outside his palace, where only his dogs now recognise him.

Equestrian Saints
They are usually depicted on the north wall of the Holy of Holies and may include Fasiladas, Claudius, Mercurius, Menas, Theodorus and George.

Mary
Very popular and little known outside Ethiopia are the numerous and charming legends and miracles concerning Mary, as well as the childhood of Jesus and the flight to Egypt. A tree is often depicted hiding the holy family – and the donkey – from Herod's soldiers during the flight to Egypt; the soldiers are confused by the sound of the donkey braying. Sometimes a furious Mary is shown scolding Jesus, who's managed to break a clay water jug. He later redeems himself a bit by fixing it.

Dega Estefanos This is one of the most sacred monasteries and was rebuilt in the mid-19th century. It houses a 16th-century painting of the Madonna, and mummified remains in glass coffins of five former emperors of Ethiopia (13th to 17th centuries). Dega Estefanos is set on a hill nearly 100m above the lake, 30 to 45 minutes' walk one way. It lies beside Narga Selassie (see following). The monastery is open to men only. Admission prices are negotiable, and depend on the size of the group (eg, Birr100 for one person; Birr50 per person for two to five people).

Kebran Gabriel One of the most beautiful and atmospheric of the monasteries, Kebran Gabriel dates from the 17th century. It features a 12-columned portico and good paintings on the *maqdas* (inner sanctuary). Look out for the depiction of Iyasu before Christ. It's half an hour away by boat and a short walk from the landing stage. Open to men only. Admission is Birr20.

Mitsele Fasiladas Most of this monastery's treasures were stolen in the early 1990s but it's still worth visiting if you're in the vicinity. It has an attractive setting and the foundations of the old church remain. It's around two hours away by boat and a short walk from the landing stage. Admission is Birr20.

Narga Selassie Built in the mid-18th century in the style of the Gonder castles in a very beautiful location. Effigies of Mentewab and James Bruce are engraved on the exterior of the church, as are fine 18th-century paintings and crosses. Little visited, peaceful and atmospheric, the monastery is highly recommended. It's 2½ hours by boat and a two-minute walk from the landing stage. Admission is Birr20.

Tana Cherkos This monastery attached to the mainland is one of the most mysterious and one of the most important historically – the Ark of the Covenant is said to have been hidden here for 800 years. The present modest church dates from the 19th century. It's around 2½ hours away by boat plus a 45-minute walk uphill and is open to men only. Admission is as for Dega Estefanos.

Ura Kidane Meret This is the most famous of the Zege Peninsula monasteries and has a very beautiful painted *maqdas*. It is practically a compendium of Ethiopian religious iconography (see the boxed text 'Know Your Ethiopian Saints'), and holds an important collection of old crosses and crowns, said to date from the 16th to 18th centuries. It's on the Zege Peninsula, 30 to 40 minutes by boat plus 10 to 15 minutes' walk from the landing stage. Admission is Birr20. As the most-visited monastery, it also attracts the most souvenir sellers, hustlers and guides. It's a good idea to take a guide or the boatman to discourage them.

Getting There & Away At least six licensed boat operators now rent out boats (for up to 12 people). Prices are not fixed, and you'll need to negotiate hard; in the low season, you'll get good discounts. It normally takes between 15 and 30 minutes to organise a short trip; overnight to organise longer trips.

Boat 'agents' can be found hanging around the Ghion and Tana Hotels (see Places to Stay under Bahar Dar earlier). If not, ask at the hotel receptions. A boat (with captain, fuel and sometimes guide included, but not monastery admission fees) should cost from Birr100 to Birr200 for one to four people, Birr300 for five to 10 people (depending on the monasteries you want to visit). It costs around Birr200 to Birr300 for half a day (say to four monasteries on the Zege Peninsula), and Birr600 to Birr700 for a full day (say to Narga Selassie via the Zege Peninsula). If time is of the essence, you can usually find a

speedboat (Birr1200 for one to three people). Guides, if they're not included, charge Birr150 per day (for one to 10 people).

The **Marine Authority** (☎ 20 07 30, fax 20 07 18; open 8am-noon & 1.30pm-5.30pm Mon-Fri, 8am-noon Sat) charges Birr200 for a trip to two or three nearby monasteries in a small boat (up to five people), or rents out boats (with radio, life jackets, fuel and captain, but no guide) for Birr136 per hour.

Check that your boat has life jackets (it can become stormy in the afternoon) and spare fuel. Bring a raincoat or umbrella and something warm.

For the adventurous, *tankwas* can also be hired (Birr50 per person per day), though it will take you a good three hours to reach the Zege Peninsula! Basic fishing equipment can also be rented (Birr5 to Birr10 per day).

The Zege Peninsula can also be reached by road. It lies around 25km from Bahar Dar. To get there, you can hire a car or bicycle from Bahar Dar.

A ferry service connects Bahar Dar to Gorgora on the northern shore of the lake, via the Zege Peninsula (see Gorgora under Around Gonder later in this chapter). However, it operates just once a week.

Blue Nile Falls (Tis Isat)
ጢስ እሳት

Known locally by the more evocative names of Tis Isat (Smoking Water) or Tis Abay (Smoking Nile), the Blue Nile Falls is one of the most spectacular falls in Africa. When in full flood, it is as impressive for its sheer width (measuring over 400m) as for its depth (45m). Dropping over a sheer chasm, the thunderous noise can be heard long before arrival, and the spray that is thrown up can be felt up to a kilometre away.

James Bruce, the 18th-century Scottish traveller who was one of the first Europeans to describe the falls, called it 'a magnificent sight, that ages, added to the greatest length of human life, would not efface or eradicate from my memory'.

Unfortunately, the sight today is no longer so magnificent. Following the construction in recent years of a series of dams upstream near Bahar Dar, the volume of water flowing over the falls has decreased significantly. Though the hydroelectricity project is an important one, the aesthetic impact on the falls is unquestionable. Though occasionally – and erratically – the dams are temporarily 'opened', many visitors are disappointed.

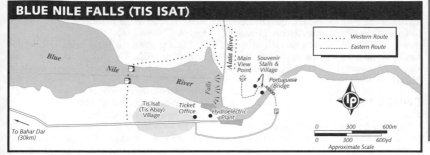

Sadly too, the perennial mini-rainforest that once thrived in the microclimate created by the falls, has also dwindled; birds, though still plentiful, are less abundant (but still keep an eye out for parrots, bee-eaters, lovebirds or turacos). Look out for vervet monkeys as well.

The falls lies 32km southeast of Bahar Dar, just beyond the village of Tis Isat. The **ticket office** *(adults/students Birr15/5, video cameras Birr100; open 6am-6pm daily)* is at the far end of the village.

You'll get plenty of offers of guides. Engaging a guide (around Birr10 per person depending on your group size and skills of negotiation) may not prove too illuminating, but at least it will deter the others.

From the car park (1.5km from the village), follow the rocky path along the so-called eastern route down into a gorge across the 17th-century Portuguese bridge, then climb up past the little settlement towards the falls. The walk takes 20 to 30 minutes. Though not difficult, the initial descent is a little steep; make sure you have decent walking shoes.

From the main viewpoint, you can continue along a path that leads over a tributary of the Nile to the base of the falls. The walk takes about 20 minutes. The path can be muddy, particularly during the rainy season, so take care. Bird life is abundant here.

From here you can complete the circuit (in around 20 to 30 minutes) by winding up along the path to the river above the falls and crossing its banks by motorboat (following the so-called western route). The **boat service** *(Birr20 return)* operates daily, in theory from 6.30am to 6pm. Trips in local *tankwas* are no longer allowed. If you're on the river early in the morning, look out for crocs.

Less energetic or mobile people may want to approach and return from the falls this way, crossing the Nile twice. The walk is gentler. The base of the falls is a great place

for a picnic. In places, the spray generated by the falls is so dense it's like walking through a car wash. Undertake the walk in the morning when it's cooler.

If you need accommodation in Tis Isat because you've missed the last bus, the dirt floor of the **Jaguar Hotel** *(rooms with bucket shower for Birr10)* is the best bet!

Camping (free) is permitted anywhere around the falls. Within the next couple of years, there are plans to install some bungalows (around Birr200) near the falls.

Getting There & Away From Bahar Dar, buses leave every hour (from 6am to 4pm) for Tis Isat village (Birr3.60, one hour), which is also known as Tis Abay.

From Tis Isat, one bus usually runs every two to three hours to Bahar Dar from the centre of town, the last between 3pm and 4pm. If you miss it, you may be able to hitch with one of the tour operators or hotel vehicles returning to Bahar Dar (particularly if you offer to contribute something), but don't count on it. On Fridays, fewer buses run.

A simpler but more expensive option is to take a tour with one of the Bahar Dar tour operators (half-day excursions cost around Birr200 per person).

Also, most mornings (around 8am), a 10-seat minibus is chartered by travellers from the Ghion Hotel (Birr100 to Birr300 for the whole bus, depending on numbers).

Debre Tabor
ደብረ ታቦር

About 100km by road northeast of Bahar Dar is the town of Debre Tabor. Though not so illustrious now, during the 18th and 19th centuries it was the site of an important Ethiopian capital, including that of the ill-fated Emperor Tewodros II (see History in the Facts about Ethiopia chapter).

Today, only the ruins of the old palace remain, along with the old churches of Debre Tabor and the 19th-century Heruy Giyorgis. However, if you're passing through on your way to Woldia, it's worth a leg-stretch. Buses run daily between Bahar Dar and Debre Tabor (Birr12.70, three hours).

GONDER
ጎንደር

☎ 08 • pop 112,249 • elevation 2210m

Gonder has been called Africa's Camelot, and with its series of castles and churches is one of the major attractions of the historical route.

Surrounded on all sides by fertile and well-watered land, and at the intersection of three major caravan routes, Gonder was the perfect place for a capital. To the southwest lay rich sources of gold, civet, ivory and slaves, to the northeast lay Massawa and access to the Red Sea, and to the northwest lay Sudan and Egypt.

The Emperor Fasiladas made Gonder his capital in 1636. The city became the country's first permanent capital since Lalibela, and flourished for the next 200 years. By the time of the emperor's death in 1667, Gonder's population exceeded 65,000 and its wealth and splendour had become a local legend.

The Gonderine period is one of the most colourful in Ethiopia's history, and drifting through the old palaces, banqueting halls and former gardens, it's not difficult to imagine the courtly pageantry, ceremony and intrigue that went on here.

It is still not certain who built the castles. Scholars currently believe that Portuguese and Indian craftsmen (possibly brought here

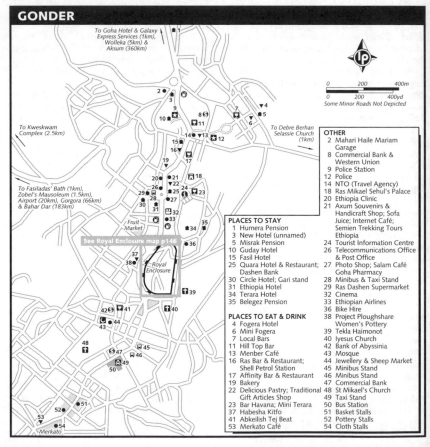

GONDER

To Goha Hotel & Galaxy
Express Services (1km),
Wolleka (5km) &
Aksum (360km)

To Kweskwam
Complex (2.5km)

To Debre Berhan
Selassie Church
(1km)

To Fasiladas' Bath (1km),
Zobel's Mausoleum (1.5km),
Airport (20km), Gorgora (66km)
& Bahar Dar (183km)

Fruit
Market

See Royal Enclosure map p146

Royal
Enclosure

Merkato

0   200   400m
0   200   400yd
Some Minor Roads Not Depicted

PLACES TO STAY
1 Humera Pension
3 New Hotel (unnamed)
5 Misrak Pension
10 Guday Hotel
15 Fasil Hotel
25 Quara Hotel & Restaurant;
   Dashen Bank
30 Circle Hotel; Gari stand
31 Ethiopia Hotel
34 Terara Hotel
35 Belegez Pension

PLACES TO EAT & DRINK
4 Fogera Hotel
6 Mini Fogera
7 Local Bars
11 Hill Top Bar
13 Menber Café
16 Ras Bar & Restaurant;
   Shell Petrol Station
17 Affinity Bar & Restaurant
19 Bakery
22 Delicious Pastry; Traditional
   Gift Articles Shop
23 Bar Havana; Mini Terara
37 Habesha Kitfo
41 Abkeilish Tej Beat
53 Merkato Café

OTHER
2 Mahari Haile Mariam
   Garage
8 Commercial Bank &
   Western Union
9 Police Station
12 Police
14 NTO (Travel Agency)
18 Ras Mikael Sehul's Palace
20 Ethiopia Clinic
21 Axum Souvenirs &
   Handicraft Shop; Sofa
   Juice; Internet Café;
   Semien Trekking Tours
   Ethiopia
24 Tourist Information Centre
26 Telecommunications Office
   & Post Office
27 Photo Shop; Salam Café
   Goha Pharmacy
28 Minibus & Taxi Stand
29 Ras Dashen Supermarket
32 Cinema
33 Ethiopian Airlines
36 Bike Hire
38 Project Ploughshare
   Women's Pottery
39 Tekla Haimonot
40 Iyesus Church
42 Bank of Abyssinia
43 Mosque
44 Jewellery & Sheep Market
45 Minibus Stand
46 Minibus Stand
47 Commercial Bank
48 St Mikael's Church
49 Taxi Stand
50 Bus Station
51 Basket Stalls
52 Pottery Stalls
54 Cloth Stalls

by the Portuguese) who remained after the expulsion of the Jesuits were probably responsible.

Though extensively looted in the 1880s by the Sudanese Dervishes and damaged by British bombs during the liberation campaign of 1941, most of Gonder remains amazingly well preserved.

Around town, look out also for the fascinating and outstanding examples of Italian Fascist Art Deco architecture, such as the cinema, the telecommunications building and the Quara and Ethiopia Hotels. If you wander some of the streets on the outskirts of town, you may come across some beautiful, old Italian villas.

For more information on the city's history see History in the Facts about Ethiopia chapter.

Information

A little **tourist information centre** run by the Ethiopian Tourism Commission (ETC) was closed at the time of writing, but is promising to reopen soon.

Particularly good times to visit Gonder are during the festivals of Leddet (Christmas) and Timkat (see under Public Holidays in the Facts for the Visitor chapter).

Guides (free at the Royal Enclosure) can give city tours for around Birr150 per day, and can be organised through the tourist information centre, or, if it is still closed, at the Royal Enclosure. Alternatively, the NTO has good guides for Birr150 per day. Be wary of the many unofficial guides. All sites charge Birr50 to Birr75 for a video camera.

Good souvenir shops (including the charitable Project Ploughshare Women's Pottery) are marked on the map. There's an **Internet café** *(Birr1 per minute)* next door to Sofa Juice as well as in the Quara Hotel. The **merkato** in the south of town is also worth a wander. Traditional cloth, pottery and baskets can be bought here.

Gonder and its vicinity are a good spot for birds. Species such as the African paradise flycatcher and mousebirds can be spotted here.

A few travellers have complained of hassle from children soliciting money with improbable 'sob stories'. A good local initiative is the Peace of Mind project (which helps the genuinely hungry). Peace of Mind food tokens (Birr5 for ten) can be bought at the Habesha Kitfo restaurant.

Water supply problems sometimes affect Gonder.

The World Bank plans to fund a kind of interpretive centre in the Royal Enclosure. Work should be completed (in theory) by 2008, and will include a new historical/ethnographical museum (due to open in 2005 or 2006), perhaps in Fasiladas' Palace.

Royal Enclosure

Gonder's Royal Enclosure *(admission per day Birr50, video camera Birr75; open 8.30am-12.30pm & 1.30pm-5.30pm daily)* covers an area of over 75,000 sq metres. The admission price includes entry to Fasiladas' Bath, 2km from the city centre. Guided tours (free, but tips will be expected) are available and last around 1½ hours. Ato Addisu, in particular, is recommended.

The enclosure is surrounded by high stone walls and is connected by a series of tunnels and raised walkways. The recently restored **Fasiladas' Palace** is the oldest and perhaps most impressive of the castles. It stands two storeys high and has a crenellated parapet and four small, domed towers. Made of roughly hewn brown basalt stones, it is reputedly the work of an Indian architect, and shows an unusual synthesis of Indian, Portuguese and Moorish as well as Aksumite influences. From the rectangular tower in the southwest corner, there's a terrific view over the enclosure all the way to Lake Tana.

The ground floor of the castle was used as a dining hall and formal reception area. On the first floor, Fasiladas' prayer room has four windows in four directions, each with a view of one of the city's many churches. On the roof, religious ceremonies were held, and it was from here that the emperor addressed his people. The 2nd-floor rooms include Fasiladas' bedroom.

Behind the castle are various ruined buildings, including what is thought to be the remains of a **bathing pool**. Nearby is the two-storeyed quadrangular **library** of Fasiladas' son, Yohannes I (r. 1667–82), and a **chancellery**, topped by a tower, once an impressive palace decorated with ivory.

Next door to the palace is the two-storeyed saddle-shaped palace of Iyasu I. The son of Yohannes I, Iyasu (r. 1682–1706) is considered the greatest ruler of the Gonderine period. **Iyasu's Palace** is unusual for its vaulted ceiling. In former times, the palace was sumptuously decorated. Gilded Venetian mirrors and chairs made up the furnishings; gold leaf, ivory and beautiful paintings adorned the walls. Visiting travellers described the palace

ETHIOPIA

ROYAL ENCLOSURE

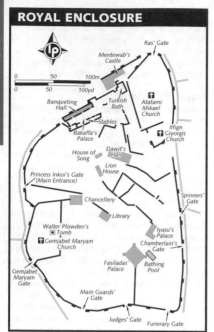

Ras' Gate
Mentewab's Castle
Banqueting Hall
Turkish Bath
Atatami Mikael Church
Stables
Ilfign Giyorgis Church
Bakaffa's Palace
Dawit's Hall
House of Song
Lion House
Princess Inkoi's Gate (Main Entrance)
Chancellery
Spinners' Gate
Library
Walter Plowden's Tomb
Gemjabet Maryam Church
Iyasu's Palace
Chamberlain's Gate
Fasiladas' Palace
Bathing Pool
Gemjabet Maryam Gate
Main Guards' Gate
Judges' Gate
Funerary Gate

as 'more beautiful than Solomon's house'. Sadly, the 1704 earthquake as well as British bombing in the 1940s have done away with the interior.

Also in the compound are the remains of the Emperor **Dawit's Hall** and **House of Song**, in which many religious and secular ceremonies and lavish entertainments took place. Dawit (r. 1716–21) also built the **Lion House**, where, until recently, Abyssinian lions were kept. Other buildings in the compound included a House of Assembly, a House of Mourning and two public squares used for proclamations and public executions.

When Dawit came to a sticky end (he was poisoned in 1721), the Emperor Bakaffa (r. 1721–30) took up the reins of power and built the huge **banqueting hall**, the scene of vast feasts and lavish entertainments (in the future, this may undergo restoration by the World Bank). He also built the nearby **stables**.

Next door was a *wesheba* (Turkish bath), which operated in the same way as a Roman bath, and which apparently worked wonders for those suffering from syphilis!

Bakaffa's consort was responsible for the last castle, known as **Mentewab's Castle**, a two-storeyed structure that is now used as a

public library. The Gonder cross is used as a decorative motif.

Also in the enclosure is **Walter Plowden's Tomb**. Plowden served for a time as British consul and became a close friend of the Emperor Tewodros before he was murdered journeying to the coast.

Fasiladas' Bath
ፋሲል መዋኛ

Around 2km northwest of the city centre lies Fasiladas' Bath *(admission included in Royal Enclosure ticket; open 8.30am-12.30pm & 1.30pm-5.30pm daily)*, which is, in fact, attributed to both Fasiladas and Iyasu I. A large, rectangular sunken pool is overlooked by a small but charming two-storeyed tower, surrounded by a stone wall. It's a peaceful, shady and beautiful spot, and is well worth a visit. A five-year project to fully restore the complex (financed by the Norwegian government at a cost of 6.4 million birr) should commence in 2003.

Although the complex is popularly known as a bathing palace, most probably it was constructed for important religious celebrations, the likes of which still go on today. Once a year, Fasiladas' Bath is filled with water for the important *Timkat* ceremony. After being blessed by a priest, the pool becomes a riot of spraying water, shouts and laughter as the crowd jumps in. The ceremony replicates Christ's baptism in the Jordan River, and is seen as an important renewal of faith.

Just beyond the wall of the compound is a small pavilion known as **Zobel's Mausoleum**, after a horse which, Nero-style, was honoured by Fasiladas or Iyasu.

If you don't want to walk to the bath, you can hop on one of the town minibuses (85c) that leave from near the Ras Dashen Supermarket in the centre. Admission to the compound is included in the Royal Enclosure ticket; note that tickets can't be bought at the bath.

Kweskwam Complex
ቄስቋም ደብር

Lying in the hills about 3.5km northwest of the town centre is the royal compound known as Kweskwam *(admission Birr15; open 8.30am-12.30pm & 1.30pm-5.30pm daily)*, which was built by the Empress Mentewab, redoubtable wife of the Emperor Bakaffa.

Though less well preserved than the Royal Enclosure, it too is made up of a series of buildings including a long, two-storeyed, castellated palace used for state receptions and also for housing the royal garrison. Like the empress' other palace, its exterior is decorated with red volcanic tuff. Look out for the figures of crosses and Ethiopian characters and animals, such as St Samuel riding his lion, all said to have belonged to a bishop of the time.

The nearby smaller building is said to have been the empress' private residence. To the west of the palace there was once a fine church which was rebuilt after damage by British bombs. A tiny crypt contains the mummified bodies of the empress, her son and her grandson, the Emperors Iyasu II and Iyo'as. There's also a good view of the town from here.

Ras Mikael Sehul's Palace
ራስ ሚካኤል ሳህል ቤተ መንግስት

Located north of the Royal Enclosure, this palace is like a small version of Fasiladas' palace, but has a slightly foreboding air. Perhaps it's because it was the residence of Ras Mikael, the dictator who usurped power at the end of the 18th century, as the monarchy became increasingly impotent and ineffectual. Later, the building was used – more chillingly – as a prison during the Derg, and is said to have been the site of untold brutality and torture. It's currently closed to visitors.

Debre Berhan Selassie Church
ደብረ ብርሃን ስላሴ ቤተ ክርስቲያን

Lying around 2km to the northeast of the Royal Enclosure is probably the country's most famous church and one of the highlights of Gonder – and Ethiopia. Debre Berhan Selassie (admission Birr15; open 5am-6pm daily), meaning 'Trinity at the Mount of Light', is familiar to many long before they arrive from the endlessly reproduced photographs of its ceiling. The winged heads of 80 Ethiopian cherubs entirely cover the ceiling; all have slightly different expressions.

No less impressive than the ceiling are the paintings on the walls attributed to the same artist, Haile Meskel. Full of all the colour, life, wit and humanity of Ethiopian art at its best, they provide practically a compendium of Ethiopian saints, martyrs and lore.

Look out for the 'portrait' of Emperor Iyasu I, the church's founder; the depiction of the Prophet Mohammed on a camel being led by a devil; and the almost Bosch-like depiction of Hell.

The building itself is rectangular in design and dates from the reign of Yohannes I.

According to local tradition, the church was saved from the sacking of the Dervishes by a timely swarm of bees.

Some have claimed that the emperor planned to bring the Ark of the Covenant here from its reputed resting place at Aksum, and that the church was in effect especially designed to house such a prestigious relic.

Flash photography inside the church is not permitted. If you can visit the church on a feast day, when it comes alive with the ancient tradition and ceremonies of the Orthodox church, do. Priests offer tours but a small contribution for the church should be left afterwards.

Places to Stay

Camping (Birr20 per person) is possible at the Terara Hotel. Tents (Birr62/100 for one/two people) can be hired from the Goha Hotel, north of town.

Ethiopia Hotel (☎ 11 02 03; doubles/twins with shared shower Birr15/25) is basic, but about the best for those on their last cent.

Fasil Hotel (☎ 11 02 21; basic doubles/twins with sink and shared hot shower Birr30/40) is a better choice.

Guday Hotel (☎ 11 09 59; singles/doubles with shower Birr40/50) is also basic but is cleaner. It lies off the main road beyond the police station.

Belegez Pension (☎ 11 43 56; rooms with hot shower Birr60.50) is a new, good-value place with small, but clean rooms set around a central courtyard.

Quara Hotel (☎ 11 00 40; singles/doubles Birr62.50/75, with hot shower Birr75/87.50) is an old colonial-built institution with adequate rooms, right on the central square.

Misrak Pension (☎ 11 00 69; rooms without/with private cold shower Birr60/80), though peaceful, is no longer the bargain it was.

Humera Pension (☎ 11 07 87; doubles without/with shower Birr50/100) is a decent, new place, though a bit overpriced. Discounts are sometimes possible.

Terara Hotel (☎ 11 01 53; singles/doubles Birr54/72, doubles with shower Birr108) dates from the days of the Italians and, though a bit faded, is clean and peaceful and set in pleasant grounds.

Circle Hotel (☎ 11 19 91; singles/doubles with shower and TV Birr80/100) is a new place offering not bad value in this category.

Fogera Hotel (☎ 11 04 05; tukuls for one/two people Birr160.70/214.25) has rather overpriced rooms, but the tukuls (conical thatched huts), set in gardens, are quite attractive

Goha Hotel (☎ 11 06 34, fax 11 19 20; camping for 1/2 people Birr50/72; singles/doubles/suites US$37.50/50/75), government-run, is top of the range. Like its 'brother' the Tana Hotel in Bahar Dar, its greatest asset is its location. Lying 2km north of Gonder, it's perched on a high natural balcony overlooking the town.

If there's one hotel worth a splurge in Ethiopia, this might be it, particularly after a hard trek in the Simien Mountains. If you can't afford a room, a sunset drink (beer costs Birr5.50) or dawn stroll on the lovely terrace is almost as good. The restaurant and its service can let it down; you may prefer to eat in the town.

At the time of writing a large, new hotel was being built close to the roundabout near the Total petrol station. Rooms with bathrooms and satellite TV should cost from Birr100.

Places to Eat & Drink

Mini Fogera (also known as Zewdetu Yilma) is a local favourite and serves both Ethiopian and *faranji* food.

Fogera Hotel has a good reputation for *faranji* food, as does the **Circle Hotel**.

Ras Bar & Restaurant is the new local favourite and is good value (Birr5 to Birr12). Head for the bamboo-constructed tent at the back. It's next door to the Shell petrol station (the restaurant is signposted in Amharic only).

Habesha Kitfo, lovingly decked out in the traditional style, serves good food in a great setting. *Faranji* food can be ordered in advance.

Decent pastry shops include **Delicious Pastry** (with a good selection of pastries) and **Menber Café**. **Affinity Bar & Restaurant** has outdoor seating; **Sofa Juice** has good juices.

Salam Café on the main roundabout (signposted in Amharic only) is good for a local breakfast.

Ras Dashen Supermarket (open 8am-9pm daily) is good for stocking up for treks in the Simien Mountains.

Mini Terara is one of several small, loud and lugubrious local bars, but it's open until 1am or 2am.

Bar Havana, next door, has live *azmari* (itinerant minstrel) performances (see the boxed text 'Mincing Minstrels' in the Addis Ababa chapter) nightly.

Hill Top Bar (open 6pm-1am daily) is American-inspired but insuppressibly Ethiopian. Try, if you dare, a *gin fir fir* (gin mixed with beer), or, for women, wine diluted with Coca-Cola!

Abkeilish Tej Beat is a well-known *tej beat* (a kind of local wine bar) opposite the Bank of Abyssinia. You'll probably need a local to help you find it. Other local bars are marked on the map.

Getting There & Away

Ethiopian Airlines (☎ 11 01 29) flies twice daily to Addis Ababa and once daily to Lalibela, Aksum and (sometimes twice daily) Bahar Dar.

One bus leaves daily for Addis Ababa (Birr78, 1½ days via Debre Markos), Debre Tabor (Birr20, five to six hours). Two buses depart for Bahar Dar (Birr 20, four hours), Debark (Birr12.35, four hours) and Woldia (Birr51, two days). For Aksum, go first to Shire (Birr37, 12 hours). For Gorgora (Birr7.80, 3½ hours), two buses leave daily. For longer journeys, buy your ticket one day in advance. If you're with a vehicle, fill up on fuel the night before; occasionally there are shortages.

For Sudan, one bus leaves daily to Shihedi (Birr48, eight to 10 hours). Buy the ticket early in the morning (around 7am) of the previous day, as the route is popular. From there, pick-up trucks (Birr7) cover the last 40km or so to Metema.

From Metema, you can walk across the border into the Sudanese town of Gallabat. From Gallabat, you can catch a truck to the nearest large town of Gedaref (Dinar 1500, eight to 10 hours). Stay overnight at Shihedi (it has better facilities than Metema).

If you're coming from Sudan, stay overnight in Gedaref (better than Gallabat) then catch a dawn truck straight though to Shihedi via Gallabat. The bus from Shihedi to Gonder departs at around 7am. See also Sudan in the Getting There & Away chapter.

Getting Around

The airport is 21km from the town. A taxi costs around Birr40 to the airport, and Birr50 from it (add Birr10 for the Goha Hotel). Taxis for half a day cost around Birr200 and a whole day costs around Birr300, including airport pick-up, but negotiate hard. Minibuses charge between Birr0.50 and Birr1.75 for hops around town; *garis* (horse-drawn carts) cost around Birr1 to Birr5.

The **NTO** (☎ 11 03 79) and **Galaxy Express Services** (☎ 11 15 46) rent out vehicles, though this should be prearranged.

The newly opened **Semien Trekking Tours Ethiopia** *(fax 11 07 05;* e *nega_eth@ freemail.et)* offers an airport transfer and city tour (including admission fees and guides) for Birr550/650 for one/two people, but needs 24 hours' notice. Day trips to Gorgora (Birr600, one or two people) are also offered and so are treks to the Simien Mountains (see that section later in this chapter). The NTO offers similar tours, but prices are high.

Bicycles can be hired from near the Terara Hotel and cost Birr5 per hour, or Birr4 per hour for a half-day or whole-day hire.

AROUND GONDER
Gorgora
ጎርጎራ

The little town of Gorgora, 67km south of Gonder on the northern shore of Lake Tana, makes a pleasant excursion from Gonder for those with time, particularly for travellers interested in birds.

The most interesting relic of Gorgora's former days as capital is the attractive, round **Church of Debre Sina** *(admission Birr15)*, built in 1608 by the Emperor Susenyos' son. It's decorated with fine frescoes. Look out for the so-called 'Egyptian St Mary'. A self-appointed guide, Tesfaye Mekonnen, will take you around or help you locate birds.

Nearby, the ruins of **Susenyos' old palace** can be visited by boat (30 minutes from Gorgora) or car (30 to 40 minutes), as can various churches, including **Birgida Maryam** and the monastery of **Mendaba Medhane Alem** (both closed to women), around 20 minutes from Gorgora (see the Lake Tana & its Monasteries map).

A speedboat (Birr136 per hour for one to five people, including captain and fuel) can be hired from the nearby **Lake Tana Transport Enterprise office** *(*☎ *20 00 06; open 8am-noon & 2pm-5.30pm Mon-Fri, 8am-noon Sat)*.

Gorgora Port Hotel *(*☎ *07 via operator; camping per tent Birr28; doubles/twins/suite with shower Birr105/157/210)* is a bit run-down and 1970s, but it's a good choice if you're looking for peace and quiet in pleasant, lakeside gardens. It's an excellent place for bird-watching.

A cheaper option is the **Berhane Hotel** *(rooms with shared shower Birr20-30)*, just outside the entrance gate to the Gorgora Port Hotel. Its rooms are clean but basic.

Two buses daily ply the Gonder–Gorgora route (Birr7.80, 3½ hours). A weekly ferry service runs from Bahar Dar to Gorgora

(Birr122.50 first class, 1½ days) via the Zege village on the peninsula (overnighting at Konzola).

The ferry sails from Bahar Dar every Sunday between 6am and 7am (arriving in Bahar Dar at 3pm the following day). From Gorgora to Bahar Dar, the ferry leaves between 6am and 7am on Thursday (overnighting in Konzola).

Buy tickets the night before and bring food and water, as there's no restaurant or café on board (though there are stops at restaurants en route).

Getahun Abay Hotel *(singles/doubles Birr15-20)* is probably the best bet in Konzola.

Wolleka (Falasha Village)
ወለቃ

Around 6km north of Gonder is the little village of Wolleka, once the home of a thriving population of Falashas or Ethiopian Jews. Before Christianity arrived, Judaism was for centuries the dominant religion of most of northwestern Ethiopia.

After the adoption of Christianity as the state religion, the Falashas were sometimes persecuted. The punishment for refusing to convert was the confiscation of land. Many Falashas then became skilled craftsmen. Recent research suggests that it may have been the Falashas who provided the labour for the construction and decoration of the castles.

From 1985 to 1991 many Falashas were airlifted to Israel, and today only a handful remain. Sadly, the pottery for which they were once famous has degenerated into clumsy, half-hearted affairs, produced to feed the demand from tourists (mainly depicting King Solomon in bed with the Queen of Sheba). However, the Project Ploughshare Women's Crafts Training Center, which helps disadvantaged women learn a craft, is worth supporting (see the Gonder map). Items cost around Birr5 to Birr20.

The old synagogue and Falasha homes can be visited, but a special trip to the village can't be called worthwhile. To get here from Gonder, you can take a taxi (Birr40 return) or a *gari* (Birr10 return).

SIMIEN MOUNTAINS
የሲሜን ተራሮች

The traveller Rosita Forbes, in Ethiopia in 1925, described these mountains as 'the most marvellous of all Abyssinian landscapes'. By any standards the scenery is spectacular; in places it's breathtaking.

The Simien Mountains, north of Gonder and east of the main road to Aksum, make a terrific break from the monument-bashing on the historical route. They'll also give you a taste of Ethiopia's remarkable wildlife. Home to a variety of endemic mammals, birds and plants, including the beautiful walia ibex (a type of goat) found only here, the park has been declared a World Heritage Site by Unesco.

Although facilities for trekkers are few (the undeveloped state of the park is actually one of its attractions), the mountains are nevertheless easily accessible and treks can be quickly organised (see Organised Treks). Most demands can be met, from casual strolls and a picnic to several weeks' trekking and hard-core rock climbing.

For anyone remotely interested in walking, wildlife or scenery, the Simien Mountains are not to be missed; they undoubtedly rank among the most beautiful mountain ranges in Africa.

Geography & Geology
Comprising one of the principal mountain massifs of Africa, the Simien Mountains are made up of several plateaus, separated by broad river valleys. A number of peaks rise above 4000m, including Ras Dashen, the fourth-highest mountain in Africa.

The dramatic landscape of the Simien Mountains is the result of massive seismic activity in the area about 40 million years ago. Molten lava poured out of the Earth's core, reaching a thickness of 3000m. Subsequent erosion over the millennia has left behind the Simiens' jagged landscape of spectacular gorges, chasms and precipices.

The famous pinnacles – the sharp spires that rise abruptly from the surrounding landscape – are volcanic necks: the solidified lava that is the last remnant of ancient volcanoes.

The park itself stretches over 179 sq km and lies at an altitude of between 1900m and 4543m, in the 'Afro-Alpine' zone. A typical trek takes you through tiny villages and fields of barley in the lower valleys to the steep gorges and sheer escarpments of the lower slopes. Beyond lies the wild and sometimes bleak landscape of the upper slopes, including those around Ras Dashen.

Climate
The average daily temperature of the Simien Mountains ranges between 11.5°C and 18°C. At night, the temperature drops to around 3°C; during the coldest period, from October to December, it can dip several degrees below freezing point.

Flora & Fauna
The mountains are home to three of Ethiopia's larger endemic mammals: the walia ibex (numbers are estimated at between 514 and 520 according to a 2002 census), the more

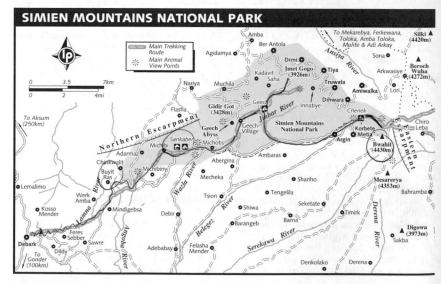

SIMIEN MOUNTAINS NATIONAL PARK

common gelada baboon (estimated between 7000 to 10,000), and the very rarely seen Ethiopian wolf (estimated at just 42). Other mammals sometimes seen are rock hyraxes, jackals, bushbucks and klipspringers.

Endemic bird species include the commonly seen thick-billed raven, and the less common black-headed siskin, white-collared pigeon, white-billed starling, wattled ibis, spot-breasted plover and white-backed black tit. One of the most memorable sights is the huge, soaring lammergeyer – easily seen in the Simien Mountains.

Along the roadside on the approach to Sankaber, look out for the ivory-coloured, endemic Abyssinian rose.

Planning

Organising trekking yourself in Debark is straightforward. Camping equipment can be hired (enquire at the park headquarters). Mattresses cost from Birr7, sleeping bags from Birr10 and two-person tents from Birr25 (all per day). Cooking equipment and gas stoves can also be hired. Kerosene can be bought from the petrol station in Debark. The park headquarters in Debark now also has a 4WD available for hire.

Organised Treks In Gonder there are more and more freelance 'agents' offering to organise treks for you. If you're in a hurry, this may save you some time. They charge only a

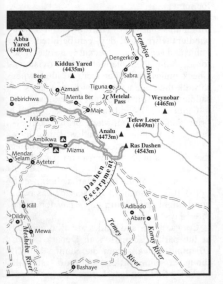

nominal commission. They can organise both car and equipment rental (to hire mattresses costs around Birr10, sleeping bags Birr20, tents Birr30 and cooking equipment Birr100 per day) and can even buy food.

Two **agents** to be particularly recommended are Habteselassie Asemare (e *exploresimens@ yahoo.com*) and Fasil Mesfin (☎ *11 00 40;* e *fasilm675@yahoo.com*). They have just opened an office at the Quara Hotel in Gonder. Another guide highly recommended by several travellers is Bedassa Jote (☎ *11 50 73;* e *bejgobena@yahoo.com*).

A newly opened agency in Gonder is **Semien Trekking Tours Ethiopia** (fax *11 07 05;* e *nega_eth@freemail.et*), run by a freelance guide. The company offers four-day treks to Geech camp (all food, transport and equipment included) for around Birr4500 for one person and Birr5000 for two people. At least half a day's notice is required.

Maps A new brochure, which includes a map as well as a good overview of the park, is available from Park Headquarters (Birr5).

The most useful trekking map is still that produced by the well-respected Institute of Geography, University of Berne, Switzerland – the *Simen* [sic] Mountains *Trekking Map* (1980; 1:100,000). Occasionally it's available in Debark priced from Birr120 to Birr150, but it's best to get it before leaving home.

A new map (more comprehensive and at a larger scale) is apparently under preparation (also by Berne University) and should be available sometime in 2003–04.

When to Go December to March is the driest time, but October, after the rainy season, is when the scenery is greenest and the wildflowers are out.

During the main rainy season, between June and September, mist often obscures the views and the trails can be slippery underfoot. However, you're still assured of several hours of clear, dry weather for walking; the rain tends to come in short, sharp downpours.

Park Fees Fees for the park (admission per 48h Birr50, camping Birr20, vehicle fee depending on size Birr10/15/20) are payable at the **park headquarters** (☎ *11 34 82;* open *8.30am-12.30pm & 1.30pm-5.30pm Mon-Fri)*. On weekends, you'll have to dig out the cashier or Tourist Officer. In the future, the entry time limit may be reduced to a 24-hour period.

Vanishing Wolves

Though it derived its name from the mountains, the Ethiopian wolf (previously known as the Simien fox or jackal) is close to extinction in the area. Officially, the population is estimated at 42.

Many wolves have died from diseases caught from local dogs, others have died after eating rats poisoned by villagers to protect their crops, or in traps. Hybridisation with dogs is another threat to the species' survival. Fortunately, the endemic animal is faring far better in the Bale Mountains to the south (see the boxed text 'The Ethiopian Wolf' in the Southern Ethiopia chapter).

It takes at least two hours to arrange everything. The best plan is to arrive in the afternoon and arrange everything for an early start the following morning.

Note that entrance and camping fees will not be refunded once paid. However, if mules, cooks, guides and scouts are not used (because of problems such as bad weather or acclimatisation difficulties), their fees can be refunded – but make sure this is clearly agreed before setting off.

Supplies Outside Debark, there are no shops, although you can buy eggs (Birr1 for three eggs), chickens (Birr7 to Birr15), sheep (Birr65 to Birr120) and potatoes (Birr3 for 1kg) from villages on the mountain. Your guide will negotiate prices, and mule handlers will gladly kill, skin and roast a sheep if they get to tuck in too. If you leave the carcass a little way outside camp, it may well attract a lammergeyer.

Debark's food supplies are limited to a few tin cans, biscuits, pasta, tomato sauce and milk powder, plus some fresh fruit and vegetables from the market. Gonder is a better place for stocking up. Stoves, lanterns and kerosene (paraffin) are also available in Gonder. Anything 'specialised', such as packet soups, should be bought in Addis Ababa (where things are also cheaper).

Water is available in various places on the mountain but should be treated. Make sure the cook, if you have one, boils the water sufficiently, rather than just warming it up.

Though eucalyptus wood (sold by villagers on the mountain) is permitted for fires, it's best to bring a stove. Burning wood from indigenous trees is strictly forbidden.

If you're worried about warmth, do as the locals do: buy a *gabi* (Birr40 to Birr80 depending on the size) at Debark market, which makes a great blanket, sheet, pillow, shawl or cushion.

Guides, Cooks & Mules At the time of writing, price increments were as good as confirmed by the park headquarters. The proposed new prices are quoted.

Guides (Birr100 per day) are recommended by the park headquarters. Although they are freelancers, the guides are trained by the national park on courses established by an Austrian team. Most are excellent, a few are less so. Guides now work by rota, so there's little point recommending any by name. However, don't be afraid to ask for another guide if you're not happy with the one assigned to you (see also the boxed text 'Guidelines for Guides' in the Facts for the Visitor chapter). Be aware that unofficial guides or cooks may approach you on the street. If you want official ones, head for the park headquarters.

'Scouts' (armed park rangers) are compulsory (Birr50 per day). Few speak English, but what they lack in conversation they make up for in willingness to help. Some scouts, though fit, are quite old; a tip at the end is particularly appreciated.

Cooks can also be hired for Birr50 per day, a welcome and not-too-costly luxury for some.

Porters are not available in the Simien Mountains, but mules (Birr50 per day) with handlers (Birr30 per day) can be hired. The guide and scout will expect at least one mule for carrying their blankets and provisions. Check mules for tender feet (ask the owner to walk the mule up and down) and signs of saddle sores. If in doubt, ask for another.

Guides, cooks and mule handlers should bring their own food. Many bring token offerings or nothing at all and will then look to you for sustenance. Either check that they have enough or bring extra packets of rice etc.

At the end of the trek, staff will expect a tip. A rule of thumb if the service has been good might be an extra day's pay for every three days' work.

Cooks, mules and guides are all organised at the park headquarters in Debark (about 10 minutes' walk from the Simien Hotel), though a guide, official or unofficial, will probably find you long before you get there.

Treks

All treks begin and end in Debark, where the park headquarters (and the nearest medical assistance) are located.

A new gravel road now winds all the way up to Chenek camp and beyond (though Unesco, concerned about the impact on wildlife, may conceivably reroute it in the future). Paths crisscross the rest of the mountainside. For centuries these paths have connected villages with pasture lands, and they make terrific trekking routes. The walking itself is generally not challenging and gradients are not too steep.

Don't forget to allow time for acclimatisation when planning your routes, particularly if you're aiming to reach Ras Dashen.

The most popular trekking routes are along the western side of the massif; these take in the most impressive sections of the famous escarpment. The park 'camps' of Sankaber, Chenek and Geech make convenient spots at which to overnight.

With two days you could walk from Debark to Sankaber and back. With four days you could reach Geech; with five you could get to Chenek, taking in Mt Bwahit; and with around ten days you could bag Ras Dashen (possible in seven if you hitch or hire a vehicle to and from Sankaber and continue the same day to Geech). All times include the return journey to Debark. A vehicle obviously speeds up access to and from the camps (see Getting There & Away later) and trekking times.

The foot that is restless, will tread on a turd.
Ethiopian proverb

Choosing a Trekking Route In a nutshell, if it's spectacular scenery you're after, head for Geech. If it's the walia ibex, Chenek is good (but be sure to be here early – no later than 9am). If it's the gelada baboon, opt for Buyit Ras, though Chenek, Geech and particularly Sankaber are also good. If it's pleasant walking, the stretch between Geech and Chenek is good. If it's the lammergeyer you're after, they're almost guaranteed at Chenek.

Ras Dashen, frankly, doesn't offer a great deal beyond the satisfaction of 'bagging it'. The going can be tedious, and gradients are steep in parts.

The following is a classic route, though, with the new road, the lower camps can be bypassed and trekking times dramatically cut by driving or hitching the first part. For those very short on time, for example, you could just reach Mt Bwahit and travel back in three days by hitching or hiring a vehicle from Debark to Sankaber and trekking the same day to Geech, trekking on day two from Geech to Chenek, and on day three from Chenek to Mt Bwahit, then back to Ambaras, from where the main road to Sankaber and Debark can be reached (to be collected by vehicle).

Note that trekking times vary from individual to individual, and also depend on whether exact routes are followed. The following routes and times have been devised in consultation with local guides.

Debark to Ras Dashen Trek
Debark to Buyit Ras (10km, three to four hours) Sankaber can be reached in a single day, but many trekkers prefer to break the first day at Buyit Ras, where there's an attractive camping spot with beautiful views. It's also a good place to see gelada baboons. If you do want to push on to Sankaber, it's another 13km (around three to four hours).

Buyit Ras to Geech Camp via Sankaber (25km, seven to eight hours) The dirt road and your guide will take you straight to Sankaber, but a more scenic route is to follow the narrow path that keeps close to the escarpment edge. There are particularly good views between Michibi and Sankaber. Look out for gelada baboons.

From Sankaber to Geech it's between four and five hours' walk. At Geech there's a long-drop toilet and a small shower house.

Monkey Trouble

Now the focus of international scientific studies, including a BBC documentary by David Attenborough, the extraordinary endemic gelada baboon is yet little appreciated by the locals. Resented for its alleged damage to village crops and pasture, it has become the scapegoat for more sinister goings-on, too. According to local police reports in Sankaber, gelada baboons are responsible for local thefts, burglaries, rapes and even murders – in one case bursting into a house to drag an adult man 1.5km before shoving him off a cliff face! If in doubt, blame the gelada! See also the boxed text 'The Bleeding Heart Baboon' in the Facts about Ethiopia chapter.

Geech Camp to Chenek via Imet Gogo (20km, seven to nine hours)

Geech to Chenek takes about five to six hours, but a very worthwhile diversion is the promontory of Imet Gogo, around 5km northeast of Geech. It takes 1½ to two hours one way.

The promontory, at 3926m, affords some of the most spectacular views of the Simien Mountains. To make a day of it, you could continue to the viewpoint known as Saha. From Saha, you can head for the viewpoint at Kadavit (2.5km, 30 to 40 minutes), then return to camp.

You can also trek to Chenek via Imet Gogo using Saha as a starting point (eight to nine hours). Saha lies around 3km from Geech.

From Imet Gogo you have two choices: the first is to return to Geech by your outward route, then head directly south, back across the Jinbar River and up to an area called Ambaras where you meet the dirt road and follow it all the way to Chenek. The alternative, which is harder but more scenic, is to follow the escarpment edge south by way of another promontory viewpoint called Innatiye (represented on some maps as Gedadere).

Just before arrival at Chenek, look out for a spot known as Korbete Metia. Although it provides stunning views of the lowlands, there is a sinister side: it was here that some regional officials were executed. *Korbete Metia (korbat mataya)* means loosely 'the place where skin was thrown down'. Lammergeyers are often seen here.

Chenek is probably the best spot in the Simien Mountains for wildlife.

For those who want to return to Sankaber from Chenek (seven to eight hours) but avoid most of the dirt road, a scenic local trail up to Ambaras through the village of Argin can be followed. The trail affords good views of the escarpment and the foothills of Mt Bwahit.

Chenek to Mt Bwahit & Return (6km, two to three hours)

The summit of Mt Bwahit (4430m) lies to the southeast of the camp. From the top, you can see a tiny piece of Ras Dashen.

Around 20 minutes from the camp towards Mt Bwahit, there's a spot that affords one of the best opportunities for glimpsing, at long range (around 300m to 400m), the walia ibex. This animal, a member of the wild goat family, lives on the crags of the steep escarpment above 3000m. Don't miss it, but come very early in the morning or late in the afternoon (after 4pm) with binoculars.

Chenek to Ambikwa (22km, eight to nine hours)

From Chenek, a track leads eastward then southeastward up towards a good viewpoint on the eastern escarpment, to the north of Mt Bwahit. To the east, across the vast valley of the Mesheba River, you can see the bulk of Ras Dashen.

Ambikwa to Ras Dashen & Return (17km, eight to ten hours)

Most trekkers stay two nights at Ambikwa and go up to the summit of Ras Dashen on the day in between. It's a good idea to start at first light.

At Ras Dashen there are three distinct points, and much debate about which is the true summit. Whichever peak you go for, the total walk from Ambikwa to reach one summit is about five to six hours. If you want to knock off the others, add two to three hours for each one. Returning by the same route takes about three to four hours.

Ambikwa to Debark (77km, three days)

Most trekkers return from Ambikwa to Debark along the same route via Chenek and Sankaber. If you are tired or have had enough, you may be able to hitch a lift (Birr30) with one of the trucks that ply the route daily.

Ambikwa to Adi Arkay (about 65km, three to five days)

One interesting alternative return route is to trek from Ambikwa to Arkwasiye, to the northeast of Chenek, taking in the nearby peaks of Beroch Wuha (4272m) and Silki (4420m).

From Arkwasiye to Adi Arkay will take another two to three days of strenuous walking, via Sona (three hours from Arkwasiye) and Mekarebya (seven hours from Sona).

From Adi Arkay, which lies about 80km north of Debark, you can continue northward to Aksum.

Other Routes

There are endless alternatives for keen trekkers or rock climbers, such as a return route from Ras Dashen back to Ambikwa and Chenek, via the east and north sides of the Mesheba River.

One slightly more challenging route which will give you a taste of the highlands as well as the lowlands, and bags some 4000m on the way (and is much more interesting than climbing Ras Dashen), is from Debark to Adi Arkay via Sankaber, Geech, Chenek (climbing Mt Bwahit at 4430m), Arkwasiye (climbing Beroch Wuha at 4272m), Sona (climbing Silki

ETHIOPIA

at 4420m), Mekarebya, Mulite and Adi Arkay. The route should take around nine to 10 days, though it can be done in as few as six if Sona and Mulite are missed out. Note that, since it takes the guides, mules and other members of your trekking entourage two further days to return to Debark from Adi Arkay, you must pay two days' extra fee.

Places to Stay & Eat

Debark Beyond the park headquarters, **Simien Park Hotel** (*☎ 11 34 81; singles/ doubles/twins with shared shower Birr25/ 35/45, one room with private shower Birr60*) is the best bet and, though simple, is reasonably clean. Reservations are advised; it's sometimes booked with groups, particularly in January. There's also a safe box and small souvenir shop. A bar/restaurant serves local and *faranji* food (Birr6 to Birr10) and drink. Boxed lunches can be prepared for Birr8.

Simen Hotel (*doubles/twins with bucket shower Birr15/30*) is an alternative if the Simien Park Hotel is full. It's set a block back from the main street and a short walk from the bus stop and market. Rooms are basic, but it's set in pleasant grounds.

Ras Dashen, two minutes from the Simien Park Hotel towards the bus station, is considered the best restaurant in town (though it's basic) if you're keen to escape the confines of the hotel.

On the Mountains The stone huts at Sankaber, Geech and Chenek are reserved for the park rangers.

Recently, two new, but spartan **'lodges'** (*huts; Birr40*) were built at Sankaber. Don't expect more than a rickety bed, blanket, some bed linen and possibly the odd flea. The lodges sleep nine to 10 people, dormitory style. The toilet is in a hut outside and a nearby stream serves as the shower. There is an electrical generator, but no kitchen facilities.

Cooking equipment can be rented from the park headquarters (Birr30 for one to two people). More lodges are planned for both Sankaber and Chenek in the future.

The camping sites at Geech and Chenek provide flat ground, water (from nearby streams) and, at Geech, a basic shower.

If you don't have camping equipment (and don't want to rent it) you can do as the guides do: stay in the local huts (but you should contribute about Birr10 per night). Don't expect luxuries. A floor or wooden platform covered

with a goatskin serves as your bedroom; any number and combination of animals, children, chickens and especially fleas will be your roommates.

Getting There & Away

One bus runs daily to Gonder (Birr12.35, four hours). A local taxi from Gonder to Debark should cost Birr450 to Birr500 for one to four people (2½ hours).

The new gravel road allows access right up to Chenek camp (which can be visited in a day from Debark if you leave early enough), which means that even nontrekkers can visit the park. There are plans to continue the road all the way to Lalibela eventually.

Usually at least one supply truck plies the road daily to Chenek and beyond (leaving Debark at around 6am and returning the same day). You may be able to hitch a lift in the back (though a contribution of around Birr30 will be expected). As a result of local pressure, a bus service may soon run along this road. Keep an ear out for developments.

Private vehicles can sometimes be contracted. Enquire at the bus station or ask at your hotel reception. Private pick-up trucks and larger trucks expect from Birr400 to Birr800 depending on your destination and if it's one way or return.

In both Gonder and Debark, 4WD vehicles can now be hired. If you're short of time, you can arrange for a vehicle to drop you off and pick you up later. During the rainy season (June to August), the road can be difficult to navigate even in a 4WD.

From Debark to Aksum, you'll need to get to Shire first. The Shire bus coming from Gonder (from Birr37, six to seven hours from Debark), is often full, so it may be easier to return to Gonder and start from there. Coming the other way, catch the Gonder bus from Shire and ask to be dropped at Debark.

SHIRE

ሺሬ

Shire, marked on some maps as Inda Selassie, is of interest to travellers only because it provides a link with Aksum, 60km to the east. However, the journey from Debark to Shire (and in particular the stretch of road between Debark and Adi Arkay) is one of the most dramatic in Ethiopia.

The beautifully constructed Italian road cuts its way through the mountains in a series of neat loops and bends and provides impressive views along the way. Around Adi Arkay, look out for the peak known as Awaza (represented on the back of Ethiopian Airlines tickets).

If you get stuck in Shire (and you will if you miss the early morning onward buses), the **Andet Hotel** (☎ 44 04 84; rooms without/ with cold shower Birr15/25, with hot shower & TV Birr45) is probably the best bet and has a restaurant.

From Shire, there are three or four buses daily to Aksum (Birr8, 1½ to two hours) and two or three minibuses (Birr10, 1½ to two hours). To Gonder, one bus leaves daily (Birr37, 10 to 11 hours). For Debark (Birr37, six to seven hours), take the bus to Gonder and ask to be dropped off en route.

The plains on the outskirts of Shire were the scene of fighting between the Tigrayans and advancing Italians in the 1930s, and later against Mengistu's army in the civil war. Keep an eye out for war relics. The *sho-ruba* hairstyle of the Tigrayan women has remained unchanged for centuries.

AKSUM
አክሱም
☎ 04 • pop 27,148 • elevation 2130m

Sprawling, dusty, and rural – Aksum is modest almost to a fault. On first sight, it's hard to imagine that the town was ever the site of a great civilisation. Yet Aksum is one of Ethiopia's star attractions. Littered with the ruins of palaces, underground tombs, stelae and inscriptions, the town once formed part of the great Aksumite kingdom that Dr Neville Chittick described as 'the last of the great civilisations of Antiquity to be revealed to modern knowledge' (see the History section in the Facts about Ethiopia chapter). Aksum is undoubtedly one of the most important and spectacular ancients sites in sub-Saharan Africa. Unesco lists it as a World Heritage site.

Aksum was known to the ancient Greeks and Romans, was featured in Byzantine and Arab literature, and was reported with wonder by European visitors in the 16th to 18th centuries. Yet it remained almost unknown to the wider world right up to the 19th century. It was not until the beginning of the 20th century that the first archaeological dig took place, carried out by the Deutsche Aksum-Expedition (DAE) in 1906.

Remarkably, 98% of Aksum still remains unexcavated. At the time of writing, a University of Hamburg team (due to wind up excavations in 2004) had just discovered what is believed to be a new palace at a site known as Barihi Awdi.

Perhaps the 'undiscovered' nature of Aksum is part of its charm. Though no longer a wealthy metropolis, the town continues to flourish as a centre of local trade; life continues as it has for millennia. Around the crumbling palaces, farmers go on ploughing their land, women continue to wash their clothes in the Queen of Sheba's Bath, and market-goers and their donkeys hurry past the towering stelae. You won't find pyramid-parking coaches or sound-and-light shows here. And inextricably interwoven with the archaeological evidence is the local tradition – the legends, myths and fables.

A particularly good time to visit is during one of the major religious festivals or for the celebration of Maryam Zion in late November (see under Public Holidays in the Facts for the Visitor chapter). To do the town justice, you should schedule a bare minimum of two days, or one full day if you have a vehicle.

History
According to local legend, Aksum was the Queen of Sheba's capital in the 10th century BC. More fantasy than fact that may be, but what is certain is that a high civilisation had arisen here around the 1st century AD.

By the 1st century AD, Greek merchants knew Aksum as a great city and the powerful capital of an extensive empire. For close to 1000 years, Aksum dominated the vital seaborne trade between Africa and Asia. The kingdom numbered among the greatest states of the ancient world.

Even after its rapid and somewhat mysterious decline, the town retained considerable prestige and status. Today Aksum serves as a kind of unofficial religious capital, and many kings have been crowned here.

Pilgrims still journey to Aksum and important festivals are celebrated here. The great majority of Ethiopians believe passionately that the Ark of the Covenant resides within the town.

Aksum has a vibrancy, life and continuing national importance very rarely found on ancient sites. Sadly, however, the sites are threatened by the expansion of the town. Unless funds can be found, much archaeological evidence may be lost.

Information
The **Tourist Office** (☎ 75 39 24; open 8.30am-12.30pm & 1.30pm-5.30pm Mon-Sat) is operated by the Tigray Tourism Commission, and can provide a basic map of Aksum (Birr3),

AKSUM

PLACES TO STAY
8 Yeha Hotel; NTO;
  Galaxy Express Services
28 Ghenet Hotel
29 Bazen Hotel
30 Kaleb Hotel
33 Sheferoch Hotel
39 Axum Touring Hotel; Experience
  Ethiopia Travel Agency
45 Ark Hotel
46 Africa Hotel; Internet Café
48 Remhai Hotel

PLACES TO EAT
31 Mini Pastry
32 Marta Hotel
43 Vanilla Cafeteria
44 Habesha Restaurant

49 Café Abyssinia

OTHER
1 Abba Pentalewon
  Monastery
2 Abba Liqanos
  Monastery
3 Tombs of Kings Kaleb &
  Gebre Meskel
4 King Ezana's Inscription
5 Queen of Sheba's Bath
6 Abuna Aregawi Church
7 View Point
9 Souvenir Shops
10 New Church of St Mary
  of Zion
11 Ark of the Covenant Chapel
  & Museum

12 Archaeological Museum &
  Tickets to Sites
13 Old Church of St Mary
  of Zion
14 Arbatu Ensessa Church
15 Dungur (Queen of Sheba's
  Palace)
16 Gudit Stelae Field
17 Ta'akha Maryam (Ruins)
18 Ethnographical Museum
19 Ethio-Cultural Heritage
  Project
20 Souvenir & Photo Shops
21 Tourist Office;
  Post Office
22 Old Palace (Library)
23 Taxi & Gari Stand
24 Police

25 Bike Hire
26 King Ezana Hotel
27 School
34 Telecommunications
  Office
35 King Bazen's Tomb
36 Ethiopian Airlines;
  Handicrafts &
  Jewellery Shops
37 Photo Shop
38 Kahsay Supermarket
40 Axumait Handicraft
  Center; Souvenir
  Shops
41 Commercial Bank
42 Garage
47 St Gebreal Drugstore
50 St Mary Hospital

quite an interesting, Italian-produced brochure entitled a 'A Guide to Aksum Historical
Site' [sic] (Birr3) and, most usefully, official
guides (free but you should tip afterwards; a
minimum of Birr50 per group is fair).

David Phillipson's new *Aksum: an archaeological introduction and guide* promises to be
an excellent compendium to Aksum's history,
archaeology and major sites and monuments,
when it's published at the end of 2003. In the
meantime, *The Monuments of Aksum* by the
same author details many of the sites.

Although you can see the monuments
on your own (or in the company of street
boys who will offer to guide you), an official guide is recommended. All are trained
and many are history students, so you'll get
much more out of your visit. Bring a torch
for the tombs.

Tickets can be bought from the **Archaeological Museum** *(adults/students Birr50/25)*.
They are valid for the duration of your stay
and allow entry to all the historical sites within
the immediate vicinity of Aksum, except for
the St Mary of Zion church compound.

Aksum's **main market** is on Saturday. Also
worth a peek are some of Aksum's **souvenir
shops**.

By the end of 2004 a new **artisanal centre**,
an ethio-cultural heritage project funded by the
World Bank, should open in a traditional-style
Aksumite house and compound, not far from
the Ethnographical Museum. Local craftsmen
will be trained in ancient Aksumite techniques
to produce, exhibit and sell arts and crafts.

To see craftsmen at work, try the **Axumait
Handicraft Center**, which also houses a large
collection of good-quality, but not cheap

ETHIOPIA

A Quick Guide to Aksum's Stelae

For perhaps as long as 5000 years, monoliths (stelae) have been used in northeast Africa as a kind of tombstone-cum-monument to local rulers. In Aksum, this tradition reached its apogee. Like Egypt's pyramids, Aksum's stelae were like great billboards announcing to the world the authority, power and greatness of the ruling families. The more finely carved the stele, the more splendid and complex the tomb underneath. Aksum's astonishing stelae are striking for their huge size, their incredible, almost pristine, state of preservation, and their curiously modern look. Sculpted from single pieces of granite to look like multistoreyed buildings, they more closely resemble Manhattan skyscrapers than 2000-year-old obelisks. Despite the stone being famously hard, Aksum's masons worked it superbly, often following a set design.

Six of the stelae imitate multistoreyed buildings complete with little windows, doors and sometimes even door handles or locks. The architectural design mirrors the traditional Aksumite style of the time, used to construct the city's houses and palaces (see Architecture in the Facts about Ethiopia chapter).

In former times, metal plates, perhaps in the form of a crescent moon and disc, are thought to have been riveted to the top of the stelae both at the front and back. The crescent is an ancient pagan symbol, originating from southern Arabia. In 1996 a broken plate that perfectly matched the rivet holes at the top of the stelae was excavated. It bore the effigy of a face, perhaps that of the ruler to whom the plate's stele was dedicated.

At the base of the stelae is a stone platform thought to have served as an altar. The little carved cavities probably held sacrificial offerings. In King Ezana's stele, look out also for the *gabeta* board game, carved into the platform by bored ancients clearly unimpressed by what towered above them!

Many aspects of the stelae are still shrouded in mystery. It is uncertain why they were designed in this way. And no one has yet figured out how the massive blocks of granite were transported at least 4km from the quarries, then stood upright; the largest weighed no less than 517 tonnes. Traditionally it is believed that the celestial powers of the Ark of the Covenant were harnessed for the feat; archaeologists believe that the earthly forces of elephants, rollers and winches were probably used.

Northern Stelae Park

The Northern Stelae Park, lying to the northeast of town, is the biggest and most important stelae field in Aksum and contains over 120 stelae. The original number would have been more – some have been removed, others probably lie buried.

The stelae range from 1m to over 30m in height and from simple slabs of stone (the majority) to finely dressed blocks of a rectangular shape, usually with flat sides and a rounded or conical apex. Though they were undoubtedly connected with the practice of human burial, it is not yet certain if every stele marks a tomb.

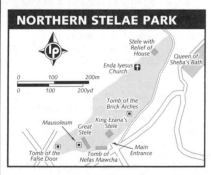

The biggest stele here, the Great Stele, measures a massive 33m. It believed to be the largest single block of stone that humans have ever attempted to erect, and overshadows even the Egyptian obelisks in its conception and ambition.

The stele near the entrance is popularly known as King Ezana's stele (though it's almost certainly significantly earlier than Ezana), and is now the biggest still standing, measuring 24m in height. Henry Salt, the British traveller and first foreigner to describe it in 1805, proclaimed it 'the most admirable and perfect monument of its kind'.

A Quick Guide to Aksum's Stelae

In the courtyards of Enda Iyesus, a stele decorated with a disc (the pagan symbols of the sun) and a crescent moon can be seen. In 1997 another huge stele (18m) was discovered near the church. If you haven't already seen Ethiopian church painting, the church itself is a worth a peek for its colourful murals (see also the boxed text 'Know Your Ethiopian Saints' earlier in this chapter).

Among the various other stelae in the area is one that boasts a unique decoration. It lies on the ground around 200m to the north of King Ezana's stele. Measuring around 9m in length, its upper section is carved like a pointed arch. Near the top, a small house-like object is carved in relief (on one side of the stone, supported by a pillar), formed by a rectangle surmounted by a triangle. Some have claimed that this is early proof of Aksum's claim to house the Ark of the Covenant!

The Great Stele

At one time this stele was believed to have stood but, following further investigations in 1998, scholars now believe that the monolith never did stand – that it toppled over as it was being erected sometime in the second quarter of the 4th century. It now lies like a broken soldier. Look out for the unworked 'root', which contrasts dramatically with the sleek, carved base; it gives you a vivid idea of the precision, finesse and technical competence of the Aksumite stone workers.

When the Great Stele crashed to the ground, it sounded the knell not only on the long tradition of obelisk erection in Aksum, but also on the old religion. Some scholars have suggested that the disastrous collapse of the massive stele may actually have contributed to the people's conversion to Christianity – like a kind of Ethiopian Tower of Babel – or even that it was sabotaged deliberately to feign a sign of God. Whatever the origin of its downfall, the stele remains exactly where it fell 1600 years ago, a permanent reminder of the defeat of paganism by Christianity.

The Rome Stele

The second-largest stele, at 25m high, was shipped to Italy in 1937 during the Italian occupation, on the personal orders of Mussolini. It stands to this day in the Piazza di Porta Capena in Rome, and is sometimes known as the Rome stele. After decades of negotiation and feet-dragging, it should be returned to Ethiopia in the near future – possibly by the end of 2003, or 2004…

But that's easier said than done. The stele will have to be lowered onto its side, cut into two pieces, then flown back in a special plane – probably US-supplied – large enough to take it. Then there's the problem of road transportation and re-erection when it arrives; archaeologists believe that the proposed site, where underground tombs are also found, may not be stable enough to hold it.

While all the head-scratching continues, the achievement of the ancient Aksumites is rather thrown into perspective: the stele was transported and erected at Aksum in the first place – without chopping it up, without US planes and without advice from technicians – around 2000 years ago.

Gudit Stelae Field

Though less immediately arresting than those found in town, the stelae in the Gudit Stelae Field, on the south side of Dungur (the Queen of Sheba's Palace), are still worth a visit.

Named after Queen Gudit, who is said to have sacked Aksum in around the 10th century, the area covers some 500m by 200m and contains several hundred stelae. Most are small, undressed and lie on the ground. Local guides like to point out the largest stele in the field, which is said to mark the Queen of Sheba's grave.

Excavations were carried out in 1973 and 1974, and from 1994 to 1996, but little is known about the stelae field. Though some are known to mark graves, neither rock-hewn nor constructed tombs have been found around them. One pit did contain, among other things, a set of fine glass goblets, probably dating from the early 3rd century, which has led scholars to suggest that perhaps the place was the burial site of the lesser nobles of Aksumite society.

The walk to the complex is lovely at dusk, when you'll meet the farmers and their animals returning home before nightfall.

ETHIOPIA

(by local standards) handicrafts. Ask for the energetic and well-informed Haile, himself a carver for more than 20 years.

There is an **Internet café** (Birr2 per minute) at the Africa Hotel.

Tombs

Aksumite tombs were first dug out from under the ground, then lined with very large, often beautifully worked, blocks of granite.

To the east of the largest obelisk in the Northern Stelae Field is the **Tomb of the Brick Arches**. It dates from the 4th century and is remarkably well preserved. Eighteen stone steps lead down to a horseshoe brick arch, which gives access to the tomb. The latter is made up of four rock-cut chambers, subdivided by a series of brick arches built with lime mortar.

The tomb is just one of two so far excavated that have avoided wholesale robbery. Among the many finds were the remains of at least two skeletons, finely carved ivory including two beautiful tusks, pottery, fragments of glass vessels, and, in a pit in the first chamber, a large quantity of bronze, including decorative panels.

Particular excitement surrounded the discovery of a cast circular plaque, upon which a human head had been represented, framed by an inscription. The holes in the plate have led to speculation that it may once have been riveted to the top of a stele. It's currently closed to the public, but there are plans to open the tomb by the end of 2004.

In 1972 the unique **Tomb of the False Door** was discovered (known locally as the Tomb of King Ramhai). It lies in the western extremity of the Northern Stelae Field and is thought to date from around the 4th or 5th century AD. More complex in structure, its stone blocks are also larger and more finely dressed than those found in some other tombs. Comprising an antechamber and inner chamber, it is surrounded on three sides by a passage.

Above the tomb, at ground level, a rectangular, probably flat-roofed building would once have stood (measuring some 12 sq metres by 2.8m high). Above the stairs leading down into the tomb was a stone slab carved with a false door (from which the tomb gets its name) almost identical to those found on the stelae. Look out for the iron clamps fixing blocks of stone together like a kind of giant staple.

All the tomb's contents were stolen in antiquity and, judging from the lengths to which the robbers went to gain access, it is thought to have contained objects of great value. The much-mutilated single stone sarcophagus can still be seen.

Other tombs include the megalithic **Tomb of Nefas Mawcha**. Covering an area of some 16m by 23m, the tomb consists of a large rectangular central chamber surrounded on three sides by a passage. The tomb is unusual for its large size, the sophistication of the structure and the size of the stones used for its construction (the stone which roofs the central chamber measures 17.3m by 6.4m and weighs some 360 tonnes!).

The so-called **mausoleum** was discovered in 1974, but not excavated until the mid-1990s. A monumental portal (hewn from a single slab of granite) marked the entrance to the tomb and was also carved with the curious false door motifs of the stelae. The portal leads into a passageway and on each side, five chambers. Part of the tomb had been disfigured at some unknown date by robbers, who succeeded in digging through 1.5m of solid masonry! The mausoleum is currently closed to visitors, but should open eventually.

In some places in the stelae field you can hear the sound of an unopened tomb echoing below your feet. This is part of Aksum's appeal – the thought that fascinating finds, secrets and maybe even treasures lie waiting to be discovered. The temptation to return in the night with a shovel is almost unbearable.

Most other tombs so far excavated have been pillaged by robbers, so very little is yet understood about Aksumite burial customs, nor the identities and personalities of those buried. Though it's unlikely that anything as spectacular as an Ethiopian Tutankhamen will turn up, the importance of the kingdom of Aksum in the ancient world, and the potential for discovery of future excavations, should not be dismissed. The world awaits.

St Mary of Zion Churches

Opposite the Northern Stelae Field in a walled compound lie the two churches of St Mary of Zion (admission Birr60, video cameras Birr100).

The rectangular **old church** was built by the Emperor Fasiladas, the founder of Gonder, in 1665. Look out for the old podium on which it sits – it may well belong to the original church erected by King Ezana or King Kaleb in the 4th or 6th century after the adoption of Christianity. This would have been the very first church on African soil. Unfortunately, the building was destroyed during the incursions of Mohammed

ARIADNE VAN ZANDBERGEN

Afro-alpine moorland at 4000m altitude in the Sanetti Plateau, Bale Mountains National Park

FRANCES LINZEE GORDON

Hamer woman, Lower Omo Valley

FRANCES LINZEE GORDON

Local man, Lower Omo Valley

Tsemai girl, Lower Omo Valley

Galeb warrior, Lower Omo Valley

Red-hot poker plant

Burchell's zebra, Nechisar National Park

Mursi woman

Gragn the Left-Handed in 1535 (see History in the Facts about Ethiopia chapter). The present church is, nonetheless, a remarkable example of traditional architecture.

Inside there are some fine murals, including a painting of the Nine Saints, and a collection of musical instruments used in church ceremonies.

A carefully guarded chapel in the church compound is said to contain the famous **Ark of the Covenant**. Don't think you can take a peek: just one specially chosen guardian has access to the Ark. And many the unfortunate onlooker who has 'burst into fire' just for getting close!

The little **museum** in the same building contains an unsurpassed collection of crowns belonging to former Ethiopian rulers. Neither the chapel nor the museum is open to women, but some of the crowns can be brought out by obliging priests; you should tip them afterwards. The chapel is not always open; try and get here early in the morning.

The huge **new church** of St Mary of Zion, which now dominates the Aksum skyline, may get the 'hideous carbuncle' prize from some. Haile Selassie, displaying his usual unusual taste, had it erected in the 1960s. It somewhat resembles public swimming baths. Beside it, a disproportionately tall bell tower, shaped to resemble the biggest stele of all, sprouts heavenwards.

In the church courtyard, as well as in various other spots around town, look out for the remains of the **old thrones** probably used for important ceremonial occasions and assemblies. Of the two dozen remaining, just the bases survive.

Archaeological Museum
አርኪዮሎጂ ሙ-ዚየም

The Archaeological Museum (open 8am-noon & 2pm-6pm daily) contains some fine and well-preserved ancient Sabaean and early Ge'ez **inscriptions** and an interesting variety of **objects found in tombs**, ranging from ordinary household objects such as drinking cups, lamps and incense burners, to quite sophisticated glassware including perfume bottles. There are also ancient amphorae imported from the Mediterranean.

Look out particularly for the collection of **Aksumite coins** dating from the 4th to 6th centuries AD (though those housed in the Ethnological Museum in Addis Ababa are finer).

Keep an eye out also for the beautiful lion **gargoyles**, and the charming **pot** shaped like

---

Aksumite Coins

Aksumite coinage provides a vital and fascinating source of information on the ancient kingdom. The coins bears the names, effigies and sometimes lineage of no fewer than 20 different kings, and probably served propagandist purposes.

Beautifully struck, the coins depict the royal crowns, clothing and jewellery of the kings – even the large earrings worn by some monarchs. A curiosity still unexplained by historians is the fact that almost all the coins are double-headed: on one side the king is depicted with his crown, on the other, he dons a modest head-cloth.

In the mid-1990s a find near the little town of Hastings in southern England caused a mild sensation: an original Aksumite bronze coin was unearthed. In fact, the coin almost certainly arrived on English shores not through ancient trade with Britain, but through modern tourism.

---

a three-legged bird. Much of the pottery was produced in ancient Aksum and the tradition continues today.

Posted in each room are a series of interesting information panels prepared by an Italian archaeological team. The free guided tours (15 to 20 minutes) are comprehensive though not wildly inspiring; tips are expected.

Ezana Garden
ኢዛና መናፈሻ

Lying in a garden or park in the centre of town is the famous stone of the 4th-century King Ezana. Ezana's kingdom stretched from eastern Sudan all the way to modern-day Yemen across the Red Sea.

It may not look much, but the stone is of great historical value. The inscription records the honorary titles and military victories of the king over his 'enemies and rebels'. In ancient Aksumite time, it was placed by the roadside at the eastern entrance of the town. When the Italians widened the road in the 1930s, the stone was moved to its present location.

The stone's significance lies in the fact that the inscription is written in three ancient scripts (Sabaean, Ge'ez and Greek) like a kind of Ethiopian Rosetta stone, as well as recording the king's conversion to Christianity. The inscribed stone is actually one of several in Aksum.

ETHIOPIA

King Bazen's Tomb
የንጉስ ባዜን መቃብር

In contrast to the beautifully dressed blocks used to construct the tombs of the kings in the stelae fields, King Bazen's tomb is hewn out of solid rock, perhaps suggesting that it may be older. According to local tradition, the king is thought to have reigned at the time of the birth of Christ.

Sixteen rock-hewn steps lead down towards an arched doorway. Around a central room, there are four main burial chambers.

Near the entrance to the tomb, look out for the rock-hewn rectangular pit containing a row of smaller burial chambers (including a few which appear to be unfinished). Judging from the number of tombs and stelae found in the area, the burial site may once have been quite large and important.

The Queen of Sheba

Ethiopia's most famous legend is that of the Queen of Sheba. According to the *Kebra Negast* (Ethiopia's national epic), the Ethiopian queen once undertook a long journey to visit the wise King Solomon of Israel.

At the great palace, Solomon assured the queen that he would take nothing from her so long as she took nothing from him. However, the crafty king had placed at her bedside a glass of water. During the night, awaking thirsty after the spicy food served to her, the queen reached for a drink.

Solomon wasted little time demanding his side of the deal, and the queen returned to Ethiopia carrying his child, the future king Menelik.

Menelik later visited his father in Jerusalem, but as he left the Holy Land, he made off with the Ark of the Covenant (it seems Solomon got his comeuppance after all). He returned with it to Ethiopia, where he later established a dynasty that would reign for the next 3000 years.

Though there are serious anachronisms in the legend – the queen is thought to have lived a thousand years before this period – many Ethiopians believe it passionately, at least in parts. Haile Selassie himself, the last Ethiopian emperor, claimed direct descent from King Solomon, and therefore the divine right to rule.

Queen of Sheba's Bath
የንግስት ሳባ መዋኛ

Though impressive for its sheer size, this reservoir, hewn out of solid rock, is thought to postdate the queen by at least a millennium! Still, it remains an outstanding piece of ancient engineering. For the ancient Aksumites, it was an important source of water. Today, local women come to fetch water and wash clothes. Locals claim that the waters are cursed; local boys occasionally drown here.

The reservoir is bowl-shaped and measures around 67m in diameter and 5m in depth. A broad dyke is formed by the curving part of the bank, which is supported on the inside by a wall of small, dry stones.

Ta'akha Maryam
ተኣካ ማርያም

Early excavations revealed that Ta'akha Maryam was a magnificent palace, probably dating from the 4th or 5th century AD. Unfortunately, much of the stone has been removed. What did remain was as good as obliterated in 1937 when the Italians cut a road straight through it.

Today, little more than a few piles of rubble and a couple of dressed blocks of stone remain, strewn about on each side of the road.

Covering a vast area of some 120m by 80m, Ta'akha Maryam would have been far larger than medieval European palaces of the time, and contained at least 50 rooms. Encircling the whole complex was a huge stone wall reinforced with towers. Monumental stairs on the north and south sides led to the main entrances of the building, which would have comprised at least one storey.

Dungur (Queen of Sheba's Palace)
ዱንጉር (የንግስት ሳባ ቤተ መንግስት)

The structure at Dungur, popularly known as the Queen of Sheba's Palace, is similar to Ta'akha Maryam, but much better preserved (though smaller), and fully excavated (in places rather clumsily restored).

The architectural style – the small undressed stones set in a timber framework with the walls recessed at intervals and tapering with height – are typically Aksumite. The **stairwells** suggest the existence of at least one upper storey. The well-preserved **flagstone floor** is thought to have belonged to a throne room. The palace also contains a private bathing area and a kitchen, where two large **brick ovens** can still be seen.

Despite the colourful legends, archaeologists now date the palace to some 1500 years after the Queen of Sheba's time in the 10th century BC, to around the 6th or 7th century AD.

Tombs of Kings Kaleb & Gebre Meskel

On a small hill 1.8km from town lie two monumental tombs. Lying side by side, they are attributed to the 6th-century King Kaleb and his successor, King Gebre Meskel. Kaleb was one of Aksum's most important rulers; he succeeded in bringing southern Arabia under Aksumite rule.

The tombs are a great example of the sheer sophistication of Aksumite architecture and building techniques. The 19th-century British traveller Theodore Bent exclaimed magnanimously that the tombs were 'built with a regularity which if found in Greece would at once make one assign them to a good period'!

The tombs are similar in design. A steep stairway leads into the interior, which is constructed with massive and beautifully dressed slabs of stone that fit perfectly against one another. Each has been worked individually to fit its place.

King Gebre Meskel's tomb, which consists of one chamber and five rooms, is a little more sophisticated and better preserved than that of King Kaleb. Look out for the three sarcophagi (one broken into four pieces, probably by robbers) contained in one room and the exceptionally finely carved portal which leads into it.

Ask your guide – if you have one – to shine a torch on the carvings in relief of several crosses inside the tombs and on one of the sarcophagi. Similar to the Christian crosses found on Aksumite coins, these may provide some clue to the dating of the tombs – perhaps around the 6th century (which, very interestingly, corresponds with the local tradition).

Above ground, a kind of raised 'courtyard' combines the two tombs. Some scholars have suggested that two parallel churches with a basilica plan lay here, probably postdating the tombs.

According to local sources, 5000 elephants were used to transport the great blocks of these structures.

A visit is well worthwhile and involves a lovely walk through the *tef* (cereal grass) fields that have been cultivated here for millennia.

The walk will also take you through the side of Aksum, where the 'other half' lived: the workers, farmers and craftsmen. Just as important and as fascinating as the great palaces and tombs, the area is only now receiving attention from archaeologists.

There are also good views to be had from close to the tombs: southwards over Aksum, north towards Eritrea, and east to the distinct jagged profile of the mountains of Adwa.

King Ezana's Inscription

On the way up to the tombs of Kings Kaleb and Gebre Meskel, you'll pass a little shack containing a remarkable find stumbled upon by a farmer in 1981. It was another trilingual inscription dating from King Ezana's time and giving thanks to God for conquests in Saudi Arabia. It is almost identical to the inscription in King Ezana's Garden and dates from between AD 330 and 350.

The inscription apparently contains a curse: 'the person who should dare to move the tablet will meet an untimely death'. The tablet remains exactly where it was found! You should tip the guardian a small amount for opening the hut.

Abba Pentalewon & Abba Liqanos Monasteries

Around 2km from the tombs of Kings Kaleb and Gebre Meskel lies the Abba Pentalewon Monastery, thought to date from the 6th century. It's open to men only, but some fine illuminated **manuscripts** and **church regalia** (such as metal crosses, censers and sistra) can be brought out by the priests. Admission costs Birr20.

From Abba Pentalewon, it's around 20 minutes by foot to the Abba Liqanos Monastery (which contains similar religious paraphernalia). Ask to see the so-called crowns of King Kaleb and Gebre Meskel. The church is also open to men only, but boasts excellent views of the surrounding countryside.

Neither church is a must-see, but the walk to them is pleasant.

Arbatu Ensessa Church

The little church of Arbatu Ensessa boasts some interesting and colourful **murals** and church regalia. More importantly, it provides a good example of traditional architecture.

Ethnographical Museum

Keen to conserve the old ways of living, an elderly woman has recently opened her home to visitors. The house is a showcase of eclectic arts and crafts (from the proprietor's wedding dress to fine basketry and other household objects), and gives a tangible glimpse into life 'in the old days'. Admission is free, but you should leave a contribution towards upkeep (Birr10 is fair). The house lies right next door to Arbatu Ensessa Church.

Lioness of Gobedra

Though often overlooked by visitors, the mysterious lioness, around 3km west of the city (7km from the centre) off the Gonder road, is worth a visit. It is etched on one of the large fallen rocks that cover the slopes of Gobedra.

Measuring 3.27m from nose to tail, it prowls across the southern face of the boulder. Look out for the cross etched in the rock around 50cm in front of the jaws of the animal (and which probably dates from a later period).

It is not known who is responsible for the work, nor why a lioness is depicted on this spot. According to local tradition, the Archangel Mikael fought a tremendous battle with the beast. However, goodness prevailed and the saint, mustering all his force, threw the animal against the rock with such violence that its outline lies imprinted on the stone forever.

It's quite a rough walk from the road over boulders and through scrub, and you'll need a guide or one of the – all too willing – local children to help you find it.

The Lost City

Aksum's relatively rapid decline and disappearance is still a mystery, though many explanations have been offered.

The environmental argument suggests that Aksum's ever-increasing population led to overcropping of the land, deforestation and eventually soil erosion. The climatic explanation claims that a kind of 'global warming' took place, which finished Aksum's agriculture and led eventually to drought and famine. The military argument claims that Aksum was undermined by continual incursions from neighbouring tribes, such as the Beja from the northwest of the country.

According to the traditional explanation, Aksumite power was usurped around the 9th century by the dreaded warrior queen, Gudit (or Judit), a Pagan or Jew, who killed the ruling king, burnt down the city and sabotaged the stelae. Intriguingly, this legend seems to be born out by at least two documents written at about this time.

Ancient Quarries

Near the lioness, at a site on Gobedra Hill known as Wuchate Golo, have a look for the ancient quarries, where much granite for the **stelae** was cut. Mystery still surrounds the tools that were used by the master craftsmen of Aksum, but you can see clearly, in one area, the process by which they cut the hard stone from the rock. After the intended break was mapped out, a row of rectangular sockets were cut. Wooden wedges were next inserted into the sockets and made to expand either by the use of water, by percussion or by hammering in metal wedges, which caused the rock to fracture.

In another place, you'll see a stele almost completely freed from the rock, but strangely abandoned. It's a fascinating place.

Places to Stay

Aksum suffers from water shortages so don't waste what little there is.

Sheferoch Hotel *(rooms Birr12)* is rock-bottom, but clean.

Bazen Hotel *(☎ 75 02 98; rooms with hot shared shower Birr20-25)* is cheap but clean.

Ghenet Hotel *(☎ 75 22 17; doubles/twins Birr25/50, with private shower Birr50)* is the best bet in this price range.

Kaleb Hotel *(☎ 75 22 22; doubles/twins Birr30/40, with private hot shower Birr50/70)* is a peaceful place set in a grassy compound. Discounts of Birr5 to Birr10 are offered for students with ID.

Africa Hotel *(☎ 753700; e africaho@telecom .net.et; doubles/twins Birr20/30, with private shower Birr50/70)* is clean, well run and good value. It has a pleasant garden/courtyard.

Ark Hotel *(☎ 75 26 76; singles/doubles/ twins with bathroom Birr75/80/100)* is a new, comfortable and pleasant middle-range hotel.

Axum Touring Hotel *(☎ 75 02 05; singles/ doubles with bathroom US$24/36)* is an old Italian *albergo* set in attractive gardens. The rooms are overpriced, and the plumbing looks its age, but discounts are readily available.

Remhai Hotel *(☎ 75 15 01, fax 75 28 94; singles Birr119-170, doubles Birr153-221, suites Birr340)* is a large, new hotel. Rooms have satellite TV and telephones, and a swimming pool is planned.

Yeha Hotel *(☎ 75 23 78, fax 75 23 82; singles/doubles/suites US$37.50/50/75)* can seem a little lugubrious. Like its state-owned brothers, the Tana Hotel in Bahar Dar and the Goha Hotel in Gonder, its best asset is its location – on a hill overlooking town.

Places to Eat & Drink

The evening draws to a close early in Aksum. Make sure you eat before 8pm. Hotels can prepare picnics which you can enjoy among the ruins.

Habesha Restaurant, set in a simple but attractive *tukul*, serves good local food. Try the *zilzil tibs* (fried strips of beef).

Sheferoch Hotel is popular locally and is known for its *kitfo* (raw or warmed minced beef) and raw meat.

Marta Hotel is another local favourite.

Axum Touring Hotel offers quite respectable three-course *faranji* menus for Birr23. The garden is a good place for breakfast or an evening drink.

Yeha Hotel has a three-course set dinner for Birr28.75. Its terrace is also good for breakfast (Birr12 for continental, Birr18 for full) or – even better – a drink at sunset; a soft drink costs Birr5, a beer Birr6.60.

Mini Pastry has a good selection of pastries and fruit juices (Birr3). The little garden is a pleasant spot for breakfast. At night it transforms itself into a bar. **Vanilla Cafeteria** is also good.

Café Abyssinia, right in front of the hospital, is a new place and already a firm local favourite, serving as café, bar and restaurant. Good Ethiopian and *faranji* mains cost from Birr8 to Birr12.

Seek out the **tella beat** (local beer houses) in the tiny streets around town; they're great places for Tigrayan dancing. The locals will help you find one.

Getting There & Away

Ethiopian Airlines (☎ 75 23 00) has one or two flights daily to Addis Ababa via Lalibela, Gonder and Bahar Dar (then does the route in reverse). There are three flights weekly to Mekele.

For buses to Gonder, Debark and the Simien Mountains, you'll need to go to Shire first. One bus (Birr10, two hours) and two minibuses (Birr15) depart daily. One bus runs daily to Mekele (Birr27.60, eight to nine hours), and one to Adigrat (Birr20, five hours).

For Adwa, more than 10 minibuses ply the route daily (Birr5, 30 minutes). For Debre Damo see that section. For Yeha, a contract minibus should cost around Birr400 to Birr450 (around two hours).

The border crossing to Asmara in Eritrea is currently closed, but two buses used to run daily (Birr25, six hours).

Getting Around

A taxi to the new airport, 7km from town, costs Birr40, or Birr10 'shared'. Wait under the tree in the square opposite the old palace.

Taxis elsewhere charge foreigners from Birr5 to Birr10 for short hops; longer journeys cost Birr8 to Birr15, and further afield Birr20 to Birr25. To hire a taxi for a half day costs around Birr100 low season, Birr150 high season; for a full day Birr150 low season, Birr250 in the high season. Negotiate the rate.

Garis cost around Birr2 to Birr5 for short journeys, Birr20 per hour, or Birr50 for half a day. For Dungur they cost Birr15; for the Lioness of Gobedra they cost Birr20. Again, you'll need to negotiate hard.

If you're short of time and want to make day trips to Yeha, cars can be hired from the local travel agencies if you make arrangements in advance in Addis Ababa (see the Aksum map for their locations). The tourist office can also help you find (unofficial) local operators, as well as privately owned vehicles (usually minibuses and 4WDs with driver).

Full-day city tours of Aksum (including all sites) cost from Birr300, tours to Yeha cost Birr400 to Birr600, and to Debre Damo Birr800 to Birr1000. A three-day tour of the rock-hewn churches of Tigray costs Birr2300 to Birr3000. Prices are for the whole vehicle; try and find a group. These tours are organised through the unofficial, local operators.

Bicycles (Birr6 per hour) can be hired from diagonally opposite the King Ezana Hotel.

ADWA

አድዋ

☎ 08 • pop 24,519 • elevation 1907m

Like Aksum, unassuming, urban Adwa belies its status. For Ethiopians, the town holds huge significance. It was in the hills surrounding Adwa that the Emperor Menelik II inflicted the biggest defeat ever on a colonial army in Africa and Ethiopia was saved from colonisation (see the boxed text 'The Battle of Adwa').

Though Adwa is a pleasant enough town, there's not much to see here besides a couple of churches (the Selassie Church contains some good murals), but you may want to use the town as a base from which to visit Yeha or Debre Damo.

About 11km east of Adwa is the **monastery of Abba Garima**, said to have been founded by one of the Nine Saints in the 6th century. The monastery is known for its collection of religious artefacts including three illuminated gospels from the 10th century, thought to number among the oldest extant manuscripts in the country. It makes a great day's hike (around six hours' walk), but bring lots of water and food.

Teferi Hotel (*☎ 71 18 28; rooms without/ with shared shower Birr25/35*) is a good bet if you get stuck in Adwa. It's right next door to the bus station.

Around 10 minibuses daily ply the route between Adwa and Aksum (Birr5, 30 minutes). For Adigrat (Birr15, three hours) three to four buses run daily. For Yeha, catch a bus to Enticcio (four or five run daily), and ask to be dropped off at the signpost for Yeha (Birr6, 30 to 40 minutes) on the main Adwa–Adigrat road. From there it's a 5km walk. Go early to be sure of return transport, and bring water and a hat – the walk is very hot and dusty. Contract taxis cost around Birr200 to Birr300 to Yeha and Birr400 to Birr500 to Debre Damo.

YEHA
 የሃ

Yeha (*admission Birr50, video cameras Birr100*), 58km northeast of Adwa, is a little-visited but very peaceful and evocative spot. Of all Ethiopia's historical sites, Yeha is perhaps the most enigmatic. The journey there also takes you through some attractive Tigrayan scenery. Food and drink are not readily available so bring your own.

Yeha was Ethiopia's first known capital, and is considered the birthplace of the country's earliest civilisation. It is believed to have been established by colonists from southern Arabia. The immense, windowless, sandstone walls of the ruins do indeed look like something straight out of Yemen, and, in the late afternoon light, the fawn-coloured temple could easily feature in a David Roberts painting. You can get here via Aksum or Adwa (see Getting There & Away under those headings).

Things to See

Apart from the massive walls of a pre-Christian, so-called **temple**, little remains of the old capital. Yet Yeha's ruins are impressive for their sheer age, dating from around the 5th century BC – some experts have dated them as early as the 8th century BC – and for their stunning construction. Some of the sandstone building blocks of the temple measure over 3m in length and are so perfectly dressed and fitted together – without a trace of mortar – that it's impossible to insert so much as a 5c coin between them. The whole temple is a grid of perfect lines and geometry.

The Battle of Adwa

In September 1895, as the rains began to dwindle, the Emperor Menelik II issued a decree: All the able-bodied men of his empire should gather together and await his arrival at fixed points across the country. Once assembled, the vast army began its march north; behind it trundled 40 cannons, as well as mules with 100,000 rifles on their backs. In the north, the Italians were ready.

In the initial skirmishes that followed, the Ethiopians succeeded in capturing the Italian strongholds at Amba Alage and Enda Iyesus. However, because of the serious shortage of food, the two sides agreed to sue for peace. Yet the Italians continued to insist on Italy's protectorate claim, and an agreement could not be reached.

In February 1896 Crispi, the Italian prime minister, sent his famous telegram to General Baratieri. In it he declared the motherland was 'ready for any sacrifice to save the honour of the army and the prestige of the monarchy'.

Four days later, at dawn, the Italians made a surprise attack. Stumbling in the darkness over difficult terrain, with inaccurate maps and with no communication between the three offensive brigades, the attack was a disaster. Menelik, whose spies had long before informed him of the forthcoming attack, was ready to meet the Italians on every front. A thunderous artillery duel followed, then a bout of fierce fighting.

Nearly half the Italian fighting force was wiped out – over 6000 soldiers – and of the five Italian field commanders, three were killed, one was wounded, and another was captured. Finally, laying down their arms, the Italians ran. Though the Ethiopians had lost almost equal numbers, the day was clearly theirs.

To this day the battle of Adwa is celebrated annually and, like the Battle of Hastings in Britain or the War of Independence in America, it is the one date every Ethiopian child can quote.

Near the temple is the modern **Church of Abuna Aftse**, which replaced a church dating from the 6th century. Inside, there is a little 'museum', containing an outstanding collection of beautifully incised ancient Sabaean inscriptions, believed to originate from the temple, as well as some good (and unusually large) **manuscripts** and silver and gold crosses.

Incorporated into the walls of the church are stones removed from the original temple. In the west wall, look out for the famous and exceptional **relief of ibexes**, stylised and with lowered horns; the ibex was a sacred animal of southern Arabia. The National Museum in Addis Ababa contains many other important finds unearthed at Yeha.

Nearby lie various other ruins including, 200m to the northeast, the remains of a monumental structure known as **Grat Beal Gebri**, distinguished for its unusual, square-sectioned, monolithic pillars (such features are also found in the Temple of the Moon in Ma'rib in Yemen). Important rock-hewn tombs have also been found in the vicinity.

DEBRE DAMO
ደብረ ዳሞ

Around 86km northeast of Aksum lies one of the most important religious sites in Ethiopia. Debre Damo (open to male visitors only) dates back to Aksumite times and the reign of King Gebre Meskel, successor to King Kaleb. It boasts the oldest standing church in the country, and is the best surviving example of the ancient Aksumite building style. The monastery's exact age, however, is the subject of endless debate, since the buildings have been repeatedly rebuilt.

The monastery is equally famous for its position, perched on a 2800m-high *amba* or flat-topped mountain surrounded on all sides by vertical cliffs. How the solid stones of the monastery were carted up has also been the subject of much speculation.

According to local tradition, the monastery was founded by Abuna Aregawi, one of the Nine Saints of the 6th century, with a little help from a snake (see the boxed text 'Know Your Ethiopian Saints' earlier).

During Aksumite times, the place was used – in the Ethiopian way – to coop up excess male members of the royal family, who might have posed a threat to the reigning monarch.

Some 80 monks live in the monastery, which comprises a total area of around half a square kilometre. The inhabitants are entirely

---

Rope Tricks

Access up the 24m-high rock face to the monastery is by rope – in fact two ropes. One is tied around your waist and is used by the monks above to assist in trying to hoist you up; the second is fixed to the rock, and you use it in combination with the footholds to scramble up. The priests use just the second rope and flash up like spiders. See also the boxed text 'Toeholds in Tigray' later in this chapter.

The ascent is not difficult, but requires some nerve and a bit of biceps. Women are not allowed to visit the monastery, but the priests may let you have a dangle on the rope if you really want to. Shouts of '*becka, becka!*' (enough!) will soon make it clear you've come far enough!

---

self-sufficient (though gifts of coffee, sugar or honey are greatly appreciated), and even have their own livestock, and reservoirs of water hewn deep into the cliff.

For male travellers, a visit to Debre Damo is well worthwhile, and gives you an idea of the extraordinary artistic heritage Ethiopia might have had, had it not been for the devastation of the Muslim–Christian wars. An admission fee of Birr60 is now charged.

If you get stuck here, men can spend the night at the monastery, and women can find accommodation with the nuns at the foot of the monastery.

Things to See

From the top of the monastery there are great **views** over the countryside all the way to Eritrea. The largest of the two **churches**, located in the easternmost part of the *amba*, is especially remarkable as an almost prototypical example of Aksumite architecture. One window, with its wooden tracery, is virtually a replica of that depicted in stone on the largest of the Aksumite stelae. Look out for the famous Aksumite **frieze** – a row of false window openings constructed of wood. Also notable are the beams and ceiling, famously decorated with carved **wooden panels** depicting Ethiopian wild animals such as elephants, lions, gazelles, rhinos, giraffes and snakes. Various recent **paintings** can be seen too.

The monastery has long been used as a safeguard for religious treasures. It now has an outstanding collection of at least 50

ETHIOPIA

illuminated manuscripts, among them the oldest surviving fragments in the country, though they are rarely brought out to visitors (don't insist).

At the base of the cliff, look out for the minute **caves** still inhabited by seven hermits (two of them women). They rely entirely on the food and water brought to them from the monastery and the village.

Getting There & Away

There is currently no public transport to Debre Damo. Buses travelling the Aksum–Adigrat road pass by the junction to Debre Damo. Ask to be dropped off here (5km southeast of the village of Bizet if you're travelling from Adwa to Adigrat). From there it's an 11km uphill and quite strenuous walk to Debre Damo (around three hours). To avoid the heat of the day, travel early, and bring lots of water and a hat – it gets very hot and dusty.

There's a bus stop close to the junction. Wait there to catch a bus on the way back. Note that you'll probably have to spend the night at Debre Damo (as the last bus will have gone). The best option is to get a group together and hire a 4WD from Aksum and make a day trip of it, departing from Aksum at around 6am and returning via Yeha at around 5pm. Cheaper, if there are a few of you, is a contract minibus (Birr700 to Birr800); this can take you as far as the river, from where you walk the remaining 4km to 5km.

ADIGRAT
አዲግራት

☎ 04 • pop 37,417 • elevation 2473m

Adigrat is the largest town in Tigray after Mekele, and is situated on what was, until recently, an important junction linking Ethiopia with Eritrea. It lacks any must-see attractions, but makes a useful and pleasant enough stop-off point to or from Aksum, and additionally makes a good base from which to explore some of the northern rock-hewn churches of Tigray.

Things to See

If you're filling in time, a couple of churches are worth a peek: the 19th-century **Adigrat Chirkos** south of the town centre, and the 20th-century **Medhane Alem** in the north of town.

The large dome on the skyline belongs to the **Holy Saviour Catholic cathedral**. Completed in 1916, it's Italian-designed, but with a distinctly Ethiopian flavour. Look out for the paintings by Afewerk Tekle.

There's also a peaceful **Italian war cemetery** 4km north of town on the Asmara road. It commemorates some 765 Italian soldiers, many of them *caduti ignoti* (the unknown fallen) of 1935–38.

The **market** is also worth a wander. Look out for the locally produced pale honey, and the *beles* (prickly pears), which cost just Birr1 for 10; they're deliciously refreshing.

Travelling south from Adigrat, look out for the attractive Tigrayan stone farmsteads

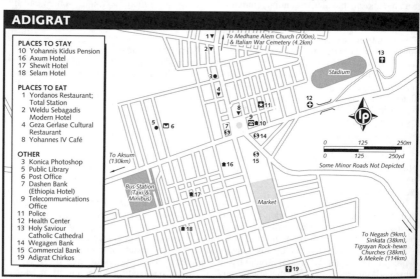

ADIGRAT

PLACES TO STAY
10 Yohannis Kidus Pension
16 Axum Hotel
17 Shewit Hotel
18 Selam Hotel

PLACES TO EAT
1 Yordanos Restaurant;
  Total Station
2 Weldu Sebagadis
  Modern Hotel
4 Geza Gerlase Cultural
  Restaurant
8 Yohannes IV Café

OTHER
3 Konica Photoshop
5 Public Library
6 Post Office
7 Dashen Bank
  (Ethiopia Hotel)
9 Telecommunications
  Office
11 Police
12 Health Center
13 Holy Saviour
  Catholic Cathedral
14 Wegagen Bank
15 Commercial Bank
19 Adigrat Chirkos

To Medhane Alem Church (700m),
& Italian War Cemetery (4.2km)

Stadium

To Aksum
(130km)

Bus Station
(Taxi &
Minibus)

Market

0   125   250m
0   125   250yd
Some Minor Roads Not Depicted

To Negash (9km),
Sinkata (38km),
Tigrayan Rock-hewn
Churches (38km),
& Mekele (114km)

with their **dry-stone walls**. The houses have few windows; those they do have are small to keep the interior cool.

Places to Stay & Eat

Yohannis Kidus Pension *(☎ 45 02 84; rooms with shared shower Birr12-15)* is the best budget hotel. Look for the sign 'Pension'.

Axum Hotel *(☎ 45 23 56; rooms with shared shower Birr12-15)* makes a good second choice.

Selam Hotel *(☎ 45 03 85; rooms with hot shared shower Birr20)* is simple but clean.

Shewit Hotel *(☎ 45 30 28; singles/doubles Birr40/60, with hot shower Birr60/80)* has quite good, clean rooms.

Yohannes IV Café is the best place for a snack, cake, breakfast or a fruit juice. A new Yohannes IV Hotel should open soon and promises to be the best in town. Ask here for progress and directions.

Yordanos Restaurant is new and modern, serving local (Birr8 to Birr15) and *faranji* fare (including pizzas Birr25 to Birr30).

Weldu Sebagadis Modern Hotel is a favourite local place. Try the speciality, *ta'ilo* (a sorghum-made dough dipped in spicy meat and tomato sauce).

Geza Gerlase Cultural Restaurant offers great local food in a great local setting – a large, well-decorated *tukul*.

Getting There & Away

At least 10 buses run daily to Mekele (Birr13.15, around 2½ to three hours); two to three go to Aksum (Birr15.65, four to five hours); one bus goes daily to Shire (Birr25, five to six hours). For Addis Ababa, go to Mekele first. For Wukro (Birr8, 1½ hours) and Negash (Birr8, 1½ hours), take the Mekele bus.

Minibuses run to Sinkata (Birr5, one hour), Daga Hamus (Birr3, 30 minutes) and Wukro (Birr10, 1½ hours).

When the border with Eritrea was open, two buses ran daily to Asmara (Birr23, seven hours).

NEGASH

ነጋሽ

On a small hill around 10km north of Wukro is the tiny town of Negash, which, like Aksum and Adwa, belies its prestigious past.

Negash was the first site of Muslim settlement in Ethiopia. Fleeing persecution in Saudi Arabia in Mohammed's own lifetime, a community of Muslims took refuge here. The current mosque is said to stand on the site of the 7th-century original. An ancient cemetery, also believed to date from the 7th century, was found recently.

Every year an important festival takes place at Negash, attracting pilgrims from all around. Just 3% of Tigray is Muslim; the little mosque sits amid a sea of Christian churches.

The basic **Negash Hotel** *(rooms with bucket shower Birr10)* is the best bet.

Minibuses that ply the route between Adigrat and Mekele stop here.

ROCK-HEWN CHURCHES OF TIGRAY

Far less famous than their prestigious cousins in Lalibela, the **rock-hewn churches of Tigray** are no less significant or interesting.

Some of the churches may even predate those at Lalibela, and possibly represent a crucial link between Aksum and Lalibela – chronologically, artistically and technically. The architectural features, though less perfect than at Lalibela, where the rock-hewing tradition reached its zenith, are just as remarkable and intriguing.

Between the Tigrayan towns of Adigrat and Mekele lie a veritable rash of churches. It is still unknown exactly how many exist – at least 120 at the last count. Unlike many of the churches of Lalibela, which were carved out of the ground, the Tigrayan churches are generally sculpted into cliff faces or into pre-existing caves.

Many are pretty inaccessible; it's thought that security was the major concern. In other words, the more remote the church was, the better its chance of survival. Visiting some churches involves quite a steep climb; visiting others involves a scramble up almost sheer rock faces using just footholds in the rock.

All this somehow adds to the churches' attraction. To come across an absolute jewel

---

Heavenly Visions

One day, St Gabriel appeared in a dream to a farmer. The saint commanded the man to build a new church that would replace the old one, and gave his messenger careful instructions as to its location and construction.

Yet another Ethiopian legend? Yes, only the day in question was in 1982, and the 'new church' replaced the current one of Petros & Paulos, near Sinkata. In Ethiopia, legends are made every day.

hidden for centuries in the mountains, after a long and arduous toil through the arid and rocky landscape of Tigray, makes for a very rewarding excursion. For those who want to combine trekking with terrific art and history, this may be just the ticket. The Tigrayan churches may well prove to be Orthodox Ethiopia's best-kept secret.

History

Right up until the mid-1960s, the churches were almost unknown outside Tigray – even to Ethiopians. Even today very little is known about their origins, their history or the architects who designed them.

Local tradition attributes most of the churches to the 4th-century Aksumite kings, Abreha and Atsbeha, as well as to the 6th-century rulers. The first historians to visit the churches placed them in a period no earlier than the 11th or 12th century.

Currently, the most popular thinking is that they date from between the 9th and 15th centuries, though some argue for both before and after these dates. There are few documentary records, and little research has yet been carried out. However, it is almost certain that many do indeed predate their more famous and glamorous cousins in Lalibela.

Much work remains to be done on the churches. Sadly, many are in a very sorry state of repair and are rapidly deteriorating further; in places, seepage is ruining the frescoes. In the next two years, Abraha Atsbeha, Petros & Paulos and Debre Tsion Abraham should undergo restoration.

Orientation & Information

Mekele makes the best base from which to explore the churches. The helpful staff at the Tigray Tourism Commission in Mekele can advise on itineraries (see Mekele following). By the end of 2003, a new tourism office should have opened in Wukro, where guides will be available (Birr50 to Birr75 per day plus tips if guiding outside Wukro).

The brochure *Tigrai: The Open-Air Museum*, has a small map on the back and a brief description of the churches. A new map of both Mekele and Tigray (including the churches) is being prepared by the Tourism Commission. Little other information exists. Ivy Pearce and David R Buxton have written on the churches following visits there; the Tourism Commission can give references.

Guides (available through Mekele travel agencies – see under Getting There & Around later) are essential, not only to locate the remoter churches, but also to act as interpreters for tracking down the often elusive priests, keepers of the all-important church keys. The Tourist Commission recommends a daily fee of Birr150 to Birr200 for guides.

Many of the churches are located in groups, referred to as 'clusters'. The most famous clusters are Gheralta, Takatisfi, Tembien and Atsbi. The Gheralta cluster is considered the most important (with the highest number of churches), and the Takatisfi cluster is the most accessible (around 3km east of the Mekele–Adigrat road).

Churches are supposed to charge Birr20 for admission. If you're asked for more, simply hand over Birr20, firmly but politely. Don't forget, however, that a small tip or donation after a trip is usual and greatly appreciated.

CHURCHES OF TIGRAY

1	Petros & Paulos	11	Yohannes Maequdi
2	Mikael Milhaizengi	12	Debre Tsion Abraham
3	Medhane Alem Kesho	13	Dugem Selassie
4	Zarema Giyorgis	14	Giyorgis Debre Mahar
5	Cherkos (Agobo)	15	Maryam Korkor & Daniel
6	Debre Selam		Korkor
7	Mikael Imba	16	Abuna Yemata Guh
8	Mikael Barka	17	Abuna Gebre Mikael
9	Chirkos	18	Gebriel Wukien
10	Abraha Atsbeha	19	Abba Yohanni

To Asmara (Eritrea)
(border currently closed)

· · · · · · Scenic Route
=== Unfinished Road
- - - Broken Road

To Adwa (22km)
& Aksum (46km)   Debre Damo

Yeha

Adigrat   Edaga Hamus

Edaga Arbi

Nebelet   Sinkata   Takatisfi Cluster

Hawsien   Teka Tesfay   Atsbi Cluster
Megab   Gheralta Cluster   Negash
Tembien Cluster   Dugem   Wukro Cluster   Atsbi

Workamba

Abi Addi

Hagere Selan

Abi Agbe   Abraha Atsbeha   Wukro

Agula

Mai Makdem

Mekele   Airport

Quiha

0   15   30km
0   10   20mi
Approximate Scale Only

Chelekot

Sekota   To the South

Many priests (who receive no salary) drop work in the fields to open churches for you; additionally the journeys there can be long and arduous. The tourist office recommends Birr5 to Birr10.

Good walking shoes are essential. Bring a torch, lots of small notes for tips and admission fees, and water. You'll also need a lot of patience. It can often take between 30 and 60 minutes to locate the priests, particularly during the rainy season.

Highlights

Abraha Atsbeha አብርሃ አጽብሃ (Gheralta) Said to date from the 10th century, this is a large cruciform church with interesting architectural features such as cruciform pillars and step capitals plus well-preserved 17th- and 18th-century murals. It's one of most accessible churches. It lies just off the road, halfway between Dugem and Wukro.

Abuna Yemata Guh አቡነ የማታ ጉህ (Gheralta) Is less impressive architecturally, but famous for its beautiful and well-preserved frescoes which adorn two cupolas. It has stunning views from the top and is well worth the climb. It lies around 4km west of Megab. The climb is considered the most challenging and takes one hour, using footholds up a sheer ascent for at least 20 minutes and crossing a narrow ledge.

Debre Tsion Abraham ደብረ ጽዮን አብርሃም (Gheralta) Rectangular in shape, with six massive freestanding pillars, this church is known for its diverse architectural features including decorated cupolas, bas-reliefs and carved crosses on the walls and ceiling. It also has beautiful, though faded and damaged, 16th-century murals and an unusual, large 15th-century ceremonial fan. It sits like a fortress on a hill about 500m south of Dugem; quite a steep 50-minute walk.

Maryam Korkor ማርያም ቆርቆር (Gheralta) This impressive, cross-shaped church is one of the largest in the area, known for its rich decoration – carving, architectural features (columns, arches and cupolas) and fine frescoes which cover its interior – and for its church treasures. The smaller Daniel Korkor Church, with less refined murals, is a few minutes away, and can also be visited. The church is around 500m from Megab and involves a fairly steep 50-minute ascent.

Dugem Selassie ዱገም ስላሴ (Gheralta) This tiny, older church lies within the newer one. Its large, double-tomb chamber has three 'shelves'; look out for the beautifully carved ceiling above the maqdas. It was probably converted to a church later. It's on the southern edge of the village of Dugem, just off the road.

Yohannes Maequdi ዮሃንስ መኹዳይ (Gheralta) This rectangular chapel has six freestanding pillars which support a ceiling carved with geometrical designs. It's best known for its well-preserved murals which cover the walls. From the village of Matari it's around a 40-minute walk (about 1km south of Dugem) via a steep footpath.

Abune Gebre Mikael አቡነ ገብረ ሚካኤል (Gheralta) Considered one of finest churches in the cluster, this church has a cruciform plan hewn into a dome-like rock. It features carefully carved columns, pillars, cupolas and arches, and four windows and two doors. It also has good frescoes covering the interior. It's around 15km south of Abuna Yemata Guh and requires a steep climb, negotiating a few obstacles on way.

Medhane Alem Kesho መድኃኔዓለም ኬሾ (Takatisfi) Also known as Adi Kesho, this is one of the oldest and finest churches in Tigray, known for its architectural features, particularly the elaborately carved coffered ceiling. It can be found 40 to 60 minutes' walk from Mikael Milhaizengi (see following).

Mikael Milhaizengi ሚካኤል ምልኃዘንጊ (Takatisfi) This tiny church is known for its carved ceiling and dome that is nearly 3m high; it is thought to date from the 8th century. It's around 15 to 20 minutes' walk from Petros & Paulos (see following).

Petros & Paulos ጴጥሮስ ና ጳውሎስ (Takatisfi) Only partly hewn, this church is built on a ledge and has delightful old murals, but is very rapidly deteriorating. From Wukro, or Adigrat, take a minibus to Teka Tesfay and walk about 3km from the junction. It's a five-minute climb to the church using footholds up one part.

Chirkos ጨርቆስ (Wukro) This is a three-quarter sandstone monolith, perhaps dating from the 8th century. It has very unusual and interesting architecture, with cubical capitals, an outstanding Aksumite frieze and a barrel-vaulted ceiling. It lies around 500m from Wukro and is the most easily accessible church.

Abba Yohanni አባ ዮሃኒ (Tembien) This church has a very impressive location set in a 300m-high sheer cliff face. It has a three-aisled and four-bayed interior, eight finely hewn cruciform pillars which support the ceiling, and 10 vaults. Interesting church treasures are kept here. It lies 15km from Abi Addi, including a 1km walk and a short climb with footholds.

Gebriel Wukien ገብርኤል ውቄን (Tembien) Architecturally interesting, this church has three aisles and four bays. It features well-carved, interesting details; six massive, finely hewn freestanding pillars and three cupolas. It's 16km northwest of Abi Addi and involves a 15-minute easy walk, then a 10-minute climb up a mountain.

Mikael Barka ሚካኤል ባርካ (Atsbi) This small church is shaped like a cross and probably dates from the 13th century. It is 17km from Wukro, and reaching it involves a 10-minute climb.

Mikael Imba ሚካኤል እምባ (Atsbi) This church has Aksumite features, some lovely barrel vaulting and a good view from the top. It's 9km south of Atsbi and has a quite easy 20-minute ascent with ladder.

Debre Selam ደብረ ሰላም (Atsbi) This is a 'church within a church'. It has exceptional architecture and paintings – look out for a beautiful carved arch leading into the maqdas. The setting is lovely and there are good views from the top. It's close to Atsbi and involves a quite easy 20-minute ascent.

Other churches that are architecturally interesting, and well worth visiting if you have time, are Giyorgis Debre Mahar and the church of Tekla Haimanot in Hawsien. Two newly 'discovered' churches in the Atsbi cluster are Cherkos at Agobo and Zarema Giyorgis. Enquire at the Tourist Commission in Mekele for details. All churches are marked on the map.

Places to Stay & Eat

Accommodation in the nearby villages is spartan to put it mildly; many are without electricity and have only limited supplies of water. Many are also noisy, the haunt of bar girls and sometimes flea-infested. The best option is to camp and to be fully self-sufficient.

In Wukro the **Fikra Selam** *(rooms without shower 12Birr)* is basic but clean and has a good restaurant.

In Hawsien the **Hawsien Hotel** *(rooms without shower Birr25)* is the only option; it's overpriced.

Megab has no hotels. **Fitsum's Buna Bet** *(3 basic rooms Birr8)* can accommodate and feed you.

Toeholds in Tigray

Though daunting at first sight, the ascents up rock faces required to reach some of the Tigrayan churches are not difficult if taken carefully. Just focus on the footholds, get a good grip, don't stop and don't look down. If you're having trouble, or finding that your nerves are getting the better of you, get someone to climb in front showing you the footholds. Sometimes the holds are very small, hewn by the bare feet of generations of priests. In which case, do as they do and take off your shoes. It's amazing the grip a toe can get!

In Sinkata, **Walwalu Hotel** *(singles/doubles Birr6/10)* is basic but fairly clean.

In Abi Addi, **Abyssinia Hotel** *(rooms with shared shower Birr15-20)* is adequate.

In Dugum, **Andenet Buna Bet** and **Abraha** can each provide basic rooms (for Birr20). By 2004, some tourist lodges should have opened.

In Atsbi, the new **Medre Genet** *(doubles with shared shower Birr20)* has small but decent rooms around a green compound. Food and boxed lunches (Birr3) can be ordered.

Abraha Atsebha has no hotels.

Getting There & Around

Many of the churches are in remote places – between 20km and 30km off the main road. A private vehicle is the easiest way of reaching them, and cuts down considerably on travel time between them. However, if you have camping equipment and lots of time, an exploration by bus and foot is both possible and very enjoyable (see also Getting There & Around in Mekele later).

Quite good gravel roads now connect the villages with most of the churches. New roads are planned for the future, such as linking Edaga Hagus with Atsbi (by 2006). Unfortunately, the road linking Megab with Abi Addi (shown on most maps) is currently impassable and there are no immediate plans to repair it.

The alternative is to take a tour, which solves the problem of organising transport and guides (see Organised Tours in the Getting Around chapter). A few tour operators can also be found in Mekele. **Goh Tour & Travel Agency** *(☎ 40 64 66, fax 40 26 48; e rasbisrat2002@yahoo.com)*, close to the Aksum Hotel, has a good reputation.

A guide's services cost Birr200 per day. On a three-day tour you could hope to see most of the churches in the Atsbi, Takatisfi and Gheralta clusters. On a four-day tour you could see the Tembien cluster too. Excursions to the Afar region can also be organised (minimum one week's notice required to organise permission papers), though car hire here is expensive (US$170 per day all-inclusive).

Hiring a 4WD costs Birr1000 to Birr1200 per day (all-inclusive with driver). Currently 4WD rental is not available in Adigrat. However, travel agents based in Addis Ababa and Mekele can arrange for a vehicle to meet you there.

If you can't afford either a tour or a vehicle, there are still around a dozen churches that can be easily reached with a combination of public transport and walking. The towns or villages of Adigrat, Mekele, Hawsien, Edaga Hamus, Wukro, Atsbi, Abi Addi and Sinkata are all served by minibuses. Some villages (such as Megab and Hawsien) are only well served on market days. If you can't coincide with a market day and you're desperate, you can always contract a minibus (usually Birr100 to Birr300 per day for the whole vehicle depending on distance). Ask at the town bus stations.

Although a 4WD will take you close to the churches, there's almost always a climb to the top of a hill or rock. The climbs are not especially difficult, but the gradients can be a little steep and some require short ascents up almost sheer rock faces, using just footholds in the rock. See the boxed text 'Toeholds in Tigray' earlier.

MEKELE
 መቀሌ

☎ 04 • pop 96,938 • elevation 2062m

Mekele, Tigray's capital, owes its importance to the Emperor Yohannes IV, who made it his capital in the late 19th century. For the traveller, it provides a useful base for visits to the nearby rock-hewn churches of Tigray.

The **Tigray Tourism Commission** (*☎/fax 40 10 32; e tigrai.tourism@telecom.net.et; Commercial Bank bldg, 5th floor; open 8.30am-12.30pm & 1.30pm-5.30pm Mon-Thur; 8.30am-12.30pm Fri*) can advise you on your itinerary.

There's Internet access (Birr0.75 per minute) at the **El Fami Business Center** (*open 8.30am-noon & 2pm-8.30pm daily*) beside the Aksum Hotel.

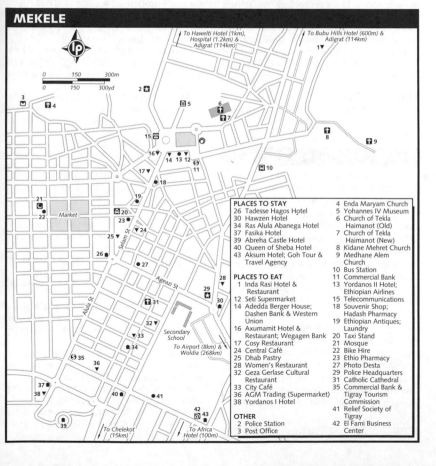

MEKELE

PLACES TO STAY
26 Tadesse Hagos Hotel
30 Hawzen Hotel
34 Ras Alula Abanega Hotel
37 Fasika Hotel
39 Abreha Castle Hotel
40 Queen of Sheba Hotel
43 Aksum Hotel; Goh Tour & Travel Agency

PLACES TO EAT
1 Inda Rasi Hotel & Restaurant
12 Seti Supermarket
14 Adedda Berger House; Dashen Bank & Western Union
16 Axumamit Hotel & Restaurant; Wegagen Bank
17 Cosy Restaurant
24 Central Café
25 Dhab Pastry
28 Women's Restaurant
32 Geza Gerlase Cultural Restaurant
33 City Café
36 AGM Trading (Supermarket)
38 Yordanos I Hotel

OTHER
2 Police Station
3 Post Office
4 Enda Maryam Church
5 Yohannes IV Museum
6 Church of Tekla Haimanot (Old)
7 Church of Tekla Haimanot (New)
8 Kidane Mehret Church
9 Medhane Alem Church
10 Bus Station
11 Commercial Bank
13 Yordanos II Hotel; Ethiopian Airlines
15 Telecommunications
18 Souvenir Shop; Hadash Pharmacy
19 Ethiopian Antiques; Laundry
20 Taxi Stand
21 Mosque
22 Bike Hire
23 Ethio Pharmacy
27 Photo Desta
29 Police Headquarters
31 Catholic Cathedral
35 Commercial Bank & Tigray Tourism Commission
41 Relief Society of Tigray
42 El Fami Business Center

Things to See

Like Adigrat, Mekele boasts little major sightseeing, but is nevertheless a pleasant town with good facilities and hotels.

The very lively **market** is definitely worth a stroll, particularly on Saturday, the main market day – get there by 10am. Look out for the salt bars brought in by camel from the Danakil Desert, and sawn into little blocks (see the boxed text 'Salt for Gold'); Mekele's market is the largest market for salt in the country.

The **spice market** (within the main market) is also interesting. A large variety of roots, bark and herbs is used in traditional medicine.

The Italian-designed **Yohannes IV museum** was built for the emperor in 1873 and gives a good overview of the sites and points of interest in the region. It also houses furniture and manuscripts that date from the days of the emperor. From the roof, there's quite a good view of Mekele. In 2001 a significant collection of Ethiopian manuscripts, crosses and icons (that had formed part of a private collection in France) were handed over to the Tigray Cultural Association. They're now on display here.

Places to Stay

Queen of Sheba Hotel (☎ 40 13 87; singles/doubles with shared hot shower Birr15/20) is basic but spotless.

Salt for Gold

Since earliest times and right up to the present day, salt, a precious commodity for men and their animals, has been used as a kind of currency in Ethiopia. According to Kosmos, a 6th-century Egyptian writing in Greek, the kings of Aksum sent expeditions west to barter salt, among other things, for hunks of gold!

Mined in the Danakil Depression, the mineral was transported hundreds of kilometres west across the country to the Ethiopian court in Shoa. Later, the salt was cut into small, rectangular blocks, which came to be known as *amole*; their value grew with every kilometre that they travelled further from the mine.

To this day, Afar nomads and their camels continue to follow this ancient salt route. Cutting the bars by hand from the salt lakes in western Ethiopia, they spend weeks travelling by caravan to market, where the bars will be bartered.

Fasika Hotel (☎ 40 00 47; rooms with shared shower Birr20) is second-best.

Tadesse Hagos Hotel (☎ 40 26 98; rooms without shower Birr20, with shower Birr30-35), south of the town centre, offers good value.

Africa Hotel (☎ 40 44 43; rooms without/with shower Birr30/50) also offers good value.

Hawelti Hotel (☎ 40 10 86; rooms Birr40, with hot shower Birr50-60) is peaceful with two pleasant terraces, though it's a little way north of the centre.

Ras Alula Abanega Hotel (☎ 40 66 75; rooms with shower Birr30-50) is a new and pleasant hotel offering the best value in its range (though prices may soon increase by around Birr10).

Abreha Castle Hotel (☎ 40 65 55; singles/doubles US$25/30, with shower US$30/46) is an old, state-run establishment. Even with the freely proffered discounts of 20% to 30%, it still seems overpriced. But its terrace overlooking the whole town is a lovely place for a drink (beer Birr5.50) at sunset.

Hawzen Hotel (☎ 40 69 55, fax 40 43 49; doubles/twins with satellite TV Birr90/108) is a modern, comfortable and good-value place that also has a nightclub.

Aksum Hotel (☎ 40 51 55, fax 40 61 15; singles/twins Birr201.60/235) is a large, new hotel, and a swimming pool is planned for the future. Rooms have TV and telephone.

Bubu Hills Hotel, north of the town centre, tops the top-end. Set on a hill above the town, it has recently changed hands, but should reopen in 2003. Facilities should include a swimming pool and tennis court.

Places to Eat

Adedda Berger House, despite the name, is a good place for breakfast (from 6.30am), snacks and fruit juices.

Dhab Pastry, Central Café and **City Café** are good for coffee and a cake.

Cosy Restaurant is not bad for good-value snacks and meals (from Birr6).

Yordanos I Hotel, with seating in a pleasant compound, serves good local and *faranji* food (including pizzas Birr20 to Birr25). Try the delicious *tsahli* (meat stew).

Yordanos II Hotel is also good, with an extensive menu of local and *faranji* food for similar prices to Yordanos I Hotel.

Axumamit Hotel & Restaurant has a rooftop terrace and is also good for *faranji* food.

Women's Restaurant, run by unemployed widows, is a pleasant, traditional-style place serving good food.

Geza Gerlase Cultural Restaurant serves great traditional food in a great traditional setting (a large *tukul*). The *zilzil tibs* (Birr7), *kitfo* (Birr14) and shish kebab (Birr15) are particularly recommended. On Thursday and Saturday (from 8.30pm) there's usually traditional singing and dancing.

Inda Rasi Hotel & Restaurant has a traditional restaurant in the huge 100-year-old *tukul*, which should reopen soon.

Seti Supermarket and **AGM Trading** are the best places to stock up for camping.

Getting There & Around
Ethiopian Airlines (☎ 40 00 55) flies twice daily to Addis Ababa and three times weekly to Aksum and Shire. For Bahar Dar and Lalibela, fly to Aksum and change flights.

A contract taxi to the airport, 8km out of town, costs Birr30 to Birr50. You can also take a minibus (Birr2, 20 minutes) to the village of Quiha and ask to be dropped off en route; from the road, it's a two- to three-minute walk to the airport. The new airport should open in 2003.

Around 20 buses run daily to Adigrat (Birr13.15, 2½ to three hours); three buses to Addis Ababa (Birr78, 1½ days via Kombolcha); one or two buses to Aksum (Birr27.50, seven to nine hours); for Woldia (Birr30, six hours) take the Addis Ababa bus; for Lalibela, go to Woldia.

For the churches, minibuses or 4WDs leave (from the bus station) daily for Abi Addi (Birr15, two to three hours, three or four daily), Wukro (Birr8, one hour, 10 daily) and, on Wednesday only, Hawsien (Birr15, 2½ hours). For Atsbi, go to Wukro first; for Sinkata, take the Adigrat bus (Birr8, 1½ hours).

Short hops in a share-taxi cost Birr5, contract taxis cost Birr10 to Birr20. Bikes can be hired (diagonally opposite the mosque in the market) for Birr2 per hour.

DANAKIL DESERT
ደንከል በርሃ
With several points lying more than 100m below sea level, the Danakil Desert has acquired a reputation as one of the hottest, most inhospitable places on Earth; temperatures can soar to 50°C. The region, due east of Mekele, is nevertheless home to the fascinating Afar people, a nomadic ethnic group known in the past for their legendary ferocity (see the boxed texts 'Peoples of Ethiopia' in the Facts about Ethiopia chapter and 'The Dreaded Danakils' in the Eastern Ethiopia chapter).

For centuries the Afars have mined and transported salt from the great Danakil salt lakes to highland markets in Ethiopia (see the boxed text 'Salt for Gold' earlier).

Though little more than a wasteland, the area is strangely beautiful in parts and, more surprisingly, is home to some interesting wildlife including gazelles, zebras and the now extremely rare wild ass.

An excursion into the region is best organised through a tour operator in Addis Ababa (see Organised Tours in the Getting Around chapter) or Mekele.

The Tourism Commission in Mekele hopes to develop trips into the region with camel caravans in the next two years. Enquire there. Otherwise, you'll need to treat a journey here in full expedition style: people have perished within a matter of hours here. The region is cooler from December to February.

Berahile, east of the Adigrat–Mekele road, is the most usual jumping-off point. Currently a new road is being constructed. Occasionally, local conflicts cause security problems in the region; check out the situation with the Tourism Commission in Mekele first.

WOLDIA
ወልድያ
The town of Woldia provides a springboard for visits to its famous neighbour, Lalibela, 120km to the northwest. You should stock up here on petrol, batteries, birr, snacks and drinks (if you're planning long treks), and anything you might need from a pharmacy. Lalibela, despite its fame, is still the back of beyond.

Genet Hotel (☎ 31 07 27; *rooms without/ with hot shower Birr12/27*) is good value with simple but clean rooms. It lies 1.5km from the bus station on the Dessie–Addis Ababa road.

Roha Hotel (☎ 31 02 12; *rooms without/ with cold shower Birr15/20*) is adequate and lies bang opposite the bus station.

Lal Hotel (☎ 31 03 14; *singles/doubles/twins with private bathroom Birr70/87.10/104.50*) is a large hotel with plans to renovate its rooms in the near future. There's also a good restaurant serving both *faranji* and local food. Camping is possible. It lies 1.2km from the bus station on the Dessie–Addis Ababa road.

Manen Restaurant, a local favourite, lies – unnamed – on the main Dessie–Addis Ababa road, next door to the Photo Addis shop.

Getting There & Away
Local demand for transport to Lalibela is low; you may find yourself waiting some

ETHIOPIA

hours for buses to fill and leave. One bus leaves daily for Lalibela (Birr25, seven to eight hours). If you miss it, try finding a seat on the bus coming from Addis Ababa (stopping in Woldia around 9am).

Two buses leave daily for Dessie (Birr11, three hours); try also for seats on the buses coming from Maychew, Bahar Dar or Debre Tabor. For Mekele, try for a seat on the Addis Ababa bus (Birr30, eight hours). For Bahar Dar and Gonder go to Dessie first.

If there are several of you, you could consider taking a contract minibus to Lalibela (Birr800 to Birr1000 for the whole vehicle).

Usually at least one aid truck, government pick-up, or 4WD also makes the journey (Birr30 to Birr40, up to 11 hours). Ask at the Total station or around the Lal Hotel.

LALIBELA
ላሊበላ

☎ 03 • pop 8484 • elevation 2630m

Also known as 'Africa's Petra', Lalibela and its rock-hewn churches are arguably Ethiopia's top attraction. Though the town has drawn 'tourists' since the 16th century, it remains remarkably undeveloped. Until recently there was no electricity, and there are still no banks or pharmacies. In 1998 the tourist office unceremoniously opened – and then closed again.

Lying in the rugged Lasta Mountains at an altitude of 2630m, Lalibela also remains a very isolated place. Right up until 1997, the main road leading to the town was impassable during the wet season. Today, the journey overland is still quite long and arduous – the sense of arrival at the little town is rather like that after making a great pilgrimage.

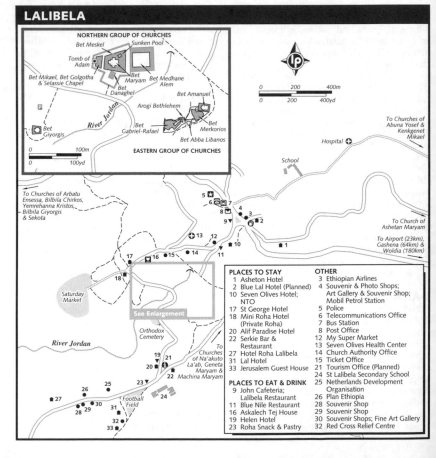

LALIBELA

PLACES TO STAY
1 Asheton Hotel
2 Blue Lal Hotel (Planned)
10 Seven Olives Hotel; NTO
17 St George Hotel
18 Mini Roha Hotel (Private Roha)
20 Alif Paradise Hotel
22 Serkie Bar & Restaurant
27 Hotel Roha Lalibela
31 Lal Hotel
33 Jerusalem Guest House

PLACES TO EAT & DRINK
9 John Cafeteria; Lalibela Restaurant
11 Blue Nile Restaurant
16 Askalech Tej House
19 Helen Hotel
23 Roha Snack & Pastry

OTHER
3 Ethiopian Airlines
4 Souvenir & Photo Shops; Art Gallery & Souvenir Shop; Mobil Petrol Station
5 Police
6 Telecommunications Office
7 Bus Station
8 Post Office
12 My Super Market
13 Seven Olives Health Center
14 Church Authority Office
15 Ticket Office
21 Tourism Office (Planned)
24 St Lalibela Secondary School
25 Netherlands Development Organisation
26 Plan Ethiopia
28 Souvenir Shop
29 Souvenir Shop
30 Souvenir Shops; Fine Art Gallery
32 Red Cross Relief Centre

In fact, Lalibela *is* a centre of pilgrimage. Among the dimly lit passageways and tunnels of the medieval churches, robed priests and monks still float; from hidden crypts and grottoes comes the sound of chanting, and in the deep, cool recesses of the interiors, the smell of incense and beeswax candles still pervades.

Lalibela undoubtedly ranks among the greatest religio-historical sites, not only on the African continent, but in the Christian world. Just as remarkable, however, is its total disregard for this status. Medieval Lalibela just goes about its business. Here, more than anywhere in Ethiopia, one has the impression of landing in a time at least seven centuries behind our own.

Probably the best time to visit is during a major festival (see Public Holidays in the Facts for the Visitor chapter), though you should book hotel rooms and flights way in advance. If you have a chance, it's also worth attending one of the church services.

History

Lalibela was the capital of the Zagwe dynasty in the 12th and 13th centuries, but was known initially as Roha. On the death of King Lalibela, the ruler credited with the construction of the churches, the town was named after him.

The churches are thought, in accordance with local tradition, to date from the 12th or 13th century – during King Lalibela's reign. Legend has it that King Lalibela was exiled or – in fear of persecution from his half-brother – fled to Jerusalem. There he wondered at the buildings he found, and vowed to build a new holy city when he returned to his own kingdom. Another legend claims that it was, in fact, a heavenly vision that Lalibela saw.

Perhaps King Lalibela was making a deliberate attempt to create a new Jerusalem on African soil, far from Muslim usurpers, and accessible to all Ethiopians. Even the names of Lalibela's features echo those of Jerusalem: the River Jordan, Calvary, and the Tomb of Adam, for example.

In fact, the buildings are so different from each other in style, craftsmanship and state of preservation that they may well span a much longer period than Lalibela's reign.

Lalibela's churches are remarkable for three main reasons: because many are not carved into the rock, but freed entirely from it; because the buildings are so refined; and because there are so many within such a small area. Alvares, the early-16th-century Portuguese writer, described them as 'edifices, the like of which – and so many – cannot be found anywhere else in the world'.

During construction, first a large area was marked out. Trenches were then cut on all four sides until a solid rock remained. This was then chiselled out from inside. The relatively soft red volcanic tuff was quite conducive to the hewing.

But who built the churches? Some scholars have estimated that it would have taken a workforce of some 40,000 to construct the churches. The locals claim that, toiling all the hours of daylight, the earthly workforce was then replaced by a celestial one, who toiled all the hours of darkness. In this way, the churches rose at a miraculous speed!

However, foreign intervention, whether celestial or mortal, can almost certainly be ruled out. Long a victim of the usual 'it can't be African' chauvinism, Lalibela in fact almost certainly represents the pinnacle of a very longstanding Ethiopian building tradition.

Exceptional masonry skills had long been in existence during the days of Aksum, and indeed most of the churches show clear characteristics of the ancient Aksumite style. If angels did build the churches, they were almost certainly Ethiopian angels!

Orientation

The churches can be divided into three main groups. The first two groups lie within a short distance of the town centre, one to the north of the canalised watercourse known as the 'River Jordan', and another to the east. The third group lies outside town.

Information

The tourism office is scheduled to reopen soon. In the meantime, the hotels are the best bet for information. The Alif Paradise Hotel recently opened a little information office and also offers organised excursions outside Lalibela.

The Ethiopian Tourism Commission (ETC) does a useful publication on Lalibela that's sometimes available in souvenir shops for Birr30 to Birr50. *Lalibela: World Wonder Heritage* by Tilahun Assefa may be available at the Hotel Roha Lalibela.

Take a torch when visiting the churches. Beware the fleas that infest the rugs; if you brought flea powder (see the What to Bring list in the Facts for the Visitor chapter) this is the time for it! If not, try two pairs of socks.

Money There are still no banks in Lalibela – the nearest is 185km away in Woldia – so come prepared. The Hotel Roha Lalibela and the Seven Olives Hotel do change cash and travellers cheques, but in US dollars only, and only for guests. If you're desperate, you may be able to persuade the Hotel Roha. If not, a black market operates in a couple of the souvenir shops.

Communications There are currently no Internet facilities in Lalibela, though Ethiopian Telecommunications plans to extend its service to Lalibela in the future.

Tickets The ticket office *(open 8am-noon & 2pm-5pm daily; admission Birr100)* lies beside the path leading to the northern group of churches and Bet Medhane Alem. Tickets give access to all churches in town (but not to those outside) for the duration of your stay.

Admission to each of the churches outside town costs Birr20 (unless otherwise indicated). For these, pay at the churches.

The fee for video cameras is Birr150 in town and usually Birr50 per church out of town (larger video cameras or film equipment may cost up to Birr1000). Note that a camera flash can cause great damage to the murals and frescoes so try to resist using one. Many priests are happy to show off their church's treasures and pose obligingly beside them for photos. It is customary and polite to tip them something small afterwards.

Guides A guide is recommended, as much for finding your way around as for keeping other guides at bay. In recent years the standard has greatly improved, but see the boxed text 'Guidelines for Guides' in the Facts for the Visitor chapter.

Official guides can be obtained through the hotels. Generally, their services cost around Birr100 per day for a small group (say one to three people), and Birr120 to Birr150 for a larger group. Tips of Birr5 to Birr10 per person are also expected if the service is good. The Lal Hotel has set up a Guide Service offering guides for Birr150 per day for one to 15 people. Reduced rates are usually available in the low season. Elsewhere, you may be asked more, particularly during the major festivals. Be prepared for an onslaught of guides and touts at the airport.

Because unemployment is high, the prospect of money earned from guiding is attractive, to children as well as adults. Using children as guides encourages them to play truant at school, encourages migration to the town, and anyway contributes little to your visit; few children know much about the churches.

The self-appointed shoe bearers should be tipped Birr2 to Birr5 per church per person. Priests will expect a small tip too (Birr5).

Mule Hire Mules, a useful addition on the longer or steeper treks, can be hired for Birr35 to Birr40 for Asheta Maryam and Na'akuto La'ab, and Birr50 to Birr70 for churches further afield, per mule and driver, per day.

Local residents recommend tipping Birr15 per mule driver per day for shorter distances, and Birr30 for longer distances, or Birr100 to Birr200 at the end of, say, three days. The mule drivers are obliging and work hard. They also earn very little, and tipping is greatly appreciated. If you want mules, ask at your hotel.

When to Visit A good time to visit Lalibela is during the country's major religious festivals (see Public Holidays in the Facts for the Visitor chapter). However, flight and hotel reservations are recommended six months in advance for Timkat and Leddet, and three or four months in advance for Fasika. Meskel and Kiddus Yohannes are also busy.

Note that some hotels raise their rates during the high season of the festivals and European Christmas. Conversely, you can normally negotiate good discounts during the low season, from May to August.

Outside these periods, find out from your hotel if any of the local churches are celebrating their saint's day; these are well worth attending. You'll need at least one full day to see the town churches and two days to do those outside town justice.

Northern Group of Churches

Bet Medhane Alem (ቤተ መድኃኔዓለም)
Bet Medhane Alem (Saviour of the World) is said to be the largest rock-hewn church in the world, measuring 33.5m by 23.5m. It's as impressive for its size as for its majesty, and in design and proportions it resembles much more a Greek temple than a traditional Ethiopian church.

Some scholars have suggested that the church may have been a copy in rock of the original St Mary of Zion church in Aksum.

The building is supported by 72 pillars – 34 large, square columns on the outside (many actually replicas of the originals), and a further 38 inside which support the gabled roof.

The interior of the church consists of a barrel-vaulted nave and four aisles. Look out for the three empty graves in one corner, said to have been prepared symbolically for Abraham, Isaac and Jacob. Pierced stone 'panels' fill the windows, each of which is decorated with different central crosses. You may be allowed to see the famous 7kg gold Lalibela cross. In 1997 it was stolen by an Ethiopian antique dealer and sold to a Belgian tourist for US$25,000, but was fortunately recovered.

Bet Maryam (ቤተ ማርያም) Connected to Bet Medhane Alem by a tunnel is a large courtyard containing three churches. The first, Bet Maryam, is small, yet designed and decorated to an exceptionally high standard. It's unusual for its three projected porches, which lead into a triple aisle.

The ceilings and upper walls are painted with very early frescoes, and the columns, capital and arches are covered in beautifully carved details such as birds, animals and foliage, including a curious two-headed eagle and two fighting bulls, one white, one black (thought to represent good and evil). Look out also for the Aksumite frieze (row of false windows).

At the eastern end of the nave is a column that is kept permanently wrapped in cloth. One local tradition has it that Christ leant against it as he appeared in a vision to King Lalibela. Under the cloth are said to be inscribed the words 'past and future of the world'. Above the western porch, look for the rare and beautifully carved bas-relief of St George fighting the dragon.

The church is dedicated to the Virgin, who is particularly venerated in Ethiopia. To this day, it remains one of the most popular churches among pilgrims. Some believe it may have been the first church built by Lalibela.

In the courtyard there is a deep sunken pool, of which the water is said to have miraculous properties. On certain days, infertile women come here to bathe.

Bet Meskel (ቤተ መስቀል) Carved into the northern wall of the courtyard of Bet Maryam is the tiny chapel of Bet Meskel. Four pillars divide the gallery into two aisles spanned by arcades.

Keep an eye out for the cross carved in relief beneath stylised foliage on one of the spandrels of the arches.

Some of the large caves in the chapel are still inhabited by hermits.

Bet Danaghel (ቤተ ድንግል) To the south of the Bet Maryam courtyard is the chapel of Bet Danaghel, said to have been constructed in memory of the 136 maiden nuns martyred on the orders of the 4th-century Roman emperor Julian in Edessa (modern-day Turkey). Many of its features – the cruciform pillars and bracket capitals – are typical architectural features of the churches.

Bet Golgotha (ቤተ ጎልጎታ), **Bet Mikael & Selassie Chapel** (ቤተ ሚካኤል ና ስላሴ የጸሎት ቤት) A tunnel at the southern end of the Bet Maryam courtyard connects it to the twin churches of Bet Golgotha and Bet Mikael (also known as Bet Debre Sina).

Bet Mikael serves as an anteroom to the Selassie Chapel, one of the holiest sanctuaries in Lalibela. It contains three monolithic altars. One is decorated with a beautiful relief of four winged creatures with their hands held up in prayer; it is thought to represent the four evangelists. Unfortunately, the chapel is very rarely open to the public.

Bet Golgotha is known for containing some of the best early examples of Christian art in Ethiopia. On the so-called Tomb of Christ – an arched recess in the northeast of the church – a recumbent figure is carved in high relief; above it, in low relief, hovers an angel. Look out for the exceptional, life-sized depiction of seven saints carved into the niches of the walls.

The two churches also boast among the most important religious treasures in Lalibela, such as some fine processional crosses. You may be shown a blackened but richly decorated metal cross, thought to have belonged to the founding king.

Close to the Tomb of Christ is a movable slab of stone, said to cover the most secret place in the holy city, the tomb of King Lalibela himself. Such is the importance and sanctity of Golgotha that a visit is said to assure your place in heaven!

Standing in a deep trench in front of the western facade of Bet Golgotha is the so-called Tomb of Adam. It consists of a giant, hollowed-out block of stone. On the upper floor there's a hermit's cell; the ground floor serves as an entrance to the nearby churches.

Bet Giyorgis (ቤተ ጊዮርጊስ) Lying slightly apart from the main northern cluster – towards the southwest of town – is the church of Bet Giyorgis. The most famous and photographed of all Lalibela's churches, it represents the apogee of the rock-hewn tradition:

it is the most visually perfect of all. It is also exceptionally well preserved.

The church is constructed on a three-tiered plinth and is shaped like a Greek cross. Though considered the most recent church, it still incorporates many features of Aksumite architecture.

Inside, an old olive-wood box is said to have been carved by King Lalibela himself, and used by him for storing his famous tools. See also the boxed text 'St George' later in this chapter.

Eastern Group of Churches

Bet Amanuel (ቤተ አማኑኤል) The free-standing, monolithic church of Bet Amanuel is considered one of the most finely carved churches in Lalibela; some have suggested that it was used by the royal family as their private chapel.

In style it is typically Aksumite, perhaps more than any other church in Lalibela, with its projecting and recessed walls, monkey heads, and carved windows and doorways. A spiral staircase connects the four-pillared walls to an upper gallery.

The most striking feature of the interior is the double Aksumite frieze in the nave. In the southern aisle, a hole in the floor leads to a long, subterranean tunnel (one of three) which connects the church to Bet Merkorios.

In the courtyard outside, look out for the little cavities hewn in the wall to attract the sacred bees. Throughout Ethiopia, honey produced in churches is believed to possess special healing properties.

The chambers in the walls are the old graves of pilgrims who requested to be buried here.

Bet Merkorios (ቤተ መርቆሪዮስ) This may not in fact have served as a church at all. The discovery of ankle shackles among other objects has led scholars to believe that the building may once have served as the town's prison, or house of justice. It was not until much later that the building was converted to a church.

On the northeastern wall, there's a fading but beautiful fresco thought to represent the three wise men. With their little flipper hands and eyes that look askance, they are delightfully depicted; it may date from the 15th century. The Twelve Apostles are also represented in a less attractive fresco, probably of a later date. The painting on cotton fabric is believed to date from the 16th century. Formerly, such paintings were plastered to the church walls with a mixture of straw, ox blood and mud.

Bet Abba Libanos (ቤተ አባ ሊባኖስ) This is unique among the town-based churches in that it's a hypogeous church – that is, only the roof remains attached to the overhead rock.

Like Bet Amanuel, many of its architectural features, such as the friezes, are Aksumite. Curiously, although it looks large from the outside, the interior is actually very small.

The church is said to have been constructed in a single night by Lalibela's wife, Meskel Kebra – with a little help from the angels. Three-quarter cut, the church seems to grow from the rock; it gives you a vivid idea of the work required to hew out one of these churches.

A tunnel leads off the church to the tiny chapel of Bet Lehem.

Near the church is the monastery-village of Lalibela, where 12 monks and six nuns continue to live in tiny caves (4m by 3m) hewn out of the rock. You can visit them, but you should leave something for the community.

Bet Gabriel-Rufael (ቤተ ገብርኤል ሩፋኤል) Because of its curious, irregular plan, it is thought that Bet Gabriel-Rufael served another function before its conversion to a church – perhaps as a residence of the royal family.

The complex is made up of three halls and two courtyards. King Lalibela is said to have addressed his people from the top. Its monumental facade is its most interesting feature. Look out for the very unusual Aksumite windows with little pointed arches. Inside, the decoration is quite plain – just three Latin crosses.

A tunnel leads to the so-called Arogi Bethlehem, a bakery for making the holy bread.

St George

Just as King Lalibela was finishing off his series of churches, he was suddenly paid an unexpected visit. Astride a white horse and decked out in full armour came the country's patron saint, George. However, the saint turned out to be severely piqued: not one of the churches had been dedicated to him.

Lalibela – profusely apologetic – promised to make amends immediately by building him the most beautiful church of all.

Today, the priests of Bet Giyorgis (meaning 'Place of George') point out the hoof prints left behind by the saint's horse, permanently imprinted in stone on the side of the trench.

Churches Outside Town

Many other churches lie within a day's journey of Lalibela. Some of them require quite long walks, or rides by mule. Many are well worth a visit; some may predate those in the town.

The journey to the churches can take you through some beautiful countryside. Some are quite tucked away, and none of them are currently listed on any maps, so you'll need a guide to find them. Ask your hotel to prepare you a boxed lunch as the church sites make great places for a picnic.

The churches vary greatly in style, age and design. Sadly, many are in a very sorry state of repair, crumbling and flaking visibly. Ashetan Maryam, Bilbila Chirkos, Bilbila Giyorgis and Kenkgenet Mikael are all in urgent need of restoration.

Yemrehanna Kristos (የምረሃና ክርስቶስ)

Lying 42km by road (around 20km by mule) northeast of Lalibela, Yemrehanna Kristos *(admission Birr50)* is undoubtedly the finest church outside the town.

The ugly brick wall, built in 1985 to improve the church's security, conceals the jewel within. Unusually, the church is built – rather than excavated – within a cave. Very much in the Aksumite style, it may well predate Lalibela, some say by up to 80 years. According to local tradition, the church was built by King Yemrehanna Kristos between 1087 and 1127.

There are surprises everywhere. The exterior of the church is decorated with whitewashed marble panels, and the whole church sits on a foundation of carefully laid olive-wood panels, which 'float' it perfectly above the marshy ground below. The carving and decoration are exceptional; look out for the elaborate nave ceiling.

At the back of the church, under an overhanging rock, are the bones of countless pilgrims who have chosen to be buried here, as well as a tomb said to contain the remains of Yemrehanna Kristos.

It takes about five hours to get here by foot or mule from Lalibela. Recently, the road has been improved. Around 75% of tourists never get here – but it's well worth the effort.

Arbatu Ensessa (አርባቱ እንሳሳ)

Around 35km from Lalibela is the church of Arbatu Ensessa *(admission Birr30)*, one of the most easily accessible churches. Its a three-quarter monolith in a wild, overgrown, but rather beautiful setting. It is thought to have been built by King Kaleb in AD 518. *Arbatu*

ensessa means 'the four beasts' after the four Evangelists, Matthew, Mark, Luke and John, whom the beasts represent.

Bilbila Chirkos (ቢልቢላ ጨርቆስ)

Close to Arbatu Ensessa, around 35km from Lalibela, is Bilbila Chirkos *(admission Birr30)*. An interesting three-quarter monolith, it is known particularly for its ancient frescoes. Also attributed to King Kaleb, it is thought to date from AD 523. It's a three-minute walk from the road.

Bilbila Giyorgis (ቢልቢላ ጊዮርጊስ)

Lying to the west of Arbatu Ensessa, around 32km from Lalibela, Bilbila Giyorgis *(admission Birr30)* is also attributed to King Kaleb, but resembles Bet Abba Libanos in design.

According to tradition, five swarms of bees took up residence shortly after the church was completed and still reside here! Their sacred honey is said to have curative properties, particularly for psychological disorders and skin problems. The priest will let you taste it. It's 20 to 30 minutes' walk up the hill to the church from the road.

Ashetan Maryam (አሼታን ማርያም)

At an altitude of 3150m, Ashetan Maryam *(admission Birr20)* sits atop a mountain that rises above Lalibela. There are commanding views in all directions. The local priests believe they are 'closer to heaven and to God' here, and it's easy to see why.

The monastery's construction is believed to have been started during King Lalibela's reign, but finished between the years of 1207 and 1247 under King Na'akuto La'ab. Some claim King Na'akuto La'ab lies buried in the chapel. Church treasures include parchment and some icons.

The architecture compares pretty poorly with what lies below in Lalibela. Nevertheless, the journey takes you through lovely country. Listen out for the witchlike cackle of the francolins resounding around the valley.

The 1½-hour climb (one way) to reach it is quite steep. Many travellers take mules, though you'll still need to walk over the rockiest parts.

Na'akuto La'ab (ናቁቶ ላአብ)

Lying 7km from Lalibela, this church *(admission Birr20)* was built by King Lalibela's successor of the same name. It is a simple but attractive little church (apart from the outer security wall), built under a natural cave. It was almost certainly the site of a much older shrine.

Empress Zewditu built the ugly inner red-brick building. Some very old stone receptacles collect the precious holy water as it drips from the cave roof.

The church boasts various treasures said to have belonged to its founder, including crosses, crowns, gold-painted drums and an illuminated Bible. It's just a 10- to 15-minute walk from the village of the same name. Birdlife in the area is good.

Geneta Maryam (ገነታ ማርያም)

Near the source of the Tekeze River, 31km from Lalibela, lies Geneta Maryam (admission Birr20). It is thought to have been built in around 1270 by Yekuno Amlak, who restored the Solomonic line (see History in the Facts about Ethiopia chapter). With its rectangular shape and 20 massive rectangular pillars that support it, it more resembles Bet Medhane Alem in Lalibela. It is also known for its remarkable 13th-century paintings.

On the western wall, look out for the face of Christ, shaped like a moon, and on the southern side, the very grumpy-looking elephants. Geneta Maryam is about four hours by foot from Lalibela, or 1½ hours by vehicle, with a five-minute walk from the road.

Machina Maryam (መጭና ማርያም)

Two hours' walk from Geneta Maryam and six hours' walk from Lalibela is the remote church of Machina Maryam (also known as Emachina Lideta Maryam; admission Birr20), said traditionally to have been constructed by three virgins during the reign of King Gebre Meskel in AD 537.

The church is constructed under an overhanging rock in a natural cave. It rather resembles Yemrehanna Kristos in design, and many features are Aksumite, but its beautiful frescoes are the main attraction – look out for the hunting scenes with the many one-eyed lions. It also contains a good number of church treasures.

There are many bricked-up tombs in the church. Bodies buried under the rock are said to be preserved forever. The church is little visited, but is well worth the long – and in parts steep – ascent; mules are probably a good idea (but not in the wet season when it is slippery).

Abuna Yosef (አቡነ ዮሴፍ)

It's an eight-hour walk (one way) from Lalibela to reach Abuna Yosef, which lies at an altitude of around 3750m. Little more than a cave, albeit an old one, it is devoid of both paintings and architectural details. But it does make a great trek through beautiful country, and Ethiopian wolves have been seen here in the past couple of years.

Nearby is a holy spring, said to have sprung up from the blood of Abuna Yosef, who cut his leg when the devil pushed him over.

It's possible to overnight in a nearby mountain village (don't expect more than a goatskin on an earthen floor). Otherwise you'll need to bring camping equipment and food for two days. Leave a tip at the cave (for the visit) and the village (if you overnight there).

Kenkgenet Mikael (ቀንክገነት ሚካኤል)

Lying around three hours' walk from Abuna Yosef and around six hours from Lalibela,

---

Donkey Lore

Ever wondered why donkeys nuzzle and sniff one another when they meet?

Once upon a time, long ago, the donkeys became tired of their role as beasts of burden. So they called a big meeting and decided to send a representative to God to plead their cause, and to end their suffering at the hands of people.

Although the years have passed, their representative has not yet returned. The donkeys go on waiting patiently and submissively, but every time they meet one another, they put their heads together to ask 'Has our envoy returned yet?'.

For so it is that all living things yearn for freedom.

A traditional Ethiopian tale

the rock-hewn church of Kenkgenet Mikael (*admission Birr20*) is much more interesting architecturally.

It is thought to have been built by the monk Abba Muses between AD 633 and 648. Many of its features are similar to those found in the Tigrayan rock-hewn churches, and it contains some interesting church treasures including a royal seal.

Places to Stay

Lalibela still suffers from water shortages, particularly in the dry season and high tourism season. You may have to shower at a certain time (usually early mornings and evenings) or may be given a bucket of warm water. Recently, electrical cuts (sometimes lasting the whole day) have been a problem.

In the low season, discounts are negotiable in most of the mid-range and top-end hotels. Conversely, prices may go up in the peak season. Shop around.

If you want to camp, tents can be hired from the Alif Paradise Hotel (Birr25 per tent per night) or the **Church Authority office** (☎ 36 00 21; *Birr50 per tent*). Cooking utensils (but not stoves) are also available. You can pitch a tent at various hotels in Lalibela (see their listing following).

Budget hotels are not Lalibela's strong point.

St George Hotel (*rooms with shared shower Birr10*) is the least awful, but has cell-like rooms – two of which have rather beautiful views. A chicken was occupying one when we visited.

Serkie Bar & Restaurant (☎ 39 00 40; *rooms with shared shower Birr20*) is probably Lalibela's best-kept budget secret. Though basic, rooms are clean.

Mini Roha Hotel (☎ 36 00 94; *singles/ doubles with shared hot shower Birr30/45*), also known as Private Roha, is simple but clean and welcoming, with a pleasant patio. Some rooms – and loos! – have good views over town.

Alif Paradise Hotel (☎ 36 00 23; e elsameft@ freemail.et; *doubles/twins Birr80/120*) is a new, pleasant, family-run place in a cosy compound. The helpful manager, Solomon, is a good source of local information. Travellers have written to recommend the ice-cold beers.

Asheton Hotel (☎ 36 00 30; *singles/ doubles Birr30/70, with private bathroom Birr60/70*) has clean rooms around a pleasant courtyard. It has its own water supply.

Soon to open in the mid-range category is the new **Blue Lal Hotel**. Rooms will have private showers. There will also be a traditional restaurant (which promises good food) as well as barbecue facilities.

Jerusalem Guest House (☎ 36 00 47; *camping per tent US$6-10, singles/doubles with private shower US$25/35*) is a pleasant and peaceful place with a beautiful traditional *tukul* restaurant. Rooms have attractive balconies and new rooms are in the works. Discounts of up to 30% are available in the low season.

Seven Olives Hotel (☎ 36 00 20; *singles/ doubles US$25/37.50*) is government-run and boasts an attractive setting. Rooms, though clean and peaceful, are overpriced, but rates should soon drop by around US$5 to US$10. If not, enquire about discounts, which are negotiable (up to 25%).

Lal Hotel (☎ 36 00 08; *camping per person Birr25, singles/doubles low season Birr160/ 240, high season Birr240/320*) has quite comfortable rooms set in a pleasant compound. Campers have access to hot showers. New rooms are being built. Discounts are usually negotiable and a free airport transfer is offered. It's also a source of local information.

Hotel Roha Lalibela (☎ 36 00 09, fax 36 01 56; *camping per person US$6.25, singles/ doubles/suites US$37.50/50/75*) lies 2km from the centre and belongs to the same government chain (Ghion Hotels) as the Goha in Gonder. Campers have access to hot showers and the hotel has its own generator. Discounts of 15% are negotiable in the low season.

Places to Eat & Drink

Don't leave Lalibela without tasting *tej* (honey mead). A *birille* (little flask) costs from Birr4 to Birr5

Helen Hotel brews its own *tej* (Birr5 for a *birille*) and the restaurant's food has a good reputation. *Azmaris* usually perform here nightly from 9pm to 11pm.

Serkie Bar & Restaurant is a local favourite and serves decent, good-value food.

Blue Nile Restaurant is a pleasant place and one of the best for *faranji* food (Birr8 to Birr15) with pizzas (Birr15 to Birr20) and veggie options. The **Asheton Hotel** is also good.

Lalibela Restaurant is a good place for breakfast.

Roha Snack & Pastry is considered the best pastry shop in town and is also good for breakfast. In the northern end of the town, **John Cafeteria** isn't bad.

Askalech Tej House *(open until 10pm daily)*, also known as 'torpedo', is considered one of the best *tej* watering holes in town. From 7pm to 10pm it often has *azmaris*.

The grounds of the **Seven Olives Hotel** are a lovely place for a drink at sunset or for breakfast.

Shopping

Lalibela's **souvenir shops** sell the usual artefacts. A more unusual shop is the **Fine Art Gallery**, where attractive watercolours and pen-and-ink drawings of Lalibela can be purchased (from Birr100 to Birr150). Also worth a peek is the **Art Gallery & Souvenir Shop**, which sells prayer books, icons and traditional skin paintings (Birr150 to Birr250). A skin postcard might surprise the relatives back home!

Getting There & Away

Ethiopian Airlines (☎ 36 00 46) flies at least once daily to Addis Ababa (via Gonder and Bahar Dar), and to Aksum.

Overland, the best approach currently is via Woldia. There are two routes from Woldia, one via Kulmesk and Dilb (120km) and another along a new road via Gashema (180km). The former, though currently impassable, should be repaired by a Dutch project in the near future. When it is, it will be the quickest route. The former route (via Kulmesk) will eventually form part of a new road connecting Lalibela directly with Addis Ababa. Though begun in 1997, the road may take until 2006 to complete.

Two buses leave daily for Woldia (Birr25, six hours). One bus leaves daily for Addis Ababa (Birr73.30, two days), overnighting in Dessie (Birr36, 10 hours), via Gashena, Woldia, Kombolcha and Debre Berhan. Tickets are best bought the afternoon before travel (after 4pm) when the bus arrives from Addis Ababa.

Going west, a couple of pick-up trucks usually depart daily from Lalibela for Gashena (Birr10). From there, you should be able to hop on transport coming from Woldia to Debre Tabor and beyond. Travelling the other way, ask to be dropped at Gashena, and hop on a pick-up truck or bus on its way to Lalibela.

Getting Around

The new airport lies 23km from town. The NTO and various hotels offer an airport transfer service (from Birr25 to Birr30 one way). Fuel is now available in Lalibela.

Ethiopian Magic

Despite the deep roots of Christianity, a surprising amount of magic and superstition still persists in Ethiopia.

You'll notice that many children wear charms or talismans around their necks attached to a *matab* (cord given at baptism). These are said to deter evil spirits and terrible diseases. In the country, many believe in the *zar* (spirits or genies), both good and bad. The *buda* is the evil eye, which can turn people by night into mischievous hyenas – like the European werewolf.

Various hotels (including the Lal Hotel, Hotel Roha Lalibela, Jerusalem Guest House and Alif Paradise Hotel) can organise car hire or all-inclusive excursions to the churches outside town for one to four people (return). Examples of trips and prices include: Na'akuto La'ab, Birr150; Yemrehanna Kristos, Birr500; Geneta Maryam, Birr500; Bilbala Chirkos and Yemrehanna Kristos, Birr600 to Birr700.

The Lal Htel also has a minibus for hire. Transfer to the churches in town and other short hops cost Birr10 one way. The **NTO** (☎ 36 04 10) offers not a bad City Tour of all 11 churches over half a day for US$6 per person (including guide; minimum three people).

DESSIE
ደሴ

☎ 03 • pop 97,314 • elevation 2470m

Though it's quite attractively set amid eucalyptus-forested hills, Wolo's capital wouldn't win a beauty contest. However, it's a major transport hub, makes a good stopover point on your way to or from Lalibela, Hayk or Maqdala, and has a good range of reasonably priced hotels and restaurants. Pickpockets can be a problem in the streets and around the bus station. Be vigilant.

Next door to the Stadium Cafeteria, **ACAS Computer** *(open 8am-noon & 2pm-8pm Mon-Sat)* has Internet access for Birr1 per minute.

In 1998 a **museum** *(admission Birr7; open 9am-12pm & 2pm-5pm daily; 9am-12pm Sat & Sun)* opened in the curious, Indian-built palace. Originally it was home to the Ethiopian noble, Dejazmach Yoseph Biru. Exhibits include musical instruments, local arts and crafts, and regal and religious regalia. Photos of the building are not allowed.

Places to Stay & Eat

Mazzagaja Hotel & Restaurant *(☎ 11 25 98; rooms with shared shower Birr15)* is close to the bus station. It's also a local favourite for food. The sign is in Amharic only.

Fasika Hotel No1 *(☎ 11 29 30; rooms without hot shower Birr25, with hot shower Birr30-40)* is much the best-value hotel in town. The more expensive rooms have telephones. It's often full so make a reservation.

Fasika Hotel No2 *(☎ 11 77 05; doubles with shower Birr60-75, twins with shower Birr90)* is a more expensive but quieter alternative to No 1. Rooms have telephones.

Royal Pension *(☎ 11 49 39; doubles without/with hot shower Birr20/50)* is not so 'royal', but its rooms are adequate if the Fasikas are full (though one traveller wrote to complain of fleas).

Blue Nile Restaurant is a cosy place and a local favourite for food, Ethiopian and *faranji* (Birr5 to Birr10).

Stadium Cafeteria is great for breakfast. Try the *special ful* (chickpea puree)

Addis Pastry is a pleasant café and is good for fruit juices and cakes.

Getting There & Away

Ethiopian Airlines *(☎ 11 25 71)* flies once daily to Addis Ababa. Flights depart from the airport at Kombolcha, 23km from Dessie. Shared taxis to the airport cost Birr10, contract taxis cost Birr80.

Five buses leave daily for Addis Ababa (Birr37.50, eight to 10 hours); one bus leaves daily for Lalibela (Birr37, 10 to 11 hours) and to Mekele (Birr41.05, 12 hours); three buses leave daily to Woldia (Birr12, four hours). Buses and minibuses also run at least every half-hour to Kombolcha (Birr3, 30 minutes).

HAYK
ሃይቅ

Lying 28km north of Dessie on a peninsula is the little town of Hayk, known for its monastery and lake.

The monastery dates from the mid-13th century and was founded by Abba Iyasus Moa. Between the 13th and 15th centuries it was among the most important monasteries in the country, and it contains the oldest known manuscript to record its own date: the book of the four gospels produced for the monastery between 1280 and 1281. It is open to men only.

The lake and its environs, 3km from town, is an excellent spot for birders.

DESSIE

PLACES TO STAY & EAT
4 Blue Nile Restaurant
5 Royal Pension
6 Fasika Hotel No2
7 Stadium Cafeteria; ACAS Computer
9 Fasika Hotel No1
11 Mazzagaja Hotel & Restaurant
16 Addis Pastry

OTHER
1 Parini Garage
2 Beza General Hospital
3 Municipality
8 Kana Zegellila Pharmacy

10 Mosque
12 Dashen Bank
13 Ekram Clinic
14 Photo Addis
15 Honey Supermarket
17 Telecommunications; Post Office
18 Medhane Alem Church
19 Kañaw Hotel (Tej Beat)
20 Commercial Bank & Western Union
21 Police
22 Ethiopian Airlines
23 Goldsmiths
24 Museum
25 Mosque

At least 15 minibuses or buses (Birr4, one hour) run daily to the village of Hayk.

KOMBOLCHA
ኮምቦልቻ

Dessie's twin town, Kombolcha, lies 25km from Dessie. Like Dessie, it has quite good facilities, and is closer to the airport (2km). The hotels are all between 1.5km and 2.5km from the bus station. If you don't want to walk, take a *gari* (Birr1 to Birr2).

Lem Hotel *(☎ 51 05 29; rooms without/ with shower Birr15/25)*, off the main Kombolcha–Addis Ababa road, has rather peeling, but clean and good-value rooms.

Kombolcha Wein Hotel *(doubles without shower Birr30, with shower Birr40-50)*, just past the Mobil station on the main road, has simple, but clean rooms and a popular

Battle of Maqdala

Northeast of Dessie, near the tiny village of Tenta, are the remains of the Emperor Tewodros' fortress and the site of the famous 1867 battle of Maqdala. Though little remains of the fortress – it lies strewn across the plateau since the British flattened it – a visit makes a terrific walk, and there are stunning views of the surrounding countryside from the windswept top.

Maqdala is rather a mournful place – still haunted, some say, by the unhappy Emperor. Find a villager who will show you where Tewodros killed himself, and the location, not far away, of his famous cannon, Sebastopol.

The walk involves a 700m descent from Tenta before a steep ascent up the mountain, which lies at around 3000m. It's not difficult, but takes around 3½ hours from Tenta to Tewodros' fortress. Mules can be hired, and are advised for the last ascent.

You'll need to stop at the administration office in Ajibara (10km before Tenta) to get papers giving you permission to visit Maqdala . The office is open from 8am to 12.30pm and from 1.30pm to 5pm on weekdays.

The Roman Hotel in Ajibara is better than anything Tenta has to offer, and has rooms for Birr10.

One 4WD and one bus run from Dessie to Tenta each morning at around 8am (Birr25). Though it's only 140km, the journey can take up to five hours. The service will stop at Ajibara so you can get permission papers. With your own vehicle, the same journey is possible in just under two hours.

restaurant. Try the *bazana shiro* (chickpea puree with meat).

Tekle Hotel (*☎ 51 00 56; doubles/twins with hot shower Birr50/70*) offers the best deal in town with spotless rooms in pleasant grounds.

Hikma on the piazza is the best pastry shop. **Kingo Pasty** opposite is good for breakfast.

The Looting of Maqdala

The capture of Emperor Tewodros' citadel of Maqdala by British troops on 13 April 1868, was accompanied by extensive looting. Articles carried off to Britain included the royal crown, seal, drum, tent and archives. The nearby church did not escape the looting either. Processional crosses, no less than 10 altar slabs and over 500 church manuscripts now reside in museums and private collections across Britain.

A few of these articles have now been returned to Ethiopia, including (in 2002) Tewodros' amulet, torn from the dead emperor's body. More extensive repatriation is, however, demanded by AFROMET (the Association of the Return of Ethiopia's Maqdala Treasures, W www.afromet.org), which argues that the looting had no basis in law and was an act of sacrilege.

Professor Richard Pankhurst
(Vice-Chair of AFROMET)

Most intercity transport leaves from Dessie; frequent buses connect the two towns (Birr3, 30 to 40 minutes). One bus leaves daily for Addis Ababa (Birr34.06, 10 to 11 hours).

AROUND KOMBOLCHA

The little town of **Bati**, 41km east of Kombolcha, is known for its large, colourful Monday market (from around 9am to 3pm), which attracts up to 10,000 Afars, Oromos and Amharas from all around.

Bati is the largest market in the country after Merkato in Addis Ababa. It's lively and interesting, but perhaps not quite as spectacular as the tourist literature makes out. But if you're in the area, it's well worth trying to catch it. The market is at its busiest around 11am. Look out for the old gallows (dating from the emperor's day). If you're planning to take photos, come armed with Birr1 notes. An Ethiopian companion is a good idea to keep curious children, as well as pickpockets, away.

At least one bus and 10 to 15 minibuses leave for, and arrive from, Dessie daily (Birr6 to Birr10, 1½ to two hours). For Mille (Birr10 to Birr12) and Asaita (Birr23, four to five hours), catch the bus coming from Dessie.

DEBRE BERHAN
ደብረ ብርሃን
☎ 01 • pop 38,717 • elevation 2840m

Lying 130km northeast of Addis Ababa, the town of Debre Berhan makes another useful stopping point on the road to or from the northern destinations. It boasts a church believed to date from the 15th century, and is known for its woven woollen rugs. However, most are exported to Addis Ababa.

Girma Hotel *(☎ 81 13 00; rooms without/ with shower Birr20/30)* has adequate and clean rooms and its restaurant is considered the best in town. The **Helen Hotel** opposite has a good bar.

Akalu Hotel *(☎ 81 11 15; rooms without/ with hot shower Birr30/40)* lies around 800m beyond the Girma Hotel on the road to Addis Ababa. It's well run, pleasant, clean and has a good restaurant. The new **Amanuel Pastry** is the best place for a cake or fruit juices.

At least 10 buses run daily between Debre Berhan and Addis Ababa (Birr11, three hours). One bus leaves daily for Kombolcha (Birr24, seven hours), and for Dessie (Birr27, eight hours). You may also be able to find a seat on one of the buses coming from Addis Ababa.

Around 65km to the south, the village of Shano is famous throughout the country for its high-quality butter (Birr24 for 1kg), an essential ingredient of Ethiopian cooking.

ANKOBER
አንኮበር

The little town of Ankober lies 40km southeast of Debre Berhan. Right up until the late 19th century, when Addis Ababa was founded, it was the capital of the Shoan princes.

The 2km ascent up to the ruins of the old fort, perched on a hill above town, makes for a great walk. The area is also a very good place for birding and is the official home of a very rare endemic, the Ankober serin.

On the way, several historic churches and their treasures can also be visited (Ankober Mikael, St Maryam and Medhane Alem). With your own vehicle, you can drive to the foot of the fort.

If you want to stay the night, **Getachew Tekle Selassie Hotel** *(rooms with bucket shower Birr6)* is basic but clean. Food can be had at **Shibirey Kurs Beat**.

Two buses depart every morning to Debre Berhan (Birr6, two hours). The churches are usually open just from 6am to 8am, so you'll have to make an early start from Debre Berhan.

Southern Ethiopia

If the north is known for its historical attractions, then the south is known for its natural attractions. With scenic landscapes, interesting wildlife and some of the most diverse and fascinating peoples of the country, the south represents the other side of Ethiopia – almost the antithesis of the northern highlands. In some ways, it is also the most 'African' region of Ethiopia.

The African Rift Valley dominates the south. Africa's largest and most famous geographical feature, it runs from Djibouti all the way down to Mozambique, and is home to a string of lakes known for their birdlife. The national parks, also running in a string from north to south, are nevertheless quite different from each other, offering different scenery, different birds and different mammals.

Quite distinct from one another too are the vast numbers of ethnic groups inhabiting the area; no less than 45 languages are spoken. The Omo region in the southwest has been called the last great wilderness on the African continent, and is home not just to Ethiopia's few remaining large mammals including lion and elephant, but also to its last 'untouched' peoples, including the famous Mursi lip stretchers and body-painting Karo.

Travellers planning a trip to the southwest should note that the main rains occur from March to May or June, and the light rains from October to December. In the wet season many roads in the Omo Valley become impassable.

To the southeast of Addis Ababa, the Bale Mountains rise high above the surrounding pastures of the Oromo people, and dominate the landscape for miles around. Within these peaks and hills, there lies a very beautiful national park. One of the largest mountain parks in Africa, it boasts the most extensive area of Afro-alpine habitat on the continent. Though less well known than the Simien Mountains, the Bale Mountains provide some of the most scenic walking in the country. In the rain and among the heather, the landscape can resemble Scotland or New Zealand.

Warning

Note that all bus journey duration times in this chapter are indications only. Times vary greatly according to individual vehicles, weather and road conditions.

Highlights

- Take your camera and zoom in on the zebras and giant crocs at one of East Africa's prettiest national parks, Nechisar

- Take a stroll or trek through the hills and high plateau of the Bale Mountains, home to prolific birdlife and endemic wildlife including the famous Ethiopian wolf

- Venture into the remote heartland of the Lower Omo Valley, home to some of the most fascinating peoples on the continent, such as the Mursi lip stretchers and body-painting Karo

- Watch the pelicans take a dip at dusk in the silvery waters of Lake Abiata, home to the most important breeding colony of great white pelicans in Africa

- Relax at the oasis-like hot-spring resort of Wondo Genet, set among dense forest and resonating with bird song

- Taste the fresh tilapia of Lake Langano, and have a splash at sunset in its waters, the colour of English tea

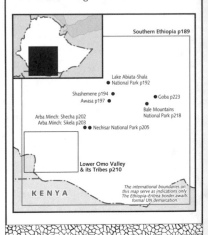

Southern Ethiopia p189

Lake Abiata-Shala National Park p192

Shashemene p194
Awasa p197

Goba p223

Bale Mountains National Park p218

Arba Minch: Shecha p202
Arba Minch: Sikela p203

Nechisar National Park p205

Lower Omo Valley & its Tribes p210

The international boundaries on this map serve as indications only. The Ethiopia–Eritrea border awaits formal UN demarcation.

KENYA

Without a doubt, the Bale Mountains National Park is the best place in the country to see endemic wildlife. The Ethiopian wolf, the rarest canid in the world and near extinction in most other areas of Ethiopia, is quite easily spotted here. The park is also home to no fewer than 16 endemic bird species; sightings are so common that there is a saying in the park that 'in Bale, every bird is endemic'.

The great majority of Oromos in the southeast are Muslim. Two very important Muslim shrines can be found in the region: Sheikh Hussein, the centre of the most important annual Muslim pilgrimage in Ethiopia; and the Sof Omar Caves, an important natural attraction.

ADDIS ABABA TO ZIWAY
Via Meki
Of the two routes south to Lake Ziway, the quickest is via Debre Zeyit and Meki, and most transport heading south comes this way.

Along the road, 20km south of Mojo, look out for the **Koka Dam**. Part of a hydroelectric power station, it supplies most of Addis Ababa with electricity. Birdlife is good near the water and hippos can sometimes be seen.

Continuing southwards, keep an eye out for the **Oromo tombs** that dot the countryside, decorated with bright murals, some of elephants and warriors on horses. In season, delicious watermelons (just Birr2 to Birr5) are sold on the roadside.

Via Butajira
The second route south from Addis Ababa to Lake Ziway, via Butajira, is slower, but more interesting, and takes you past several important historical sites. Access is easy: just hop on a bus to Butajira from the Autobus Terra in Merkato, Addis Ababa, and ask to be dropped off at the sites. A day or weekend trip from Addis Ababa is possible.

Melka Kunture *(open 9am-5pm daily)*, 1.5km southwest of Melka Awash (signposted off the main Addis Ababa–Butajira road), is

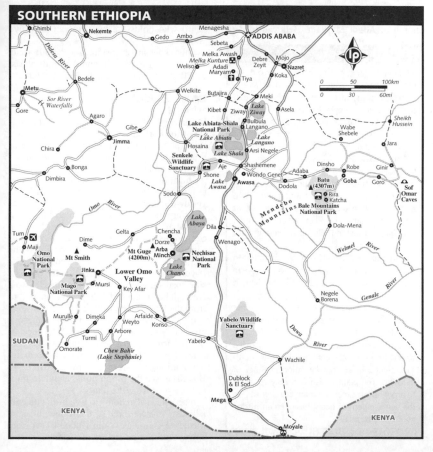

SOUTHERN ETHIOPIA

famous for the remarkable prehistoric stone-tool factory discovered in the 1960s. Extending over 5km on both sides of the river Awash, it encompasses more than 50 prehistoric sites dating as early as 1.7 million years ago.

A series of explanatory panels are posted around the site and a *tukul* (hut) displays some well-captioned finds, including the tools used by the *homo erectus/homo sapiens* who once inhabited the area. Outside opening hours, see the guard in the hut beside the site. A five-minute walk will take you to one of the sites currently under excavation where animal bones and tools can clearly be seen. It's a fascinating place.

The nearest accommodation is in Melka Awash. **Awash Ber Hotel** *(rooms with shared shower Birr8)* is basic but adequate.

Around 18km south of Melka Kunture is the village of Adadi. A five-minute walk will take you to the impressive rock-hewn church of **Adadi Maryam**. Believed to date

Enduring Enset

When travelling in the south, look out for the false banana *(Musa ensete)*, which as the name suggests, resembles a single-stemmed banana plant. Known locally as *enset*, this ancient plant has been cultivated in Ethiopia for millennia and is eaten by over a third of the population.

The preparation of *enset* for cooking is a laborious process. After the plant is cut, it must be trimmed and scraped to remove all excess fibre, then chopped and beaten into a starchy white pulp (often seen for sale at markets). Finally, the plant is buried in an underground pit and allowed to ferment for at least a month.

And the final result? For the uninitiated traveller, a kind of sticky, unleavened bread that closely resembles a fibrous carpet liner. It also makes a very chewy porridge.

Despite its appearance, texture and rather lowly status as a food staple, *enset* may well provide the solution to an age-old Ethiopian problem: the threat of famine. *Enset* can be stored for up to 20 years, providing its cultivators with an emergency ration in times of hardship. The plant is also famously resistant to drought. An American team of scientists, to the bemusement of locals, has been enthusing about its potential.

from the 12th or 13th century, the church is a three-quarter monolith. It is only worth a special stop if you're not visiting the rock-hewn churches of Lalibela or Tigray (see the Northern Ethiopia chapter).

A place that is worth a stop is **Tiya** *(admission Birr10)*. The site contains around 40 ancient stelae, the largest of which stands up to 2m high. They are as intriguing and as mysterious as any of the standing stones found in Europe. They form only one cluster among the many that dot the countryside all the way down to Dila, south of Awasa.

Almost nothing is known about the monoliths' carvers or their purpose. Most of the stones are engraved with enigmatic symbols, notably swords. French excavations have revealed that the stelae mark mass graves of individuals aged between 18 and 30.

The stelae lie 500m from the village of Tiya, where you should go first to locate the guard who holds the key. He can also give you a tour.

Other sites in the area include the Silti stele, 9km south of Kibet. Around 2.8km northeast of Kibet is the crater lake of Hare Shetan.

LAKE ZIWAY
ዝዋይ ሐይቅ

Measuring 400 sq m, Lake Ziway is the largest of the northern group of Rift Valley lakes. It lies about 1.5km east of the town of Ziway. Surrounded by blue volcanic hills, it's an attractive enough place, but it's best known for its **birdlife**, attracted by the teeming tilapia population. White pelicans, saddlebill and yellowbill storks are all seen here, as well as a variety of kingfishers and waterfowl.

One of the best spots to see birds is from the earthen 'jetty' to the east of town, which serves Ziway's fishermen. It's known locally as the 'Cafeteria' after the much neglected park there. If you're coming from Addis Ababa, take the side road immediately after the Bekele Mola Hotel; it lies 1.5km from the main road, not far from the Santa Maria church.

The birds are particularly numerous around 4pm, when they gather to pick at the fishermen's cast-offs. You can also take a local punt (Birr25 per person after hefty negotiation) or pay a fisherman (Birr15 to Birr20) to see the **hippo pods**, about 15 minutes by boat from the jetty.

The lake is also home to five little volcanic islands. At least three of them once boasted medieval churches. Tullu Gudo, 14km from Ziway and the largest of the islands, is still home to three monasteries. **Debre Sion**, the most famous, has a long and enigmatic history. According to local tradition, the church once housed the Ark of the Covenant. Priests, fleeing the destruction of the city of Aksum at the hands of Queen Gudit in the 9th century, brought it here. The original church now lies in ruins and a new one has been built. Interestingly, the oldest written documents on Aksum were discovered here.

Tullo Gudo is a beautiful, little-visited place. The walk to the church through the *tef* (an indigenous grass), wheat and barley fields is pleasant and there are very good views from the top of the church on the top of the hill. You can also bath in hot springs; the islanders have created a little tub near the shore front. A brief exploration of the island takes around two hours.

Currently a couple of rather slow (15hp) motorboats can be hired from private operators in Ziway (but be warned that they lack radios or life jackets). Head for 'Cafeteria' (see earlier) and enquire there. A return trip to Tullo Gudo in a 20- or 30-seater boat costs Birr500 officially, but try negotiating. It takes around two hours one way. A boat operator highly recommended by one reader was **Eshetu Beresa** (☎ 41 21 51, PO Box 41, Ziway).

A trip to the nearer islands, such as Debre Sina, Galila and Bird Island (appropriately named for the birds that nest there) costs from Birr100 each, or Birr150 to Birr200 to visit all three (for one to six people).

Camping is permitted on the islands, as is fishing on the lake.

ZIWAY
ዝዋይ

☎ 06 • pop 20,056 • elevation 1846m

The town of Ziway, 158km south of Addis Ababa, is home to a fishery centre, a caustic soda factory and a prison! It's also home to some important horticultural gardens, which export fruit and vegetables (including the well-known Ziway strawberries) to, eg, Belgium and Germany. It's a pleasant, laid-back little place, with good, reasonably-priced hotels, restaurants and cafés.

Places to Stay & Eat
Lulaa Hotel (☎ 41 26 37; rooms Birr15, with shower Birr20) off the main street, close to the Agip station, has spotless rooms.

Park Hotel (☎ 41 26 71; rooms with cold/hot shower Birr17/33-44), past the Mobil petrol station, represents the best value.

Jemaneh (rooms with hot shower Birr25-35), in the town centre, around 150m from the Telecom, is probably second choice and has a pleasant compound and a popular local restaurant.

Bekele Mola Hotel (☎ 41 25 71; rooms with hot shower Birr25-30) behind the Agip station, has only adequate rooms, but its pleasant and peaceful grounds (brimful of birds) compensate.

Ziway Tourist Hotel, towards the southern end of town, is a pleasant and popular place for a drink and dinner in the evening.

About 30km south of Ziway, the new, up-market **Abule Bassuma Lodge** (☎ 01-61 55 93, fax 62 07 27; bungalows Birr230, villas Birr460-690) can be found. It lies 13km off the main Addis Ababa–Moyale road (from the junction at the village of Bulbula) on the northern tip of Lake Langano. Facilities include a tennis court, boats, horses and a pool.

Firehiwot Pastry in the town centre is the best place for breakfast and fruit juices.

Getting There & Around
Two buses leave daily for Shashemene (Birr8, 1½ to two hours); five or six buses leave for Butajira (Birr6, 1½ to two hours); and three depart for Addis Ababa (Birr14, three hours). For Debre Zeyit or Nazret, go to Mojo first (Birr8, 1½ hours, three to four buses daily).

For Lake Langano, take the bus to Shashemene or a minibus to Arsi Negele (Birr7, 45 to 50 min); ask to be dropped at the junction to the Bekele Mola or Langano Resort (Wabe Shebele) hotels (see Lake Langano).

Bikes can be hired in Ziway for Birr3 per hour from beside the bus drop-off point near the Jemaneh Hotel.

LAKE LANGANO
ላንጋኖ ሐይቅ

☎ 09

Set against the blue Arsi Mountains which rise above the lake to 4000m, Lake Langano is a scenic sort of place. But its location – a stone's throw from Addis Ababa – attracts hoards of weekenders. During the week Langano is more peaceful, and is not a bad stop-off for road-weary travellers. It also makes a convenient base for a visit to the nearby Lake Abiata-Shala National Park.

Although its curious colour resembles a cup of strong, English tea (with a dash of milk), the lake's waters are clean and it's one of the few lakes in Ethiopia to have been declared bilharzia-free.

Places to Stay & Eat

Bekele Mola Hotel *(Lake Abiata-Shala NP map; ☎ 19 00 11; camping per 2-person tent Birr30, rooms with twin beds Sun-Thur/Fri-Sat Birr172.50/207, bungalows Birr287.50/373.75)* is 3km down a road off the main Addis Ababa–Shashemene road. The turn-off is opposite the main entrance to Abiata-Shala park. It boasts a better beach than its rival the Langano Resort Hotel (Wabe Shebele), though it's still coarse and pretty grey. It can also be noisy and crowded, particularly at the weekend when young Addis Ababans come to party and chew chat (a mildly intoxicating leaf). Facilities include horse-riding (Birr60 per hour), tour boats (Birr300 for 30 minutes; up to 30 people) and pedal boats (Birr30 for 30 minutes). It also hires out four-people tents (Birr80).

If you're after a change of scene and cheaper beer (Birr3.50), the rough and ready **Jungle Bar**, 50m down the road from the Bekele Mola Hotel, provides both.

Langano Resort Hotel *(Wabe Shebele Hotel; Lake Abiata-Shala NP map; ☎ 19 01 31; camping per 2-person tent Birr25, 1-/2-/3-room bungalows Sun-Thur Birr146.25/253.75/351.25, Fri-Sat Birr183/328.75/463.75)* lies 16km north of the park main entrance, 10.3km south of Bulbula (including the 3km walk down the track east of the main road). It's less attractively designed and situated than the Bekele Mola (and the 'beach' is pebbly rather than sandy), but it's much more peaceful, particularly at weekends. Motorboats (maximum five people) can be hired (Birr2.50 per minute!) for visits to the hot springs (20 minutes one way) and for lake tours.

Both hotels serve delicious fresh tilapia (fresh-water fish), though Bekela Mola in particular is expensive (Birr25 to Birr30 for mains). If you're on a budget, bring your own food.

About 235km from Addis Ababa, close to Asela on the eastern shore of Lake Langano, is the new **Bishangari Lodge** *(☎ 09-19 02 75, in Addis Ababa ☎ 01-62 71 60, fax 62 08 26; e bishangari@telecom.com; w www .bishangari.com; bungalow twins with private shower per person weekday/weekend US$78.25/95.25, for 2 people US$137.50/167.50)*. The camp is set in 12 hectares and is a beautiful and peaceful place. It's also a terrific spot for birds (300 species recorded and eight endemics) and other wildlife. Facilities include boat, horse, mountain-bike and fishing equipment rental; guides for trekking and bird-watching; a bar set in a tree house; and a French *maître de cuisine*! Prices include meals. In 2003–04, Greenland Tours in Addis Ababa will build a further camp in Bishangari. Reservations should be made via email.

Getting There & Away

To get to/from Lake Langano, take any bus plying the Addis Ababa–Shashemene road, and ask to be dropped off/picked up (just signal) at the turn-off to your hotel. From both turn-offs it's a 3km walk to the hotel.

LAKE ABIATA-SHALA NATIONAL PARK

አባያታ ሻላ ሐይቅ ብሔራዊ ፓርክ

Of much greater interest than Lake Langano are the twin lakes of Abiata and Shala, which form part of the 887 sq km Lake Abiata-Shala National Park *(admission per 48h Birr50; vehicles of up to 5 seats Birr10, pay at main entrance)*. Mt Fike (2075m), which sits atop the 3km-wide strip of land separating the two lakes, dominates the landscape.

Lake Abiata provides the main source of food for the colonies of great white pelicans on the nearby Lake Shala islands. The latter is one of seven nesting sites of the bird in the whole of Africa.

Unfortunately, the park has suffered greatly at the hands of humans. Much of the thick acacia woodland surrounding Lake

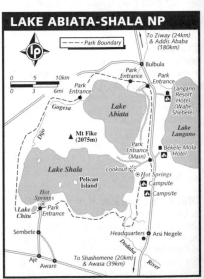

LAKE ABIATA-SHALA NP

Arab architecture in Massawa

Coffee served the traditional way, Dahlak Kebir

Catholic cathedral, Asmara

Shop doorway in Dankalia region

Red Sea coast near Assab

A woman winnowing, Senafe

Monastery of Debre Libanos, near Senafe

The Dankalia region, one of the most desolate places on earth

Abiata has been turned into charcoal. Commercial farms and a mined soda-ash factory near Lake Abiata have caused much pollution. A decrease in the fish population has also led to a dramatic fall in the populations of pelicans and flamingos. Additionally, large numbers of local people have illegally settled in the park and their domestic animals and plantations have taken over much of it.

Despite all these disturbances the park is worth a visit. Some of the scenery is very beautiful; at dusk, the sight of pelicans dipping into the silver waters of Lake Abiata is unforgettable.

Information
Armed scouts (Birr30/100 for short vehicle trips/whole day by foot) are advised, as robberies and car break-ins have occurred. They can also act as guides; you find them at the main entrance. If you have a vehicle, don't leave it unattended; guards can be hired.

If you're particularly keen to see flamingos and pelicans, head for Lake Abiata. January and February are the best months. Go early in the morning or late in the afternoon; the wildlife is better and you'll avoid the heat of the day.

Things to See
Although they are called 'twin' lakes, Abiata and Shala could not be more different from one another. Lake Abiata is a shallow, brackish pan, just 14m deep. Its natural level fluctuates periodically, leaving mud banks and grass flats exposed, which attract many birds, including colonies of **flamingos**.

Lake Shala, on the other hand, is a crater lake. With a depth of around 260m, it's the deepest in the Ethiopian Rift Valley. A few volcanic islands dot its surface, and around about, several **sulphurous springs** bubble up. A kind of local resort has grown up to the northeast of the lake. Amid the steaming springs people bathe, wash clothes and seek cures for rheumatic ailments. Since the water of the lake has a high saline content, fish are not found here.

The islands on Lake Shala are home to the most important breeding colony of **great white pelicans** in Africa. Because of the lack of fish in the lake, the birds are obliged to feed at Lake Abiata. The islands are protected sanctuaries and can't be visited. There are good views over both lakes from the **lookout point**.

Other birds seen on the lake include ·African fish eagles, various waders and water birds including several species of duck. In the surrounding acacia woodland, various species of weaver bird, the red-billed hornbill, Didric's cuckoo, the Abyssinian roller and the superb starling can be seen.

According to the tourist literature, the park is also home to various mammals including greater kudus, warthogs, golden jackals and oribi antelopes. Unfortunately, because of the many disturbances to the park, very few of these are in evidence. Beautiful **Grant's gazelles** are quite often seen just beyond the park barrier.

Places to Stay & Eat
Camping (adult/child per 48h Birr20/5) is permitted anywhere, but three main sites are suggested by the park.

Lake Langano makes a good base from which to visit these lakes (see Lake Langano earlier).

For budget hotels, head for the town of Arsi Negele. **Tsaday Hotel** (doubles with shared shower Birr7-15), 400m south of the bus station on the main Addis Ababa–Shashemene road, is the best bet.

Getting There & Around
The main entrance to the park is signposted on the main Addis Ababa–Moyale road. Any bus doing the Addis Ababa–Shashemene run can drop you off at the entrance gate.

From the main park entrance to Lake Abiata-Shala National Park (up to the hot springs) is around 8km. A circuit is between 14km and 18km. If you're driving, road conditions usually make a 4WD essential.

SHASHEMENE
ሻ ሸመኔ
☎ 06 • pop 52,080 • elevation 1700m
Lying at an important crossroads connecting the north to the south and the east to the west, Shashemene bustles with traffic and trade. Like all crossroads towns, it's grubby, noisy and shambolic. With bars cheek by jowl with brothels, blaring music shops and truckers' cafés, Shashemene is a strong contender for the least-attractive-town-in-Ethiopia award. Both Wondo Genet and Awasa are much more pleasant places to stay. However, some travellers may be obliged to overnight here, particularly if catching early buses.

In the town, keep an eye out for pick pockets and petty thieves. Some travellers have also reported – very unusual in Ethiopia – hostility towards faranjis.

SHASHEMENE

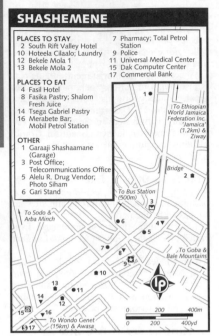

PLACES TO STAY
2 South Rift Valley Hotel
10 Hoteela Cilaalo; Laundry
12 Bekele Mola 1
13 Bekele Mola 2

PLACES TO EAT
4 Fasil Hotel
8 Fasika Pastry; Shalom
    Fresh Juice
14 Tsega Gabriel Pastry
16 Merabete Bar;
    Mobil Petrol Station

OTHER
1 Garaaji Shashaamane
    (Garage)
3 Post Office;
    Telecommunications Office
5 Alelu R. Drug Vendor;
    Photo Siham
6 Gari Stand

7 Pharmacy; Total Petrol
    Station
9 Police
11 Universal Medical Center
15 Dak Computer Center
17 Commercial Bank

To Ethiopian World Jamaica Federation Inc. 'Jamaica' (1.2km) & Ziway

Bridge

To Bus Station (500m)

To Sodo & Arba Minch

To Goba & Bale Mountains

To Wondo Genet (15km) & Awasa

0   200   400m
0   200   400yd

There is Internet access (Birr0.75) at the **Dak Computer Center** in the same building as the Awash International Bank.

Jamaica

Shashemene can boast one claim: it is the unofficial capital of the Ethiopian Rastafarian community. The community's official name is the **Ethiopian World Jamaica Federation Inc** (☎ 10 27 51), but the locals know it simply as 'Jamaica'. It lies on the main Addis Ababa road, 1.7km north of the Agip petrol station (north of Shashemene).

Though usually hospitable and welcoming, the community is understandably reluctant to be viewed either as a tourist attraction or as a source of marijuana (illegal anyway in Ethiopia and the cause of recent police raids). If you're genuinely interested in the movement, it's possible to share a meal with the community and learn about its history, but contributions or donations are expected. There's also a gift shop. Camping in its compound is permitted.

Places to Stay & Eat

Hoteela Cilaalo (☎ 10 37 20; doubles with shared shower Birr15) is probably the best budget place.

Bekele Mola 2 (☎ 10 33 48; doubles/twins with private shower Birr30-35/40) is quiet, clean and good value. It also serves quite good faranji food including fresh fish.

Bekele Mola 1 (☎ 10 33 44; rooms with private shower Birr40) is currently undergoing renovation.

South Rift Valley Hotel (☎ 10 37 25; doubles with private bathroom Birr30-60) lies on the outskirts of town and has an extensive and well-designed garden. Rooms have TV. It also serves good faranji food.

Fasil Hotel is rated highly by Shashemenites for its local food. **Merabete Bar** is also good.

Fasika Pastry, **Tsega Pastry** and **Shalom Fresh Juice** are all good for snacks.

Rastafarians

When the Emperor Haile Selassie was crowned in 1930, he assumed subjects who lived far beyond the confines of his own kingdom. In Jamaica, where Marcus Garvey's 'return to Africa' movement had been established, many saw the emperor's coronation as fulfilment of the ancient biblical prophesy that 'Kings will come out of Africa'.

Identifying themselves passionately with the new Ethiopian monarch, as well as with Ethiopia's status as an independent African state, Garvey's followers rejected European Christianity and created a new religion of their own.

In it, the emperor was accorded divinity – the Messiah of African redemption. The new faith's name was derived from the emperor's name before he assumed the crown: Ras Tafari. The emperor, meanwhile, was said to have been a bit embarrassed by all this unexpected adulation.

Rastafarians follow strict dietary taboos: pork, milk and coffee are forbidden. Ganga (marijuana) is held to be a sacrament.

Today, the Rastas patiently await the restoration of the Ethiopian monarchy. The Ethiopian–Eritrean War at the end of the 1990s was seen as a punishment visited on the country for having killed its king – the chosen one of God.

Getting There & Away

Shashemene is the principal transport hub of the south, and you can catch buses from it, in any direction.

Around ten buses leave daily for Addis Ababa (Birr20 to Birr23, 5½ hours); one to Arba Minch (Birr24, five to six hours); two to Goba (Birr25.35, six to seven hours); eight to 10 buses to Ziway (Birr8 to Birr10, two hours); one to Moyale (Birr40, 1½ days, overnight in Yabelo). Six buses/minibuses run daily to Dila (Birr12 to Birr17, three hours) and leave every 15 minutes or so to Awasa (Birr3 to Birr4, 30 min).

If you're planning an early start, try and get the ticket by 5.30am, or you may find yourself stuck in Shashemene for another day.

Getting Around

The bus station lies 500m off the main road; a gari to your hotel costs Birr1. Bikes can be hired for Birr10 per half day, Birr12 for a full day.

AROUND SHASHEMENE
Wondo Genet
ወንዶ ገነት

A worthwhile detour off the main north–south route is to the hot-springs resort of Wondo Genet, around 15km southeast of Shashemene. Surrounded by dense forest, filled with bird song, and – in season – overflowing with fruit and honey, it's like arriving in the Promised Land. If you've spent too much time in Addis Ababa, if you've taken one bus too many or if you're just after some peace and quiet, Wondo Genet may be just the ticket. It's also rather a romantic place, and may provide a timely panacea for jaded and bickering couples! Be aware that the resort is 50% busier at weekends, so choose a weekday if you possibly can – it's also cheaper then.

The Wondo Genet Resort Hotel (see Places to Stay & Eat following), set amid citrus orchards and flowering gardens, sits on a natural balcony overlooking the Rift Valley. In the hotel grounds, a couple of swimming pools fed with natural hot-spring water can be used any time of day or night. Next to the pools, the spring water is piped over the cliff face to make a waterfall-type shower.

There's great hiking to be had in the surrounding forest. Birdlife in the forest is abundant. Bushbucks, hyena and Anubis baboons are also found here. In the gardens, colobus and vervet monkeys are easily seen.

The nearby Wondo Genet Agricultural College (☎ 20 23 19, fax 20 24 90; admission free; open 8.30am-12.30pm & 1.30pm-5.30pm Mon-Fri) can also be visited. It lies 2km down the road from the springs. In its beautiful forests, many indigenous tree species have been replanted. Parts of the ancient forest also remain, and give a great insight into how Ethiopia's countryside must once have looked. There's also an arboretum with over 124 species of trees. Six endemic birds are found in the forest.

The hot springs and pool (admission Birr3.45) lie 300m from the hotel. The main pool is emptied for cleaning every Wednesday.

Guides to the surrounding forests can be organised by the hotel (half day Birr100, full day Birr150). Guided walks include excursions to local villages and plantations, and bird- or wildlife-spotting trips. You can also follow the springs upstream. A 10-minute walk immediately above the springs will take you to their source, where you can see the cooling system in action. In the boiling water upstream, local cowherds cook their lunch: 17 minutes for potatoes, 35 minutes for maize!

If you've come without your bathers, costumes and trunks can be bought at the shop near the entrance to the springs.

Places to Stay & Eat The only accommodation in Wondo Genet is at the Wondo Genet Resort Hotel (☎ 20 37 63; camping per person Birr37.50, doubles weekday/weekend Birr146.25/183.75, Menelik suite Birr327.85/421.60). Campers have access to pools and showers. Prices are a little high for what you get: the usual 1970s decor and rundown bathroom, typical of Ethiopian government hotels. It's the location you're paying for. Reservations (advised at the weekend) should be made through the Wabe Shebele head office (☎ 01-51 71 87, fax 51 84 77; e washo.et@telecom.net.et).

A restaurant and a snack bar near the springs (snacks and mains from Birr6 to Birr16 plus tax) serve both faranji and Ethiopian food. For a picnic, lunch boxes (around Birr30) can be prepared. If there are several of you, a barbeque around a campfire (including a whole roasted sheep) can be arranged (Birr375 for up to 10 people).

Delicious fruit can be bought from along the road leading to the springs, including in season papaya, avocado, banana and mango. Try a local favourite, the kazmir. The area is

ETHIOPIA

also known for its *chat* (see the boxed text 'Chat Among the Pigeons' in the Eastern Ethiopia chapter). This may be the perfect place for a chew, if you fancy it!

A cheaper alternative is to use the facilities at Wondo Genet but stay at the nearby village of Washa. **Abyssinia Hotel** *(camping per tent Birr10, doubles with shared shower Birr15)* is the best budget bet with quite a pleasant garden and a reasonable restaurant.

Getting There & Away From Shashemene, buses and minibuses (Birr3 to Birr4, 30 minutes) run about every half hour (to around 5.30pm) to and from Wondo Genet (in fact to the village of Wondo Washa, not far from the springs). The turn-off to the springs is in the middle of the village on the left, from where it's a 3km walk.

At the weekend, you can sometimes find minibuses (Birr5) travelling all the way to the springs.

For a bus back, wait on the Shashemene road opposite the junction to the springs in Wondo Washa. It's possible to take a *gari* (Birr7 to Birr10) from the village to the springs.

A contract minibus (up to 10 people) from Shashemene costs Birr250 to Birr300 return (including waiting time). Bikes – great for reaching the springs – can also be hired in Shashemene.

Senkele Wildlife Sanctuary
ሰንከሌ የዱር አራዊት ፓርከ

The Senkele Wildlife Sanctuary *(admission per person Birr50, per vehicle Birr20)*, 28km west of Shashemene, stretches over 36 sq km and was originally established to protect the Swayne's hartebeest (an endemic race of hartebeest).

Other mammals found in the park include Bohor reedbucks, greater kudus, spotted hyenas, serval and civet cats, caracals, warthogs, common jackals and oribi antelopes, as well as 91 species of bird.

The open acacia woodland of the park is quite scenic and some of the animals are fairly easily spotted, particularly the Swayne's hartebeest, the population of which is currently estimated at between 400 and 500.

The park is worth a visit if you're in the vicinity. There's a 65km track around the park, but not all of it is maintained. From the Borana Hill, around 6km east of the park office, there are good panoramic views.

Until recently, the park was overrun with livestock. In 2001, however, following an agreement between Aje administration elders and park officials, most settlements were cleared. The future is looking brighter for wildlife here, and numbers (particularly of hartebeest) already appear to be on the increase.

Visitors must contact the **Administration Office** (☎ 10 34 46; open 8.30am-12.30pm & 1.30pm-5.30pm Mon-Fri) in Aje before visiting the park, where a guide can be provided. The best time to visit is early in the morning or after 4pm.

Zed Hotel *(doubles with bucket shower Birr6)* is basic but about the best if you get stuck in Aje. Diagonally opposite is **Tinsae**, the best restaurant.

The road leading to the park lies 5km west of the town of Aje. From the turn-off to the park gate, it's another 17.5km to the park headquarters. To and from Shashemene around 20 minibuses run daily (Birr3, 25 to 30 minutes). A contract minibus to the park from Aje should cost around Birr200 to Birr300 return, including around two hours waiting time; in the dry season, it's possible to drive around parts of the park.

If you're continuing on towards Arba Minch, you'll pass through some of the most fertile land in Ethiopia, where abundant fruit and cotton is grown. If the bus stops, don't miss the bananas – no bigger than your middle finger, but as sweet as honey (just Birr1 for around 1kg!). A local favourite, *gishta*, is worth tasting! Look out for the Wolaita 'haircut houses' too, with neatly trimmed eaves that look just like fringes.

AWASA
አዋሳ

☎ 06 • pop 69,169 • elevation 1708m

Awasa is the capital of the old Sidamo province. Poised at the edge of Lake Awasa, it's an attractive town in a beautiful setting. There's not much to see in the town, but it's a pleasant place to break the north–south journey and is well equipped with places to stay and eat.

A small **tourist office** (☎ 20 09 28) operates inside the bus station, which can give information on nearby sites of interest. Another usually operates in the grounds of the Wabe Shebele Hotel.

Internet access (Birr0.50 per minute) can be had at **City Business Computers** *(CBC, ☎ 20 40 94)* in the office block next to the Post Rendez-Vous Café, and at **Router** (☎ 20 63 15) on the third floor of the crescent-shaped Gudumaale House shopping complex.

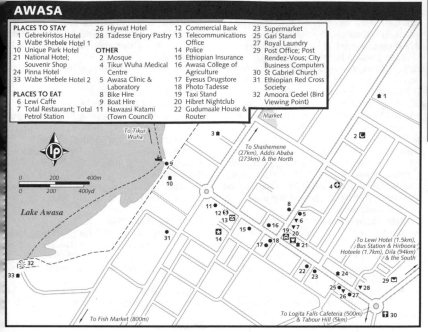

AWASA

PLACES TO STAY
1 Gebrekiristos Hotel
3 Wabe Shebele Hotel 1
10 Unique Park Hotel
21 National Hotel;
   Souvenir Shop
24 Pinna Hotel
33 Wabe Shebele Hotel 2

PLACES TO EAT
6 Lewi Caffe
7 Total Restaurant; Total
   Petrol Station

26 Hiywat Hotel
28 Tadesse Enjory Pastry

OTHER
2 Mosque
4 Tikur Wuha Medical
   Centre
8 Awasa Clinic &
   Laboratory
9 Boat Hire
11 Hawaasi Katami
   (Town Council)

12 Commercial Bank
13 Telecommunications
   Office
14 Police
15 Ethiopian Insurance
16 Awasa College of
   Agriculture
17 Eyesus Drugstore
18 Photo Tadesse
19 Taxi Stand
20 Hibret Nightclub
22 Gudumaale House &
   Router

23 Supermarket
25 Gari Stand
27 Royal Laundry
29 Post Office; Post
   Rendez-Vous; City
   Business Computers
30 St Gabriel Church
31 Ethiopian Red Cross
   Society
32 Amoora Gedel (Bird
   Viewing Point)

Things to See & Do

Though there isn't a great deal to see or do in Awasa, a boat trip on the lake in the late afternoon makes a pleasant excursion. **Rowing boats, with rower** *(per hour for 1-5 people Birr50)* can be hired at the small pier just beyond the Unique Park Hotel.

The waters, teeming with tilapia, catfish and barbus, attract good birdlife. Kingfishers, herons, storks, crakes, darters and plovers are among the species commonly seen on the waters' edge. The fig forest and scrub around parts of the lake attract weavers and hornbills, as well as the endemic black-winged lovebird.

Possible boat trips include: to **Tikur Wuha** (Black Water) to see the hippos and birds (around three hours return), and to **Amoora Gedel** (Crow Valley), behind the Wabe Shebele Hotel 2 (1½ to two hours return), one of the best places for birds. If you want to make an early start to see birds, organise the boat the night before.

If you fancy some fishing, do what the locals do and take a boat to the wooden platform out on the lake. Hooks and line can be bought in various shops in town (such as around the Eyesus Drugstore), or ask a local lad to fetch you some. You can also fish from a boat.

A pleasant walk is along the footpath at the edge of the lake, leading southwards from Wabe Shebele Hotel 1. For a good view of the lake, you can climb Tabour Hill, around 5km south of town.

The town **market** *(Mon & Thur)* and the **fish market** *(open 6.30am-9am daily)* are worth a wander. Sidama, Amharas and Gurages come in from all around. Straw hats, baskets and mats are all typical Sidama products. A shop selling some traditional clothes and scarves can be found next door to the National Hotel.

Places to Stay

National Hotel *(☎ 20 13 10; doubles with cold shared shower Birr12)* has small but clean rooms around a courtyard.

Unique Park Hotel *(☎ 20 13 18; doubles with cold/hot shower Birr20/25)*, situated close to the lakefront, is probably the best value in town. Simple but comfortable rooms are set around an attractive garden, which teems with birds. It's also a pleasant place for a drink.

Lewi Hotel *(☎ 20 01 28; doubles with hot shower/satellite TV Birr35/60)* just up from the bus station (going west along the main road) is a new place with quite comfortable rooms and its own pastry shop and restaurant.

ETHIOPIA

Gebrekiristos Hotel (☎ 20 27 80; doubles Birr40-75.90) has comfortable and quiet rooms, if a little characterless. More expensive rooms have telephone, TV and fridge.

Wabe Shebele Hotel 2 (☎ 20 53 97; camping per tent Birr40, twins/doubles in bungalows Birr78.25/93.75) offers the usual government 1970s-style, overpriced rooms. But the beautiful, shady grounds compensate. An outdoor pool is filled from Friday to Sunday (Birr8.75 for nonguests). The grounds teem with birds and the breezy terrace by the lake is a lovely place for an evening drink (coffee/beer Birr2/ 5.10). Boats can be hired for Birr72 per hour.

Pinna Hotel (☎ 20 24 11, fax 20 23 43; doubles/twins Birr156/186) is modern and pleasantly furnished. Rooms have TV, veranda and telephone.

Wabe Shebele Hotel 1 (☎ 20 53 96; camping Birr40 per tent, bungalows or villas with 1/2/3 bedrooms Birr156.25/166.25/273.75) is even poorer value than Wabe Shebele Hotel 2, but has a pool (Birr10 per person) and tennis court (Birr4.50 per hour). Rooms have TV, fridge, telephone and verandah.

The new **Hirboora Hoteela** is being built opposite the bus station.

Places to Eat

Pinna Hotel has a pastry shop (with a good selection of home-baked cakes) and a restaurant (with a pleasant balcony), considered one of the best places for *faranji* food (mains from Birr8 to Birr12.50). There's also a good but pricey wine list.

Total Restaurant behind the Total station is similar but with a good selection of veggie options.

Lewi Caffe, a local favourite, is a good and cheap place for breakfast (though the menu's in Amharic).

Tadesse Enjory Pastry, with a pleasant terrace on the main drag, is a good place for cakes, fruit juices, breakfast and snacks. The sign is in Amharic only; look for the yellow-and-white striped awnings.

Post Rendez-Vous (open 6am-9pm daily), a popular local hang out, is good for an early evening drink, and also serves a variety of *faranji* food including pasta (Birr7), pizza (Birr10) and even veggie burgers (Birr4).

Hiywat Hotel is considered one of the best places in town for local food and particularly *kitfo* and fish dishes. It's got a pleasant shaded terrace.

Logita Falls Cafeteria is an atmospheric place for local food, served in a large *tukul*.

Getting There & Away

The main bus station lies 1.7km from the town, but you can ask buses to drop you off in the centre. Otherwise, *garis* are available at the station.

Usually five buses run daily to Addis Ababa (Birr25.10, five to six hours), one bus to Arba Minch (Birr25, six hours) and Moyale (Birr47, 14 hours, overnight in Dila). Buses run every 30 minutes to Shashemene (Birr4, 30 minutes). For Ziway (Birr15, two hours), take the Addis Ababa bus, if there's space, or change at Shashemene. There are usually three to five buses daily to Wondo Genet (Birr6, one hour); if not go to Shashemene and change there. Ten minibuses a day run to Dila (Birr13, 1½ hours).

Getting Around

Garis charge Birr1.50/2 for short/long journeys or Birr3/20 per hour/day. Taxis cost around Birr30 per hour, or Birr10 to Birr20 for journeys around town; you'll need to negotiate hard.

Bikes (Birr3 to Birr4 per hour) can be hired from diagonally opposite Lewi Caffe.

DILA
ዲላ

Dila, south of Awasa, represents a kind of epicentre of the southern Ethiopian tradition of **stelae** erection. Before visiting any of the monoliths, permission papers must be obtained from the Gedeo Culture & Information Office in Dila, where you can also find a guide.

Tutu Fella is probably one of the most impressive sites. It lies near the village of **Wenago**, 13km from Dila, along a track up a hill. Around 80 stones are variously carved with facial features, phalluses etc. The 'sex' of the stone is believed to represent the sex of the person buried underneath.

Tutiti, the second major site in the area, lies on a hill 2.3km from the village of **Chalba** and consists of some very large, tapering, generally uncarved standing stones, again marking graves.

Also worth strolling through is Dila's large **market**; *enset*-made parasols shelter abundant agricultural produce.

Zeleke Hotel (rooms Birr15, with hot shower Birr25) is probably the best place to stay. **Get Smart Restaurant** is considered a smart place to eat. **Delight Pasty** is good for cakes, fruit juices and breakfast.

One bus leaves daily for Yabelo (Birr24, four hours) and for Moyale (Birr34, seven hours). Four or five buses run daily to Shashemene (Birr14, three hours) via Awasa (Birr10, 2½ hours).

YABELO
ያቤሎ

Yabelo, about 5km off the main north–south road, makes a convenient base for a visit to **Yabelo Wildlife Sanctuary** and a couple of other places nearby.

If you get here on a Saturday, the local Borena market is worth a peek. Electricity is very erratic in Yabelo. The Commercial Bank currently changes cash only.

Borena Wubit Hotel *(doubles without shower Birr20)*, with no bar, is the quietest budget option.

Yavello Hotel *(☎ 31 23 27, fax 31 23 27; camping Birr10, doubles with/without shower Birr50/20)* is a new top address. Prices may rise to Birr100 with the installation of telephone and satellite TV. It lies beside the Mobil petrol station at the Yabelo–Dila–Moyale junction (ask the bus to drop you there).

Salam Restaurant is considered a good bet locally. **Kokeb Restaurant** (sign in Amharic only) has a small grocery.

One bus and two or three minibuses leave daily for Moyale (Birr20 to Birr22, three hours) and one bus and one minibus for Dila (Birr23 to Birr25, five hours). Only Isuzu pick-up trucks run to Konso (Birr20, three hours, two to three daily).

AROUND YABELO

A foray into Borena territory is worthwhile. The famous *ela* or **'singing wells'** (see the boxed text 'The Singing Wells of the Borena' following) are dotted around the nearby village of Dublock, 70km south of Yabelo. There are nine wells currently operating in the region; some have been operating for more than a century.

To find them, you'll need a guide from Dublock. Borena chieftains now charge tourists an entrance fee: Birr5 per man working in the well; Birr20 for the owner of the well and Birr10 for the 'broker' (ie, a total of about Birr80), though brokers may well ask much more initially.

To see the real water gathering (rather than a performance), come between January and March (during the dry season when the cattle come to drink).

At least nine buses ply the Addis Ababa–Moyale road from towns north and south of Dublock and can drop you off at the village. Getting to some wells involves quite long walks.

The village of El Sod, around 12km south of Dublock, lies beside one of the largest salt deposits in Ethiopia. Known as the **House of Salt**, it's famous for its 100m-deep crater lake, one of four in the region. The lake is about 800m across and is so dark, it looks like an oil slick. Valuable, muddy, black salt has been extracted from the lake for centuries. Today, donkeys laden with the mud continue to toil up the steep sides of the crater.

From the village, it's a 30-minute walk down into the crater and a one hour walk up (admission Birr50 per person and per vehicle, Birr100 for two compulsory guides). The best time to visit is in the morning, when it's not so hot. One bus runs weekly (Friday) from Dublock; otherwise you can try hitching.

Around 26km south of El Sod, a couple of kilometres north of Mega, look out for the

The Singing Wells of the Borena

Inhabiting the dry, hot plains to the east of Konso, the Borena people are semi-nomadic pastoralists whose lives revolve entirely around their cattle. During the long dry season, it is a constant struggle to keep their vast herds alive. To combat the problem, the Borena have developed their own peculiar solution: a series of wells dug deep into the earth. Each Borena family and each clan is assigned its own well.

A series of water troughs are dug close to each well's mouth. Approaching them is a long channel that drops to about 10m below the ground level, which funnels the cattle to the troughs. It's just wide enough to allow two single columns of cattle to pass one another.

When it is time to water the cattle, the men create a kind of human ladder down the well (which can be up to 30m deep), tossing buckets of water between one another from the bottom up to the top, where the troughs are gradually filled. The work is very strenuous, and the men often sing in harmony to encourage one another as well as to reassure the cattle. Several hundred or even thousand cattle come to drink at a time; it's a memorable and unique sight.

remains of an old Italian fort, dating from the time of the invasion. Though impressive from the road, there's little to see within.

YABELO WILDLIFE SANCTUARY
ያቤሎ የዱር አራዊት ፓርክ

Covering an area of 2496 sq km, the Yabelo Wildlife Sanctuary *(admission free)* was created originally to protect the endemic Swayne's hartebeest. It is now better known for its birds, and contains some 194 species including the endemic white-tailed swallow (quite commonly seen around dusk) and the commonly seen Stresemann's bush crow, which was first described in the 1930s and '40s.

The 25 mammal species inhabiting the acacia woodland and savanna grass include Burchell's zebra, the dik-dik, the greater and lesser kudus, the gerenuk and Grant's gazelle, all quite commonly seen. The golden jackal and ostrich are sometimes seen in the area.

The town of Yabelo provides the nearest accommodation. Travellers are advised to report to Yabelo Administration before a visit to the park. Scouts-cum-guides can be provided (half day/full day Birr25/50).

MOYALE
ሞያሌ

Two towns have grown up on either side of the Ethiopia–Kenya border; both are called Moyale. If you have to spend the night here, the Ethiopian Moyale is the more pleasant of the two and hotels and restaurants are better on this side of the border.

Places to Stay & Eat

Hootela Afrika *(☎ 44 00 15; doubles/twins with shared shower Birr10/13)*, tucked away off the main road around 40m from the Police Branch Office, is simple but peaceful and clean.

Hoteela Teodros *(☎ 44 00 65; rooms with/ without shower Birr20/15)*, opposite the Mobil station at the northern end of town, is good value.

Bekele Mola Hotel *(☎ 44 00 30; doubles with/without shower Birr32/20)*, also near the northern end of town, is peaceful.

Ysosadayo Borena Moyale Hotel *(doubles/twins with cold shower Birr25/37)*, 200m from the Mobil station opposite the Commercial Bank, is probably the best value, and has the most character.

Fikadu Restaurant not far from Ethiopian immigration is considered the best restaurant. It also has a lively bar.

Hotel Tawakal *(singles/twins with shared shower KSh150/300)*, on the Kenyan side 400m from the main square, is cleaner and quieter than most (alcohol and bar girls are not allowed) and serves good food.

Al-Rahma Hotel is considered the best restaurant on the Kenyan side of the border.

Getting There & Away

Ethiopia From Moyale, one to two buses leave daily for Yabelo (Birr20, five hours) and one bus leaves daily for Shashemene (Birr48, 13 hours) via Dublock, Dila and Awasa. For Addis Ababa, go first to Shashemene. A couple of pick-up trucks leave weekly for Negele Borena (Birr50).

Kenya By land, there are two routes to Nairobi, via Wajir and via Isiolo. Between five and 20 trucks leave daily from Moyale for Nairobi (KSh1500 for front seats; overnight in Marsabit and Isiolo, arriving on the third day at 8am).

If you miss the Nairobi trucks, you can hitch a ride with one of the trucks (10 per day) departing from Isiolo (KSh800 for back seats, KSh1000 for front seats, two days, overnight in Marsabit). From Isiolo, you can take one of the many minibuses or Peugeot taxis to Nairobi (from KSh350, six hours).

For Wajir, around four public Land Cruisers do the journey daily (KSh400, four to six hours). From Wajir, two buses depart every morning for Nairobi (KSh1200, around eight hours).

Aban Agencies *(☎/fax 01-85 24 55)*, 100m from the main square opposite the two-storey building, sells one-way air tickets to Nairobi for KSh8000 to KSh10,000 depending on the season. See the Getting There & Away chapter (also for immigration details).

ARBA MINCH
አርባ ምንጭ
☎ 06 • pop 40,020 • elevation 1400m to 1600m

Arba Minch, the capital of the old Gamo-Gofa province, is the largest town in southern Ethiopia. Set on an escarpment overlooking Lake Abaya to the north, Lake Chamo to the south, and the Rift Valley to the west, the town boasts a lovely position. It also makes a good base for exploring the nearby Rift Valley lakes, the beautiful Nechisar National Park and the highland towns of Dorze and Chencha.

If you've just emerged from the Omo Valley, Arba Minch will seem like a place of incredible sophistication, with its 24-hour electricity, real loos, cappuccinos and pastries.

Even so, at first sight – and after all the tourist literature – Arba Minch disappoints. On arrival you are greeted by a line of pylons and the streets are grubby and chaotic. But Arba Minch will soon start to work its charm. A bit of advice? Head straight for the terrace of the Bekele Mola Hotel near the southern entrance to the town; you'll soon see why. There is good walking in the area.

Orientation & Information

The town consists of two settlements connected by a 4km stretch of asphalt. Sikela, on the plain to the north, is the commercial and residential centre; Shecha, perched on the hill overlooking the lakes to the south, is where most of the government buildings are found, as well as the 'smarter' tourist hotels.

A few travellers wrote to complain of hustlers posing as guides. They tend to hang around the tourist hotels. For information, head for the **tourism office** (☎ 81 01 27; open 8.30am-12.30pm & 1.30-5.30pm Mon-Fri) which is situated within the Trade, Industry & Urban Development building, 100m from the Agip station. Ask for the excellent and indefatigable Kapo Kansa, who can suggest treks in the park, surrounding forests and Guge Mountains as well as cycling and bird-watching trips.

He'll also provide a guide (half day/full day Birr50/100), organise boats (from Birr300 for up to 10 people), mountain bikes (US$8 per day), car hire (from US$100 per day all-inclusive), and basic fishing equipment.

The **Sol Computer Center** (☎ 81 11 26; open 7am-8pm daily) opposite the Sol Café has Internet access (Birr0.75 per minute). The **Souvenir & Art Shop** has an eclectic collection of crafts and curios.

Lakes Abaya & Chamo

Measuring 1160 sq km, Lake Abaya is the longest and the largest of the Rift Valley lakes. Its peculiar dark red colour is caused by suspended hydroxide in its waters. The smaller Lake Chamo (551 sq km) lies to the south. Both are ringed by savanna plains. Many consider the lakes to be the most beautiful in the Rift Valley chain. The ridge of land that divides the two lakes is known as 'Bridge of God' or 'Heaven' for the commanding and beautiful views from it.

On the waters of lake Abaya, look out for the Hararus in their high-prowed *wogolo* boats. Made of *isoke*, a very light-weight local wood, the boats are capable of carrying quite heavy loads (including cattle).

Forty Springs

Arba Minch (Forty Springs) derives its name from the innumerable little springs that bubble up in the evergreen forest covering the flats below the town. It is the site of the only ground-water forest in East Africa, and the semipluvial vegetation is home to good birdlife and a variety of mammals. You can bathe in the pools around the springs.

For security reasons, a visit to the springs (the town's main water supply) requires a permission paper from the **Arba Minch Water Supplies Service** (☎ 81 02 52; open 8am-noon & 1pm-4pm Mon-Fri, 8am-noon Sat). It's a simple, quick and free procedure. Note that it's not worth while trying to sneak in – in December 2002, a guard fired a warning shot at a couple of travellers who had tried to do so!

To get to the springs, take the road towards Nechisar National Park. Where the road forks, 600m from the roundabout at Sikela, take the road that bears right. The springs are a further 2.8km away. You can camp here if you wish; it's also a great place for a picnic.

Crocodile Market

Azzo Gabaya (see the Nechisar National Park map) is said to have Africa's most impressive display of big crocodiles. Sunning themselves on the warm sand of the lakeshore at the point where the Kolfo River empties into the lake, Arba Minch's crocodiles are fat and famous.

A 15- to 30-minute boat ride (depending on weather, the level of water and the speed of the boat) takes you to the spot. A minimum of two to three hours should be allowed for the trip. The boat launching point is down a track to the east off the Konso road, 8km south of the roundabout in Shecha. The best time to go is in the late afternoon, around 4.30pm, or early in the morning, when it's cooler. Hippos can also be seen here, but they are shy since the Ganjule people hunt and eat them. Twitchers should take the trip just for the birdlife.

The crocodile market can also be approached by land through the park. However, be very careful. Fishermen continue to be taken by crocodiles (six were attacked on Lake Abaya alone in 2001–02). An armed scout from Nechisar National Park is advised. If you hire a boat, don't dangle your legs or arms in the water. Note that as the Market forms part of the Nechissar National Park,

ETHIOPIA

you should officially pay the entrance fee before visiting (see Orientation & Information under Nechisar National Park later).

The tourist office can organise boats, or you can go directly to the tour operators, among them **TEM** *(☎ 81 12 57; boats for 1/2 people Birr100/200)*. With more boats, but a little more expensive is **Arba Minch Fishery** *(☎ 81 01 97; open 6.30am-5.30pm Mon-Sat; boat hire up to 2h for 1/2-3/4-5 people Birr250/300/350)*. Life-jackets are available.

Crocodile Farm & Hippo-Viewing Platform

The government **crocodile farm** *(Nechisar National Park map; ☎ 81 17 57; admission Birr10; open 8am-noon & 1.30pm-5.30pm daily)* contains around 5000 crocs (living in rather cramped enclosures) and serves three purposes: as a commercial venture, a centre of research, and as a tourist attraction. Most of the hapless crocs will end up as handbags or belts in Middle Eastern markets.

Eggs are collected from the lakeshores, then incubated and hatched at the farm. They are slaughtered when they are around 13 years old. The guided tour (20 to 30 minutes) is free, but you should tip afterwards.

The farm lies off the Addis Ababa road past the old airport, 7km from the roundabout at Sikela. You can walk, bike or hitch part of the way or get a contract taxi here from Arba Minch for Birr40 to Birr50 one way, Birr 80 to Birr100 return.

Two to three minutes' walk from the farm on the edge of Lake Abaya is the new hippo-viewing platform. The best time to go is between 4pm and 6pm; it's also a good spot for bird-watching. An entrance fee may be charged in the future.

Markets

At the Arba Minch markets, look out for the delightful bamboo *doro beat*, tiny hen houses that look like miniature *tukuls*; they cost just Birr5 to Birr10. Good fresh fruit can also be bought including papaya and mango.

Fishing

Fishing on the lakes is permitted. Tilapia, catfish, barbus and some tigerfish are all found in Lake Chamo, as are the famously large Nile perch (which can weigh more than 100kg).

Places to Stay

There's no shortage of reasonably-priced hotels in Arba Minch, but they can be noisy. Of the Sikela and Shecha, the upper town is probably the better choice; it's a little cooler, quieter and has a better choice of restaurants. **Camping sites** are currently being prepared in the forest near the crocodile farm.

Sikela Basic but clean rooms are available at **Kemba Hotel** *(singles/doubles with shared shower Birr7/8)*.

Kayro Hotel *(☎ 81 03 23; doubles with/ without cold shower Birr25/15)* is clean and good value. Two new hotels are planned opposite.

Chamo Hotel *(☎ 81 15 71; doubles with cold shower Birr30)* nearby is also good value, and with no bar, restaurant or bar girls is a quieter bet!

Shecha The new **Andinnet Hotel** *(☎ 81 08 79; doubles with shared shower Birr15)* has clean rooms.

Abbayaa Hotel *(☎ 81 10 81; doubles with cold shower Birr30)* has simple but clean rooms in pleasant grounds, though it can be a bit noisy at night.

Wubete Hotel *(☎ 81 16 29; doubles with/ without shower Birr30/20)*, nearby, has quite pleasant rooms set in a compound.

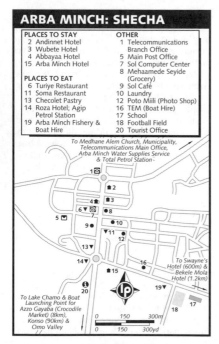

ARBA MINCH: SHECHA

PLACES TO STAY	OTHER
2 Andinnet Hotel	1 Telecommunications
3 Wubete Hotel	Branch Office
4 Abbayaa Hotel	5 Main Post Office
15 Arba Minch Hotel	7 Sol Computer Center
	8 Mehaamede Seyide
PLACES TO EAT	(Grocery)
6 Turiye Restaurant	9 Sol Café
11 Soma Restaurant	10 Laundry
13 Checolet Pastry	12 Poto Miili (Photo Shop)
14 Roza Hotel; Agip	16 TEM (Boat Hire)
Petrol Station	17 School
19 Arba Minch Fishery &	18 Football Field
Boat Hire	20 Tourist Office

To Medhane Alem Church, Municipality, Telecommunications Main Office, Arba Minch Water Supplies Service & Total Petrol Station

To Swayne's Hotel (600m) & Bekele Mola Hotel (1.2km)

To Lake Chamo & Boat Launching Point for Azzo Gayaba (Crocodile Market) (8km), Konso (90km) & Omo Valley

0 150 300m
0 150 300yd

Arba Minch Hotel (☎ 81 02 06; *doubles without shower Birr20-25, with shower Birr40-60*), is usually a little quieter than the others.

Bekele Mola Hotel (☎ 81 00 46; *camping per tent with shower Birr25, bungalow singles with private shower Birr179-220, doubles with private shower Birr265-312*) lies 2.8km from town in a beautiful position that overlooks the lakes and park. It's peaceful, cool and pleasant, but the rooms (and 'obligatory' meals, included in the price) are nothing special. It is, however, a great place for a beer (Birr4) at sunset. A contract taxi from town should cost about Birr10 to Birr15.

Swayne's Hotel (☎ 81 18 95, fax 81 22 00; e swayneshotel@yahoo.com; camping for 1/2-person tent Birr25/30, singles Birr95-120, doubles Birr120-160, 1-4 person bungalows Birr200) is an attractively designed, new complex set on a bluff overlooking the park. Future plans include a pool (by end of 2004) and car rental. It lies 1.8km from the Agip on the roundabout in Shecha (around 600m beyond the Arba Minch–Bekele Mola junction).

Places to Eat

Sikela Simple and cheap local favourites are **Abi Restaurant** (sign in Amharic only,

opposite the Maj Cafeteria) and **Guugge Zuma** (also known as Mt Guge).

Flamingo Pastry is probably the best pastry place in town, with quite good cakes and fruit juices (Birr2).

The **Zebib Pastry** has a small, but cool, garden.

Shecha A strong contender for the best provincial restaurant in Ethiopia award is **Soma Restaurant** (☎ 81 06 14). Its speciality is fresh fish dishes (accompanied by fish soup, salad and fried potatoes). Try the delicious *asa gulash*, fish served with a tomato and chilli sauce. Other styles include *goden, filetto, wat* (battered and grilled, with a hot sauce). The slightly excessive 'grilled fish' (Birr60) for one to four people is served with a lemon in its mouth!

Turiye Restaurant is also known for its fresh fish.

Roza Hotel comes in at third place, but is cheaper.

Arba Minch Fishery, next door to the Marine Authority in Shecha, is great for budget-priced fresh fish (just Birr4 to Birr6).

Checolet Pastry is a popular place in Shecha, with a pleasant, shaded terrace.

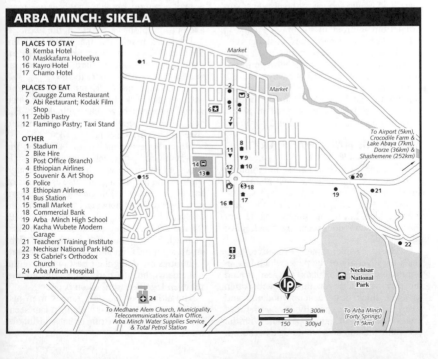

ARBA MINCH: SIKELA

PLACES TO STAY
8 Kemba Hotel
10 Maskkafarra Hoteeliya
16 Kayro Hotel
17 Chamo Hotel

PLACES TO EAT
7 Guugge Zuma Restaurant
9 Abi Restaurant; Kodak Film Shop
11 Zebib Pastry
12 Flamingo Pastry; Taxi Stand

OTHER
1 Stadium
2 Bike Hire
3 Post Office (Branch)
4 Ethiopian Airlines
5 Souvenir & Art Shop
6 Police
13 Ethiopian Airlines
14 Bus Station
15 Small Market
18 Commercial Bank
19 Arba Minch High School
20 Kacha Wubete Modern Garage
21 Teachers' Training Institute
22 Nechisar National Park HQ
23 St Gabriel's Orthodox Church
24 Arba Minch Hospital

Market

Market

To Airport (5km),
Crocodile Farm &
Lake Abaya (7km),
Dorze (36km) &
Shashemene (252km)

Nechisar National Park

To Medhane Alem Church, Municipality,
Telecommunications Main Office,
Arba Minch Water Supplies Service
& Total Petrol Station

To Arba Minch
(Forty Springs)
(1.5km)

0   150   300m
0   150   300yd

ETHIOPIA

Getting There & Away

Ethiopian Airlines (☎ 81 06 49) in Sikela, flies twice weekly from Arba Minch to Addis Ababa via Jinka. The airport lies 5km out of town.

All buses arrive and leave from outside the Wubete Hotel in Shecha before or after going down to the bus station in Sikela. Two buses depart daily for Addis Ababa (Birr46.45, 11 hours). One leaves for Awasa (Birr25, six hours), Shashemene (Birr23.35, seven hours) and Jinka (Birr30, eight hours) via Konso (Birr10, three hours) and Weyto (Birr20, five hours). One bus leaves daily for Dorze (Birr10, three to four hours). For Chencha, take a bus from Dorze (Birr3, 20 to 30 minutes). In the early mornings, a couple of Landrover taxis (Birr12) also leave daily for Chencha from Arba Minch (and return around lunchtime).

Three trucks also run to Konso, and around three to Jinka (via Weyto and Konso), usually departing from outside the Agip and Shell petrol stations. They usually charge a bit more than buses.

Getting Around

Frequent minibuses connect the two towns (Birr1.50) from around 6am to 9pm, but there's no public service to the airport. Contract taxis (blue minibuses or 4WDs) can be hired from in front of Flamingo Pastry in Sikela. For the airport, they cost between Birr20 and Birr40, depending upon your powers of negotiation. A trip between towns should cost around Birr15 one way.

Beware the car brokers who hang around some of the hotels in Sikela looking for easy commissions. Bikes can be hired in Sikela near the post office, and cost Birr2 per hour.

NECHISAR NATIONAL PARK

ኘቻ ሳር ብሔራዊ ፓርክ

Nechisar means 'White Grass' in Amharic, in reference to the pale savanna plains that stretch over much of the park's 514 sq km. In the early morning and at dusk the grass looks golden, but in the shimmering heat of the midday sun it does seem to turn a kind of silver-white.

Nechisar's name, though evocative, conceals the diversity of the park, which has an impressive range of habitats. The road around the park will take you through wide open savanna, thick bush, acacia woodland and riverine forest. Occasionally, lovely views of Lakes Abaya and Chamo open out. With the deep blue Sidamo hills providing a backdrop, the park is very beautiful in places. It ranks among the most scenic – yet least visited – in East Africa.

Reflecting the diversity of habitats is the diversity of birds and animals – and this is what makes Nechisar special. Ninety-one mammal species are found in the park. In the forest, bushpigs, warthogs, Anubis baboons, genets, bushbucks and vervet monkeys are found. On the savanna plains (where animals are most easily seen), the Burchell's zebra is the most conspicuous animal, sometimes seen in – unusually – large herds of 100 animals or more. You can get close to them and they are a beautiful sight, bucking defiantly or baying as they canter off before the car.

Of the antelopes, the most commonly seen is the greater kudu in the cover of the bush, with its beautiful spiralling horns, and the tiny Guenther's dik-dik, which is often seen in pairs, since it is a monogamous animal. The Grant's gazelle, with its horns pointing forward, is easy to spot on the plains, as is the endemic Swayne's hartebeest.

If you're very lucky you may get to see African hunting dogs and black-backed jackals. According to the park warden, 20 to 30 Abyssinian lions inhabit Nechisar. Sightings are not common, but you may hear one roaring. In the eastern area of the park, keep an eye out for colobus monkeys in the trees.

Like the mammals, the birds here are diverse: 351 species have been counted including hornbills and bustards. The Nechisar nightjar was last seen here in 1991.

The local Guji and Koira people inhabit parts of the park. Look out for their huts, which resemble haystacks with doors. The neat piles of pebbles that look like round cheeses are burial mounds.

Officially, cattle should not be kept in the park, but you'll see plenty. Domestic animals pose a threat to the wildlife not just through competition for grazing, but also as vectors of anthrax. People who kill the wildlife receive a prison sentence of between three months and one year. However, wildlife is still killed both for food and to make crafts such as shields. Fierce local disputes also continue to flare up between the Guji and the Koira. The park authorities are doing their best to remove the settlements, but the park boundaries are not yet even legally described on paper.

The altitude of the park ranges from just 1108m to 1650m. On the plain, it can seem very hot and dusty. Bring a hat and lots of water.

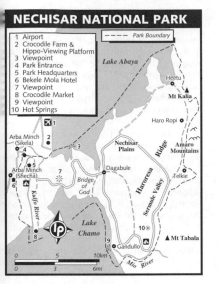

NECHISAR NATIONAL PARK

1 Airport
2 Crocodile Farm & Hippo-Viewing Platform
3 Viewpoint
4 Park Entrance
5 Park Headquarters
6 Bekele Mola Hotel
7 Viewpoint
8 Crocodile Market
9 Viewpoint
10 Hot Springs

--- Park Boundary

Lake Abaya

Heetu

Mt Kalia

Haro Ropi

Arba Minch (Sikela)

Nechisar Plains

Amaro Mountains

Haroresa Ridge

Arba Minch (Shecha)

Dagabule

Telkie

Bridge of God

Kulfo River

Sermule Valley

Lake Chamo

Gandullo

Mt Tabala

Mio River

0   5   10km
0   3   6mi

Orientation & Information

The park headquarters is 1km from the roundabout in Sikela, near the entrance to the park (see the Arba Minch map earlier). A basic map and information sheet are available at the headquarters. You can only enter the park in a vehicle. To reduce the cost of 4WD rental (around Birr800 per day), find a group, club together and enquire at the tourist office or at the park.

If a 4WD is beyond your budget, you can still explore the hot springs and dense forests surrounding the Forty Springs. Although they form part of the park, they remain accessible (and free). The tourist office in Arba Minch offers guided treks here.

Nechisar National Park *(admission per person/vehicle Birr70/20; scouts per day/day & night Birr30/50; open 6am-7.30pm daily)* is large: a complete circuit is over 120km long. A shortened version (which gives an excellent variety of landscapes, viewpoints, animals and birds) covers around 85km and takes between five to seven hours to complete (including stops).

If you're pushed for time, there's a reasonable three-hour circuit. Ask your scout to show you. Though not compulsory, scouts are recommended: they will navigate, provide security (they are armed) and provide a pair of trained eyes for animal and bird location, spotting and identification. Tips are appreciated; you will find scouts at the park headquarters.

Places to Stay

Camping *(per person Birr20)* is possible anywhere, but there are two official camping grounds, including one beside the Kulfo River, around 5km from the park headquarters. Most travellers stay in Arba Minch.

Getting Around

A 4WD vehicle is a must for exploration of the park as parts of the road are steep and rocky; in the wet season, mud is the main problem and can render some roads impassable.

DORZE & CHENCHA

ደርዜ ና ጨንቻ

High up in the Guge Mountains, 36km to the north of Arba Minch, is the cold, cloudy territory of the Dorze people. Belonging to one of the many branches of the Omotic peoples of the southwest, the Dorze are famous for their huge **beehive huts**.

The first huts can be seen around 30km from Arba Minch at the settlement known also as Dorze. The people are skilled farmers who prevent soil erosion of the mountainside with ingenious terracing.

Some of the country's best woven cotton comes from Chencha, and some fine cotton *shammas* (cotton togas) and *gabis* (thicker *shammas*) can be bought here. Traditionally, it is the men who weave and the women who spin. You can visit the **weaving cooperative** *(open 8am-5pm Mon-Sat)* at the village of Gambela Dokko, 1.2km from Chencha. You'll be expected to pay at least Birr10 to Birr20 if you want to take photos. *Gabis* cost Birr30 to Birr80, depending on their size.

Dorze Huts

Standing up to 12m high, the famous Dorze hut resembles a giant beehive. Constructed with vertical hardwood poles and woven bamboo, it is topped with a thatched roof of *enset* leaves. On the outside, a kind of nose juts out, which serves as a small reception room.

Though fragile-looking, the hut can last up to 60 years. Thanks to the vertical poles that make up the structure, the hut is easily transported to a new location. Eventually, rot or the unstoppable termites will get the better of it, and the hut will be abandoned.

Most Dorze huts also boast their own little garden containing vegetables, spices and tobacco, as well as *enset* plantations.

There's a very colourful **market** *(Tues & Sat)* at Chencha, and at Dorze *(Mon & Thur)*. Woven blankets (around Birr100), honey (Birr7), traditional woven Dorze trousers (Birr40 to Birr80) and decorated gourds (Birr15 to Birr20) can all be bought there. The piles of white, mushy dough wrapped in green leaves are *enset* (see the boxed text 'Enduring Enset' earlier in this chapter).

Getting There & Away

The journey up to Chencha affords some spectacular views over Arba Minch and the Rift Valley lakes and is worthwhile in itself. Trucks and 4WDs travel each morning between Chencha and Arba Minch (Birr10, two hours). If you're driving, check the condition of the road in advance. After rain, the road becomes a steep and slippery quagmire and is difficult to pass, even in a 4WD.

KONSO
ኮንሶ

Konso serves as a kind of frontier town and gateway to the Omo Valley and beyond. It also has an ancient, complex and fascinating culture all of its own, and is well worth a stop.

At the **markets** *(Mon & Fri)*, look out for the colourful woven cotton 'shorts' (Birr40 to Birr60) and locally woven cotton blankets (Birr15 to Birr160). You'll also find tea, millet, tobacco, raw cotton, sweet potatoes, butter, incense and cassava. Souvenirs for sale include wooden dolls (Birr25 to Birr30), local knives (Birr40 to Birr50) and miniature *wagas* (Birr30; see the boxed text 'The People of Konso' following). The giant two-handled pots are for making *tella* (home-brewed beer). If you're lucky, you may come across some lovely old Konso glass beads.

An important Ethio-Japanese archaeological venture (known as the Konso Gardula Project) is soon to resume excavations at a **site** just outside Konso (after wrapping up a 10-year project in 2002). Many fossils (unusual for their large size), human and particularly animal, have been unearthed from the site of an old lake and have been dated to between 1.3 and 1.9 million years old. By the end of 2003 or beginning 2004, it is hoped that Konso will be declared a Unesco World Heritage Site. The site can be visited (ask for a guide at the Culture, Information & Tourism Office). There are plans to build a museum to exhibit some of the finds.

On arrival in Konso, visitors should report to the **Culture, Information & Tourism Office** *(open 8.30am-12.30pm & 1.30pm-5.30pm Mon-Fri)* to pay the obligatory Birr30 'admission fee' (if you arrive at the weekend, ask one of the lads to rouse the caretaker).

The People of Konso

The pagan society of the Konso boasts a rich culture, and a highly specialised and successful agricultural economy.

Beautifully constructed, buttressed stone terraces have allowed the Konso to eke out a living from the dry, unyielding land around them. Surrounding the villages and fields are sturdy stone walls, which serve as a defence against straying cattle and flash flooding, as well as against intruders. Visitors must enter a Konso house on hands and knees, via a wooden tunnel – a compromising position should the visitor turn out to be a foe.

When Konso warriors die, they are honoured with the erection of a series of carved wooden sculptures – the famous Konso *waga*. Designed according to a strict formula, the 'hero' is usually distinguishable by the phallic ornamental *khalasha* worn on the sculpture's forehead or by its slightly larger size.

Placed on either side of the hero are between two and four of his wives (identifiable by necklaces and breasts) and the hero's slain enemies (usually smaller and without phallic symbols), or animals (such as leopards) that the hero has killed. Occasionally a monkey-like figure stands at the feet of the hero, and sometimes his spears and shields are included. The eyes of the figures are usually represented with shells or ostrich eggshells, the teeth with the bones of goats.

Unfortunately, *waga* erection is dying out. The widespread theft and removal of the statues to Addis Ababa for sale to diplomats and tourists (for between Birr15,000 and Birr30,000), as well as the work of missionaries who are against ancestor worship, has discouraged the continuance of this ancient tradition.

You're also encouraged to take a trained guide (Birr30 to Birr50). Keep the receipt of the admission fee with you; you may well be asked for it in the villages and sites outside Konso. Villagers may also demand Birr1 for photos of them or their houses.

The year 2003–04 should be a good one for Konso: electricity should arrive, and a bank and small supermarket should open (in the same building).

Travellers are free to visit the villages in and around Konso. You can also visit the Chief of Konso (including the family grave-yard and the so-called House of Mummies). Ask your guide to take you there.

Unfortunately, some Ethiopian guides now award Konso 'the worst *faranji* frenzy' accolade. Local children can make your trip around the market and the village rather trying. For advice on dealing with them, see Dangers & Annoyances in the Facts for the Visitor chapter.

Places to Stay & Eat
Camping *(Birr10)* is possible in the grounds of the Culture, Information & Tourism Office, as well as at some of the hotels.

Edget Hotel *(☎ 16 81 71; rooms with cold shower Birr30)*, is simple but clean and set in a large compound. Its outdoor tables are a good place for a meal or drink in the evening.

Kiddus Maryam Hotel *(☎ 16 81 71; doubles with shared shower Birr10-20, with cold shower Birr50)* is considered the top hotel in town and has a newly opened wing.

Konso Wubet Hotel, the Edget and the Kiddus Maryam have the best restaurants.

Hess Travel Ethiopia (see Organised Tours in the Getting Around chapter) has plans to complete a new and comfortable lodge on the hill overlooking Konso by the end of 2004.

Getting There & Away
For Yabelo (tying in with market days), two or three Isuzu trucks depart every Monday and Thursday (Birr20 to Birr30, 2½ hours). Two buses and two Isuzu trucks depart daily for Arba Minch (Birr10, three hours) and Weyto (Birr10, two hours). For Jinka (Birr25 to Birr40, five to six hours), the Arba Minch bus usually arrives in Konso between 9am and 10am daily; there are usually seats. Coming the other way, the Jinka buses arrives between 11am and noon. For Turmi, go to Key Afar first (with the Jinka bus). For Arfaide, Isuzus leave every Tuesday and Saturday (Birr5, one hour).

AROUND KONSO
If you have a vehicle, a popular excursion from Konso is to the village of Gesergio (pronounced gas-**ag**-ee-yo), popularly known as 'New York'. According to local tradition, thieves once stole some sacred drums and temporarily buried them at Gesergio. All the people of the village prayed for help to get them back, and God himself came down to retrieve them, excavating them with his own hands from the soil. New York was left – a bizarre landscape of sand pinnacles formed by the wind and rain. New York lies 18km from Konso.

You can also visit various Konso villages where the famous *wagas* can be seen, including Machekie (around 14km southwest of Konso), Arfaide (19km west of Konso) and particularly Busso (7km south of Konso). In some villages, you may be charged a Birr5 'photography fee' per person. Agree on a reasonable fee in advance.

Sadly, in the last ten years, many of the *wagas* have been stolen. In 1997 local thieves working with antique dealers in Addis Ababa stole around 60 of the villages' best statues. A French team from the Centre Français des Etudes Ethiopiennes is currently carrying out an inventory of the statues. If you want to see some statues but are short on time, the Culture, Information & Tourism Office in Konso has around 60 to 70 in a locked shed for safekeeping. In the future, it is hoped that funds will be found to build a museum in which to house them permanently.

Around Konso, look out for the lozenge-shaped beehives placed in the acacias. The sheet of metal wrapped around the trunk supposedly facilitates identification for homeward-bound honey bees! On the road to Jinka, you'll see young boys selling tennis-ball sized clumps wrapped in tree bark. It's *etan,* a kind of gum popularly used as incense for the coffee ceremony (see the boxed text 'The Coffee Ceremony' in the Eastern Ethiopia chapter).

Other roadside souvenirs for sale include black and white porcupine quill bracelets (Birr2), dangly black and orange decorations (made from the outer wings of the *tinziza* fly), miniature *wagas* (Birr5 to Birr10), calabashes (gourds), miniature wooden *gras* (lyres) and sometimes good-quality wooden headrests. Painted child-buskers leap into action with a traditional jumping dance as each tour group sweeps by.

ETHIOPIA

JINKA
ጂንካ

☎ 06 • pop 12,407 • elevation 1490m

Located 138km from Konso, Jinka is the nearest town to the Omo and Mago National Parks. At 1490m, it feels like a breath of fresh air after the close, steamy and muddy confines of the lowlands. After a foray into the Omo, Jinka can seem like Paris.

Though it serves as the administrative centre of the South Omo Zone, Jinka still retains a very small-town feel. Its grassy airstrip, in the very centre of the village, doubles as the town's football pitch and as useful extra grazing for the local sheep; both players and animals are shooed from the airstrip on the arrival of a plane. In the morning, you'll hear a dawn chorus like you've never heard before: thousands of cockerels going off like little alarm clocks across the town and country.

Although the town boasts a **bank**, its services are rather unreliable as they depend upon electricity supplies. Sometimes it's not possible to change either cash or travellers cheques. Jinka also suffers from water shortages, so try not to waste it. Some travellers have written to warn of aggressive self-appointed guides.

The large and colourful Saturday **market** is worth a visit. It's around 1km northeast of the airstrip. Expect to come across a variety of ethnic groups, among them the Ari, Hamer, Banna, Karo, Koygu and Bodi (see the boxed text 'Peoples of the Lower Omo Valley' later in this chapter); they may charge Birr1 for a photo. It's also a good place to stock up on some fresh fruit including in season the delicious *fruitish* (passion fruit), also known locally as 'fashion fruit'!

The German-funded **South-Omo Museum & Research Centre** (☎ 75 01 49; admission free; open 9am-noon & 3pm-5pm Tues-Sat), perched on a hill around 2.5km to the northeast of town, has a small but interesting exhibition on the material culture of the peoples of the region. Objects on display include calabashes, pots and headrests. Some interesting illustrated panels inform about local traditions such as divination, sacrifice, initiation ceremonies and local superstition.

From Jinka, you can do a day trip to Mursi territory, around 60km west of the town.

Places to Stay & Eat
Tour operators often book up the top hotels, so reservations are advised. Be aware that many places charge foreigners different prices for food (up to double); head for the local places if you're on a budget.

Rocky Recreation Campsite (camping per person Birr15), 1.5km from the Total petrol station in Jinka on the Konso road, is quiet, green and peaceful. It has a generator, access to showers and sells drinks, but not food.

Lucy Campsite (☎ 75 00 94; camping per person Birr15) is new and pleasant and lies 600m from the centre. Showers should be built soon.

Kokeb Hotel (☎ 75 03 58; doubles with shared shower Birr15), about 40m north of the Orit Hotel, is the cleanest and quietest of the budget hotels and has a little garden.

Goh Hotel (☎ 75 00 33; doubles with/ without cold shower Birr60/20), next to the Orit and similar to it, is the best mid-range choice.

Orit Hotel (☎ 75 00 45; camping per person Birr10, rooms with cold shower Birr60) is the top of the range. There's a pleasant compound, though it can be a little noisy. The restaurant is also good (for local and *faranji* fare). Prices are soon to increase to Birr80 when hot showers are installed. It's centrally placed on the eastern side of the airstrip.

The Orit Hotel can arrange car rental (Birr1200 per day, all-inclusive), guides (Birr80 per day) and tents (Birr50 per day). The friendly owner is happy to advise on itineraries and current road conditions. A souvenir shop should also open soon.

Ivangari is the local favourite for food, and is simple yet tasty. **Mehbub Pastry** is the place for breakfast or a cake (though *faranji* prices apply).

Hirut Hotel (also known as Busca) is good for local food; it is not far from the South Omo Transport & Communication Office.

There are several small **grocery stores**, including one opposite the Orit Hotel. If you haven't already stocked up for a camping trip, Jinka is your last chance.

Dejene Hotel (open 10pm-2am) is a popular place for music and dancing. It's centrally placed on the eastern side of the airstrip.

Getting There & Away
Ethiopian Airlines (☎ 75 01 26) flies to Addis Ababa via Arba Minch twice weekly. In the wet season, flights are sometimes postponed for 24 hours because of runway conditions.

Currently, buses arrive and depart from near the police station. A bus leaves daily for Addis Ababa (Birr76.50, two days) via Arba Minch (Birr33 to Birr40, nine hours).

Four or five trucks depart daily (from near the Orit and Omo Hotels), heading for Key Afar (Birr10 to Birr20, one hour, at least one daily, more on Sunday), Konso (Birr35 to Birr40, four hours) via Weyto (Birr20 to Birr25, 2½ hours); to Omorate (Birr50 to Birr60, eight to 10 hours, Tuesday and Saturday) via Turmi (Birr30 to Birr40, seven hours) and Dimeka (Birr25, five to six hours). You'll need your best bargaining skills to negotiate a ride; *faranjis* are often charged double or more.

Various government and missionary cars also circulate in the region; they usually give lifts, but a contribution towards fuel should be made. The Mobil and Total petrol stations are good places to look for lifts.

The **National Tour Operation** (☎ 75 01 54) has two 4WDs for hire (US$90/126.50) per day. This includes the driver, fuel and 100km (US$0.45/0.75 per additional km). Six or seven private vehicles are also available for hire, though they carry their own risks (Birr900 to Birr1000 per day, including fuel and driver). Ask at your hotel.

LOWER OMO VALLEY
ዝቅተኛው የኦም ሸለቆ

The Lower Omo Valley landscape is diverse, ranging from the dry, open savanna plains to the riverine forest that borders the Omo and Mago Rivers. The vast Omo River meanders for nearly 1000km southwest of Addis Ababa, all the way to Kenya. There it is the sole feeder of East Africa's fourth-largest lake, Lake Turkana. The river also bisects Ethiopia's largest, wildest and most inaccessible parks: the Omo National Park which lies on its west bank, and Mago National Park on its east bank.

Wild, undisturbed and little visited, the parks boast not only remarkable wildlife, but also remarkable peoples. It is here that some of the most fascinating and colourful ethnic groups of the country are to be found (see the boxed text 'Peoples of the Lower Omo Valley' later).

Many of the peoples' ancient customs and traditions have remained almost entirely intact. Animism is still the religion, and some still practise a purely pastoral economy. Hostility between neighbouring tribes is still high and internecine warfare is common. Just very recently, Galeb warriors (from Old Omo, 20km north of Omorate) made incursions into Hamer territory to steal cattle; the Hamer retaliated by invading Galeb territory. Around a dozen warriors died in the conflict.

Body Decoration

The people of the Omo may lack any form of advanced material culture, but they have developed art forms that allow them not just great artistic expression, but also serve important social and cosmetic purposes. The practice of body painting and scarification developed by the tribes is among the most ornate and extravagant seen anywhere in the world.

For most of the Omo tribes, scarification serves as a distinction for brave warriors; the men are not allowed to scarify themselves until they have killed at least one foe. For the women, the raised texture of the skin is considered highly desirable, and is said to hold sensual value for the men.

Scarification is achieved using a stone, knife, hook or razor blade. Ash is then rubbed into the wound, creating a small infection and promoting scar tissue growth. As the wound heals, the raised scar creates the desired knobbly effect on the surface of the skin.

A large number of mammals make their home here including leopards, buffaloes, elephants and lions. Unfortunately, after years of hunting and continued poaching, some animals are rare; others are shy and are not often seen. Visitors hoping for a Kenya- or Tanzania-type safari will be disappointed. But the parks do offer something unique: an unforgettable glimpse into a genuine African wilderness.

Probably the best time to visit the region is from June to September. At this time (after the harvest) many celebrations take place including harvest-home dances, marriage ceremonies, and initiation ceremonies including the famous bull-jumping.

When visiting the villages of the Lower Omo Valley, try and coincide with at least one market day (see the boxed text 'Market Day in the Omo Valley'). A good time to visit the villages is between 5pm and 6.30pm, when the workers return from the fields or from market.

Dangers & Annoyances
The Lower Omo Valley is still a very remote place which is undoubtedly one of its attractions. Road conditions are rough, and the annual rainfall at 500mm to 800mm is quite high and quickly turns the tracks into quagmires.

ETHIOPIA

Tsetse flies are a problem in some areas, particularly in the wet season or after rain. Mago National Park is probably the worst area, along with village of Makki in Mursi country. Malaria is endemic in some parts of the region, particularly south of Key Afar; precautions are essential. A doctor is available in Jinka, but the nearest hospital is in Arba Minch. There's also a clinic specialising in malaria in Turmi (which has a laboratory for tests).

For many ethnic groups, raiding is a part of life – a means of survival in a very harsh environment. In the Karo language, the word for 'thief' apparently doesn't exist, and children are encouraged to pilfer from a young age – they're only beaten if they're caught. Camps should never be left unattended, and all jewellery including watches is best removed before you mingle with some groups such as the Mursi.

Some travellers may be disappointed or even shocked by the seemingly mercenary nature of the different peoples, or the apparent voyeurism of the encounter. However, the local people have a right to benefit from tourism. In fact, it's money bargained for photos instead of money bargained for crops. Tourism may even help to preserve the groups and their traditions by assisting them economically. Many villages (such as Turmi, Dimeka and some Mursi villages) now charge an admission fee of Birr40 to Birr50 per car. If you spend a little time with the people, you'll soon discover that they're sociable and resourceful, often with a fabulous sense of humour.

Many tribes ask at least Birr1 to Birr2 for photos, and you'll probably be asked for more. Some people, particularly the Mursi, have perfected intimidation techniques – such as throwing hysterics, shouting, or even grabbing your hands and not letting go. Just be firm and polite, stay calm and keep smiling. Ideally, get your guide, if you have one, to negotiate for all photos in advance. Additionally, they have been known to give wrong directions to inexperienced drivers. No sooner is the vehicle stuck in mud, than a fee of up to Birr1000 is demanded to help pull it out!

Remember to bring with you a good stash of *new* Birr1 notes for photos (noses are often turned up at old ones), but be sensitive when taking them. Gifts such as razor blades, soap and sugar are all much appreciated.

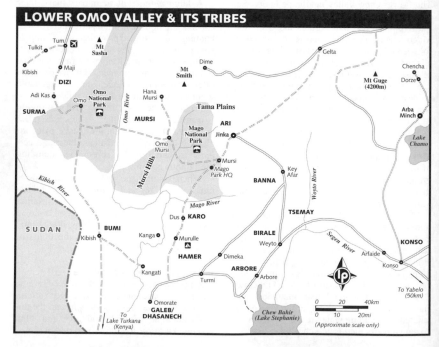

LOWER OMO VALLEY & ITS TRIBES

Omo Valley Villages

A good itinerary which gives you a glimpse of diverse ethnic groups, as well as diverse scenery, begins in Konso and takes you through the little villages of Weyto, Arbore, Turmi, Dimeka, Key Afar, Jinka and Mago National Park.

The little village of **Weyto** lies halfway between Konso and Key Afar. The Tsemay, part farmers, part pastoralists, inhabit the region.

Just after Weyto, there's a junction. Take the road that branches southwest towards the village of **Arbore**.

The Arbore people resemble the Borena people, with their beads and aluminium jewellery. To escape the notorious mosquitoes the Arbore sleep on 5m-high platforms; locals outside the village know it as 'mosquito town'.

South of Arbore, off the main Arbore–Turmi road, tracks lead to the strange saline lake of **Chew Bahir** (also known as Lake Stephanie). From Arbore to the junction of the main track is a 35km drive. From the junction to the lake is 60km. Oryx and gazelles are sometimes found near the lake. The ground around the lake is notoriously unstable. Take a policeman-guide from Arbore (Birr70 per day). January to December is the best time to visit.

After the Weyto Valley, the road enters Hamer territory. Nearly 4km east of the town of Turmi on the Weyto road, look out for the pump and well at the side of the road, close to Wadi Kaske. Local Hamer women come from miles around to fetch water from the well. The Weyto market is worth a stop if you're in the area.

At **Turmi** itself, the main town of the Hamer, the Monday **market** is a must. The main square fills with Hamer market-goers, selling vegetables, spices, butter and milk. It's a great place for picking up the beautiful incised gourds, which are used by the local women as shopping baskets and as a handbag for stashing cash. If you spot one you like, you can probably negotiate for it. Hamer villages are half an hour's walk from Turmi.

The region around Turmi particularly, and around Dimeka, is known for the famous Hamer and Banna **Jumping of the Bulls ceremony**, usually held from July to September and during the first half of December. Admission fees of Birr50 per person are asked (minimum Birr300); the ceremony lasts all day (from 11am to 6pm). The *evangadi* (Hamer night dance) can also be seen or organised. It usually costs Birr10 per person and lasts three hours. Ask locally.

Also worth a peek is **Hamer Traditional Goods**, a souvenir shop next door to the Gulilat Haile Hotel in Turmi. You can buy yourself a traditional – and fantastically smelly – goatskin decorated with beads and cowry shells. Incised calabashes (Birr15 to Birr20), head stools (Birr20) and metal arm bracelets (Birr50) are among the items on sale.

Southwest of Turmi, the road continues to **Omorate**, marked on some maps as Kelem, where there is a small but lively daily market. This is Galeb (also known as Dasanech) territory. To visit, you can take a brief ride in a dugout canoe (Birr1) to the other side of the Omo river, from where it's a five minute walk.

You could previously cross the Omo River by car ferry and enter the Omo National Park, until the ferry fell into disuse.

A worthwhile detour is to the camp of **Murulle**. Here Ethiopian Rift Valley Safaris has established a beautiful, shady camp on the banks of the Omo. The attractive and comfortable **bungalows** *(singles/doubles with private bathroom US$90/150)* are not for budget travellers, but **camping** *(per person with access to shower US$8)* is possible; reservations are required for bungalows (see Organised Tours in the Getting Around chapter). Bird and wildlife viewing excursions, boat and fishing trips, and Karo cultural shows can all be organised.

Close by are a couple of Karo villages, such as **Kolcho**, just north of Murulle. There's a lovely campsite on the plateau overlooking the Omo River and Valley, but hiring a guard from the local village (Birr50 to Birr70 per 24 hours) is essential, as theft is a problem here. Kolcho is one of the best places to see traditional dancing, though it'll cost you (Birr50 per vehicle; Birr300 to Birr700 per group depending on size). Dances last around one hour and usually take place at sunset.

Around 1km from Kolcho is Lake Deepa, which is a great spot for bird-watching or fishing in the season after the rains (it can dry up to almost nothing). The Bumi village of **Kanga**, which lies across the river from Murulle can also be visited. You should take a guide from Murulle for all these places.

At the village of **Dus**, around 20km north of Murulle, you can also arrange to see traditional dancing (same prices as Kolcho).

The road from Murulle back to Turmi traverses a beautiful savanna plain where oryx and Grant's gazelles are frequently seen. This whole area is known as the **Murulle Controlled Hunting Area**, and is the one place where

Peoples of the Lower Omo Valley

The Lower Omo Valley is almost unique in the world by being home to so many peoples in such a small area. Historians believe that the south served for millennia as a kind of cultural crossroads, where quite different ethnic peoples – Cushitic, Nilotic, Omotic and Semitic – met as they migrated from the north, west, south and east. The peoples of the Lower Omo Valley are considered among the most fascinating on the African continent.

The Ari ኣሪ

The Ari inhabit the northern border of Mago National Park and have a population of around 120,000 people. They keep large numbers of livestock and produce large amounts of honey, often used for trade. The women wear skirts made from the *enset* tree.

The Banna ባና

The Banna are believed to number around 45,000; they inhabit the higher ground to the east of Mago National Park. Most practise agriculture, though their diet is supplemented by hunting. If they manage to kill a buffalo, they decorate themselves with clay and put on a special celebration and feast for the whole village.

The Bodi ቦዲ

Numbering around 3500, the Bodi are agro-pastoralists and their language is Nilo–Saharan in origin. They inhabit the northeast edge of Omo National Park.

The Bumi ቡሚ

The Bumi, numbering around 8000, inhabit the land south of the Omo National Park, but sometimes invade the southern plains when fodder or water is scarce.

Like the Bodi, the Bumi are agro-pastoralists, growing sorghum by the Omo and Kibish Rivers as well as fishing and rearing cattle. They also hunt in the park and smoke bees out of their hives for honey. They are known as great warmongers and are at war with almost everyone, particularly the Karo, the Hamer and the Surma.

The Bumi use scarification for cosmetic purposes, tribal identification and as indications of prowess in battle. Both men and women use little *pointilles* or dots to highlight their eyes and cheekbones. The women also scarify their torsos with curvilinear and geometrical designs.

The Dizi ዲዚ

Inhabiting the northwest edge of Omo National Park, the Dizi are sedentary agriculturists, cultivating sorghum, root crops and coffee. They also practise terracing on the mountain slopes.

The Hamer ሃመር

The Hamer, who number around 50,000, are subsistence agro-pastoralists. They cultivate sorghum, vegetables, millet, tobacco and cotton, as well as rearing cattle and goats. Wild honey is an important part of their diet.

The people are known particularly for their remarkable hairstyles. The women mix together ochre, water and a binding resin, rub the mixture into their hair, then twist strands again and again to create coppery-coloured tresses known as *goscha*. These are a sign of health and welfare.

If they have recently killed an enemy or a dangerous animal, the men are permitted to don clay hair buns that sometimes support magnificent ostrich feathers. The buns – with the help of special headrests (*borkotos*) for sleeping – last from three to six months, and can be 'redone' for up to one year.

The Hamer are also considered masters of body decoration. Every adornment has an important symbolic significance; earrings for example, denote the number of wives a man has.

The women wear bead necklaces, iron coils around their arms, and decorate their skin with cowry shells. The iron torques around their necks are known as *ensente* and are worn by married or engaged

Peoples of the Lower Omo Valley

women only. They indicate the wealth and prestige of the woman's husband. Young, unmarried girls wear a metal plate in their hair that looks a bit like a platypus' bill.

The iron bracelets and armlets are an indication of the wealth and social standing of the young girl's family. When she gets married, she must remove the jewellery; it is the first gift she makes to her new family.

The Hamer territory stretches across the plains of the Lower Omo to Chew Bahir in the east, almost to the Kenyan border in the south, and to the territory of the Banna in the north.

The Karo ካሮ

The Karo people are thought to be one of the most endangered groups of the Omo, with a population of about 1500 people. They inhabit the eastern bank of the Omo. They were formerly pastoralists, but many of their cattle have been wiped out by disease, and many have turned to agriculture.

In appearance, language and tradition, they slightly resemble the Hamer, to whom they are related. The Karo are considered masters of body painting, in which they engage when preparing for a dance, feast or celebration. Most famously, chalk is used to imitate the spotted plumage of the guinea fowl.

The Karo are also great improvisers: Bic biros, nails, sweets wrappers and cartridges are all incorporated into jewellery and decoration. Yellow mineral rock, black charcoal and pulverised red iron ore are traditionally used.

The Koygu ኮይጁ

The Koygu (also known as the Muguji) inhabit the junction of the Omo and Mago Rivers. They commonly grow sorghum, and collect wild fruit, berries and honey. The Koygu are known for fishing and for hunting the hippo, which they eat. They use both guns and traps for hunting.

The Mursi ሙ-ርሲ

Perhaps the best known of the Omo peoples are the Mursi, the subject of a number of recent TV documentaries. The Mursi, thought to number around 6500, are mainly pastoralists who move according to the seasons between the lower Tama Steppe and the Mursi Hills in Mago National Park.

Some Mursi practise flood retreat cultivation, particularly in the areas where the tsetse fly prohibits cattle rearing. Honey is collected from beehives made with bark and dung. The Mursi language is Nilo-Saharan in origin.

The most famous Mursi traditions include the fierce stick fighting between the men, and the lip plate worn by the women. Made of clay and often quite large, the plates are inserted into slits in their lower lips. Anthropologists offer several theories to explain the practice: to deter slavers looking for unblemished girls; to prevent evil from entering the body by way of the mouth; or to indicate social status by showing the number of cattle required by the wearer's family for her hand in marriage.

The Surma ሱ-ርማ

Formerly nomadic pastoralists, the Surma now largely depend upon the subsistence cultivation of sorghum and maize. The Surma have a fearsome reputation as warriors, in part inspired by their continual search for grazing lands. Fights against the Bumi, their sworn enemies, still occur.

It is believed that the Surma once dominated the area, but their territory has been reduced to an area stretching along the western edges of the Omo National Park, in the hills around Maji and along the Kibish River. They are believed to number around 45,000, and are split into three subgroups: the Chai, Tirma and Bale. The Surma hunt in the park and make beehive huts. Like the Mursi, the Surma men are famous for their stick fighting, the Surma women for their lip plates.

The Surma are known for their white, almost ghostlike body painting. White chalk is mixed with water to create a kind of wash. The painting is much less ornamental than that found in other tribes and is intended to intimidate enemies in battle. Sometimes snake and wavelike patterns are painted across the torso and thighs.

wildlife reaches more normal density levels; there are far more animals reported here than at Mago National Park (which says much for the role controlled hunting now has in conservation). It is hoped that other species, such as giraffes, black rhinos and zebras, will be reintroduced in the future.

There are also 340 bird species in the region. Look out for the delightful carmine bee-eaters, which fly alongside your vehicle and snap up the insects stirred up by the wheels. Honey guides are also quite a common sight, trying to persuade you to follow them to a nearby beehive. The clouds of little quail-like birds that explode like popcorn from the grass as vehicles pass, are red-billed queleas.

The road from Turmi back to Jinka will take you through **Dimeka**, home to the Hamer and Banna people, and on to **Key Afar**, home also to the Banna people, who live quite close to the village and can be visited quite easily. From Key Afar, the road takes you north to Jinka, from where there's access to Mago National Park and the Mursi.

Mago National Park
ማጎ ብሔራዊ ፓርክ

Mago National Park (*admission per tent/person/vehicle Birr30/70/100*) measures 2162 sq km. Parts of the park are just 450m above sea level, and temperatures can reach 41°C. The park was originally created to protect the plains animals. It boasts, in theory, an exotic collection, including buffalo, lions, leopards, elephants and giraffes. In practice, widespread poaching in the area keeps populations down, so animal viewing is not what it might be – or should be according to the tourist literature. Even the park scouts rarely see the 'big' animals more than once in two months.

Mammals you can expect to see more realistically are Burchell's zebra, greater and lesser kudu, the Defassa waterbuck and the gerenuk. Topis and Lelwel hartebeest are also sometimes seen. Occasionally, large herds of buffalo are reported, usually close to sources of water. The best time to visit is from January to March.

The tiny visitors' centre at the park headquarters contains some information panels, maps and the usual animals' skulls and skins.

Hang onto your ticket; you will be asked to show it at the park barrier, 27km from the park headquarters. The headquarters also provides day and night guards (around Birr40 per 24 hours). Guards are essential if you're leaving your belongings and tents unattended, and they will also collect water and firewood, if you want. If you want to look for wildlife in the forest, such as buffalo, you can hire a scout (Birr40 per 24 hours).

The camping grounds at Mago National Park consist of little more than clearings. The so-called Buffalo Camp, beside the Neri River, is considered the most pleasant.

Mago National Park can be reached via a track from Jinka. No public transport runs here, and almost no trucks. You really need your own vehicle to reach the park; vehicles can be rented in Jinka.

Market Day in the Omo Valley

A terrific way of seeing some of the colourful Omo people is at the local markets. Try to get there between 10.30am and 2pm; some of the peoples have long journeys to or from the markets. The most interesting markets include:

Arbore	Friday
Dimeka	Tuesday & Saturday
Jinka	Tuesday & Saturday
Key Afar	Thursday
Konso	Monday & Thursday
Tum	Tuesday & Saturday
Turmi	Monday
Surma	Tuesday
Weyto	Sunday
Yabelo	Saturday

The ones at Dimeka, Key Afar and Turmi (in that order) are probably the most colourful.

Mursi Territory

About 8km from the headquarters of Mago National Park, a track to the left leads to a bridge over the Mago River (around 27km from the park) and into the Mursi Hills and into Mursi territory. The village of Haile Woha lies 33km from the river (60km from the park); from this village, which lies at a junction, it's a further 24km to Omo Mursi and 45km to Hanna Mursi.

The Mursi charge an 'admission fee' of Birr30 to Birr40 per vehicle, and at least Birr2 per photo.

If you can't get to Mursi territory, you can usually spot a few of the people at the market at Jinka on Saturday.

Omo National Park

አማ ብሔራዊ ፓርክ

In terms of habitat and the animals that make their home here, Omo National Park *(admission per tent/person/vehicle Birr30/70/100)* is very similar to Mago National Park, though its wildlife is almost certainly more prolific. Hunting is less of a problem, and with less forest cover, the animals are more easily seen.

The park staff recommend a visit of three or four days to have a realistic chance of seeing buffalo, lion, élan and giraffe. Elephants are only sometimes seen around Kibish. The black rhino was last seen here 25 years ago.

Currently, the only access to Omo National Park and the Surma region is from the north along the road to Maji or Tum. There are also twice weekly flights to Tum from Addis Ababa. There are no vehicles for hire in Maji or Tum, so walking (a three day hike from Tum) is the only option. You'll need to be totally self sufficient, but guides and mules (Birr50 per day) can be found in Tum and Maji.

You should check out the security situation in the region at the police station in Tum. After visiting the park, the usual route is to cross the Omo river by boat and have a vehicle pick you up from Omo Mursi (arrange this through travel companies based in Addis Ababa). It's sometimes possible to get a lift to the edge of the river with the park headquarters' vehicle (up to Birr500 one way).

The park was accessible by car ferry, which forded the Omo River from Omo Mursi. Unfortunately, the ferry fell into disuse several years ago, but you can inquire about its status at the **NTO** *(☎ 01-15 17 22)* in Addis Ababa. As part of a project to make the park more accessible, a road was recently constructed from Omo National Park to Maji; unfortunately, rain has damaged it and local disputes currently stall repairs. Other future (central government) plans include a road from Jimma to Kenya via Maji and Omorate (including a bridge over the Omo). Enquire about progress at the NTO.

Places to Stay & Eat

Most of the villages of the Lower Omo Valley are without electricity and have very basic hotels: rooms with dirt floors, no showers and sometimes earth 'beds'. Camping is the best bet. If you don't have a tent, some of the following villages have hotels, and can usually rustle up something to eat as well.

In Weyto, the **Mihirat Restaurant** offers camping (Birr10) or a mattress on top of the Coke crates in its open-air compound. Rooms with showers and toilets (around Birr10 to Birr15) are planned here soon.

In Key Afar, **Abebe Kebede Hotel** *(doubles with bucket shower Birr15)* is the best bet.

In Turmi, **Buska Restaurant** *(doubles Birr20; cold shower Birr2)* is currently the best budget hotel. In the future, a new hotel should be built offering rooms from Birr15 to Birr20 with shared shower.

The new **Evangadi Campsite** *(☎ 01-63 46 60; e evangadilodge@yahoo.com; camping per tent with cold showers Birr25, doubles/ twins in furnished tukul-tents Birr100/150)* is a lovely choice with a pleasant campsite amid mango trees, 24-hour security and a generator. A restaurant is planned to open soon. It's about 500m from the **Tourist Restaurant**, on the outskirts of Turmi, which is considered the best place to eat.

You can also camp (per tent Birr10, guards Birr50 per person) at a pleasant, shaded site on the Kaske river known as Wadi Kaske, 3.9km from Turmi on the road to Weyto (see Omo Valley Villages earlier). Unfortunately, a flash flood washed the camp away in 2002. Check conditions before camping here!

In Omorate, the **Tourist Hotel** *(☎ 19 01 29; doubles/twins with shared cold shower Birr20/24)* is the best choice. The **National Hotel** *(doubles Birr15)* is second choice, but has the best restaurant. If you want to camp in Omorate, the best place is inside the police compound; Turmi is a better choice.

In Dimeka, the **Ashabir Hotel** *(doubles with shared cold shower Birr15)*, though basic, has a restaurant and is often full on market day.

Getting There & Around

The best time to visit the Lower Omo Valley is during the dry season, from July to August and December to January. Roads can become impassable in the wet season. In recent years, however, the rains have been very erratic and unpredictable. Be aware that just one day of rain can render the roads temporarily impassable, so keep your itinerary flexible.

The road to Konso from Yabelo has now been improved and is usually accessible. West of Weyto, conditions depend on the rain. No public transport goes to Mago or Omo National Parks.

Bus & Truck Currently few buses and pick-up trucks connect the villages in the Omo Valley. On market days, more local transport is available and this is a good time to travel. If you're planning to use local transport, you'll need time on your hands. A bus service may be set up in the next three or four years, but crossings over the *wadis* (rivers that are dry except in the rainy season) need to be built first.

From Addis Ababa, one bus usually runs three times a week to Jinka (Birr76.50, two days) overnighting in Arba Minch (Birr33 to Birr40; nine hours) then back again, depending on weather conditions. From Arba Minch a bus runs daily to Konso, Weyto and Jinka (see Getting There & Away under Arba Minch earlier) and back again.

Pick-up trucks (from Birr5 to Birr35 though *faranjis* may be asked double), however, do link the villages more frequently. Interconnected villages include Konso, Arba Minch, Weyto, Key Afar, Arbore, Turmi, Omorate and Dimeka.

As an example of a circuit: from Jinka, there are currently pick-up trucks every two days to Turmi and Omorate (Birr40 to Birr50). From Omorate, there are usually trucks every two or three days to Turmi (Birr12 to Birr15). From Turmi, there are trucks every two days to Key Afar (Birr24). From Key Afar, there are trucks and buses every two days back to Arba Minch (Birr36).

If you want to visit the more remote Mursi, it is possible to hike to Maki (the nearest Mursi village to Jinka) and back in three days, hitching part of the way. Ask at the Orit Hotel for a guide (Birr50).

Organised Tours If you're alone or in a couple, the next cheapest alternative is to try and join a tour group. These are not scheduled, so you should check as far in advance as possible with the travel agencies in Addis Ababa, and organise your itinerary around that (see Organised Tours in the Getting Around chapter).

Tours are not cheap compared with safaris offered in other East African countries, but if you can afford one, the opportunity is not to be missed. Most tours last a minimum of seven to 10 days, but also take in the Rift Valley lakes, Awasa and Arba Minch.

4WD Rental If you're hiring a vehicle, try and go in convoy with another. If one vehicle gets stuck, the other can drag it out. Ensure the vehicle is adequately equipped with good tyres, a shovel, pick axe and a metal cable (a winch is even better). If you do get stuck, and you're within a 10km radius of Mago National Park, a tractor can help pull you out, or one of the 4WDs that are equipped with winches and ropes.

Carry between 230 and 240 litres of fuel (including the tank contents). When the going is heavy, your average speed can be as low as 6km/h, which quickly burns up the fuel. Budget four litres of drinking water per person per day. If coming from the north, fill up in Arba Minch, if from the south, in Yabelo, then fill up again in Konso or Jinka.

A knowledgeable driver or guide is essential; sometimes the roads are little more than tracks that lose themselves in the savanna or clearings through the jungle.

A local guide who knows the area quite well is Dinote Kusia Shenkere, who can be located at the Culture, Information & Tourism Office in Konso. He doesn't come cheap, and now charges Birr100 per day.

The Southeast & The Bale Mountains

ADDIS ABABA TO BALE MOUNTAINS NATIONAL PARK

The agricultural town of **Asela** makes a convenient overnight stop en route to the Bale Mountains, when coming from the capital, but if you can bus straight through to Dinsho or Goba, do so. The choice of hotels and restaurants is better.

Hooteela Beezaa (☎ *31 19 85; doubles with/without hot shower Birr18/8*), off the main Nazret–Dodola road, 500m north of the bus station, is the best budget place in Asela. The restaurant of the **Laaqaw Indaala** is considered the best place to eat.

Buses and minibuses travel from Asela to Nazret (buses Birr6 minibuses Birr9, 1½–2½ hours, every 30 minutes), Addis Ababa

(Birr14, three to four hours, one daily), Dodola (Birr16, four hours, one daily) and Dinsho (Birr32, six to seven hours, one daily).

If you get stuck in **Dodola**, the **Bale Mountain Motel** *(☎ 06-66 00 16; camping per person Birr20, doubles with/without shower Birr40/20)*, on the approach to town from Nazret, has adequate rooms. A cheaper option is **Hoteela Daneel** *(doubles with/without shower Birr10/7)* on the right after the IMEP office. Considered the best restaurant in town is the **Wayn Restaurant** about 100m from the Commercial Bank, off the main road.

From Dodola, eight to 10 buses run daily to Shashemene (Birr10, 2½ hours). For Dinsho, take the bus to Robe (Birr20, 3½ to four hours, four buses daily) and ask to be dropped off. Around 20 buses and minibuses run daily to Adaba (Birr3.50, 40 min).

BALE MOUNTAINS NATIONAL PARK
የባሌ ተራሮች ብሔራዊ ፓርክ

More than any other park in Ethiopia, the Bale Mountains are known for their wildlife. Over 60 mammal species and 260 bird species have been recorded here.

The scenery may be less spectacular than in the Simien Mountains, but it is certainly no less beautiful. Rivers cut deep gorges through the plateaus; streams, waterfalls and alpine lakes are all features of the landscape. In the lower hills, Highlanders canter along century-old paths on their richly caparisoned horses, and the noise of shepherd boys cracking their whips echoes around the valley. Among the abundant wildflowers, beautiful birds such as the malachite and Tacazze sunbirds flit about.

Geography
The national park stretches over 2400 sq km and ranges in altitude from 1500m to 4377m.

The Harenna Escarpment splits the park in two, running fracture-like from east to west. To the northeast of the escarpment lies the high-altitude plateau known as the Sanetti Plateau (4000m). The plateau is broken by a series of volcanic plugs and small peaks, including Tullu Deemtu, which at 4377m is the highest point in southern Ethiopia.

To the south, the land gradually falls away from the plateau, and a thick heather belt gives way to heavily forested areas known collectively as the Harenna Forest.

Climate
On the plateau, temperatures range from 10° to 26°C depending on the time of year. The dry season has the highest range of temperatures: it can get quite hot in the daytime, while at night, frost and even snow are sometimes reported.

The wet season has more moderate temperatures. Most rain falls between March and October, and the annual rainfall is high: an average of 1150mm.

Flora
The park can be divided into three main zones. The northern area of the park, around the park headquarters at Dinsho, consists of grassy, riverine plains and bushland of mainly sagebrush and St John's wort. From 2500m to 3300m, woodland of mainly *Hagenia abyssinica* and *Juniperus procera* is found. The abundant wildflowers in the area include geranium, lobelia and alchemilla.

Higher up, montane grassland gives way to heather. Here the plant can be found not only as little bushes, but as large and mature trees.

The second zone, the Sanetti Plateau, is home to typical Afro-alpine plants, some of which have adapted to the extreme conditions by either remaining very small or becoming very large. The best known is the curious-looking giant lobelia *(Lobelia rhynchopeta-lum)*, which can reach 5m in height. The silver *Helichrysum* or 'everlasting' flowers are the dominant wildflowers. Keep an eye out for the indigenous Abyssinian rose, with its lovely subtle scent.

The third habitat, the moist, tropical Harenna Forest, is home to tree species such as *Hagenia*, *Celtis* and *Podocarpus*.

Fauna

The Bale Mountains are known particularly for their endemic wildlife. The park was created initially to provide a stronghold for two endemic animals: the Ethiopian wolf and the mountain nyala.

The sighting of an Ethiopian wolf, the world's rarest canid, is a highlight of a trip to

the Bale Mountains, and is almost guaranteed on the Sanetti Plateau. But there are plenty of other no-less-remarkable endemics to be seen, including Menelik's bushbuck and the giant molerat.

Other large mammals commonly seen in the northern area include grey duikers, Bohor reedbucks and warthogs. Serval cats and Anubis baboons are occasionally seen.

In the Harenna Forest, giant forest hogs, bushpigs, warthogs, colobus monkeys and spotted hyena are all found, as well as leopards, lions and African hunting dogs. The last three are rarely seen.

Though most travellers can't wait to get trekking, the area around the park headquarters at Dinsho is, ironically, the one place where many of the larger mammals are easily seen. The park grounds are fenced, keeping

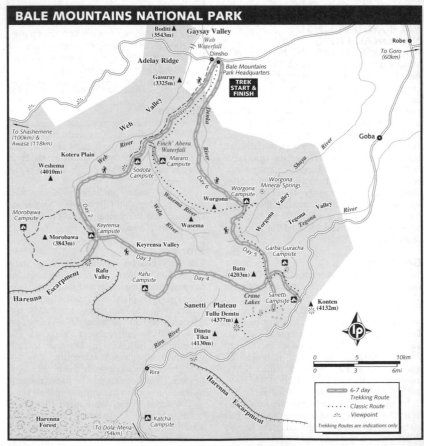

BALE MOUNTAINS NATIONAL PARK

The Ethiopian Wolf

The Ethiopian wolf (*Canis simensis*) is the rarest canid (dog family member) in the world. Found only in the Ethiopian highlands, it is thought to be on the verge of extinction. Only about 1000 wolves are believed to remain in the whole country.

Wolves are found on both sides of the Rift Valley, in the old provinces of Gonder, Wolo, Menz, Arsi and Bale. The Bale Mountains are home to by far the largest number. In Amharic, the wolf is known as *Ky Kebero* or 'red jackal'. Though the wolf does look like a kind of jackal, its connection to the wolf family has recently been established.

Living in family groups of around 13 animals, the wolves are highly territorial and family orientated. When the dominant female in the pack gives birth to her annual litter of between two and six pups, all members chip in, taking it in turns to feed, look after and play with the young. When it comes to hunting, however, the wolves forage alone. Any of the 19 rodent species found in Bale provide snacks. The giant molerats provide a feast and are the favourite food of the wolves.

The main threats to the wolves are rabies and canine distemper caught from the domestic dog population, and cross-breeding (male wolves with female dogs). In the Bale Mountains, the 1991–92 outbreak of rabies reduced the population from around 400 animals to 120. In 1995, distemper also took its toll.

Loss of habitat to livestock and cultivation (such as in north and south Wolo), and local superstition are other obstacles to be overcome. Locals believe that the antirabies vaccine changes the character of their dogs, or renders them less efficient as guard dogs. It is also considered very bad luck if a wolf crosses your path. In the past wolves have been deliberately run over or shot by truck drivers.

Current measures to try and save the animal from extinction include an antirabies vaccination, a sterilisation programme for local domestic dog populations and local education. New surveys and studies of population are currently being conducted. There is also talk of starting a captive breeding programme in the future. Though it is still threatened, the Bale population of wolves now looks healthier than it has in decades.

most of the animals in and the people out. The animals are less shy here as they are more used to people. The best times for spotting wildlife and for photos are from 6.30am to 9am and 4pm to 6pm.

Bale is also famous for its incredible number of endemic birds – 16 at the last count, though in 1998 an entirely new species of falcon may have been recorded by American researchers. Unusually, the endemics are very easily seen. No self-respecting twitcher should leave the mountains off their itinerary!

On the plateau, sightings of endemics (the blue-winged goose, wattled ibis, thick-billed raven, black-headed siskin and spot-breasted plover) are almost guaranteed. The birdlife in the juniper forests around the park headquarters is outstanding too. Ask for Idriss or Tilahun, guides who are quite good at locating birds.

Near the park headquarters, a 1km nature trail leads up to Dinsho Hill, from where there are quite good views of the surrounding park. The little **museum** (*open 8.30am-6.30pm daily*) is also worth a peek. Though tiny, it's crammed with various local stuffed animals including those not commonly seen such as the honey badger, civet cat and aardvark. There also some interesting information panels about conservation efforts, flora, fauna, and the local people.

Planning

All treks begin and end in the little highland town of Dinsho, which lies at the entrance to the park, around 30km northwest of Goba.

Maps A new and quite useful map is now available at Dinsho lodge and museum for Birr10. A small booklet about the Bale Mountains (Birr10) is also available and gives a good overview of the mountains and their environment.

When to Go December to March is the driest time, but late September to December, after the rainy season, is when the scenery is greenest and the wildflowers are out.

During the main rainy season – between June and September – mist often obscures the views and the trails can be slippery underfoot. Even in the wet season, however, you are assured of several hours a day of clear, dry weather for walking; the rain tends to come in short, sharp downpours.

Park Fees & Regulations Fees are payable at the **park headquarters** *(tourists/residents per 48h Birr50/30; vehicles per 24h Birr10-20; camping per 48h Birr20; open 8.30am-12.30pm & 1.30pm-5.30pm Mon-Fri, 8am-12.30pm Sat)* at Dinsho lodge, 2.5km from Dinsho village. If you come outside hours, someone can usually be summoned. Guides, scouts and horses are also organised at the headquarters (see later).

Fires are permitted only at campsites. Deforestation is a major problem here as in other parts of Ethiopia. Many guides and scouts like to make fires in the evening to keep warm. Try at least to use the dead erica (heather) wood. Cheap kerosene stoves can be bought in Addis Ababa.

Supplies There are just a couple of stores in Dinsho, selling little more than the basics (pasta, rice, tomato puree etc). **Mohammed Hussein Shop** on the corner of the road at the end of town as it bends upwards towards Dinsho Lodge, is considered the best. If you're planning more elaborate menus, you should stock up in Addis Ababa. You can usually barter for eggs in the local markets of the nearby villages (Birr1 for four or five) or on the mountain (Birr1 for three), and chickens (Birr10 in the markets, Birr15 in the mountain) which helps the local economy.

Water is available in various places on the mountain but should be treated.

If you don't have your own tent, you can usually hire basic ones from private individuals in the village (Birr20 per 24 hours). Ask at your hotel. As a last resort you could rely on the caves and *tukuls* in the area; ask your guide. Basic sleeping bags can also usually be hired (Birr10) in Dinsho. Or, if you're desperate, warm Dinsho blankets can be bought in the town (Birr100 to Birr120).

Trekking

Organising the 'team' (guide, scout, horses) inevitably takes time. The best plan is to arrive in Dinsho in the early afternoon, sort out your trek for the following morning, then spend the rest of the day exploring the wooded land immediately surrounding the park headquarters. A night spent in Dinsho is also a good start towards acclimatisation.

Most trekking in the Bale Mountains is fairly gentle and undemanding, following

Potent Plants

While trekking in the Bale Mountains, look out for the endemic plant *Kniphofia foliosa*, a member of the red-hot poker family, found quite commonly in the hills between 2050m and 4000m. The plant flowers from May to October and from December to January.

Long valued by the local Bale people for its medicinal properties, it's used to relieve stomach aches and cramps. Recently, a scientific investigation revealed that the plant does in fact contain several anthraquinones including islandicin, which is found in fungi such as *Penicillium islandicum*!

good, well-trodden paths or sheep tracks. But don't forget that the effects of altitude can make easy-looking terrain quite heavy going.

Trekking in Bale lacks the variety of trails and the drama of the high escarpments of the Simiens, and the most beautiful scenery is found among the hills immediately below the plateau. The plateau itself, at 4000m, can be very bleak and monotonous, though there are some scenic lakes in places. The birds and wildlife, however, more than compensate for the landscape.

Guides, Scouts & Horses According to regulations, all trekkers must be accompanied by a guide and a ranger – known as a 'scout' – though it's OK to walk around the woodland of the park headquarters without them.

Guides work as freelancers, but by rote, so there's little point recommending individuals. Few scouts speak English, but they make willing additions to the team. Guides cost Birr70 per day (one to three people), Birr90 (four to 20 people); scouts Birr40 (one to 40 people).

Porters are not available, but horses can be hired (Birr25 per day). If you're in a big group, you'll be expected to hire a horse driver as well (Birr30 per day). The guide and scout will expect at least one horse to carry their blankets and provisions.

Guides, scouts and handlers should provide food for themselves. Some bring token offerings or nothing at all and will then look to you for sustenance. Either check they have enough or bring extra. As if by compensation, the guide is happy to act as cook, and the scout to collect dead wood. Eucalyptus wood (Birr15 for an average bundle) can also be bought from the park headquarters.

At the end of the trek, staff will expect a tip. A rule of thumb, if the service has been good, tip an extra day's pay for every three days of work.

Classic Route The park covers a relatively small area, and most treks last just six days, or four days with a vehicle, though longer excursions can be planned.

Day One The four- or six-day standard trek begins at the park headquarters in Dinsho and works its way southwest up the Web and Wollo Valleys to the Finch' Abera Waterfall (two or three hours from the park headquarters). You can either camp here or continue on to Mararo (3750m), where there's a pleasant campsite beside a stream.

Day Two This day is spent walking up the Wasama Valley (six hours). A good stop on the way is the mineral springs at Worgona. Keep an eye out for the giant molerats, which are easily seen in the area. The steep ascent to the Sanetti Plateau then begins. A good campsite is beneath the crags of Mt Batu in the Shaya Valley.

Day Three Mt Batu can be climbed on day three, before you walk to the picturesque campsite situated in the Tegona Valley under the sheer cliffs beside the Garba Guracha Lake (six hours). The campsite is a terrific spot for birds of prey. Lammergeyers, buzzards and eagles are all commonly seen here.

Day Four This day is spent walking to the Crane Lakes (six hours) – marked on some maps as the 'Alpine Lakes'. These are known for their water birds, and as one of the best spots to see the Ethiopian wolf. A detour can be made to visit Tullu Deemtu. It'll then take you another day's trekking back to Dinsho. A vehicle could meet you on the Goba–Dola-Mena road.

Tullu Deemtu is little more than a very monotonous scree slope, with a pretty unattractive observatory planted on the top. However, it affords good views from the summit, over the Harenna Forest to the south, the Sanetti Plateau to the north and the town of Goba to the northeast. From the main Goba–Dola-Mena road, it's 4km to the mountain.

Other Routes The following routes are also recommended. New *tukuls* (huts) and campsites should be established in the

mountains by the end of 2003. These will further facilitate trekking in this area. Consult your guide (and the map) for details:

Wasama Valley (five days)
Day one Dinsho–Sodota (four hours)
Day two Sodota–Wasama (four to five hours)
Day three Wasama–Garba Guracha (six hours)
Day four Garba Guracha–Worgona (five hours)
Day five Worgona–Dinsho.

Garba Guracha Lake & Mineral Springs (six to seven days; see map)
Day one Dinsho–Sodota (four hours)
Day two Sodota–Keyrensa campsite (five to six hours)
Day three Keyrensa–Rafu campsite (five to six hours)
Day four Rafu–Garba Guracha (five hours)
Day five Garba Guracha–Worgona (five hours)
Day six Worgona–Dinsho (six hours).
Crane Lakes can also be visited en route. If you're short of time, you can arrange for your vehicle (if you have one) to pick you up on the Goba–Dola-Mena road.

Harenna Forest (eight to 10 days)
Day one Dinsho–Sodota (four hours)
Day two Sodota–Keyrensa campsite (five to six hours)
Day three Keyrensa–Rafu campsite (five to six hours)
Day four Rafu campsite–Rira village (six to seven hours)
Day five Rira–Katcha campsite (four hours)
Day six Katcha–Rira (six to seven hours)
Day seven Rira–Worgona (nine to 10 hours)
Day eight Worgona–Dinsho (seven to eight hours)

Alternative Routes For those very short on time, one-day excursions include walks up the Web Valley to Gasuray Peak (3325m) and Adelay Ridge. The Web Gorge takes around 1½ hours to reach, and is good for seeing colobus monkeys. Go early in the morning.

A good overnight excursion is to a spot on the Kotera Plain. It's the site of an old observation post for the Ethiopian wolf, and the animal is still often seen here. The walk takes five hours one way.

For a very pretty walk that includes birds and a good chance of seeing the Ethiopian wolf, go to the Finch' Abera Waterfall then spend the night nearby at the so-called 'French Camp'. Leopards are seen very occasionally near the waterfall.

For those who want to spend longer periods in the mountains, the almost totally unexplored Harenna Forest offers great hiking potential. Recent scientific expeditions here have discovered many new endemic species (see the boxed text 'Funny Frogs' in the Facts about Ethiopia chapter).

Nontrekkers

If you've only limited time, or can't walk far, you can still see a great deal of wildlife particularly with your own vehicle. The top of Tullu Deemtu can also be reached by 4WD, via the Sanetti Plateau.

If you go up to the plateau early enough (around 7am is ideal), you are almost guaranteed a sighting of the Ethiopian wolf. The afternoon between 3.30pm and 5.30pm is also quite good. The animal wakes up ravenous after a cold night and spends the early hours of the morning intently searching for food.

If you get out of the car and approach from downwind, you can get very close indeed. The spot where most wolves are currently sited appears to be around 1km after the first telecom satellite dish on the plateau. If you're lucky, you may spot a klipspringer here too.

A pleasant, short stroll from the Goba–Dola-Mena road is to the Crane Lakes, an excellent spot for birds (though in the dry season, some of the lakes evaporate). Wattled cranes often nest here, migrating to the lowlands during the dry season. June and September are the best months to see them.

Places to Stay & Eat

Dinsho The best bet is **Dinsho Lodge** *(camping Birr20 per person per 48h, 2-/3-/6-/8-bed dormitories with cold shared shower per person Birr50/20/15/10).*

If you want to light a fire (there's no other heating in the lodge), bundles of firewood cost Birr15. Currently (and until electricity reaches Dinsho by the end of 2003), a generator is used from 6.30pm to 10pm daily. To ease those weary limbs, a sauna (Birr10, then Birr3 to Birr4 per extra person) can be fired up.

There's no restaurant in the lodge, but you can use the lodge kitchen (Birr4 per person per day), housed in a separate block. There's just a wood fire; if you have your own stove, you can use that. Cooks can be hired (Birr20 to Birr30 per day).

During the high season, reservations should be made in advance through the **Ethiopian Wildlife Conservation Organisation** *(☎ 51 79 22; PO Box 386, Addis Ababa)* or by writing directly to: The Warden, Dinsho Lodge, PO Box 107, Goba, Ethiopia.

Camping *(per person per 48h Birr20)* is possible on Dinsho Hill behind the lodge.

The only alternatives to the lodge are the budget hotels in Dinsho town.

Hotel Tsahayi *(rooms without shower Birr10)* has rooms set off a small garden. Food *(faranji* and local) can be ordered in advance. The **Hotel Genet**, a very similar place, is second best.

The new **Wolf Den's Cafe** *(open 7am-10pm)* is the best – and almost only – place for a beer. The Hotel Tsahayi is also popular.

On the Mountains The national park has established various sites for camping, though there are not yet any huts, shelters or other facilities. You'll need to be fully independent with tent, sleeping bag and cooking gear.

Getting There & Away

Ethiopian Airlines flies from Addis Ababa to Goba (around 43km from Dinsho and the nearest large town along with Robe). See Getting There & Away under Goba, next.

Regular buses run between Addis Ababa and Goba (see next). From Goba, you can take a bus or hitch a ride with a truck to Dinsho. It's then a 2km walk to Dinsho Lodge. Buses (Birr1.50, 15 minutes) run every 30 minutes or so between Goba and Robe.

Buses also run to Goba or Robe from Shashemene, Dola-Mena, Dodola and Asela (see under those places for details of cost, duration and frequency of buses).

It's 425km from Addis Ababa to Dinsho. By private vehicle, you can get there in a single day if you make a dawn start.

Getting Around

A great way to take in a lot of the park without your own vehicle is to catch one of the buses or trucks that ply the Dinsho–Dola-Mena road (via Robe and Goba). The road takes you right through the park, up over the Sanetti Plateau and down into the Harenna Forest. You can explore the area from the road, then hitch back, which isn't too difficult, but don't leave it too late in the day.

GOBA & ROBE
ጎባ ና ሮቤ

Goba ☎ 06 • pop 28,358 • elevation 2743m
The twin towns of Goba and Robe lie 14km from one another. Goba, the old capital of the Bale region, is still the most convenient of the two. The town is larger than Robe and is the terminus for most bus travel.

ETHIOPIA

At the town markets, look out for the delicious local acacia honey, the attractive basketry and the heavy cotton *buluko* (togas). The honey and the shawls make great accompaniments to a Bale Mountains trek. Goba's market is on Wednesday (the largest) and on Saturday; Robe's is on Thursday.

Beyond the colourful markets there's little to see in either town, but you may well be obliged to spend the night here on your way to or from the Bale Mountains.

Places to Stay & Eat

Goba The **Hooteela Goobbaa Roobee** *(rooms with shared shower Birr7)* is basic but adequate.

Yilma Hotel *(☎ 61 04 82; doubles with/ without hot shower Birr40/20, twins Birr80)* has a pleasant garden. Unfortunately, prices have increased and standards dropped a bit lately; some travellers have also complained of double *faranji* prices for food. Check first.

Batu Terara Hotel *(☎ 61 07 12; doubles with/without shower Birr40/20)* with clean but simple rooms set around a garden is probably the best value now. It was undergoing refurbishment at the time of writing and wasn't yet marked. Ask for directions.

Baltena Hotel is one of the best, local restaurants in town, set in a little garden.

Mana Kitifoo Zariihuun is a popular *kitfo* (raw or partly cooked minced meat) house.

Goba Wabe Shebele Hotel *(☎ 61 00 41; singles/doubles Birr137.50/169.15)* isn't great value accommodation-wise, but does good *faranji* food (three-course set menu Birr37.50), including breakfast (Birr18.75). It is 1.7km from the Commercial Bank in the north of the town.

Shalom Pastry, **Sweet Pastry** and particularly **Nyala Bale Pastry** *(open 6.30am-9pm)* all make delicious cakes.

City Café with a pleasant garden, is a local favourite. It's good for breakfast, with fruit juices, cakes and fresh bread.

Robe In the centre of town the **Peacock Hotel** *(☎ 65 01 12; rooms with/without cold shower Birr12/10)* has adequate rooms though it can be noisy. The new **Choice Hotel** *(☎ 65 09 50)*, in front of the Total petrol station 1km from the main roundabout, has a good reputation for food locally.

Bekele Mola *(☎ 65 00 65; doubles/twins with shower Birr35/45)*, at the southern end of town (on the road towards Goba) 350m north of the bus station, has good rooms set in

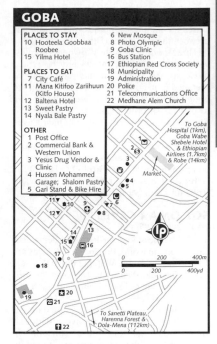

GOBA

PLACES TO STAY
10 Hooteela Goobbaa Roobee
15 Yilma Hotel

PLACES TO EAT
7 City Café
11 Mana Kitifoo Zariihuun (Kitfo House)
12 Baltena Hotel
13 Sweet Pastry
14 Nyala Bale Pastry

OTHER
1 Post Office
2 Commercial Bank & Western Union
3 Yesus Drug Vendor & Clinic
4 Hussen Mohammed Garage; Shalom Pastry
5 Gari Stand & Bike Hire
6 New Mosque
8 Photo Olympic
9 Goba Clinic
16 Bus Station
17 Ethiopian Red Cross Society
18 Municipality
19 Administration
20 Police
21 Telecommunications Office
22 Medhane Alem Church

To Goba Hospital (1km), Goba Wabe Shebele Hotel & Ethiopian Airlines (1.7km) & Robe (14km)

Market

To Sanetti Plateau, Harenna Forest & Dola-Mena (112km)

a large garden area. On the main roundabout at the southern end of town, **Fountain Café** is a good pastry shop.

Getting There & Away

Ethiopian Airlines *(☎ 61 00 16)* – based in the Goba Wabe Shebele Hotel – flies just once a week to and from Addis Ababa (currently on Sunday). The airport lies 7km from Robe and 22km from Goba.

One bus runs daily from Goba to Shashemene (Birr23.35, six to seven hours) and to Addis Ababa (Birr45.95, 11 to 12 hours). For Dola-Mena, one to two buses leave daily (Birr20, four to five hours); usually at least one truck also travels to Dola-Mena for the same price, leaving in front of the Hussen Mohammed garage in Goba. On Wednesday and Saturday (market day in Dola-Mena), usually four trucks make the journey.

For Dinsho (Birr7) buses leave only three times a week. You may be able to hitch a lift with a pick-up truck (Birr7) – ask at the bus station. Otherwise, a contract minibus would set you back Birr200 to Birr250.

For Robe, all buses travelling between Goba and Shashemene or Addis Ababa stop here; ask to be dropped off.

Getting Around

Buses and minibuses shuttle every 15 minutes between the two towns (Birr1.50, 15 mins).

Three or four privately owned vehicles, with driver and fuel, can usually be rented in Goba. Ask around the bus station and be prepared to negotiate hard. 4WDs cost in the region of Birr1000 per day; you may be able to pay for specific visits, say to the Sanetti Plateau (around Birr200) or Sof Omar Caves (Birr400).

For the Sanetti Plateau, a minibus (maximum 10 people) can be hired in Robe if there's a group of you (Birr400 to Birr500).

Bicycles can be hired in both Goba and Robe for Birr3 per hour or Birr15 per day.

SOF OMAR CAVES
የሶፍ አማር ዋሻዎች

Thought to be among the largest underground caverns in the world, the Sof Omar Caves are 135km east of Goba. Winding down the Bale Mountains, the Web River has, over the millennia, carved a 16km course through the limestone hills.

The huge caves, with their vaulted chambers, flying buttresses, massive pillars and fluted archways, resemble a cathedral; in fact, Sof Omar has long been an important religious site. Sheikh Sof Omar reportedly took refuge here in the very early days of Islam. The caves are still greatly venerated by Muslims in the area, although, curiously, many pagan rites and ceremonies seem to have carried over from the ancient past.

The highlights are the Chamber of Columns or Conference Hall, the dome and the balcony not far from the entrance to the cave. The normal 'tour' takes around 20 minutes.

The villagers at Sof Omar charge an admission fee of up to Birr100, but Birr20 ought to be adequate.

A visit to the caves takes a full day; they're probably only worth a visit if you're planning

a full exploration or want to visit the Sof Omar market too. The market is a colourful event, held every Saturday.

Getting There & Away

By public transport, you'll have to go first to Goro, 40km east of Goba. One or two buses and minibuses run there daily from Goba and Robe (Birr8 to Birr12, two hours). From Goro, you can try to hitch a lift with a pick-up truck to Sof Omar (Birr20, 1½ hours, 45km). The best time is on Saturday (market day at Sof Omar). The alternative, if you're desperate, is to take a contract minibus (one to 10 people) for Birr800 return.

SHEIKH HUSSEIN
ሸኽ ሁሴን

Located north of Sof Omar, Sheikh Hussein is Ethiopia's most important centre of Muslim pilgrimage and attracts thousands of pilgrims every year. The complex consists of an attractive little mosque, various tombs within a wall, and shrines and caves that are found within an hour's walk east of the complex. It is said Sheikh Hussein himself used the caves to seek some peace and quiet for prayer.

At least 500 years old, it is dedicated to the 13th-century holy man, who was responsible for the conversion of many Bale and Arsi Oromos to Islam. Pilgrims come here to make wishes and to offer thanks for wishes fulfilled. Feast days are during May and October, with minor ones during February and September; the exact dates depend on the lunar calendar.

This peaceful and atmospheric place is open to people of all faiths (not just Muslims). Local religious leaders will give you a tour. It's customary to leave a small contribution of Birr20 after a visit.

If you get stuck here, **Golocha Hotel** *(rooms with shared shower Birr15)* in Jara is basic but adequate.

The journey to the site takes you through some very beautiful scenery, and birdlife is abundant – a reason for going in itself.

Getting There & Away

Unless you visit the shrine during a major pilgrimage (when local transport is available from surrounding towns, including Robe), you'll need your own vehicle to visit Sheikh Hussein. A contract Land Cruiser taxi from Goba there and back would set you back at least Birr1500 (for up to six people). Bring extra fuel.

Cows & Crowns

Cattle rearing is the mainstay of the southeast's economy, and the cow is greatly prized by the local people. The animal supplies not just meat, milk, butter and blood for food, but dung for fuel and for building houses. Ownership of cattle confers great social status on Oromo men: traditionally, if a herdsman owns more than 1000, he is entitled to wear a crown.

A bus runs on Friday between Robe and Jara (Birr20 to Birr25, six hours) and a mini-bus plies the route daily (Birr2, six hours). From Jara, you'll have to try to hitch a lift with private local transport to Sheikh Hussein (57km, two hours).

DOLA-MENA
ዶላ ሜና

Dola-Mena is dreary, but the journey to the town, 110km south of Goba, is a terrific one. You traverse the eastern part of the Bale Mountains National Park, cross the Harenna Escarpment and wind up onto the lofty San-etti Plateau itself. The route is the highest all-weather road in Africa. It must also rank among the continent's most spectacular.

The road takes you through the extra-ordinary *Podocarpus* woodland known as the **Harenna Forest**. With its twisted trunks draped in 'old man beard' lichens, mosses and ferns, and with cloud swirling all around, the forest is like something straight out of a Grimm brothers fairy tale.

The forest, undoubtedly one of the most remarkable in Ethiopia, is home to a whole host of endemic plants, amphibians and insects, as well as wild coffee. Proper ex-ploration awaits. Sadly, the local demand for firewood is seriously threatening the forest. In the meantime, a Dutch World Wide Fund for Nature project awaits the signature of both the local and federal authorities.

At Katcha, 9.4km from Rira, a clearing has been made for a **campsite**, though you'll need a guide to find it; it is 10 minutes' walk off the Goba–Dola-Mena road. Look out for the colobus monkeys, which are quite often seen here. Lions are sometimes heard in the area.

Dola-Mena lies a further 31km beyond. **Makuriya Mengistu Hotel** (doubles Birr6), centrally-placed on the main drag, has very basic rooms and the **Fasika Restaurant**, not far from the mosque, serves adequate local fare.

Two or three pick-up trucks connect Goba and Dola-Mena (see under Goba earlier). From Rira, the road is currently in a poor state. After rain, it can become impassable. From Dola-Mena to Negele Borena, 179km to the south, the road is also bad. Trucks no longer travel the route as frequently as they did. At the time of writing, Mercedes trucks departed twice daily from Dola-Mena for Negele Borena (Birr35 to Birr40, 10 to 12 hours). To Goba (Birr20, four to five hours), usually one bus leaves two or three times weekly.

Note there is no fuel station in Dola-Mena, but a black market usually operates, if you're desperate.

NEGELE BORENA
ነገሌ ቦረና

Continuing south from Dola-Mena, the town of Negele Borena is the southeastern equiva-lent of Shashemene. Sitting at an important crossroads of the region, it serves as a useful transport hub. But not much else.

The journey south is pleasant enough. Birds and wildlife abound. You may well see jackals and grey duikers. Hornbills, vulturine guinea fowls, bustards, hoopoes and white-billed go-away birds are common sights.

In Negele Borena, the **Hawi Hotel** (doubles with shared shower Birr10-13) opposite the bus station is the best value. The **Green Hotel No 1** (rooms with/without shower Birr30-60/20-24) diagonally opposite the Health Centre is simple, but clean and set in a pleasant garden.

Getting There & Away
From Negele Borena, there is currently no transport to Mega, 300km to the southwest. Two pick-up trucks a week follow the rough track all the way to Moyale (Birr50, around 12 hours) on the Kenyan border.

Trucks leave twice weekly to Dola-Mena (Birr35 to Birr40, 10 to 12 hours); one bus runs daily to Shashemene (Birr39.50, 10 hours). One bus leaves daily for Addis Ababa (Birr62.60, 1½ days, overnight in Shashemene). For Yabelo, there are no direct buses currently; you'll have to travel there in short hops via Shakiso (Birr20, three hours) and Dawa.

Eastern Ethiopia

ETHIOPIA

The east of Ethiopia could be a different world. In stark contrast to the green, densely populated, Christian highlands, the east is largely arid, sparsely populated, low-lying and Muslim. But in it lies one of Ethiopia's greatest and perhaps most underestimated attractions: the old walled town of Harar.

For centuries Harar existed as an independent state and was an important centre of learning and arts. With its location at a key commercial crossroads, trade here flourished. For a time, no Christian was allowed to set foot within the city on pain of death. The town still retains a rather exotic Oriental air. At night, with the famous ritual feeding of the Harar hyenas, the place takes on a distinctly eerie air.

Easily accessible from Addis Ababa is a different sort of attraction: the Awash National Park. If you're not planning a trip to the parks in the south, an excursion here is recommended.

The road leading northeast to Eritrea, by contrast, penetrates a sparsely populated, arid, often desolate area known as the Danakil region. There are no must-see attractions here, and wildlife in Yangudi-Rassa National Park is barely visible, but the journey does take you through the heart of Afar territory. The Afar people, almost the only ones capable of surviving in these harsh conditions, have long fascinated European travellers (see boxed text 'The Dreaded Danakils' later in this chapter). For those with time, an exploration of this remote region could prove rewarding.

The east is also known as the home of some of the best coffee in the world. Almost as famous is the notorious *chat*, the mildly intoxicating leaf (see boxed text 'Chat among the Pigeons' later in this chapter); if you want to try it – here's your chance!

The road east will also take you through some pretty scenery and past lively and colourful markets. The Oromo people in particular are known for their bright finery and colourful jewellery.

Warning

Note that all bus journey duration times in this chapter are indications only. Journey times can vary greatly according to individual buses, weather and road conditions.

Highlights

- Explore the labyrinth-like streets and shrines of the old walled city of Harar, and witness the famous feeding of the hyenas after nightfall

- Take a tour of the crater lakes of Debre Zeyit, home of good birdlife and attractive scenery

- Visit the peaceful and serene mountain monastery of Mt Zuqualla Maryam, set beside a hallowed crater lake

- Take a tour of Awash National Park, home to the beautiful beisa oryx and outstanding birdlife

- Have a chew on *chat*, the mildly intoxicating stimulant, for centuries the inspiration to artists, intellectuals and warriors preparing for battle

- Encounter the Afar people, once legendary for their ferocity and still fascinating for their ancient culture

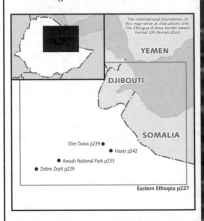

The international boundaries on this map serve as indications only. The Ethiopia–Eritrea border awaits formal UN demarcation.

YEMEN

DJIBOUTI

SOMALIA

Dire Dawa p239 ●
● Harar p242
● Awash National Park p233
● Debre Zeyit p229

Eastern Ethiopia p227

ADDIS ABABA TO DEBRE ZEYIT

The road running east from Addis Ababa is good; most travellers shoot straight though to Debre Zeyit. But for those with time or the interest, a brief stop can be made at Akaki (for the birds) or Mt Yerer (for the old volcano).

Akaki Wetlands

The Akaki wetlands, 22km southeast of Addis Ababa, attract good birdlife, drawn to the

iverse range of habitats, such as marsh, river
nd lake. The wetlands lie around 15km west
f the village of Akaki. September to October
(after the rains) is probably the best time for a
visit (note that the wetlands are seasonal).

Dese Hotel *(☎ 01-34 00 84; doubles with
shared shower Birr8-10)* in Akaki is basic,
but is the best place to stay here. Take the
first right (if approaching from Addis Ababa)
before the Commercial Bank, then first right
again, and follow the road for around 100m.
At the hotel ask for Girma, who can act as a
guide (Birr50 for a full day).

Getting There & Around Minibuses and
buses run around every 15 minutes between
Addis Ababa and Dukem, (Birr2.50, 50 to 60
minutes) and Debre Zeyit (Birr2.50 to Birr5,
around 45 minutes).

Akaki is on the Addis Ababa–Djibouti train
line. Trains from Addis to Akaki cost Birr5/
4/3 for 1st/2nd/3rd class; see Train under Djibouti in the Getting There & Away chapter.

From Akaki, a *gari* (horse-drawn cart)
is the cheapest way of getting to the wetlands (Birr5, one hour). They can be found
around the marketplace. For the return
journey, arrange for the *gari* to collect you.

In the wet season (June to September), the
track sometimes becomes impassable for
garis. A 4WD can be hired from the Dese
Hotel (Birr200 for half a day).

Dukem
ዱከም

Dukem, a roadside town serving traffic along
the Addis–Jijiga road, provides a useful base
for a trip to nearby Mt Yerer.

Menafasha Hotel *(☎ 01-32 00 10; doubles
without shower Birr8-10; with cold shower
Birr22)* is basic but clean. **Worku Bikila Hotel**
*(☎ 01-32 01 84; doubles with shower Birr30-
100)* is the new top-of-the-range place. The
more expensive rooms have TV. Its restaurant
along with that of the **Misrak Ber Hotel** are
considered the best in town.

Minibuses and buses run regularly between Dukem and Akaki (see previous) and
Debre Zeyit (Birr1, 20 minutes). Trains to or
from Addis Ababa cost Birr8/6/4 for 1st/2nd/
3rd class.

Mt Yerer
የረር ተራራ

Lying 35km east of Addis Ababa, and 10km
north of Dukem, Mt Yerer (3100m higher than

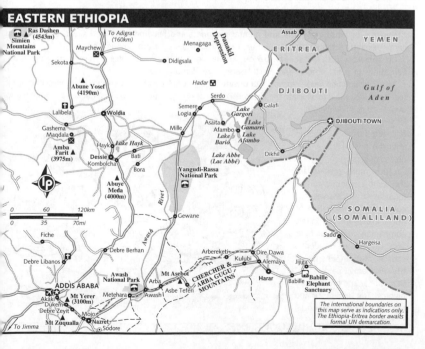

ETHIOPIA

Chat among the Pigeons

Catha edulis Forskal (chat) is an evergreen shrub averaging around 2m in height. It is found on warm, humid slopes between 1500m to 2800m. Growing wild in many eastern and southern African countries and on the Arab peninsula, it is actively cultivated in Yemen, Kenya and Ethiopia.

A natural and mildly intoxicating stimulant, it has been consumed for centuries in these regions, and is legal in Ethiopia.

According to legend, an angel one day appeared before two Muslim holy men and miraculously revealed the properties of the plant. With the help of the leaves, the holy men were able to resist sleep and continue their prayers, meditation and study deep into the night.

Whoever discovered it, it is almost certain that *chat* originated in East Africa, and that it had taken a firm hold on both sides of the Red Sea by the 15th century. Indeed, as far back as the 13th century, Arab writers were praising the plant as a panacea for melancholia. Warriors sometime took it in preparation for battle. Later, Arab historians noted its ability to stimulate intelligence and memory, as well as to suppress both appetite and sleep – all properties greatly appreciated by the intellectuals of the day!

For cautious travellers who prefer to try things vicariously, here's a quick session!

The psychological effects of *chat* can be divided into three main phases.

The first phase (which normally lasts around two hours) is known as the 'euphoric period'. Chewers quickly feel a sensation of wellbeing, optimism and excitement. Feelings of reserve or inhibition usually disappear.

The second phase is called the 'illusory period' (usually lasting around two hours). Intellectual activity appears to increase, the imagination becomes more and more active and attention seems to become sharper.

Later, chewers become reflective and introverted, and gradually lose themselves in an imaginary world where anything seems possible. All kinds of projects and plans are dreamed up during this phase, and all problems are apparently resolved! Towards the fourth hour, an increase in libido is commonly felt.

The third phase is known as the 'depressive period' (and usually lasts from five to six hours). Chewers experience a physical and mental weariness and become sullen and silent. But the brain continues in its activities. Both insomnia and a loss of appetite are experienced.

Consumers start to feel uneasy, anxious and nervous, with a sudden desire to seek other diversion. Sensations of guilt, remorse and worthlessness are also often felt.

After consumption, male impotence or unsatisfactory sexual performance is the commonest complaint (eating cloves is said to alleviate the problem!). The next day, many chewers experience a kind of hang-over. Feelings of dehydration, lethargy and tiredness are felt, often lasting right up until the next day – or the next *chat* session!

Much more serious are the socio-economic consequences of excessive *chat* consumption. Inspiration to poets, artists and musicians, companion to intellectuals and saviour of students, *chat* is also an enemy of the economy, catalyst of bankruptcy and provoker of divorce! The debate for and against the leaf rages on.

ETHIOPIA

the surrounding country) is an extinct volcano believed to date from three or four million years ago. From the top of the collapsed caldera there are good views, such as of Addis Ababa and the crater lakes of Debre Zeyit.

Timber trucks occasionally go to Yerer. Otherwise, you'll need your own vehicle and a guide (ask at the bus station). In the wet season, the road can become impassable.

DEBRE ZEYIT
ደብረ ዘይት
☎ 01 • pop 73,372 • elevation 1920m
Known in the local Oromo language as Bishoftu, Debre Zeyit serves a divergent double function: it is both the base for the Ethiopian air force and a popular weekend resort for Addis Ababans. The latter are drawn by the town's unusual position: it is set at the centre of no less than five crater lakes, and in the proximity of another three.

There is no tourist office in Debre Zeyit.

Lake Bishoftu
ቢሾፍቱ ሐይቅ
Lake Bishoftu is the most central lake. Though the area is almost totally denuded of trees, the lake still attracts quite good birdlife. The best

way to appreciate the lake is probably from the Hotel Bishoftu, a drink in hand. The view overlooking the crater rim is impressive. You can also walk around the edge if you fancy it.

Lake Hora
ሆራ ሐይቅ
Lake Hora lies 1.5km north of the centre of Debre Zeyit; follow the signposts to the Hora Recreation Center. The lake is attractively set and its birdlife is outstanding. Storks, pelicans, shovellers and grebes, as well as brightly coloured kingfishers are among the species seen here.

Along the shore, the **Hora Recreation Center** (☎ 16 71 18; admission Birr2) has opened. At the weekend it can get a bit noisy, but it's easy enough to escape the crowds: just follow the footpath around the lake as it winds through the forested slopes of the crater. A circumnavigation of the lake takes around 1½ hours. You should go accompanied, as hassle (and even theft) has been a problem.

There are plans to turn the place into an international sports centre, with a pool as well as boat trips and water sports on the lake. At the beginning of October, a big festival is held here that celebrates the start of the planting season.

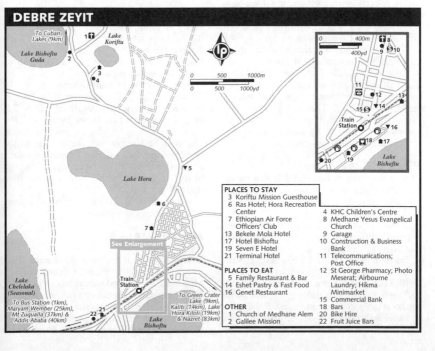

DEBRE ZEYIT

To Cuban Lakes (9km)
Lake Koriftu
Lake Bishoftu Guda
Lake Hora
Lake Chelelaka (Seasonal)
To Bus Station (1km), Maryam Wember (25km), Mt Zuqualla (37km) & Addis Ababa (40km)
Train Station
To Green Crater Lake (9km), Kaliti (14km), Lake Hora Kiloli (19km) & Nazret (83km)
Lake Bishoftu
See Enlargement
Train Station
Lake Bishoftu

PLACES TO STAY
3 Koriftu Mission Guesthouse
6 Ras Hotel; Hora Recreation Center
7 Ethiopian Air Force Officers' Club
13 Bekele Mola Hotel
17 Hotel Bishoftu
19 Seven E Hotel
21 Terminal Hotel

PLACES TO EAT
5 Family Restaurant & Bar
14 Eshet Pastry & Fast Food
16 Genet Restaurant

OTHER
1 Church of Medhane Alem
2 Galilee Mission
4 KHC Children's Centre
8 Medhane Yesus Evangelical Church
9 Garage
10 Construction & Business Bank
11 Telecommunications; Post Office
12 St George Pharmacy; Photo Meserat; Airbourne Laundry; Hikma Minimarket
15 Commercial Bank
18 Bars
20 Bike Hire
22 Fruit Juice Bars

Other Lakes

Just 3km north of Debre Zeyit is the scenic and peaceful **Lake Bishoftu Guda**. **Lake Koriftu** *(admission Birr2.50)*, nearby, is known particularly for its tilapia (fresh-water fish). The Protestant Koriftu Mission is situated here. You can stay at the **guesthouse** *(☎ 33 95 53; rooms from Birr64-100)* but it's a no-smoking no-alcohol zone. It is an additional Birr49 per person to have all meals included. To get to the mission, go through the KHC Children's Centre gates on the main Addis Ababa–Nazret road and follow the road up.

Birdlife on Lake Koriftu is quite good and fishing is permitted.

Around 14km north of town, beyond the Godino Soil Conservation and Forestry Development Nursery, are the so-called **Cuban Lakes**. In fact, they are dams but they provide one of the best places for spotting birds, including pelicans, cormorants and egrets.

Lake Chelelaka, 5km before town off the road to Addis Ababa, is in fact little more than seasonal floodwater, but the shallow mudflats usually attract excellent birdlife, including flamingos.

Green Crater Lake, 10km south of Debre Zeyit off the Nazret road, beyond the air force camp, is both large, and – as the name suggests – green (the result of algae). There is an impressive view over the lake from the crater rim. At night, flamingos often converge on the water; for the best chance of seeing them, try to get here at sunset or at dawn.

Lake Hora Kiloli lies 20km from Debre Zeyit. A side road leaves the main road just past the Oromiya water mines and energy resources complex. The lake is 5km from the village of Kaliti. It's well worth a visit for those with time; the journey takes you through some beautiful landscapes.

Place to Stay

The ex-government **Ras Hotel** is still awaiting refurbishment. Camping in the pleasant lakeside grounds is possible with the manager's permission.

Terminal Hotel *(☎ 33 88 77; doubles with/ without cold shower Birr10/8)* has clean, quiet and good-value rooms.

Seven E Hotel *(☎ 33 98 88; doubles with cold shower during weekdays/weekends Birr20/35)*, just off the main road up from the Shell station, is a decent new hotel with rooms set in a garden compound.

Hotel Bishoftu *(☎ 33 82 99; doubles/twins with hot shower Birr30/40)* has adequate rooms

in a pleasant courtyard; its attractive location above Lake Bishoftu is its main selling point.

Bekele Mola Hotel *(☎ 33 80 05; doubles with hot shower Birr30)* is similar to the Bishoftu, but cleaner and more peaceful.

Ethiopian Air Force Officers' Club *(☎ 33 14 00; doubles Birr200)* is a newly refurbished complex. Rooms have telephone and TV, but are nothing special. However, you may fancy a dip in the Olympic-sized pool (price for nonguests still undecided).

Places to Eat

Genet Restaurant, just down the road from Hotel Bishoftu, is simple but pleasant and popular.

Seven E Hotel with its pleasant garden and extensive menu is the local favourite.

Family Restaurant & Bar *(open weekends only)* next to the Defence Engineering College on the outskirts of town is modelled on an American bar. Hamburgers, ice cream and even chocolate cake are available, but prices are high.

Eshet Pastry & Fast Food is a new place serving good cakes, snacks and fruit juices.

Hotel Bishoftu is good for an evening drink or breakfast with a view.

Getting There & Around

Buses and minibuses leave every 15 minutes for Addis Ababa (Birr3, 45 to 60 minutes), Nazret (Birr6, 45 to 60 minutes), Dukem (Birr1, 20 minutes) and Akaki (Birr2.50 to Birr5, around 45 minutes).

Trains to or from Addis Ababa cost Birr10/ 7/5 for 1st/2nd/3rd class, to or from Nazret: Birr8.85/7/5, to or from Awash: Birr29.80/22/ 16 and to or from Dire Dawa: Birr67/49/37.

A *gari* is a great way to visit the lakes. They can be hired outside the bus station for Birr25/50 per half/full day. Around two days are needed to see all the lakes. Hops about the town cost Birr1 to Birr2; in a local minibus Birr0.70 to Birr0.90.

Bikes can be hired (Birr3 per hour) around 120m west of Hora Pastry.

MT ZUQUALLA

ዝቋላ ተራራ

Debre Zeyit also makes a good base from which to explore the extinct volcanic cone of Mt Zuqualla. Though only rising to just over 600m, the mountain dominates the landscape for miles around. On a clear day, the views from the top are stunning. You can see the Rift Valley to the east and the lakes to the south; Addis Ababa and the Entoto Mountains are just discernible to the northwest.

The crater, measuring 2km across and over 50m deep, contains a lake that has long been held holy by the monks of the nearby monastery. Pilgrims come here to drink the water, which is said to have great healing properties. Women are not allowed to get too close to the water (50m is considered a 'safe' distance!).

The **monastery of Mt Zuqualla Maryam** (admission Birr50) is traditionally thought to have been founded by Saint Gebre Manfus Kiddus (see the boxed text 'Know Your Ethiopian Saints' in the Northern Ethiopia chapter) in the 12th or 13th century. The site may actually date to the 4th century, when a hermit community may have been established here by Saint Mercurios.

Two churches are found in the monastery. The round basilica was built by the Emperor Menelik in 1880 (designed by the Italian architect Sebastiano Castagna). Higher up, the church of Kidane Meret was built during the reign of Haile Selassie. The monastery is entirely self-sufficient, with its own vegetable patches, weaving room, water cistern, bakery and so on. There is also a little graveyard, and hermit cells, still used today.

In March and October large festivities are held at the monastery, and pilgrims come from miles around. Try to have your visit coincide with the festivities; you can join the pilgrims on the toil up to the church and then on the circuit around the lake following the *tabot* (replica of the Ark of the Covenant, kept in the inner sanctuary of every Orthodox church); see the boxed text 'The Tabot & The Ark of the Covenant' in the Facts about Ethiopia chapter.

Because the trees populate a sacred place, they have been preserved, unlike the denuded landscape below the crater. In the beautiful hills behind the monastery, you can walk to a place known as **Wednesday and Friday Mountain** (after the days of fasting).

Here, there are two large rocks lying close to one another. Locals maintain that if you can't squeeze through them, you won't go to heaven, since you haven't done your fasting! In another place, it is believed that two rocks will clash together and crush you if you're an unrepentant sinner. If you want to risk taking these tests, it's around one hour's walk there and back which will take you through some lovely forest full of birds and colobus monkeys. Leopards (known by the priests as 'tigers') are sometimes seen here.

Places to Stay
You're welcome to spend the night at the monastery, but don't expect the Ritz. The 'guesthouse' more closely resembles a stable – albeit a rather snug one – spread with straw. You can also camp in the church compound. Any gifts such as sugar, salt, oil and especially coffee, are greatly appreciated by the monks (see also Church Etiquette under Responsible Tourism in the Ethiopia Facts for the Visitor chapter). Bring your own food.

Getting There & Away
The nearest village to Mt Zuqualla is Maryam Wember, which lies at the foot of the mountain, around 25km southwest of Debre Zeyit.

Usually one to two 4WD vehicles travel daily to Maryam Wember (Birr8, up to two hours) from Debre Zeyit (more on market day on Thursday). Supply vehicles also run there; you may be able to get a lift. From Maryam Wember, it's 12km walk (three hours up and 2½ hours down). Look out for the indigenous Abyssinian rose along the roadside.

Contract taxis are also available (a 4WD is essential) for Birr700 to Birr800 (up to 10 people). Ask at the bus station. After rain, the road can be impassable.

NAZRET
ናዝሬት
☎ 02 • pop 127,842 • elevation 1712m
With no great churches, ancient monasteries or sacred relics, Nazret's name, derived from Christ's birthplace in Israel, seems a bit of a misnomer. Large, commercial and bustling, the town is, however, an important agricultural centre.

Lying just 100km from the capital, Nazret is a popular weekend retreat for Addis Ababans, and is well-endowed with hotels and restaurants. **CPU Computer Centre** (☎ 11 19 52) opposite Frank Hotel in the Hawas building, has Internet access (Birr0.75 per minute).

Places to Stay & Eat
Africa Hotel (☎ 11 25 13; doubles with shared shower Birr8) lies around 200m north of the Total station on the road leading to the train station. It's gloomy and basic, but about the best bet of the rock-bottom budget places.

Canal Hotel (☎ 11 25 45; doubles with hot shower Birr25), opposite the bus station on the Addis road, is a good-value budget option.

Bekele Molla Hotel (☎ 11 23 12; doubles & twins with cold shower Birr30, with hot shower Birr40-80) has spotless rooms in peaceful and quiet grounds. Rooms for Birr80 have TV & fridge. It lies 400m east of the main square.

Palace Hotel (☎ *11 38 00; 3rd/2nd/1st-class doubles Birr60/80/105; prices increase by Birr5/15/25 at weekends*) lies opposite the bus station. Though a little characterless, there's a large garden. The 1st - and 2nd-class rooms have TV and balcony.

Adama Ras Hotel (☎ *11 21 88; twins Birr60-80*) on the western approach to town, is government-run and a little overpriced, but has a reasonably well-maintained outdoor pool in a garden (Birr3.45/7 per day for guests/nonguests).

Pan-Afric Hotel (☎ *12 68 88, fax 11 37 77; doubles Birr65-75, twins Birr95*) is a new hotel and has good rooms with TV in the same area.

Adama Makonnen Hotel (☎ *11 08 88, fax 11 41 79; doubles Birr92-103.50, twins Birr138*) is the best in the middle–upper range. The rooms are comfortable, well maintained and well furnished, with balconies, TV and telephone. Service is good too, as is the restaurant. It's not far from the Pan-Afric Hotel.

Rift Valley Hotel (☎ *11 44 44; fax 11 44 09; doubles weekdays/weekends Birr86.25/117.75*) is another comfortable, newish place at the western end of town, with TV and television in the rooms. Its restaurant has a good variety of *faranji* (Western) dishes, though it's a little pricey (Birr14 to Birr17 plus tax).

Safari Lodge Adama (☎ *12 20 12;* e *leila worku@hotmail.com; suites Mon-Fri/Sat-Sun Birr250/281.25*) is a new, rather exclusive set-up lying 100m off the main Addis Ababa road, just past the Pan-Afric Hotel if heading for Addis. Rooms are comfortable and set in well-designed gardens. Facilities include a swimming pool (Birr45 for nonguests), tennis court and (in future) a Jacuzzi. Its restaurants serve good international dishes, though it's not cheap (mains Birr18 to Birr37 plus 25% tax).

Frank Hotel, not far from the main square, is the local favourite with an extensive but good-value menu. Join the locals for a drink on the street-side terrace, if you can find a table. **Genet Kitfo Beat** is a popular local joint serving excellent *kitfo* (raw or lightly cooked minced meat).

Sunrise Bakery, 20m up from the Total station, is considered the best cake shop in town. **River Café** has quite pleasant outdoor seating beside the 'river' (a smelly, city outlet). Snacks include 'humberegers' if you're pining after a bit of Western stodge.

Getting There & Around

At least 20 buses leave daily for Addis Ababa (Birr8, 2½ hours), and at least 10 to Sodore (Birr3.25, 30 minutes) and to Asela '(Birr6 two to three hours). One bus leaves daily for Awash (Birr9.25, 2½ hours). For Debre Zeyit (Birr6), it's best to go to Mojo, for where buses leave every 15 minutes (Birr3, 15 minutes,) first and change.

When heading south for Bale Mountains NP, go to Asela first and change (Birr5, two hours). For Ziway and the Rift Valley lakes, go to Mojo (Birr2, 15 minutes) and change.

Trains to or from Addis Ababa cost Birr18/13/10 for 1st/2nd/3rd class; to or from Debre Zeyit cost Birr8.85/7/5; to or from Awash cost Birr22.25/17/12; and to or from Dire Dawa cost Birr68/45/34.

Garis are good for getting around. From the bus station to your hotel costs Birr1. Bikes (Birr3 per hour) can be hired from beside the *chat* sellers, 50m up from the bus station.

AROUND NAZRET
Sodore
ሶደሬ

The hot-springs resort of Sodore (*admission weekdays/weekends Birr7/10*) also attracts Addis Ababan weekenders – up to 5000 of them per day, according to the manager! During the week, it's much quieter. It's not a patch on its hot-spring cousin, Wondo Genet. Unless you're filling time or are desperate for a dip in the Olympic-sized **thermal pool** (*open Fri-Sun only; lockers Birr2.35*), it's not worth a special excursion. Note that a 'food fee' of Birr25.75 to Birr78.80 is charged for bringing in food; there's a checkpoint.

The riverine forest that lines the Awash River in the resort grounds is home to a variety of birdlife and monkeys. In the river itself, crocodiles and (rarely now) hippos can be found. Beware of the crocodiles – they have taken children from the banks. There's good hiking in the hills behind the resort. Ask the hotel to find you a local guide (Birr50 for the whole day).

Sodore Wabe Shebele Resort Hotel (☎ *11 34 00, fax 12 03 84; camping per person Birr50, rooms with bathroom Birr144-228, huts with shower Birr144, bungalow with bathroom Birr278*) is the only accommodation inside the resort. All bathrooms are fed with natural, hot, spring water. There is only one bungalow available. Tents can be hired for Birr109 per tent (two person) including the camping fee. Watch your possessions – theft is a problem.

Getting There & Away At least 10 minibuses and buses run back and forth from Nazret (Birr3.25, 30 minutes) to the resort gates. A contract taxi from Nazret costs Birr50 one way.

AWASH NATIONAL PARK
አዋሽ ብሔራዊ ፓርክ

Awash National Park, easily accessible from Addis Ababa, is one of Ethiopia's most visited parks. Visitors who come expecting Kenya-style safaris will be disappointed. Nevertheless, for those with patience and some time, the park offers quite good wildlife viewing and outstanding birdlife viewing. It also contains an interesting range of volcanic landscapes.

The park takes its name from the Awash River, the longest river in Ethiopia The river marks the park's southern boundary, then veers north before disappearing into the remote and desolate confines of the Danakil region. The salt lake, Lake Abbe (Lac Abbé) on the Ethiopia–Djiboutian border, is the river's last gesture.

Wilfred Thesiger, the well-known British explorer, set off to trace the end of the Awash in the 1920s. His account of the Afar peoples (then known as the Danakils) encountered along the way has become something of an epic (see the boxed texts 'The Dreaded Danakils' here and 'Peoples of Ethiopia' in the Facts about Ethiopia chapter). It greatly fuelled the Afars' already legendary reputation for ferocity.

Orientation & Information

The park *(per person per 48h Birr50, per vehicle up to 5 seats Birr10; open 6am-6pm daily)* covers an area of 756 sq km and mostly lies at around 1000m above sea level. The exception is the dormant volcano of Fantale, which at 2007m dominates the centre of the park.

The park's vegetation is typical of the hot, arid lowlands. To see the greatest number of animals, come first thing in the morning or late in the afternoon. At midday, many animals retire to the shade of the trees. The main gate is around 14km after the town of Metehara, 16km before Awash, if you're coming from Addis Ababa. The park headquarters lie 10km southeast of the main gate.

In the same complex as the park headquarters is a small **museum** filled with the usual stuffed animals, plus some reasonably interesting 'interpretative materials' on the area's flora, fauna and people, and some useful animal locator maps. Nearby, there's

The Dreaded Danakils

The Danakil invariably castrated any man or boy whom they killed or wounded, removing both the penis and the scrotum. An obvious trophy, it afforded irrefutable proof that the victim was male, and obtaining it gave the additional satisfaction of dishonouring the corpse...

Wilfred Thesiger
From *The Life of My Choice*
(HarperCollins, 1992)

a viewpoint over the Awash Falls, which are a good spot for birds. In season, when there's enough water, you can have a dip in the falls. Fishing is not allowed in the park.

Dangers & Annoyances

Walking is 'discouraged' (not allowed) in the park. The official explanation is because of the carnivores that inhabit the area but, in reality, robbery from local tribespeople poses the greater risk. Even if you're with a vehicle, armed scouts (from Birr50 for the whole day) are recommended. They can also act as guides.

If you're planning to travel in the northern region of the park (including the Filwoha Hot Springs), they're compulsory. Tribal conflicts between the Kereyu, Afar and Itu pastoralist

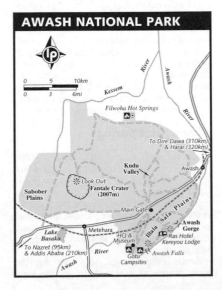

AWASH NATIONAL PARK

tribes are still common. In November 2001, 11 tribespeople died in a Kereyu–Afar conflict.

Be aware that many of the locals are sensitive about cameras, and may become very aggressive if you take photos without permission.

A park guard (Birr30/50 per day/night) is a good idea if you leave the campsite during the day, as well as providing extra security during the night. Leaving the vehicle to take photos or approach birds is permitted, but it is better to do so with a scout.

Malaria here is a major problem; make sure that you take adequate precautions. Don't drink the river water (even boiled). The sugar factory that lies upstream contaminates it. You'll need to bring all drinking water with you.

Watch out for both the baboons and the grivet monkeys, which have become adept camp pillagers.

Fantale Crater
ፋንታሴ

Towards the west of the park lies the Fantale Crater. There are impressive views down into the elliptical caldera, which measures an enormous 3.5km in diameter. The local Kereyu people can be seen grazing their animals and growing crops far below.

On the southern flank, look out for the dark lava, evidence of the last volcanic flow in 1820. Steam can be seen issuing from the vent of the crater. Animals found on its steep slopes include klipspringers and mountain reedbucks. Keep an eye out for lammergeyers soaring in the thermals above.

The crater rim lies around 25km from headquarters; it's a two-hour drive as the road – little more than a path – is very steep and rough in parts. With its terrific views, total quiet and cool air, it is a great place for a picnic. Hamadryas baboons are easily seen.

Filwoha Hot Springs
ፍል ውኃ

In the far north of the park, around 40km from the park headquarters, the Filwoha Hot Springs can be found. You can swim in the turquoise-blue pools. They're not as refreshing as they look: temperatures touch 36°C! In the cooler areas of the springs, as well as in the Awash River, crocodiles are found. Hippos are also found in the Awash River, though they are shy.

Around the springs, look out for the doum palms, much appreciated by the local

Afar people (who use them to make mats as well as a kind of wine). After 5pm, the area comes alive with birds. Lions can sometimes be heard at night. Waterbucks and hamadryas baboons are also seen here.

Wildlife

In the south of the park lies the grassy Illala Sala Plains, which attract most of the larger mammals. The beautiful beisa oryx are easily seen here (in particular between the park gate and Ras Hotel Kereyou Lodge), as are Soemmering's gazelles. Swayne's hartebeests were re-introduced to the park, but their numbers have since declined. Few remain. Salt's dik-diks prefer the acacia bushes.

In the bushland areas, particularly in the rocky valleys to the north, around the park headquarters and in the area known as 'Kudu Valley', greater and lesser kudus, defassa waterbucks (though few in numbers now) and warthogs are found. Anubis and hamadryas baboons are found in the east side of the park as well as around the Filwoha Hot Springs and Fantale.

The colobus monkey is found in the riverine forest. Leopards, lions, black-backed and golden jackals, caracals, servals and wildcats are also found in the park, but are seen pretty rarely. Striped and spotted hyenas are often heard at night. The nocturnal aardwolf also occurs.

For the past 13 years, the park has been at the centre of international research efforts on both the Anubis and hamadryas baboon.

Birds

The park lies on an important migratory route between the north and the south. Up to March 2003, 462 bird species had been recorded in the park, among them six endemics: the banded barbet, golden-backed woodpecker, white-winged cliff chat, white-tailed starling, thick-billed raven and wattled ibis.

Two especially good spots to observe birds are around Filwoha Hot Springs, and around the camping grounds near Awash River, where doves, barbets and hoopoes are all seen.

Near the river itself kingfishers and bee-eaters are found. On the plains, bustards are quite easily spotted, and sometimes secretary birds and ostriches. Among the many raptors are tawny and fish eagles, dark chanting goshawks and pygmy and lanner falcons. Another good spot is Lake Basaka, west of Metehara.

Places to Stay & Eat

At the time of writing, there was talk of establishing a private lodge near the source of the hot springs, as well as a take over of the Ras Hotel. Check on progress at the park headquarters.

Camping The best accommodation option inside the park is camping *(Birr20)*. The shady sites along the Awash River in the area known as 'Gotu', 400m south of the park headquarters, are attractive. Of the six spots, the *Gumarre* (Hippo) site is considered the most pleasant. At night you can often hear the noises of hippos, hyenas and jackals who come to the river to drink. Crocodiles are also seen here, sunbathing on the banks of the river. If you're lucky, you may hear the roar of a lion.

The area around the Filwoha Hot Springs in the northern extreme of the park, with its shady fig trees, is the other possibility. However, at the time of writing it was not recommended because of the security situation. Note also that camping outside these two areas is now forbidden for the same reason. Check the situation when you get there. Campfires are only permitted at these two sites.

Caravans Lying at the edge of the gorge, **Ras Hotel Kereyou Lodge** *(caravan doubles/twins Birr150/200)* is a rather decrepit caravan site. Lying 12km from the park gate, it offers 16 caravans with cold 'showers' (in fact buckets) that are also rather neglected. They will provide an extra bed for Birr20.

However, the restaurant has a terrace that boasts wonderful views over the gorge and the Arba River (a tributary of the Awash which marks the boundaries of West Harerge, Arsi and East Shoa). Look out for the crocs. After some early morning wildlife viewing, it's a fabulous place for a coffee or breakfast (full breakfast Birr11.50 plus tax). If you're determined to boil alive in the caravans, make reservations through the **Ras Hotel head office** *(☎ 51 60 70)* in Addis Ababa.

Getting There & Around

Walking is not allowed in the park (see Dangers & Annoyances earlier), nor are bikes or motorcycles. Most visitors hire vehicles or come with a tour, both from Addis Ababa.

A cheaper alternative if there's a group of you, is to hire a contract minibus in Awash (Birr350 to Birr400 per half day for up to 11 people) or in Metahara. Ask at the main bus stations.

A 4WD is necessary only for the Fantale Crater or during the rainy season (July–September); otherwise the roads aren't bad. The speed limit for vehicles inside the park is 40km/h.

If a taxi's beyond your budget, there's a economical solution: walk along the Awash–Metehara road. Many animals, including oryx and gazelles, can be seen on the plains from the road. You could even hop off a minibus near the main entrance gate and walk back to Awash (3½ hours). Remember to go early in the morning or late in the afternoon to maximise your chance of seeing wildlife. Bring water.

A Conflict of Interests

Awash National Park epitomises the clash of interests between the local people and conservationists in Ethiopia, and the difficulty of law enforcement. Though prohibited from grazing their animals inside the parameters of the park, the Kereyu are quite often spied there, particularly during times of drought. In 1993 the Kereyu even managed to establish villages close to Ras Hotel Kereyou Lodge; they were forcibly evicted by the authorities in 1994.

Cattle found within the parameters of some parts of the park are rounded up by the park authorities, and are only released on the payment of a fine of Birr10 per animal.

Outright conflicts with the park authorities still occur. In 1996 a warden was shot and wounded by a local herdsman, whose cattle he was trying to pen. The locals have lived on the land for centuries and see it as their own; during times of hardship, they have no other means of survival.

Additionally, the killing of a lion still bestows great prestige upon the hunter. Local superstition has it that the hunter will assume some of the lion's strength and majesty in a kind of ritual power transferral: from the king of the beasts to the king of the people.

The conflict will continue until the local people become actively involved in the park's conservation and benefit directly from its protection (see also Ecology & Environment in the Facts about Ethiopia chapter). A Care Project has recently been set up to help the local people (see **W** www.care.org).

AWASH
አዋሽ

☎ 02 • pop 5,886 • elevation 900m

The little town of Awash also takes its name from the river. After the park, however, it appears rather a dismal, scruffy place. Its *raison d'être* is more to do with the railway; the town represents a halfway stop between Addis Ababa and Dire Dawa.

On Monday there is a very colourful market that attracts both Kereyu and Afar people. Look out for the Kereyu women in skins and sandals and with braided hair. The men prefer a carefully shaped Afro, often ornamented with combs. Animal fat (like a kind of Ethiopian Brylcreem!) is used to give it a chic gloss and to keep it in condition.

Around 600m behind the station lies the Awash Gorge. There's good hiking potential here if you're filling in time. If you're in town when the old Djibouti–Addis Ababa train pulls in, it's worth a peek.

Places to Stay & Eat

Park Hotel (☎ 24 00 15; *doubles Birr10, with shower Birr30-40*) lies beside the telecom around 100m west of the Mobil station. It has clean, good-value rooms around a compound.

Genet Hotel (☎ 24 00 40; *twins & doubles Birr30, with shower Birr40-120*), on the eastern end of town, has a good restaurant and, if the Park is full, slightly overpriced beds.

Ogling the Afars

On the journey north, look out for the Afar men striding along in simple cotton *shirits* (sarongs), with their famous *jile* hanging at their side, the curved knife described by the writer Wilfred Thesiger (see the boxed text 'The Dreaded Danakils' earlier). Many also carry gourds which act as water bottles.

Many Afars still lead a nomadic existence, and when the herds are moved in search of new pasture, the huts in which the Afars live are simply packed onto the backs of camels and carted away. Look out for the wooden boughs used for the armature, which resemble great ribs curving upwards from the camels' backs. In the relatively fertile plains around the river, some Afars have turned to cultivation, growing tobacco, cotton, maize and dates. Inter-clan rivalry is still alive; conflict occasionally breaks out.

Buffet d'Aouache (☎ 24 00 08; *doubles Birr30, with shower Birr40-120*) lies south of town, beyond the railway station. Built in 1904, it's a great old relic of French railway days. Rooms are simple but spacious (some with giant baths on legs). The biggest draw is the restaurant on the veranda; the garden is brimful of birds. It's a great place to come for a drink or dinner (but not if you're in a hurry). Mains cost around Birr8 to Birr15 and Greek, Italian or French-style dishes can be ordered in advance.

A new 'ecotourism' camp, **Bilen Lodge** (*in Debre Zeyit* ☎ 01-55 22 69; *tukuls with full board per person US$60*), has been established recently at Bilen, around 9km from the park. *Tukuls* are traditional-style huts. Reservations are necessary. Camel treks through Afar territory can be organised, as well as bird- and wildlife-watching excursions. Contact Village Ethiopia (see Organised Tours in the Getting Around chapter).

Getting There & Away

One bus leaves daily for Gewane (Birr12, two hours), two buses weekly to Logia (Birr40, eight hours) via Mille (Birr35, seven hours), two buses leave daily for Nazret (Birr10.25, three hours).

For Dire Dawa, try to find a seat on one of the 10 buses that pass through Awash from Addis Ababa and Nazret. Trains to or from Addis Ababa cost Birr38/29/22 for 1st/2nd/3rd class, to or from Debre Zeyit cost Birr29.80/22/16; to or from Nazret cost Birr22.25/17/12; and to or from Dire Dawa cost Birr38/29/22.

AWASH TO ASAITA

The road north to Asaita takes you through the Yangudi-Rassa National Park via the town of Gewane. Don't expect much wildlife; there is probably less here than in any national park in Ethiopia. The journey is an interesting one, however, as it takes you through the heart of Afar country (see the boxed texts 'Peoples of Ethiopia' in the Facts about Ethiopia chapter and 'Ogling the Afars' following).

The rolled-up objects sold along the roadside are mattresses made from local rushes. They're a hit with the truck drivers on their way to and from Djibouti port, who in the heat of the region, prefer to sleep *en plein air* on top of their trucks. If you fancy one too, it'll cost you Birr10.

For the most part, the land is flat; the road just heads straight through it, like an American highway in the Midwest.

Yangudi-Rassa National Park
ያንጉዲ ራሳ ብሔራዊ ፓርክ

The 4730-sq-km Yangudi-Rassa National Park is a semidesert, and was originally founded for the protection of the extremely rare wild ass. Other mammals that you're more likely to see include Soemmering's gazelles, hamadryas baboons, and in theory, gerenuks and beisa oryx. Unfortunately, the park is so overrun with local herds, you will be lucky to see even one specimen of any species. It's certainly not worth a special visit.

There's no established entrance gate. The so-called park headquarters are found in Gewane. You can hire a scout-cum-guide for around Birr25 per day. Camping is the only accommodation option in the park.

If you want to stay overnight in the wind-swept, dusty little town of Gewane, 62km south, the **Agip Motel** (*doubles with/without shared shower Birr20/15*) has clean rooms and quite a good restaurant; try the delicious *dabbo fir fir*: torn-up bread with butter and *berbere* (spice mixture).

Malaria is a big problem in this area; make sure you take adequate precautions.

After Gewane, the country resembles Djibouti more and more: arid and desolate. Around 100km outside Mille, look out for the ostriches, bustards and Soemmering's gazelles, quite often seen here.

Getting There & Away The main Awash–Assab highway runs right through the park. One bus departs Gewane daily for Awash (Birr12, two to three hours), as do several trucks (Birr30). Buses run twice weekly to Logia (Birr15, three to four hours) via Mille (Birr12, three hours) but trucks run more frequently: to Mille (Birr20) and Logia (Birr25). For Galafi (the Djibouti border), you should be able to hitch a lift with one of the many trucks travelling that way (around Birr50); ask around at the Total station (and the café next door).

Mille
ሚሌ

Not much goes on in Mille; just sitting through the heat, with a bit of *chat*-chewing thrown in. Around Mille, look out for the little domed Afar huts, made from the interwoven leaves of the doum palm, which are light and easy to transport.

Park Hotel (*doubles/twins Birr8/12, with shower Birr20*) is clean and has a decent restaurant.

Hadar – Lucy Woz 'Ere

Around 80km northeast of Mille, a track leads to the famous archaeological site of Hadar. It was here that the hominid Lucy was discovered (see the boxed text 'Lucy in the Sky' under History in the Facts about Ethiopia chapter). The site is still being excavated, and the finds continue. Most discoveries are whisked straight off to Addis Ababa for examination, and there is little to be seen on the site itself. If you still want to visit, you should first get a permission paper from the Asaita tourist office. In the future, a museum will be build in the vicinity.

Around five buses run daily to Dessie (Birr15, four hours). For Asaita (Birr15, four hours), about two buses run daily. Two buses run weekly to Gewane (Birr12, three hours). For Galafi (around Birr50) in Djibouti, it's quite easy to hitch a lift with one of the legions of trucks. Currently a new gravel road is under construction from Mille to Djibouti.

If you're heading back to Addis Ababa, it's worth coinciding, if you can, with the colourful market at Bati (see under Around Kombolcha in the Northern Ethiopia section). Around five buses run daily to Bati (Birr10, three hours).

ASAITA
አሳይታ

☎ 03 • pop 14,392 • elevation 300m

Around 70km east of Logia is the town of Asaita, at the heart of Afar territory. It currently serves as the region's capital, but will soon be eclipsed by Semere, the development of which is scheduled to be finished by the end of 2003. Semere will also be the site of a new museum, displaying traditional Afar material culture.

Torrid, poor and dingy, and supporting a suffocating climate for nine months of the year, the town of Asaita is little visited. Around Asaita, the landscape is so bleak in parts it resembles a desolate building site. Asaita does, however, make a useful base from which to explore the 30 salt lakes in the area, the volcanic springs, Hadar and the Danakil Depression.

A **tourist office** (☎ 55 05 86; *open 8am-noon & 3pm-6pm Mon-Thur, 7am-noon & 3pm-6pm Fri*) lies just off the western side of the main square. Note that to visit the surrounding attractions (including the lakes and Hadar), you'll need to get a permission paper (Birr100 per person, valid for the whole Afar region for the length of your stay) as well as hiring a compulsory guide (Birr100 per day).

For some places, you'll also have to hire an armed policeman (Birr100 per day). Disputes over land ownership in the region sometimes result in violence between the different clans.

During the hot season (May to July in Afar), senior citizens and anyone with heart problems are discouraged (and sometimes refused permission) from extended excursions outside the town. The heat should not be underestimated.

Asaita's **Commercial Bank** (☎ 55 00 11) has foreign exchange facilities for cash only. Market day at Asaita is Tuesday; a must if you're in town. Fuel is available in the town.

Places to Stay & Eat The best hotel and restaurant in town is **Basha Hotel** (☎ 55 01 19; *doubles with shared shower Birr15*). Rooms are basic but clean. Some travellers prefer to sleep on the cooler roof terrace (Birr15), where mosquito nets are supplied. At night, you can hear the hyenas and the nomads' camels in the camps of the Afar nomads below.

Lem Hotel (☎ 55 00 50; *doubles with/ without shared shower Birr16/6*) makes a good second choice if the Basha is full, with rooms at a similar price.

Kulubi Gabriel

Every year in December, tens of thousands of pilgrims converge on the little town of Kulubi and its cathedral, Saint Gabriel, perched on a hill above town. Traditionally, the truly pious walk the whole length of the 64km-long journey from Dire Dawa. The church is one of the most significant in Orthodox Ethiopia. Pilgrims come to express thanks after the fulfilment of a wish, or in the hope of a miraculous cure. If you're in the area during the festival, it's well worth a stop.

Ras Makonnen founded a little church in thanks for the great victory over the Italians at Adwa (see the boxed text 'The Battle of Adwa' in the Northern Ethiopia chapter). In 1962 the Emperor Haile Selassie erected the huge and slightly hideous cathedral.

The **Menafasha Hotel** (*doubles with shared shower Birr12*) is the best bet. Frequent minibuses and Peugeot contract taxis connect Kulubi with Dire Dawa (Birr10, 1½ to two hours) and Harar (Birr10, 1½ hours).

Getting There & Around For Djibouti, you'll have to take a bus back to Logia. From there, try to hitch a lift (front seats only) on the steady stream of trucks travelling from Addis Ababa to Galafi (Birr20, three to four hours). With your own vehicle, Dikhil (Djibouti) can be reached from Asaita in three to four hours.

Around five buses leave daily for Dessie (Birr22, seven to eight hours) via Mille (Birr15, 2½ hours). At least three to five minibuses leave each day for Logia (Birr12, two hours).

At the time of writing there were no 4WDs available for hire in Asaita, and no contract taxis.

Salt Lakes

The salt lakes around Asaita have a stark, desolate, almost surreal beauty, and birdlife is good – storks, flamingos, ibises, vultures and raptors can be seen here. The journey also takes you through very remote Afar country where the people are magnificent. However, it takes time to reach the lakes and sometimes access is limited because of security concerns. Check the situation when you get there.

The reeds that grow along the streams are used by the Afars to make their famous mats, which serve a triple purpose: artistic, social and practical (they are used, among other purposes, as mattresses, prayer mats and mortuary cloths).

Lakes in the region that can usually be visited include Lake Gamarri (around 30km from Asaita – known for its hundreds of flamingos); Lake Afambo and Lake Bario (both near the town of Afambo); and Lake Abbe. If you have the option, Lake Abbe approached from the Djibouti side is a far better choice, for accessibility as well as for natural beauty.

See Getting There & Around under Asaita earlier for transport to the area.

AWASH TO DIRE DAWA

Going east, the landscape seems to get drier and drier, the temperature hotter and hotter. It's not too long, though, before the road once again starts to snake upwards from the arid lowlands.

This is the heart of Oromo country. The men gathered under ancient trees are attending the village assembly. Around the Chercher Mountains, the first signs of *chat* cultivation appear – look for the little bushes with shiny, dark-green leaves planted in neat rows.

ETHIOPIA

A Nomad's Toothbrush

On the roadside, look out for little boys selling 'local Colgate' – the regional version of a toothbrush. It is cut from the evergreen shrub *Salvadora persica*.

With a bit of chewing, the very fibrous and spongy wood forms into long, strong 'bristles'. And contained in the wood are chloride, various antibacterial agents and vitamin C. In other words, the little twigs are a kind of toothbrush-toothpaste neatly packaged as one.

As the road begins to climb, you're taken through some very beautiful scenery with stunning views; the last 120km or so of road before the turn off to Dire Dawa (at Alemaya) is one of the prettiest in Ethiopia. The markets along this route, such as the Thursday market at Asbe Tefari, are among the most colourful in the country. Don't miss them. Saturday is market day for many villages in the region – if you can travel east on this day, do. Many women don their best finery: very colourful skirts, headbands, waistband and beads.

The fat, sleek cows from this area are also famous and fetch high prices in Addis Ababa.

Around 8km east of Asbe Tefari, a new road is being constructed to the southeast and Bale region (home of the Bale Mountain National Park).

DIRE DAWA
ድሬዳዋ
☎ 05 • pop 164,851 • elevation 1200m

The great Addis Ababa–Djibouti railway was intended to pass through Harar, but with ever-burgeoning costs, the project was falling into difficulties. Then a momentous decision was taken: to bypass the great Chercher Mountains and keep to the lowlands. Instead of passing through the old commercial town of Harar, the railway would pass through a new town, which Menelik chose to call New Harar. In 1902 Dire Dawa – as it was known locally – was born.

Dire Dawa is now the second most populous town in Ethiopia. Cement, textile and soft drink factories are scattered all around its periphery. Unlike almost all other Ethiopian towns, Dire Dawa boasts the unusual distinction of town planning: it features straight, tree-lined streets, neat squares and some interesting colonial architecture.

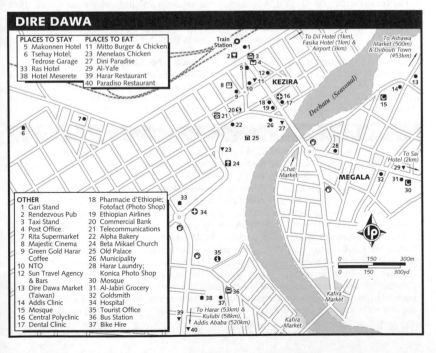

DIRE DAWA

PLACES TO STAY	PLACES TO EAT
5 Makonnen Hotel	11 Mitto Burger & Chicken
6 Tsehay Hotel; Tedrose Garage	23 Menelaos Chicken
33 Ras Hotel	27 Dini Paradise
38 Hotel Meserete	29 Al-Yafe
	39 Harar Restaurant
	40 Paradiso Restaurant

Train Station

To Dil Hotel (1km), Fasika Hotel (1km) & Airport (3km)

To Ashawa Market (500m) & Djibouti Town (453km)

KEZIRA

Dechatu (Seasonal)

MEGALA

To Sai Hotel (2km)

Chat Market

OTHER	
1 Gari Stand	18 Pharmacie d'Ethiopie; Fotofact (Photo Shop)
2 Rendezvous Pub	19 Ethiopian Airlines
3 Taxi Stand	20 Commercial Bank
4 Post Office	21 Telecommunications
7 Rita Supermarket	22 Alpha Bakery
8 Majestic Cinema	24 Beta Mikael Church
9 Green Gold Harar Coffee	25 Old Palace
10 NTO	26 Municipality
12 Sun Travel Agency & Bars	28 Harar Laundry; Konica Photo Shop
13 Dire Dawa Market (Taiwan)	30 Mosque
14 Addis Clinic	31 Al-Jabiri Grocery
15 Mosque	32 Goldsmith
16 Central Polyclinic	34 Hospital
17 Dental Clinic	35 Tourist Office
	36 Bus Station
	37 Bike Hire

To Harar (53km) & Kulubi (58km), Addis Ababa (520km)

Kafira Market

Kafira Market

0   150   300m
0   150   300yd

ETHIOPIA

Foreign influence is still much in evidence in Dire Dawa. Look for Arab, French and Italian styles in some of the architecture and design.

Apart from the markets, there's not much to see in Dire Dawa. After – or in anticipation of – Harar, Dire Dawa invariably disappoints and can seem hot, dusty and dull. However, a 'city tour' in a *gari* is a pleasant way to while away a morning or afternoon.

The mosquitoes may form part of your less pleasant recollections of Dire Dawa; remember to take adequate precautions against malaria. Unfortunately, begging has increased in the town in recent years.

Orientation & Information

The town is made up of two distinct settlements, divided by the Dechatu wadi (seasonal river). Lying to the north and west of the Dechatu is the 'new town' known as Kezira, planned and built in response to the railway.

On the southern and eastern side of the wadi is the 'old town' known as Megala, which, with its labyrinth-like streets and Arab-looking houses, has a distinctly Muslim feel. Here, Dire Dawa's enormous market, Kafira, is found (see Markets following).

The **tourist office** (☎ 11 37 63) is found inside the Trade, Transport, Industry & Tourism complex. The **Commercial Bank** (open 7.30am-11am & 3pm-4.30pm Mon-Fri, 7.30am-10.30am Sat) in Kezira changes money. There's Internet access (Birr0.50 per minute) at the **Dire Dawa Tele-Center** (☎ 12 04 34; open 8am-12.30pm & 3pm-7pm Mon-Sat) diagonally opposite Mitto Burger & Chicken, down from the Makonnen Hotel.

If you fancy taking home some Ethiopian coffee, **Green Gold Harar Coffee** in Kezira is the place to go. It sells 1kg packets of excellent quality coffee for Birr18. You can also have a tour of the roasting and grinding machines in the back.

Markets

Kafira Market (open 10am-1pm daily except Sun) in Megala has some interesting 'Moorish-style' architectural features; look out for the striking horseshoe arches that serve as entrances.

The market attracts people from miles around, including Afar herders, Somali pastoralists and Oromo farmers; sometimes, around dawn, large camel caravans march in from the Somali desert. A large variety of spices are sold here. The best time to go is around 10am.

There is also a thriving contraband market; merchandise is brought in from Djibouti either by night caravans across the remote frontiers, or carefully concealed in trucks.

Ashawa Market, on the outskirts of town, sells everything from beard trimmers to 'designer watches' and Johnson's Baby Powder.

The nearby **Dire Dawa Market** (also known as Taiwan), as its name suggests, specialises in cheap electronic goods. Both are worth a peek.

A two-hour tour of the old markets by *gari* costs Birr10.

Places to Stay

Hotel Meserete (☎ 11 33 05; doubles Birr15, with shower Birr20-25) in Kezira has small basic rooms around a courtyard, but they're not bad value.

A Dream Come True

In the 1890s, a man had a dream: to build a railway that would link Ethiopia with French Somaliland (present-day Djibouti) 800km to the east. Carved though some of the most inhospitable terrain in Ethiopia, the plan was to end forever the old isolation of the Ethiopian highlands.

Putting into practice the vision of Alfred Ilg (Emperor Menelik's Swiss technical adviser) proved easier said than done. Each kilometre of line demanded no less than 70 tonnes of rails, sleepers and telegraph poles, as well as massive quantities of cement, sand and water, and food and provisions for an army of workers. To keep the costs down, a narrow gauge of just one metre was used.

To cross the difficult terrain, several viaducts and 22 tunnels (one nearly 100m long) had to be built. In the meantime the local Afars, whose territory the 'iron monster' was penetrating, ran horrific raids on the line at every opportunity, stealing building materials and killing workers. It took no less than 20 years to complete.

Today the railway continues to play an extremely important role. Since the Eritrean–Ethiopian border dispute of the late 1990s, the railway has carried a significant part of the country's imports and exports to and from the Red Sea port of Djibouti Town. Just as Alfred Ilg had dreamt.

Makonnen Hotel (☎ *11 33 48; rooms with shared shower Birr20*), opposite the train station, is an Italian colonial hotel. With its central location and simple but spotless rooms (some with balconies overlooking the square), it's probably the best budget deal in town. The manager, Nigatu, is friendly and a good source of local knowledge.

Tsehay Hotel (☎ *11 00 23; doubles Birr24, with shower Birr30-40*), on the western side of Kezira, has adequate but clean rooms set in pleasant, hedged gardens. The restaurant is a local favourite and is good value (mains Birr5 to Birr10).

Fasika Hotel (☎ *11 12 60; doubles with shower Birr70*), off the airport road (follow the sign), is one of the best mid-range places. Rooms are simple, and set in quiet gardens.

Dil Hotel (☎ *11 41 81; doubles with TV Birr75-110*), lying 1.3km from the train station along the airport road, is a new place with comfortable and pleasant rooms. There's also a good bar and restaurant.

Ras Hotel (☎ *11 32 55; doubles Birr112.50-250*), in Kezira, has tired, overpriced rooms, but is worth a visit for its garden (full of birds) and outdoor pool (Birr6/8 for non-guests during weekdays/weekends).

Sai Hotel (☎ *11 22 85, fax 11 84 60; doubles/twins Birr140/168*), 2km east of the mosque on the Megala side of town, is comfortable, but officially couples should be married. Rooms have TV and fridge. Alcohol is not served in the hotel.

Places to Eat & Drink

Paradiso Restaurant with its half-Italian owner serves both Ethiopian and Italian food (Birr13 to Birr18 for mains), and is considered one of the best places in town. It has an attractive veranda.

Harar Restaurant (signposted in Amharic only) is diagonally opposite Paradiso Restaurant. It's a large, lively, local place. Traditional and Italian food is served inside and out.

Dini Paradise, set in a large garden, is a great place to escape the heat and dust of the town. It does good snacks (hamburgers Birr5 to Birr7, chips Birr3), cakes, fruit juices and milkshakes, if you're desperate for some Western nosh.

Menelaos Chicken in Kezira is the closest Dire Dawa gets to fast food. Its roast chickens (Birr22) are fairly finger-lickin'-good.

Mitto Burger & Chicken, in Kezira, is a new place which does a good selection of freshly baked cakes (and snacks). Try the speciality: black forest gateau.

Remote People

Stuck briefly in Dire Dawa in 1931, Evelyn Waugh wrote:

I am constitutionally a martyr to boredom, but never have I been so desperately and degradingly bored as I was during the next four days…Most of the time I thought about how awful the next day would be.

From *Remote People*
(Duckworth, London, 1931)

Al-Yafe in Megala is a simple place that does good fruit juices (Birr2). Opposite, the **Al-Jabiri Grocery** isn't bad for provisions.

For a drink, try the **Rendezvous** pub near the train station or the bars around the corner from the Sun Travel Agency.

The garden of the **Ras Hotel** (see Places to Stay earlier) is the most pleasant place for a drink in the evening. The bar inside attracts the town's big and little fish.

Getting There & Away

Trains head east from here for Djibouti town (see the Getting There & Away chapter). Trains to or from Addis Ababa cost Birr75/55/41 for 1st/2nd/3rd class, to or from Debre Zeyit cost 67/49/37, to or from Nazret cost Birr60/45/34 and to or from Awash cost Birr38/29/22. For information call the **station** (☎ *11 24 34*).

Four buses run daily to Addis Ababa (Birr71, 12 hours) via Awash (Birr61, nine hours), Nazret (Birr61, 10 hours) and Debre Zeyit (Birr71, 11 hours). Minibuses run every 15 minutes to Harar (Birr9, one hour); around five Peugeot contract taxis run daily to Kulubi (Birr15). There are no buses to Djibouti.

Ethiopian Airlines (☎ *11 30 69*) has one to three flights daily to Addis Ababa, and five weekly to Jijiga. **Sun Travel Agency** (☎ *11 40 59*) is an agent for Djibouti Airlines. Flights depart thrice weekly to Djibouti town and cost Birr505.40 one way, Birr965.40 return.

Getting Around

The **National Tourist Organisation** (*NTO; ☎ 11 11 19*) has an office in Kezira; cars can be rented for the usual rates (see under Car & Motorcycle in the Getting Around chapter). There's a travel agency in the Sai Hotel.

Garis, a great way of getting around town, cost from Birr1 to Birr3 depending on distance. A half/full day costs Birr20/40. A contract taxi to or from the airport should cost Birr5 shared and Birr30 contract. Bikes (Birr1 per hour) can be hired from outside the train station.

HARAR
ሐረር

☎ 05 • pop 76,378 • elevation 1856m

Harar, capital of the old Harerge province, lies off the southern edge of the Chercher Mountains at an altitude of 1856m. Situated just a few hundred kilometres east of the staunchly Christian highlands, Harar, like an exotic bird, might have been blown off course – either from across the waters of the Red Sea or from the northern deserts of Muslim North Africa.

For centuries, as a crossroads for every conceivable commerce, the town boomed, great dynasties of rich and powerful merchants grew up and the arts flourished. Harar became a kind of commercial meeting point of Africa, India and the Middle East. Right up until 1850, it was home to the most important market in the Horn.

Harar also spearheaded Islam's penetration into the Horn. It still holds very special significance for Ethiopia's Muslim population. Still something of an exotic bird in a country that prides itself above all on its ancient Christian heritage, this historic city is perhaps Ethiopia's most undervalued attraction.

History
In 1520 a local emir, Abu Bakr, decided to relocate his capital. The site he chose was Harar, not far from the old capital of Dakar. Five years later, however, the emir was overthrown and the new city was taken over by the legendary Ahmed Ibn Ibrahim al Ghazi, nicknamed

HARAR

PLACES TO STAY
1 Dessie Hotel
11 Ras Hotel
18 Tourist Hotel
20 Tewodros Hotel
31 Belayneh Hotel
38 Harar Hotel

PLACES TO EAT
3 Hirut Restaurant
9 Alpha Cafeteria & Restaurant; Speedy Laundry
19 Canal Cafeteria
22 Central Café
33 Mermaid Icecream; Goldsmiths
39 Cafeteria Ali Bal; Souvenir Boutique

OTHER
2 Ethiopian Red Cross Society
4 Selassie Church

5 Harari Supreme Court
6 Regional 4 Administration
7 Ras Makonnen Statue
8 Industry, Transport, Trade & Tourism Bureau (Tourist Office)
10 Old Officers' Training School & New Site of Alemaya University
12 Harar Pharmacy
13 Clinic
14 Telecommunications; Jegol Supermarket
15 Post Office
16 Harar Laundry
17 National Hotel
21 Commercial Bank
23 Konika Photo Express
24 Cottage Bar
25 City Council
26 Harari People National Regional State Administration

27 Cyber Computer Services (Grand Shopping Centre)
28 Bus Station
29 Hiwot Fana Hospital
30 Babille Mineral Water Factory
32 Asma'addin Bari Market (New Market)
34 Samsun Hotel & Bar
35 Pharmacy; Hayat Clinic
36 Regional Police Office
37 City Taxi Stand
40 Medhane Alem Cathedral
41 Emir Nur's Tomb
42 Hospital
43 Ay Abida Tomb
44 Jamia Mosque
45 St Mary's Catholic Church
46 Old Leper Colony
47 Mosque
48 Harar Clinic

49 Harari National Cultural Centre & Museum
50 Old Palace & Harari Regional Bureau of Sport & Culture
51 Ras Tafari's House
52 Rimbaud's House & Museum
53 Fatuma Safir Ahmed's House (Souvenir Shop)
54 Sitti Alawiyya Mosque
55 Said Ali Hamdogn Tomb
56 Gidir Magala (Main Market)
57 Aounsar Shrine; Site of Hyaena Feeding
58 Zeituna Yusuf Grille's Shop
59 Community Fountain
60 Sheikh Abadir's Tomb Tomb

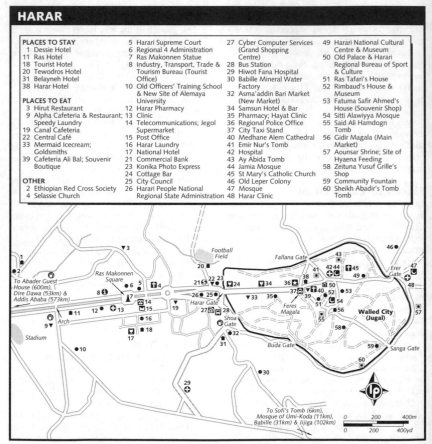

Mohammed Gragn the Left-Handed (see The Muslim–Christian Wars under History in the Facts about Ethiopia chapter).

Fourteen years of war against the Christian empire of the West followed, during which time the rich resources of the city were depleted. By the time the great leader himself had been killed, the town had fallen upon hard times. A new threat then arose: the migrations northwards of the Oromo. In response, Gragn's successor, Nur Ibn al-Wazir Mujahid, erected thick, 5m-high walls around the town, which stand to this day.

For the next three decades, Harar existed as a kind of independent city-state, sometimes ruled by a strict Muslim theocracy. Commerce continued to flourish, however, and the town even issued its own currency. Harar's merchants travelled as far afield as India, Arabia and Egypt, and both coffee and *chat* were cultivated.

In the 17th and 18th centuries, Harar become known as an important centre of Islamic scholarship. Handicrafts flourished, in particular bookbinding, weaving and basketry; the tradition continues to this day.

In 1875 Harar was again threatened, this time by the Egyptians, who dreamed of establishing an East African empire. Marching with 4000 men on a virtually defenceless city, they killed its ruler, Amir Mohammed, and occupied the town for a decade. Though he met with fierce resistance, the emir Abdullahi eventually took over, only to be defeated (in 1887) by the Emperor Menelik, who sought to expand his highland empire. Menelik, considered the great unifier by the Amharas, is to this day greatly resented by many Hararis.

For years, the city was closed to Christians. In 1854 Richard Burton, the famous British explorer, was the first non-Muslim to penetrate the city (see the boxed text 'Forbidden Footsteps' later). Later, the bustling commercial town attracted many foreign merchants from India, Armenia, England and France. The famous French poet, Arthur Rimbaud, spent some of his last years here (see the boxed text 'Arthur Rimbaud' later in this chapter).

Harar's economic fortunes, however, suffered a serious blow at the end of the 19th century when the Addis Ababa–Djibouti railway was diverted to Dire Dawa (see Dire Dawa earlier). To this day, the city retains a somewhat isolated, inward-looking feel. The Hararis have their own ethnic identity, their own language and their own culture. As Dire Dawa continues to flourish and grow, Harar

languishes somewhere in the past – for the traveller at least, this greatly contributes to the old city's charm.

With the new government and the new federal constitution of 1995, Harar won a new victory: a kind of independence, with legal recognition as a city-state among the nine regions (and two regional administrations) comprising the Federal Republic of Ethiopia. It is a major landmark in the city's history.

Orientation & Information

The **tourist office** (☎ 66 17 63; open 8am-12.30pm & 2pm-5.30pm Mon-Fri) lies on the main street. At the time of writing, a new travel agency **Trio-T** was planned. Ask at the tourist office for details and location.

The **Commercial Bank** (open 8am-11am & 2pm-4pm Mon-Fri, 8am-11am Sat) near Harar Gate, has foreign exchange facilities. Internet access is possible at the **Cyber Computer Service** (inside the Garad shopping centre, next to the Dashen Bank). Next door to Cafeteria Ali Bal, there's a boutique selling an excellent range of traditional and quite good quality arts and crafts including the famous Harari baskets.

Although you can see the major attractions in a day (and a night), two days is probably better. Harar's old town, with its 362 alleyways squeezed into just 1 sq km, is a fascinating place that begs exploration.

Dangers & Annoyances

Water shortages are a major problem in Harar and can affect the city for two or three days at a time. Try not to waste it. A new project to pipe water from Dire Dawa is underway, but it will take until 2008 to complete it. Power cuts are also a problem; city quarters are supplied by rota and do without one day a week.

Some travellers have written to complain of hassle from children in the walled city. Hiring a guide is the best deterrent. Others have reported pickpocketing in the market areas. Be vigilant.

Be wary of trekking in the area. Some places are still not officially mine free. Check with the local administration.

Guides For your first foray into Harar, it's quite a good idea to hire a guide and take a turn round the town's main attractions. Guides also know the location of less-visited corners and the best Harari houses and arts and crafts shops. If you're interested, they can take you to a traditional coffee-roasting room; Harar is, after all, famous for its coffee. Hiring a guide also deters other would-be guides.

Later, you can return to wander unaccompanied. Even if you get lost, Harar is so small you'll eventually come to a major street or wall that will lead you back to the main gate. There are plenty of small boys to show you the way too.

Currently eight official guides work in Harar (and many more unofficial ones). If you're in doubt ask to see ID. There's no official price, but the tourism office suggests a fee of Birr50 to Birr100 depending on the size of the group. Birr50/100 per half/full day is also fair. If you're happy with the service, it is polite – and kind – to tip something as well (see also the boxed text 'Guidelines for Guides' under Dangers & Annoyances in the Facts for the Visitor chapter). Two guides that can be particularly recommended are Abdul and Sebsebe (who speaks French).

Inside the Walls

The walled city of Harar covers an area of a little over 1 sq km. With over 87 **mosques** in the old town alone, Harar is said to house the largest concentration of any city in the world. **Shrines** devoted to local holy men or religious leaders are even more numerous: over 300 inside and outside the walls – no one has yet managed to count them. Many are very peaceful, beautiful and well-kept places open to both sexes and all religions.

Look out for the Adare women, known for their very colourful traditional costumes. These consist of dresses – usually black,

yellow, red or purple – worn over velvet trousers. Many also wear orange head scarves. Sometimes they carry huge bundles of cloth or baskets on their heads. You should be sensitive when trying to photograph these women.

It's well worth visiting a traditional Adare house (see Traditional Adare Houses later) but you'll probably need a guide to find one.

Walking Tour An exploration of the old walled town (known locally as Jugal), begins at the main gate. This is known as the **Harar Gate** or Duke's Gate after the first Duke of Harar, Ras Makonnen. There are seven gates in total; two were added by the Emperor Menelik in 1889 to the five original ones (which date from the 16th century).

Streets lead from each gate and converge in the centre at a little square, known as **Feres Magala** (Horse Market). It is here that you can find a guide (or a guide will find you). Radiating out from the square are a maze of little alleyways and passages.

On and around the central square are many of the old town's attractions. **Medhane Alem Cathedral** was originally an Egyptian mosque, but Haile Selassie 'converted it' in the 1940s.

On the northeast corner of the square is the seedy **Harar Hotel**. This was one of four places where the great French poet Rimbaud is said to have lived.

Further on, near the middle of the walled city, **Rimbaud's House** is (yet another) building in which the poet is said to have lived. Although he did live in the city, it is not thought to have been here. However, the building houses a new **museum** (admission Birr5; open 8am-12.30pm & 2pm-5.30pm Mon-Sat) dedicated to Rimbaud. One room in the museum contains a series of illustrated panels (mainly in French) about the poet's life, as well as housing a small collection of books, letters and writing about the poet. Another room holds changing exhibitions (often old photographs), and there's a small selection of traditional Adare arts and crafts. From the rooftop, there's a good view over Harar to the blue Chercher Mountains. A guide can give a free 30 minute tour.

Not far from the museum is **Ras Tafari's House**. The building has now been taken over by a local family including a holy man-cum-herbal healer. A sign declares that the sheikh can cure anything from STDs to diabetes, mental illness and cancer! Past patients – apparently testifying to his success – return to look after the holy man, cooking and cleaning for him for the rest of their lives.

Forbidden Footsteps

Richard Burton in 1854 became the first European to enter the forbidden Muslim stronghold of Harar. He wrote the following of the experience:

The spectacle, materially speaking, was a disappointment: nothing conspicuous appeared but two grey minarets of rude shape: many would have grudged exposing three lives to win so paltry a prize. But of all that have attempted, none ever succeeded in entering that pile of stones: the through-bred traveller…will understand my exultation.

Richard Burton
**From *First Footsteps in East Africa*
(Dover, New York, 1988)**

Arthur Rimbaud

In 1875 an unhappy young man made a decision. Discouraged both by the reception of his poetry in Paris and by increasing financial worries, Arthur Rimbaud, the great French poet, came to a bitter conclusion: to turn his back on poetry forever. He was just 21 years old.

In 1876 Rimbaud set out to see the world. In the winter of 1879, in the service of a coffee trader in Aden (Yemen), Rimbaud achieved a different kind of fame. He became the first white man to travel into the Ogaden region of southeastern Ethiopia. In October 1885, he decided to risk all his savings on a venture to run guns to King Menelik of Shoa (and may even have been involved in slave trafficking).

While in Ethiopia, Rimbaud lived like a local in a small house in Harar. His interest in the Ethiopian culture, languages and people made him popular with the locals, and his plain-speaking and integrity won the trust of the chiefs and the friendship of Menelik's nephew, the Governor of Harar.

His home became a popular destination for both Ethiopian and European visitors. In his letters to his mother written during this time, however, Rimbaud confesses to a longing for companionship, both intellectual and sentimental. This led him to plan a holiday home in order to look for a wife.

In 1891 Rimbaud developed a tumour on his right knee. Leaving Harar in early April, he endured the week's journey to the coast on a stretcher. Treatment at Aden was not a success, and Rimbaud continued on to France. Shortly after his arrival at Marseilles, his right leg was amputated, and he was diagnosed with cancer.

By the time of his return, Rimbaud's poetry was becoming increasingly known in France. But he was indifferent to his fame. He died later that year at the young age of 37.

Rimbaud's poetry has won a huge popular following for its daring imagery, verbal eccentricities and beautiful and evocative language. Few poets have been the object of more passionate study or have exercised greater influence on modern poetry.

The house was built by an Indian trader and many of its features, such as the Hindu figures on the door are Oriental. Haile Selassie spent his honeymoon here, hence the house bears his pre-coronation name.

The **Jamia Mosque** just south of the square is Harar's great mosque. It was built in the 16th century, though according to local tradition, a mosque has stood on the site since the 12th century, long before the foundation of Harar.

Just south of the square is the **Gidir Magala**, the main market (previously known as the Muslim market); it's definitely worth a stroll. On Mondays, Oromo and some Somali people come in from the surrounding areas (it's most busy from 2.30pm to 5.30pm).

The **Fallana Gate** was the one Richard Burton entered disguised as an Arab merchant (see the boxed text 'Forbidden Footsteps' earlier). *Chat* markets can be found around most of the city gates, except the Buda Gate, as well as to the south of Feres Magala.

Traditional Adare Houses Heading east towards Erer Gate (known locally as Argobari), the **museum** (*entrance Birr3; open 8am-noon & 2pm-5pm Mon-Fri*) of the Harari National Cultural Centre can be found. It is designed like a typical Adare house and contains examples of traditional arts and crafts.

In some of the Adare houses in the old town, the ever-enterprising Adares have set up **souvenir shops** displaying beautifully made baskets and silver and amber jewellery.

The house of **Fatuma Safir Ahmed**, just north of the main market is one example. Another is **Zeituna Yusuf Grille's shop**, just south of the market, which is as good as an antique shop. Amber necklaces cost around Birr560, baskets cost from Birr700 to Birr1500. Because these shops are family-run, they may not always be 'open'. The latter shop is currently closed, but should reopen soon. Ask your guide to take you to a shop, and remember to bring your sharpest bargaining skills! It's customary to tip the owner something after a tour around.

Shrines & Tombs Southwest of Gidir Magala is the **Tomb of Said Ali Hamdogn**, a former religious leader of the town. The tomb looks a little like a miniature mosque without the minaret. Local legend has it that below his tomb there lies a well that can sustain the whole city in times of siege.

Another tomb that can be visited is **Sheikh Abadir's Tomb** near the southeastern point of the old town. The sheikh was one of the most important preachers of Islam in the region and his tomb still attracts worshippers seeking solutions to daily struggles: financial concerns, illnesses, family crises and infertility. If their prayers are answered, many devotees return to make gifts to the shrine: usually rugs or expensive sandalwood. The tomb has become an important centre of pilgrimage, especially for those who cannot afford a trip to Mecca.

Emir Nur's Tomb, north of square, is devoted to the ruler who built the city's walls. It resembles a spiky beehive. The **Ay Abida Tomb** nearby is visited by those who are desirous of seeing their daughter or son soon married, as well as by those praying for health. Harari families often send big pitchers of milk or tea there, or gifts of food for pilgrims or the city's poor.

Outside the Walls

The **Asma'addin Bari Market** or New Market (also known as the Christian Market) lies outside the walls, near Shoa Gate. The market is at its peak of activity from 2.30pm to 5.30pm. Look out for the *etan* (incense) from Jijiga; it's sold for the famous coffee ceremonies (see the boxed text 'The Coffee Ceremony' under Drinks in the Facts for the Visitor chapter). The spice market is filled with bark, roots and twigs used in the preparation of traditional medicine.

In the centre of **Ras Makonnen Square** stands an Italianate equestrian statue of the *ras* (duke), cast in bronze by the well-known Amhara artist Afewerk Tekle (see the boxed text 'Afewerk Tekle' in the Addis Ababa chapter). The *ras* is said to look towards Somalia and the lands conquered there. Ras Makonnen was Emperor Menelik's cousin and was appointed first ruler of Harar after the emperor's occupation of the city. The *ras* was also the father of the Emperor Haile Selassie.

Also by Afewerk Tekle are the well-executed **stained glass windows** in the Harari Supreme Court. Unfortunately the court is closed to the general public; it is hoped that visits will be permitted soon. The windows depict different Ethiopian rulers of the past.

Hyena Feeding

Possibly Harar's greatest attraction and certainly its most famous one (shown recently on a CNN clip of 'world culture'), are the hyena men of Harar. As night falls (from around 7pm), the last remaining hyena men (just two) set themselves up just outside the city walls. Sometimes the hyena men risks feeding the animals from their own mouths – you can have a go at this, too, if you like!

Though the tradition of feeding spotted hyenas like this has existed for no more that 35 years, the ritual is less of a tourist show than some travellers imagine. The Hararis have long had a strange relationship with the hyena, and some rituals remarkably similar to this one have existed for at least 700 to 800 years (see the boxed text 'Hyena Porridge' later).

It's a memorable spectacle. The hyena men know the animals as individuals and

---

Adare Houses

The traditional Adare house, the *gegar*, is a rectangular, two-storey structure with a flat roof. The house is carefully constructed to remain cool whatever the outside temperature: clay reinforced with wooden beams is whitewashed. Sometimes bright green, blue or ochre murals adorn the facades. A small courtyard conceals the interior of the house from curious passers-by.

The upstairs room used to serve as a storeroom; today it acts as a bedroom. The main living room consists of five raised platforms of different levels, which are covered in well-made rugs, cushions and stools. Guests and members of the household sit on the platform befitting their status.

The walls are usually painted bright red or ochre – said to symbolise the blood that every Harari was prepared to shed during the resistance against Menelik. Hung on the walls are woven cloths or carpets. Eleven niches are carved into the wall. In these, cups, pots and plates made by the Adare women themselves are proudly displayed.

From the grills above the main entrance door, carpets can be hung to advertise that a girl of marriageable age resides within the household.

After marriage, newlyweds retire to a tiny, windowless, cell-like room that lies to the side of the living quarters. They remain there for one whole week, during which time they are passed food and water through a hatch by relatives.

call them by the names they have given them, such as *Krincaiyo* (Grinder), *Cha'ala* (Big Girl), *Defkinater* (Not Fussy) or *Gelaa* (Crooked – after his crooked leg).

If you want to see the feeding, just let your guide know. One feeding takes place near Sanga Gate in the east of the old town. Be sure to establish the fee in advance; the tourism office advises paying a minimum of Birr50 per 'show', but if there are a few of you (say four) Birr25 per person is sufficient. Usually you can expect to see between 15 and 20 hyenas. Be there from around 7pm to 8pm to be sure of seeing the spectacle (though it can go on to 9pm). If you just turn up, you'll still be expected to contribute something.

Some guides recommending hiring a taxi to provide a kind of floodlight for the show (and to assist taking photos). Taxis now propose a 'hyena feeding programme' (Birr50), which includes transfers to and from your hotel.

Places to Stay

Unfortunately, the places on the square in the old town are rough, ready and rowdy.

Harar Hotel (☎ 66 00 25; *doubles with shared shower Birr10-15)* is the best one on the square if you're desperate to stay here. But it's far from spotless. Rooms vary; check several.

Tewodros Hotel (☎ 66 02 17; *doubles Birr15-25, with cold shower Birr35)* lies near Harar Gate. The Birr15 rooms are very basic, but four rooms for Birr25 have a special value. At night, from the balconies, you can watch hyenas stealing about in the shadows. In the early hours, when the town is quiet, the animals try and sneak into the city to scavenge. The city's dog population does its best to keep the intruders out. It's your very own hyena show and is fascinating to watch. Rooms 13 and 14 have the best views; 15 and 16 are second best (though check first, the hotel sometimes renumbers rooms!).

Dessie Hotel (☎ 66 07 68; *doubles with/ without cold shower Birr20/15)*, west of the new town, is peaceful, clean and simple if the Tewodros is full.

Tourist Hotel (☎ 66 08 24; *doubles with/ without cold shower Birr25/20)* in the new town has clean rooms around a courtyard, though it can be noisy.

Abader Guest House (☎ 66 07 21; *doubles with/without hot shower Birr60/50)*, offers quite good-value rooms, but lies outside the centre, 600m from the stadium.

Belayneh Hotel (☎ 66 20 30, fax 66 62 22; *doubles Birr120)*, a pleasant place near the bus station, is probably the best mid–upper range place. Rooms have TV and telephone.

Ras Hotel (☎ 66 02 27; *doubles Birr100, doubles/twins with shower Birr112.50/ 162.50)* with its long, bare, white corridors and dour, smocked staff, isn't unlike a psychiatric institution. Built by the Italians, it's fading a bit and the plumbing could do with an overhaul. Like other government hotels, it's overpriced, but it does have a pleasant terrace, which is a nice place for a drink.

Places to Eat & Drink

Hirut Restaurant is cosy and serves excellent food at reasonable prices (Birr5 to Birr20 for mains plus tax). Try the delicious *tibs shekla* (special tibs). *Faranji* food is also available.

Belayneh Hotel is also good. You can have lunch on the pleasant and cool roof terrace, which has a good view over the town.

Ras Hotel has a *faranji* menu which is more varied than most. Three-course fixed menus cost Birr31.25.

Canal Cafeteria near Harar Gate serves tasty cakes and fruit juices (Birr3) as well as milkshakes, yoghurt and spicy tea. Try the Harari speciality *hasher ka'ah* (a kind of tea made from coffee husks). It's a good place for breakfast (open from 6am daily).

Central Café, near Canal Cafeteria, has quite appetising cakes as well as delicious samosas and *fatira* (savoury pastries).

Cafeteria Ali Bal, inside the old town, is a local favourite.

Alpha Café & Restaurant in the new town is a good place for traditional snacks and simple mains.

Outside the Harar Hotel, you can find *fatiras* cooked to order on a griddle. They're cheap (Birr2.50 to Birr4.50 depending on size), filling and delicious. The *fatira* maker 'opens' from 6am to 10am and from 5pm to 8.30pm.

Mermaid Icecream sells vanilla ice cream (Birr4) from a machine.

Harar is well known for its beer. Among the brands to try are the light Harar beer, Hakim stout and Hakim, a kind of lager. Sofi is non-alcoholic, designed for Harar's Muslims. Bars around town include **Samsun Hotel & Bar** and the **Cottage Bar**, both inside the old town. **National Hotel** in the new town is a kind of nightclub. Bands play Thursday to Sunday from around 9.30pm to 2am or

3am. The music is a mixture of Ethiopian/ Middle Eastern pop, with some traditional tunes thrown in.

Getting There & Around

Minibuses leave every 15 minutes for Dire Dawa (Birr9, one hour). Around six to seven buses leave for Jijiga (Birr13, 2½ to three hours) via Babille (Birr7). Two buses leave daily for Addis Ababa (Birr53.65, 1½ days). Tickets for the capital should be bought from 10am the previous day.

Shared/contract taxis cost Birr1/4 for a short hop about town. The Belayneh Hotel can organise vehicle hire for excursions outside Harar (Birr650/800 for half/full day). Ask for the manager, Makonnen Tesfaye. Rental bikes (Birr3 per hour) can usually be found around the new town. Ask your guide. All transport leaves from the bus station near Harar Gate.

Driving in the area is not advised at night due to *shifta* (bandit) activity.

Hyena Porridge

Once upon a time, many years back, there was a terrible famine in the city of Harar. Both people and animals went hungry. One day the hyenas outside the town began to prey on the people. That night, a man 'pure of heart' had a dream. In it, he was instructed by God to make a pact with the hyenas and feed them a special porridge. The man did so, and from that day on both man and beast have remained in harmony.

To this day, the agreement is renewed annually by the people of Harar. On the seventh day of Muharram, during the religious festival of Al-Ashura, a special porridge is prepared with different cereals and served with abundant melted butter.

The hyena king (actually the dominant female), the leader of the pack, always comes forward to taste the porridge first. If the hyena eats more than half the bowl, the year will be plentiful and good. But if, on the other hand, the hyena only picks at the porridge or refuses it, the omens augur ill: pestilence may be on the horizon. If the king devours the whole bowl, famine may be around the corner.

With thanks to Ahmed Zekaria for this local legend

AROUND HARAR

A number of important mosques and shrines lie around Harar, including that of the holy man and teacher, Sofi, who lived nearly 1000 years ago. **Sofi's Tomb**, an important centre of pilgrimage, lies 7km from Harar. It's a simple and peaceful place.

Lying east of the Harar–Jijiga road, around 5km beyond Sofi's Tomb is the **Mosque of Umi-Koda** which is thought to date back a millennium. It was erected by Nur Hussein, but was largely rebuilt in the 15th century by the Turks. The building, which resembles a Turkish mosque has recently been restored. Women who are infertile come here to pray for children. Food is left for the local hyenas here.

See also the boxed text 'Valley of Marvels' later .

BABILLE
ባቢሌ

The little town of Babille is famous as the site of hot springs and is the source of the Babille bottled water distributed all over eastern Ethiopia.

Biruke Hotel *(doubles with shared shower Birr8)* on the main road around 100m west of the Mobil station, has adequate rooms and a decent restaurant. The **Anwar** restaurant serves good food.

Around five to six minibuses leave daily for Harar (Birr5, 45 minutes). For Jijiga (Birr12, 2½ hours) you can hop on a bus coming from Harar if there's space.

Babille Elephant Sanctuary
ባቢሌ የዝሆን ጣቢh

This sanctuary was established originally for the protection of the endemic race of elephant, *Loxodonta africana orleansi*. Spreading over 6982 sq km, the park is also officially home to kudus and lions.

Unfortunately, it has been taken over by local people and their livestock, and wildlife here suffers at the hands of poachers. It is unlikely that you will see any animals and a special visit is not worthwhile. There is no formal park headquarters or entrance gate.

JIJIGA
ጂጂጋ

☎ 05 • pop 58,360 • elevation 1696m

Lying 102km east of Harar is the town of Jijiga. It is an important administrative and commercial centre and has been colonised by various international aid organisations, but contains little of particular interest to the traveller.

However, if you're killing time, the large market is definitely worth exploration. You can sometimes find intricately woven mats as well as silver jewellery and yellow amber necklaces. Most of it is little more than heaps of contraband 'junk'. Look out for the pick-up trucks with mudguards trailing on the ground; they're contraband vehicles (often with souped-up engines too); the mudguards conveniently cover incriminating tracks in the sand. The camel and livestock market is also very interesting.

Adom Hotel (*☎ 75 30 77; doubles Birr15, with shower Birr25-40*) has clean rooms set round a courtyard. Its restaurant is considered one of the best in town. It lies 100m off the main road; take the first left after the Shell station if coming from Addis Ababa.

Getting There & Away
Around 10 buses leave daily for Harar (Birr13, 2½ to three hours). One leaves for Addis Ababa (Birr65, 1½ days); book tickets the day before (after 1pm). One bus leaves for Dire Dawa (Birr18, four hours)

Valley of Marvels

About 4km from Babille, the road passes through the Dakhata Valley, now better known as the Valley of Marvels. The Italians rechristened the place for the strange volcanic formations found here. Tall rocks have been sculpted into strange shapes by the elements. Some are topped by precariously balanced boulders, including one that's formed like an arch. The valley stretches for some 13km.

The birds in the area are particularly diverse and colourful. Look out also for the cylindrical beehives placed high in the acacia trees.

Only trucks travel to Hargeisa in Somalia (Birr50, one day); go to the market known as Kutra (100m to the south of the bus station), and ask around there. In theory, at least five should leave daily.

Ethiopian Airlines (*☎ 75 20 30*) flies five times a week to Addis Ababa via Dire Dawa, and to Gore three times a week. The airport lies 3km out of town.

Western Ethiopia

The Anuak people in western Ethiopia believe that if you keep walking, you will eventually fall off the end of the world. In western Ethiopia, if you keep walking, you fall into another world. Where the old provinces of Wolega end and Ilubador begins, the landscape changes abruptly. The highland plateau gives way to lowland plains; fields of golden *tef* (local cereal) to plantations of verdant banana and mango; Semitic people to dark Nilotic people, and a bracing climate to the torrid humidity of the tropics. Geographically, climatically and ethnically, the far west has much more to do with Sudan than with Ethiopia.

Of all of Ethiopia's regions, the west remains the least known and the least explored by travellers. Though lacking the historical attractions of the north and east, and the wildlife of the south, the region is still rich in both culture and natural beauty. Gentle hills, fertile valleys, montane forest and little streams make up most of the area; birdlife and wildlife abound, and fruit, crops and vegetables seem to grow from every corner. As you wind your way through the west, the region seems like an Ethiopian Arcadia.

The area, specifically the old province of Kafa, is also said to be the original home of coffee (consumed here as early as AD 1000). When visiting the province, it is easy to see why; quite a lot of coffee still grows wild. It was this plant that was responsible for opening up the once almost impenetrable region: some quite good roads now ford the great rivers and gorges, which for so long isolated the area from the rest of Ethiopia.

The west is quite well served by public transport, and a road connects all the major towns in a convenient loop which begins and ends in Addis Ababa. However, the torrential rain during the wet season can still quickly put paid to all that.

The best time to visit the region is between mid-November and mid-January, when the

Highlights

- Pack a picnic for the very beautiful crater lake of Mt Wenchi and travel by boat to its island monastery and hot springs
- Explore the colonial river port of Gambela, home to the Nilotic peoples, the Anuak and Nuer
- Set off in search of the elusive Ethiopian elephant in Gambela's rambling National Park
- Take a tour of one of the vast state-owned coffee plantations, and get a fascinating insight into Ethiopia's top export
- Look in at the interesting museums of Jimma and Nekemte, and learn about the ancient traditions of the Kafa and Wolega peoples

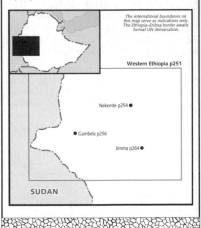

The international boundaries on this map serve as indications only. The Ethiopia–Eritrea border awaits formal UN demarcation.

Western Ethiopia p251

Nekemte p254 ●

● Gambela p256

Jimma p264 ●

SUDAN

weather is driest. A tour of the west comprising a loop to Gambela, Nekemte and Jimma takes at least a week; 10 days is better.

ADDIS ABABA TO NEKEMTE

Lying 18km west of Addis Ababa, the **Gefersa Reservoir** is fed by the Akaki River and supplies the capital with its water. It attracts a good number of birds including Egyptian geese and sometimes pelicans.

Coming into view not far after the reservoir is the domed profile of **Mt Menagesha**. According to local tradition, the mountain was the site of an ancient coronation place for many of Ethiopia's kings. To hike to it from the main road will take you about an hour one way.

At the base of **Mt Wuchacha**, 20km from the village of Menagesha (29km from Addis Ababa), is the beautiful **Menagesha Forest**. On the western slopes of the crater, you can get a good idea of how Ethiopia's ancient, indigenous forest must once have looked before the arrival of the eucalyptus and mass settlement. Some trees, among them giant juniper and *wanza* (Podocarpus) are over 400 years old.

The forest forms part of a state park that is protected. Colobus monkeys, the endemic Menelik's bushbuck, duikers and, higher up near the crater rim, klipspringer are all found here (though the last three animals are rarely seen). Unless you have time on your hands and camping equipment, the forest is best visited with a rented vehicle.

Addis Alem
አዲስ አለም

The unprepossessing agricultural town of Addis Alem is 55km west of Addis Ababa. It was here that the Emperor Menelik II once thought of establishing a new capital at the end of the 19th century, when Addis Ababa was as good as crippled by fuel shortages. Menelik went as far as to send engineers and builders to Addis Alem to start construction of this 'new world'.

Of the buildings that remain (clustered on a small hill to the south of the present-day village), **St Maryam Church** *(admission Birr20)* is the most interesting. It stands out for its lavish decoration: the exterior of the basilica church, as well as the *maqdas* (inner sanctuary), is entirely covered with murals (including Ethiopian rulers, saints, landscapes, plants and wild animals – look out for the grumpy-looking lions of Juddah). Apparently Menelik wished to create here a kind of new St Mary of Aksum. If you're not going north, and haven't yet seen examples of Ethiopian painting, the church is well worth a visit.

Unfortunately, a fire in 1989 destroyed the museum and many of the church's old treasures that it housed. A new museum is scheduled to open in 2004. Items on display will include a crown and clothing belonging to Menelik and Haile Selassie, and relics from the Battle of Adwa. The remains of the royal dining room and kitchen will also be opened.

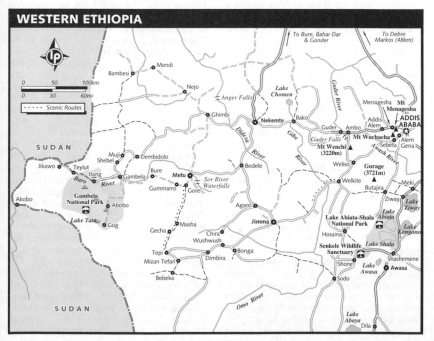

WESTERN ETHIOPIA

Outside the village, look out for the shepherd boys selling models including amazingly complex models of St Maryam Church made from the local river reeds. The bunches of green pods contain *shimbara* (chickpeas), a popular snack for Ethiopian motorists.

Just east of Addis Alem on the road to Addis Ababa, there's a new high-tech flower farm. The export of flowers is thought to have good economic potential for Ethiopia.

Getting There & Away At least 10 buses run daily to and from Addis Ababa (Birr5, 1½ to two hours). Three minibuses run daily to Ambo (Birr8, two to three hours). You can also try hopping on one of the Addis Ababa buses travelling west – as you can also do for Nekemte (Birr31, eight hours).

Ambo
አምቦ
☎ 01

Ambo's claim to fame is its thermal mineral water **pool** *(admission Birr5.70; open 8am-5pm Mon-Fri, 8am-6pm Sat-Sun)*. Lacking the facilities of Sodore in the east or the scenic beauty of Wondo Genet in the south, it's only worth a stop if you're desperate for a dip. Despite the murky green colour, the pool is cleaned weekly. Avoid the weekends when it gets very busy.

Ambo also makes a good base for a trip to Mt Wenchi, a beautiful and impressive crater that lies nearby (see later). A trip is well worthwhile.

In Ambo itself, look out for the fine Italian 1930s architecture of the post office, police headquarters and some of the hotels. If you come to Ambo on a Saturday, the market is worth a stroll; you can pick up the brightly coloured Ambo baskets here.

The famous Ambo **mineral water factory** lies 5km west of town but can't be visited without special permission.

Places to Stay & Eat Just west of the Commercial Bank, **Taddese Abebe Hotel** *(☎ 36 12 95; doubles Birr8-12, with bathroom Birr17)* is adequate and clean.

Jebatna Wecha Hotel *(☎ 36 22 53; doubles with bathroom Birr20)*, located diagonally opposite the Commercial Bank, is clean, good value and set in pleasant grounds. The restaurant, with seating on a shady veranda, is very popular locally. Try the *shekla tibs* (sautéed meat served on a hot

clay pot) and the delicious home-brewed *tej* (honey wine).

Ambo Ethiopia Hotel *(☎ 36 20 07; doubles Birr51.25, twins/doubles with shower Birr78.85/102.50)* is an old colonial place set around a leafy garden. It's peaceful but overpriced. The restaurant has a good selection of *faranji* food.

Abebech Metaferia Hotel *(☎ 36 23 65; doubles/twins with shower Birr50/60)* is a new hotel cascading with marble, which offers good value. It's set in pleasant, grassy grounds.

Getting There & Away Ten buses run daily to and from Addis Ababa (Birr10, three to 3½ hours). One bus runs to Nekemte (Birr16.40, six to seven hours). For Guder (Birr1.50, 15 minutes) minibuses run around every 20 to 30 minutes.

For Mt Wenchi, privately owned 4WDs can usually be hired (Birr400 for the return journey including driver). Ask around at the bus station.

Mt Wenchi
የወንጪ ተራራ

Mt Wenchi, 31km south of Ambo, rises 3220m (though measurements vary). At the bottom of the steep-sided and very beautiful crater there is a lake (20m to 68m deep) and in the middle there's an island with a church. There are also some mineral springs in the vicinity. A small village has grown up beside the lake, and its inhabitants cultivate the fields inside the crater. A good day trip from Addis Ababa might include a picnic lunch at the crater, followed by an afternoon swim in Ambo.

To get to Mt Wenchi you can hike from Ambo, or take one of the Landrover taxis from Ambo to Weliso and ask to be dropped at the turn-off to Mt Wenchi. From there, it's a 3km walk to the crater rim. It can be a problem finding space in a taxi on the return journey, so make sure you don't return too late in the day. Alternatively, you can bring camping equipment with you. By 2005 a new road leading directly to the lake should be open. A hotel will also eventually open on the crater site.

At the weekend, you can occasionally hitch a lift with a private vehicle coming from Ambo; ask at the Ambo Ethiopia Hotel. The top of the crater can usually be reached with a 4WD (around one hour from Ambo) though the last bit of road can be difficult after rain.

Guides (Tadessa Hailu has been recommended) can be found at the Abebech Metaferia Hotel and cost Birr100 per day.

Tadessa can also organise car hire or contract taxis from Ambo to Wenchi (Birr250 to Birr300 return all inclusive) and will suggest trips to surrounding attractions.

From the little village near the top of the crater rim, horses can be hired for the steep descent and ascent (Birr20 return per horse). You'll need to negotiate the price. The self-appointed guide who helps organise the horses (this may take up to an hour) and accompanies you will expect at least Birr5. Even if you prefer to walk down, you may be grateful for the horses on the way back up. It takes 30 minutes to descend and about one hour to ascend.

At the lakeside, you can hire a dugout canoe (Birr10 per person, one way) for the five-minute journey to the peaceful island church of Cherkos. At the **church**, ask to see the large 'Gonder bell', which once belonged, according to local tradition, to the Emperor Fasiladas and was brought here by Menelik.

A good time to visit the church is on Sunday before 10am when the main church service takes place. There's no official entrance fee. A fair price is Birr10 per person (though you may well be asked much more). On the way back from the church, you can ask the boatman to take you to the hot springs (Birr30 per person for the whole trip including to and from the church).

Water birds are found on the lake; raptors soar above the crater. On the paths up and down, look out for the monkeys and baboons. The lakeside makes a great spot for a picnic.

Around Ambo

There are a few natural attractions outside Ambo, including the Guder Falls, 1km beyond Guder (12km from Ambo) outside the town on the Nekemte road. More impressive, but less visited, are the **Huluka Falls**, 2km northwest from Ambo. You can walk to both or use local minibuses. Ask the Ambo guides (see earlier) for details and other suggestions for treks and trips in the area.

The Guder River is an important tributary of the Blue Nile. The ubiquitous Ethiopian red wine, Guder, was named after the river, and a few **vineyards** can still be seen covering the surrounding area. Vineyards soon give way to **coffee plantations**, however.

The old province of Wolega is known as the home of some of Ethiopia's gold reserves and precious frankincense. Both still fetch high prices in Middle Eastern and Egyptian markets.

Ethiopian Houses

Ethiopian houses are famously diverse; each ethnic group has developed its own design according to its own lifestyle and own resources.

In general, the round *tukul* (hut) forms the basis of most designs. Circular structures and conical thatched roofs better resist the wind and heavy rain. Windows and chimneys are usually absent. The smoke, which escapes through the thatch, fumigates the building, protecting it against insect infestations such as termites.

Sometimes the huts are shared: the right side for the family, the left for the animals. Livestock are not only protected from predators but in some regions they also provide a kind of central heating.

NEKEMTE
ነቀምት
☎ 07 • pop 47,258 • elevation 2101m

Some 187km beyond Guder is the large, sprawling commercial centre of Nekemte, which serves as an important coffee-forwarding centre. There's not much to detain the traveller, but markets (which bustle most on Wednesday, Thursday and Saturday) are worth a wander.

The town does boast a well put-together museum which is worth a visit if you're spending the night. Look out for the many star and sickle emblems around town, which are leftovers of the Marxist Derg. The old palace is not open to visitors. The **Commercial Bank** has foreign exchange facilities.

Museum

Muziiyema Wallagga (admission Birr5; open 9am-noon & 3pm-6pm Tues-Sun) was entirely financed by the people of Wolega, and gives a good insight into the Wolega Oromo life and culture. It contains a collection of traditional musical instruments as well as displays on local industries such as spinning, carving and basket weaving. Look out for the marvellous *berchuma* (high-backed chair) carved from a single piece of *wanza*. Also keep an eye out for the wooden coffin – according to traditional Oromo culture, men must prepare their own. Other exhibits include a reconstruction of an Oromo hut and a good collection of arms including a traditional hippo- and buffalo-hide shield. Guided tours are available.

Places to Stay & Eat

Nekemte's hotels cater to truckers and come complete with bar, bar girls and load music.

Wallaggaa Hotel (☎ *61 17 09; doubles with shared shower Birr10*) offers the best budget deal (despite its unpromising appearance). Its restaurant is considered the best place for local fare.

Wolega Ethiopia Hotel (☎ *61 10 88; twins with hot shower Birr62.50*) is government run and as usual rather overpriced, but offers *faranji* food.

Wugagen Hotel (☎ *61 15 08; doubles with cold shower Birr48, with hot shower Birr53-63*) offers better value and about the best range of *faranji* food.

Mana Keekii Kaliid, known locally as 'Ephrem', is a great place for a local breakfast. Try spicy, tomato-based *sils* or pureed chickpea *ful*. There's also a selection of cakes and fruit juices. **Central Pastry** is also good.

Getting There & Around

Around five buses leave daily for Addis Ababa (Birr30.15, eight to nine hours). One bus goes to Ambo (Birr18.80, 6½ hours); to Dembidolo (Birr38.45, 12 to 13 hours); to Jimma (Birr40, 10 hours) and to Bedele (Birr20; four to five hours). For Gambela, go to Dembidolo first.

Contract taxis can be hired and cost Birr10 to Birr15 for short hops about town.

DEMBIDOLO
ደንቢዶሎ

The little commercial town of Dembidolo is 215km west of Ghimbi. The town is known for two things in particular: its goldsmiths and its *tej* (honey wine). The former can be seen at work, the latter can be tasted in any of Dembidolo's numerous *tej beats* (wine bars).

Shell Hotel (*rooms Birr15, with hot shower Birr25*) is on the main road right next to its namesake the Shell station. Brand new, it still awaits its own name and will soon have a restaurant.

From Dembidolo, one bus leaves daily for Nekemte (Birr34, 11 hours). Trucks run to Gambela (Birr30, five hours) on Thursday and Sunday only.

After Muji, the road narrows and is uneven and slow. It descends quite steadily and temperatures start to rise. Birds are abundant in the area; look out for the widow birds. Fruit is also abundant: 30 *habesha muz* (Ethiopian bananas) will set you back just Birr1!

GAMBELA
ጋምቤላ

☎ 04 • pop 18,263 • elevation 526m

Muggy, swampy, sweaty, at an altitude of 526m, Gambela is unlike any other town in Ethiopia. So is its history. Situated on the banks of the Baro River, just a few kilometres upstream from Sudan, Gambela's strategic

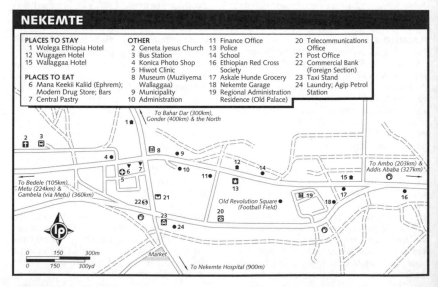

NEKEMTE

PLACES TO STAY
1 Wolega Ethiopia Hotel
12 Wugagen Hotel
15 Wallaggaa Hotel

PLACES TO EAT
6 Mana Keekii Kaliid (Ephrem);
    Modern Drug Store; Bars
7 Central Pastry

OTHER
2 Geneta Iyesus Church
3 Bus Station
4 Konica Photo Shop
5 Hiwot Clinic
8 Museum (Muziiyema
    Wallaggaa)
9 Municipality
10 Administration
11 Finance Office
13 Police
14 School
16 Ethiopian Red Cross
    Society
17 Askale Hunde Grocery
18 Nekemte Garage
19 Regional Administration
    Residence (Old Palace)
20 Telecommunications
    Office
21 Post Office
22 Commercial Bank
    (Foreign Section)
23 Taxi Stand
24 Laundry; Agip Petrol
    Station

To Bahar Dar (300km),
Gonder (400km) & the North

To Ambo (203km) &
Addis Ababa (327km)

To Bedele (105km),
Metu (224km) &
Gambela (via Metu) (360km)

Old Revolution Square ●
(Football Field)

0   150   300m
0   150   300yd

Market

To Nekemte Hospital (900km)

and commercial importance began to be noticed only at the end of the 19th century.

At this time, Menelik II dreamed of linking Ethiopia with Egypt to the north and Sudan to the west. A great inland shipping service was to be formed connecting the Baro with Sudan's capital Khartoum. To help develop the site, the emperor agreed to grant the British an enclave on the Baro River and in 1907, Gambela, the site eventually chosen, was formally inaugurated as a port and customs station.

Soon steamers were chugging up and down the wide river, laden with valuables ranging from coffee, salt and beeswax to skins, liquors and cotton. Commerce flourished and Gambela boomed.

The Italians briefly captured Gambela in 1936, during which time a fort was built which now lies in ruins. In 1941 the British won the river port back again and in 1951 it became part of Sudan. When Sudan gained its independence, the enclave reverted to Ethiopian ownership. In 1955 the old shipping service formally ceased to be.

Currently the Ethiopian government is considering plans to revive the river port and thus the region's economic fortunes. In the meantime, Gambela slowly sinks back into the mud.

The Baro is the only truly navigable river in Ethiopia. It was also along this watercourse that the raiding slave parties transported thousands of captured men.

Wildlife in the area, though not as prolific as it once was, is still quite good and birdlife is particularly interesting. Gambela serves as a base from which to visit the Gambela National Park.

Orientation & Information

Gambela is rather amorphous in shape and is littered rather untidily around the old, colonial grid imposed upon it. A large roundabout marks the colonial area; the heart of the town lies between the main road and the river.

The **Tourist Office** (☎ 51 10 29; open 7am-12.30pm & 3pm-5.30pm Mon-Fri) does its best, and can usually dig up a guide if you want one. It is threatening to shift location; if it does, head for the **Gambela Culture, Tourism & Information Bureau**.

The **Commercial Bank** (open 7.30am-10.30am & 3pm-5pm Mon-Fri, 7.30am-10.30am Sat) can change travellers cheques (in dollars only), but not cash. There is currently no Internet access in Gambela.

Shifty Shiftas

Some stretches of road around Gambela (such as between Shebel and Gambela) have, in the past, been targeted by shiftas (bandits).

It's pretty unlikely, but should you be unlucky enough to encounter gun-toting shiftas, here's a quick survival guide. Stop at once, stay very calm and hand over a respectable wad of money as calmly and quickly as possible (keeping an easily accessible stash somewhere nearby is a good idea). If you're driving, don't attempt to move until the shiftas have disappeared back into the bush. Accidents only happen when drivers panic and try to do a runner. If you have a driver, make sure he understands the plan of action too. Tourists are not targeted; if anything, they're avoided because of the repercussions.

Dangers & Annoyances

Malaria is a major problem in Gambela, killing an extraordinarily high percentage of the population. Adequate precautions are essential. Giardia is also common.

Currently Gambela suffers from water shortages, though a government water project is under construction.

Swimming is possible in the Baro River, but keep to the places frequented by the locals. The crocs are a problem. A local was taken not long before our last visit.

Photographers should show even more sensitivity and caution than normal (see Taking Photographs under Social Graces in the Facts for the Visitor chapter). It is strictly forbidden to take photos of, or from, the bridge. The Anuak and Nuer people are also notoriously camera-shy. Always ask permission before taking photos (even for people's houses and animals); if you don't, you may provoke real upset, anger and aggression, including stone throwing.

The Ethiopian Slave Trade

Ethiopia's slave trade was a lucrative one. From the 16th century right up to the 19th century, the country's main source of foreign revenue was from slaves. At the height of the trade, it is estimated that 25,000 Ethiopian slaves were sold every year for markets across the world.

ETHIOPIA

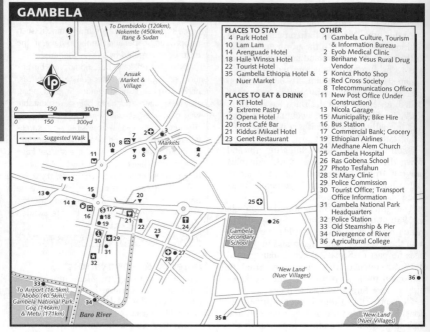

GAMBELA

To Dembidolo (120km),
Nekemte (450km),
Itang & Sudan

Anuak
Market &
Village

0   150   300m
0   150   300yd

····· Suggested Walk

Markets

Gambela
Secondary
School

'New Land'
(Nuer Villages)

To Airport (16.5km),
Abobo (40.5km),
Gambela National Park,
Gog (146km)
& Metu (171km)   Baro River

'New Land'
(Nuer Villages)

PLACES TO STAY
4 Park Hotel
10 Lam Lam
14 Arenguade Hotel
18 Haile Winssa Hotel
22 Tourist Hotel
35 Gambella Ethiopia Hotel &
    Nuer Market

PLACES TO EAT & DRINK
7 KT Hotel
9 Extreme Pastry
12 Opena Hotel
20 Frost Café Bar
21 Kiddus Mikael Hotel
23 Genet Restaurant

OTHER
1 Gambela Culture, Tourism
   & Information Bureau
2 Eyob Medical Clinic
3 Berihane Yesus Rural Drug
   Vendor
5 Konica Photo Shop
6 Red Cross Society
8 Telecommunications Office
11 New Post Office (Under
    Construction)
13 Nicola Garage
15 Municipality; Bike Hire
16 Bus Station
17 Commercial Bank; Grocery
19 Ethiopian Airlines
24 Medhane Alem Church
25 Gambela Hospital
26 Ras Gobena School
27 Photo Tesfahun
28 St Mary Clinic
29 Police Commission
30 Tourist Office; Transport
    Office Information
31 Gambela National Park
    Headquarters
32 Police Station
33 Old Steamship & Pier
34 Divergence of River
36 Agricultural College

Although they appear reticent and deeply suspicious, the locals soon reveal themselves as a warm, gentle and friendly people. Using *'daricho'*, the Anuak greeting, or *'male'*, *the* Nuer greeting, helps break the ice.

Things to See & Do
A pleasant **walk** around Gambela includes the riverside, the old steamship and pier (visible from the riverbank), the bridge and the markets. You may well come across an old colonial warehouse, bungalow or merchant villa too. See the map for one suggested walk.

At sunset, many locals gather at the **point where the river diverges**. People come to bathe, walk or catch up on gossip. It's a colourful scene. The **Nuer villages** on the outskirts of town, known as 'New Land', can also be visited; a Nuer guide is a good idea. A **Nuer market** can be found near the Gambella Ethiopia Hotel.

In the north of the town is the **Anuak market**. Vendors sit in the shade of the trees selling cereals, firewood, large Nile perch and tobacco. To pass the time, many indulge in *akowyo* (water pipe) smoking. You can taste the traditional 'beer', *borde*, served to thirsty market-goers from metal buckets.

Fishing is permitted all along the river. An Anuak recently landed a 150kg Nile perch!

Places to Stay
Decent hotels are not Gambela's forte. The mid-range old-timers, the Tourist Hotel and Openo, closed at the time of writing, should reopen in the future. Check out the situation.

Park Hotel (☎ 51 01 53; *doubles with shared shower Birr15*) has basic but clean rooms around a large courtyard. Though it can be rather noisy, it's currently the best budget bet.

Arenguade Hotel (☎ 51 04 26; *doubles with shared shower Birr15*) is a new place, though its walls are already looking grubby.

Haile Winssa (☎ 51 12 33; *doubles with shared shower Birr10-15*) will do if the others are full.

The **Lam Lam** (☎ 51 00 89; *rooms Birr13*) is centrally placed.

Gambella Ethiopia Hotel (☎ 51 00 44; *twins with shower & ventilator fans Birr102.48-150.63*) is the biggest hotel in town. Rooms are clean but fairly Spartan and rundown. Like the majority of government hotels in Ethiopia, it's faded and overpriced.

Places to Eat & Drink

KT Hotel is the new local favourite and offers reasonably-priced Ethiopian food (Birr5 to Birr 6).

Genet Restaurant, also popular locally, is unmarked (at the time of writing, it was painted bright green).

Park Hotel has a good restaurant and is known for its *kitfo* and *tere sega* (raw meat).

Gambella Ethiopia Hotel serves local and *faranji* food (such as steak and shish kebab) inside a pleasant and fan-cooled traditional *tukul* (Birr7 to Birr12 plus 15% tax).

Extreme Pastry, a new place, is the best cake shop in town, though the selection isn't enormous. It also does breakfast. Try the delicious *ful* (chickpea puree) and *sils* (spicy tomatoes).

Frost Café Bar, bizarrely-named and also new, has good fruit juices and a few cakes.

If you're looking for camping provisions, there's a grocery next door to the Commercial Bank.

For a drink, **Kiddus Mikael Hotel** *(open 6pm-midnight)*, opposite the old Tourist Hotel, has a pleasant terrace. **Haile Winssa Hotel** is popular locally.

Getting There & Around

From Gambela, one bus leaves daily for Addis Ababa (Birr78.80, two days) overnighting at Bedele (Birr31, 11 hours) via Gore (Birr20, six hours), Metu (Birr20 to Birr30, 6½ hours) and Welkite (Birr78.80).

For Nekemte, go first to Dembidolo. Trucks leave three times a week for Dembidolo (Birr30, 5½ hours). Isuzu trucks also run to Metu (Birr30). For Itang (Birr10, two hours), one bus departs daily, a truck every two days.

During the wet season (July to end of September), the road from Nekemte to Gambela is sometimes impassable; check conditions in advance. If it is, you can reach Gambela via Bedele to the south of Nekemte. By bus, the journey from Nekemte to Gambela takes around 2½ days.

Ethiopian Airlines *(☎ 51 00 99)* flies four times weekly to Addis Ababa via Jimma and Asosa. The airport lies 16.5km outside town. Note that there are no taxis in Gambela. To get to the airport, ask Ethiopian Airlines to arrange a lift for you with other passengers.

In the past, during the wet season, cargo boats occasionally ran the Baro River from Gambela all the way to Akobo on the Sudanese border (330km). Now only one small boat (the cargo/passenger boat *Baronesh*) –remains in operation. There are no scheduled or regular services currently, but in future there may be. If you're desperate to navigate the Baro, you may be able to charter the *Baronesh*. Enquire at the tourist office.

The Transport Office also has plans to offer a cargo and passenger service, which will be designed to run in conjunction with a food distribution aid project.

Bikes (Birr6 per hour) can be hired from in front of the Administration building. No 4WDs are available for hire. There are no taxis and no *garis*.

AROUND GAMBELA
Gambela National Park
ጋምቤላ ብሔራዊ ፓርክ

Less than 50 years ago, Gambela National Park, spreading over 5061 sq km, was one of the richest places for large mammals in the country. Elephants, lions, leopards, giraffes, buffaloes, topis, tiangs, roan antelopes, white-eared kob, hartebeests, Nile lechwe and waterbucks were all found here. The park was home to species not found elsewhere in Ethiopia. The Nile lechwe and white-eared kob are more typical of neighbouring Sudan.

Today, however, the ever-growing need for shelter, firewood, food and land for farming, as well as the influx of Sudanese refugees has dramatically reduced the wildlife's habitat and numbers by reducing the size of the park. A few years ago, the Alwero dam project (47km from Gambela) was constructed in

The Anuak

Fishing is the main means of survival for the Anuak people, though some grow crops such as sorghum. Most live in extended family groups, rather than villages, composed of a cluster of huts in a small compound.

Anuak huts are characterised by low doorways and thickly thatched roofs. The eaves, which stretch almost to the ground, keep out both the torrential rain and baking sun. The walls of the houses are often decorated with engraved designs including animals, magical symbols and geometrical patterns.

A common practice among many Nilotic peoples of Ethiopia and Sudan, including the Anuak, is extraction of the front six teeth of the lower jaw at around the age of 12. This is said to have served originally as a precaution against the effects of tetanus or 'lockjaw'.

the very middle of the park. At Fengudo, 90km from Gambela, a very large refugee centre has been built.

The lack of funds is a big obstacle to the park, too. Despite budget increases in 2001 and the recent national and international interest in the park, Gambela remains one of the most neglected and threatened parks in Ethiopia.

Geography With an altitude ranging from 500m to 768m, temperatures in the park are high. So is rainfall – 1500mm annually, mostly between April and October. Vegetation consists largely of woodland and grassland, with large areas of swamp in between.

Fauna Animals you might realistically hope to see are the common bushbuck, oribi, lesser kudu and around Jor (69km from Gambela), the white-eared kob. Poaching limits elephant numbers, but the best place to spot them is around the Mekoy river (around 56km south of Abobo on the road to Gog). Around the Nimert river is also good. To get to either area, you'll need a vehicle, scout and camping equipment and you'll have to trek the final 30km to 40km. The best place to spot lions is around Gog, particularly near Abobo, where villagers have complained of livestock being taken.

Birdlife is plentiful, both in the forest and around the swamps. Gog is particularly good for woodland birds, and Itang and Jor for water birds (including the pink-backed pelican). The whale-headed stork was last seen in 1996, around Gog.

The Nuer

The Nuer people, the largest ethnic group in Gambela, are largely cattle herders, though like the Anuak, they also fish. The people's affection for their cattle is legendary and much Nuer oral literature, including traditional songs and poetry, celebrates their beasts.

Unlike the Anuak, the people like to live together in large villages on the banks of the Baro River. Very tall and dark, the Nuer women are fond of ornamentation, including bright bead necklaces, heavy bangles of ivory or bone and, particularly, a spike of brass or ivory which pierces the lower lip and extends over the chin. Cicatrizing (considered sensual) is also widely practised; the skin is raised in patterns used to decorate the face, chest and stomach. Rows of dots are often traced on the forehead.

Park Fees & Regulations Next door to the Police Commission in Gambela, the **Gambela National Park Headquarters** (☎ 51 09 12; admission per 48h Birr35; open 7am-12.30pm & 3pm-5.30pm Mon-Fri) can be found. Guides cost Birr20 per day. Scouts (Birr50 per 48 hours) are obligatory for security reasons.

Places to Stay Camping (a fee will be introduced in the future) is permitted in the park, but a scout is compulsory. Skirmishes between the Anuak and Nuer still occur, particularly around the Itang area. Two weeks before we visited, five men were killed in ethnic skirmishes around Itang, though tourists have not been targeted. Steer clear of the border area with Sudan. Without camping equipment, you can stay in the village of Gog (see following).

Gog
ጎግ

A trip to Abobo, 40.5km from Gambela, and Gog, 96km south of Gambela, will take you through the middle of Gambela National Park. Gog was once the best place to see elephants, and some sightings have been made in recent years (see Fauna earlier). The best time to see them is from January to April, when they cross from the southern areas of the park to the east in search of food.

With your own vehicle, you can drive to the nearby Lake Tata, 9.3km northwest of Gog. The spot is outstanding for water birds, with 230 species recorded here or in the vicinity, including saddle-billed, open-billed and woolly-necked storks, white-backed and pink-backed pelican, as well as abundant raptors.

Before visiting Gog, you should visit the park headquarters in Gambela, where you'll be given a (compulsory) scout.

Neguse Hotel (doubles with shared shower Birr15) is the best bet if you want to stay the night at Gog. **Imabet** restaurant, around 100m from Neguse, is the best place to eat.

The road to Abobo and Gog has been improved; a few buses now make the trip to Gog (Birr15, three to 3½ hours). A truck also usually runs daily from Gambela to Gog (Birr20, three hours) and Abobo (Birr10, one hour).

Itang
ኢታ·ንግ

The area west of Gambela is very remote, populated by sparse groups of Anuak and Nuer people.

Though the area continues to see fighting between the Anuak and Nuer, the region is

Arts & Crafts

Ethiopia boasts a particularly rich tradition of arts and crafts. This is partly due to the wide range of raw materials available, from gold to good hardwood and fine highland wool. Additionally, the number and diversity of the country's ethnic groups (64 according to some reckonings), and the differing needs arising from the different environments, has ensured this.

Traditional arts and crafts include basketware (Harar is considered the centre), paintings (including the well known animal-skin paintings), musical instruments (see Music in the Facts about Ethiopia chapter), pottery, hornwork, leatherwork (Ethiopia is second in Africa for numbers of cattle) and woodcarving. The best woodwork traditionally comes from Jimma in western Ethiopia, where forests of tropical and temperate hardwoods once flourished. The Gurage and Sidamo also work wood.

Other crafts include metalwork (materials range from gold and silver to brass, copper and iron, and products include the famous and diverse Ethiopian crosses) as well as weaving. The Konso are known for woollen products; the Gurage and Dorze for their cotton products, which include the famous *kemis* (traditional women's dresses) and *shamma* (togas) of the highlander men. Special skills are particularly required for making the ornate and beautifully coloured *tibeb* (borders) of the women's *natala* (shawls). Debre Berhan is considered the capital of rug making.

---

considered relatively safe for tourists, though you should check the situation at the Gambela tourist office first. In the rainy season, the roads west can be impassable.

As with Gambela, life revolves around the river and markets. The remains of the old British wharves can still also be seen.

GAMBELA TO BEDELE

The road to Gore takes you across the Baro River via the longest single-spanned bridge in the country, built by Mengistu in the 1970s. The bridge affords great views over the town and the river, but don't forget that photography is strictly prohibited. A good variety of mammals (including colobus monkeys and lesser kudu) are often seen along the road; keep your eyes peeled.

The road then gradually winds its way a thousand metres up onto the escarpment. Around 10km before Gore, look out for the tea plantations lining the road. The (now privately owned) Gummarro plantation is the biggest in Ethiopia, with 800 hectares given over to the little plants. A kiosk at the side of road sells packets of tea for Birr1.40. Colobus monkeys are also seen here.

Gore

The old town of Gore, 146km east of Gambela, is set on the edge of an escarpment which rises 1500m above the lowlands.

The town rose to importance in the 19th century when it became the base of one of the Emperor Menelik's main commanders, Ras Tessema Nadew. In the town, the Ras' old palace can still be seen. Gore was also an important collecting point for the region's coffee.

If you get a chance, taste the local honey (for sale at the market), for which the little town is famous locally.

Tewodros Hotel *(doubles Birr10)* is a bit of a truckers' stopover, but is probably the best bet here. A common shower is being built. **Alif Cafeteria** serves food as well as fruit juices, cakes and snacks.

Six to eight minibuses run daily from Gore to Metu (Birr5, 30 to 40 min). For Gambela (Birr20, four hours), it can be difficult finding a seat on the bus coming from Addis Ababa; it's probably better to go to Metu first.

Metu

መቱ

☎ 07 • pop 19,298

Spreading over the slope of a small hill, 25km beyond Gore, is the town of Metu, the capital of the old Ilubador province. Metu has an interesting market where everything from coffee and berries to wild honey can be found.

Antena Hotel *(☎ 41 10 02; doubles Birr15, with cold/hot shower Birr25/40)*, around 100m from the bus station, is a new place. Though basic, it's clean and good value.

Luci Hotel *(☎ 41 17 75; doubles Birr15, with hot shower Birr30)* situated 1.4km from the bus station at the eastern end of town, is similar, but noisier, but it's a good place for a drink or meal. **Fili Yanus Andenet** ('Snack & Bakery' written in English) is good for fruit juices and breakfast.

ETHIOPIA

Getting There & Away One bus departs daily for Gambela (Birr19.60, six hours); three buses depart for Bedele (Birr11 to Birr 20, four hours), and for Addis Ababa (Birr57.65, 1½ to two days, overnight at Jimma); two buses leave for Jimma (Birr26, nine hours). Minibuses run regularly to Gore (Birr5, around 30 to 40 min).

To reach Mizan Tefari from Metu, there are no direct buses or trucks; you'll have to hop in stages via Masha (75km) and Tepi (45km) and on to Mizan Tefari (56km). If you start early enough, you can reach Mizan Tefari in a day.

Sor River Waterfalls
የሶር ወንዝ ፏፏቴ

A worthwhile excursion from Metu is to the Sor River Waterfalls, one of the most beautiful falls in Ethiopia. It lies close to the village of Bechu, 13km south of Metu. The one-hour walk to the falls takes you, for the last 15 minutes, through some dense forest that absolutely teems with birds and monkeys. In a small opening, the Sor River suddenly drops 100m, over the lip of a wide chasm.

Getting There & Away A Land Cruiser or Toyota station wagon leaves Metu every morning for Bechu (Birr10, 1½ to two hours from around 7am. Coming back, they depart around 2pm. You may have to walk back to Metu. For a guide, ask at the bus station or hotels of Metu. At Bechu, it's best to enlist the help of a villager (Birr10).

BEDELE
በደሌ

☎ 07 • pop 11,907 • elevation 2162m

Lying 115km east of Metu, Bedele isn't the most attractive town; additionally, *faranj* frenzy (unwanted attention from local children) registers pretty high here. The town is best known for its beer.

The **beer factory** (☎ 61 20 04; *admission free; open 8am-4pm Mon-Fri*) is the largest in Ethiopia and churns out around 36,000 little

A Scream so Strong it Would Shake the Earth

The practice of female genital mutilation, or female genital cutting as it is now officially known, is practised in 30 countries worldwide. In Africa and parts of Asia, it is believed that two million women are cut each year; in other words, 6000 women every day.

However, female genital mutilation is neither a modern phenomenon nor one restricted to Africa and Asia. According to modern sociology, the practice is just the 'natural continuation of the ancient patriarchal repression of female sexuality'. From the Romans (using genital rings on their slave girls) and the Crusaders (literally keeping their wives under lock and key in chastity belts) to the doctors in 19th-century Europe and America (counselling operations on the female genitalia to treat a variety of antisocial conditions including nymphomania, insanity, hysterics and depression), the West has seen many forms of this kind of repression.

In no other continent, however, has female genital mutilation taken such hold as on the continent of Africa. In theory there are three types of mutilation. 'Circumcision' (the name often given confusingly to all types of mutilation) involves the removal of the prepuce or hood of the clitoris. 'Excision' involves the removal of all or some of the clitoris and all or part of the inner genitals (labia minora). It is the commonest form of mutilation, accounting for 80% of cases. 'Infibulation' is the severest form of circumcision and requires the removal of the clitoris, the inner genitals and most or all of the outer genitals (labia majora). The two sides of the vulva are then stitched together with catgut, thread, reed or thorns. A tiny opening is preserved by the insertion of some small object such as a twig, allowing for the passing of urine. The girl's legs are then bound together from hip to ankle and she is kept immobile for a period of up to 40 days to allow the formation of scar tissue.

Operations are carried out with a variety of instruments including special knives, scissors, pieces of glass or, as they become more available, razor blades. Sometimes sharp stones have been used or, in Ethiopia, cauterisation (burning). The operation is normally the special responsibility of one woman in the tribal group, who may also be credited with special powers such as knowledge of the occult. Except for very rich families in the hospitals of big cities, no anaesthesia is ever employed.

The area known as the Horn of Africa, encompassing Ethiopia, Eritrea, Djibouti and Somalia, is home to a particularly rampant tradition of female circumcision. These customs are deeply entrenched and are inextricably tied up with the cultural, religious and social lives of the

brown bottles daily. The equipment and 'know-how' are Czech. The factory is 3km from the town centre on the Metu road, west of town.

Bedele lies at an important crossroads and so is furnished with a selection of hotels and restaurants; the best is probably the **Hoteela Ka'umsaa Fi Ga'umsaa** *(rooms Birr15, with hot shower Birr20)*, on the main road. It also has a good restaurant.

From Bedele, four buses go daily to Jimma (Birr15, 3½ hours), two buses to Nekemte (Birr20, four to five hours), two buses to Metu (Birr11 to Birr20, four hours) and one bus leaves at dawn for Addis Ababa (Birr75, via Welkite, arriving 10am the next morning).

SOUTH OF METU

A recommended alternative to the usual Gambela–Bedele–Jimma route is to make a short deviation via the town of Mizan Tefari. The route will take you through perhaps the wildest, most beautiful scenery in the whole of the west, characterised by densely forested

hills. After Gore, you'll see many colobus monkeys near the roadside.

Lying close to both Tepi and Mizan Tefari are vast state-owned **coffee plantations**. Visits are permitted and give a fascinating insight into Ethiopia's most important export (see Economy in the Facts about Ethiopia chapter). The forest plantations are also very beautiful, and provide good walking and bird-watching. Bebeka is the oldest and largest, but Tepi is much more accessible.

Visitors are welcome to turn up, but it's a good idea to arrange for a proper tour of either estate in advance. You can do this by contacting the **Coffee Plantation Development Enterprise Jimma** *(☎ 11 01 99, fax 11 59 18)* in Jimma first. The coffee harvest, from May to October, is a particularly good time to visit.

Tepi
ፒፒ

Tepi is famous for its coffee plantation. The second-largest in Ethiopia, it stretches over a

---

A Scream so Strong it would Shake the Earth

inhabitants who practise them. Reasons given for the practice include hygiene (where water for washing is scarce) and aesthetics (where the result is considered more pleasing to the touch and sight). Superstition also plays a part.; some believe that an uncircumcised woman cannot conceive; others that if she does, the unexcised clitoris is capable of killing the first born child just be coming in contact with it. The practice also contributes to maintaining social cohesion within groups. By conforming to a community's rules and regulations, members expect to reap the benefits of group protection and interaction. This sense of belonging and identification plays an extremely important part in the lives of most Africans (and is the issue probably least understood by non-Africans). Just as male circumcision is seen as crucial to Jewish tradition, so female circumcision is seen as crucial to some African traditions.

Another common defence for genital cutting is the claim that it prevents female promiscuity. Circumcision is seen as a means to protect against rape and a way to guarantee virginity – a prerequisite for marriage in all traditional African societies. Virginity reflects the moral prestige of the girl's family, ensures a good 'market value' for the bride and establishes the paternity of future children.

There is no doubt that female genital mutilation brings enormous physical and psychological pain and suffering. Postoperative complications include haemorrhage, damage to other organs or bones, and septicaemia. Doctors have estimated that 15% of girls die postoperatively of infections or bleeding. Those who survive often suffer ongoing complications such as infections or abscesses, or even, after infibulation, an inability to empty the bladder fully because of the narrowness of the opening left after the operation.

The next chapters in a girl's life, the marriage night and childbirth, bring repeat experiences of unbearable pain and sometimes life-threatening danger. Though little studied to date, the psychological damage of the operation is considered no less serious. Cases of severe depression, frigidity, anxiety and very low self-worth have often been reported. As one doctor put it: 'These women are holding back a scream so strong, it would shake the earth'.

If elimination of the practice is to be brought about, however, a grassroots campaign is required that seeks to understand as well as to confront the deeply ingrained traditions of the local people. Above all, it will depend on the will and the courage of African women.

huge 6205 hectares. The plantation headquarters can be found in the same complex as the Coffee Plantation Guesthouse (see Places to Stay & Eat following).

The plantation is state run and produces an average of 3000 tonnes of raw arabica coffee per year.

Because Ethiopia lies so near the equator, the coffee requires extra protection from the sunlight. The natural trees of the forest (*Gravilia robusta*, *Melia*, *Cordia africana Cuperessus* and rubber trees) give natural protection, providing the plants with 70% shade.

The very beautiful and shady forest is brimful of birds and makes a lovely walk or drive. However, because of the size, a vehicle is really required for a proper tour. To cover all the sites (the plantation itself, the crater lake, experimental spice and fruit plantations and the pulping and processing stations), you'll need about eight hours. A morning and afternoon tour is ideal.

Places to Stay & Eat Around the corner from the bus station, **Felege-Ghion Hotel** (☎ 56 00 15; *doubles with shared shower Birr7-10*) has basic rooms set around a large compound.

Coffee Plantation Guesthouse (☎ 56 00 62; *rooms with cold shower Birr30-40*) is 600m beyond the main roundabout at the edge of Tepi town on the Jimma road. It's good value and is set in pleasant gardens. Reservations are advised (see under Coffee Plantation Development Enterprise under Jimma later). It also has a good restaurant (*faranji* fare can be ordered in advance).

Ethiopian Hairstyles

Hairstyles in all societies form an important part of tribal identification. Reflecting the large number of ethnic groups, Ethiopian hairstyles are particularly diverse and colourful. Hair is cut, shaved, trimmed, plaited, braided, sculpted with clay, rubbed with mud, put in buns and tied in countless different fashions. In the Omo Valley, hairstyles are sometimes so elaborate and valued that special wooden head-rests are used as pillows to preserve them.

In rural areas, the heads of children are often shaved to discourage lice. Sometimes a single topknot or tail plait is left so that 'God should have a handle with which to lift them unto Heaven', should he decide to call them!

Getting There & Away From Tepi, around eight buses run daily to Masha (Birr15, three hours). For Metu, go to Masha first. For Mizan Tefari (Birr10, 1½ hours), buses and minibuses run daily.

Ethiopian Airlines flies once a week from Tepi to Mizan Tefari, Jimma and Addis.

Mizan Tefari
ሚዛን ተፈሪ

Mizan Tefari, the old capital of the Bench people, serves as a base for a visit to the nearby Bebeka coffee plantation. On Tuesday, there's quite a colourful market.

Aden Hotel (☎ 35 05 42; *doubles with/ without shower Birr40/26*) has basic but clean rooms, a 'park' and a restaurant.

Around three buses run daily to Tepi (Birr10, two hours); for Metu go to Tepi and Masha first. Two buses leave daily for Bonga (Birr20, five hours), and for Jimma (Birr25, seven to eight hours). Two buses go to Addis Ababa (Birr57, 1½ days) staying overnight in Jimma. On the Mizan Tefari–Wushwush road, look out for the mango sellers. Stop if you can; 30 cost just Birr5!

Around Mizan Tefari
Bebeka Coffee Plantation Covering 6537 hectares, 30km from Mizan Tefari is Ethiopia's largest and oldest coffee plantation. Almost 240km of roads wind around it and a tour of the plantations takes about six hours, which is well worth it.

Around 15,000 quintals of arabica coffee are produced annually; during the harvest, up to 7000 workers are employed. Beehives have also been established on the plantation and now produce up to 4500kg of forest honey a year. It's delicious and costs just Birr15 for a kilogram; pots can normally be provided. Bananas cost just Birr0.50 a kilogram.

Experimental spice and fruit plantations have also been established, as well as an organic coffee plantation and an interesting coffee arboretum, with around 40 different coffee species originating from all corners of the world including Brazil, Cuba and India.

Bebeka has a comfortable and very attractive **guesthouse** (*camping per 2-person tent Birr25, bungalows for 1/2 people Birr40/50, large bungalows with private shower Birr75*) set in the thick of the plantations. The lodge is also a fantastic place for birds, and you're free to explore the surrounding forests. Temperatures are muggy – Bebeka lies at an altitude of between 920m and 1394m.

Reservations are strongly advised (through the Coffee Plantation Development Enterprise in Jimma). Food can be ordered in advance at the 'canteen'.

No public transport runs to Bebeka. The only option is to try and hitch a lift (if there are seats) with the workers' minibuses. One minibus leaves daily from the main roundabout in Tepi between 10am and noon. Another one collects workers from the Jimma bus at Mizan Tefari bus station before departing for Bebeka around 2pm to 3pm. You'll be asked between Birr6 and Birr10 for the ride.

Wushwush
ዉ-ሽዉ-ሽ

A 1242 hectare tea plantation (open 8am-12.30pm & 2pm-5.30pm Mon-Fri, 8am-1pm Sat), lies 92km east of Mizan Tefari, 5km west of the village of Wushwush and 2.3km off the main Mizan Tefari–Jimma road. The privatised plantation makes an interesting excursion for those with time. Tours of the plantation and packaging factory are possible.

Wushwush Guest Lodge (rooms Birr10, with hot shower Birr20) is 200m off the main Mizan Tefari–Jimma road. Take the first right after the road to the plantation if heading for Jimma. It's a comfortable place and is set in pleasant grounds. You'll need to register with the **Administration Office** (☎ 11 29 79) in the factory complex itself first.

Around 1km from the lodge, there's a simple **restaurant and bar** used by the plantation workers, or you can use the lodge kitchen. Camping in the lodge grounds is also possible; there's currently no charge.

Bonga
ቦንጋ

☎ 07 • pop 10,851

In the past, Bonga formed part of the great kingdom of Kafa. In the surrounding area are a number of unexcavated historical sites, including what is thought to be an ancient burial site for kings, defensive ditches believed to date from the 14th century, some churches possibly 500 years old and various old battle sites.

There's also terrific potential for hiking in the surrounding hills. Caves, waterfalls, natural bridges, hot springs, natural forest, wildlife and birdlife are all found not far from town.

For more information on this almost totally unexplored but fascinating and beautiful area, you can visit the little Bonga **Tourist Office** (PO Box 6, Bonga, Kafa). Guides can be provided.

Biherawi Hotel (☎ 31 00 51; doubles with cold shared shower Birr15-20), 50m up the hill from the telecom (150m from the bus station), has basic but clean rooms. Its restaurant is considered the best in town.

Supak Guesthouse (☎ 31 01 95; camping per tent with hot shower Birr35, rooms for 1/2 people with shared shower Birr80/120) is a pleasant, comfortable place just 2km from the centre on the hill above town. You can also use the kitchen or employ a local cook. Guides and mules for excursions can be provided.

From Bonga, one bus leaves daily for Jimma (Birr15; four hours), and for Mizan Tefari (Birr20 to Birr25; five hours). One Land Cruiser goes to Wushwush (Birr5, 30 min).

JIMMA
ጂማ

☎ 07 • pop 88,867 • elevation 1678m

Jimma, the capital of the old province of Kafa, is the largest town in western Ethiopia. After a foray west, Jimma can seem like a place of great sophistication and gentility. Cake shops, topiary hedges, city planning and fat policemen are among the city's attributes, and there's no shortage of decent hotels and restaurants.

The region (now known as Jimma zone) lies to the west of the Great Rift Valley at an altitude of between 1300m and 2100m. With a temperate, frost-free climate that never exceeds 29°C, and an ample annual rainfall of 1600mm, the area provides the perfect conditions for growing not just coffee, but cereals and root crops too. The region is like an Ethiopian Promised Land.

Jimma also has a distinguished history. For centuries, a powerful Oromo monarchy ruled the region from their capital at Jiren (part of present-day Jimma). The region owed its wealth to its situation at the crux of several major trade routes. At its height, the kingdom stretched over 13,000 sq km. When Menelik came to power in the late 1800s, he required the region to pay high tribute.

As the capital of the most fertile region in the country, the Italians in the 1930s had great hopes for the town and planned the construction of a great new city. The town today boasts some good examples of 1930s Italian Fascist architecture. Take a peek at the cinema, post office, the old hotels and the municipality.

Jimma's markets are also worth a wander; Thursday is the main market day. Look out for the famous three-legged Jimma stools. Good-quality basketware can also be found. The Jimma honey is well known and costs from

Birr10 to Birr12 per kilo. You can find it in the warren of shacks opposite the grain market.

Ibrahim Adem (☎ 11 15 80) was closed at the time of writing, but should reopen. It's the best souvenir shop in town and specialises in Jimma woodwork. It was possible to watch the carvers at work in the workshop in the back of the shop. A kind of woodwork market also exists near Ethiopian Airlines where prices are cheaper.

Well provided with hotels, restaurants and other facilities, Jimma makes a good overnight stop en route to or from Gambela (423km to the west) or Addis Ababa (330km to the east).

In the vicinity of Jimma, there are various caves, hot springs and a hippo pool (at the Boye Dam, 5km from town) that can be visited. For more information, ask at the Tourist Office.

Information & Orientation

The **Tourist Office** (*open 8.30am-12.30pm & 1.30pm-5.30pm Mon-Fri*) is in the Department of Culture, Information and Tourism building.

If you want to visit or stay at one of the coffee plantations in the region (such as Tepi or Bebeka), it's a good idea to contact first the **Coffee Plantation Development Enterprise Jimma** (*☎ 11 01 99, fax 11 59 18, open 8am-noon & 1pm-4pm Mon-Fri, 8am-noon Sat*). If you fax in advance (with details of your name, nationality, passport number, purpose and date of the trip and the size of your group) staff can make reservations for you and assign an official guide.

Jimma's **Commercial Bank** (*open 8am-4pm Mon-Fri, 8am-noon Sat*) has foreign exchange facilities. Internet access can be had

JIMMA

PLACES TO STAY
1 Jimma Degitu Hotel
16 Jimma Gibe Hotel
28 Befikadu Hotel
40 Wolde Aregaw & Family's Hotel
41 Temky Pension
42 Pensionii Haamidayaan

PLACES TO EAT
5 Beimnet Pastry; Fruit Sellers
7 Hooteela Mollaa
9 Melat Pastry; Jiffar Engineering & Business Services (Internet Access)
17 Taq'a Hotel; Souvenir Shops

24 Mulu Supermarket
29 Oromiya Brothers' Pastry; Awash M. Clinic

OTHER
2 Cinema
3 Muuziyemii Jimmaa (Jimma Museum)
4 Photo Solar
6 Zenith Laundry
8 Ethiopian Red Cross Society
10 Ibrahim Adem (Souvenir Shop)
11 Telecommunications Office
12 Post Office
13 Ethiopian Insurance Corporation

14 Municipality
15 Coffee Plantation Development Enterprise Jimma
18 Department of Culture, Information & Tourism (Tourist Office)
19 Woodwork Market
20 Ethiopian Airlines
21 Central Clinic
22 Commercial Bank
23 Hooteela Jokaa Bar & Nightclub
25 Hiwot Rural Drug Vendor
26 Bars
27 Poolisii (Police Station)

30 Taxi Stand
31 Dashen Bank
32 Souvenir Sellers (Baskets etc)
33 Honey (Wax & Butter) Vendors
34 Mosque
35 Grain Market
36 Telecommunications (Branch)
37 Minibus & Gari Stand
38 Bike Hire
39 Bike Hire
43 Sharif Garage; Spare Parts Shops
44 Gari Stand

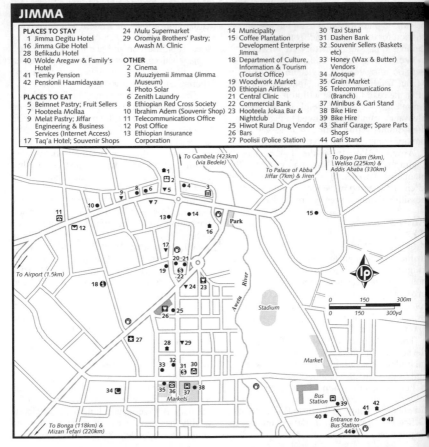

at **Jiffar Engineering & Business Services** (☎ 11 11 49; 8am-8pm daily) near Melat Pastry, for Birr0.50 per minute. **Souvenir shops** can be found inside the Wolde Aregaw & Family hotel and near the Taq'a Hotel.

Jimma Museum
ጇማ ሙዚየም

The **Muuziyemii Jimmaa** (admission Birr10; open 9am-noon & 2pm-5.30pm Mon-Fri, 2pm-5.30pm Sat-Sun & holidays) houses examples of Jimma's traditional arts and crafts, and includes some fine examples of woodwork, musical instruments and traditional and more modern weapons. The old rickety-looking machine gun is Italian and dates to 1936. Look out for the Italian-made walking stick-cum-gun! The bark skirts and the grass raincoats are still worn in the country today.

The museum also contains a collection of possessions belonging to the Kafa king, including a carved wooden throne and – in contrast – the king's loo, which looks like a frying pan with a hole in it.

Look out for the massive and magnificent wooden urn, used as a kind of royal clothes chest, with a circumference of 3.16m. The enormous drum (1.3m in diameter) was used to summon the people to war.

In the future, the historical artefacts of the collection will be transferred to the palace museum; cultural artefacts will remain here.

Palace of Abba Jiffar
የአባ ጇፋር ቤተ መንግስት

King Jiffar (1852–1933), one of the most important local lords of the Kafa kingdom, ruled at the end of the 19th century. His two-storey, 150-year-old Palace of Abba Jiffar (admission Birr10; open 9am-noon & 2pm-5.30pm Mon-Fri, 2pm-5.30pm Sat-Sun & holidays) lies 7km northeast of the town centre, on a hill near the village of Jiren.

The palace has been recently restored. There are also good views; come in the late afternoon. Soon, free guided tours should be available.

The palace contains a private family mosque (which is still in use) which once boasted a library, as well as rooms said to have served as a throne room, reception chamber, king's guard room, sentry tower, courthouse and guesthouse.

The house adjoining the palace is said to have belonged to the king's grandson, the sultan. From the balcony overlooking the courtyard, the royal family watched musicians, wrestlers, singers and poets. Nearby, 1.6km from the palace on the road back to Jimma, lies the tomb of the king.

If you don't want to walk to the museum, you can catch one of the shared taxis (Birr1 to Birr2) heading for Jiren village on Tuesday and Thursday. Alternatively, buses or minibuses (Birr0.50) will take you to the end of the asphalt (about half way), from where it's a one-hour walk. A contract taxi the whole way should cost from Birr40 to Birr50.

Places to Stay

Jimma boasts a handsome collection of squalid little hotels.

Department of Culture, Information & Tourism (☎ 11 06 94; doubles with shared shower Birr10) has 13 cheap, clean and above all quiet rooms, which at the time of writing were open to travellers. If they still are, they're Jimma's best-kept secret.

Befikadu Hotel (☎ 11 17 57; doubles Birr18, with hot shower Birr30) has good-value, clean rooms, despite first appearances. Ask for the rooms at the back; they're less noisy.

Temky Pension (☎ 11 08 44; doubles without shower Birr42-46, with shower Birr69) is a new and quite pleasant place set in a large grassy compound.

Pensionii Haamidayaan (☎ 11 60 14; doubles without shower Birr30 with shower Birr50-60) is similar if the Temky is full.

Wolde Aregaw & Family's Hotel (☎ 11 27 31; doubles with shared shower Birr50-60, doubles with shower Birr66.07-92, twins with shower Birr150-184), directly opposite the bus station, is set in quite large grounds. The more expensive rooms have fridge, TV and telephone.

Jimma Degitu Hotel (☎ 11 05 93; doubles/twins/suites with shower Birr70/92/132), recently privatised, is comfortable. Its biggest asset is the pleasant and peaceful grounds.

Jimma Gibe Hotel (☎ 11 00 71; rooms Birr80.04) is, like many government hotels, a bit dank, run-down and gloomy, but rooms are quiet, very clean and a good size.

Places to Eat

Befikadu Hotel is a local favourite.

Hooteela Mollaa has simple but tasty food, especially its doro arrosto (roast chicken).

Wolde Aregaw & Family's Hotel restaurant serves both Ethiopian and faranji food, including breakfast (Birr7/12 plus tax for continental/full).

ETHIOPIA

Melat Pastry is a new place with a pleasant shaded terrace. It boasts the best selection of cakes and fruit juices in town.

Beimnet Pastry is popular with local students. Other pastry shops are marked on the map.

Jimma Degitu Hotel is also good.

Mulu Supermarket is the best place to stock up if camping, heading west or into the Surma region.

Try tasting the local *besso* drink, made from ground barley. Some of Jimma's swinging bars – or rather dinghy dives – are marked on the map.

Getting There & Away
Ethiopian Airlines (☎ *11 00 30*) flies five times weekly to Addis Ababa, four times weekly to Gambela and Asosa, and once weekly to Tepi and Mizan Tefari. Note that during the rainy season, flights are particularly subject to delays or cancellations.

Three buses leave daily for Addis Ababa (Birr31.80, 8½ to 10 hours) and for Tepi (Birr29.60, seven to eight hours). One bus leaves for Bedele (Birr14.50, four hours); two for Mizan Tefari (Birr24.65, seven to eight hours); and around six minibuses go to Welkite (Birr25, five hours).

Getting Around
Garis (horse-drawn carts) cost Birr0.50 to Birr2 for hops around town depending on the distance; a half/full day's hire costs Birr25/50. Bikes can be hired (Birr3 per hour) outside the bus station opposite the Wolde Aregaw & Family's Hotel.

No buses or minibuses go to the airport; to get there you'll need to take a contract taxi (Birr50). See the map for taxi and *gari* stand locations.

JIMMA TO ADDIS ABABA
After Jimma, the road begins to wind back in a northeasterly direction towards Addis Ababa. Approximately 57km out of town, the road passes the Gibe river dam which, when finished, will be the second largest hydroelectric plant in Ethiopia (after the one on the Tekeze, begun in 2002). Anubis baboons are commonly seen along the road.

Between Welkite and Indibir, there are terrific views of the highland plateau and surrounding valleys. If you get stuck at **Welkite**, the **Tefera Hotel** (☎ *291 through the operator; doubles Birr15, with shower Birr20*) has simple but clean rooms and a pleasant restaurant. Around four buses leave daily for Addis Ababa (Birr13 to Birr20, three to four hours) and to Jimma (Birr15 to Birr20, 4½ to five hours), and one bus for Hosaina (Birr15 to Birr20, four hours).

The little town of **Weliso**, 43km northeast of Welkite, is known for its hot springs. A naturally heated **swimming pool** (*nonguests Birr4.60; filled 8am Fri-6pm Mon only; indoor pool open daily except Mon*) can be found at the **Wollisso Ethiopia Hotel** (☎ *41 00 02; doubles with cold/hot shower Birr75/103.75*). The hotel is 1.4km from the town centre; you can hop on a *gari* for Birr0.50. Camping is permitted. The grounds are full of birds and vervet monkeys.

A budget option is the **Refera Hotel No 2** (☎ *41 02 94; rooms Birr12, with shower Birr20-35*), next to the Mobil station. It has clean rooms set in quite large and pleasant gardens. Ten buses travel daily to Addis Ababa (Birr10, 2½ to three hours) and to Welkite (Birr5, one hour). For Jimma, go to Welkite.

Around Weliso is Gurage country (see the boxed text 'Peoples of Ethiopia' in the Facts about Ethiopia chapter). From the village of **Sebeta**, a solid 3½ hour trek (one way) takes you up to the top of Mogli, one of the peaks of Wuchacha.

Turning left at the junction just beyond Alem Gena, not far from Sebeta, the road leads south to **Butajira**. Continuing south, on the main Alem Gena–Butajira road are some falls near the bridge over the Awash River.

Just as you enter Addis Ababa on the Jimma road (7.5km from Meskel Square), there's a leprosarium, the **All Africa Leprosy and Rehabilitation Training Center** (*ALERT; open 8am-4pm Mon-Fri, 8am-noon Sat*), on the right, which sells various handicrafts such as cushion and bed covers produced by patients.

Eritrea

Eritrea's history should inspire and restore your sense of fair play. It has all the hallmarks of a mythical story from a heroic past. For 30 years, a tiny nation struggled against giants, baddies and powerful outside forces to win its freedom. Every family fought; every family made sacrifices. But justice ultimately triumphed and the diminutive goodies finally won. Then a legendary political tale began, with the building of a Utopian nation in which corruption was unheard of and crime was unknown. Ministers rode bicycles, women walked freely and everyone lived happily and in harmony.

But one day, two old friends and fighting buddies had a squabble and things began to turn nasty. The bloody dispute which broke out in May 1998 between President Isaias of Eritrea and Prime Minister Meles Zenawi of Ethiopia over a tiny stretch of barren borderland has been likened to two bald men fighting over a comb. Hundreds of thousands of lives were lost, the Eritrean economy was ruined and political credibility abroad evaporated. The country's fairy tale had turned into a horror story.

However, the tragic and wasteful conflict between the former allies appears to have been resolved. And although the extraordinary – and highly infectious – mood of optimism, excitement and hope that once prevailed in Eritrea's streets has waned somewhat, the country is still a fascinating and rewarding place to visit.

The capital, Asmara, is like a film set from an early Italian movie. Old chrome espresso machines churn out cups of *macchiato*, Cinquecento taxis putt-putt about and all over town you can see outstanding examples of Art Deco architecture. Asmara is without doubt one of the safest, cleanest and most attractive capital cities in Africa.

Eritrea's landscape, though often arid, can be beautiful in its starkness and has a peculiar appeal. The Sahel Mountains in the north, for a long time the home of the guerilla fighters, have a wild and bleak quality. The apocalyptic wasteland of Dankalia stretching to the south is considered one of the most inhospitable places on earth.

Eritrea's nine colourful ethnic groups have had to adapt to these different environmental conditions and are correspondingly diverse and individual. Many have ancient and

Eritrea at a Glance

Capital City: Asmara

Population: 4.4 million

Time: 3 hours ahead of GMT

Land Area: 124,320 sq km

International Telephone Code: ☎ 291

GDP per Capita: US$740

Currency: Nakfa (Nfa10.50 = US$1 official; Nfa20 = US$1 parallel)

Official Languages: Tigrinya, Arabic, English

Greeting: *Selam* (Tigrinya)

Massawa p332
Massawa p334
Taulud Island p335
Asmara p310 ☉
Asmara Walking Tours p303
Central Asmara p314
Dahlak Islands p339

The international boundaries on this map serve as indications only. The Ethiopia-Eritrea border awaits formal UN demarcation.

Highlights

- Strap on your snorkel or scuba-diving gear and marvel at the unspoilt underwater treasures around the Dahlak Islands

- Explore Eritrea's remarkable archaeological ruins in Qohaito

- Take a tour of war-torn Nakfa, once the heart of Eritrean resistance

- Discover the lunar landscape of Dankalia, one of the most desolate areas on earth

- Hang out in one of Asmara's Italian-style cafés and enjoy a coffee or a pastry

- Admire Asmara's superb colonial architecture

- Climb up to one of the isolated Orthodox monasteries, set amidst spectacular scenery

- Savour the distinctly Arabic flavour of Massawa, and sample a grilled fish at an outdoor restaurant on Massawa Island at dusk

intriguing cultures. The Afars and Rashaida in particular, have fascinated European travellers for centuries.

On the coast, the sultry town of Mas???? is redolent with Islamic influence. It ? the starting point for visits t? ??? Islands – Eritrea's coral reef? ??? among the richest, least ???? known in the Red Sea.

Though not as sp?? ??? historical sites, tho? ?? ??? important. With ??? ??? count, Eritrea has one ? ????est densities of archaeological sit? ?? Africa. Finds that call into question key aspects of the region's history are unearthed almost every day.

Perhaps Eritrea's greatest resource is its people. Though impoverished, the nation has from the outset showed self-reliance, vigour and independence. Eritrea is not about to become anyone's vassal and this attitude has elicited both passionate admiration and furious exasperation from visitors, aid workers and international organisations alike. Towards the traveller, Eritreans show exceptional politeness, hospitality and friendliness. The inhospitality of the countryside in which most of the people live as nomads may well contribute to this keen sense of the importance of hospitality.

In practical terms, the country has many attractions too. The cost of living is low, hustling and hassling is practically unknown and travel around the country is reasonably easy and cheap. Above all, tourism is still almost unknown.

ts about Eritrea

y

ry

???ral well-preserved hominid fossils ??? ???thed near Buya in the Dubub ??? ???and Adi Keyh in southern Eritrea). ??? are thought to date from around two million years ago. To date, 51 prehistoric sites have been found in Eritrea, including the Karora site in the northeast of the country and the Beylul site in the southeast.

Tools found in the Barka Valley dating from 8000 BC appear to offer the first concrete evidence of human settlement. Numerous rock paintings have been found throughout the country, particularly in the southern Dubub area. The latter date from at least 2000 BC, and appear to be the work of a nomadic or seminomadic people who bred cattle.

Eritrea's earliest inhabitants are thought to have been related to the Pygmies of Central Africa. Later, they intermingled with Nilotic, Hamitic and finally Semitic peoples migrating from across Africa and Arabia. By around 2000 BC, close contacts had been established with the people of the Nubian lowlands to the west and those from the Tihama coast of southern Arabia to the east. Some ruins in Eritrea are thought to date from the Pre-Aksumite Civilisation – for more information see that section in the Facts about Ethiopia chapter.

Aksumite Civilisation

Around the 1st century AD (or even earlier), the powerful kingdom of Aksum began to

ERITREA

The Land of Punt

Since the dawn of history, the Horn of Africa has been a source of fascination for the outside world. Lying on the African side of the Red Sea, the area provided a crucial trade link, connecting Egypt and the Mediterranean with India and the Far East.

However, this wasn't the region's only asset. Known to the Egyptian Pharaohs as 'Land of the Gods' or 'Land of Punt' (together with what is now Djibouti), the area yielded a seemingly limitless supply of precious commodities. Gold, frankincense, myrrh, slaves, ostrich feathers, antelopes, ebony and ivory were all loaded onto foreign ships jostling in the region's ports.

Egyptian accounts of this land accorded it almost legendary status and provide the earliest glimpse of the region. Expeditions are thought to date from the First or Second Dynasties (2920–2649 BC). At Queen Hatshepsut's famous Theban temple of Deir al-Bahri (built around 1490 BC), dramatic pictorial reliefs recount the departure of an entire fleet to the magical land.

For scholars today, the Land of Punt retains its legendary aura. Thought to lie somewhere between the lands to the south of Nubia and those just north of present-day Somalia, no one knows its exact location. Eritrea, Djibouti, Yemen, Somalia and even Kenya have all made claims to the title of the Land of Punt.

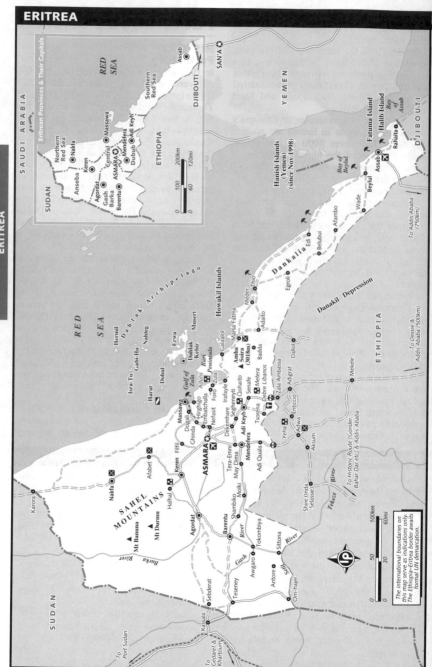

ERITREA

Eritrean Provinces & Their Capitals

SAUDI ARABIA

RED SEA

SUDAN

Anseba Agordat Gash Barka Barentu

Northern Red Sea

Nakfa Keren Central ASMARA Mendefera Dubub Adi Keyh

Southern Red Sea

Massawa

ETHIOPIA

DJIBOUTI

SAN'A

0   100   200km
0   60   120mi

YEMEN

Hanish Islands (Yemen) (since Nov 1998)

Fatuma Island Halib Island

Bay of Assab

Assab

Rahaita

DJIBOUTI

Beylul

Wade

Afambo

Belubui

Edi

Bay of Beylul

To Addis Ababa (750km)

RED SEA

Hermil

Isra-Tu Gabi-Hu Nahleg

Dohul

Harat

Dahlak Archipelago

Dahlak Kebir

Erwa

Museri

Howakil Islands

Gulf of Zula

Adulis Zula

Buri Peninsula

Foro

Galaalol

Marsa Fatma

Meder Tho

Egroli

Adaito

Badda

DANKALIA

Danakil Depression

ETHIOPIA

Dallol

Mekele

To Dessie & Addis Ababa (500km)

Amba Soira (3018m)

Senafe

Metera Debre Libanos

Zala Ambassa

Adigrat

Adwa

Aksum

Yeha

Eritcico

Tsorona

Massawa

Dogali Chinda

Hirghigo Embatchalla

Nefasit Dekemhare Segheneyti

Adi Keyh Dohaito

Irafayle

ASMARA

Filfil

Keren

Halhal

Afabet

Nakfa

SAHEL MOUNTAINS

Mt Bamua Mt Durmu

Agordat

Barka River

Karora

SUDAN

To Port Sudan

Kassala

To Gedaref & Khartoum

Sebderat

Teseney

Antore

Om-hajer

Awgaro

Tokombya

Barentu

Gash River

Shambiko

Molki

Tera-Emni

May Dima

Mendefera

Adi Quala

Tekeze River

Shire (Inda Selassie)

Setit River

Siitona

To Historic Route (Gonder, Bahar Dar etc) & Addis Ababa

0   50   100km
0   30   60mi

The international boundaries on this map serve as indications only. The Ethiopia–Eritrea border awaits formal UN demarcation.

ETHIOPIA

develop. Situated in Tigray, in the north of modern Ethiopia (around 50km from present-day Eritrea), Aksum lay just 170km from the Red Sea. Much foreign trade – on which Aksum's prosperity depended – was seaborne, and came to be handled by the ancient port of Adulis in Eritrea.

On the way to Adulis (a 12- to 15-day journey from Aksum) many exports, including rhinoceros horn, gold, hippopotamus hide, slaves, apes and particularly ivory, passed through Eritrean towns, including Koloe (thought to be present-day Qohaito in the south).

Some of the goods exported were Eritrean in origin. Obsidian, a black volcanic rock, came from the waters of the Red Sea, and was highly prized by the ancients for the manufacture of jewellery and votive offerings. Red Sea tortoiseshell was another export much valued by the ancients.

Arrival of Christianity

Christianity was undoubtedly the most significant 'import' into the region during the Aksumite period. According to the Byzantine ecclesiastical historian Rufinus, the religion was brought to the region by accident when Christian Syrian merchants travelling home from India were shipwrecked on the Red Sea coast. Whatever its origin, by the 4th century AD Christianity had become the Aksumite state religion, and King Ezana began to mint coins bearing the cross of Christ.

The new religion had a profound impact on Eritrea's culture, influencing much of the country's art and literature, as well as shaping the spiritual and moral lives of the Christian population.

Islam & the Decline of Aksum

Islam, the arrival of which coincided with Christian Aksum's decline in the 7th century, was the other great influence on the region. Though not directly responsible for the empire's collapse, the expansion of the religion was concomitant with the increasing power of the Arabs, who fast became the new masters of the Red Sea. Aksum's commercial domination of the region was over.

Islam made the greatest inroads in the Dahlak Islands, some of which later sprouted a significant kingdom in their own right. Muslims traders also settled in nearby Massawa on the mainland.

Aksumite authority had long been challenged by other forces too, with incursions, attacks, rebellions and even mass migration

The Red, Red Sea

Eritrea is said to derive its name from the Greek word *erythrea*, meaning red. It was coined from the famous *Periplus of the Erythrean Sea*, a trade or shipping manual written by a Greek-speaking Egyptian sailor or merchant around the 1st century AD. The *erythrea* (or red of the sea) is so named because the water turns a vermilion shade as a result of newly spored algae during certain periods.

by neighbouring tribes. The Beja tribe, a Cushitic people originating from present-day Sudan, were particularly active. From the 4th century onwards, most of the northern coast, the highlands and the northwest of Eritrea were settled by the Beja. Five kingdoms were established, and to this day their influence can be felt in the traditions and beliefs of the local people of the region.

After the settlement of the Beja in the interior of the country, and the Arabs on the coast, the Ethiopians were unable to recover the influence the Aksumites held over the region for another thousand years. Several attempts were made by later kings who tried to regain the vital access to the Red Sea, but all of them failed.

Turks & Egyptians

The Turks first arrived in the Red Sea at the beginning of the 16th century. For the next 300 years (with a few short-lived intervals) the coast, including the port of Massawa, belonged to the Ottomans.

By the middle of the 19th century, new powers were casting covetous eyes over the region. The Egyptians, under Ali Pasha (Mohammed Ali), invaded modern-day Sudan and occupied parts of Ethiopia. Soon after, the western lowlands of modern-day Eritrea were also taken, including the port of Massawa.

Under threat, the Ethiopian King Yohannes eventually forced a battle. In 1875 at Ghundet, near Adi Quala in modern-day southern Eritrea, and later at Gura, near Dekemhare, Yohannes inflicted resounding defeats on the Egyptian armies. Although the invaders' influence lingered on along the coast and particularly in the region of Keren, Yohannes' victories stamped out forever Egyptian designs on the territory.

At the same time, Egyptian rule in Sudan was overthrown by Mohammed Ahmed,

ERITREA

known as the Mahdi. His successor Khalifa Abduhalli and his dervishes then threatened the west of modern-day Eritrea. The power vacuum left by the departing Egyptians was soon to be filled by yet another meddling foreign power – Italy.

The Italians Arrive

During the 'Scramble for Africa' (see the boxed text later) in the second half of the 19th century, France grabbed Djibouti (which then became known as French Somaliland) and Britain snatched Aden in Yemen, as well as a stretch of Somali coastline. Italy wasn't going to miss out on a piece of the pie.

In November 1869 an Italian shipping company bought up a piece of land near Assab in what is now southern Eritrea. In 1882, the Italian government arrived, buying out the shipping company, installing a local administration and setting up a permanent garrison. Colonisation had begun. In 1885 the Italians occupied Massawa.

Alarmed by further expansion and the threat it posed to his kingdom, Yohannes challenged the Italians, but was killed in battle with the Mahadists in 1889.

As the struggle against the Mahadists preoccupied the Ethiopians, the Italians were left to get on with the realisation of their military ambitions. First they took the highland town of Keren, then Asmara. Soon they began a march southwards.

Relations were at first good with the new Ethiopian emperor, Menelik, and in 1889 the Treaty of Wechale was signed. In exchange for granting Italy the region that was to later become Eritrea, the Italians recognised Menelik's sovereignty and gave him the right to import arms freely though Ethiopia. However, a dispute over a discrepancy in the purportedly identical Amharic and Italian texts later led to the treaty's dissolution, and relations began to sour. In the meantime, Italian campaigns continued in the west.

Towards the end of 1889 the Italians turned their attention to the south. In 1890, they took Adwa and Mekele in Ethiopian territory. The Italians then made attempts to subvert the local chiefs of Tigray, but in a rare act of unity, the chiefs sided with the Ethiopian emperor, Menelik.

The Italians managed to defeat Ras Mangasha and his Tigrayan forces at Adwa in 1894, and proceeded to annex further important Ethiopian towns, including Aksum, Adigrat and Mekele.

In 1896 the battle lines were drawn again. To international shock and amazement, the Ethiopians resoundingly defeated the Italian armies. The Battle of Adwa was one of the very few occasions when a colonial power was defeated by an African force (for more details, see the boxed text 'The Battle of Adwa' in the Northern Ethiopia chapter).

In the months that followed new international boundaries were drawn up: Ethiopia remained independent and Eritrea became, for the first time, a separate territory – and an Italian colony.

Italian Colonial Rule

Of all Italy's colonies (Eritrea, Libya and Italian Somaliland), Eritrea was considered the jewel in the crown. Apart from providing a strategic base for imperial ambitions (particularly against Ethiopia), it boasted vital access to the Red Sea, as well as potential for mineral and agricultural exploitation. For this reason, much effort was put into industrialising the little country, and major schemes began to be developed, including the building of the great railway between Massawa and Asmara in 1909 (which was later extended to Keren) and the construction of a national network of roads.

By the end of the 1930s, Eritrea – albeit on a diminutive scale – was one of the most highly industrialised colonies in Africa. By 1930 Massawa had become the largest port on the East African coast. The population of the country numbered a staggering 760,000 in 1941.

The Italians initially governed Eritrea indirectly through local chieftains. Later, a series of provinces were created, administered by a large body of Italian civil servants, headed by a governor.

During this period, much land was expropriated from Eritreans and handed over to Italian private enterprise. This policy was deeply resented, and opposition to Italian rule simmered and sometimes erupted, as it did in 1894 in Akele Guzay.

Dispossessed of their land, many Eritreans moved to the towns. Urban populations swelled, resulting in the establishment of a substantial working class and an urban-based 'intelligentsia'.

British Administration

In May 1936 Italy avenged itself for the defeat at Adwa and triumphed over the Ethiopians. In 1940, with the outbreak of WWII, Italy declared war on Britain, and soon became embroiled in conflicts in what was then Anglo-Egyptian Sudan. Though initially successful, Italian campaigns in this area were soon repulsed by reinforced British armies.

Soon British forces were giving chase to the Italians, pursuing them into Eritrea, and capturing Agordat. In 1941 the British took the strategically important town of Keren and killed the Italian general Lorenzini. On 1 April 1941 the Italians surrendered in Asmara and the colony became an Administration of the British.

The British attempted to maintain the status quo in the territory largely due to practical constraints. They left in place the old Italian administration, but the colony inevitably sank into a state of demoralisation and decline.

Eventually the loss of Italian state subsidies forced the colony towards a more self-reliant stance. In the early 1940s, the economy experienced a brief revival. The ports of Massawa and Assab became important imperial

The Scramble for Africa

At the beginning of the 19th century, European maps of Africa showed little more than huge, blank spaces. Fifty years later, these gaps began to be filled with the continent's major physical features: the great African lakes, mountains and rivers. European explorers, keen to win kudos for themselves, their religion and their country, fell over one another in the rush to 'discover' them. Within a decade, more than 25 million sq km of Africa and over 100 million Africans had been swallowed up by the European powers. The 'Scramble for Africa', as the partition of the continent is more luridly known, was the most dramatic instance of the carving up of the world by foreign powers in the history of mankind.

There are various 'explanations' for the partition. Commercially, Africa was seen as a vast tropical treasure house that would yield huge quantities of valuable commodities such as ivory and slaves. The development of new markets abroad was seen as essential to the newly industrialised capitalist states of Europe. Also, ignorance about the continent of Africa was seen as rather shameful, and many Europeans became increasingly fascinated by the natural sciences as a whole, and in particular by the new and fashionable research on ethnology, the study of races and peoples.

In political and diplomatic terms, the partition was a grand power play between the competing European countries. Statesmen could use overseas territories as bargaining chips in a ruthless game of global diplomacy. Others have suggested that colonial policies were used to distract attention from irksome tensions at home. Italy, for example, was encouraged to dream of re-creating the great Roman Empire. In Germany, Bismarck is said to have staged colonial advances in Africa in 1884 purely as an electioneering stunt. Missionaries, convinced of their divine mission to save souls and convert the world, were another important influence. New technologies such as the train and the steamship, and the discovery of the antimalarial quinine facilitated European invasion of the 'deep, dark' African continent.

Although the causes of the partition can be debated, the results are more obvious. The divisions sent out political, economic and social shock waves that are felt in Africa to this day. As Dr WEB Dubois put it:

There came to Africa an end of industry…Cheap European goods pushed in and threw the native products out of competition…Methods of work were lost and forgotten. The authority of the family was broken up; the authority and tradition of the clan disappeared; the power of the chief was transmuted into the rule of the white district commissioner…The old religion was held up to ridicule, the old culture and ethical standards were degraded or disappeared, and gradually all over Africa spread the inferiority complex, the fear of colour, the worship of white skin, the imitation of white ways of doing and thinking, whether good, bad or indifferent. By the end of the 19th century the degradation of Africa was as complete as organised human means could make it.

Dr WEB DuBois
From *The World and Africa*
(International Publishers, New York, 1965)

The old imperial chauvinism seems to have been replaced by a new cultural one. And, with the proliferation of aid and financial packages, many would argue an economic one, too.

staging posts and many of the big industrial names known today established themselves – Melotti beer, Tabacchi cement, Sava glass and Maderni matches.

However, the fortunes of the colony were pinned to larger events unfolding beyond it. When the course of WWII changed, the territory lost its strategic importance and in 1945 the British began a slow withdrawal.

Unfortunately, the British decided to take most of the colony with them, cleaning the place out lock, stock and barrel. Everything was dismantled and removed. With the British went Eritrea's extensive infrastructure.

By 1946 the country was in trouble. The economy was floundering, unemployment was soaring, and unrest was brewing.

Federation with Ethiopia

In 1948 Eritrea's fate was pondered by a four-powers commission consisting of the UK, the USA, France and the Soviet Union. Unable to reach a decision, the commission passed the issue on to the United Nation's General Assembly.

In 1947 a commission of inquiry found the population divided into three main factions: the pro-Ethiopian Unionists (mainly Christian), the anti-Unionists (mainly Muslims in favour of a Muslim League) and members of a Pro-Italia party (many of them Italian pensioners). The commissioners, whose findings reflected the political interests of their respective governments, produced totally different conclusions and recommendations.

In 1950 the very contentious Resolution 390 A (V) was passed. Eritrea became Ethiopia's fourteenth province and disappeared from the map of Africa.

Annexation by Ethiopia

This 'shotgun wedding', as it has been described, between Eritrea and Ethiopia was never a happy one. Little by little, Ethiopia began to exert an ever-tighter hold over Eritrea, as both industry and political control were shifted to Ethiopia's capital, Addis Ababa. The Eritrean economy stagnated and the province's autonomy dwindled. Eritrean politicians and leaders were soon ousted, Ethiopian Amharic replaced Tigrinya as the official language in schools, and protests against the regime were suppressed with brutality. During the General Strike of 1958, several protesters were killed or wounded.

The repeated appeals by the Eritrean people to the UN fell on deaf ears. With the start of the Cold War in the 1950s, the Americans had set their sights on establishing a communications centre in Asmara. When, in the early 1960s, Ethiopia formally annexed Eritrea in violation of international law, Cold War politics ensured that both the US and the UN kept silent.

With no recourse to the international community, the frustration of the Eritrean people grew. In 1961, the inevitable happened. In the little town of Amba Adal in the western lowlands, a small group of men led by Hamid Idriss Awate assailed one of the much-resented Ethiopian police stations and stole some pistols. The fight for independence had begun.

Eritrean Resistance

The Struggle, as resistance to Ethiopian rule became popularly known, was an extraordinary event in the history of the Horn. Lasting for 30 years, it shaped – physically and psychologically – the Eritrean nation and its people. For the first time, a real sense of national identity was forged.

The first resistance movements on the scene included the ELM (Eritrean Liberation Movement), the (Christian) People's Liberation Front (PLF), and the (Muslim) Eritrean Liberation Front (ELF). From the latter two, a splinter group emerged, the Eritrean People's Liberation Front (EPLF), which called for social revolution as well as national independence. Continual conflict between the various groups, particularly the ELF and the EPLF, considerably undermined the nationalist movement throughout its history. It was only after periods of bloody civil war and the defeat of the ELF in 1981, that the EPLF emerged as the leader of unified forces.

Nevertheless, the resistance continued to make progress, and in 1978 the Eritreans were on the brink of winning back their country. However, just on the point of victory, yet another foreign power decided to intervene.

In 1974 Colonel Mengistu Haile Mariam, a communist dictator, had come to power in Ethiopia. Three years later the Soviet Union began to arm his troops. In the face of massive aerial bombardment and an army bristling with modern weaponry, the EPLF was obliged to retreat. The famous 'Strategic Withdrawal', as it is known, later proved to be crucial to the movement's survival.

Eight major offensives were carried out against the Eritrean fighters from 1978 to 1986, all of which were repulsed. From 1988, the EPLF began to inflict major losses on the Ethiopian army, capturing first its northern headquarters in Afabet, then the large highland town of Keren. In 1990, amid some of the fiercest fighting of the war, the EPLF took the strategically important port of Massawa.

By this time, however, Mengistu Haile Mariam's regime was threatened from within, and civil war had broken out in Ethiopia. In 1991 Mengistu was overthrown and fled to Zimbabwe. His 140,000 Ethiopian troops laid down their weapons and ran. The EPLF walked into Asmara without having to fire a single bullet.

The New State

In April 1993 the Provisional Government of Eritrea held a referendum on Eritrean independence. More than 99.81% of voters opted for full Eritrean sovereignty, and on 24 May 1993, independence was declared. Eritrea was back on the African map.

In early 1994 the EPLF dissolved itself and re-formed as the People's Front for Democracy and Justice (PFDJ) under the chairmanship of the head of state, President Isaias Afewerki. Some members of the old ELF were also invited to join the team.

After the war, the little nation worked hard to rebuild its infrastructure, repair the economy and improve conditions for its people.

Wide-ranging laws, policies and constitutional rights were drawn up, from protection of the environment and positive discrimination towards people with disabilities at work, to the rights of women and the fight against AIDS.

Eritrea was also at pains to establish good international relations with, among others, Ethiopia, the Gulf States, Asia, the USA and Europe.

However, this progress was seriously undermined in 1998, when war broke out with Ethiopia. For the history of the recent war and ongoing tensions with Ethiopia, see History in the Facts about Ethiopia chapter.

In December 2002 the Ethiopian embassy in Asmara was closed. Relations with Ethiopia are likely to remain tense until the border demarcation is completed, probably sometime in 2003–04. The psychological war between the two countries is ongoing.

Relations with most of Eritrea's other neighbours have not been cordial either. In 1998 Eritrea was obliged to hand back the Hanish archipelago to Yemen, following a long-standing dispute.

In September 2000 the return of the Djiboutian ambassador to Asmara formally marked an improvement in relations between these two countries. Relations had been broken off after President Isaias accused Djibouti of supporting Ethiopia in its dispute with Eritrea.

After a five-year impasse, relations with Sudan were formally resumed in January 2000. However, in January 2003, the Eritrean leadership accused Ethiopia, Yemen and Sudan of embarking on a policy of deliberate isolation of Eritrea, referring to them as an 'axis of belligerence'. In the meantime, disputes continue with Sudan over antigovernment forces based

ERITREA

A Super Struggle

The price of Eritrea's freedom was high. Africa's longest war of the 20th century, the Struggle for Freedom lasted 30 years, wrecked the country's infrastructure and economy, cost 65,000 lives and drove at least a third of the population into exile.

The war was not a story of vast armies, brilliant leadership and sweeping conquests. For three decades, a tiny guerrilla force (which numbered at most 40,000 during its last days), was able to thwart the might of a country 10 times its size, that was backed by two superpowers and had all the modern weaponry of the 20th century.

Initially a ragbag bandit force, the resistance fighters were gradually converted into what was described by a BBC journalist in the 1980s as 'the best guerrilla army in the world'. The fighters operated in tightly organised cells, taught their soldiers to read and write, history, philosophy and political economy, as well as guerrilla tactics. Equality of all people was advocated; soldiers had to respect the gender (many soldiers were women), ethnic group, religion and race of their fellow fighters.

In response to the devastating blanket bombing inflicted by the Ethiopians, whole villages were constructed underground, with schools, hospitals, factories, printing presses, mills, pharmacies, workshops and entertainment halls. The remains of these 'towns' can be seen today in the village of Nakfa in the north of Eritrea. The workshops became places of remarkable ingenuity and resourcefulness. Everything was put to use or recycled. The Eritrean Struggle for Freedom is without doubt one of the most remarkable in modern history.

in Eritrea, and with Yemen over fishing rights in the Red Sea.

At the end of 2002 and beginning of 2003, various military officials, including the US Defence Secretary, Donald Rumsfeld, visited Eritrea. The country's strategic importance in the US-led global 'war against terrorism' is obvious. Eritrea may well benefit economically and politically, as President Isaias is well aware. The Americans have been offered the use of Eritrean bases to back up its forces in neighbouring Djibouti. However, in early 2003 the US Secretary of State, Colin Powell, expressed concern over human rights and democratic conditions in Eritrea, and threatened the withdrawal of aid. This will undoubtedly prove a sticking point in future military cooperation between Eritrea and the USA.

GEOGRAPHY

With a land area of 124,320 sq km, Eritrea is about the size of England or the state of Pennsylvania in the USA. The coastline measures around 1000km and off it there are over 350 islands.

Eritrea has three main geographical zones: the eastern escarpment and coastal plains, the central highland region, and the western lowlands.

The eastern zone consists of desert or semidesert, with little arable land. The people inhabiting the region are generally nomadic pastoralists or fishing communities.

The northern end of the East African Rift Valley opens into the infamous Dankalia region in the east, one of the hottest places on earth. This semidesert lies in a depression up to 120m below sea level, and is home to several salt lakes.

The central highland region is more fertile, and it is intensively cultivated by farming communities.

The western lowlands, lying between Keren and the Sudanese border, are watered by the Gash and Barka Rivers. Farming is practised, but less intensively than in the highlands.

CLIMATE

Eritrea's climate corresponds to its geography.

The low, eastern zone is by far the hottest area. Temperatures range from a torrid 30° to 39°C during the hot season (June to September) and from 25° to 32°C during the cooler season (October to May).

Rainfall on the coast is less than 200mm per year, and occurs mostly from December to February. The high humidity in the coastal

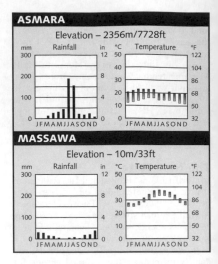

region can make temperatures seem much higher than those further inland.

In the Dankalia region, temperatures can reach 50°C in the shade! Rainfall is practically zero.

In the highland zone, the average annual temperature is 18°C (17°C in Asmara). May is the hottest month, when daily temperatures can reach around 30°C. The coldest months are from December to February when lows can approach freezing point. Temperatures can vary by up to 20°C between day and night. Mists are also prevalent at this time. Light rains fall from March to April, with heavy rains from the end of June to the beginning of September. The average annual rainfall is 540mm.

In the western zone, temperatures range from 30° to 41°C in the hot season (April to June). December is the coolest month (13° to 25°C). Rainfall mirrors that in the highland zone.

ECOLOGY & ENVIRONMENT

Eritrea's environment has been greatly impacted by war, famine and demographic pressure. When the new government came to power in 1994 it quickly realised that Eritrea's economic future was inextricably linked to its environment. Much of Eritrea's farming is still subsistence or semi-subsistence, so land productivity is vital to the population's survival.

Today, population growth is the biggest problem, placing increased demands on the land and leading to overgrazing and overcropping. The practice of 'shifting cultivation' in the southwestern lowlands (in which whole areas of vegetation are burnt before planting) is also seriously detrimental to the region's flora.

In the mid-1990s various international conventions were signed, including the 1973 Convention on International Trade in Endangered Species (Cites) and the 1992 Convention on Biological Diversity (CBD).

The Forests

Eritrea's forests supply products such as gum and traditional rural medicine, as well as firewood and wood for construction. In times of famine, trees provide emergency rations for the people and their livestock. Above all, the trees prevent soil erosion. Eritrea's current water shortages and low-yielding land are directly linked to the destruction of the forests.

Less than 1% of the country is covered by woodland, as against 30% a century ago. During colonial times Italian colonialists cleared 300,000 hectares of forest for farming. During the war with Ethiopia troops on both sides cleared forests for the construction of shelters, trenches and other fortifications. Today the demand for firewood is the biggest threat. The traditional *hidmo* (hut) also requires large quantities of wood.

Measures to combat deforestation include a nationwide programme of tree planting and the establishment of nearly 100 nurseries nationwide. In the 1990s, a policy of 'hillside closure' was introduced. In these areas, all logging, grazing and crop cultivation is banned. Currently, around 100,000 hectares are protected in this way.

FLORA

The eastern landscape is characterised by acacia woodland (several species), brushland and thicket, semidesert vegetation, riverine vegetation and mangrove swamp. Around Massawa, small plantations of *Conocarpus lancifolius* exist, and along the roadsides of major towns are kassod tree *(Cassia siamea)* and flame tree *(Delonix regia)*.

The highland region is dominated by an indigenous species of juniper *(Juniperus procera)* and wild olive *(Olea africana)*. Various species of acacia are also found. In degraded areas, various pioneer species have been introduced including East African laburnum *(Calpurnia aurea)* and native hops *(Dodonaea viscosa)*. Various eucalyptus plantations have also been established.

The Semenawi Bahri, or Green Belt area, is in the northeast of Asmara, around the village and valleys of Filfil. It contains the last remnant of mixed, evergreen, tropical woodland in Eritrea. At an elevation of between 900m and 2400m, it stretches north to south for about 20km.

The landscape to the west is made up mainly of woodland savanna, brushland, thicket and grasslands *(Aristida)*. Around 50% of the firewood needed for the population of Asmara is collected from this area, resulting in serious deforestation. Species include the doum palm *(Hyphaenea thebaica)*, found particularly along the Barka River, eucalypts and various acacia species. Other species include baobab *(Adansonia digitata)*, toothbrush tree *(Salvadora persica)* and tamarisk *(Tamarix aphylla)*.

Endangered species of flora include the eucalypt *(Boswellia papyrifera)*, the baobab and the tamarind tree *(Tamarindus indica)*.

FAUNA
Mammals & Reptiles

In the past, Eritrea was home to a large range of animals, including buffaloes, cheetahs, elephants, giraffes and lions. With the loss of the forests and the decades of civil war, many of these animals have disappeared.

Mammals commonly seen today include the Abyssinian hare, African wild cat, black-backed jackal, common jackal, genet, ground squirrel, pale fox, Soemmering's gazelle and warthog. Primates include the vervet monkey and hamadryas baboon.

Lions, greater kudus and Tora hartebeests are said to inhabit the mountains of Gash-Barka province, north of Barentu. In the Bure peninsula, dik-diks and dorcas gazelles can be seen. In the area between Awgaro and Antore, Eritrea's last population of elephants is said to roam.

Birds

Eritrea's range of habitats is surprisingly diverse, and its birdlife is correspondingly rich. A total of 537 species of birds have been recorded, including the rare blue saw-wing.

The isolated and uninhabited Dahlak Islands, and the rich feeding grounds which surround them, attract large numbers of nesting sea birds from all over the Red Sea (and from the Mediterranean and the Gulf). Some 109 species have been recorded on the islands, including the Arabian bustard and osprey.

Eritrea also lies within a popular migratory fly way. Hundreds of species of wintering and migratory coastal and sea birds can

ERITREA

be seen crossing between the continents of Africa and Arabia.

On the Bure peninsula, the ostrich and Arabian bustard are commonly seen. Sea birds include gulls, terns, boobies and, on the coastline and islands, many species of wader.

In the lush, evergreen, tropical forests in the Semenawi Bahri area northeast of Asmara, birdlife is particularly abundant. Species include the near-endemic white-cheeked turaco and the Narina trogon.

Marine Life

Major Eritrean marine ecosystems include the coral reefs, sea-grass beds and mangrove forests.

In the Red Sea at least 350 species of coral are known to exist. Eritrea's coral is mainly found as 'patch reef' extending from the surface to a depth of around 15m to 18m; below this, coral development tends to be limited.

Eritrea is home to at least three species of mangrove, despite its location on the northerly limits of the mangrove ranges. They are found along the coast and on the Dahlak Islands.

Five species of marine turtle have been recorded. Most common are the green and hawksbill turtles. The green turtle is quite often spotted around the Dahlak Islands, as are dolphins and sharks.

The Red Sea: An Oasis of Life

The Red Sea possesses physical characteristics found nowhere else in the world. Geologically, it is classed as a basin, ie, a partially enclosed area of water. The Gulf of Suez in Egypt and the Gulf of Aqaba in Jordan mark the northern limits, and the Straits of Bal al Mandab in Djibouti, 2350km away, mark the southern limits.

Isolation for the past 2.5 million years in such a semi-enclosed environment has given rise to an incredibly rich marine life, as well as high proportion of endemism – nearly 20% of the fish in the Red Sea are found nowhere else. The variety of coral is also enormous, with over 350 species recorded.

The reefs of the Red Sea are renowned for their vibrant marine life. The reef is home to more major animal groups than any other ecosystem in the world. It teems with creatures of all shapes, sizes and colours – including fish, echinoderms, crustaceans, molluscs, sponges, reptiles and visiting mammals.

The Eritrean and Sudanese coastlines are thought to be home to at least half the 4000 to 5000 endangered dugong (sea cow) estimated to inhabit the Red Sea.

Collecting coral, shells or plant life from the beaches and waters is forbidden in the Dahlak Islands. See also the boxed text 'The Joys of Diving in Eritrea' under Activities later in this chapter.

Endangered Species

The greatest threat to wildlife in Eritrea is the loss or degradation of habitat. Almost all of Eritrea's animals (with the exception of the baboon, ostrich and gazelle) are considered endangered within the country's own national perimeters. Internationally, the Nubian ibex (which has probably disappeared from Eritrea) is considered dangerously threatened. In recent years, concerns have also been expressed for Eritrea's elephant populations. A century ago, significant numbers inhabited Gash-Barka province. Today it is thought that no more that 100 elephants exist, in a tiny pocket near Omhajer and Antore.

An even rarer animal is the African wild ass *(Equus africanus)*. The ass is found between Dankalia and the Buri Peninsula, but numbers are extremely low.

National Parks

There are no formal national reserves or parks in Eritrea, although their establishment is expected sooner or later.

At present, there are no marine parks either, but several islands in the Dahlak group have been proposed.

GOVERNMENT & POLITICS

The head of state, the president, holds wide powers and is elected for a five-year term, which is renewable once only.

The government is made of two branches: an executive branch composed of a 17-member cabinet; and a legislative branch, comprising the national assembly (parliament). Of the 150 seats in parliament, 75 belong to the Central Council of the ruling party, the PFDJ, and 75 to nonparty members (including representatives of the Eritreans living abroad). Thirty percent of all seats are earmarked for women.

Reflecting the Eritrean ethos of multiculturalism, the judiciary comprises judges in both the provincial and sharia (Islamic law) courts, as well as the overall head of the High Court. New criminal and civil codes are still being drafted to replace the old Ethiopian ones.

Domestic politics remain largely the domain of the ruling PFDJ, which sees itself less as a party and more as a broad popular front, representing all spheres of the population. In May 1997 a pluralist constitution was promulgated, though opposition political parties remained illegal.

The brief period of strong nationalist sentiment sparked by the Ethiopian–Eritrean war has now waned. A post-war malaise has set in (aggravated by the sickly state of the economy), and the mood is increasingly against the government. Moreover, a full transition to a parliamentary democracy is still awaited.

In January 2002 the National Assembly at last ratified a law that would allow for national elections. However, the long-awaited draft law on political parties and organisations has been postponed.

Additionally, the president has shown signs of turning government into a one-man show and of resorting to increasingly repressive measures to silence the rising voices of opposition. In September 2001 tensions finally came to a head and a long-rumoured split within the PFDJ was confirmed when 15 party members formally called on the president to introduce greater democracy. The government responded by arresting 11 members of its party. A crackdown on the media and journalists was also launched. To date, 11 dissidents and 14 journalists remain jailed and no formal charges have been brought. It seems that political freedom is in abeyance in Eritrea.

Various dissident groups operate outside Eritrea, including in Ethiopia and Sudan; outspoken and influential critics are also found among Eritrea's large diaspora.

Immediate future political agendas include the demobilisation of Eritrea's army (which increased with mass conscription during the recent war to an estimated 250,000).

In early 2003 the escalating food crisis began to overshadow political concerns and will continue to do so. A huge one quarter of the population face severe food shortages (see the boxed text 'Famine' in the Facts about Ethiopia chapter).

ECONOMY

After independence, Eritrea began to enjoy strong economic growth and low inflation. However, the high cost of the war with Ethiopia put a swift stop to this. In addition, the war caused Eritrea to lose vital revenue from its port, Assab, where previously 90% of business was Ethiopian.

About 70% of the population are farmers, pastoralists or fishers. A major government priority – along with development of the infrastructure – has been to improve food security. Obstacles to the development of agriculture include serious soil erosion, outdated technology and lack of irrigation. Some horticultural projects are flourishing in the highlands, and may soon be developed in the western lowlands.

Other economic hopes include the huge resources of the Red Sea, especially high-value species such as lobster, fish and crab. Fishery cooperatives are currently being developed in Massawa.

Eritrea's main exports are salt, flowers, textiles, leather and livestock. Imports include fertilisers, machinery, spare parts and tools and construction materials.

Oil and gas reserves are estimated to be substantial but they have yet to be explored and exploited. The signing of a deal in 2001 with a US company should eventually bring some tangible results. Other potentialities include the developing exports of high-quality marble to the Middle East and Europe. Eritrea's traditional light industries continue to fill the shops of the capital with knitwear and sweaters, cotton, leather, glass, salt and processed food.

There are also moves to develop the private sector. Several government hotels have been sold and it is hoped that Eritreans living abroad will invest in new businesses in the country, which should foster economic growth. Another axis of development could be external aid to finance infrastructure, though the government has long avoided this solution for philosophical reasons.

When the border dispute with Ethiopia is finally resolved, tourism could also be a growing sector. Eritrea boasts many assets, including unspoiled reefs, untouched landscapes, colonial architecture and archaeological remains. The launching of Eritrean Airlines in April 2003 could also open new perspectives.

POPULATION & PEOPLE

The population of Eritrea is estimated to be 4.4 million. There are nine ethnic groups: Tigrinya (the largest group), Afar, Bilen, Hedareb, Kunama, Nara, Rashaida, Saho and Tigré, each with their own language and customs (see the special section 'A Museum of Peoples' in this chapter). It is estimated that 1100 Italians live in Eritrea, 750 of whom live in Asmara.

Approximately 35% of the population are nomadic or seminomadic and around 80%

live in the country. Just 13% of Eritreans have access to sanitation and waste disposal, and healthcare outside the capital is low. Only 22% has access to safe drinking water.

Women enjoy far greater equality in Eritrea than in most other African countries. This liberal national attitude has been won by Eritrea's women, who themselves contributed more than one-third of troops in both the recent wars against Ethiopia. However, Eritrea remains a deeply conservative country and the 'double liberation' (for their country and for their gender) expected after independence has not been as forthcoming as some had hoped. In rural areas, prejudices remain deeply rooted.

In the towns several active, well-organised women's groups have sprung up in the last years (for more details, see Women Travellers under Facts for the Visitor in this chapter).

In theory, Tigrinya, Arabic and English are all official languages of Eritrea. In practice, Tigrinya is mainly confined to the highlands, Arabic to the coastal regions and along the Sudanese border and English to the educated urban populations (particularly in Asmara).

Until independence only Arabic, Tigré and Tigrinya had a written form. Nowadays, Eritrea is developing a Latin-based alphabet for the remaining six languages as a way of reinforcing regional culture and identity.

As English is the medium of instruction at secondary and tertiary level, travellers to Eritrea will find English useful. Also, some Italian words for greetings, food and beverage are spoken.

If you know a few words of Tigrinya, you'll amaze and delight the Eritreans and quickly win friends. See the Language chapter for useful words and phrases in Arabic and Tigrinya.

Wiles & Ways

For weddings, religious festivals and special occasions, Tigré and Tigrinya women love to get their hair done. The mass of tiny plaits go right up to the scalp, and can take a whole morning to prepare.

Married women can additionally have the palms of their hands and their feet tattooed with curvilinear patterns of henna. Fashionable teenagers prefer to have their gums tattooed. Pricked until they bleed, the gums are rubbed with charcoal. The resulting blue colour sets off a dazzling set of teeth, and is considered a mark of great beauty.

EDUCATION

Education is divided into three categories and is free to all: primary (for five years), middle (two years) and upper (four years). Some students then go on to university.

The government has made improvements in education a high priority. Despite this, 80% of the population remain illiterate (though more can read than write). The capital is well provided with primary and secondary schools, as well as a university with the capacity for 1300 students a year. Outside the capital, schools are few and far between, and enrolment is low anyway – with 45% in the primary schools, falling to just 10% in the upper schools.

Local languages are the medium for teaching at primary schools; English is used at secondary schools and above.

ARTS

Eritrean arts reflect the diversity of the country's many peoples. See Arts in the Facts about Ethiopia chapter for more on the subject.

Dance

Dance plays a very important social role in Eritrea. It marks the major events of life, such as births and marriages, and celebrating special occasions and religious festivals. Dances traditionally permitted young girls and boys to meet, and warriors to show off their prowess.

The dances of the Kunama and Hedareb are particularly exuberant. Well-known Eritrean dancers include Dahab Fatinga.

Music

Traditional musical instruments of Eritrea have their roots in Ethiopia (see Arts in the Facts about Ethiopia chapter). They include the *krar* and *wata*, both string instruments; the *shambko*, a type of flute; and the *embilta*, a wind instrument.

Though sharing some similarities, each of the nine ethnic groups has its own distinct melodies and rhythms.

Atewebrhan Segid is considered one of the leading traditional musicians and singers in Eritrea today. The famous Eritrean singer Yemane Gebremichael, known as the 'father of the poor', died in 1997.

Others singers, both traditional and modern, include Faytinga, Berekhet Mengisteab, Osman Abdel Rahim, Idriss Mohammed Ali, Teklé Kiflemariam, Tesfay Mehari and Samuel Berhane.

[Continued on page 285]

ERITREA

A MUSEUM OF PEOPLES

Since the beginning of time, Eritrea has attracted migrants, merchants and meddlesome foreign powers. Today, these influences are reflected in the country's diverse ethnic population. The Italian historian Conti Rossini described Abyssinia (an area comprising both Ethiopia and Eritrea) as *'un museo di populi'* (a museum of peoples).

Tigrinya ትግርኛ

The Tigrinya make up approximately 50% of the Eritrean population and inhabit the densely populated central highlands, extending over the provinces of Dubub, Central and the area of Adi Keyh. They are settled farmers and are largely Orthodox Christian, with just a small minority of Muslims who are known as Jiberti. The very distinct plaited hairstyle of the women has for centuries been depicted in local art.

The Tigrinya have always been fiercely attached to their land, which has been the cause of many a dispute, and their community is traditionally tightly knit and deeply conservative. Tigrinya is one of the country's official languages.

Tigré ትግሬ

The Tigré make up about 30% of the population, and inhabit the northern lowlands, from the Sudanese frontier to the western limits of the Danakil.

A heterogeneous people, the Tigré are divided into groups and clans. Most Tigreans are Muslim, and they are both sedentary and nomadic. The sedentary farmers cultivate maize, *durra* (sorghum) and other cereals.

Tigrean society is traditionally hierarchical, with a small aristocracy known as *shemagille* ruling the masses. When the village leader dies, his power passes to his offspring.

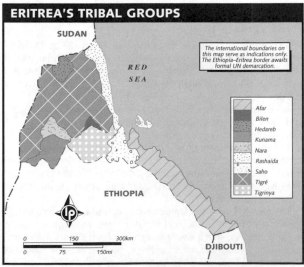

ERITREA'S TRIBAL GROUPS

SUDAN

RED SEA

The international boundaries on this map serve as indications only. The Ethiopia–Eritrea border awaits formal UN demarcation.

Afar
Bilen
Hedareb
Kunama
Nara
Rashaida
Saho
Tigré
Tigrinya

ETHIOPIA

0   150   300km
0   75   150mi

DJIBOUTI

Tigrean oral literature is rich. Fables, riddles, poetry, funeral dirges, war cries and supernatural stories colour the different elements of Tigrean life. The Tigré are also known for their love of singing and dancing, usually to the accompaniment of a drum and a *mesenko* (a type of guitar). Dances are used to celebrate many occasions, such as the discovery of a new waterhole.

Saho ሳሆ

The Saho make up 5% of the population. They inhabit the coast and the hinterland south of Asmara and Massawa. Towards the end of April, when the rains stop in the lowlands, many Saho leave the coastal area and trek with their livestock up to the highlands near Adi Keyh. When the rains stop in September, they return for the wet season on the coastal lowlands.

The Saho people are predominantly Muslim, and feelings of ethnic identity are less strong among them than other groups. Known as great pastoralists, they fought for centuries with the highlanders over the pastures of the mountains. Today they often tend other people's cattle, including those of the Tigrinya, in exchange for grain. Many Saho children (up to the age of 16) wear little leather pouches around their neck, which are full of herbs and spices to ward off evil spirits.

Some Saho are farmers who have settled in the highlands south of the country. Honey is an important part of the Saho diet and they are known as good beekeepers. In the past they were also reputed as warriors, and were often enlisted to escort trade caravans between central Ethiopia and the port of Massawa.

The Saho are organised in patrilineal descent groups. The leaders, elected by the male assembly, are known as *rezantos*, and were formerly the military chief in times of war.

Afar አፋር

The Eritrean Afars, also known as the Danakils, make up 5% of the population and inhabit the long coastal strip stretching from the Gulf of Zula into Djibouti. Predominantly nomadic pastoralists, the Afar people are Muslim, though elements of ancient ancestor-worship still persist.

Since early times the Afar territory has been divided into kingdoms and ruled by individual sultans who have always remained fiercely independent of any foreign power.

The sole inhabitants of one of the most inhospitable regions on earth, the Afars have acquired a fearsome reputation among Western travellers and explorers during the last 100 years. In 1934 Nesbitt, an English engineer, declared, 'The Danakil are ready to kill any stranger whom they come across'.

The men still carry the famous *jile* or curved knife, and some file their teeth to points. Afar oral literature reveals a high esteem for military prowess, with a whole repertoire of war chants. Today their songs tend to extol the virtues of the camel. See also the boxed text 'The Dreaded Danakils' in the Eastern Ethiopia chapter.

Hedareb ሄዳረብ

The Hedareb, along with their 'brother' tribes the Beni Amer and Beja, make up 2.5% of the population, and inhabit the northwestern valleys of Eritrea, straddling the border with Sudan.

Most Hedarebs are nomadic and travel great distances in search of pasture. They are Cushitic in origin (probably directly descended from the ancient Beja tribe) and speak mainly Tigré and an ancient Beja language (though this is in decline, as it is replaced by more dominant languages).

The **Beni Amer** are a strongly patriarchal, socially stratified, almost feudal people. Their skills as camel drivers and rearers are legendary. Many of the men scarify their cheeks with three short, vertical strokes – the Italians called them the '111 tribe'.

Bilen ብሊን

The Bilen inhabit the environs of Keren and make up approximately 2% of the population. Cushitic in origin, the Bilen are either settled Christian farmers or Muslim cattle rearers.

Bilen traditional society is organised into kinship groups. The women are known for their brightly coloured clothes and their gold, silver or copper nose rings which indicate their means and social status. Like the Beja language, Bilen is slowly being replaced by Tigré, Tigrinya and Arabic, due to intermarriage, economic interactions and because Arabic is taught in local schools. Henna tattoos that mimic diamond necklaces or little freckles are fashionable among the women.

Kunama ኩናማ

The Kunama inhabit the Gash Barka province in the southwestern corner of Eritrea, close to the Ethiopian and Sudanese border, and make up 2% of the population. Barentu is their 'capital'. The Kunama are Nilotic in origin, and very dark skinned. They are the original inhabitants of the region.

A few Kunama are Muslim, some are Christian, but the great majority are animist. According to their beliefs, the higher divinity, Anna, created the sky and the earth but is largely indifferent to human fate. The spirits, by contrast, must be placated before every event, even ploughing a field.

Kunama society is patriarchal, but contains certain matriarchal elements, including inheritance through the female side. The Kunanma only recognise the authority of the elders and the village assemblies. The community is closely knit, and many educated Kunama abandon the city to return to their traditional home.

Land is often farmed cooperatively and, after the work is finished, the village unites to celebrate with feasting and dancing. The Kunama are known for their dances, and have developed more than 25 dance forms, often re-enacting great historical events or victories. This tradition was particularly well suited to the resistance movement against Ethiopia, when the dances were greatly popularised.

Nara ናራ

The Nara, also known as the Baria, make up about 1.5% of the population and inhabit the Barka Valley near the Sudanese border. Along with the Kunama, they are the only Nilotic Eritrean tribe, and are mainly Muslim.

The Nara practice mixed farming and share many customs with their neighbours, the Kunama. In the past, skirmishes and raids from other tribes have forced many of the people to flee.

Rashaida ራሻኢዳ

The Rashaida are the only true Eritrean nomads. Making up just 0.5% of the population, they roam the northern coasts of Eritrea and Sudan, as well as the southern reaches of the Nubian desert. Like their neighbours, the Beja (related to the Hedareb), they live by raising cattle and are Muslim.

The Rashaida were the last of the Semitic people to arrive in Eritrea in the middle of the 19th century. Their language is Arabic.

The magnificent Rashaida women are famous for their black-and-red geometrically patterned dresses, and their long, heavy veils *(burkas)* elaborately embroidered with silver thread, beads and sometimes seed pearls.

The Rashaida are known for their great pride; marriage is only permitted within their own clan. They are expert goat and cattle rearers, as well as merchants and traders along the Red Sea coasts.

[Continued from page 280]

Literature

Eritrea's oral literature – in the form of folk tales, ballads, poetry, laudations etc – is rich and diverse (see the boxed text 'Oral Literature – Tales Tall & True' in the Facts about Ethiopia chapter).

Though Eritrean inscriptions date from the 7th century, written works are said to date from about the 15th century, with the *Adkeme Melgaë* (a collection of rules and laws), as well as some Arabic writings.

The Italians imposed their own language and literature (and Latin alphabet) on the country, as did the British and Ethiopians. Woldeab Woldemariam is especially venerated for his part in fighting the supression of the local languages. His *Zanta Quedamot* is a collection of children's stories designed to make the Tigrinyan alphabet more easily understood by children. Other works of the 1950s and '60s included *Embafrash*, *Awet dehri Sequay* and *Merab Melash*.

During the Struggle for Independence from Ethiopia, writing in the vernacular was encouraged through such publications as the fighters' magazine *Mahta* (Spark) and *Fitewrari* (Avant Garde).

Today Eritrean writers are publishing and producing increasing amounts of poetry, fiction and drama (mainly in Tigrinya and Arabic). Current novelists include Alemseged Tesfai, Solomon Drar and Bruk Habtemikael.

In recent times, the nine languages of the nine ethnic groups have adopted written scripts: six have adopted the Latin alphabet and one Arabic. The other two, Tigrinya and Tigré, have always used the Ge'ez-derived script of ancient Aksum.

Architecture

Eritrean vernacular architecture depends on both its ethnic and geographical origin. In the cool highlands, the traditional house is the *hidmo*. Built on a rectangular plan, the house is constructed with dry-stone walls topped with a thick, earthen roof, supported both inside and out with strong wooden pillars.

In the lowlands, where warmth is less of a concern, people traditionally live in huts. Depending on the ethnic group, the hut walls are made of adobe (sun-dried brick), wood or stone, and have thatched roofs.

In Asmara and many of the larger towns such as Keren, Massawa and Dekemhare the colonial heritage can be seen in the Italian-style buildings (see the boxed text 'An Exceptional Architectural Legacy' under Asmara later in this chapter). Many of them, in Asmara and Massawa in particular, are remarkable historical and artistic pieces, but most of them are in urgent need of restoration. There are plans to protect and restore some of them.

Painting

The country's ancient orthodox church has long provided an outlet for painting. Most church walls are painted with colourful and dramatic murals. Canvas and parchment manuscripts, some several hundred years old, are illustrated with delightful and sometimes very beautiful biblical scenes.

Painters in various media today include Mikael Adonai, Tesfay Gebremikael, Ygzaw Mikael and Giorgis Abraham.

Pottery

Pottery is one of Eritrea's oldest arts. In rural areas, earthenware pots are still commonly used for cooking, food preparation and storage.

Even in the towns, earthenware pots are preferred over metal ones for the cooking of the traditional *zigni* (meat sauce).

Theatre

Eritrean theatre is an ancient art and, like painting, has its roots in Ethiopia. Traditionally, it was staged to celebrate religious festivals, and involved music, singing, dance and acting.

During federation with Ethiopia, censorship was one of the principal constraints restricting the development of local theatre. With the emergence of the EPLF in the 1980s, new works began to appear. One of them, *The Other War* by Alemseged Tesfay, has appeared in an English anthology of contemporary African plays.

SOCIETY & CONDUCT

Given the close links between the two countries, Eritrea and Ethiopia share many traditional customs and ceremonies. For more information see this heading in the Facts about Ethiopia chapter.

It is considered impolite to ask an Eritrean his ethnic origin, religion or whether or not he was a 'fighter' (in the Struggle for Independence). There is still a bit of a stigma attached to those who weren't – even if they made sacrifices in other ways.

ERITREA

RELIGION

The population of Eritrea is almost equally divided between Christians and Muslims. Christians are primarily Orthodox – the Eritrean Orthodox church has its roots in the Ethiopian one (see Religion in the Facts about Ethiopia chapter for more details). There are also small numbers of Roman Catholics and Protestants, as a result of missionary activity. The Muslims are primarily Sunnis, with a Sufi minority.

Roughly speaking, the agriculturalist Orthodox Christians inhabit the highland region and the Muslims are concentrated in the lowlands, the coastal areas and towards the Sudanese border. Some animists inhabit the southwestern lowlands.

There are at least 18 monasteries in Eritrea. Following the raids of the famous 16th-century Muslim leader, Mohammed Gragn the Left-Handed, almost all of them were safely tucked away in very remote and inaccessible places. Three of the oldest and most important are Debre Bizen (near Nefasit), Hamm (near Senafe) and Debre Sina (near Keren).

Facts for the Visitor

SUGGESTED ITINERARIES

Though Eritrea is a small country, you should bear in mind that travelling anywhere takes time. In Dankalia, the going can be as slow as 20km/h. From Asmara to Nakfa (around 200km to the north), count on a whole day's travel. Consider Asmara as a good base for excursions into the country.

Historical Sites

Eritrea has a fair share of historical sites. In Asmara, you can spend a day or two discovering the architectural wonders of the colonial era. Lying 115km to the east of Asmara is the old Turkish port of Massawa, which is worth a visit in itself, although it's better known as the starting point for visits to the Dahlak Islands. Sooner or later the old Italian railway track will again reconnect Asmara and Massawa, and will make for one of the most spectacular train journeys on the African continent. It is worth spending two or three days exploring Massawa. The attractive and cheerful town of Keren also deserves a day or two for its colonial architecture. You could head then for Nakfa in the far north, for years the centre of the Struggle, to immerse yourself in the country's scenery and history.

South of Asmara lie the ancient ruins of Qohaito and Metara – allow at least two days there and back to visit both sites.

The Orthodox monasteries are also worth a trip for their historical importance, especially the monasteries of Debre Bizen (allow one day) and Debre Libanos (allow two to three days from Asmara and back). Remember though that most of them are off-limits to women. It is still worth the trip for women, because the monasteries are set amidst breathtaking landscapes.

Natural Sites

If you're after breathtaking landscapes, the lowland savanna of the west and far north can be explored, giving a fascinating glimpse of some of Eritrea's most colourful inhabitants, though you'll need to hire a decent 4WD to get you there. Allow at least four days for the western region, and four days for the northern region.

The tropical forest near Filfil (a must for bird-watchers and wildlife enthusiasts) is another wild area and makes a good day trip. There is good potential for hiking.

Penetration into the famously inhospitable Dankalia region to the south makes for an epic journey. It's possible by bus but it takes at least a day and a half (more if the road conditions are bad). With your own vehicle, it's only possible with a 4WD.

The Orthodox monasteries are set in remote areas offering breathtaking scenery. There are some good hiking possibilities amidst spectacular landscapes around the monastery of Debre Libanos in the south.

Diving & Snorkelling

The Dahlak Islands are still virtually untouched and are a diver's dream. There is at least one good dive centre in Massawa offering regular diving trips to the islands. With more days and money at your disposal, you could plan a diving cruise off the Dahlak Islands. Be sure to book it in advance. (See Diving under the Dahlak Islands later in this chapter.) Allow three days to a week here.

PLANNING
When to Go

Although Eritrea can be visited any time of year, the ideal time climate-wise is September to October and March to April (for more details, see Climate in the Facts about Eritrea section). If you can, avoid travelling during June to August, when it is the rainy season in the highlands and western lowlands, and the hot, torrid season in the eastern lowlands.

It's also worth trying to coincide with one or more of the country's colourful religious festivals. The most spectacular are Timkat (19 January) and Meskel (27 September) – for more details, see Public Holidays & Special Events later in this chapter. Though it can have its drawbacks, the other major religious event to look out for is the Muslim fasting month of Ramadan, which takes place during the ninth month of the Islamic calendar.

The effects of Ramadan are most felt in the Muslim-dominated areas along the coast and around the Sudanese border. It hardly features in the Christian-dominated areas such as the capital.

Maps

The best map currently available is the one produced by ITMB Publishing in Canada (1: 9,000,000). Most map suppliers should stock it, including **Stanfords** (☎ 020-7836 1321, fax 7836 0189; W www.stanfords.co.uk), in London.

A reasonable government-produced map of Eritrea (1:1,000,000) is sold in Asmara (about Nfa95), but it's hard to find. If you know you'll need a map, it's best to get one before leaving home.

If you need navigational charts of the islands or ports, the ones produced by the British Admiralty are unsurpassed. Stanfords can order these for you, and delivery takes up to one week.

What to Bring

High-factor sunscreen, hat, mosquito net, and water bottle are probably the most important things for a trip to Eritrea. A torch is essential also; many towns have electricity until midnight only, and many villages have none at all. Reasonable snorkelling equipment can be hired in Massawa. Personal items such as contact lens fluid and tampons are very difficult to find in Eritrea.

RESPONSIBLE TOURISM

The country receives relatively few tourists, so the impact on the environment has so far been fairly minimal.

The beautiful coral reefs around the Dahlak Islands are perhaps most vulnerable to damage, and in addition receive more tourists (local and foreign) than many areas.

Eritrea is a party to Cites, and it is therefore illegal to export any endangered species or their products, such as turtle or ivory. You may find turtle meat in restaurants, and turtle and elephant souvenirs in shops (particularly in Asmara); hawkers may offer you turtle eggs (particularly in Massawa). It's best to avoid these, as all species of marine turtle are currently threatened. Coral and shell collection is now discouraged too.

Try to resist the temptation to buy any genuinely old artefacts, such as manuscripts, scrolls and Bibles, found in some of the shops in the capital. Eritrea has already lost a huge amount of its heritage, particularly during the Italian era. Such exports will soon be illegal anyway.

Water is an extremely precious and scarce resource in Eritrea. Take care not to waste it.

See this heading in the Facts for the Visitor chapter under Ethiopia for more information.

TOURIST OFFICES

The best places to go for information are **Travel House International** (☎ 20 18 81/2, fax 12 07 51; e soloabr@eol.com.er; PO Box 5579, Asmara) and **Explore Eritrea Travel & Tours** (☎ 12 12 42, 12 55 55, fax 12 79 08; e explore@tse.com.er; PO Box 2061, Asmara). These travel agencies will help you, but their interests obviously lie in selling you a tour.

Outside Eritrea, the Eritrean embassy or consulate in your home country (the few that exist) is your best bet, but tourist literature is generally limited.

In France contact the **Association France-Erythrée** (e asmaraparis@hotmail.com; 6 rue Charles Bassée, 94120 Fontenay-sous-Bois).

VISAS & DOCUMENTS

For general information on travel insurance, see the Facts for the Visitor chapter under Ethiopia. You'll need an international driving permit if you are planning to drive in Eritrea.

Visas

All foreign nationals require visas for entry to Eritrea. Requirements tend to vary arbitrarily from one Eritrean embassy or consulate to another. Eritrea is also a very young country, and visa requirements are likely to change, so check with the relevant embassy.

Visas should be obtained from the Eritrean embassy or consulate before you leave your home country. If there isn't any diplomatic representation in your home country, obtain a visa from the nearest one. If this is inconvenient, you can contact the consular section of the **Ministry of Foreign Affairs** (☎ 12 71 08,

ERITREA

fax 12 37 88; PO Box 190, Asmara) in Asmara. Normally, you'll be asked to fax your details to immigration in advance of your arrival. You'll then be issued with a visa at your port of entry. If you're planning to visit neighbouring countries first, it might be easier to get a visa there, although it's not possible in Ethiopia.

You can also contact the two best travel agencies in Asmara (see Tourist Offices earlier). They can offer a tourist visa service for about US$20. You'll need to fax them details of your passport pages and give them at least two weeks to organise the visa, which will then be faxed back to you.

For visa applications, you'll need your passport (valid for at least three months) and one passport photo. Some embassies also require some or all of the following: a valid return air ticket, travellers cheques worth US$40 per day for the duration of your visit, and an up-to-date yellow-fever vaccination certificate.

The visa application form may require an address in Eritrea and a 'reference'. If you don't have any, find a hotel and tour operator later in this chapter, and use these names. Applications can be made by post, and normally take 48 hours to process.

You usually have to travel within three months of the date of issue of the visa.

Tourist visas are for single entry only, and are valid for 30 days from the date of arrival in Eritrea. They cost around €48.

To get a business visa, you'll need a letter from your sponsoring company stating the purpose of the trip. Business visas cost US$170 or US$194 (single/multiple entry, valid for three months).

Visa Extensions In Asmara, the **Department of Immigration** *(☎ 20 00 33; Denden St)* will extend your visa twice for a further 30 days. This costs US$40 (except for US citizens, who pay US$25) and you will need one photo, photocopies of your passport details and visa page, and a 20¢ stamp. Payment must be made in cash and with exact change. Applications must be made before the old visa expires.

Travel Permits

Eritrea's 'national treasures' are protected by paperwork. To visit many places, you'll need to get a special permit from the capital. Though this is a bit time-consuming and irksome, it means that the sites attract only those really interested in them. If you're taking a tour, your agency should do this for you. Bring your passport.

To obtain a permit to visit any of the archaeological sites of Eritrea, contact the **National Museum office** *(☎ 11 99 02; PO Box 5284, Asmara)* in the old school building next door to the Comboni Sisters' convent school and opposite the Department of Water Resources. It keeps normal business hours. You'll need your passport and Nfa50 per site. The paper can be issued immediately; the staff are helpful and efficient. You can walk there in 15 minutes from Harnet Ave or take a taxi (Nfa25). Tell the driver it's next to the Barka school.

To visit the Dahlak Islands, obtain permission from the **Eritrean Shipping Lines office** *(☎ 55 24 75, 55 27 20, fax 55 23 91)* in Massawa. Note that you'll need US dollars cash to pay for the permit, so plan ahead.

To visit the monasteries obtain a permit from the **Orthodox Tewahedo Church Headquarters** *(☎ 18 20 98, 18 65 44)* in Asmara (ask for the 'monastery tour application'). It costs about Nfa70 per monastery.

To go to Filfil, you will need a permission paper from the Ministry of Tourism in Asmara. It's free.

At the time of writing, a permit was also necessary to go to Nakfa. It is obtainable from the Ministry of Tourism (though you might be redirected to the police headquarters).

EMBASSIES & CONSULATES
Eritrean Embassies & Consulates

The Eritrean embassy in Addis Ababa, Ethiopia, was closed when this edition went to print. Eritrean embassies and consulates include the following:

Australia (☎ 02-6290 1991, fax 6282 1984) 16 Bulwarra Close O'Malley, ACT 2606
Canada (☎ 613-234 3989, fax 234 6213) Suite 610, 75 Albert St, Ottawa K1P 5E7
Djibouti (☎ 35-86-06, fax 25-02-12) Rue de Kampala, Djibouti town
Egypt (☎ 34411955, fax 3030516) 6 El Fallah St, Al Muhandesein, PO Box 2624 Cairo
France (☎ 01 43 06 15 56, fax 43 06 07 51) 31-33 rue Lecourbe, 75015 Paris
Germany (☎ 30-4467460, fax 44674621) Stavanger Str 18, 10439 Berlin
Italy (☎ 06-4274 1293, fax 4208 6806) Via Boncompagni No 16 Int 6, 00187 Roma
Kenya (☎ 444 3164, fax 444 3165) New Rehema House, Raphta Rd, 2nd floor, Westlands, PO Box 38651, Nairobi
Sudan (☎ 11-483834, fax 483835) Khartoum 2-St 39, PO Box 11618

Old Russian tank outside Keren

Shepherd, Senafe

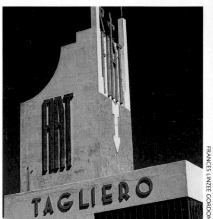

Fiat Tagliero Building, Asmara

Archaeologists surveying the remains of a 3rd-century city near Adi Keyh

Priest at the festival of Meskal, Asmara

Yellow Fiat taxis ply the streets of Asmara

Goatherd, Sittona

UK (☎ 207-713 0096, fax 713 0161) 96 White Lion St, London N1 9PF

US (☎ 202-319 1991, fax 319 1304) 1708 New Hampshire Ave, NW Washington DC 20009

Yemen (☎ 1-209422, fax 214088) Western Safia, Algeria St, Building No 68, PO Box 11040 San'a

Embassies & Consulates in Eritrea

Street names are given when they are reliable, definitive (there was a major renaming process at the time of writing) and useful. Otherwise, check on the map or ring your embassy for directions. All embassies and consulates are based in Asmara, and include the following:

Djibouti (☎ 12 59 90)

Egypt (☎ 12 00 56) Marsa Fatuma St

Ethiopia Franklin Roosevelt St. Closed at the time of writing.

France (☎ 12 65 99) Nakfa Ave

Germany (☎ 18 66 70) Saba Building, Andinet Ave

Italy (☎ 12 01 60) Keskese St

Sudan (☎ 12 06 72) Hazemo St

UK (☎ 12 01 45) BDHO Ave

USA (☎ 12 00 04) Franklin Roosevelt St

Yemen (☎ 18 13 99)

CUSTOMS

On arrival at the airport, any major electronic items (such as expensive cameras, laptops, video cameras) must be registered at customs. This is to deter black-market business. On departure the items will be signed off. If anything is stolen during your stay in Eritrea, make sure you immediately obtain a police statement registering the loss.

Duty-free allowances include 1L of alcohol and 200 cigarettes. Rifles and shotguns for hunting require an import permit.

Declaration of foreign currency is not required. It is strictly forbidden in theory to export any nakfa from Eritrea. In practice, an allowance of up to Nfa50 is permitted to allow for any problems or needs.

MONEY

For general advice on safety issues, see Security in the Facts for the Visitor chapter under Ethiopia.

Currency

The nakfa (Nfa) was introduced in November 1997 to replace the old Ethiopian birr. It is divided into 100 cents, and is available in 5, 10, 25, 50 and 100 cent pieces, and in 1, 5, 10, 20, 50 and 100 nakfa notes.

Exchange Rates

The nakfa was initially valued on a par with the Ethiopian birr. Since it was floated in mid-1998, military expenditure on the war greatly weakened the economy, and the nakfa suffered correspondingly.

Note that foreign exchange bureaus and banks in Asmara charge an intermediary rate, about 30% better than the official rate, but still much lower than the black-market rate. Official exchange rates at the time of writing were as follows:

Australia	A$1	=	Nfa6.37
Canada	C$1	=	Nfa6.89
euro zone	€1	=	Nfa11.01
Kenya	KSh100	=	Nfa12.63
New Zealand	NZ$1	=	Nfa5.63
UK	UK£1	=	Nfa15.50
USA	US$1	=	Nfa9.61

Exchanging Money

US dollars (cash or travellers cheques) are the best currency to carry. Not only are US dollars easier to exchange outside the capital, but you have to pay for certain things in US dollars, including the government hotels, a permit to visit the Dahlak Islands, visa extensions, some air tickets and the departure tax. The rate of exchange for US dollars is also better than for other currencies.

Currently the only bank authorised to issue US dollars cash is the Commercial Bank in the capital, so be careful not to get stuck with cheques only.

There is one bank at Asmara airport and several in Asmara, as well as several exchange bureaus. Some of the larger hotels in Asmara also exchange money or travellers cheques.

Outside the capital, there are banking facilities in the main towns.

Banks Remember to take your passport to the bank; sometimes it's needed even for exchanging cash. Because of queues and bureaucracy, the process can be lengthy (particularly in the smaller rural branches, which have to telephone Asmara for the exchange rate). In Asmara, there are a number of foreign exchange bureaus that offer speedy exchange facilities at fairly worthwhile rates. They have shorter queues than banks and keep longer hours.

All major currencies can be exchanged in the capital; in rural areas, sometimes only US dollars are exchanged. Banks charge a commission of around 1.3% for dollars and 1.5% for other currencies.

There are currently no ATMs in Eritrea.

ERITREA

Black Market You'll meet plenty of unofficial moneychangers around the main post office in Asmara, but exchanging money outside the banks or exchange bureaus is illegal. If you do indulge, make the transaction with people you know, and not in the street. Be aware that you're taking a big risk.

Travellers Cheques Most of the capital's major banks and hotels, some airline offices and some travel agencies accept travellers cheques. Most exchange bureaus don't charge any commission on travellers cheques, but they might apply a slightly inferior rate than for cash. Shop around.

As with cash, travellers cheques are best carried in US dollars, although most major currencies can be exchanged in the banks in the capital and some banks elsewhere.

Credit Cards The larger hotels in the capital, some airlines and, increasingly, some travel agents now accept credit cards. A commission of up to 7% is sometimes charged – check in advance. There are plans to introduce facilities for cash withdrawals with credit cards at the Commercial Bank of Eritrea – check on progress when you get there.

International Transfers If you need a transfer urgently, the Western Union is the probably the best bet, though it's not cheap. You will need someone at home to deposit the money; it will then be transferred immediately via a computer to the recipient bank. The whole process should take no more than a day (the transfer itself will take around 20 minutes). In Asmara, the Commercial Bank of Eritrea in Harnet Ave acts as an agent of Western Union. The Himbol Exchange office on Bahti Meskerem Square can also handle money transfers.

Costs

In general, Eritrea is a very cheap country to visit. The only expensive activities are car hire, some tours, and getting to and around the islands. Because of transportation costs, food and beer in the towns in the hinterland are a little more expensive than in Asmara.

At the time of writing, some sample prices were Nfa4.92 for a litre of diesel fuel, Nfa0.40 for a local phone call, Nfa50/20 for a meal in a town/country restaurant (without alcohol), and Nfa5 for a beer. Budget rooms without bathroom cost from Nfa20 to Nfa50; midrange rooms cost from Nfa120 to Nfa160.

Tipping & Bargaining

The practice of tipping has been introduced in Eritrea recently and is expected in the towns only. In the rural areas, you may even have your tip returned to you.

In the smaller restaurants in the towns, service is included, and Eritreans don't tip unless the service has been exceptional (in this case, Nfa2 to Nfa5 would be an appropriate amount to leave). In bars and cafés, loose coins are sometimes left. However, in the larger restaurants accustomed to tourists, at least 10% will be expected, and in the larger hotels, staff will expect a bare minimum of Nfa5 to Nfa10.

Unlike in other places in Africa, corruption is not the norm in Eritrea. Overcharging of tourists is very rare in the country, and prices are usually firmly fixed; haggling can offend Eritreans. However, all the usual discounts apply, and it's always worth asking for them – for long stays in hotels, extended car hire and the like.

The one exception where haggling is almost expected is in the local shops and markets; there are no fixed prices. In shops, prices are rarely displayed.

POST & COMMUNICATIONS
Post

The Eritrean postal service is considered quite reliable, albeit not the speediest. Postage for the first 200g is Nfa3 worldwide, except for neighbouring countries, which are cheaper. Postcards cost Nfa2 worldwide.

Express Mail Service (EMS; ☎ 12 50 29; near the post office) offers worldwide delivery of both letters and parcels, but it's relatively expensive. It costs Nfa170 to Nfa187 to send a 0.5kg parcel to Europe, the USA or Australia, and Nfa50 for each additional 0.5kg. Courier services, such as **DHL** (☎ 12 02 10), are available in the capital.

There is a free poste restante service in the capital; you'll need to show your passport to collect mail. Address mail to Poste Restante, Post Office, Asmara, Eritrea.

Telephone & Fax

When calling Eritrea from abroad, the country code is ☎ 291. The major towns (Asmara, Massawa, Dekemhare and Mendefera) must be prefixed by the number 1, followed by the six-figure number.

When calling abroad from Eritrea, call ☎ 00 followed by the country code. Direct dialling from main towns in Eritrea (Asmara, Dekemhare, Barentu, Adi Keyh, Teseney and Mendefera) is only possible to Europe and the USA. For all other countries, you'll need to go through the operator.

International calls are best made from the telecommunications office found in all the main towns. Faxes can be sent and received from some of the telecommunications offices.

International rates are the same all day, and costs are calculated per minute: Nfa17 for the USA, the UK, Italy, Germany and Sweden; and Nfa22.40 for Australia, Canada and New Zealand.

National calls cost between Nfa1.15 and Nfa5.45 (40¢ within Asmara). Telephone cards are available in denominations of Nfa25, Nfa50 and Nfa100.

It is possible to make calls and send or receive faxes from the larger hotels, but rates are much more expensive than from telecommunications offices.

For directory assistance call ☎ 97. For the international operator call ☎ 98.

Email & Internet Access
Internet centres have mushroomed in Asmara. The cost is usually around Nfa10 per minute. Connections were pretty slow at the time of writing, but you can expect this to improve. Outside the capital Internet access is harder to find. There are a few outlets with Internet access in Massawa and Keren.

DIGITAL RESOURCES
There are a few websites with useful information on Eritrea, including the following:

Awate (W www.awate.com) This is a political opposition site, based in the US

All Africa (W www.allafrica.com/eritrea) Specialising in Africa, this site has a page on Eritrea, with updated news about the country

CIA (W www.cia.gov/cia/publications/factbook/geos/er.html) This site has (brief) information on the country's main sectors (geography, people, government etc)

Dehai (W www.dehai.org) Compiled by Eritreans based in the US, Dehai is a well-informed site. It has much information on politics and history, with daily updated news on Eritrea gathered from various sources.

Eritrea1 (W www.eritrea1.org) This is useful for those seeking a point of view different from the official stance about Eritrea

Shaebia (W www.shaebia.org) This is the site of the People's Front for Democracy and Justice (PFDJ). Various topics are covered, including a couple of pages devoted to tourism and culture. There's also a link to the *Eritrean Profile*.

BOOKS
Few books on Eritrea are available, at least in European languages. Italian is the one exception: colonial histories, travel accounts and novels of the late 19th and early 20th centuries abound. Some older books written about Abyssinia include the area covered by Eritrea (see the Books section in the Facts for the Visitor chapter under Ethiopia).

Guidebooks
Eritrea at a Glance, edited by Mary Houdek and Leonardo Oriolo, is an excellent, locally produced book. Despite its title, it's really a guide to Asmara rather than Eritrea, making it a good choice if you're going to be spending any length of time in the capital. Try also to get hold of *Eritrea – A Country Handbook* published by the Ministry of Information of Eritrea. A recent valuable book is *Massawa and the Red Sea*, published by Alliance Française in Asmara. It features pictures of Massawa along with comments written by historians.

If you read Italian, *Eritrea* by Andrea Semplici is a very comprehensive, if rather idiosyncratic, guide to Eritrea. Though practical details and maps are a bit lacking, the depth of research and sheer enthusiasm for the country more than compensate. The best German guide is *Eritrea Ein Reiseführer*.

History & Politics
The Struggle has inspired a rash of gripping stories, many of them eyewitness accounts. Three of the best-known are *Against All Odds* by Dan Connell, *Even the Stones Are Burning* by Roy Pateman, and *Revolution at Dusk* by Robert Papstein. Sadly, no account in English by an Eritrean fighter or historian has so far emerged. *Women and the Eritrean Revolution* by A Wilon recounts the important role of women throughout the Struggle. All these books can be found in Asmara.

NEWSPAPERS & MAGAZINES
The best-known local publication is the widely read *Hadas Eritrea* (New Eritrea), a newspaper published daily except Sunday and Monday in both Tigrinya and Arabic.

The *Eritrea Profile* is also published weekly by the Ministry of Information. It's popular with the expat community in Asmara and is available every Saturday from roaming street vendors. It's a good source of local information, including weather forecasts, pharmacies that do 'night duty' and so on.

ERITREA

ERITREA

RADIO & TV

Eritrean national radio, known as 'Voice of the Broad Masses', broadcasts three times a day in at least four of Eritrea's national languages (on 945 kHz medium wave and 41 and 49 metre bands short wave).

The BBC World Service can be picked up on short-wave radios.

Eritrean television broadcasts every evening from around 6.30pm in Tigray, Arabic, Tigrinya and English. You can tune in to the English programmes at 9.30pm.

PHOTOGRAPHY & VIDEO

Eritrea, like Italy, uses the PAL system. It differs from France (which uses the SECAM system), and the USA, Canada and Japan (which use NTSC). The three systems are not compatible.

Decent print film is quite widely available in the capital and costs around Nfa35 for a 36-exposure Kodak film. Some slide film is also available, but only in the capital. Outside Asmara, it's difficult to find film except in the larger towns, and it may not always be within its use-by date.

Photographic equipment is very limited in Asmara, but photo development is of a good quality and fast (it can be done in around 30 minutes for about Nfa110).

For technical tips on photographing in the Horn of Africa, see the boxed text 'Tips for Photographers in the Horn' in the Ethiopia Facts for the Visitor chapter.

Restrictions

After 30 years of war, certain subjects in Eritrea are considered 'sensitive'. Avoid military and police installations and personnel, and even airports and bridges. Civil engineering and government buildings are off-limits too.

Outside the capital, it's fine to take pictures of war relics. You'll use up a whole film on your first burnt-out tank, but by the end of the journey, they won't even turn your head.

Photographing People

In some areas, people such as the colourful Rashaida and enigmatic Afars are more accustomed to photographers and understandably want to benefit by it too. They may ask for money. The fee should always be agreed in advance. In some places, you may be charged a fee for video cameras, though this seems to be randomly applied.

See also Photographing People in the Ethiopia Facts for the Visitor chapter.

TIME

Eritrea is three hours ahead of GMT/UTC.

ELECTRICITY

Confusingly, Eritrea uses both 110V and 220V at both 50Hz and 60Hz AC. If you're planning to take a laptop with you, make sure you have something to protect it against the variations in current, as power surges occur frequently. Alternatively, a UPS (Uninterrupted Power Supply) will protect it and can be bought locally.

A variety of electrical sockets are found around the country. Many are like the Italian type and take plugs with two round prongs rated at 600W. It's a good idea to bring an adapter; visitors from the US and Canada (with 120V at 60Hz) should be careful to choose one appropriate for their equipment.

LAUNDRY

Laundries are found mainly in Asmara; they offer efficient and cheap services (see Information under Asmara later in this chapter).

The larger hotels offer laundry services, but at expensive prices.

TOILETS

Both the sit-down and squat types of toilet are found in Eritrea, reflecting Italian and Arab influences, respectively.

In the highlands, the sit-down type tends to prevail. In the Muslim lowlands such as in Massawa, the squat style is more commonly found (but only in the cheaper hotels). Toilet paper is very rare in either, so carry your own.

In the small villages of the lowlands, you'll be lucky to find a bush. The inhabitants simply demarcate an area outside the village, point you in that direction, and off you trot.

If you're caught short in the towns, the hotels are the best places to head, and unlike in Europe, wouldn't dream of turning you away in your moment of need. Some of the Italian-designed cafés also have toilets.

HEALTH

Asmara is reasonably well endowed with medical facilities, though it's always best to bring your own supplies of any prescription drugs you use, as these may not be available locally. Outside the capital, facilities are lacking.

Environmental Hazards

Don't forget that the closer you get to the equator, the more vicious the sun becomes. If you're spending time outdoors, use a hat, sunglasses and high-protection sunscreen.

The risk of skin infection is high in the heat, particularly in coastal areas such as Massawa, where humidity is also high.

If you're a diver, you should note that there is currently no decompression chamber in Eritrea.

Infectious Diseases

Common conditions travellers encounter in Eritrea are diarrhoea, giardia, dehydration and worm infestations. For more information on these and other health issues, see Health in the Facts for the Visitor chapter in Ethiopia.

HIV is a growing problem. UNAIDS estimates that at least 2.9% of the population are HIV positive. In 2001 AIDS was the second leading cause of death (it was only the 10th highest in 1996). Public awareness campaigns are limited by the deep conservatism of Eritrean society.

Insect-Borne Diseases

Malaria is endemic on the coastal plain, in the western lowlands and around Keren (anywhere less than 2000m above sea level), particularly during the dry season. Get advice on malaria prevention before you go, but if you need to stock up on antimalarials, the drugs (with the exception of mefloquine or Lariam) are widely available in Asmara.

Dengue fever is also prevalent, so wherever you go it's important to take steps to prevent mosquito bites.

WOMEN TRAVELLERS

With a very low national crime rate and an unusually liberal policy towards women, Eritrea must be one of the safest and least restrictive countries on the continent for women travellers.

Women NGO workers report few hassles in Eritrea, and in Asmara they happily stroll the streets after dark. Use your common sense, though – all the usual precautions apply, such as safety in numbers.

Smoking or drinking and wearing lots of make-up are sometimes construed by the nation's less enlightened males as signs of promiscuity (as this is also the way the local prostitutes behave). As a result of Hollywood cinematic glamour, foreign women are sometimes considered easier 'prey' than local women. An invitation to the cinema, for example, isn't necessarily to watch a film.

There are a number of women's organisations in Eritrea. In Asmara, the **National Union of Eritrean Women** (NUEW; ☎ 11 95 14, fax

12 06 28) welcomes visitors at its headquarters. It has a small library with a collection of books on women.

GAY & LESBIAN TRAVELLERS

Homosexuality is severely condemned by both traditional and religious cultures and remains a topic of absolute taboo. Eritrea's penal code concerning homosexuality is currently still based on Ethiopian law (see Gay & Lesbian Travellers in the Ethiopia chapter). Although homosexuality obviously exists in Eritrea, local gays behave with extreme discretion and caution. Gay and lesbian travellers are advised to do likewise.

SENIOR TRAVELLERS

Traditionally, older citizens are accorded great respect in Eritrea, and senior travellers will be made to be feel very welcome. Eritrea's capital is well equipped with good-quality hotels, restaurants and medical care and should cater to most senior travellers' needs. Outside the capital, facilities are much more limited. Although most tourist sites can be visited in one- to three-day trips from the capital, roads are very rough in parts, and journeys are long, hot and hard (particularly on the back), even in the best 4WD.

DISABLED TRAVELLERS

Taxis are widely available in towns and are good for getting around, though none have wheelchair access. Car rental with a driver is easy to organise, if expensive. In Asmara, at least one hotel (Intercontinental Hotel) has facilities for travellers with wheelchairs. A few hotels have lifts.

Eritrea's Struggle for Independence left many of its inhabitants disabled. Land mines continue to maim the population. Disabled visitors can expect to find a sympathetic and accommodating attitude from Eritreans.

TRAVEL WITH CHILDREN

Eritreans are very welcoming and open towards children. However, many useful facilities for children – such as cots in hotels, safety seats in hired cars, and highchairs in restaurants – are almost totally lacking.

Items such as nappies, baby food and mineral water are available in the expat supermarkets of Asmara, but they are quite expensive.

Should you need them, there are a few good medical facilities in the capital. See also Travel with Children in the Ethiopia Facts for the Visitor chapter.

DANGERS & ANNOYANCES
Crime
After independence, Eritrea's capital Asmara became known as the most peaceful capital on the continent. Muggings were unheard of, pickpocketings rare and everyone lets everyone else get on with their business.

Asmara is still an extremely peaceful place and the crime rate is incredibly low, but minor incidents of street crime are now occasionally reported. With the economy squeezed ever tighter by the war with Ethiopia, such incidents will inevitably become more common. By 2000 begging had certainly increased, particularly in Asmara. Markets all over the world attract pickpockets, and no less so in Asmara, so take some basic precautions. Outside the capital, the crime rate is even lower.

In the far western and northern areas bordering Sudan, a few incidents of bandit and terrorist attacks against Eritrean civilians were reported in the late 1990s. The Eritrean Islamic Jihad (EIJ) was blamed for some attacks. However, there is no evidence that foreign travellers are being targeted specifically. Foreign embassies are a good source of up-to-date information on security issues in the country.

Land Mines
After 30 years of war, the biggest threat outside the capital is the risk of land mines and unexploded munitions. Despite the government's best efforts, thousands still litter the countryside; they continue sporadically to kill and maim the population.

Most mines are confined to the sites of major battle fronts but there is some element of risk anywhere fighting has occurred. Areas north and west of Keren and around Ghinda are still thought to be heavily mined.

Maiming Mines

During the Struggle, two million land mines were laid, which works out at almost one for every Eritrean inhabitant. However, the guerrillas quickly learnt to turn the deadly weapons against those who had laid them. Replanted up to 10 or 12 times, the mines accounted for 30% of all EPLF victories.

Since independence, the government has tried hard to rid the land of mines, but thousands still remain. Between 1995 and 1998, 3500 antitank and antipersonnel mines exploded. Almost all victims were children.

Check with local government and local village officials before travelling in less-frequented areas. Never stray off the road. If you're walking, keep to well-trodden tracks and avoid hiking in river beds. Forget about 'war souvenirs' – you shouldn't touch anything. A useful phrase when out walking is *Fenjy allo?* (Are there mines here?).

LEGAL MATTERS
Foreign visitors are subject to the laws of the country in which they are travelling. Penalties for possession, use or trafficking of illegal drugs are strictly enforced in Eritrea. Convicted offenders can expect long jail sentences, fines and possible confiscation of personal property.

Note that consumption of the mildly intoxicating leaf *chat* is not permitted in Eritrea.

BUSINESS HOURS
Private businesses and shops keep various hours. In general, most open from 8am to noon and 2pm to 6pm Monday to Friday, and on Saturday morning. Many shops in the capital stay open until 7.30pm.

Most banks open from 8am to 11am and from 2pm to 4pm Monday to Friday, and from 8am to 12.30pm on Saturday.

In Massawa and Assab, government offices open from 6am to 2.30pm Monday to Friday during the hot season (June to September) and from 8am to noon and 4pm to 6.30pm Monday to Friday the rest of the year. Private businesses open from 6am to noon and 3pm to 6pm Monday to Friday the whole year.

In Muslim areas, business hours are shorter during Ramadan, and cafés and restaurants may be closed during the day.

PUBLIC HOLIDAYS & SPECIAL EVENTS
Eritrea's public holidays can be divided into three categories: national (secular) holidays, Christian Orthodox holidays and Islamic holidays.

The country follows the Gregorian (European) calendar, with 12 months to the year. However, the Eritrean Orthodox church, which is derived from the Ethiopian Orthodox church, follows the Julian calendar, which has 13 months (see the boxed text 'Be Seven Years Younger' in the Ethiopia Facts for the Visitor chapter). Some events, therefore, trail those of the Gregorian calendar by around one week. Muslim holidays are based on the Hejira calendar, which is 10 or 11 days shorter than the Gregorian calendar, so these holidays fall 10 or 11 days earlier each year. The precise dates are determined by the sighting of the moon.

National holidays include the following:

New Year's Day 1 January
International Women's Day 8 March
Workers' Day 1 May
Liberation Day 24 May
Martyrs' Day 20 June
Start of the Armed Struggle 1 September

The main Christian Orthodox holidays are:

Leddet (Christmas) 7 January
Timkat (Epiphany) 19 January
Tensae (Easter) March/April (variable)
Kiddus Yohannes (Orthodox New Year) 11 September
Meskel (Finding of the True Cross) 27 September

Islamic holidays include Lailat al-Miraji, Eid al-Fitr, Eid al-Adha Arafa (the Muslim New Year), Al-Ashura, and Eid Mawlid al-Nabi (the Prophet's birthday).

For more information on the religious holidays listed in this section, see Public Holidays & Special Events in the Facts for the Visitor chapter in Ethiopia.

ACTIVITIES
Hiking & Camel Trekking
Eritrea has good potential for hiking in the various hills and mountain ranges in the east of the country. Another good place is the tropical forest around Filfil. However, because of the recent war, travellers should carefully check the safety of the areas they wish to visit with the local authorities (for risk of land mines etc) and should consider hiring a local guide.

Some travel agents in the capital now offer treks into the hinterland by camel (for details, see Organised Tours under Getting Around later in this chapter).

Water Activities
Eritrea's best-known activity is diving in the Red Sea. The Dahlak Islands off the coast near Massawa is currently the only place where organised diving and snorkelling takes place.

Diving is principally organised through various charter boats that tour the Dahlak Islands. Tours generally last a week, but occasionally two- or three-day trips are possible. If you're interested you should book well in advance through a travel agency in Asmara (see Organised Tours under Getting Around

later in this chapter). You can also organise your own day trips by motorboat. Diving equipment can be hired in Massawa.

Though the islands are opening up, access is still a little limited, monopolised by a few boat companies charging high prices. This may well serve to protect the reefs from too many tourists in the future. At the moment, most destinations are out of the reach of budget travellers. If you can afford a trip – even just snorkelling – the opportunity is not to be missed. When you're prepared for the conditions and the demands, you're likely to be rewarded with some of the best diving of your life. Get there before the crowds do.

Water-skiing is possible in Massawa.

For more information on water activities, see the Dahlak Islands later in this chapter, and also the boxed text 'The Red Sea: An Oasis of Life', earlier in this chapter.

The Joys of Diving in Eritrea

The southern waters of the Red Sea around Eritrea are known principally for four things: the huge shoals of fish, the large size of individual specimens of fish, the fishes' apparent lack of fear of humans and the significant number of unusual species, even by Red Sea standards.

Snappers, jackfish, sweetlips, unicorn fish and fusiliers all form enormous schools. Giant specimens of groper are quite frequently seen, and large Napoleons, bumphead parrotfish and lyretail cod are common sightings.

The southern Red Sea was once famous for its shark population but shark life is not as abundant as it once was due to commercial shark fishing. However, reef, grey, hammerhead and nurse sharks, turtles, stingrays and dolphins are all common. Manta rays and dugongs are occasionally seen.

Divers should be aware that the reef is a very fragile ecosystem. Avoid touching living organisms or dragging equipment across the reef. Polyps can be damaged by even the gentlest contact. Maintain proper buoyancy control. Resist also the temptation to collect or buy corals or shells, and ensure that you take home all your rubbish, especially plastics.

Water temperatures range from 27° to 29°C, so a swimskin or 3mm tropical wetsuit offers more than adequate protection.

For more information, refer to Lonely Planet's *Diving & Snorkeling Red Sea*.

Fishing

Boats can be hired in Massawa for fishing trips in the Red Sea. Rods and gaffs can be borrowed free from the boat operators, but you'll need to bring your own hooks and lures.

ACCOMMODATION

Tourism is still in its infancy in Eritrea, and accommodation is limited. During the war, many of the old Italian hotels were destroyed. Those that remain are badly in need of decoration and, in some cases, serious restoration.

The Eritreans are a very polite, soft-spoken people; what's missing in amenities is made up for in their hospitality and friendliness. Theft from hotels is very rare here.

Camping

There are no official camping grounds in Eritrea. In theory, if you have your own tent, you are free to camp anywhere, apart from near the obvious off-limits sites, such as military installations. Be very careful to check that the area you are in is free of land mines (see Dangers & Annoyances earlier in this chapter). Take care not to start fires, and take all your litter away with you.

Hotels

Asmara has hotels of all categories, though some of the popular medium-priced hotels are often booked up, and reservations are strongly advised. Currently, the government is trying to sell the dozen or so state-owned hotels in the capital.

Many of the country's cheaper hotels double as brothels. Conversely, a few of the Muslim-run hotels allow only married or single-sex couples to share rooms. Many budget hotels also have cold water only (not a worry in the lowlands). Though breakfast is provided by some, you will usually be charged extra for it.

All the small towns have hotels. They're often pretty basic affairs. Often rooms contain up to six beds (though you can pay for the whole room) and many lack running water (you get a bucket shower instead).

In the torrid lowlands, including Massawa, many people sleep on beds in the courtyards and on the verandas or rooftops. The cheap hotels, which don't have air-conditioning or ceiling fans, usually have similar arrangements.

In the rural areas, accommodation is sometimes little more than a bed in a hut, without running water, electricity or even washing facilities.

In Eritrea, a room with a double bed is usually called a 'single', and a room with twin beds a 'double'. Prices for one and two people are often the same.

Prices for budget accommodation averages US$6 to US$10 for singles and US$8 to US$15 for doubles. For mid-range hotels, you'll pay about US$15 to US$30 for singles and US$20 to US$60 for doubles. A five-star place to stay will set you back up to US$210. These prices apply to hotels in the capital. In the rest of the country, rates are usually cheaper.

FOOD

Eritrea is not exactly the gastronomic capital of Africa. It's unusual to have a half-heated reaction to local food – you'll either love it or loathe it. Many travellers will find that they loathe it initially but grow to love it.

More important than the style or quality of the food is the ceremony. You won't forget your first meal, shared from a large plate with fellow diners. If you don't take to it, you could always try the ubiquitous, if rather bland and overcooked, pasta dishes.

Most types of food are very reasonably priced, the only exception being imported food in some of the capital's supermarkets. A dinner for two comes to around Nfa60. People eat early in Eritrea (usually between 6.30pm and 8pm).

Italian

Along with their roads, towns and bridges, the Italians left another legacy: *macchiato* and spaghetti. Italian dishes are available in all restaurants throughout Eritrea. Outside the capital, these may be limited to just one dish: lasagne or spaghetti bolognese. However, it fills the gap.

In the capital, the choice is much more extensive, with both *primi piatti* (first courses), usually pasta, and *secondi piatti* (main dishes), usually fish or meat, on offer.

Traditional

Traditional Eritrean cuisine is the same as in Ethiopia – see the Food section in the Facts for the Visitor chapter under Ethiopia for a complete rundown of typical local dishes, ingredients and food etiquette, and see the Language chapter for a glossary of food terms. Most of the terms used are the same as in Ethiopia, except for *wat*, the fiery and ubiquitous sauce, which is known as *tsebhi* in Tigrinya; *injera*, which is sometimes called *taita* in Tigrinya; *tibsi* (fried meat with garlic and onion); and *kai wat* (meat in spicy sauce), known as *zigni* in Tigrinya.

If you like hot food, try the delicious *silsi*, a peppery fried tomato and onion sauce served for breakfast. Another very popular breakfast dish is *ful* (based on chickpea puree), with *frittata*, omelette or scrambled egg jazzed up with a bit of pepper.

Capretto often features on menus. It's roast goat, sometimes served like a rack of lamb.

Desserts aren't a traditional part of the diet and usually consist of fruit salad or synthetic creme caramel. Eritrean yoghurt (served in a glass) and the mild local cheeses are a much better bet. The latter are sometimes served with bread and exquisite local honey, which makes for a terrific and easily prepared picnic.

In the western lowlands, look out for little boys selling *legamat*, a deep-fried dough sold hot in newspaper cones in the early morning; it's delicious for an early breakfast.

In the far west, the food is heavily influenced by the proximity of Sudan. One popular and very tasty dish is *sheia*, lamb drizzled with oil and herbs then barbecued on very hot stones until it sizzles. It's delicious. It's usually served with a lentil dish *ades*, and a stock-like soup known as *merek*.

In Massawa, the Arabic influence is evident. Kebabs and Yemeni-style charcoal-baked fish are both widely available.

A useful Tigrinya word that will please your host is *te-oom* (delicious).

Vegetarian
If you're after vegetarian food, ask for *nai tsom*, a selection of vegetable dishes traditionally served during times of fasting.

Self-Catering
The capital is well equipped with supermarkets, some stocked with a good selection of European imports. Outside the towns, local shops have a very limited selection of food products for sale.

DRINKS
Nonalcoholic Drinks
In Asmara and, to a lesser degree, the larger towns, innumerable little cafés and bars dot the centre. In true Italian style, *macchiato*, espresso and cappuccino are all served, along with a selection of pastries and cakes.

The Eritreans seem to get a fix from large amounts of sugar, which is copiously applied to all hot drinks and even fresh fruit juices. If you don't want sugar, you'll have to make that clear when you order. Ask for *beze sukkar*.

Outside the capital and in the country, sweet black tea is the most common drink. Following Islamic traditions, it is often offered as a gesture of welcome to guests. In the lowlands, cloves are often added. In the west, near the Sudanese border, coffee is sometimes spiced with ginger. If you don't want it, ask for *beze gingebel*.

The water in Asmara is considered safe to drink but, as in many places, new arrivals may experience problems with it. Various makes of bottled water (known in Tigrinya as *mai gas*) can be bought in all the towns and some villages. Local brands include Dongollo and Sabarguma (which has a lighter fizz).

Fresh fruit juices (most commonly mango, papaya, pineapple and banana) are sold in Asmara and some of the larger towns.

Various fizzy soft drinks are widely available, even in Dankalia, where without refrigeration they are served at room temperature, which in some places is as warm as tepid tea.

Glass bottles are recycled; save them and you can exchange them for full ones.

Alcoholic Drinks
In the capital and towns, all the usual favourites are available, including whisky, gin, vodka and beer. As many are imported, they tend to be expensive.

Local varieties include Asmara gin (also known as *ouzo*), which is a bit rough around the edges (as you will be the morning after drinking it), but it is soon knocked back. A shot of gin (about Nfa5) is only slightly more expensive than Coke or mineral water (Nfa3 to Nfa4).

The local beer, Melotti, is popular among both Eritreans and aid workers. It's manufactured in Asmara, and has a mild, quite smooth flavour and is very drinkable. It's also cheap at about Nfa5.

As for the red Asmara wine – it is no huge cause for celebration. Local wines are very reasonably priced in restaurants, usually between Nfa15 and Nfa30 per bottle. Imported wine starts at about Nfa90.

If you're not catching an early bus out of town the next morning, try the local *araki*, a distilled aniseed drink, a little like the Greek ouzo. *Mies* is a delicious local wine made from honey, and comes in varying degrees of sweetness (the drier it is, the more

ERITREA

alcoholic). Don't miss it. If you're in Afar territory in Dankalia, try the delicious – but very powerful – *doma* palm wine (see the boxed text 'Popular Palms' under Assab later in this chapter).

ENTERTAINMENT

Most of the country's facilities for leisure and entertainment are in Asmara. Here, you'll find decent cinemas (showing films in English and sometimes Italian), nightclubs and bars. There's also a theatre (though plays are usually in Tigrinya).

Music in the bars is for the most part local (Tigrinya and Amharic pop), which, like the food, takes a bit of getting used to. Western music and some reggae are also played. Most bars close around 10pm or 11pm during the week, but stay open until at least 2am on Friday and Saturday.

Locals love to dance. Traditional dancing features a lot of shaking of body parts (some of which is hard to imagine, until you see it). It's certainly unique in style. If you can give it a go, you'll win a lot of friends, however inept and awkward you may feel. Men should be aware that most of the women in the smaller bars and nightclubs are prostitutes.

A few of the larger hotels in the capital occasionally stage shows with local musicians and dancers.

Outside the capital, entertainment is limited to a few bars and cafés. Many of these have *biliardo* (Italian billiards) tables.

Spectator Sports

Bicycle races take place in many of the larger towns. Streets are cordoned off, and everyone comes to watch.

SHOPPING

Eritrea's tourism industry is not yet greatly developed, and you won't find a many shops catering to tourists. Most curios are imported from other countries (such as the wooden carvings and sculptures from Kenya).

Shops sell intricate silver and gold jewellery (priced by weight), fabrics, ceramics and basketware. Quality (and some might say taste) is variable, so it's worth taking a good look around before you buy.

More unusual and interesting souvenirs include little pewter crosses, which are often crudely fashioned. Although they are neither very old nor silver as some shopkeepers like to make out, they are attractive, and don't constitute a national treasure.

The *gabi*, the equivalent of a toga worn by the local men, are also available. They are quite bulky, but can be turned to a multitude of uses – blankets, ground sheets, pillows and wraps – while you're travelling.

In some shops along Harnet Ave, ivory carvings and turtle shells are still available. Apart from the environmental arguments against buying these, it is also illegal to import them into most Western countries.

Outside the capital, simple pottery, basketware and combs can be found in local markets.

Getting There & Away

Eritrea's conflict with Ethiopia has taken a heavy toll on its international land, sea and air links. Ethiopian Airlines used to provide a crucial link between Eritrea and the rest of the world but no longer does. The Eritrean ports have lost much traffic, and the roads connecting Eritrea and Ethiopia were still closed at the time of writing. The most convenient way to get to Ethiopia is to go through Djibouti.

For general information on travel and prices, see the Ethiopia Getting There & Away chapter.

AIR

Travel during the month of August, and over Easter, Christmas and New Year should be booked well in advance. Eritreans living abroad tend to visit their families during this time and some flights are more expensive.

Airports & Airlines

Eritrea's one international airport lies 6km from the capital. A second airport is being built in Massawa but was not operational at the time of writing.

Departure Tax

International departure tax is US$15. All foreign nationals except those with residence permits are charged in US dollars.

USA

United Airlines and Lufthansa fly on a codeshare basis six times a week from Washington to Asmara (via Frankfurt), and a return trip costs US$1600. From the west coast, the same airlines fly from San Francisco six times a week for US$1800.

Eritrean Airlines, in conjunction with Delta Airlines, operates flights to/from the USA via Amsterdam, Frankfurt or Rome. Return trips cost US$1350 to US$1500 in low season (depending on which US city you depart from) and US$1600 to US$1800 in high season.

Australia & New Zealand
There are no direct flights from Australia and New Zealand to Eritrea. The best routing is through Cairo (via Singapore) or via Sana'a (Yemen). You can also try to fly to Dubai (United Arab Emirates), and then continue to Djibouti and Eritrea. In any case, be prepared for a time-consuming journey. Expect to pay between A$1800 and A$2000.

UK & Europe
Eritrean Airlines has just begun regular services to Frankfurt, Rome, Milan and Amsterdam, on a twice-weekly basis. Expect to pay around €800 return to/from Frankfurt, €1000 return to/from Amsterdam, and €720 to/from Rome or Milan.

Other international airlines connecting Asmara to Europe include Lufthansa, which currently flies six times a week from Frankfurt for around €1200. About the cheapest deal is offered by Daallo Airlines, which flies from London to Djibouti (via Paris) twice a week, with a connecting flight to Asmara, for £520 (from London) or €776 (from Paris). Other options include EgyptAir, which flies to Asmara (via Cairo) from London or Paris once a week for around €565; and Yemenia Yemen Airways, which has flights from Paris, Frankfurt and Rome to Asmara (via San'a) for around €700.

Africa & Middle East
Before the war, Ethiopian Airlines had daily flights from Addis Ababa to Asmara. These should resume eventually, but it is difficult to predict when.

EgyptAir has one flight a week between Asmara and Cairo for US$583/640 one way/return.

Sudan Airways has two flights a week between Asmara and Khartoum for US$259/280 one way/return.

Regional Airlines has three flights a week between Asmara and Nairobi for US$508/730 one way/return (one via Djibouti). Eritrean Airlines also has three weekly flights to/from Nairobi for around US$680 return. From Nairobi, there are numerous connecting flights to many destinations in the rest of Africa.

Daallo Airlines connects Asmara with Djibouti twice a week for Dfr25,300/30,800 one way/return. Another option to fly to/from Djibouti is Regional Airlines, once a week, for US$190/232.

Saudi Arabian Airlines has two flights a week between Asmara and Riyadh via Jeddah (US$538 return).

Yemenia flies three times a week between Asmara and Sana'a (US$245 return).

At the time of writing, Eritrean Airlines was planning to operate flights to several destinations in the Middle East. Check with your travel agent.

LAND
Border Crossings
Travellers should note that there is no formal border crossing established on the border in the south between Eritrea and Djibouti. You'll have to go to the immigration office in Assab.

Two posts on the border between Eritrea and Ethiopia serve as formal border crossings: Senafe and Adi Quala. As long as the dispute between the two countries is not settled, they will remain closed.

Djibouti
Only tracks and dirt roads lead south of the town of Assab to Djibouti.

Very little traffic heads south, except for some shared taxis that go to Moulhoulé, the first town after the border, to collect passengers arriving from Obock in other taxis. In theory, this service operates on the same days as the Djibouti–Obock ferry, but check the current situation in Assab before setting off.

It's now possible to take your own vehicle south. Be warned, though: if you do have a mechanical problem, you're unlikely to meet another living soul for a couple of days. It's advisable to check with the Djiboutian embassy and Immigration Department in Asmara before setting off. Once in Djibouti, go to the Service d'Immigration or immigration office in Djibouti town.

Ethiopia
Of the three sealed roads connecting Eritrea with Ethiopia, the first goes from Asmara via Mendefera and Adi Quala to Aksum in Ethiopia; the second route goes from Asmara via Dekemhare and Adi Keyh in Eritrea to Adigrat in Ethiopia; and the third route connects Assab in the south with Addis Ababa in Ethiopia. Since the outbreak of the conflict with Ethiopia, these roads have been closed.

ERITREA

Sudan

At the time of writing, it was possible to cross the border from Eritrea to Sudan but not the other way. Check the current situation when you get there.

The road is now sealed from Asmara to Barentu and there are plans to extend it to Teseney on the Eritrea side of the border. There are no regular bus services between the two countries.

SEA

Eritrea has two ports, Massawa and Assab. There are no scheduled passenger services, but many cargo ships from other Red Sea countries use the ports, particularly the one at Massawa. It's sometimes possible to hitch lifts.

Getting Around

While the conflict with Ethiopia remains unresolved, travel around Eritrea may be slightly restricted, particularly at border towns. At the time of research, a permit was required for travel to Nakfa in the north. However, check the situation when you get to Asmara.

The Italians were responsible for the construction of a small, but beautifully built, network of roads connecting Asmara to the north, south, east and west. During the Struggle for Independence, most of these roads were destroyed. After independence, the reconstruction of the network became one of the government's prime objectives. Much progress has been made, including

The Old Railway

The old Italian railway, which climbed from Massawa 2128m up the escarpment to Asmara, passing through three climate zones, 30 tunnels and 65 bridges, is a masterpiece of civil engineering.

At independence, Eritrea appealed for help to rehabilitate the old line. 'Impossible,' said most. 'Too expensive,' said some; 'It depends,' said others.

Undeterred, the Eritreans pulled the old railway workers, metal forgers and blacksmiths out of retirement, called for volunteers and set to work.

The great line reopened in 2003 and will make for one of the most spectacular train journeys on the African continent.

the constructions of good roads connecting Asmara with Keren, Massawa, Adi Quala, Barentu and Ethiopia's Adigrat.

Recent projects include the extension of the sealed road from Barentu to Teseney (it should be completed by the time this book is published), and the construction of sealed roads between Keren and Nakfa, Massawa and Nakfa and, eventually, Massawa and Assab in the south.

Some roads are in a very bad state of repair. However, the track between Massawa and Assab has been much improved.

Garis (horse-drawn carts) are used for short hops around the towns (see Ethiopia Getting Around chapter) but their numbers are dwindling.

AIR

Eritrean Airlines, based in the capital, flies to just one domestic destination: Assab. Flights leave from Asmara once a week on Wednesday (US$42/84 one way/return).

When relations with Ethiopia normalise, flights from Assab to Addis Ababa should resume.

BUS

The bus service in Eritrea is reasonably efficient, comfortable and extensive. There are usually at least two buses a day between the larger towns (Asmara, Massawa and Keren), and at least one bus a day between the smaller ones. Fares are cheap, and services run between 6am and 4.30pm or 6pm. For long-distance journeys (those taking three hours or longer), two buses often leave within an hour of each other, between 5.30am and 6.30am.

The major drawback of bus travel is that it's time-consuming. Progress on the road is often slow. Additionally, buses don't adhere to fixed timetables; they depart when they're full. For long-distance journeys, you need to be at the bus station by 6am to buy a ticket and be guaranteed a seat. It's not usually possible to buy tickets in advance, except for the journey between Asmara and Teseney and between Asmara and Assab. From 6am, you then wait any time up to 9am for the bus to fill and depart.

TRAIN

The old Italian railway that stretched between Massawa, Asmara, Keren and Agordat was another casualty of war. Many of its tracks were pulled up to reinforce trenches.

However, the stretch has now been repaired. There are no regular services as yet, and the people in charge of the train are currently looking for a new locomotive. When this new locomotive is found, regular services will be offered. At the time of writing, the train only offered charter services. Ask at the railway station in Asmara (☎ 12 33 65).

CAR & MOTORCYCLE

Over long distances in Eritrea, cars can be twice as quick as buses. If you're trying to calculate journey times by car, see the bus journey durations in each destination's Getting There & Away section, and cut the time given by about a third for short journeys and half for long journeys. For information on taxis see Getting Around in the Asmara section.

If you're taking your own car or motorcycle into Eritrea, you should always carry your passport, a valid international driving licence, the vehicle ownership papers and proof of insurance (third-party insurance is mandatory) covering all the countries you are visiting. Cars can be imported duty-free for a period of four months.

Road Rules

Since Italian colonial days, driving has been on the right-hand side of the road.

The road hazards that exist in Ethiopia also apply in Eritrea – precipitous roads, curfews, children playing, livestock wandering, land mines and roads impassable in the rainy season. (For detailed information see Road Rules in the Ethiopia Getting Around chapter.)

Fuel (both petrol and diesel) is quite widely available, apart from in the north beyond Keren, and south of Massawa into Dankalia. For travel in these places, it's essential to carry plenty of extra fuel.

Rental

Vehicle rental is not cheap in Eritrea. The condition of many roads makes 4WDs obligatory, though cars are adequate for Massawa and Keren.

Fortunately, the country is small and, with your own wheels, most of its attractions can be seen in quite a short period. If you're travelling solo, or as a couple, you can reduce the cost of vehicle rental by joining up with other travellers to hire a car plus a driver/guide. Most vehicles accommodate around five passengers, though some have extra benches in the back and can take about 10.

Cars can be rented from various agencies in Asmara (see Getting Around under Asmara; see also Organised Tours). To hire a car, you must have a valid international driving licence and be over 25 years old.

Prices vary and are usually open to negotiation, so shop around. You should ask for a discount if you're hiring for more than a week. A deposit of around Nfa2000 is required to rent a 4WD; for a car it's around Nfa1000.

A driver is usually supplied for your 4WD. Sometimes there's an additional charge if you want the driver to work more than eight hours in a day – check in advance.

Cars cost Nfa250 to Nfa350 per day; a 4WD costs Nfa1000 to Nfa1800 per day, including third-party insurance. The first 50km to 90km are free, and each additional kilometre costs between Nfa1.50 and Nfa3. If you want to hire a car with a driver, add Nfa100 per day.

ORGANISED TOURS

In Asmara there are various reputable travel agencies that organise tours around the country. Tours can be tailored to your time, means and interests: from one-day birdwatching excursions from Asmara or weekend trips to the beach in Massawa, to four-day elephant safaris in Antore or six-day expeditions through the Dankalia region to Assab. They also offer hotel and flight reservations and car hire.

Explore Eritrea Travel & Tours (☎ 12 12 42, 12 55 55, fax 12 79 08; e explore@tse.com.er; PO Box 2061, Asmara) has competent and enterprising management and staff. They can organise camping, diving and bicycling trips, as well as excursions by camel. Tailor-made trips using public as well as private transport can be arranged, which can cut costs a little. Credit cards are accepted.

The excellent agency **Travel House International** (☎ 20 18 81/2, fax 12 07 51; e soloabr@eol.com.er; PO Box 5579, Asmara) is run by the efficient and very helpful Solomon Abraha, and offers similar services. Credit cards are accepted.

Asmara አስመራ

pop 500,000 • elevation 2347m

With a perfect climate, remarkable architecture and spotless, safe streets, Asmara ranks among the most pleasant capitals on the African continent. Perched on the eastern edge of the highland plateau, some 2356m above sea level, Asmara boasts a climate classed as 'tropical highland' – in other words, balmy and temperate, with cloudless blue skies for about eight months of the year.

ERITREA

Italian Apartheid

From 1922 to 1941, a system of discrimination existed in Eritrea and Ethiopia that was remarkably similar to the apartheid system of South Africa.

Local and Italian children were educated at different schools, with different textbooks, and to different levels. Non-Italian adults were prevented from learning basic skills or professions, or from opening shops, restaurants or businesses; they were expected to work as menials for the Italians.

On buses and in cinemas, Italian passengers sat in the front, whereas locals were obliged to sit at the back. Marriage between Italians and locals was forbidden by law, with a punishment of up to five years in prison for offenders. Following a decree in 1940, children of mixed Italian and local parentage were not considered Italian.

Thousands of locals were evicted from their houses and resettled in reservations far from where the Italians lived. The best agricultural land was seized, rent for town houses was not paid and there were continual abuses of law in which locals were punished, fined and even killed without cause.

With a population of half a million inhabitants, Asmara is easily the largest city in Eritrea, though compared to most African capitals it's tiny. Following a government policy of 'positive discrimination' in favour of settlement of the countryside, Asmara has generally been spared the litter-strewn, sprawling ghettos of many developing-world cities and the bleak, Western-style high-rise office and apartment buildings of post-colonial Africa.

The town has long evoked clichéd comparisons to 'southern Italian towns'. In some ways, Asmara is very Italian, not just in the tangible remnants of colonial days, such as the Cinquecento taxis and Art Deco architecture, but also in the way of life – the morning cappuccino, the evening *passeggiata* (stroll) around town and the relaxed, unhurried pace of life.

But that is just one facet of Asmara. The city also exudes an undeniably African and Arab atmosphere. In the morning you'll hear the sound of the cathedral bells and the footsteps of the Orthodox monks on their way to mass as well as the Muslim call to prayer.

These sounds are symbolic of the remarkable harmony that reigns in the city and throughout the country among the four different religions and nine ethnic groups. Apart from the Catholic cathedral, Asmara is home to 28 mosques and a thriving Muslim market, 12 Orthodox churches and a Jewish synagogue.

HISTORY

The town was settled in the 12th century by shepherds from the Akele Guzay region, southeast of the country. Encouraged by the plentiful supplies of water, they founded four villages on the hill that are now the site of the Orthodox church of Enda Mariam. The site became known as Arbate Asmere (Four Villages), from which the name Asmara is derived.

The little village then became a staging post for travellers making the long and arduous journey between the sea and the mountains. Soon it developed into a small but bustling trading centre.

At the end of the 19th century, Ras Alula, the dashing Tigrinya *negus* (prince) made it his capital and the centre of a flourishing caravan trade. By 1884 the town was home to some 2000 inhabitants and 300 houses.

The town then caught the eye of Baldissera, the Italian general, and in 1889 he took it over. A fort was constructed and a square building (which later became the Governor's Palace) for the *comando* (commander) Truppe. Italian architects and engineers got to work and had soon laid the foundations of the new town – Piccola Roma, as it was dubbed, was born.

In 1897 the first governor of Eritrea, Governor Martini, chose Asmara (in preference to Massawa) as the future capital of the Italian East African empire. Amid dreams of great military conquests in Abyssinia during the Mussolini era, the town was greatly enlarged and a military base was installed.

During the Struggle, Asmara was the last town held by the occupying Ethiopian army and, from 1990, it was besieged by the (EPLF). By a fortuitous turn of events, the Ethiopian dictator Mengistu was overthrown in 1991, his troops fled Eritrea and a final confrontation in the capital was avoided. Asmara was left intact. It was one of the very few Eritrean towns to survive the war undamaged.

[Continued on page 309]

WALKING TOURS IN ASMARA

Asmara's greatest attraction is undoubtedly its stunning collection of buildings, a legacy of the Italian colonial era (for more details, see Architecture in the Facts about Eritrea section and the boxed text 'An Exceptional Architectural Legacy' in the Asmara section). As you walk around the town, you will see remarkable examples of the Art Deco, International, Cubist, Expressionist, Functionalist, Futurist, Rationalist and Neoclassical architectural styles. Don't expect to see perfect architectural gems, though. Many buildings are in need of restoration, but there are plans to protect and rehabilitate them.

There was a major street-renaming process at the time of writing. Street names are given when relevant and confirmed.

Tour 1 – Harnet Avenue

This short walk starts at the western end of Harnet Ave and ends at the Cinema Impero, about 500m further east.

At the western end of Harnet Ave is the old Governor's Palace. With its pediment supported by Corinthian columns and its spacious,

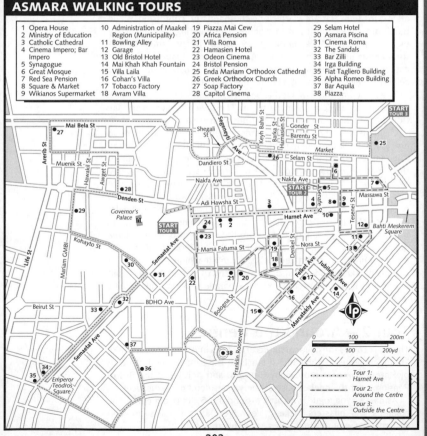

ASMARA WALKING TOURS

1 Opera House	10 Administration of Maakel	19 Piazza Mai Cew
2 Ministry of Education	Region (Municipality)	20 Africa Pension
3 Catholic Cathedral	11 Bowling Alley	21 Villa Roma
4 Cinema Impero; Bar	12 Garage	22 Hamasien Hotel
Impero	13 Old Bristol Hotel	23 Odeon Cinema
5 Synagogue	14 Mai Khah Khah Fountain	24 Bristol Pension
6 Great Mosque	15 Villa Laila	25 Enda Mariam Orthodox Cathedral
7 Red Sea Pension	16 Cohan's Villa	26 Greek Orthodox Church
8 Square & Market	17 Tobacco Factory	27 Soap Factory
9 Wikianos Supermarket	18 Avram Villa	28 Capitol Cinema

29 Selam Hotel
30 Asmara Piscina
31 Cinema Roma
32 The Sandals
33 Bar Zilli
34 Irga Building
35 Fiat Tagliero Building
36 Alpha Romeo Building
37 Bar Aquila
38 Piazza

elegant interior, it is thought to be one of the finest Neoclassical buildings in Africa. Unfortunately, it is not currently possible to go near the building.

Heading east down Harnet Ave, you'll see the old Opera House on your right, near the telecommunications building. The Opera House is one of Asmara's most elegant early-20th-century buildings. Designed by Cavagnari and completed around 1920, this eclectic building combines a Renaissance scallop-shell fountain, a Romanesque portico supported by Classical columns and inside, above multitiered balconies, a spectacular Art Nouveau ceiling painted by Saviero Fresa.

Next door is the Ministry of Education. Built during the 1930s as the Casa del Fascio (the Fascist Party headquarters), it mixes the Classical (the right-hand section) with the monumental and Fascist. Its massive stepped tower has strong vertical elements, including three gun-slit windows. The steps, string courses (projecting bands of bricks) and mouldings give the building harmony.

Head eastwards along the avenue until you get to the Catholic cathedral. This building, consecrated in 1923, is thought to be one of the finest Lombard-Romanesque-style churches outside Italy. The altar is made of Carrara marble and the baptistry, confessionals and pulpit are carved from Italian walnut. The painting of Saint Mary by Carlo Maratta di Camerano (1625–1713) was presented by Vittorio Emmanuel III, king of Italy. According to a plaque inside the cathedral, Mussolini himself was a patron of its construction. Mass is celebrated every Sunday at 11am in the cathedral.

The cathedral's narrow, Gothic bell tower makes a useful landmark and offers great views over the town. The tower is open every day from 8am to 12.30pm and 2pm to 6pm; entry is Nfa10.

Continue heading east down Harnet Ave for another 100m or so and you will see the Cinema Impero and Bar Impero, part of a grand Rationalist terrace built in 1938. The imposing cinema is made up of three massive windows which combine strong vertical and horizontal elements with 45 porthole lamps. In the lobby, all the marble, chrome and glass features are original. The cavernous auditorium seats 1800 people and is decorated with motifs such as lions, nyalas and palm trees depicted in Art Deco style. The Bar Impero, where cinema-goers traditionally enjoyed an aperitif before the film, is also original. Look out for the bevelled-glass cake cabinet, the porthole windows, the 'zinc' bar and the ancient *gelato* (ice cream) machine.

Bahti Meskerem Square at the eastern end of Harnet Ave was built during the Ethiopian occupation as a parade ground and remains half-finished.

Tour 2 – Around the Centre

This walk covers the major architectural styles in Asmara and will take about 2½ hours to complete. It starts at the synagogue, just north of Harnet Ave near the Cinema Impero, and finishes at the Bristol Pension, near the opera house at the western end of Harnet Ave.

Asmara's synagogue was built around 1905. Its pediment, Doric columns and pilasters make it very Neoclassical. As is usual in Asmara, the wrought-iron gates are handcrafted.

Turn right as you leave the synagogue, then right again at the first junction, then take a left turn at the next. This should bring you to the Great Mosque (Kulafah Al Rashidin). Completed in 1938 by Guido Ferrazza, this grand complex combines Rationalist, Classical and Islamic styles. The symmetry of the mosque is enhanced by the minaret, which rises at one side like a fluted Roman column above Islamic domes and arches. The mihrab (niche indicating the direction of Mecca) inside consists of mosaics and columns made from Carrara marble.

Ferrazza's style is also seen in the great square and market complex surrounding the mosque.

Head east from the mosque, back to Nafka Ave, and walk two blocks along Nafka Ave until you reach a square. On the edge of the square, the Red Sea Pension with its sweeping facade is typical of the Moderne style.

Past the square turn right into Massawa St, back towards the synagogue. Take the third turn to the left, and head south towards Harnet Ave. On the way look out for Wikianos Supermarket, formerly the Palazzo Mutton (residential palace), on Harnet Ave. This shop represents the curious 'corner solution' first used in Italy by Giuseppe Terragni, a founder of the Rationalist movement. The cleverly curved corner entrance is studded with massive porthole windows.

Across the street from Wikianos you'll see the Municipality building. Though built in the 1950s, the Municipality is firmly Rationalist. The two geometric wings are 'stripped Palladian' in style, and are dominated by a soaring central tower. The windows are beautifully detailed. Look out for the 'crazy majolica' facade in green and beige.

Head south from Harnet Ave down the street on the eastern side of the Municipality and take the first left. The bowling alley here is one of the few genuine 1950s alleys left in the world. It was probably built for US servicemen when they were manning military bases in the region. The reloading system is still manual. Look out also for the bowling motifs on the balustrades and the carved wooden benches. The colourful early 'pop art' window is spectacular at sunset.

Across the road from the bowling alley is a garage possibly built in the 1950s. The roof of the building features zigzags.

Take a right turn down Marsatekly Ave. About 50m from the junction, on your right, opposite the Saudi Arabian embassy, you'll see the Old Bristol Hotel (now the Ministry of Land, Water and Environment). Built in the 1930s, this very unusual and innovative building was once a bordello. Its solid mass is still light and harmonious through the use of the Neoclassical 'rule of thirds': wing – loggia (porch) – wing. The windows and doors are in perfect proportion, too. The front part of the building is in the side street on the right.

On Jubilee Ave, close to the corner with Marsatekly Ave, is one of the most elegant pieces of architecture in Asmara – the Mai Khah Khah fountain, which cascades down the hillside in a series of rectangular steps. Above the fountain is the attractive suburb of Gezzabanda, which is full of impressive villas.

From the fountain, head northwest and take the first street on the left. As you walk up this street, look out for the numerous villas standing in shady gardens. The Italian urban planners responsible for this area were honouring the Classical tradition of *rus in urbe* (bringing a piece of the countryside into the town).

At the southern end of Felket Ave is Villa Laila, one of Asmara's finest Moderne villas.

Heading downhill on Felket Ave past a row of old shops and 1950s Formica bars with fly-bead doors, you'll see at the next block the attractive Cohan's Villa, with blue wraparound windows – a feature often used by architects in Miami, USA. You won't see much of if because the building is partially hidden by vegetation. The villa was built by one of the prominent Jewish trading families in the 1930s.

Still on Felket Ave, a block downhill from Cohan's Villa is the tobacco factory, one of the most adventurous Art Deco buildings in Asmara. Look out for the very odd 'unfinished' pilasters, the tall, slim windows and the massive cornice leading to the curved cantilever wings that give the building balance.

Across from the tobacco factory, take the street that turns left (westwards). You'll pass Ras Alula Hill, where the Tigrean Negus (prince) once had a fort. The hill is now covered with lovely old villas including the Villa Grazia, a Cuban-style Moderne building.

The piazza nearby, which features a lone palm and a tear-drop island, is beautifully designed. Heading east again along Bologna St, look out on the left for one of Asmara's grandest residences. The three-storey Avram Villa (also known as the Turreted Villa) was built by the L'Atilla family in the 1930s. The roof terrace is topped by an unusual 'surfboard' loggia.

Head north towards Harnet Ave until you reach the Piazza Mai Cew, which was once the heart of the Greek community. On the corner on the east side is an old school (now the Greek consulate) that resembles a Greek temple.

From the Piazza Mai Cew, head west through the next square (which has a palm tree in the middle) and up the hill. Near the top of the hill you reach the Africa Pension. This huge Cubist villa was built in the 1920s by a spaghetti millionaire. The villa is characterised by its elegant marble staircase and the ring of 40 marble urns. Today a solemn and slightly ludicrous bronze bust of Augustus Caesar stands guard in the once-formal garden. The villa is now a hotel (see Places to Stay – Budget under Asmara in this chapter).

Opposite the Africa Pension is Villa Roma. This beautiful villa, built in 1919 by Gaetano L'Atilla, epitomises the Roman style. The marble staircases, louvred shutters, curving balustrades, shady portico, fountain and loggia with cascading purple bougainvillea are typical features of the ideal Roman villa. Today it is the residence of the Italian ambassador.

Heading west from Villa Roma brings you to the Hamasien Hotel, designed by the architect Reviglio around 1920. The quirky chimney pots are designed to resemble miniature classical temples.

About 100m north, and just off Harnet Ave, is the Odeon Cinema with its authentic Art Deco interior. The box office, bar, bevelled mirrors, black *terrazzo* and Deco strip lights are a good introduction to the large auditorium.

Opposite the cinema is the Bristol Pension. Built in 1941, this former hotel, with its central stairwell tower surmounting geometric wings, is an example of classic Rationalist design. The strip-course separates the top-floor windows from the well-proportioned and well-made shutters and the plain concrete balconies below.

Tour 3 – Outside The Centre

Listed in this section are some buildings that are outside the town centre.

The Enda Mariam Orthodox Cathedral, one block north of Red Sea Pension, was built in 1938 and is a curious blend of Italian and Eritrean architecture. Its central block is flanked by large square towers. Rather garish mosaics of stylised Christian figures are framed vertically above the entrance. Traditional elements of Aksumite architecture can be seen, such as the massive horizontal stone beams. The four objects that look like broken elephant tusks suspended on the northern side of the compound are century-old 'bells'. These make a surprisingly musical sound when 'rung' (beaten with a stick).

Head west along Dekemhare St. Walk past the market until you reach Keyh Bahri St, on the western side of the market. Turn left here, then left again, and the entrance of the Greek Orthodox Church will come into view. The church has frescoes, carved wood and candles. Walk back till you reach Keyh Bahri St and look for Segeneyti Ave, just beyond. Head northwest and turn left into Shegali St, then right into Dandiero St. You'll soon reach Mai Bela St, a main artery that runs east–west.

The old soap factory, on Mai Bela St past the university, is typical of the International style, except that its dilapidated glass tower is nonfunctional. In Asmara, it was common for successful businesses to broadcast their wealth with such follies.

Turn left into Arerib St, and take the first left. Walk past Hawakil St and Awget St and turn right at the next intersection, then continue until you reach Denden St. On your left lies the Capitol Cinema, next to the Department of Immigration and north of the Governor's Palace. It was built in 1937. The massive horizontal elements and sweeping curves are typical of the Expressionist movement. Unfortunately the building is rather dilapidated.

From here, head west along Denden St then turn left into Mariam GMBI, where you'll come across the Selam Hotel. Built in the 1930s, it was one of a chain constructed by the Italian company Compagnia Immobiliare Alberghi Africa Orientale (CIAAO). Interesting interior details include the Arts and Crafts serving cabinets and the 'disc'-type lamps in the dining room, the old murals and the purple 'beehive' lamps in the rear courtyard. It's still run as a hotel (see Places to Stay – Mid-Range under Asmara in this chapter).

Take the first street on your left (Kohayto St). Walking down Kohayto St, you'll see the 1930s Asmara Piscina (swimming pool) on your right, housed in a yellow building (the entrance is south, next to the little square). Take a peek inside – interior details include the 'Leonardo' sporting figures on the walls.

Kohayto St leads into Semaetat Ave. You can't miss the Cinema Roma, across the avenue. It's another fine example of Italian architecture.

Turn right into Semaetat Ave and walk until you see the Sandals, in the middle of the roundabout. It commemorates the victory of the Eritrean fighters in the Struggle. At the junction of Beirut St and Semaetat Ave, you'll see the facade of the Bar Zilli. This building looks like a 1930s radio. The porthole windows and nautical balconies are separated into sections by mock-marble columns. Unfortunately, the facade is peeling.

Further south down Semaetat Ave, the beautiful Irga Building is both Neoclassical in its proportions and very modern.

Perhaps the best-known building in Asmara is the Fiat Tagliero building. This Futuristic *l'aeroplano* (aeroplane), on Emperor Teodros Square, was built in 1938 by the engineer Pettazzi. The central tower with its glass 'cockpit' is similar to many structures in Miami, USA.

Cross the square and follow the street opposite until you reach a church. Turn left. Turn left again into the third street and the dilapidated Alpha Romeo building will soon come into view. With its Palladian proportions, striking bevelled arch and Futuristic antennas, the building is a strange mix of the old and the new.

About 100m further north, the corner Bar Aquila makes a good stop to have a rest and a drink. While there, admire the original Art Deco bar. Note the shelving, mirrors, chequered floor, rare antique billiard cue stand and scoring board.

If you head east from Bar Aquila, you'll get to an intersection. Turn left, walk about 50 metres until the next fork. Take the street in the middle that goes diagonally, then the first right. You'll reach a large piazza at the top of a hill. The piazza is surrounded by an incredible collection of Art Deco architecture, including two small Lubetkin-inspired villas, a crumbling 'Tuscan' tower and the Villa Venezia with its scored walls and Lion of Saint Mark in red and gold mosaics. Look out also for the vast and curious 'ocean liner' villa.

[Continued from Page 302]

ORIENTATION

Like most colonial towns, Asmara was built according to a strict urban plan, and divided into four main areas: the administrative centre, the colonial residential quarter, the 'native' quarter and the outbuildings.

The administrative centre encompasses the area on and just north of Harnet Ave, marked by Bahti Meskerem Square at the eastern end of Harnet Ave and the Governor's Palace in the west.

To the south of Harnet Ave was once the Italian residential quarter, at a safe distance from both the centre of town and the local quarter. Many Art Deco villas can be found in this area.

The area to the northeast, and well outside the confines of the town centre, are the residential quarters of the local population. To this day, this is still the poorest area, and it lies out of sight of most tourists.

The former outbuildings – the larger garages, factories and assembly plants – are positioned outside the boundaries of the city, where they form a kind of industrial belt. Many of the old Italian factories can be found here.

Maps

The **Ministry of Tourism** produces an adequate town map (Nfa40), which is available in some bookshops, souvenir shops and travel agencies in Asmara. The central part of the map is a bit cramped, but it's good for general orientation as it shows the whole town.

INFORMATION
Tourist Offices

A new **tourist office** (☎ 12 48 71, fax 12 69 49; open 7am-11am & 2pm-6pm Mon-Fri)

Street Names

Street names have changed at least three or four times in the last 20 years. At the time of writing, there was another major renaming process; all street names with Ethiopian references were being changed. In fact, street names are not really used for giving directions. Most people go by local landmarks such as government buildings, hotels or bars. In this book, only the new, confirmed street names are mentioned.

---

has opened on the corner of Harnet Ave and Denkel Street, next to Asmara Caffe.

The most reliable sources of information in the capital are the two leading travel agencies, **Travel House International** (☎ 20 18 81/2, fax 12 07 51) near the restaurant Casa degli Italiani and, nearby, **Explore Eritrea Travel & Tours** (☎ 12 55 55, fax 12 79 08; *Adi Hawsha St*).

Money

There are various banks in Asmara, mosty on and around Harnet Ave. Most of them change major foreign currencies as well as travellers cheques. There are also a number of foreign exchange bureaus that offer speedy exchange facilities at fairly interesting rates. They have shorter queues than banks and keep longer hours. It is worth shopping around since their rates vary slightly.

There are currently no ATMs in Asmara but the main office of **Himbol** (☎ 12 07 88; *Bahti Meskerem Square*) can do cash advances on your credit card for a commission of 7% plus Nfa30. Himbol can also handle money transfers.

There is a **Housing & Commerce Bank of Eritrea** (*open 6.30am-2am daily*) near the exit of the airport. It changes cash only.

Post

The **main post office** (*open 8am-noon & 2pm-6pm Mon-Fri, 8am-12.30pm Sat*) is just north of the western end of Harnet Ave.

Telephone & Fax

The **telecommunications building** (*open 8am-9pm Mon-Fri, 8am-8pm Sat, Sun & public holidays*) is at the western end of Harnet Ave. You can make international calls in the special cabins or local calls. Phonecards (Nfa25, Nfa50 or Nfa100 denominations) are also available.

There's a **fax office** (*open 8am-8pm Mon-Sat, 8am-noon & 3pm-7pm Sun & public holidays*) to the left of the entrance of the telecommunications building. Faxes cost between Nfa26 and Nfa34 for one minute's transmission, depending on the destination. You can also receive faxes here.

Email & Internet Access

There is a rapidly expanding number of places offering Internet access in Asmara. Among the more convenient ones are **Tekseb Internet Cafe** off the western end

ERITREA

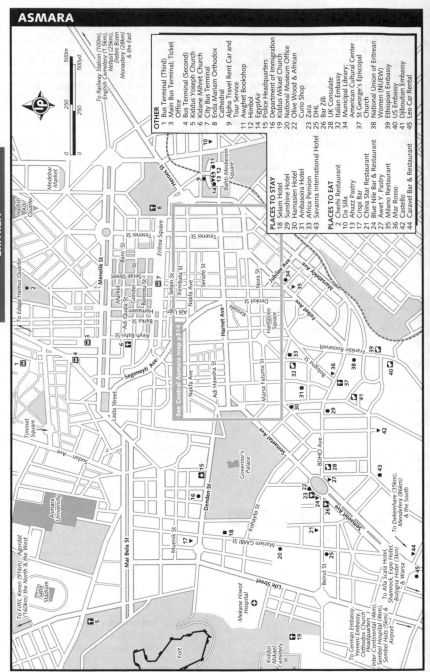

ASMARA

See Central Asmara map p314

OTHER
1 Bus Terminal (Third)
3 Main Bus Terminal; Ticket Office
4 Kiddus Yoseph Church
6 Kidane Mihret Church
7 City Bus Terminal
8 Enda Mariam Orthodox Cathedral
9 Alpha Travel Rent Car and Tour Service
11 Awghet Bookshop
12 Himbol
14 EgyptAir
15 Police Headquarters
16 Department of Immigration
19 Kiddus Mikael Church
20 National Museum Office
22 Olive Wood & African Curio Shop
23 Zara
25 DHL
26 Bar Zilli
28 UK Consulate
32 Italian Embassy
34 Municipal Library;
American Cultural Center
37 St George's Episcopal Church
38 National Union of Eritrean Women (NUEW)
39 Ethiopian Embassy
40 US Embassy
41 Djiboutian Embassy
45 Leo Car Rental

PLACES TO STAY
18 Selam Hotel
29 Sunshine Hotel
30 Hamasien Hotel
31 Ambasoira Hotel
33 Africa Pension
43 Savanna International Hotel

PLACES TO EAT
2 Cherhi Restaurant
10 Da Silla
13 Ahazz Pastry
17 Crispi Bar
21 China Star Restaurant
24 Blue Nile Bar & Restaurant
27 Awet Y. Pastry
35 Milano Restaurant
36 Mar Rosso
42 Castello
44 Caravel Bar & Restaurant

of Harnet Ave, **PCS** in Denkel Street and **Double M Internet Cafe** near Wikianos Supermarket at the eastern end of Harnet Ave. Most places are open from 8am until 10pm and charge Nfa10 per hour. Be warned that connections can be painfully slow, so you will need to figure in some extra time and be patient.

Travel Agencies

The three main travel agencies in Asmara are **Explore Travel & Tours** (☎ 12 55 55, 12 12 42, fax 12 79 08; e explore@tse.com.er), not far from the presidential office; **Travel House International** (☎ 20 18 81/2/3, fax 12 07 51; e soloabr@eol.com.er), opposite the Casa degli Italiani restaurant, near the main post office; and **Alpha Travel Rent Car and Tour Service** (☎ 20 13 55, 12 19 68; e alpha_tr@gemel.com; Bahti Meskerem Square). For details of the sort of tours they offer, see Organised Tours in the Getting Around section earlier in this chapter. Flights can be booked through these agencies or through the various airline offices in Asmara.

Bookshops

The **Awghet Bookshop** (Bahti Meskerem Square) has the widest selection of books on Eritrea, including history, politics and anthropology. It also stocks some novels by African writers, town maps, postcards, cassettes and CDs.

Libraries & Cultural Centres

Alliance Française (☎ 12 65 99, fax 12 10 36) The alliance is in the same building as the French Embassy. The library is separate from the main alliance building, behind the Ambassador Hotel off Harnet Ave. Occasionally, at the library or at the Casa degli Italiani restaurant, local artists put on exhibitions or concerts and once a week films in French are shown (free) at 7pm.

American Cultural Center Above the Municipal Library, the centre shows films every Friday at 6pm, but you should get there early, as seating is limited.

British Council (☎ 12 34 15, fax 12 72 30) In the centre, not far from the presidential office, the British Council has a respectable library, as well as a reading room stocked with British newspapers and magazines.

Municipal Library (☎ 12 70 44) Felket Ave. The library, near the Milano Restaurant, has a good selection of books as well as American magazines and journals.

Medical Services

The most reputable hospital is the new **Sembel Hospital** (☎ 15 02 30, 15 02 31), near the Intercontinental Hotel on the road to the airport. The standard fee is Nfa75 per consultation. It also offers dental services.

There are numerous pharmacies around town, including the **Cathedral Pharmacy** (Harnet Ave) opposite the Catholic cathedral and near Pensione Pisa.

Other Services

There's no shortage of laundries in the centre. Normal service takes 72 hours; express service takes 24 hours and costs double.

You'll find several photo shops on and around Harnet Ave. As an indication of price, a 36-exposure colour-print film costs Nfa35. Developing can be done in 45 minutes and costs about Nfa110.

Emergency

Emergency numbers (24 hour) include:

Ambulance (☎ 12 22 44)
Fire Brigade (☎ 11 77 77)
Police (☎ 11 55 55)

Dangers & Annoyances

Asmara is fundamentally a very safe city, especially compared with other African cities. It's generally safe to stroll around day or night in the centre. However, women should use their common sense and avoid walking alone in deserted and dark streets.

It used to be rare to see beggars in central Asmara, due to a government campaign to 'discourage' it. However, the numbers of beggars on the streets of Asmara appears to be on the increase. The odd little street urchin creeps in – a favourite game is to try to extract money, usually successfully, from gullible tourists. If you want to give alms, it is preferable to go to one of the Orthodox churches.

MARKETS

The vibrant market, just north of Eritrea Square, is one of Asmara's major attractions. It takes place every morning except Sunday, but the best time to visit is early on Saturday (from 7am), when people come in from all over the country. Highlights include the **spice market**, filled with colourful women from different ethnic groups.

The **souvenir market** is a great place to browse too, and is more interesting than the

ERITREA

shops in the town. You can find, among other things, local basketwork, wooden masks, musical instruments, decorated gourds, warrior knives and skin paintings.

Medebar (located northeast of the main market) is like an open-air workshop where absolutely everything is recycled. The Medebar is a fascinating place. The air is filled with hammering, sawing and cutting; old tyres are made into sandals, corrugated iron is flattened and made into metal buckets, and olive tins from Italy made into coffeepots and tiny scoopers. It's a salutary lesson in waste management.

NATIONAL MUSEUM
ሃገራዊ ቤተ መዘክር

East of the Governor's Palace is the National Museum *(Mariam GMBI St; admission free; open 9am-11am & 3pm-5pm daily)* includes exhibits on the ethnic groups of Eritrea and the main archaeological sites of the country. It's a bit disappointing in its present state but there are plans to upgrade it and to move it to a more suitable place in the city centre.

CITY PARK
ህዝባዊ መናፈሻ

This park *(open 6.30am-10.30pm daily)* is a pleasant place for a walk and an ice cream in the afternoon, or for a beer in the evening.

ENGLISH CEMETERY
ናይ እንግሊዝ መካነ - መቓብር

On the road to Massawa on the periphery of Asmara (2km from the centre), is the beautifully tended English Cemetery, dating from 1941. Interred here are 280 men killed during the Ethiopian campaign. There is also a Hindu burial ground for the Indian soldiers who fought alongside the British.

PLACES TO STAY

Asmara boasts a cluster of accommodation options, from very affordable, homey guesthouses and mid-range, good-value options to luxury hotels. Most places are rather featureless but well-equipped.

Most of Asmara's accommodation is concentrated in and around the centre, but there are several good mid-range places further afield on the road to the airport.

PLACES TO STAY – BUDGET

Avoid the cheapest hotels, usually known as 'pensions', dotted around the market place. Most of them double as brothels and can't be seriously recommended. Much better are those just off Harnet Ave. The following places (all with shared shower) are the pick of the bunch.

Pensione Pisa (☎ 12 44 91; Harnet Ave; singles/doubles Nfa85/100) is a friendly guesthouse opposite the Catholic cathedral

---

An Exceptional Architectural Legacy

When Mussolini came to power in Italy in 1922, he nursed two ambitions relating to Italy's role in the Horn: to avenge Italy's defeat at Adwa (see the boxed text 'The Battle of Adwa' in the Northern Ethiopia chapter) and to create a new Roman Empire in Africa. To realise these dreams he needed a strong industrial base. Labour, resources and lire were thus poured into the new colony and, by the 1930s, it was booming. By 1940 Eritrea had become the second-most industrialised country in sub-Saharan Africa.

At the same time – and encouraged by Il Duce – a new and daring architectural movement called Rationalism was springing up in Italy. It was led by an alliance of young architects based in Milan known as the Gruppo 7.

Eritrea, in common with many colonies, became an experimental architectural laboratory in which new and exciting ideas could be tested. Asmara, or Piccola Roma (Little Rome), soon came to epitomise the new philosophy: it was not just beautiful, but was well planned, well built and, above all, functional.

Isolated for nearly 30 years during its war with Ethiopia, Asmara escaped both the trend to build post-colonial piles and the push towards developing-world urbanisation. Today it remains a model Art Deco town, though some buildings are decaying for lack of funds. It is hoped that some of them will be rehabilitated in the near future.

The best way to discover Asmara's built heritage is to walk around the town (see the special section 'Walking Tours in Asmara'). You will see examples of the Art Deco, International, Cubist, Expressionist, Functionalist, Futurist, Rationalist and Neoclassical architectural styles.

and one of the better value central cheapies. It has seven spotless rooms and small but clean toilets. Ask for a room at the back.

The well-kept **Bristol Pension** (☎ 12 16 88; singles/doubles Nfa77/110) near the telecommunications building is another good choice. It has tiny but very decent rooms.

Pensione Stella (Adi Hawsha St; singles/doubles Nfa50/70) off the western end of Harnet Ave can also be recommended. It has hot showers and clean rooms and boasts a central, quiet location.

Red Sea Pension (☎ 12 67 78; singles/doubles Nfa45/55) off the eastern end of Nakfa Ave isn't bad, with modest but tidy rooms arranged around a roof terrace. The hot communal showers are not scrupulously clean.

Ghennet Hotel (☎ 12 49 68; singles/doubles Nfa80/100), opposite the Ministry of Agriculture, about a 10-minute walk from the Catholic cathedral, is a reasonable option in this category. Rooms are far from flash but they are adequate.

Africa Pension (☎ 12 14 36; singles/doubles Nfa120/160), opposite the Italian embassy, has long been a favourite among travellers thanks to its peaceful and attractive setting. A converted villa with a pleasant little garden, it's a rather impoverished aristocrat, with 10 adequate, large rooms. The communal toilets and showers are of a more dubious cleanliness than the rooms. It's not a bad place overall, but it's overpriced.

PLACES TO STAY – MID-RANGE

Sheghay Hotel (☎ 12 65 62; singles/doubles with shower Nfa140/165), a block south of the cathedral, is good value with decent, tidy rooms. It has a roof terrace with great views over the town. It can be noisy at night.

Also worth considering is **Khartoum Hotel** (☎ 12 80 08; singles & doubles with/without shower Nfa230/198). This well-kept hotel one block south of Harnet Ave offers very clean rooms and boasts a central location. The rooms with shower are unsurprisingly more cheerful and have satellite TV.

Ambassador Hotel (☎ 12 65 44, fax 12 63 65; Harnet Ave; singles with shower US$17-28, doubles US$29-39), though a bit aged, is still good value. Some of the newer hotels may have better facilities, but few can beat the Ambassador's brilliant, albeit slightly noisy spot in the heart of town. The cheaper singles are fairly plain, but the other rooms have more character. There's a good **restaurant** on the premises, with European and

Eritrean specialities on offer. Prices include breakfast. Credit cards are accepted.

Top Five Hotel (☎ 12 49 22, 12 49 19, fax 12 49 31; Marsatekly Ave; singles with shower Nfa165-330, doubles Nfa200-400) is a reliable and great-value option not far from the centre. It has neat rooms with satellite TV and telephone. An added bonus is the **restaurant** (mains Nfa25-50 plus taxes) featuring excellent local and European specialities in an attractive setting.

Selam Hotel (☎ 12 72 44, fax 12 06 62; Mariam GMBI St; singles/doubles with shower Nfa180/240, deluxe rooms Nfa300, suites Nfa360), just west of the Governor's Palace, is still a fine example of Art Deco architecture, though it's getting on a bit. The rooms don't win any prizes for modernity but are good value, especially the large suites. There's a quiet garden at the back and a restaurant.

Hamasien Hotel (☎ 12 34 11, 12 02 33, fax 12 25 95; e embasera_hamasien@tse.com.er; singles/doubles with shower US$28/38, suites US$36/49) lies in peaceful surroundings south of Harnet Ave. The ageing colonial building has lost much of its character and has drab, 1970s-style rooms with satellite TV and telephone. Credit cards are accepted, but there's a 7% commission.

Ambasoira Hotel (☎ 12 32 22, 12 34 11, fax 12 25 95; e embasera_hamasien@tse.com.er; singles/doubles with shower US$40/57, suites US$48/68). Very close to the Hamasien, it has similar standards (read: it's another overpriced government-run place), but it remains popular. The rooms are time-warped but relatively well-equipped. Prices include breakfast. Credit cards are accepted, but there's a 7% commission.

The towering **Alla Scala Hotel** (☎ 15 16 10, 15 15 40, fax 15 15 41; singles/doubles with shower US$33/66), about 4km from the city centre on the road to the airport, caters to business travellers and tourists alike. Standards are more than acceptable, with 28 well-appointed rooms, a bar and a restaurant. Prices include breakfast. Credit cards are accepted.

ERITREA

PLACES TO STAY – TOP END

The following hotels all offer rooms with bathroom.

Albergo Italia, formerly known as Keren Hotel, a couple of blocks north of the western end of Harnet Ave, is housed in an old colonial building with lots of character. It was undergoing a major revamp at the time of writing. It should feature 19 superbly decorated suites with all the mod cons and two high-class restaurants.

Expo Hotel (☎ *18 27 08, 18 66 95, fax 18 66 86; singles or doubles US$24, singles/doubles US$42/48, doubles first class US$60)*, in the vicinity of the Alla Scala Hotel, is one of the best deals in this bracket. It is professionally run, with smart modern rooms and good facilities, including a sauna, a decent restaurant and a bar. Rooms have satellite

TV and the bathrooms are spotlessly clean. The cheaper rooms are featureless but make a worthwhile budget option. It's a bit out of the way – in the Tiravolo district, a five-minute taxi ride from the centre.

Almost next door to the Expo is the **Bologna Hotel** (☎ *18 66 95, 18 13 60, fax 18 26 86; singles or doubles US$48-72)*, another modern establishment featuring good facilities, a bar and a restaurant. The rooms are bright and well-appointed and have satellite TV. That said, it's fairly pricey for what you get, although discounts of up to 30% are routinely offered during slack times.

Savanna International Hotel (☎ *11 61 83, 20 21 41, fax 20 21 46; singles US$30-70, doubles US$45-85)*. Housed in an unexceptional, white, cubic building, this hotel offers clean and well-appointed rooms with TV and

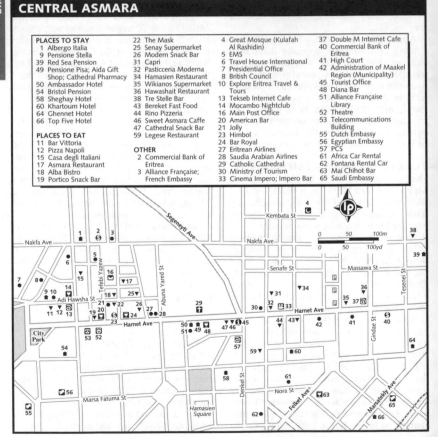

CENTRAL ASMARA

PLACES TO STAY
1 Albergo Italia
9 Pensione Stella
39 Red Sea Pension
49 Pensione Pisa; Aida Gift Shop; Cathedral Pharmacy
50 Ambassador Hotel
54 Bristol Pension
58 Sheghay Hotel
60 Khartoum Hotel
64 Ghennet Hotel
66 Top Five Hotel

PLACES TO EAT
11 Bar Vittoria
12 Pizza Napoli
15 Casa degli Italiani
17 Asmara Restaurant
18 Alba Bistro
19 Portico Snack Bar

22 The Mask
25 Senay Supermarket
26 Modern Snack Bar
31 Capri
32 Pasticceria Moderna
34 Hamasien Restaurant
35 Wikianos Supermarket
36 Hawashait Restaurant
38 Tre Stelle Bar
43 Bereket Fast Food
44 Rino Pizzeria
46 Sweet Asmara Caffe
47 Cathedral Snack Bar
59 Legese Restaurant

OTHER
2 Commercial Bank of Eritrea
3 Alliance Française; French Embassy

4 Great Mosque (Kulafah Al Rashidin)
5 EMS
6 Travel House International
7 Presidential Office
8 British Council
10 Explore Eritrea Travel & Tours
13 Tekseb Internet Cafe
14 Mocambo Nightclub
16 Main Post Office
20 American Bar
21 Jolly
23 Himbol
24 Bar Royal
27 Eritrean Airlines
28 Saudia Arabian Airlines
29 Catholic Cathedral
30 Ministry of Tourism
33 Cinema Impero; Impero Bar

37 Double M Internet Cafe
40 Commercial Bank of Eritrea
41 High Court
42 Administration of Maakel Region (Municipality)
45 Tourist Office
48 Diana Bar
51 Alliance Française Library
52 Theatre
53 Telecommunications Building
55 Dutch Embassy
56 Egyptian Embassy
57 PCS
61 Africa Car Rental
62 Fontana Rental Car
63 Mai Chihot Bar
65 Saudi Embassy

telephone. There's also a bar and restaurant. The drawcard here is the quiet location, southwest of Harnet Ave but still within walking distance of the centre. Rates include breakfast.

Sunshine Hotel (☎ *12 78 80, 12 78 82, fax 12 78 66; BDHO Ave; singles/doubles US$67/85, suites US$102/131*), west of the centre, is a modern establishment offering comfortable if rather small rooms. All rooms have satellite TV and some have balconies. There is also an attractive garden at the back where you can enjoy a drink. The **restaurant** (*mains Nfa35-110 plus taxes*) has an eclectic menu that includes veal escalope and chicken curry. Internet access is also available. Rates include breakfast.

Opened in 2000, the massive **Hotel Inter-Continental Asmara** (☎ *15 04 00, fax 15 04 01;* e *intercon@eaol.com.er; rooms US$210*) is *the* top-of-the-range hotel of Asmara and the only five-star hotel in the country. It lies 4km from the town centre on the airport road.

The hotel has all the facilities you'd expect from an international-class hotel, including conference rooms, various cafés and bars, a business centre with Internet access, a fitness centre, a nightclub and a superb swimming pool. The 170 luxurious rooms come with balconies, TV and phone. It also hosts two **restaurants** (*mains Nfa40-95 plus tax*) serving tasty, but expensive, international food.

PLACES TO EAT

Many Asmara restaurants – particularly the more upmarket ones – add a tax of up to 15% to bills. Unless otherwise specified, most places are open every day. Note that most of the larger restaurants close around 10pm.

Apart from the smart places, most restaurants charge about the same for drinks with your meal: Nfa6 to Nfa25 for local wine or Nfa90 to Nfa150 for imported wine. Beer costs around Nfa5/15 for local/imported varieties.

Street names are mentioned here where appropriate.

Restaurants

Local & Italian The market area is home to a cluster of little restaurants. They're nothing fancy, but they offer authentic fare at very moderate prices.

Pizza Napoli (*pizzas Nfa18-35*), at the western end of Harnet Ave, is a simple but authentic place well-known for its tasty pizzas. Try the *pizza della casa* which has 'a little of everything'. There's also a great *pizza vegetariana* for Nfa19/22 for small/large size.

Hamasien Restaurant (*mains Nfa20-30*); tucked off Harnet Ave, this little joint with red tablecloths is a good place to sample Eritrean specialities as well as meat dishes, pasta and soups.

Asmara Restaurant (*mains Nfa20-40*), near the main post office, is popular with locals. It's simple, reasonably priced and the food is consistently good.

Hawashait Restaurant (*Gindae St; pizzas Nfa20-40*), just off the eastern end of Harnet Ave, is a cheerful little place. As well as pizzas, it does a good selection of Eritrean dishes at moderate prices.

Castello (*mains Nfa20-40 plus tax*), southwest of the centre, is not easy to locate (take a taxi) but has a friendly outdoor seating area. The interior has an old-fashioned charm. You can enjoy Italian dishes, including cannelloni here.

Milano Restaurant (*Felket Ave; mains Nfa25-50 plus tax*) is a long-standing favourite in Asmara. It has two rooms. The one at the back serves excellent local food in a great, traditional setting. The one at the front is a more classic option in unexceptional surrounds with standard Italian and Eritrean dishes. Try the house speciality, *tibs zil zil* (sizzling lamb).

Casa degli Italiani (*mains Nfa20-60; closed Sun dinner*) at the western end of Harnet Ave, a block north of the avenue, is a small trattoria-like eatery, with good pasta and meat dishes.

Blue Nile Bar & Restaurant (☎ *11 79 65; Semaeat Ave; mains Nfa30-95 plus tax*) is a very atmospheric place popular with well-heeled locals and expats alike. It is regarded as the best restaurant in town and offers delicious local dishes, including fried lamb and minced meat in a traditionally decorated room. It has prices to match, but it is a true delight to the palate. If you want to stick to Western-style food, there is also a good selection of pasta and burgers. Bookings are essential for dinner.

Caravel Bar & Restaurant (☎ *12 38 30; Semaetat Ave; mains Nfa25-60 plus tax*), just off the southern end of Semaetat Ave, has a good reputation, but the setting lacks a bit of atmosphere. The menu offers a good choice of soups, pasta, pizzas, meat dishes, fish and local food.

Rino Pizzeria (*pizzas Nfa22-45*), tucked in a side street off Harnet Ave, opposite Cinema Impero, is a decent place to taste pizzas and some Eritrean dishes. It stays open late.

ERITREA

Mar Rosso *(☎ 20 19 59; set menu lunch/dinner Nfa40/45 plus tax; open Mon-Sat)*, opposite St George's Episcopal Church, is a well-established restaurant offering decent Italian fare. The set menu changes daily and is good value.

Da Silla *(mains Nfa40-60 plus tax; open Mon-Sat)*, about 200m east of Bahti Meskerem Square, is fairly upmarket and fashionable. It serves enticing pasta dishes, such as penne or *farfalle al pesto*, along with some Eritrean specialities.

Sembel Huts *(☎ 18 15 54; mains Nfa25-42 plus tax)* is a complex on the airport road about 6km southwest of town and 500m from the Hotel Inter-Continental. It serves a wide array of mains to suit all tastes, as well as snacks. The Sunday barbecue (Nfa60) is quite popular.

Other Tucked off Harnet Avenue, **Legese Restaurant** *(☎ 12 00 41; Mata St; mains Nfa35-55 plus tax)* is something of an institution in Asmara. It offers excellent cooking, including meat dishes, pasta, fish and imaginative chef's suggestions. It's popular with well-heeled locals as well as expats.

Cherhi Bar & Restaurant *(☎ 11 50 54; mains Nfa25-50 plus tax)* is a set on a hill around 1.5km from Harnet Ave north of the centre of town. The building looks like an air-traffic control tower but it's got great panoramic views over Asmara. The food is authentic and good, with a wide assortment of pasta, fish and meat dishes.

Bereket Fast Food *(Harnet Ave; mains Nfa15-40)*, near the Municipality, is the best place in town for a fast feed and is very busy at lunchtime. It's a clean place, serving not only burgers and sandwiches but also fish, beef, chicken and pasta. In addition, it does excellent fruit juices for about Nfa10 and delicious yoghurts. Breakfast fare includes omelettes, scrambled eggs and cornflakes.

Cathedral Snack Bar *(Harnet Ave; mains Nfa17-40)* just opposite the Catholic cathedral is a modern eatery offering various snacks, burgers, fruit juices and pastries.

Portico Snack Bar *(Harnet Ave; mains Nfa20-25)*, opposite the theatre, is popular with students and has burgers and sandwiches. It's a great place for juices and milkshakes.

Alba Bistro *(Adi Hawsha St; mains Nfa15-45)* is a snazzy, busy place near Mocambo nightclub. It's good spot for a snack or a quick meal any time of the day, or for a full breakfast (Nfa37).

The Mask Place *(Adi Hawsha St; mains Nfa25-40 plus tax)* off the western end of Harnet Ave, opposite Alba Bistro, is a newish place with a Western feel. It's a good place if you just want some grilled meat with french fries or a burger.

If you fancy a change from Eritrean or Italian food, head to **China Star Restaurant** *(☎ 12 58 53; Beirut St; mains Nfa20-110 plus tax; closed Sun lunch)*, southeast of the centre, off Semaetat Ave. This Chinese restaurant is much appreciated by the staff of the Chinese embassy, and is well known for its wide-ranging menu. The braised fish with soy sauce is worth a try. There's a popular buffet lunch on Thursday.

Some of the smarter hotels have their own restaurants and serve average to excellent local and international food, though at more expensive prices than elsewhere (see Places to Stay earlier).

Cafés & Pastry Shops

Most places listed in this section serve pastries (usually made on the premises) and fruit juices, and are great for breakfast. Most are open by 7am, some earlier.

Ahazz Pastry *(Bahti Meskerem Square)* is probably one of the best places in town for quality and choice. Pastries include finger-licking chocolate éclairs, meringues and doughnuts and cost about Nfa2. The smoky cappuccinos make a great accompaniment.

Tre Stelle Bar *(Nakfa Ave)*, at the eastern end of Nakfa Ave, is a modest and old-fashioned place brimming with *macchiato*-sipping regulars.

Bar Vittoria *(Adi Hawsha St)* is an unpretentious and cheap place, with a good selection of cakes and great cappuccino (Nfa1.50).

Casa degli Italiani (see Local & Italian earlier) is one of the most agreeable places in town. It has a pleasant, palm-shaded courtyard and is a great place to scribble a postcard or two over a coffee or a cocktail (Nfa12).

Modern Snack Bar, off Harnet Ave, does great local breakfasts, and has excellent yoghurt.

Crispi Bar, west of the centre, is a finely restored old Italian bar with a touch of character.

Awet Y. Pastry, near the British Consulate, has a great selection of freshly baked pastries to take away for a picnic.

Sweet Asmara Caffe *(Harnet Ave)*, almost opposite the Catholic cathedral, is a bright, modern place that attracts a fair crowd of people at peak times, thanks to a wide selection of tempting pastries.

Pasticceria Moderna *(Harnet Ave)* and **Impero Bar** *(Harnet Ave)*, almost next door to Cinema Impero, are both very popular. When it's warm, the outdoor tables fill up. These two snazzy places are perfect to watch the world go by while enjoying a treat or sipping a *macchiato*. Impero Bar is more traditional, while Pasticceria Moderna has a modern, trendy feel.

Capri *(Mata St)* is a large, unassuming place near the cathedral but comes recommended for its exquisite fruit juices (Nfa6 to Nfa8).

Self-Catering
Wikianos supermarket opposite the municipality has the best selection of products, and is a favourite with European expats. Most food is imported, so prices are much higher than in local supermarkets.

Senay Supermarket, near Modern Snack Bar, is a cheaper option than Wikianos.

ENTERTAINMENT
Asmara does not have a real nightlife district yet. Places are scattered in various parts of the city and are fairly safe for single women travellers (at least in comparison with other African cities), but expect to be the focus of attention.

Pubs & Bars
Most bars stay open until 10pm or 11pm during the week, and until at least 2am at the weekend.

American Bar at the western end of Harnet Ave is a bit rough and ready but it has outside tables.

Diana Bar *(Harnet Ave)* opposite the Catholic cathedral is a cheerful, down-to-earth little spot, popular for its Western music and lively atmosphere.

Mai Chihot Bar *(Felket Ave)* is more 'local' than the others but just as lively. It's usually crammed with local bar girls, but it's fun and the music is diverse.

Bar Zilli *(Semaetat Ave)* near Blue Nile Restaurant, is a bit out of the way but is the perfect place to sample a draught beer.

Bar Royal *(Harnet Ave)* towards the western end of Harnet Ave is considered one of the most chic places in town, but it's a bit Westernised. It gets lively late in the afternoon. You can sip a coffee, a beer or a freshly squeezed orange juice (Nfa15).

Zara *(Semaetat Ave)* is the city's top-notch address for a cocktail (Nfa40). The dimly lit interior and the sofas create a rather cosy atmosphere. It draws a mixed set of locals tending towards the beautiful people, as well as numerous expats.

The Mask Place (see Places to Eat earlier) is also a convenient hangout in the evening.

The bars of the larger hotels are also worth a try (see Places to Stay earlier).

Discos & Nightclubs
Most clubs open only on Friday and Saturday (from around midnight to 5am). Entrance costs between Nfa30 and Nfa75, depending on the venue and on the day, and local beer costs between Nfa10 to Nfa20. Transport is not a problem; taxis usually line up outside the nightclubs.

Mocambo *(Adi Hawsha St)*, with its modern black and white decor, is regarded as one of the most hip nightclubs. During the week, it functions as a bar and entrance is free. It's a good place for live music, both traditional and Western.

Shamrock, about 150m from Alla Scala Hotel, inside Expo Park, is not the most sophisticated dance venue in town, but is also worth a try.

Warsa is a new complex in Godaif district, towards the airport. It can get packed at weekends, mostly with wealthy Eritreans and adventurous expats, and is quite atmospheric. Music is predominantly local, with a live band on stage.

Sembel Huts (see Places to Eat earlier), another complex out towards the airport, is a popular dance venue from Thursday to Saturday. Music is a mix of Eritrean and international hits.

The Green Pub in Hotel Inter-Continental Asmara (see Places to Stay earlier) becomes a disco on Wednesday, Friday and Saturday (admission free). It is one of the favourite haunts of expats, and can get frantic at weekends.

Traditional Music
The larger hotels and restaurants sometimes put on reasonable performances by local musicians and dancers. The best time to see traditional performances is during the Orthodox Christian festivals. Check out the listings in local papers such as the *Eritrea Profile*.

Cinema
Impero *(Harnet Ave)* is one of the best places in town. It shows action-packed American, Italian and Saudi films (in the original language).

ERITREA

ERITREA

SHOPPING

There are a limited number of souvenir shops in Asmara. For variety and colour, your best bet is to head for the market – see Markets earlier in this section.

A couple of souvenir shops worth mentioning include **Aida Gift Articles Shop** *(Harnet Ave)*, in the same building as Pensione Pisa, and **Jolly** *(Adi Hawsha Ave)*, one block north of Harnet Ave. Items range from traditional paintings to carved figures, jewellery and pottery. For musical instruments, **Olive Wood & African Curio Shop** *(Semaetat Ave, at the Sandals)* is recommended.

There are goldsmiths and leather shops in the street running parallel to Harnet Ave, a block north. Gold goes for Nfa200 to Nfa250 per gram; silver is Nfa20 per gram.

GETTING THERE & AWAY
Air

The airport is 6km southwest of Asmara.

For details of international and national flights to/from Asmara airport, see the Getting There & Away and Getting Around sections earlier in this chapter.

Departure tax is Nfa15 for national flights and US$15 for international flights. The latter can only be paid in US dollars in cash, so make sure you have some with you, as they're unobtainable at the airport bank.

Airlines with offices in Asmara include the following:

Daallo Airlines (☎ 12 48 48, 12 56 56) Represented by Adulis Shipping Line/Afro Gulf Travel Agency, near Sunshine Hotel

EgyptAir (☎ 12 74 92, fax 12 74 73) Just off Bahti Meskerem Square

Eritrean Airlines (☎ 12 41 11, 12 55 00; ⓔ ersales@cts.com.er) Harnet Ave. Also acts as agent for Regional Airlines (flights to Djibouti and Nairobi).

Lufthansa (☎ 18 69 04, fax 18 12 26) Saba Building, Andinet Ave (towards the airport)

Saudi Arabian Airlines (☎ 12 01 56) Harnet Ave

Sudan Airways (☎ 20 21 61, fax 20 23 78) BDHO Ave, near the British consulate

Yemenia Yemen Airways (☎ 12 00 59, fax 12 01 07) Harnet Ave, near Wikianos supermarket

Bus

The **city bus terminal** lies next to the central market on Eritrea Square. The **long-distance bus station** is about 10 minutes' walk due north of Harnet Ave, and is split into three different terminals. The **ticket office** at the main bus terminal is open from 5am to 6pm daily.

Buses to Nefasit (Nfa4), Massawa (Nfa14, 3½ hours), Ghinda (Nfa6), Assab (Nfa103), Agordat (Nfa20, four to five hours), Barentu (Nfa28) and Teseney (Nfa44, one day) leave from the main bus station. There are numerous buses to Massawa until late in the afternoon. For the other destinations, buses leave early in the morning. Tickets to Barentu, Teseney and Assab should be bought one day in advance. For Assab, there are three buses per week.

Buses to Keren (Nfa11, 1½ hours) leave every half hour from the second bus station. If you want to continue to Nakfa, you must change at Keren.

Southbound buses to Dekemhare (Nfa4.75, one hour), Mendefera (Nfa7, 1½ hours), Adi Quala (Nfa11, 2½ hours), Senafe (Nfa16, four hours) and Adi Keyh (Nfa13, four hours) leave from the third bus terminal. There is no fixed schedule. Most buses leave early in the morning and when they are full. Tickets are sold on the bus.

GETTING AROUND

Central Asmara is so small that almost all places can be reached within 20 minutes on foot.

To/From the Airport

A taxi from the town to the airport should cost around Nfa50.

You can also take the city bus No 1, which passes in front of the cathedral on Harnet Ave; it costs Nfa1. Buses normally come every 20 to 25 minutes, but the service is erratic and you can wait up to 40 minutes.

From the airport, taxis may demand Nfa50 or more. To catch the bus, bear left at the airport exit; the bus stop is a two-minute walk to the far end of the airport compound. The bus service runs from 6am to 7.30pm.

Bus

Red Mercedes buses serve all parts of the town. It costs 50¢ for journeys within town, and Nfa1 for journeys to the periphery and beyond. The No 1 bus, which runs along Harnet Ave and out to the airport, passing the Hotel Inter-Continental and Sembel Huts complex, is probably the most useful for travellers.

Car Rental

The most reliable car rental companies include:

Africa Car Rental (☎ 12 17 55, fax 12 65 36)
Alpha Travel Rent Car (☎ 15 19 70, fax 15 06 32)

Fontana Rental Car (☎ 12 00 52, fax 12 79 05, e fontana@gemel.com.er)

Leo Car Rental (☎ 12 58 59, 20 23 07, fax 20 23 06, e dilorenzo@cts.com.er)

Taxi

Taxis are used rather like buses. If you are on a main route, such as Harnet Ave, just flag one down. If there's space, it will stop, and you'll pay a shared price of Nfa2 per person.

If you hire the taxi for yourself, or take it off the main routes, it will cost Nfa20 to Nfa40. There are no meters, so you should always agree a fare in advance. At night, fares usually double. On Harnet Ave, taxis can be found 24 hours a day.

If you are planning on a few trips around town, or if you're out partying for the evening, you can hire a taxi for a few hours for a set rate of around Nfa200 (negotiable).

Around Asmara

Asmara is a good base to explore the country, and there are some excellent places within a day's trip of Asmara, such as Filfil, renowned for its superb landscape, and Debre Bizen monastery, which gives an enlightening glimpse of the religious heritage of the country.

FILFIL
ፍልፍል

The area around Filfil, north of Asmara, is home to Eritrea's last remnant of tropical forest. It forms part of the Semenawi Bahri or 'Green Belt' area and, amid the arid starkness of the surrounding landscape, rises up oasis-like before you, cool, lush and verdant. There are also plantations of coffee and fruit trees. The forest is evergreen, so it's good to visit any time of year, but it's particularly lush from October to February, after the heavy rains.

Filfil is one of the best places in Eritrea to see birds and mammals. Vervet monkeys and hamadryas baboons are easily seen, and gazelles, duikers, bushbucks, klipspringers and even leopards have been reported.

Getting There & Away

Filfil lies 61km due north of Asmara, and the only way to reach it is along a dirt road. The road has been upgraded, but a 4WD (ideally with a driver to guide you), is still needed. The journey should take around two hours (one way) from Asmara, and makes a great half-day trip. There are beautiful views along the way.

If you have more time, you could consider following the road south all the way down to the coastal plain, where it joins the road from Massawa to Asmara. The whole circuit takes around six hours (without a stop). The route is known as the Pendice Orientali, and takes you through some of the most dramatic and diverse landscape in Eritrea. It makes a great day excursion.

If your budget doesn't stretch to car hire, the only option is to take a bus to Keren – ask to be dropped off at the junction for Filfil, and try to hitch a lift with one of the trucks taking supplies to the village. There's very little traffic so it's a bit risky, but if you leave early enough you might be in luck.

DEBRE BIZEN MONASTERY
ደብረ ቢዜን ገዳም

The monastery of Debre Bizen, near Nefasit, lies 2400m above sea level. It was founded in 1368 by Abuna Philippos. The library at the monastery contains over 1000 manuscripts as well as various church relics, including crowns, robes and incense burners. On a clear day, the view from the monastery is breathtaking – you can see the Dahlak Islands in the Red Sea. The birdlife is good in the woodlands around the monastery.

As with many Orthodox monasteries, Debre Bizen is not open to women (or any female creatures, including hens and female donkeys!). But even if you can't enter the monastery, the journey still makes a great hike.

Men need to obtain a permit to visit the monastery (see Travel Permits under Facts for the Visitor earlier in this chapter) or they will be turned back. Bring lots of water (only rainwater is available). You will be welcomed with *sewa* (home-brewed beer) and bread when you arrive.

Men are welcome to stay at the simple monastery guesthouse (with just a bed or goatskin) for a couple of days. There's no charge but it's normal to make a contribution to the upkeep of the monastery. Simple gifts are a good idea too (sugar, coffee, candles etc).

Warning

Note that all bus journey duration times in this chapter are indications only. Times vary greatly according to individual vehicles, weather and road conditions.

Getting There & Away

To get to Debre Bizen, take the bus to Ghinda and get off at Nefasit (Nfa4, 30 to 45 min). A taxi costs around Nfa250. From Nefasit, it's a 1½- to two-hour steep walk. A local will show you the start of the path up to the monastery.

Northern Eritrea

With its interesting people, landscape and history, the north is one of the most rewarding – albeit demanding – travel destinations in Eritrea.

Easily accessible from Asmara is the attractive market town of Keren, long a crossroads for people of different religions, ethnic groups and languages.

Less accessible, in the remote and wild province of Sahel, is the town of Nakfa. The journey alone is a lesson in Eritrean history. During the Struggle for Independence, every inch of the road was fought over, and the carcasses of the tanks that line the road testify to the ferocity of the fighting. Few travellers ever get here, but Nakfa, like the site of a pilgrimage, is worth the long, gruelling journey.

Though arid, eroded and bleak, the landscape of the north can be incredibly beautiful. Ancient baobab and acacia trees dot the plains, and at dusk, the Sahel mountains turn a shade of blue. Camels – sometimes making up huge caravans – far outnumber vehicles. The patchwork tents of the Tigré nomads are visible everywhere, and around Keren the beautiful Bilen women, adorned with large gold rings in their noses and henna tattoos on their necks and faces, can be seen squatting in the shade of acacia trees.

During the rains from July to September, the roads north can become impassable. Rivers rise quickly, leaving incredible debris on the roads. You should check road conditions before you set out.

KEREN
ከረን

pop 75,000 • elevation 1392m
Set on a small plateau at 1392m above sea level, and surrounded by mountains, Keren is one of Eritrea's most attractive towns.

Trade blossomed once Keren was connected to Asmara by the old Italian railway, and the little town grew rapidly. Today it is the third-largest town in the country and is still an important centre of commerce.

Nevertheless Keren remains firmly small-town in flavour, and this is largely its attraction. Since Italian colonial days, the town has been a popular weekend retreat for the inhabitants of Asmara.

Controlling the northern gateway to Asmara, and the western route to Agordat, Keren's strategic position has always been very important. During WWII, it was the scene of bitter fighting between the Italians and the British. From the 1970s to the 1990s, it was fiercely contested during the Struggle for Independence.

On the roadside look out for the evergreen shrub known locally as *adaï* that is used as a natural toothbrush.

Information

The centre of Keren is marked by the Giro Fiori (Circle of Flowers) roundabout.

Travellers cheques can be cashed at the **Commercial Bank** *(open 8am-11am & 2pm-4pm Mon-Fri, 8am-11am Sat)*.

There's a **post office** *(open 8am-noon & 2pm-6pm Mon-Fri, 8am-noon Sat)* and the **telecommunications office** *(open 8am-8pm daily)*, both opposite Keren Hotel.

Internet access at **TSM Cybercafé** *(open 8am-10pm daily)*, opposite Mackerel Seafood Restaurant, costs Nfa10 an hour.

Things to See & Do

The scene of much fighting in the past, Keren is home to a number of graveyards. The **British War Cemetery** lies off the Agordat road, about 2.5km northwest of the centre. In it, 440 Commonwealth troops lie buried, including the Hindu soldier Subadar Richpal Ram of the Sixth Rajputana Rifles, who was posthumously awarded the Victoria Cross, Britain's highest military decoration for bravery.

Just past the cemetery, a small **statue of the Madonna** watches over the road from Agordat in the west.

The well-tended **Italian Cemetery** lies close to the market, and if you continue on foot a further 20 minutes, you come to the shrine of **St Maryam Dearit** (see the boxed text 'Madonna of the Baobab'), 2.3km out of town. On 29 May every year, there's a pilgrimage to the site, and hundreds of people congregate to dance and sing; if you're in the region at this time, don't miss it.

The old Italian **railway station** (now a bus station) and the old **residential area** testify to Keren's Italian heritage. As in Asmara, some of the architecture is exceptional for

Cinema Impero, an example of Italian Art Deco architecture in Asmara

Prehistoric paintings near Senafe

Italian-style chemist, Asmara

Dolphin, Red Sea

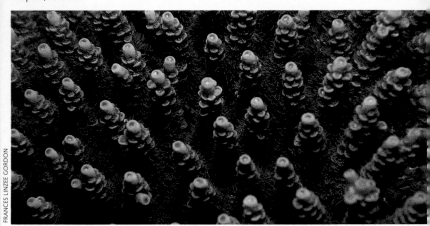

Colourful Red Sea coral

Hawksbill turtle

the period. Several Italian Roman Catholic churches dot the town, including **St Antonio** and **St Michael**.

Overlooking the town to the northeast is the **Tigu**, the Egyptian fort at 1460m, dating from the 19th century. At its foot lie the ruins of the old Imperial Palace, which were destroyed during the Struggle in 1977. There are good views from the top of the fort.

For information on Keren's markets, including the camel market, see Shopping later in this section.

Places to Stay

Bottom of the heap is **Eritrea Hotel** *(singles/ doubles with shared shower Nfa30/40)* near Sicilia Pension. **Senhit Hotel** *(rooms Nfa30)*, opposite Keren Hotel, is another cheapie. Both have basic rooms and pongy communal showers and toilets.

One notch up, **Sicilia Pension** *(☎ 40 10 59; singles or doubles without shower Nfa30-50, with shower Nfa65)* is an old colonial place with a leafy courtyard and is a good choice in the budget category. The rooms are adequate.

Yohannes Hotel *(☎ 40 14 22; rooms Nfa60)*, very close to Sicilia Pension, offers 22 clean but rather cramped rooms.

Barka Hotel *(☎ 40 13 50; singles/doubles with shared shower Nfa20/40)*, behind Albergo Sicilia, has reasonable rooms set around a pleasant leafy courtyard. The sign is in Tigrinya and Arabic only.

The central **Keren Hotel** *(☎ 40 10 14; singles or doubles with shared shower Nfa60-100, with shower Nfa104)* has seen better days and offers rather overpriced rooms. Some are better than others, so ask to see a few. Its main drawcard is its restaurant. It also has a roof terrace with good views of the town, and an unusual 'observation tower'.

On the outskirts of town on the Agordat road is the well-run **Shege Hotel** *(☎ 40 19 71; singles/doubles with shower Nfa80/130)*. Even though the location is not so convenient, it is probably the most reliable option in Keren. It boasts an inviting courtyard and neat rooms with balcony and the small restaurant offers mains for less than Nfa25.

Places to Eat

Most hotels have their own restaurant, but the menus tend to be standard and a little unimaginative.

Keren Hotel *(mains Nfa15-30)* is a decent place to eat. The menu mixes up Italian and local dishes.

Madonna of the Baobab

Close to Keren's market area there stands an ancient and gnarled baobab tree. Long venerated by the locals, it is believed to mark the spot from which fertility springs.

In the late 19th century, the Sisters of Charity built a small chapel in the tree, in the place where the city's orphans played, and it became known as St Maryam Dearit – the Madonna of the Baobab.

In 1941, some Italian soldiers took refuge in the tree from British planes. Though the tree was hit, it, the Italians and the shrine survived.

Today, according to local tradition, if a women desires a husband or a child, she must prepare coffee in the shade of the tree. If a traveller passes by and accepts a cup, her wish will be granted.

Estifanos Memorial Cafe & Restaurant *(mains Nfa10-20)*, opposite Keren Hotel, offers both Italian and local dishes at moderate prices. It also has a shady terrace.

Not surprisingly, **Mackerel Seafood Restaurant** *(mains Nfa12-25)*, off the Giro Fiori, specialises in seafood dishes. The simple but light dining room upstairs looks onto the mosque. A grilled fish or a *zigni* fish (fish cooked in a hot sauce) with cooked vegetables will set you back about Nfa35.

Restaurant Peace & Love *(mains Nfa15-25)* is an informal eatery right on the Giro Fiori. It serves pasta, *capretto*, chicken and rice.

Heran Pastry, next to Red Sea Hotel, serves delicious yoghurts and is probably the best pastry place in town.

Entertainment

The veranda of **Estifanos Bar** is a good place to drink in the evening while watching the world go by. The **Red Sea Hotel** is another popular spot and boasts a pleasant, shady outdoor area. The terrace of **Keren Hotel** is also an ideal place to sip a beer or a juice.

Shopping

Keren's markets are some of the most interesting in the country and are great for an afternoon's exploration. The covered area immediately behind Keren Hotel sells fruit, vegetables, baskets and other household objects. Branching off the covered market are narrow alleyways, columns and low porticoes filled with the whirring machines of tailors and

ERITREA

cloth merchants. Beyond, descending towards the Italian cemetery, lies the grain market.

In another quarter off the covered market, the workshops and boutiques of the silver-smiths can be found. Keren is traditionally the place to buy silver. Although it's a little cheaper than in Asmara (Nfa60 to Nfa80 per gram), the choice may not be as good. The filigree jewellery is particularly sought after.

If you're in town on a Monday between 9am and 3pm, don't miss the clamour of the camel market, 2km out of town on the road to Nakfa. It attracts people from all over the area.

Getting There & Away

Keren lies 91km northwest of Asmara. The road is in good condition.

For Nakfa, one bus leaves each morning at 5am (Nfa40, five to six hours). To Asmara, nearly 30 buses depart daily (Nfa10.75, 2½ hours). For Massawa, change at Asmara. For Barentu, three buses leave each morning (Nfa17.50, three hours). For Teseney, two buses depart each morning (Nfa33, seven hours); for Agordat there are seven daily buses (Nfa9.50, 2½ hours).

Getting Around

If you're short of time, taxis are available. The main taxi stand is close to the Keren Hotel. Most individual journeys cost between Nfa15 and Nfa30 (Nfa15 for the Italian cemetery; Nfa30 for Maryam Dearit or Shege Hotel), or you can hire a taxi for an hour (around Nfa100).

AROUND KEREN

There are a couple of monasteries around Keren, including the **Debre Sina monastery**, thought to date from the 6th century. The older, inner part of the church (which unlike many monasteries in Eritrea is open to both men and women) is hewn from the rock and, according to local tradition, is 2100 years old. The troglodyte dwellings of the 60 nuns and priests who live there can also be visited. The monastery lies around 35km east of Keren on the Gheleb road. You'll need a 4WD, then it's a 15-minute walk to the monastery. Without a vehicle, you could hitch to the approach, then walk from the main road.

AFABET
አፍዓበት

Afabet is best known for the battle which took place in and around the town, and which was the most decisive confrontation of the entire 30-year war. Around the town, you can still see the square-shaped trenches of the Ethiopian soldiers.

Although Afabet is the largest town north of Keren, it doesn't offer much to do. However, if you're travelling north to Nakfa, you may get stuck here overnight. Afabet has a bank and a post office just off the main square.

Accommodation in Afabet is very basic – dirt floors, grill windows and no showers. **Semhar Hotel** (beds Nfa10) is the best of a sorry bunch. Try also **Eritrea Hotel** (beds Nfa10), with similar facilities to the Semhar.

Buses going to Nakfa usually stop in Afabet; as do buses going south from Nakfa to Keren.

NAKFA
ናቕፋ

Lying some 221km from Asmara, at 1780m above sea level, Nakfa is little more than a tiny, remote village perched high in the mountains.

In 1978, after the famous 'Strategic Withdrawal', Nakfa became the EPLF's centre of resistance (see Eritrean Resistance under History in the Facts about Eritrea section). The town lies in a shallow dish at the edge of a mountain ridge that drops several thousand feet to the plain below. Facing south, the town guarded not only the headquarters of the EPLF, but also the essential trade and supply routes to Sudan. For this reason, Nakfa received some of the most intense and continuous assaults of the entire war.

At first sight, the corrugated-iron shacks of the village are hard to reconcile with the legendary Nakfa so venerated by Eritreans. However, Nakfa has become the symbol of the Eritrean resistance, and very recently even gave its name to the country's new currency.

With a little exploration, the town's special history soon reveals itself. Nakfa is a fascinating place, even for those who are not normally military-minded. Some sites are an incredible – and living – memorial to human endurance and courage.

Few travellers get to Nakfa. Your interest in the town will really please the locals, who are among the friendliest and most hospitable people in the country.

Information

Presently, Nakfa resembles a large building site. New constructions are going up fast. Nakfa also has a fuel station.

Electricity shuts off in the whole town at 12.30am; there are no telephones (radio contact only), and no running water except in the one big hotel. There is no public transport around Nakfa either. If you arrive by bus, you'll have to walk to those sites that can be reached on foot. It takes around two hours to get to the trenches on Mt Den Den.

Things to See

To get the most out of the place, you'll need at least half a day's touring with a good local guide. The local administration office can provide visitors with guides who are also ex-fighters. To tour a battlefield with one of the soldiers who fought on it is a worthy experience; but make sure the guide speaks adequate English – not all do.

Nakfa Mosque (ናቅፋ መስጊድ) Nakfa was flattened by the continual Ethiopian bombardments. The mosque was the only building left standing with more than two walls. The first sight of the building, standing tall and resolute amid the ruins, with a gaping hole blown in its cupola, is a memorable experience.

For many Eritreans, the mosque symbolised the unwavering faith of the fighters throughout the Struggle. The building is a beautiful sight at dawn or dusk; its maimed, very distinct profile has made it a favourite subject of Eritrean photographers and artists. It's currently undergoing reconstruction.

Den Den (ደንደን) On the approach to Nakfa, look out for the distinct twin-peaked mountain known as Den Den. It was from here that the fighters broadcast news of the Struggle every day. The radio contact contributed – perhaps more than anything else – to maintaining the morale of the fighters, even when the odds against them looked insurmountable.

You can climb to the top of the mountain (around 1½ hours), from where the views are great. All around, the countryside is bare – denuded, not just by the continual aerial bombardments of the Ethiopians, but by demands for firewood and for the construction of the trenches. To the southwest, the plain is known as Furnello (furnace in Italian), because of the incessant bombing by Soviet-supplied MIGs.

Underground Towns Around the trenches, constructed underground, and carefully camouflaged from the Ethiopian planes, were a series of buildings: the famous underground towns. The functions of these buildings

The Trenches

The shoulder-deep trenches that run warren-like all over the southern ridges of the Den Den mountain give a vivid idea of the daily life of the fighters. Take a peek at the underground bunkers. In these tiny holes, measuring no more than 1m by 2m, five to six fighters ate, slept and fought their war for up to 18 months at a time without a break. The trenches are beautifully constructed, hewn into the stony ground and reinforced with neat, dry-stone walls. Stretching for over 25 miles, the trenches meander across the hillside in an apparently random manner. In fact, these irregular patterns made accurate targeting by Ethiopian long-range artillery almost impossible (see also the boxed text 'A Super Struggle' under History earlier in this chapter).

Until quite recently, the trenches were littered with the bleached bones of soldiers from both sides. Most have now been buried. Shells of every type do still litter the landscape: rockets, mortar bombs, bullets…even napalm casings.

To the north of the trenches, on a peaceful spot overlooking the hillside, lies Dig Dig, the fighters' cemetery. Graves are marked with simple painted metal plaques, with the fighter's name and date of death given in Tigrinya.

ranged from manufacturing weapons to printing literature (see the boxed text 'A Super Struggle' under History earlier in this chapter). At the time of writing, many of these sites were closed because of lack of access. In future, the roads to them will be repaired and the sites will reopen.

The **Tsa'abraha Underground Hospital**, 12.5km from Nakfa on the road to Winna, can be visited. Between 1973 and 1991, at least 100 patients a day were treated in the hospital by five doctors working full time. The wounded were brought here by donkey, mule or camel and important medical equipment was smuggled in from Sudan. The hospital was less sophisticated than the famous Orotta hospital, where even open-heart surgery was performed, but hundreds of lives were nevertheless saved here. Though little more than the dug-out foundations of two hospital buildings and a pharmacy remain, the site is still worth a visit. The 600m walk from the road to the hospital takes you through some beautiful woodland, teeming with birds.

ERITREA

Around 1.5km from the hospital lie the remains of some school buildings. The **Winna Technical College** was another installation dug into the mountainside. It will shortly be relocated to Nakfa. Today, students from all over the country compete for the 85 scholarship places available here.

Places to Stay & Eat

Barring one hotel, most accommodation in Nakfa is spartan – just dirt floors, corrugated-iron walls and no showers. It can get cold at night; if you haven't already got a *shamma* (a light cotton toga, worn by men) or a *gabi* (a slightly thicker version of the *shamma*), now might be the time to buy one.

Apollo Hotel *(singles/doubles with bathroom Nfa115/155)* is the only proper hotel in town, with 22 adequate rooms. When there are enough guests, an electrical generator is switched on and there is hot water at night. The rooms have balconies with beautiful views over the whole town.

You'll find several cheap eateries in the centre of town. They offer basic local and Italian fare.

Getting There & Away

Although Nakfa is just 221km north of Asmara, the journey from the capital takes around 8½ hours. The road after Afabet is very rough in parts and winds through the mountains. Add the heat to this equation and you're in for a tiring journey. One bus leaves each day for Keren at 6am. You can change there for other destinations.

Southern Eritrea

Southern Eritrea is like a vast, open-air archaeological site.

Many of the country's 8000 or so sites are located here, just a fraction of which have been excavated. Though less spectacular than the more famous ruins found to the south in Ethiopia, some ruins are no less important. It is hoped that Qohaito and Metera will eventually be declared Unesco World Heritage Sites.

Even the local settlements – the farmsteads, wells and terraces – are just a continuation of those settled millennia earlier. In the same way, many of the Tigré and Saho peoples' traditions and customs remain completely unchanged. The yoke and plough used to break up the dry, stony, unyielding soil hasn't changed since its development millennia ago. The autumn winnowing – when the chaff is thrown high in the air and trampled by a wheeling team of oxen – is a beautiful, almost biblical, sight.

This interweaving of past and present, along with the new discoveries made almost every day and the mystery that still surrounds Eritrea's ancient past, makes the south a fascinating place to explore. Unfortunately, at the time of writing there was no written information available on the sites themselves, and there were no official guides.

The south is the most densely populated area of Eritrea as well as one of the most cultivated. Euphorbia, eucalyptus and the prickly pear cactus are the most common natural vegetation; the Orthodox churches perched on the hilltops are among the most common built features.

There are two roads leading south to the Ethiopian frontier. One goes to Dekemhare, Segheneyti, Adi Keyh and finally to Senafe; the other goes south via Mendefera and Adi Quala. The roads are generally good, apart from the odd pothole.

If the border crossing with Ethiopia reopens, a good excursion would be around the historical Aksumite sites of the area: the trip from Asmara to Aksum, Adigrat, Senafe and back to Asmara amounts to just 514km, and could be done in three days.

DEKEMHARE
ደቀምሓረ
pop 26,000 • elevation 2060m

The Italians had planned to make Dekemhare the industrial capital of Eritrea. Bypassing Asmara, a road ran directly from the port of Massawa to the uplands, and Dekemhare became an important industrial centre where offices, warehouses and factories were concentrated. During the war of independence, however, the town suffered much damage, and today just two of the old factories still operate: a pasta factory and the biscuit factory Red Sea General Mills. Other remains of colonial days include the old market with its iron roof to protect the fruit, vegetables and grain.

Dekemhare was also famous for its wine industry, and grapes feature in the decorations adorning many balconies around town.

Information

The **Commercial Bank of Eritrea** *(open 8am-11.30am & 2pm-5pm Mon-Fri, 8am-11.30am Sat)* cannot change travellers cheques, but does change cash.

There's a **post office** *(open 8am-noon & 2pm-5.30pm Mon-Fri, mornings 8am-noon Sat)* and a **telecom office** *(open 8am-noon, 2pm-7pm daily)*.

Places to Stay & Eat

Dekemhare's cheapies in the centre tend to be grungy places with little to recommend them except low prices. Safer bets include the recent **Feka Hotel** *(☎ 64 14 35; singles/doubles with shared shower Nfa30, with private shower Nfa60/80)*, on the northern edge of the town, near the bus station, with plain but clean rooms, and the slightly overpriced but centrally located **Paradise Hotel** *(☎ 64 13 16; singles/doubles with shower Nfa 100/150)*, with rather small singles but spacious doubles.

Bana Hotel *(singles or doubles with private shower Nfa40)* is also a good bargain. It features 10 well-kept rooms and is run by welcoming staff.

There's no shortage of cheap eating options in the centre, but the places mentioned earlier have better restaurants where you can tuck into local dishes or pasta for about Nfa30. If you want to treat yourself, the **Castello Bakery & Pastry**, opposite the cinema in the centre, has tempting pastries. There's an adjacent bar.

Getting There & Away

For Asmara there are about 40 buses a day (Nfa4.75, one hour); Adi Keyh has about five buses daily (Nfa10.50, two hours); for Senafe, you'll need to change at Adi Keyh.

There's a rough road that winds from Dekemhare to just north of Mendefera. Three buses travel to Mendefera daily (Nfa7.75, around two hours).

AROUND DEKEMHARE

At the exit from a gorge, at the approach to some experimental agricultural nurseries, is the village of **Segheneyti**, 57km from Asmara. It is dominated by the huge Catholic Church of Saint Michael and two forts from which there are good views.

In season (mid-June to mid-September), Segheneyti and the surrounding area is known for the delicious and surprisingly thirst-quenching *beles* (prickly pear fruit). Little boys sell them for just 10¢ each. Watch out for the skins – they're notorious for their almost invisible thorns.

Continuing south of Segheneyti, the road traverses the plain of Deghera, known popularly as the **Valley of the Sycamores** for the magnificent sycamore figs which march

across the plain. At dusk, the trees make one of the most beautiful natural sights in all of Eritrea. Many are at least 300 years old and there are hopes to declare the whole valley a protected site in the future.

ADI KEYH
ዓዲ ቀይሕ
pop 23,000 • elevation 2390m

Adi Keyh, 104km from Asmara, boasts one green mosque and a chaotic afternoon market. Otherwise it's little more than a staging post for visiting the archaeological ruins of Qohaito.

The **Commercial Bank of Eritrea** *(open 8am-noon & 2pm-8pm Mon-Fri, 8am-noon Sat)* is close to the Catholic church. The **post office** *(open 7am-noon & 2pm-5pm Mon-Fri, 8am-noon Sat)* is just north of the market and the **telecom office** *(open 8am-noon & 2pm-8pm daily)* is on the northern edge of the town.

The town's electricity is switched off at midnight.

Places to Stay & Eat

The rock-bottom hotels around the main square right in the centre are best avoided. Your best bet is to choose one of the places north of the centre. **Adi Key Hotel** *(singles/doubles with shared bathroom Nfa50/80)* has

Stately Sycamores

The sycamore fig *(Ficus sycomoros)* is one of the most common but also most beautiful figs in the Horn. Growing at an altitude of between 500m and 2400m high, it is found along rivers and lake margins, in woodlands, evergreen bushlands, forest edges and forest clearings.

Many people in the Horn consider the tree sacred. The Oromo people in Ethiopia have the tree blazoned on their ethnic flag.

The sycamore is used by the local people in many ways: the wood is used for carvings, the fruit is eaten during times of hardship, and the bark is used in traditional medicine.

The tree also serves a very important social purpose: under its branches in many regions of the Horn, village assemblies take place, as well as popular tribunals, community debates and disputes and advisory sessions from the elders.

The tree is also greatly appreciated for its beauty, its generous shade, and as a fruitful home for beehives.

ዓዲ ቀይሕ

plain and cramped, but acceptable, rooms. **Quohayto Hotel** (*singles or doubles with shared bathroom Nfa30*), off the main road, offers spacious rooms in peaceful surroundings, and **Garden Hotel** (*singles/doubles Nfa30/40*), a block behind the Commercial Bank of Eritrea, is close to the Shell petrol station. It has dull but adequate rooms.

Two other modest but good-value options include **Sami Hotel** (*singles/doubles with shared bathroom Nfa30/40*) and **Midre Ghenet Hotel** (*singles or doubles with shared bathroom Nfa30*), northwest of the centre, near the hospital. Both have clean and quiet rooms.

Most of these hotels serve local food on request, with limited choice. Expect to pay around Nfa20 for a dish.

Getting There & Away

Around 30 buses leave daily for Senafe (Nfa3, 45 min); five go to Dekemhare (Nfa9, three hours); and five go to Asmara (Nfa13, four hours). When the border reopens, services to Zala Ambassa on the Ethiopian border will probably resume.

QOHAITO
ቋሓይቶ

In the 2nd century AD, the famous Egyptian geographer Claudius Ptolemy (who wrote in Greek) made reference to an important ancient town named Koloe. This town flourished at the time of the great Aksumite kingdom (see Aksumite Civilisation under Facts about Eritrea earlier in this chapter) and provided a staging post between the ancient port of Adulis in the north and the capital of the kingdom, Aksum, in the south. It has long been thought that Qohaito was that town.

Even if it was not (some modern scholars favour nearby Metera), Qohaito's importance in the ancient world during this time is obvious.

Very little is known about the exact history of the settlement. A few ancient chronicles record that Qohaito was still flourishing in the 6th century AD. However, like Adulis and Metera, it then vanished very suddenly in the next one or two hundred years.

At an altitude of 2700m, Qohaito lies high above the port of Adulis and the baking lowlands, and may also once have served as a summer retreat for the Aksumite merchants. The traces of cultivated areas found between the buildings have led to the belief that Qohaito was once a garden city.

Orientation & Information

Lying some 121km south of Asmara, Qohaito's impressive ruins are spread over a large area measuring 2.5km wide by 15km long. You'll need a good half day to see all the sites. As much as 90% of the ruins remain unexcavated, and information – even the age of the sites – remains scarce.

A short walk from Qohaito takes you to the edge of a vast canyon that drops away dramatically. The views of the surrounding mountains, including Mt Ambasoira (3013m) to the south (the highest peak in Eritrea), are stunning. Far below, you can make out the terraced fields and tiny *tukuls* (thatched conical huts) of a seemingly inaccessible Saho settlement. Get to the canyon early in the morning, as it tends to cloud over later.

If you want to visit the rock art sites (described later in this section) or the viewpoint, you should ask at the village of Qohaito for a guide. One guide who speaks English is Ibrahim.

Temple of Mariam Wakiro
ማሪያም ዋቂሮ ቤተ - መቕደስ

Among Qohaito's most important ruins is the Temple of Mariam Wakiro, where four columns rise out of a mass of stones and fallen pillars. One of the columns is topped by an unusual four-sided capital. The temple was built on a rectangular plan on a solid platform, and may have been the site of a very early Christian church or even a pre-Christian temple. Nearby, other pilasters and platforms attest to the existence of at least half a dozen other temples. In the local language this site has long been referred to as 'abode of the prestigious ones'.

Egyptian Tomb
ሓወልቲ መቓብር ግብጻውያን

To the north, a little less than a kilometre from the ruins of Mariam Wakiro, lies an ancient underground tomb dug out of sandstone. Discovered in 1894, the tomb was nicknamed 'Meqabir Ghibtsi' or the Egyptian Tomb because of its impressive size. The tomb faces east, overlooking the Hedamo River. Rectangular and built with large blocks of stones, its most distinctive features are the two quatrefoil (flower-shaped) crosses carved on the inside walls.

Saphira Dam
ሳፊራ ግድብ

This remarkable structure, lying just beyond the new village mosque, is Qohaito's greatest claim to fame. Measuring 67m long and 16m deep, the dam is constructed of large rectangular blocks of stone that measure close to 1m by 0.5m. The masonry is quite beautifully dressed – one of the reasons perhaps for the dam's incredible longevity. For around 1000 years, it has served the local Saho people as the main source of water.

A team of German archaeologists has suggested – amid hot controversy – that the structure may actually be a water cistern dating to the Aksumite period, and not a dam dating to the pre-Aksumite period as had previously been thought. However, until the site is properly excavated and investigated, most theories concerning Qohaito are likely to remain just that.

On one of the walls inside the dam are some inscriptions in ancient Ge'ez, the religious language of ancient Aksum. The inscription, made up of 79 words, is the longest yet found in Ge'ez.

Rock Art Sites

At Iyago, near Qohaito, southeast of Mt Faquiti, an open shelter around 9m long is covered in rock paintings dating from approximately 4000 BC to 5000 BC. Nearly 100 figures painted in ochre, black and reddish-brown adorn the rock face, depicting cattle, antelopes and perhaps lions. To get there, it's an easy 15-minute walk from Qohaito.

Another site that's easily accessible is the cave of Adi Alauti. Getting there involves a beautiful 30-minute walk along a mule path down the edge of a gorge. A large number of animals, including camels and gazelles, are depicted in ochre and white.

Other rock shelters in the area include Ba'atti Abager, Zebanona Libanos and Mai Ayni, where figures include warriors with long spears and oval-shaped shields, and Ona Addi Qantsa, where masked dancers wearing animal skins seem to be indulging in a ritual dance.

Getting There & Away

From Adi Keyh, it's an 11km drive south until you reach the left-hand turn-off from the main road, marked by a signpost; then it's a further 10km along a dirt road to the village of Qohaito.

Your best bet is to book a tour with one of the travel agencies in Asmara (see Organised Tours earlier in this chapter). They should provide you with a knowledgeable guide.

AROUND QOHAITO
Toconda
ቶኾንዳ

The Aksumite ruins of Toconda lie 4km south of Adi Keyh in a wide valley. The ground is littered with potsherds, broken pillars and chiselled stones. Close to the dirt road there are two pillars: one standing, another with a curious rounded head. On a hill west of the site, there is an early inscription curved on a large basalt rock. Toconda is unexcavated and very little is known about it.

Keskese
ከስከስ

Keskese lies in a small valley about 400m from the main road, 128km south of Asmara. This huge, unexcavated site is considered exceptional for its pre-Christian and pre-Islamic remains, which include the ancient tomb of a local prince or lord.

Lying among the barley fields like elongated, upturned boats are various huge monoliths, one measuring a giant 14m long. Some stelae bear ancient inscriptions in Ge'ez; from their style, it is believed that they are at least 2500 years old. Elephants are offered as the most likely explanation for the way the immense stones were transported, though this, like everything else here, is shrouded in mystery.

SENAFE
ሰንዓፈ

Lying 139km from Asmara, Senafe is the last Eritrean town of any size before the Ethiopian border. It is famous as the gateway to the ancient city of Metera which is clearly visible on a large plain to the east of the road, 2km south of Senafe. The town was devastated during the war with Ethiopia and many buildings had not been rebuilt at the time of writing. Thousands of people were made homeless and still live in refugee camps on the outskirts of town.

The town has no bank. There's a **post office** *(open 8am-noon & 2pm-6pm Mon-Fri)* and a **telecom office** *(open 8am-8pm daily)*.

Things to See & Do

Apart from the site of Metera, Senafe is known for the huge rocky outcrops that dominate the plain. You can **hike** to the top of Amba Metera, one of the outcrops, in about an hour, though there are several routes with varying degrees of difficulty. Local boys soon appear and will guide you for a small tip. The most popular route takes 45 to 60 minutes and is in parts a scramble over boulders; in

ERITREA

one place, a fixed rope helps you up a short section in which grooves are chiselled into the rock. Heavy or bulky camera equipment should be left behind. From the top there is a great panoramic view that recalls Senafe's name, which is supposedly derived from the Arabic: 'Can you see San'a?'.

Make sure you go early in the morning, as it gets very hazy later on. If you want to walk further in the area, guides can be easily found around the bus station.

The Senafe **market**, located just over a kilometre outside town, is worth a peek, particularly on Saturday, the major market day.

Places to Stay & Eat

Senafe Hotel *(singles/doubles with shared shower Nfa30/50)*, in the centre, near the main intersection, has spartan and cramped rooms.

The no-sign **Embasoira Hotel** *(singles or doubles with shared shower Nfa30)*, almost opposite Senafe Hotel, offers 11 rooms set around a courtyard. They are basic and on the smallish side but the showers are kept cleaner here than at the Senafe.

Momona Hotel *(mains Nfa18-28)* was the only decent hotel before the war but was destroyed by the Ethiopians. There are plans to rebuild it in the near future. The restaurant at the back of the compound is open, though. It has *capretto*, pasta, *zigni* (meat cooked in a hot sauce) and sandwiches.

Getting There & Away

Buses from Senafe go to Adi Keyh at least every hour (Nfa3, 45 min). To Asmara, five or six buses run every day (Nfa16, four hours); to Dekemhare, four or five buses leave daily (Nfa10.50, 3½ hours).

When the border with Ethiopia was open, there were regular buses to Zala Ambessa, the first village after the border.

AROUND SENAFE
Enda-Tsadqan
እንዳጸድቃን

The rock-hewn church of Enda-Tsadqan near the village of Bareknaha, 17km due south of Metera, makes an interesting half-day excursion. You'll need a guide from Senafe to show you the rough track to the village (ask at one of the hotels or the bus station). The church recalls the ancient architectural tradition of Lalibela in Ethiopia (see the Northern Ethiopia chapter). According to tradition it dates from AD 486, when it was built by Gebre Meskel, the son of King Kaleb.

Monastery of Debre Libanos

An excursion to the monastery of Debre Libanos (also known as Debre Hawariyat) is strongly recommended. Debre Libanos is the oldest church in Eritrea, and is accessible from the very remote village of Hamm, perched dramatically on a high plateau, with sweeping views all around.

The monastery is thought to date from the 6th century. It is open only to men (a rule that is strictly enforced) but other parts on the other side of the valley can be visited by women, including a collection of 60 mummified bodies (supposed to date from the 4th century).

The walk from Haaz (see later) is worthwhile for its scenery of dramatic peaks and valleys and views south into Ethiopia. There is a **guesthouse** some 10 minutes from the monastery where you can stay for free (on a goat skin on the floor). Remember to leave a contribution for the monastery. You'll be offered bread and *sewa* (home-brewed beer).

Hamm can be reached in less than two hours by foot from the village of Haaz. To get to Haaz from Senafe, follow the road to the south for about 15km until you reach a turn-off. Then take a dirt track on the right for about 9km – a 4WD is essential. In Haaz, you'll need a guide to show you the way (about Nfa50). From Hamm, a steep and fairly difficult descent takes you down to the monastery (around 50 minutes down). From the monastery, it's a one-hour walk across the valley to reach the site of the mummified bodies. From there your guide can show you a quicker way back to Hamm (about one hour), but expect a steep ascent. Altogether, it's a six-hour loop from Haaz.

A fun alternative is to approach Debre Libanos from Tsorena, about 30km to the northwest. Most travel agencies in Asmara (see Organised Tours under Getting Around earlier in this chapter) can organise camel safaris there.

METERA
መተራ

Situated 2km south of Senafe, near the little village of Metera, are some of Eritrea's most important historical sites. Like Qohaito, Metera flourished around the time of the ancient civilisation of Aksum. (For more information on the Aksumite civilisation, see History in the Facts about Eritrea section.) The scattered ruins testify to the existence of a once large and prosperous town.

Metera *(admission free)* is important for three main reasons: for its age – some of it, from about the 5th century BC, actually pre-dates Aksum; for its huge size – it spreads over at least 20 hectares, making it the largest Aksumite site after Aksum itself and Aksum's port, Adulis; and for its unusual character – it is the only place in the Aksumite civilisation where a large bourgeois community is known to have thrived.

If you've visited Aksum in Ethiopia, you'll soon recognise the typical Aksumite architectural features present at Metera, such as construction in tiers. There are also big differences from Aksum, such as the plan and layout of the buildings. Nevertheless, it is clear that there were very strong cultural ties between Aksum, Adulis and Metera, not just during the Aksumite period, but earlier too.

A word of warning: if you're not an archaeology buff, this historical site is not striking at first sight. Your best bet is to visit the site with a knowledgeable guide. Contact one of the travel agencies in Asmara.

The Stele
ሐወልቲ - ሕልፊ እምነ መኇብር

One of Metera's most important objects is its enigmatic stele. Unique in Eritrea, the stele is known for its pagan, pre-Christian symbol of the sun over the crescent moon, engraved on the top of the eastern face. Like the famous Aksum stelae, it faces eastward.

Standing 2.5m tall, the stele has an inscription near the middle in Ge'ez. An unknown king dedicates the stele to his ancestors who had subjugated the 'mighty people of Awanjalon, Tsebelan'.

Inexplicably, the stele was uprooted from its original position on the hill, and was at one time broken into two pieces. Today it is at the foot of the hill Amba Saim, in front of the open plain. Unfortunately, it fell down during the war, but it should be returned to its upright position soon.

Excavations

Metera was 'discovered' in 1868, when Frenchman Denis de Rivoire reported its existence. In 1903 an Italian officer made a few amateur excavations in two places. The first scientific survey was carried out by the German Aksum Expedition in 1906. In 1959 the Ethiopian Institute of Archaeology began major excavations under the French archaeologist Francis Anfray.

From 1959 to 1965 Anfray excavated various sites. A large mound 100m northwest of the stele revealed a large central building – perhaps a **royal palace** or a villa – attached to an annexe of living quarters. A huge wall surrounds the whole complex. Excavations revealed several burial chambers in the larger building; in one of them, the skeleton of a chained prisoner was discovered.

Between 1961 and 1962, two additional mounds were investigated. Excavations exposed a large, square, multiroomed complex, built on a sturdy podium. A **tomb chamber** was also unearthed – but, curiously, it was empty. During the 1964 excavations the focus was on a cluster of rock-cut tombs on the Amba Saim hill south of the site.

Anfray's excavations also uncovered four large villas, some smaller houses, three Christian churches and a residential quarter – perhaps for the common people.

In the middle of the ruins, one of the building structures, made from finely chiselled, large blocks of limestone, contains a stairway that descends into a corridor. Though collapsed, the remains of what seems to be an **underground tunnel** are visible. According to local legend, this tunnel dates from the time of King Kaleb, and leads all the way to Aksum, hundreds of kilometres to the south. Curiously, a similar entrance is said to exist in Aksum, but it is blocked by a large boulder. A more modern hypothesis – and almost as exciting – is that the 'tunnel' is a deep burial chamber containing great sarcophagi.

Objects unearthed at Metera in the last 50 years include some beautiful and amazingly well-preserved **gold objects** – two crosses, two chains, a brooch, necklaces and 14 Roman coins dating from between the 2nd and 3rd centuries AD – found in a bronze vase. **Bronze coins** minted by the great Aksumite kings have also been found, as have many 'household' items including bronze lamps, needles and daggers, Mediterranean amphorae, and the remains of large marble plates.

Only a tiny part of Metera has been excavated. Big mounds lie tantalisingly untouched all around. The ancient people's tombs – hidden somewhere among the rocks – still await exploration, and may yield remarkable finds.

Getting There & Around

Metera lies just 2km from Senafe, so is easily reached on foot.

ERITREA

MENDEFERA

መንደፈራ

pop 65,000 • elevation 1980m

Mendefera, the capital of Dubub province, is a bustling market town. Reflecting an old rivalry, the town is dominated by two churches: the Orthodox San Giorgio and the Catholic church school, situated on hills opposite one another.

The town's name refers to the hill around which the town grew up. Mendefera (literally meaning 'No One Dared') is a reference to the fierce resistance put up by the local people against Italian colonialisation. The hill was never taken.

Today the town makes a convenient stop-off point on your way to or from the south.

Information

The **Commercial Bank** (open 8am-11am & 2pm-5pm Mon-Fri, 8am-11am Sat) can change travellers cheques.

The **post office** (open 8am-noon & 2pm-6pm Mon-Fri, 8am-noon Sat) is near the main roundabout. There's also a **telecom office** (open 8am-noon & 2pm-8pm daily).

Places to Stay

Mendefera is well endowed with places to stay. Most hotels are scattered along the road to Adi Quala, on the southern outskirts of town.

Semhar Hotel (☎ 61 13 56; singles/doubles with shared shower Nfa30/40) is quite a popular option and is good value. It boasts a pleasant setting with nine rooms arranged around an attractive leafy courtyard.

Tsehay Berki (☎ 61 14 79; singles/doubles with shared shower Nfa25/30) has an intimate feel, with only eight rooms at the back. This modest place will suit budget travellers. The rooms aren't fancy, but they're adequate and the atmosphere is laid-back.

Awet Hotel (☎ 61 10 63; singles/doubles with shared shower Nfa30/40) is a relatively well-maintained place, with 19 rooms set around a courtyard.

Mereb Hotel (☎ 61 14 43, 61 16 36; singles with private shower Nfa72-120, doubles with private shower Nfa96-144) is not only the southernmost place to stay, but it is also the best in town, with three types of clean rooms. The more expensive ones are reasonably cheerful and have TV and telephone. The hotel lies about 800m from the post office.

Merkeb Hotel (☎ 61 10 44; singles/doubles with shared shower Nfa25/45) is the only hotel in the centre. It's about 200m north of the post office, on the road to Asmara. It features adequate rooms but is noisier than its competitors.

Places to Eat

There's a decent range of restaurants here. Most hotels have their own restaurant and welcome nonguests. The cheapest meals are offered by the **Tsehay Berki** (mains Nfa10-19). The **Merkeb Hotel** (mains Nfa17-35) has a good restaurant upstairs. The menu features burgers, pasta, grilled fish and Eritrean specialities served in a modern, if somewhat styleless dining room. Another reliable option is **N Bar-Restaurant** (mains Nfa 10-25), on the road to Asmara, 100m from the Mobil petrol station. It serves local and Italian dishes and a few snacks at moderate prices. The **St George Bar & Restaurant** (mains Nfa20-25) is also on the road to Asmara, a few doors away from the Merkeb Hotel. It is worth a try.

Getting There & Away

Mendefera's bus station lies around 20 minutes' walk from the town centre. If your bus is continuing south, ask to be dropped off at one of the hotels on the main street.

To Adi Quala, 20 buses leave daily (Nfa4, 45 mins); for Barentu, you'll have to hop between towns: first to Shambiko (12.75, two hours), then to Mai Dima (Nfa17, two hours) and Barentu (Nfa7.75, one hour). To Dekemhare, two buses go daily (Nfa5.50, two hours); to Asmara, around 50 buses depart daily (Nfa7, 1½ hours).

The road west to Barentu is a gravel track, and there's just one fuel station, at Shambiko. If you're driving, make sure you fill up before setting off.

AROUND MENDEFERA

Green Island Hotel (☎ 15 98 26; singles & doubles with private shower Nfa55) is at Tera-Emni, 32km north of Mendefera. The hotel has an outdoor swimming pool and a verdant garden. It makes for a peaceful retreat and at weekends is popular with families from Asmara. It has a restaurant.

To get there from Asmara, take a bus heading for Mendefera, and ask to be dropped off at the hotel in Tera-Emni.

ADI QUALA

ዓዲ ኳላ

elevation 2054m

Adi Quala functions as a frontier town (it's the last town of any size before the Ethiopian border). At the time of writing there was

no bank in Adi Quala. There's a **post office** *(open 8am-noon & 2pm-6pm Mon-Fri,
8am-noon Sat)*. The **telecom office** was not
in operation at the time of writing.

Things to See

Adi Quala's most distinctive feature is the
attractive **tukul church** on the southern edge
of the city. The church has some interesting
frescoes, including a depiction of the battle
of Adwa painted on the eastern face of the
its *maqdas* (inner sanctuary). Look out for
General Baratieri (see the boxed text 'The
Battle of Adwa' in the Northern Ethiopia
chapter) with moustache and striped jodh-
purs. It's a good place to see traditional
Eritrean religious painting if you haven't
already; if you want a guided tour of the
frescoes, ask for the resident priest Gebremichael. He'll expect a small tip.

A few kilometres west of town lies the
Italian mausoleum in honour of those who
fell at Adwa. There are good views from
the top.

Adi Quala is also a market town, with a
brand new **market building** off the main road.

Places to Stay & Eat

There are a number of cheap options to
choose from if you plan to stay overnight.
Facilities are rudimentary.

The most reliable place is the **Gash Hotel**
*(singles/doubles with shared shower Nfa20/
25, with private shower Nfa30/40)* in a side
street off the main road, close to the bus station. It has 18 ordinary rooms ranged around
a peaceful courtyard and serves decent local
food, albeit limited in variety, for around
Nfa20.

If Gash Hotel is full, opt for **Tourist Hotel**
*(rooms with shared shower Nfa10, with pri-
vate shower Nfa25)* on the main road, with
small but adequate rooms clustered around a
pleasant shady courtyard. Meals are available
on request. Further south you'll come across
Mareb Hotel *(singles/doubles with shared
shower Nfa10/20)*, with shoebox-sized
rooms, and **Ghenet Hotel** *(rooms with shared
bathroom Nfa15)*, another basic place with
tiny rooms set around an inner courtyard.

Getting There & Away

To Mendefera, around 10 buses leave daily
(Nfa4, 45 mins); to Asmara, at least 10 buses
run daily (Nfa11, 2½ hours). When the border
with Ethiopia reopens, there will be regular
services to Adwa.

Eastern Eritrea

The east of the country has two main attractions: the town of Massawa, Eritrea's largest port after Assab, and the nearby Dahlak
Islands, which offer some of the best diving
in the Red Sea.

Massawa is built on two coral islands
rising from the Red Sea. It looks not west
towards Asmara but east across the water
towards Arabia. Massawa's ancient connections with the Arab world represent the other
face of Eritrea's past. The town boasts some
remarkable Islamic architecture but, like an
old museum, the exhibits are spread out, covered in dust and gradually disintegrating. It is
hoped that in the future funds will be found to
restore these historical buildings.

The Dahlak Islands near Massawa give
access to Eritrea's beautiful coral reefs.
Though the dive-cruises around them are
quite expensive, snorkelling is cheaper and
easier to arrange, and is not to be missed.
The islands are a very strange, unique environment, and a couple of days sailing around
them or camping on their beaches makes for a
memorable experience. Although it's hard to
imagine a bleaker, more desolate landscape,
the islands boast an enigmatic people and a
surprising amount of life, including various
wild animals and abundant birdlife. Some
islands, such as Dahlak Kebir, also have an
interesting and ancient history.

The far eastern arm of Eritrea is covered
under Dankalia later in this chapter.

ASMARA TO MASSAWA

The journey from Asmara to Massawa is
one of the most dramatic in Eritrea. In just
115km, the road descends nearly 2500m,
plummeting through mountains often clad in
mist, around hairpin bends and over old Italian bridges. Built by the Italians in 1935–36,
the road was the most important in the country, linking the capital with the coast.

After leaving Asmara, the first village you
come to is **Sheghrini**. Meaning roughly 'I've
got a problem' in Tigrinya, these were supposedly the words uttered during the colonial
era by an Italian whose car, like so many
other vehicles, finally gave out at the top of
the steep climb from Massawa.

Around 9km outside Asmara, the **Bar
Durfo** and the **Seidici Restaurant** both make
good places to stop, if you want to admire the
views or take some photos.

Three kilometres further on from the Seidici is the little village of **Arborobu**. Its name means 'Wednesday-Friday' after its market days. The town is known for its *beles* (prickly pears), in season from mid-June to mid-September.

Around 25km east of Asmara lies the little town of **Nefasit**, the starting point for trips to the **Debre Bizen Monastery** (see Around Asmara earlier in this chapter). The monastery, perched high above the town, is just visible from the road.

Ghinda is 47km from Asmara and halfway to Massawa. It lies in a little valley that traps the warm, moist air from the coast. Rainfall is much higher than normal here and its green, terraced hillsides supply the fruit and vegetable markets of Asmara and Massawa. The Jiberti – Tigrinya Muslims – inhabit the area. Prohibited in the past from owning and cultivating land, they became instead great craftspeople, artists and scholars.

Dongollo
ድንጎሎ

Dongollo and the springs of **Sabarguma**, 15km towards Massawa from Ghinda, are the sources of the Eritrean mineral waters that bear their names.

Nearby, across the River Dongollo is the triple-arched **Italian bridge** with the inscription in Italian Piedmontese *Ca Custa Lon Ca Custa* (Whatever It Costs), said to be a reference to the Italian purchase of the Bay of Assab in the late 1860s.

MASSAWA
ባጽዕ

pop 35,000

Though only about 100km to the east of Asmara, Massawa could not be more different from the capital. The history, climate, architecture and atmosphere of the town seem to come from another world. With its low, whitewashed buildings, porticoes and arcades, Massawa has a more Arab feel to it, reflecting its centuries-old connection with Arabia across the other side of the Red Sea.

Massawa's natural deep harbour and its position close to the mouth of the Red Sea and the Indian Ocean have long made it the target of foreign powers. It was occupied by the Portuguese, Arabs, Egyptians and Turks; finally, the British held it for a time before they all but handed it over to the Italians in 1885. Trade in Massawa flourished throughout these occupations; everything – slaves, pearls, giraffes, incense, ostriches and myrrh – passed through the port.

Massawa's buildings reflect its history of occupation. The Ottoman Turks, who occupied the city for nearly 300 years, had the biggest influence on the architecture. Their successors, the Egyptians, also left a legacy of buildings and public works, including the elevated causeways, an aqueduct and the governor's palace. In 1885 the Italians occupied Massawa, and the town became their capital until it was superseded by Asmara in 1897. During this time, many of the fabulous villas were built.

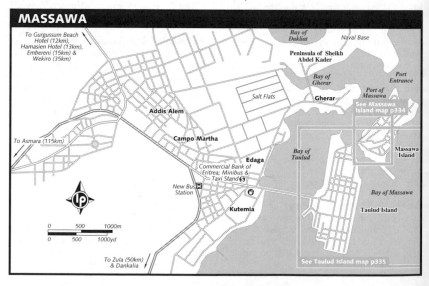

MASSAWA

To Gurgussum Beach Hotel (12km), Hamasien Hotel (13km), Embereni (15km) & Wekiro (35km)

Bay of Dakliat

Naval Base

Peninsula of Sheikh Abdel Kader

Bay of Gherar

Port Entrance

Salt Flats

Gherar

Port of Massawa

See Massawa Island map p334

Addis Alem

To Asmara (115km)

Campo Martha

Massawa Island

Commercial Bank of Eritrea; Minibus & Taxi Stand

Edaga

Bay of Taulud

New Bus Station

Bay of Massawa

Kutemia

Taulud Island

0   500   1000m
0   500   1000yd

To Zula (50km) & Dankalia

See Taulud Island map p335

Indefatigable Dhows

Since the 15th century, the ancient trading vessel, the dhow, has provided a link between Africa and Asia. Unmistakable on the sea for its single lateen (triangular) sail, the dhow is painted with multicoloured patterns, particularly around the castellated stern. Today many dhows are also fitted with engines.

Three types of dhow are found in Eritrea – sizes range from the *zaroug* (the largest), to the *zeima* and the *sambuk* (the smallest). The boats are traditionally constucted (without the aid of a plan) entirely from the expertise and memory of the master craftspeople who make them. Many Yemeni builders have inherited the art directly from the legendary builders of Mukallah. A *sambuk* costs from US$19,000 new, and takes around three months to build.

The vessel is lined with large planks of teak, impregnated with shark oil to prevent rot. A mixture of shark fat and lime is boiled together to make an extremely efficient, airtight filler, which still outperforms any modern equivalent. Weighing between 30 and 500 tonnes and measuring from 15m to 40m, the boats ply the waters between Eritrea, Djibouti, Sudan, Somalia, the Arabian Peninsula and the Gulf. The boats attain a maximum speed of only about 5 to 6 knots, even with a favourable wind.

The holds of the boats are crammed with every merchandise imaginable, from salt, cigarettes, animal hides and coffee, to dates, shark fins, electronic goods and dried fish. Even vehicles have been loaded – with the help of a lorry. Stories and rumours still abound of dhows filled with other cargo – smuggled goods, arms and even slaves.

Navigation is always without maps. Most sailors have plied the sea routes since their childhood days. The boats' captains continue to fear the storms of the Red Sea – the dhows, though beautiful, are notoriously unstable. Pirates are said to scour the seas. In 1997 various boats were attacked off the coast near Assab by machine-gun-wielding pirates in the guise of fishermen selling fish.

ERITREA

Once one of the most beautiful cities on the Red Sea, Massawa was all but flattened during the Struggle for Independence. Around 90% of the town was blitzed by Ethiopian blanket bombing, and great scars are still visible. Many visitors are shocked by the derelict state of a number of historical buildings. Rehabilitation has started but the process is slow for lack of funds. Various restoration schemes are under investigation and there should be decisive changes in the forthcoming years due to the financial support of the World Bank and Unesco, among others.

Although Massawa now far from warrants its former accolade of 'Pearl of the Red Sea', it retains an engaging, exotic character, which makes it an interesting place to explore. It's also hassle-free and pretty safe – no mean feat for a modern, international port. One major drawback is the heat. The average annual temperature is 29.5°C, though it often far exceeds that, sometimes reaching 46.5°C. With the high coastal humidity, the town can seem like a furnace, and there's marginal variation between day and night-time temperatures. The best time to visit Massawa is from October to May.

Orientation

The town of Massawa consists of two islands, Taulud and Massawa, and a mainland area. The mainland area, called Massawa, is largely residential, and a long causeway connects it to Taulud Island. Taulud is home to some old Italian villas, the administrative buildings, and a few of the town's smarter hotels.

A shorter causeway connects Taulud to the second island, Wushti Batsi, known simply as Batsi or Massawa Island. This is the oldest part of town and is in many ways its heart. Here the port can be found, along with most of the restaurants and bars.

Information

Note that business hours in Massawa differ from those in the rest of the country. Government offices open from 6am to 2.30pm Monday to Friday from June to September and from 8am to noon and 4pm to 6.30pm Monday to Friday from October to May. Private businesses open from 6am to noon and 3pm to 6pm Monday to Friday the whole year.

The **Commercial Bank of Eritrea** (*open 7am-11.30am & 4pm-5.30pm Mon-Fri, 7am-10.30am Sat*) on Massawa Island changes travellers cheques, US dollars, pounds and euros.

ERITREA

The **post office** (open 7am-noon & 4pm-6pm Mon-Fri, 7am-noon Sat) is on Massawa Island. The **telecommunications office** (open 7am-10pm daily) is in the same building.

Internet access is available at **BIT Internet Cafe** (open 8am-noon & 4pm-10pm daily), under the arcades on the seafront. It costs Nfa10 per hour.

Dangers & Annoyances

Massawa is a pretty safe place day or night. One of the biggest problems travellers face is infected wounds (from coral cuts or mosquito bites). The usual precautions against malaria apply. (See also Health in the Facts for the Visitor chapter in Ethiopia.)

Walking Tour – Massawa Island

Even if many buildings are in a very bad shape, Massawa Island is a great place to explore. It's a maze of little streets, but you're never lost for long. It has some interesting buildings, but they have to be ferreted out.

As you come over the causeway from Taulud Island, a broad sweep of white, arcaded **palazzi** (palaces) stretches out before you. On the corner, opposite the transport office, you'll see the **Hotel Savoiya**, with its long gallery.

Keep left and head down the road along the harbour towards the port entrance, near which there is a good example of a 17th-century **coral-block house**. For centuries, coral was the local building stone. Heading back towards

the causeway, you'll pass the **Banco d'Italia** an exact copy of its 1920s original and a mishmash of styles, including Gothic windows and towers. Unfortunately, the building is rather dilapidated and awaits restoration. In a square beyond the Banco is a rare example of a **Turkish house** with a domed roof, now impressively restored. Turn back towards the port entrance, passing by the **Shaafi Mosque** Founded in the 11th century but rebuilt several times since, it's worth a quick look.

As you keep heading towards the port, you'll come across the ancient house of **Mammub Mohammed Nahari** with soaring Ottoman-style windows on every side. Unfortunately they are particularly decrepit. Around this area are some large and ornate 18th-century Armenian and Jewish **merchant houses**.

Turn right at the port entrance and head towards the southern tip of the island. On your right, about 150m from the port entrance, is the **house of Abu Hamdum**, with its *mashrabiyya* (trellised) balcony, which allowed cool breezes to enter and the air inside to circulate. It's a remarkable example of Turkish Ottoman architecture, but it is almost crumbling and needs urgent restoration. Continue on until you get to the Piazza degli Incendi (meaning 'Square of the Fire', after it was the scene of a great fire in 1885), in the centre of which is the **Sheikh Hanafi Mosque**. At over 500 years old, this mosque is one of the oldest surviving

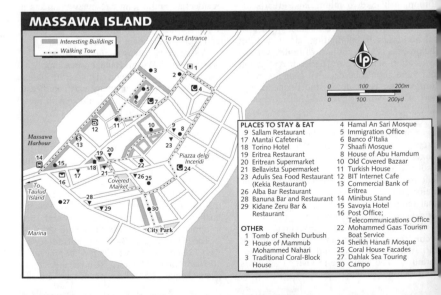

MASSAWA ISLAND

Interesting Buildings
Walking Tour

To Port Entrance

Massawa Harbour

Piazza degli Incendi

To Taulud Island

Covered Market

Marina

City Park

PLACES TO STAY & EAT		OTHER	
9	Sallam Restaurant	1	Tomb of Sheikh Durbush
17	Mantai Cafeteria	2	House of Mammub Mohammed Nahari
18	Torino Hotel	3	Traditional Coral-Block House
19	Eritrea Restaurant	4	Hamal An Sari Mosque
20	Eritrean Supermarket	5	Immigration Office
21	Bellavista Supermarket	6	Banco d'Italia
23	Adulis Sea Food Restaurant (Kekia Restaurant)	7	Shaafi Mosque
26	Alba Bar Restaurant	8	House of Abu Hamdum
28	Banuna Bar and Restaurant	10	Old Covered Bazaar
29	Kidane Zeru Bar & Restaurant	11	Turkish House
		12	BIT Internet Cafe
		13	Commercial Bank of Eritrea
		14	Minibus Stand
		15	Savoyia Hotel
		16	Post Office; Telecommunications Office
		22	Mohammed Gaas Tourism Boat Service
		24	Sheikh Hanafi Mosque
		25	Coral House Facades
		27	Dahlak Sea Touring
		30	Campo

0   100   200m
0   100   200yd

structures in the city. Sheikh Hanafi was a great teacher, who funded his students' studies in Egypt. The walls of the courtyard are decorated with stuccowork and inside hangs a remarkable chandelier from the glassworks of Murano near Venice in Italy.

Passing through the piazza, notice the small group of **coral-block houses** with finely detailed facades on your right. Then turn left into the **Campo**, a huge square lined on all sides by houses with trellised balconies and finely carved wooden doors and shutters of Turkish or Egyptian origin.

To the north of the Campo is the **covered market**. Behind and to the north of the market lies the Massawa Hotel, bringing you into the main commercial artery of the town. Turn right towards the heart of the old town then take the first left. This area was the old **covered bazaar**. Its ancient roof – in the Turkish style – was beamed like an upturned boat; at the time of writing, there was only a small section remaining. There are plans to rebuild it.

Walking Tour – Taulud Island

A good way to start the walk is to have breakfast or lunch in the circular dining room of the **Dahlak Hotel** at the northern tip of the island, with its great views of the harbour. Just north of the gates of the Dahlak Hotel is the old **Imperial Palace** overlooking the harbour. The original palace was built by the Turkish Osdemir Pasha in the 16th cen-

tury. The present building dates from 1872, when it was built for the Swiss adventurer Werner Munzinger. During the federation with Ethiopia, it was used as a winter palace by Emperor Haile Selassie, whose heraldic lions still decorate the gates. The palace also contained the first elevator in Eritrea. Look out for the beautifully carved wooden doors, said to come from India. The palace was badly damaged during the Struggle for Independence. In its present state, it gives a very vivid idea of how all Massawa looked shortly after the war. It's usually possible to wander around the grounds.

Back on the causeway road, you'll see to your right the old Italian municipal buildings. Head south down the tree-lined road, past the Dahlak Hotel. Hotels and villas line the eastern shore. Some of the villas are exceptionally beautiful, combining elements of Art Deco style with traditional Moorish arcades and huge *mashrabiyya* balconies. After about 500m you'll find yourself at the Orthodox **St Mariam Cathedral**, which is at the end of the causeway from the mainland. Opposite the cathedral is the massive **monument** to the Eritrean Struggle for Independence. Three huge tanks are preserved where they stopped in the final assault on the town in 1990, and now stand on a black marble base which is lovingly cleaned each morning.

South of the cathedral is the famous **Red Sea Hotel**, scene of many glamorous balls in

ERITREA

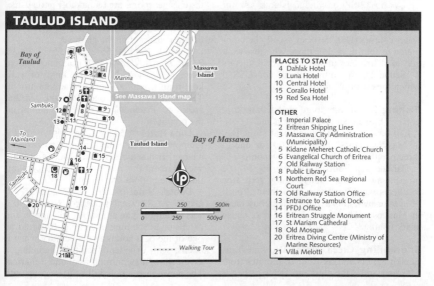

TAULUD ISLAND

Bay of Taulud

Massawa Island

Marina

See Massawa Island map

Sambuks

To Mainland

Taulud Island

Bay of Massawa

Sambuks

0   250   500m
0   250   500yd

······ Walking Tour

PLACES TO STAY
4 Dahlak Hotel
9 Luna Hotel
10 Central Hotel
15 Corallo Hotel
19 Red Sea Hotel

OTHER
1 Imperial Palace
2 Eritrean Shipping Lines
3 Massawa City Administration (Municipality)
5 Kidane Meheret Catholic Church
6 Evangelical Church of Eritrea
7 Old Railway Station
8 Public Library
11 Northern Red Sea Regional Court
12 Old Railway Station Office
13 Entrance to Sambuk Dock
14 PFDJ Office
16 Eritrean Struggle Monument
17 St Mariam Cathedral
18 Old Mosque
20 Eritrea Diving Centre (Ministry of Marine Resources)
21 Villa Melotti

the 1960s and 1970s. Devastated in the war, it has been rebuilt and is now a reputable hotel.

At the southern tip of the island is the beautiful 1930s **Villa Melotti**, built by the owners of the Asmara brewery. Much of its original furniture is preserved in the villa's huge vaulted rooms. With its stunning setting on the seafront, gardens and swimming pools, it has the decadent grandeur of a Fellini film set.

From the villa, take the road on the western side of Taulud and head north, passing by the causeway leading to the mainland. Look out for birds in the mud flats around the causeway. Pelicans are quite common visitors. Continuing north, you'll pass the original **railway station**, built during the Italian occupation, with its columns and elegant facade. There is access to the *sambuk* (dhow) **docks** just south of the train station, and it's worth taking a look at these beautiful traditional boats. There are always at least a couple around – the boats require a lot of maintenance (see the boxed text 'Indefatigable Dhows').

Activities

Diving Massawa is the starting point for trips to the Dahlak Islands, Eritrea's main diving destination. Trips to the islands and equipment hire can be organised in Massawa. For full details on boat and equipment hire, see the Dahlak Islands section later in this chapter.

If you want to learn to dive, you can contact the **Eritrea Diving Center** (☎ 55 26 88, fax 55 12 87) on Taulud Island. Ask for the helpful English-speaking Osman, who can organise the usual PADI courses. Open-water courses (US$350) can usually be completed in four days. For those who just want a taste of Eritrea's underwater world, there's a 'Scuba Diving Introduction' for US$50 which runs over a half day.

Fishing If you want to go on a fishing trip, you can hire a boat and a captain and set off. A half-day's rental of a small boat in the Bay of Massawa costs about Nfa800 for one to three people, including the boat captain.

Dahlak Sea Touring (☎/fax 55 24 89) on Massawa Island lends fishing rods free to clients who rent boats from them. You'll need your own hooks, but you can buy these in Massawa. The agency can also organise shark fishing.

Snorkelling Green Island (also known as Sheikh Saïd Island) is 10 to 20 minutes from Massawa and is the most accessible place for decent snorkelling and good beaches (see Getting There & Away under Dahlak Islands later in this section). If you rent a boat from Dahlak Sea Touring, snorkelling equipment is included. The Eritrea Diving Center organises snorkelling trips to the Dahlak Islands.

Swimming In town, the beach off the Dahlak Hotel on Taulud Island is about the best bet. If you're not a guest, then it's polite at least to buy a drink or a snack on the premises.

On the mainland, the beach at the Gurgussum Beach Hotel is OK, though it suffers a bit from litter and algae due to tidal fluctuations. It can get crowded at weekends. The beach at the nearby Hamasien Hotel is a bit better.

Water-skiing It's possible to water-ski through Dahlak Sea Touring at the cost of Nfa1000 per hour, including all equipment and instruction, for one to three people.

Places to Stay

It's best to avoid the hotels on Massawa Island. They are noisy and decrepit and none of them can be seriously recommended. Though less central, Taulud is much quieter and offers better standards.

Corallo Hotel (☎ 55 24 06; singles Nfa75-180, doubles Nfa100-240) is a good place, with three kinds of rooms to suit most budgets. It's a popular place with tour groups, and reservations are a good idea. Though very simple, the cheaper rooms are remarkably good value. The more expensive ones have bathroom, air-con and balcony with sea views. There is a decent restaurant on the premises.

Central Hotel (☎ 55 20 02, 55 22 18, 55 26 08; rooms Nfa240-480) is a better option, close to the shore. It has three kinds of well-kept rooms, with air-con, TV and bathroom. The more expensive ones face the sea and are more spacious. There's a restaurant on the premises.

Luna Hotel (☎ 55 22 72; rooms with bathroom Nfa170) has unexceptional rooms with air-con. It has a restaurant. There's nothing special about this place, but it's a decent option if the bottom line counts.

Dahlak Hotel (☎ 55 11 71/2, 55 28 18, fax 55 12 82; singles/doubles Nfa225/300) was undergoing an ambitious restoration and extension at the time of writing. It should be one of the best hotels in the country when it opens, with excellent facilities, including a dive centre, a swimming pool and a marina. The new construction will be in keeping with local style. The owner also plans to build a new hotel on Dissei Island, which will likely be called Dahlak Village Resort.

Red Sea Hotel (☎ 55 28 39, fax 55 25 44; *rooms with bathroom Nfa324*). Opened in 2000, this Italian-designed hotel is regarded as one of the best options in Massawa. It is well designed and has 50 tidy, if slightly ageing rooms with air-con, TV and balcony. All rooms enjoy a view of the sea. Facilities include a restaurant, a worn tennis court and private jetty.

If you do want to stay on Massawa Island, try the **Torino Hotel** (☎ 55 28 55; *doubles or twins with private shower Nfa165*). Rooms are short of being comfortable and are overpriced. What's more, the place is noisy – there's a nightclub on the rooftop.

On the mainland, you'll find the **Gurgussum Beach Hotel** (☎ 55 19 01, 55 19 04, fax 55 19 02; *rooms with bathroom Nfa180-576*), 12km from Massawa on a moderate stretch of beach. It's very popular with Eritrean families at the weekend and the beach is usually crowded at that time. It has a wide range of rooms to suit most budgets, from plain, older rooms to more comfortable and spacious family cottages and suites. All rooms have air-con and TV. There's a decent restaurant and an open-air bar on the premises. There are plans to renovate and upgrade the hotel in the near future. To get there from Massawa Island, hire a taxi (Nfa70) or take a minibus on Saturday or Sunday (Nfa5).

Hamasien Hotel (☎ 55 27 25; *doubles or twins with/without shower Nfa180/144*), about 1km from Gurgussum Beach Hotel, has a better beach but the rooms are spartan and tired-looking and the building is in need of a radical facelift.

Places to Eat

Most restaurants, except the ones at the big hotels, are on Massawa Island.

Massawa Island (ባጽዕ ደሴት) You'll find a row of cheap eateries on and around the main street. The pick of the bunch include:

Sallam Restaurant (*fish dishes Nfa40-70; open dinner*) doesn't look like much from the outside and actually looks worse inside but, believe it or not, it is a culinary gem. Here you can relish the Yemeni speciality of fresh fish sprinkled with hot pepper baked in a tandoori oven. The fish, served with a *chapati* flat bread, is served in two sizes: medium (Nfa40) and big (Nfa60). It's absolutely superb! Ask also for the *mokbusa*,

the traditional accompaniment made with honey, butter and either dates or bananas. It's deservedly popular with Asmarans and gets crowded at weekends.

Adulis Sea Food Restaurant (*fish dishes around Nfa50; open dinner*) opposite the mosque is also a great option if you fancy Yemeni and Middle-Eastern dishes, including the Yemeni baked fish dish and *bokhari* (meat and rice). Despite the name, seafood needs to be ordered in advance. Alcohol is not served.

Several cafeterias line the street between the post office and the Torino Hotel, including **Mantai Cafeteria**, which serves an invigorating orange juice and decent coffee.

Eritrea Restaurant (☎ 55 26 40; *mains Nfa15-30*) is considered to be the best place for Italian food in Massawa Island. It has a pleasant covered terrace, and offers a varied local and Italian menu, including vegetarian dishes. The barbecued fish kebabs are delicious.

The new **Alba Bar Restaurant** (*mains Nfa15-40*), a few paces from the covered market, features a cheerful partially covered terrace and has a cosy atmosphere. It is a good place for breakfast, lunch or dinner. The food is varied, with meat dishes, pasta, sandwiches and, of course, a wide selection of fish dishes. It also has a great fruit juices (Nfa10).

Closer to the seafront, you'll find **Banuna Bar and Restaurant** (*mains Nfa17-60*) and, opposite, **Kidane Zeru Bar and Restaurant** (*mains Nfa15-60*). These siblings have an outdoor terrace and serve good seafood, including lobster, calamari and shrimps, along with pasta and the usual *zilzil* and *zigni*.

For self-catering, **Eritrean Supermarket** is the best stocked if you're preparing for a picnic, a camping trip to the islands or an expedition through Dankalia. **Bellavista Supermarket** opposite Eritrean Supermarket is another worthwhile option.

Taulud Island & Mainland There's no choice on Taulud Island other than the big hotels. They serve reasonable if somewhat bland food. Try the **Central Hotel** (*mains Nfa30-100*) or the **Red Sea Hotel** (*mains Nfa20-85*). When the new **Dahlak Hotel** is completed, you can expect high-quality food in one of its restaurants.

On the mainland, the **Gurgussum Beach Hotel** (*mains Nfa25-50 plus tax*) is a reliable option. On the menu you'll find items such as meat, pasta and seafood. The lunch buffet at weekends is popular with families (Nfa100).

ERITREA

Entertainment

There are plenty of lively but rather seedy little bars on Massawa Island. Single male travellers will soon find they have plenty of local female company.

Kidane Zeru Bar and Restaurant, **Banuna Bar and Restaurant** and **Alba Bar Restaurant** on Massawa Island are cheerful places with large terraces in which to idle away hours in the late evening.

Torino Hotel *(admission Nfa30; open 10pm-3am daily)*, on Massawa island, has a nightclub which is a long-time favourite. It has an airy roof terrace as well as a dancing area inside with the obligatory mirror ball. Depending on the day and the clientele, the atmosphere can vary from fun and relaxed to rather seedy.

Gurgussum Beach Hotel, on the mainland, has a nightclub at weekends.

Getting There & Away

Air A new international airport is currently being built and should open soon.

Bus There are buses leaving from the new bus station on the mainland for Asmara (Nfa14, 3½ to four hours) every hour from around 4am to 5pm. For Assab, you will have to go to Asmara and catch the bus there, as the buses pass through Massawa but don't stop. For Zula (to visit Adulis) in the south, one bus leaves daily, at 1pm (Nfa13, 3½ to four hours). Buses leave from the new bus station on the mainland.

Car The road to Massawa is sealed and in good condition. A normal car can make the journey in around three hours.

Train The old Italian train linking Massawa to Asmara has begun functioning again in 2003, and at the time of writing only offered charter services; check with travel agencies in Asmara. (See also the boxed text 'The Old Railway' under Getting Around earlier in this chapter.)

Boat Cargo boats leave from Massawa to Assab every five to 14 days. The journey takes 24 to 48 hours depending on the boat. Passage costs Nfa98. Bring food, water and a blanket for sleeping on the deck. Ask at the Eritrean Shipping Lines office on Taulud Island.

Getting Around

Taxi Share-taxis for short hops around town cost Nfa2; if you take a taxi by yourself it costs Nfa30. You'll need to negotiate to get these fares. To the Gurgussum Beach Hotel a taxi costs Nfa70. An unofficial taxi stand can be found outside the Savoiya Hotel on Massawa Island.

Bus The city buses cost 50¢ and bus stops are clearly marked around town.

Minibus The town minibuses (with 'Taxi' written on the front) are plentiful, fast and efficient. They can be flagged down anywhere, and are great for hopping between the islands and getting to Gurgussum (Nfa5) at weekends. Short journeys around town cost Nfa1.

AROUND MASSAWA

North of Massawa, stretching along the sandy coast into Sudan, lies the traditional territory of the enigmatic Rashaida people (for more information, see the special section 'A Museum of Peoples'). Around 4km out of Gurgussum, a track branches right off the Massawa road. A few Rashaida camps are visible between the villages of Emberemi and Wekiro.

You'll need a 4WD and, if you want to visit the Rashaida, a local guide who speaks Arabic. It's essential to show respect towards the people and not attempt to take any photos until you have clear permission. It's a good idea to bring some simple gifts, such as tea and sugar. You may well be expected to buy something, such as the traditional silver jewellery, and it's normal to haggle over the prices.

DAHLAK ISLANDS
ዳህላክ ደሴት

Some 350 islands lie off the Eritrean coast, the majority – 209 – of which make up the Dahlak Archipelago. Largely arid, barren and flat, the islands have a maximum altitude of 15m. Fresh water is very scarce, and very few of the islands are inhabited (only three within the Dahlak Archipelago). The nine islands most popularly visited are Green Island (near Massawa), Dahlak Kebir (the largest island), Dissei, Madote, Seil, Dur Ghella, Dur Gaam, Dohul, Harat and Enteara. Note that these islands are not the tropical paradises you may be hoping for!

You need a permit to visit any of the Dahlak Islands, except Green Island. The permit costs US$20 per person for the first three days, then US$10 for each day after that. The fee has to be paid in US dollars (cash). If you have to organise it yourself, go to the **Eritrean Shipping Lines office** *(☎ 55 24 75, 55 27 20, fax 55 23 91)* just beyond the Imperial Palace on Taulud Island. It keeps normal government office hours, and is open until noon on Saturday. You need to fill out a form and pay the fee. Don't forget your passport. The papers are then taken to the Ministry of Tourism on Taulud Island. The whole process takes between 30 minutes and an hour. If you're joining a tour or hiring a boat, the permit should be organised for you.

Dahlak Kebir
ዳህላክ ከቢር

This is the largest island (over 650 sq km) in the archipelago, with nine villages and a population of 2300. The island has been inhabited for at least 2000 years and is known for its archaeological ruins. It may be declared a Unesco World Heritage Site in the future. The islanders speak their own dialect, *dahalik*, guard their own customs and traditions, and seem to use the same centuries-old building techniques as their ancestors. Most islanders make a living from the sea, either fishing in village cooperatives or collecting sea cucumbers and shark fins for the Middle East, India, the Philippines and China.

The Luul Hotel, the only hotel in the archipelago, is on this island. There's a post office on the island not far from the hotel, and a wonderful old wind-up Italian telephone, which even does for international calls (via Asmara).

On the southern coast of the island, 300m southeast of the village of Dahlak Kebir, lie some of Eritrea's most ancient relics, including 360 or so **underground cisterns**, cut from the madreporic (coral) limestone. According to local tradition, there was a different well for every day of the year. The cisterns catch rainwater and are the main source of water for the islanders, though the water from some is not drinkable now. Water was the reason for the island's importance in the past: for centuries, with fresh water limited in Massawa, passing ships were obliged to call on the island.

Around 50m southwest of the cisterns lies a huge and ancient necropolis, with literally thousands of **tombs** marked by small, upright basalt stones, beautifully inscribed with Kufic (ancient Arabic) script. The tombs are thought to date from at least AD 912 to the 15th century. Look out for the fossils scattered everywhere. Needless to say, nothing should be removed from the site.

Adel (አደል) This is a fascinating and totally unexcavated site near the village of Selawit, around 30km north of Dahlak Kebir village,

ERITREA

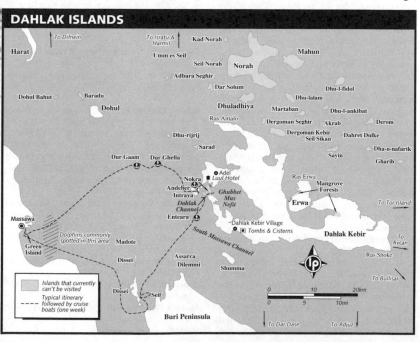

DAHLAK ISLANDS

on the journey back to the Luul Hotel. Very little is known about the mysterious ruined buildings, but the site may be even older than Dahlak Kebir, possibly dating from pre-Islamic times. There is also a necropolis with uninscribed tombstones. The buildings are beautifully constructed, with very straight, thick walls, arches and some columns.

Currently the only way of getting to the sites is by hiring a car from the Luul Hotel. From the hotel, it's a 44km journey (around 1½ to two hours) to the village of Dahlak Kebir, along a bumpy road. Keep an eye out for gazelles on the way (several hundred are said to inhabit the island); it's also a good place to see raptors (birds of prey). It's polite to stop at the village (before or after a visit to the ruins), where you'll be offered tea and biscuits. You should leave a tip. Though not expected, any income is much appreciated – life is tough here for the islanders.

A fishing trip on a traditional *sambuk* can usually be arranged through the Luul Hotel.

Diving

There's a huge potential for diving in the Dahlak Islands, but it's still in its infancy because of the lack of facilities and tourists.

One of the very few positive effects of the Struggle for Independence is that Eritrea's reefs have been allowed to flourish. During the war, the fishing industry ground almost to a halt. The reefs were also spared pollution from industry and marine traffic, and the invasions of tour boats and divers. As a result, the fish population has grown to an incredibly dense level and the reefs may well be home to one of the last pristine subaquatic coral environments in the Red Sea. The variety of wreck diving around the Dahlak Islands is also good, ranging from well-preserved Ethiopian cargo boats and WWII Italian warships to rusting Russian tankers. At least 67 wrecks are known to lie off the islands, although the true figure is probably three times this. Currently, only a few are 'open' to divers; more will become accessible in the future.

To really appreciate the reefs, you need to bear a few things in mind. Because it lies on a shallow continental shelf, there are no vertical drop-offs or 'deep blues' around the Dahlak Islands and the coral growth is not as profuse here as in the northern Red Sea. During the summer, the water temperatures on the plateau rise to the upper limit of coral tolerance. Dense algae, plankton spore and sediment are also thought to inhibit growth. Most coral is found as fringing 'patch' reefs, ranging from the surface to a depth of around 15m to 18m. At greater depths, coral colonies tend to drop off. Although the abundant plankton does attracts pelagic species such as manta ray and whale shark, these species, along with other 'crowd-pullers' such as dugongs, tiger sharks and hammerhead sharks, are only very occasionally seen.

The biggest cause of disappointment – particularly for underwater photographers – is visibility, which is notoriously erratic. The clarity of the water depends on the influx of cooler waters and plankton and nutrients from the Indian Ocean. Visibility frequently drops to between 10m and 13m, or even less. The best time for water visibility seems to be during the summer months (end of June to end of August), when temperatures outside touch 45°C. At this time, the sea can seem like a bath – surface temperatures of up to 36°C have been reported. Many cruise boats are not, or not adequately, air-conditioned, and sleeping on deck is the only option.

All divers must be certified (you will be asked for evidence), and each dive must be accompanied by a local dive master.

See also the boxed text 'The Red Sea: An Oasis of Life' under Fauna earlier in this chapter.

Diving & Snorkelling Areas The following locations are good for diving, but they come nowhere near exhausting the possibilities.

Dahlak Channel Excellent drift diving; August is the best month for manta rays

Dahlak Kebir Gropers inhabit the Ras Degan wreck

Dissei Better for diving than snorkelling; the reef is slightly deeper than other areas (20m); particularly good diving off northern tip; visibility can be very poor

Dur Gaam Currents around western side attract some sharks; good for snorkelling and diving

Dur Ghella Soft corals are generally found in the north, hard corals in the south (to 10m); waves and wind can limit access

Enteara Shallow diving (around 10m); good for snorkelling

Green Island The most accessible island, good for snorkelling

Madote Good snorkelling and diving to the east and west of island

Harat Good for snorkelling

Diving Services At the time of writing, the **Eritrea Diving Centre** (☎ 55 26 88, fax 55 12 87) at the Ministry of Marine Resources on Taulud Island was the only reliable diving operation organising diving trips to the islands.

When the extension of the **Dahlak Hotel** is completed, the hotel will have facilities for diving.

If you want to hire snorkelling gear, check also with the Eritrea Diving Centre. **Dahlak Sea Touring** provides equipment for its clients.

Organised Tours

Cruises around the islands, usually lasting a week, can be organised through the best travel agencies in Asmara (see Travel Agencies in the Asmara section for contact details). Boats range from beautiful Turkish *caiques* with private cabins and bathrooms to converted *sambuks*. Chefs, dive masters and crew are provided, as are air cylinders (boats have their own compressors). Some have diving and fishing equipment for hire. Prices depend on the type of boat and the number of persons. The bigger the group, the cheaper it is. Be prepared to spend at least US$100 per day per person.

Places to Stay

It's possible to **camp** on some of the islands, including Dissei, Madote, Dur Gaam and Dahlak Kebir. Some boat operators hire out full camping equipment; fresh water for showering is included in the price. Dissei (the east or north of the island) and Madote are probably the best for camping.

Luul Hotel (*bungalows US$50*) on Dahlak Kebir, is the only hotel on the islands and is owned by Eritrean Shipping Lines. There are small bungalows, as well as suites. Add another US$20 per person for food. You can also use the kitchen for a small fee (all provisions must be brought from the mainland). Prices must be paid in cash in US dollars.

Getting There & Away

Unless you've got your own boat, you'll need to hire one. The journey from Massawa to most of the islands takes between 1½ and two hours by motorboat.

Boats can be hired for picnic excursions, fishing, snorkelling or diving trips to the islands. It's worth shopping around, as prices vary from company to company and also depend on the season (low season is from October to February). If you come in the low season, you should be able to get a discount. Boat operators advise reservations one week to

10 days in advance. However, if you just turn up, something can almost always be organised within 24 hours. If a boat is available, it takes about an hour to get it ready. The services of a boat captain are always included in the price. You may be offered cheaper deals for *sambuks*; check that they look reasonably seaworthy (some are very rickety) and are carrying sufficient life jackets and supplies of water. Most are infested with mice and cockroaches.

No boats are currently fitted with compressors. A maximum of 10 air cylinders can be carried at one time.

Eritrean Shipping Lines (☎ 55 24 75, 55 27 20, fax 55 23 91) on Taulud Island in Massawa can organise transport to the Luul Hotel on Dahlak Kebir. A round trip costs US$330. It also has two motorboats for hire, and can supply tour guides and dive masters. A trip to one of the other islands costs between US$235 and US$390 for one to five people, depending on the distance. Mattresses, gas stove and cooking equipment are included in the price of the boats.

Eritrea Diving Centre (☎ 55 26 88, fax 55 12 87) on Taulud Island charges from Nfa500 to Nfa1200 for a trip to Green Island, depending on the boat, and from Nfa3200 to Nfa6000 for the other islands.

Dahlak Sea Touring (☎/fax 55 24 89; open 7am-6pm daily) on Massawa Island, run by Btzuamlak Gebre Selassie who is better known as 'Maik', has various boats for hire. A trip to Green Island costs Nfa400 for one to three people. Boats for one to five people to all the other islands cost Nfa3500, except to Dohul and Harat (Nfa4000) and Dahlak Kebir (Nfa4000). Bigger boats (for up to 10 people) can also be organised. Maik also has ice boxes, gas stoves, cutlery and dishes for hire.

Mohammed Gaas Tourism Boat Service (☎ 55 26 67) on Massawa Island can supply bigger boats (traditional *sambuks*) for up to 20 people for Nfa4000 per day, including a cook, but facilities are basic: just mattresses to sleep on below deck, a toilet and a stove.

Most travel agencies (see Travel Agencies in the Asmara section) offer tours to the islands. Prices depend on the number of islands visited and on the number of people.

Getting Around

Boats can be hired from the Luul Hotel for trips to the surrounding islands and cost between Nfa800 and Nfa3000 (depending on the distance) for round trips with up to two hours spent on the island.

ERITREA

ERITREA

A couple of village cars can usually be hired on Dahlak Kebir Island for about Nfa600 per day, including driver, petrol and mileage. The villagers have a monopoly so they can ask what they like but you can try bargaining. You'll need to give two to three days' notice to organise a car.

Dankalia ደንካልያ

If there's one place in Eritrea where travel is for travel's sake, it's Dankalia. Dankalia is the name given to the narrow strip of land about 50km wide that stretches south of Massawa down to Djibouti (about 600km), along the coastline. You can't miss it on the map: it looks like a long peninsula protruding from the south of the country. It's a volcanic desert where you'll be overwhelmed by breathtaking, lunar landscapes. It is known as one of the hottest and most inhospitable on earth: there's little to see, nothing to do, and no great destination awaiting you at the other end. The journey is hot, tiring and demanding; few travellers come here. But the sense of exploration is real, even on the rickety old bus. If you drive, the journey is likely to be one of the most memorable and challenging of your life. You'll feel like you're on another planet.

Dankalia is the territory of the legendary Afar people, described as one of the fiercest tribes on earth (see special section 'A Museum of Peoples'). A journey into Dankalia gives a fascinating glimpse into their way of life.

The best time to go is from November to December or from March to April. At the height of summer, the heat is unbearable; in winter, the sparse rain can quickly turn the tracks and wadis (valleys) into a mire.

If your time and budget are limited, an excursion as far as Thio will give you a good idea of the region, and the Buri Peninsula will give you a good idea of the wildlife. A trip taking in Adulis and going as far as Irafayle (87km from Massawa) at the start of the Buri Peninsula is just possible in a day.

ADULIS
አዶሊስ

Lying 59km to the south of Massawa, near the village of Foro, are the ancient Aksumite ruins of Adulis. Once numbering among the greatest ports of the ancient world, Adulis was the site of large and elegant buildings and a bustling international port. Inhabited since at least the 6th century BC, the site is the oldest in Eritrea.

Adulis' present condition belies its former grandeur, and many travellers are disappointed. It remains around 98% unexcavated; almost everything remains underground.

Like modern-day Massawa, Adulis' importance lay in its port, and by the 3rd century AD the port had grown to become one of the most important on the Red Sea. Trade at this time flourished from the Mediterranean all the way to India.

Adulis' fortunes waxed and waned with the ancient kingdom of Aksum (see Aksumite Civilisation under Facts about Eritrea earlier in this chapter). Like Aksum, its heyday came during the 3rd and 4th centuries AD. It then went into decline, before a brief revival in the 7th century. The town supplied all the major Aksumite towns of the interior: Aksum, Qohaito, Metera and Keskese.

Orientation & Information
To visit Adulis, it's best to pick up a guide at Foro. Try asking for Salhé, who has long accompanied the archaeologists working on the site. He speaks quite good Italian and Arabic, but no English; ask for him at one of the cafés or bars. From Foro it's around 8km to Adulis, in the direction of Zula.

Don't forget that you need a permit from the National Museum Office in Asmara to visit the site (see Travel Permits under Facts for the Visitor earlier in this chapter).

If you have to overnight in Zula, there's at least one no-name place where a bed can be had (Nfa10). Ask any of the locals to show you the way.

Getting There & Away
The road from Massawa as far as Zula and Adulis is quite good. If you're driving, you can usually find a guide at Foro.

From Massawa, one bus leaves daily for Zula at 1pm (Nfa13, four hours). You'll need a guide to take you to the ruins, which lie a few kilometres northeast of Zula. To return to Massawa, there's a bus from Zula at 6am. Sometimes bush taxis also make the journey. Ask around at Zula.

ADULIS TO ASSAB
Most villages on the Danakil coast survive from a mixed economy of fishing, salt mining and animal husbandry. The millennia-old trading contact with the Arabian peninsula still thrives; in some places smuggling with Yemeni merchants has proved a more lucrative means of income.

The little fishing village of **Irafayle** (meaning 'Place of Elephants' – slim chance now) lies 87km from Massawa and marks the boundary between the provinces of Akele Guzay and Dankalia. Here Afar territory and its desolate landscape begins. The village offers simple refreshments and accommodation.

The bay around the **Gulf of Zula** is the site of Napier's landing in 1868, during the expedition to rescue the hostages held by the Emperor Tewodros (see History in the Facts about Ethiopia chapter). It has good sandy beaches and snorkelling, and birdlife is plentiful along the shore.

The **Buri Peninsula** is probably one of the best places in Eritrea for wildlife. Ostriches, hamadryas baboons, and gazelles (Soemmering's and Dorca) are all quite frequently seen. The wild ass is also reported, though it's now very rare. Mangroves, good beaches and huge salt flats also characterise the area. If you have the time, a detour into the peninsula is worthwhile. Ask for a guide at Ghela'elo (about Nfa50), some 70km from Zula.

Marsa Fatma
ማርሳ ፋጡማ

Marsa Fatma, 158km from Massawa, is the starting point for a visit to the crater lake known as **Lake Badda**, around two hours (43km) west of the village of **Adaito**. Lying below sea level, seasonal water from the Tigré Mountains collects here, feeding the

Popular Palms

Situated on a large plain dotted with *amba* (flat-topped mountains), the village of Wade, around 70km southeast of Afambo, is the site of an oasis of *doum* palms. The whole area from Wade to Beylul is known for its production of the very alcoholic *doum* palm 'wine', called *doma*. You'll see old lemonade bottles in the villages frothing over with a milky liquid.

Don't miss the chance to try some; you may be invited into one of the local 'pubs' – discreet enclosures made from the wood and palms of the *doum* palms. A litre bottle costs between Nfa1.5 and Nfa7, depending on the quality.

In Wade, the drink has become almost a village addiction, and the authorities have tried to ban consumption! Fines of up to Nfa100 have been introduced.

agricultural plantations. Unless you have lots of time, it's probably not worth a special excursion.

South of Marsa Fatma, the fishing village of **Thio** (245km from Massawa) offers food and accommodation. The village, with its brightly painted wooden huts, is worth a stroll.

Edi
ዕዲ

Edi, 130km from Thio, is another Afar fishing village and also offers food and accommodation. Some 70km south of Edi, the **Bay of Beraesoli** features a stunning lunar landscape. There are several islands off the coast.

Some 60km further south, you'll reach the village of **Beylul** (515km from Massawa), surrounded by palms. You'll be offered the *doma*, a local palm wine. From Beylul, it is another 61km until Assab.

ASSAB
ዓሰብ

pop 70,000

Assab, Eritrea's largest port, is hot, windy and industrial, and has none of the charm of small-town Massawa. Lying less than 100km from Ethiopia, at the southern extremity of the desolate and inaccessible Dankalia region, Assab has always been a bit of an outpost. Tourism facilities are almost totally lacking.

Assab was Italy's first foothold in Eritrea, bought by the Rubattino Shipping Company in 1882 and taken over soon afterwards by the Italian government. For centuries up until recently, it was Ethiopia's principal port of access to the Red Sea. However, the dispute with Eritrea in 1998 ended that. The deviation of all Ethiopian commerce via Djibouti has made Assab even more of a backwater, and a feeling of dereliction emanates from the town.

Assab's average annual temperature is 29.5°C, though it can reach 46.5°C. Annual rainfall is just 58mm. The coolest time is between November and February.

Orientation & Information

The town can be divided into three parts. To the northeast lies Assab Seghir (little Assab), home to the large Yemeni community with their many restaurants, fruit sellers and small shops. In the centre lies Assab Kebhir (big Assab), which makes up the administrative

ERITREA

centre and includes the port. Most of the hotels are located here. To the west lies Campo Sudan, formerly the residential quarter for many of the town's Ethiopians and the main area for 'nightlife'.

There is no tourist office in Assab.

The **Commercial Bank of Eritrea** *(open 7am-noon & 4pm-6.30pm Mon-Fri, 7am-11.30am Sat)* accepts travellers cheques.

The **post office**, in front of the Municipality of Assab, keeps regular business hours.

The **telecom office** *(open 7am-1pm & 4pm-6pm Mon-Fri, 7am-1pm Sat)* is next to the Commercial Bank of Eritrea. International calls are possible from here.

Dangers & Annoyances

There are significant red-light districts, requiring vigilance, around both Campo Sudan and the port. These are poorer areas with many bars and the atmosphere can get rough and ready at times.

Heat rash is a common problem here and is best relieved by cold showers. Sometimes there are electrical power cuts.

Things to See & Do

To **swim** in town, head for the Ras Gembo Hotel. Alternatively, the pleasant and sandy **Bayeta beach** lies 4km to 5km from town on the airport road. A contract taxi to here costs around Nfa40.

Places to Stay

In most of the hotels in Assab, the showers are cold.

Assab Pension *(doubles without shower Nfa25, doubles with shower Nfa30-40, with air-con Nfa90)*, opposite Kebal International Hotel, is a reasonable option for budget travellers. This old colonial place has small but adequate rooms with fan.

Kebal International Hotel *(☎ 66 17 00; e kebal@aol.com.er; doubles or twins with shower Nfa55-165)* is often still known by its old name, the Nino. It's a bargain, with three types of spacious and well-kept rooms to suit most budgets. The more expensive ones are fairly bright and comfortable and come with air-con, TV and fridge.

When Assab was a busy town, **Ras Gembo Hotel** *(☎ 66 05 21, 66 11 14; singles with shower Nfa71-132, doubles with shower Nfa93-172)*, near St Michael's Church outside the main port area, was the most famous hotel in town. It's now a rather ageing establishment that lacks atmosphere and

customers. Still, it remains relatively good value with decent rooms amidst a leafy compound. All rooms have air-con. Its greatest advantage is its beach.

Places to Eat

There's no shortage of cheap eateries in Assab, serving the usual *tibsi* (fried meat with garlic and onion), *zigni*, steak or pasta for less than Nfa25. Most are much of a muchness. Campo Sudan also has its fair share of simple restaurants. Dependable places worth mentioning include **Stella Restaurant**, close to the post office, with an attractive and shady courtyard, and **Portico Park**, a bit out of the way on the northern edge of Campo Sudan, with an inviting open-air terrace and good *tibsi*.

Moving up the scale is **Aurora Restaurant** *(mains Nfa18-25)* in Assab Kebir. It's run by Signora Giuseppina Fracasso, whose Italian father built the telephone line in Assab. Although customers are few and far between, it's still the best place to enjoy pasta or grilled fish. **Kebal International Hotel** *(mains Nfa15-20)* is not bad either and has a large, open restaurant.

For self-catering, **Dankalia Provision Supplies**, one street behind Aurora Restaurant, is one of the best-stocked places. The shop has no sign.

As Assab Seghir is a Muslim area, no alcohol is served at restaurants.

Entertainment

Kebal International Hotel is a popular place for an evening drink. If you're after something more authentic, head for Campo Sudan, where local joints and outdoor 'beer gardens' (usually a gravel or cement courtyard plus a single tree decorated with Christmas lights) abound. It is a lively area at night, though you'll need to take care: bring with you the minimum amount of money, and women should be accompanied.

Getting There & Away

Air The airport is little more than a shack with a few wooden tables set up inside.

Eritrean Airlines *(☎ 66 00 28, 66 06 65)* is closed Wednesday and Sunday. There's one flight a week to Asmara (US$42 one way), on Wednesday.

Bus & Truck Incredibly, a bus service (of sorts) connects Assab to Massawa. The track between the two cities has been improved and the service is now relatively reliable, though still tiring and uncomfortable. After heavy rain, when the track becomes too muddy, services might be cancelled. The journey usually takes one day. Bring all the food and water you can carry. Three buses a week (usually Monday, Thursday and Saturday) depart for Asmara (Nfa103) at 4am; the journey takes approximately one and a half days. Tickets should be bought one day in advance. There is no bus station, but the bus departs from the Shell petrol station, near Kebal International Hotel.

If you are catching trucks don't forget that hitching always carries a risk (see Hitching in the Getting Around chapter in Ethiopia).

Ethiopia When the border with Ethiopia was open, two buses a week ran to Addis Ababa via Awash and Nazret.

Before the border dispute, many trucks ran from Assab port to Addis Ababa (1½ days). Lifts (for one to three people) were easy to organise and were faster, more comfortable and cheaper than the buses. Adi Nefas, 2km from central Assab on the Assab–Addis Ababa road, is the best place to find a truck. Get an update of the situation before planning any trip of this kind.

Djibouti The border between Eritrea and Djibouti is open but there are no buses between Assab and Djibouti. Before the recent Ethiopia–Eritrea war, the best option for Djibouti was to go to Adi Nefas then hitch a lift with a truck towards Addis Ababa and get off at the junction to Galafi on the border between Ethiopia and Djibouti; from there, it was an easy hitch to Djibouti town.

The alternative route via Rahaita (around 112km from Assab) in the south is now possible, though traffic between the two towns is limited. From Assab, shared taxis sometimes go as far as Moulhoulé in Djibouti to pick up passengers coming from Obock. Check the situation while in Assab, as this service is unreliable. Another option is to hire a 4WD to the border and then try and hitch to Obock; from there, you can take the ferry to Djibouti town.

Boat A cargo boat goes from Assab to Massawa once a week, and accepts passengers (Nfa75 one way). You can book a place at the **Eritrean Shipping Lines** (☎ 66 04 77) next door to the Ministry of Finance in Assab Kebir. You should bring food, water and a blanket for sleeping on the deck.

Currently it's not possible to hitch a ride on boats to Yemen (special permission is needed).

Getting Around

To/From the Airport Ignore the taxis jostling for custom at the exit; you can take a minibus, which costs Nfa15, into town.

Minibus The yellow minibuses serve as taxis about town. Journeys cost between Nfa1 and Nfa2 depending on the distance. You can also hire the whole bus (Nfa30).

Western Eritrea

Must-see tourist attractions are few and far between in the west. It's hot, dusty and hard going on the roads, and facilities for travellers are basic.

However, the region seeing so few travellers is a major part of its attraction. Some of the ethnic groups inhabiting the west – such as the Kunama – are among the more enigmatic and 'untouched' in Eritrea (see the special section 'A Museum of Peoples').

The towns of the west are all easily accessible by bus. Many have an interesting character, and some seem to have more in common with the Muslim parts of Sudan than the neighbouring highlands of Eritrea. In climate, geography, religion, industry, people and way of life, Eritrea's Muslim lowlands could not be more different from the Christian highlands.

Undisturbed by people or traffic, wildlife is abundant, and includes several Eritrean–Ethiopian endemics. Gash-Setit province boasts more wildlife than any other province in Eritrea. Near the town of Antore, Eritrea's last remaining elephants roam.

With your own 4WD, the west is a great place to explore. However, the roads are very rough in places, and during the rainy season can become impassable. Fuel is easily obtained in the big towns, but extra jerry cans of fuel are useful for exploring more remote areas.

During the Struggle, many towns in the west witnessed some bloody fighting. The relics of war are visible everywhere: tank carcasses, blown-up bridges, rubble and bullet holes. Along these roads, thousands of Ethiopian soldiers tragically perished while fleeing in panic to Sudan at the end of the war. Most just collapsed on the roadside from thirst, hunger and exhaustion.

Like all Muslim peoples, western Eritreans honour the Islamic tradition of hospitality: they are friendly, and genuinely pleased to see the few visitors who come their way.

AGORDAT
አቆርደት
pop 25,000 • elevation 615m
Lying 160km west of Asmara, Agordat is the capital of Gash Barka province.

Like most towns in the west, Agordat has an overwhelmingly Arab feel to it – even the colonial governor's **palace** is Moorish-inspired. Other major Muslim landmarks include the **mosque** – the second-largest in Eritrea – and the bustling **marketplace**, one of the most important in the lowlands.

Information
The **Commercial Bank** *(open 8am-noon & 4pm-5.30pm Mon-Fri, 8am-11.30am Sat)* cashes travellers cheques.

The **post office** *(open 8am-2pm Mon-Sat)* is near the old Italian railway station. The **telecom building** *(open 7am-6pm daily)* is near the police station.

Places to Stay & Eat
BG Sellassie Pension *(singles or doubles with shared shower Nfa60)*, better known as 'Belamberas', near the Commercial Bank, is acceptable. It has six unadorned rooms with ceiling fan and an attractive garden patio. Almas, the owner, is friendly and speaks adequate English.

A little out of town, near the main junction, **Beilul Hotel** *(☎ 71 12 28; singles or doubles with shared shower Nfa30)* is a reasonable and peaceful option. It has four decent rooms with ceiling fan and mosquito net. There's also one room with a private shower (Nfa50). Meals are available on request.

You'll find several cheap eateries around the market and the bus station, including **Ambaswera Restaurant**, popular for *sheia* (lamb drizzled with oil and flavoured with herbs, then barbecued), and **Tsinat Bar and Restaurant**. Most places have a small terrace where you can unwind and have a drink in the evening.

Getting There & Away
Buses leave from the main square, close to the ticket office. One to three buses depart early each morning for Asmara (Nfa20, four to five hours); six to eight buses travel daily to Keren between 6am and 4pm (Nfa9.50, two hour); one bus goes to Barentu (Nfa8, one hour). For Teseney, you should go to Barentu and change buses there.

If you have your own vehicle, you must be off the roads outside the town by 6pm.

BARENTU
ባረንቱ
pop 16,200 • elevation 980m
Lying 65km southwest of Agordat, Barentu is the heartland of the Kunama people, one of the most fascinating of Eritrea's ethnic groups (see the special section 'A Museum of Peoples').

Barentu serves three main purposes: it is a small market town for the local Kunama, it is the site of a military camp (at the top of the hill it sits on) and it provides a stopover for buses on their way to and from the west. Many local travellers stay overnight here. Though it offers little to do, Barentu is a very peaceful, laid-back sort of place.

The **Commercial Bank of Eritrea** *(open 7am-11.30am & 4pm-6pm Mon-Fri, 7am-10am Sat)* accepts travellers cheques and cash in the major currencies.

There's a **post office** *(open 7am-2.30pm Mon-Sat, 7am-2pm Sat)* and a **telecom office** *(open 8am-6pm daily)* which is found in the same building. Thursday is the main market day in Barentu, but Saturday is also good; both days are busiest around lunchtime.

Places to Stay & Eat
There are a number of ultrabasic options in the centre, but none can be seriously recommended.

The only decent option is the yellowish **Merhaba Hotel** *(☎ 73 11 01; rooms with shared/private bathroom Nfa80/100)* opposite the bus station at the southern edge of the town. It has 16 simple but acceptable rooms, with mosquito net and fan. There's a restaurant here which serves local fare for less than Nfa20.

You'll find several cheap eateries in the centre.

Getting There & Away
The bus station is in the main square. For Mendefera (Nfa16), you'll have to hop between towns: first go to Shambiko (Nfa12.75, five daily, two hours) and then take a minibus to May Dima (Nfa17, three daily, two hours) and another to Mendefera (Nfa7.75, two or three daily, one hour).

For Asmara, two buses leave daily between 6am and 6.30am (Nfa28.25, five hours). Seven buses go daily to Keren (Nfa17.50, three hours). To Teseney, five buses leave daily (Nfa15.50, four to five hours). For Agordat (Nfa8, one hour), take the bus to Keren or Asmara.

If you have your own vehicle, the night curfew comes into effect here too: be off the road by 6pm.

TESENEY
ተሰነይ

pop 15,000 • elevation 585m

Situated 119km west of Barentu, and just 45km from the Sudanese border, Teseney is a large frontier town.

At first sight the town seems like a large, sprawling, rubble-strewn conglomeration, devoid of trees, beautiful architecture or anything of interest. But Teseney has an intriguing character and is unlike any other town in Eritrea.

A crossroads between Eritrea and Sudan, the town has long been a meeting place, trading station and smuggling post for various ethnic groups from both countries.

During the war, the town was hotly contested – lost and won again and again by the Eritrean fighters. It was liberated finally in 1988, but not before it had suffered serious damage. Gradually the town is rebuilding itself.

Information

There's the **Commercial Bank** *(open 7am-11.30am & 4pm-5.30pm Mon-Fri, 7am-10.30am Sat)*. Cash can be changed here.

The **post office** *(open 7.30am-noon & 3pm-5pm Mon-Fri, 8am-noon Sat)* is near the Nacfa Hotel. Diagonally opposite is the **telecom building** *(open 7am-noon & 2pm-5pm daily)*.

Dangers & Annoyances The border with Sudan is now open – at least to foreigners – but the situation remains volatile. If you're thinking of crossing, you should first check out the situation while you're in Asmara.

Land mines were laid in the hills and plains all around the town during the war, so hiking in these areas is not advised. In the late 1990s, there was a bit of terrorist activity in the area (see Dangers & Annoyances in the Facts for the Visitor section). The situation seems to have stabilised now; if you're concerned, check with your embassy in the capital.

Malaria is rife here; take precautions.

Places to Stay & Eat

There are a number of cheapies in Teseney. They all offer spartan accommodation. Try **Shafaray Hotel** *(outside beds Nfa10, quads Nfa40)*, with a pleasant little garden, **Africa Hotel** *(Nfa20 per bed)* or **Luna Hotel** *(doubles Nfa40)*.

The **souq** area, known locally as 'Shuk al Shab' ('Market of the Masses' in Arabic) is straight out of Sudan. It's home to a huge open-air restaurant; you just join the rabble (most of them truck drivers from Sudan) at the long wooden tables and wait to be served. It's lively and fun and the evening air fills with the smoking and sizzling of the *sheia*. Beer is not available.

From June to August, watermelons are sold by the roads around the town.

Getting There & Away

At the time of writing, the sealing works between Barentu and Teseney had started – it should be completed by the time you read this. Teseney will therefore be much more easily accessible.

Teseney's bus station lies 1.4km from the town centre. Five buses run daily to Barentu (Nfa15.50, five hours); three go every morning to Omhajer (Nfa14, five hours); one goes to Agordat (Nfa20, five hours); and two buses go every morning to Asmara (Nfa30, 1½ day), overnighting at either Agordat or Keren. To Keren two buses depart daily (Nfa33, seven hours).

With your own vehicle, you could consider looping back to Agordat via Sebderat, north of Teseney. There's a hard (bumpy) road as far as Sebderat, then it's a dirt track. It will take you through hot, open plains, then, just outside Agordat, acres of banana plantations, irrigated by the Barka River. As around Barentu and Agordat, you must be safely off the roads by 6pm.

ERITREA

Language

Ethiopian Amharic

Amharic is the national language of Ethiopia. It belongs to the Afro-Asiatic language family, in the Semitic language sub-group that includes Arabic, Hebrew and Assyrian.

While regional languages such as Oromo, Somali and Tigrinya are also important, Amharic is the most widely used and understood language throughout the country. It is the mother tongue of the 12 million or so Amhara people in the country's central and northwestern regions, and a second language for about one third of the total population.

Amharic word endings vary according to the gender and number of people you're speaking to. This is indicated in this guide by the abbreviations 'm' (to a male), 'f' (to a female) and 'pl' (to more than one person, regardless of gender). There are also general modes of address that can be either informal or polite; these are indicated by the abbreviations 'inf' and 'pol' respectively.

For a more comprehensive guide to the language, get a copy of Lonely Planet's *Ethiopian Amharic phrasebook*. It has useful introductory sections on pronunciation and grammar, and includes Amharic script throughout.

Pronunciation

While many of the sounds of Amharic will be familiar to you, there are some sounds for which there are no English equivalents. Keep your ears tuned to the way Ethiopians pronounce their language – this will be a good start in mastering pronunciation.

In general, stress falls equally on each syllable. Like English, a raised tone at the end of a sentence signifies a question.

Vowels

a	as in 'mamma'
e	as in 'let'
ë	as the 'a' in 'ago'; shorter and flatter than **eu** below
eu	as the 'e' in 'her', with no 'r' sound; similar to the 'eu' in French *neuf*
i	as in 'bit'
o	as in 'hot'
ō	a cross between the 'oa' in 'coat' and the 'au' in 'haul'; similar to the 'au' in French *faut*
u	as in 'flute' but shorter
ay	as the 'ai' in 'bait'
ai	as in 'aisle'

Consonants

ch	as in 'church'
g	as in 'get'
gw	as in 'Gwen'
h	as in 'hit'; at the end of a sentence it's like a short puff of breath
kw	as the 'q' in 'queen'
j	as in 'jump'
s	as in 'plus' (never a 'z' sound)
sh	as in 'shirt'
z	as in 'zoo'
ny	as the 'ni' in 'onion'
r	a rolled 'r'
'	a glottal stop, ie, a momentary closing of the throat, like the 'tt' in the Cockney pronunciation of 'bottle'

You should also be aware of the Amharic consonant sounds that have no English equivalents – 'glottalic' or 'explosive' variants of some consonants, made by tightening and releasing the vocal chords. Explaining these sounds in any depth would take more space than we have here so they haven't been included in this guide. Instead, their nearest English equivalents have been used.

Greetings & Civilities

Hello/Greetings.	*tenastëllën* (lit: 'may you be given health')
Hello.	*seulam* (lit: 'peace be with you')
Hello.	*tadiyass* (inf)

The Ethiopic Syllabary

The unique Ethiopic script is the basis for the alphabets of Amharic, Tigrinya and Tigré. The basic Ethiopic syllabary has 26 characters; Amharic includes another seven, and Tigrinya another five characters to cover sounds that are specific to those languages.

The alphabet is made up of root characters representing consonants. By adding lines or circles (representing the vowel sounds) to these characters, seven different syllables can be generated for each consonant (eg, *ha, he, hë, heu, hi, ho, hu*). As with Roman script, the characters are written from left to right on a page.

How are you?	*deuhna neuh?* (m)
	deuhna neush? (f)
	deuhna not? (pol)
	deuhna nachu? (pl)
I'm fine.	*deuhna*
Good night.	*deuhna deur* (m)
	deuhna deuri (f)
	deuhna yideuru (pol)
	deuhna deuru (pl)
Goodbye.	*deuhna seunbët* (m)
	deuhna seunbëch (f)
	deuhna yiseunbëtu (pol)
	deuhna seunbëtu (pl)
Goodbye/See you.	*chow* (inf, as in Italian *ciao*)
Have a nice trip.	*meulkam guzo*
Yes.	*awo*
OK.	*ëshi*
No. (not the case/ not true)	*ai* (pronounced 'eye')
No. (not there/ not available)	*yeulleum*
Maybe.	*mënalbut*
Please.	*ëbakëh* (m)
	ëbakësh (f)
	ëbakon (pol)
	ëbakachu (pl)
Thank you.	*ameuseugënallō*
Thank you very much.	*beutam ameuseugënallō*
Don't mention it.	*mënëm aideuleuhm*
Excuse me.	*yikërta*
Sorry.	*aznallō*

Small Talk

What's your name?	*sëmëh man nō?* (m)
	sëmësh man nō? (f)
	sëmëwot man nō? (pol)
My name is ...	*sëme ... nō*
What country are you from?	*keu yet ageur neuh?* (m)
	keu yet ageur neush? (f)
	keu yet ageur not? (pol)

I'm from ...	*keu ...*
Africa	*afrika*
America/USA	*amerika*
Australia	*awstraliya*
Canada	*kanada*
Djibouti	*jëbuti*
Egypt	*gëbs*
Eritrea	*erëtra*
Ethiopia	*itëyopiya*
Europe	*irop*
South Africa	*deubub afrika*

| Are you married? | *ageubtëhal?* (m) |
| | *ageubtëshal?* (f) |

I'm married.	*agëbëchallō*
I'm not married.	*alageubahum*
May I take your photograph?	*(anteun/anchën/ërswōn) foto mansat yichalal?* (m/f/pol)

Language difficulties

Do you speak ...?	*... tëchëlalleuh?* (m)
	... tëchëyalleush? (f)
	... yichëlallu? (pol)
English	*ënglizënya*
Amharic	*amarënya*

Yes, I speak (English).	*aow, (ënglizënya) ëchëlallō*
I don't speak (Amharic).	*(amarënya) alchëllëm*
Do you understand?	*geubbah?* (m)
	geubbash? (f)
	geubbawot? (pol)
I don't understand.	*algeubanyëm*
I understand.	*geubëtonyal*
Do you have/Is there a translator?	*asteurgwami alleu?*
Does anyone here speak English?	*ënglizënya yeumichël alleu?*
Please speak slowly.	*ëbakëh keuss bëleuh teunageur* (m)
	ëbakësh keuss bëleush teunageuri (f)
	ëbakon keuss bëlō yinageuru (pol)
Please write it in Roman script.	*ëbakon beu ënglizënya alfabet yisafuliny*

Getting Around

Where is the ...?	*yet ... nō?*
airport	*awroplan mareufiyaw*
bus station	*awtobës tabiyaw*
bus stop	*awtobës makomiyaw*
city centre	*meuhal keuteumaw*
taxi stand	*taksi makomiyaw*
ticket office	*tiket biro/ tiket meushchaw*
train station	*babur tabiyaw*

Which bus goes to ...?	*yetënyaw awtobës weudeu ... yihedal?*
Does it go to ...?	*weudeu ... yihedal?*
Please tell me when we get to ...?	*ëbakon ... sënëdeurss yinëgeuruny?* (pol)
I want to get off here.	*ëzzih mōreud ëfeullëgallō*

What time does the ... arrive/leave?	*... meuche yideursal/ yineusal?*
boat	*jeulba*
bus	*awtobës*

Signs – Ethiopian

Open	ክፍት ነው
Closed	ተዘግቷል
Entrance	መግቢያ
Exit	መውጫ
Information	ማስታወቂያ
Danger	አደጋኛ
No Smoking	ማጨስ ክልክል ነው
Toilets	ሽንት ቤት
Men	የወንዶች
Women	የሴቶች

car	meukina
minibus	wëyëyët
plane	awroplan
train	babur
truck	yeu chëneut meukina

next	yeumikeutëllō
How much is it to ...?	weudeu ... sënt(ë) nō?
I'd like to reserve a ticket to ...	weudeu ... tiket beukëd miya meugzat ëfeullë gallō
I'd like a one way ticket to ...	weudeu ... meuheja tiket ëfeullëgallō
I'd like a return ticket to ...	weudeu ... deurso meuls tiket ëfeullëgallō

I want to rent a ...	... meukeurayeut ëfeullëgallō
bicycle	bësklet
car	meukina

Directions

I want to go to ...	weudeu ... meuhed ëfeullëgallō
How do I get to ...?	weudeu ... ëndet ëhedallō?
Is it near/far?	kërb/ruk nō?
Can I walk there?	beugër yaskedal?
Can you show me on the map?	kartaw lai yasayunyal? (pol)
Where?	yet?
Turn ...	beu ... beukul tateuf (m)/ tateufi (f)
Go straight ahead.	beukeutëta hid (m)/ hij (f)
on the (left/right)	beu (gra/keuny) beukul
at the next corner	yeumikeutëllō meuta-teufiya
to the north	weudeu seumen
to the south	weudeu deubub
to the east	weudeu mësrak
to the west	weudeu më'ërab
in front of/behind	fit leu fit/beuholla

highway	awra godana
main road	wanna meungeud
street	meungeud
village	meuneudeur

Around town

Where is a/the ...?	... yet nō?
bank	bank
church	beteu kërëstëyan
city centre	meuhal keuteuma
... embassy	yeu ... embassi
hotel	hotel
market	geubeuya
mosque	meusgid
pharmacy	farmasi/ meudhanit bet
police station	polis tabiya
post office	posta bet
public toilet	shënt bet
restaurant	mëgëb bet
tourist office	yeu turist biro
university	yuniveursiti

What time does it open/close?
sënt seu'at yikeufeutal/yizzeugal?
I want to change money/travellers cheques.
geunzeub/travleurs cheks meukeuyeur ëfeullëgallō
I want to make a (local/international) call.
(ageur wëst/wëch ageur) sëlk meudeuweul ëfeullëgallō

Accommodation

Where is a ...?	... yet nō?
hotel	hotel
good hotel	tëru hotel
cheap hotel	rëkash hotel
bed	alga
room	këfël

Do you have/ Is there ...?	... alleu?
a room/bed	alga
a single room	and alga
a room with two beds	baleu huleutt alga
a quiet room	seut yaleu këfël
showers	shaweur
water for bathing	meutateubiya wuha
hot water	muk wuha

How much is the room/bed for ...?	alga leu ... sëntë nō?
one night	and mata
one week	and samënt

Does it include breakfast?	kursënëm yicheumëral?

Food Glossary

Some terms, such as *arrosto* (roasted), *bistecca ai ferri* (grilled steak), *cabretto* (goat or kid), *costata* (chop), *cotoletta* (cutlet), *manzo* (beef), *scaloppina* (escalope) and *trippa* (tripe), are leftovers from the Italian Occupation.

All of the following are served with good-old *injera* unless indicated otherwise.

asa wat – freshwater fish served as a hot stew

atkilt-b-dabbo *(vegie)* – vegetables with bread

awazi – a kind of mustard and chilli sauce

berbere – as many as 16 spices or more go into making the famous red powder responsible for giving much Ethiopian food its kick. Most women prepare their own special recipe, often passed down from mother to daughter through successive generations, and proudly adhered to.

beyainatu – literally 'of every type' – a small portion of all dishes on the menu; also known by its Italian name *secondo misto*

dabbo fir fir *(vegie)* – torn up bits of bread mixed with butter and *berbere*

derek tibs – meat (usually lamb) fried and served *derek* ('dry' – without sauce)

doro wat – chicken drumstick or wing accompanied by a hard-boiled egg served in a hot sauce of butter, onion, chilli, cardamom and *berbere* . Considered the most sophisticated of the *wat* dishes, it's almost become the national dish of Ethiopia – the best of them are outstanding!

dulet – minced tripe, liver and lean beef fried in butter, onions, chilli, cardamom and pepper (often eaten for breakfast)

enkulal tibs *(vegie)* – literally 'egg tibs', a kind of Ethiopian scrambled eggs made with a combination of green and red peppers, tomatoes and sometimes onions, served with *dabbo* (bread). Great for breakfast.

enset *(vegie)* – false-banana 'bread'; a staple food (see the boxed text 'Enduring Enset' in the Southern Ethiopia chapter)

fatira – savoury pastries

ful *(vegie)* – chick pea and butter puree eaten for breakfast

genfo *(vegie)* – barley or wheat porridge served with butter and *berbere*

injera *(vegie)* – kind of large pancake (see the boxed text 'Edible Cutlery' in the Facts for the Visitor chapter)

kai wat – lamb, goat or beef cooked in a hot *berbere* sauce

kekel – boiled meat

kitfo – minced beef or lamb like the French steak tartare, usually warmed (but not cooked) in butter, *berbere* and sometimes thyme

kotcho *(vegie)* – *enset*; served with *kitfo*

kwalima – sausage served during ceremonial occasions

kwanta – strips of beef rubbed in chilli, butter, salt and *berbere* then usually hung up and dried

mahabaroui – a mixture of dishes including half a roast chicken

melasena senber tibs – beef tongue and tripe fried with *berbere* and onion

messer *(vegie)* – a kind of lentil curry made with onions, chillies and various spices

minchet abesh – minced beef or lamb in a hot *berbere* sauce

shiro *(vegie)* – chickpea or bean puree lightly spiced, served on fasting days

sils *(vegie)* – hot tomato and onion sauce eaten for breakfast

tere sega – raw meat served with a couple of spicy accompaniments

tibs – sliced lamb, pan fried in butter, garlic, onion and sometimes tomato

tibs sheukla – *tibs* served sizzling in a clay pot above hot coals

tilapia – freshwater fish

wat – stew

ye som megeb *(vegie)* – a selection of different vegetable dishes, served on fasting days

yinjera fir fir *(vegie)* – torn-up bits of *injera* mixed with butter and *berbere*

zilzil tibs – strips of beef, fried and served slightly crunchy with *awazi* sauce

I'd like to see the room.	*këflun mayet ëfeullë gallō*	Is there a cheap (restaurant) near here?	*ëzzih akababi, rëkash (mëgëb bet) alleu?*
Can I see a different room?	*lela këfël mayet ëchëlallō?*		
I leave tomorrow.	*neugeu ëhedallō*	I want to eat ... food.	*yeu ... mëgëb ëfeullëfallō*

Food

		Ethiopian	*itëyopiya*
		Arab	*arab*
breakfast	*kurs*	Italian	*talyan*
lunch	*mësa*	Western	*faranji*
dinner	*ërat*		

I'm a vegetarian/ I don't eat meat.	*sëga albeullam*
Can I have it mild?	*alëcha yimëtallëny?*

bread/bread rolls	*dabbo*
round bread	*ambasha*
chips	*yeu dënëch tëbs*
salad	*seulata*
sandwich	*sandwich* (usually spicy meat in plain bread)
soup	*meureuk* (usually a spicy lamb or beef broth)
yoghurt	*ërgo*

water	*wuha*
water (boiled)	*yeu feula wuha*
water (sterilised)	*yeu teutara wuha*
mineral water	*ambo wuha*
soda/soft drink	*leuslassa*
juice	*chëmaki*
milk	*weuteut*
tea	*shai*
coffee	*buna*
strong/weak	*weufram/keuchën*
with/without	*beu/yaleu*
honey	*mar*
sugar	*sëkwar*
beer	*bira*

Shopping

Where is a/an ...?	*... yet nō?*
bakery	*dabbo bet*
bookshop	*meusëhaf bet*
clothes shop	*yeu lëbs suk*
general store	*sheukeuta sheukeut meudeubër*
market	*geubeuya*
stationers	*stesheunari*
shop	*suk*

Where can I buy ...?	*... yet yigeunyal?*
I'm just looking.	*ëyayo nō*
I want a (larger/ smaller) ...	*(tëllëk yaleu/anneus yaleu) ... ëfeullë-gallō*
How much is it?	*sëntë nō?*
That's (very) expensive.	*(beutam) wëdd nō*
Do you have anything cheaper?	*rëkash alleu?*

Health

I'm sick.	*amonyal*
(Please) help me.	*(ëbakon) yeueurduny*
I need a doctor (immediately).	*hakim (baschëkwai) ëfeullëgallō*

Help!	*ërduny!*
It's an emergency!	*aschëkwai nō!*
There's been an accident!	*adeuga neubbeur!*
Danger!	*adeugeunya!*
Fire!	*ësat!*
Thief!	*leba!*
Go away!/Leave me alone!	*teumeulleuss!*
I'm lost.	*meungeud teufto-bënyal*
Where is the toilet?	*shënt betu yeuht nō?*
Call ...!	*... tëra/tëri!* (m/f)
the police	*polis*
an ambulance	*ambulans*

doctor	*hakim*
hospital	*hospital*
medical centre	*yeu hëkëmëna tabiya*

I'm allergic to ...	*... ais-mamanyëm*
antibiotics	*antibiotiks*
penicillin	*peunisillin*

I have ...	*... alleubëny*
diabetes	*sëkwar beushëta*
epilepsy	*yeumitël beushëta*
nausea/vomiting	*yasmeulëseunyal*
stomachache	*hoden yameunyal*

Time & Dates

When?	*meuche?*
What time is it?	*sënt seu'at nō?*
It's (one) o'clock.	*(and) seu'at nō*
It's a quarter past (one).	*(and) seu'at keurub nō*
It's half past (one).	*(and) seu'at teukul nō*
the morning	*tëwatu*
the evening	*mëshëtu*
the night	*lelitu*

now	*ahun*
today	*zare*
tonight	*zare mata*
tomorrow	*neugeu*
yesterday	*tënantëna*

Monday	*seunyo*
Tuesday	*makseunyo*
Wednesday	*rob*
Thursday	*hamus*
Friday	*arb*
Saturday	*këdame*
Sunday	*ëhud*

Numbers
Although there are Amharic script numerals, Arabic numerals (ie, those used in English) are now commonly used throughout Ethiopia. Amharic is used when referring to numbers in speech.

½	*gëmash*
1	*and*
2	*huleutt*
3	*sost*
4	*arat*
5	*amëst*
6	*sëdëst*
7	*seubat*
8	*sëmënt*
9	*zeuteuny*
10	*assër*
11	*assra and*
12	*assra huleutt*
13	*assra sost*
14	*assra arat*
15	*assra amëst*
16	*assra sëdëst*
17	*assra seubat*
18	*assra sëmënt*
19	*assra zeuteuny*
20	*haya*
21	*haya and*
30	*seulassa*
31	*seulassa and*
40	*arba*
50	*hamsa*
60	*sëlsa*
70	*seuba*
80	*seumanya*
90	*zeuteuna*
100	*meuto*
101	*meuto and*
200	*huleutt meuto*
1,000	*and shi*
2,000	*huleutt shi*
100,000	*meuto shi*

Tigrinya

Tigrinya is the principal language of Eritrea and is also widely spoken in Tigray province in Ethiopia. It belongs to the Ethiopic branch of the Semitic language family. Like Amharic, it uses the syllabic alphabet of classical Ethiopic or Ge'ez (see the boxed text 'The Ethiopic Syllabary' earlier in this chapter).

Tigrinya word endings vary according to the gender of the person you are speaking to; this is indicated in this guide where relevant by the abbreviations 'm' (to a male) and 'f' (to a female).

Pronunciation
Vowels

a	as in 'mamma'
e	as in 'men'
ee	as in 'heed'
i	as in 'bit'
o	as in 'or', with no 'r' sound
oo	as in 'cool'
u	as in 'put'
ay	as in 'bait'
ai	as in 'aisle'
ō	a cross between the 'oa' in 'coat' and the 'au' in 'haul'; similar to French *au*

Consonants
Most consonants are pronounced as per their English counterparts but, like Amharic, there are some consonant sounds not found in English. The transliterations in this guide are designed for ease of use and are not meant as a detailed phonetic representation of all the consonant sounds in Tigrinya. By pronouncing the words and phrases clearly you should be able to make yourself understood. Listening to the everyday speech of the people is the best way to master some of the more complex sounds of the language.

ch	as in 'church'
g	as in 'get'
h	as in 'him'
j	as in 'jump'
ny	as the 'ni' in 'onion'
q	like a 'k' from far back in the throat
r	as in 'run'
s	as in 'plus' (never a 'z' sound)
sh	as in 'shirt'
ts	as the 'ts' in 'its'
z	as in 'zoo'

Greetings & Useful Phrases

Hello.	*selam*
Welcome.	*merhaba*
Good morning.	*dehaando hadirka* (m)
	dehaando hadirkee (f)
Good afternoon.	*dehaando weelka* (m)
	dehaando weelkee (f)
Good evening.	*dehaando amsika* (m)
	dehaando amsikee (f)
Good night.	*dehaan hideru*
Goodbye.	*dehaan kun* (also Italian *ciao*)
Yes.	*u-we*
No.	*aykonen*
Please.	*bejaka* (m)
	bejakee (f)
Thank you.	*yekanyeley/yemesgin*

That's fine, you're welcome. — *genzebka* (m)
genzebkee (f)
Excuse me. — *yikrai-ta*
I'm sorry. — *aytehazeley*
How are you? — *kemay aleka?* (m)
kemay alekee? (f)
I'm fine, thanks. — *tsebuk, yekeniyeley*
Pleased to meet you. — *tsebuk afleto/ leila yigberelna*
What's your name? — *men semka?* (m)
men semkee? (f)
My name is ... — *shemey ... iyu*
Where are you from? — *kabey metsika?* (m)
kabey metsikee? (f)
I'm from ... — *a-nne kab ... iye*
Are you married? — *temereka dikha?* (m)
temerekee dikhee? (f)
How many children do you have? — *kenday kolu-oot (deki) alowuka?* (m)
kenday kolu-oot (deki) alowukee? (f)
I don't have any children. — *deki yebeleyn.*
I have a son. — *wedi aloni*
I have a daughter. — *gual alatni*
May I take your photograph? — *kese-alekado?*

Language difficulties
Do you speak (English)? — *(engiliznya) tezarebdo/ tezarebido?* (m/f)
I don't speak Tigrinya. — *a-nne tigrinya ayzareben*
I understand. — *yirede-anee iyu/ teredioonee*
I don't understand. — *ayeterede-anen*

Getting Around
Where is the ...? — *abey alo ...?*
 airport — *aryaporto/maerefi nefarit*
 bus station — *maerefi autobus*
 bus stop — *autobus tetew tiblelu*

When does the next ... leave/arrive? — *tikitsil ... saat kenday tinekel/te-atu?*
 boat — *jelba*
 bus (city) — *autobus (ketema)*
 car — *mekina*
 plane — *auroplan/nefarit*
 taxi — *taksi*
 train — *babur*

I want to go to ... — *nab ... kikeid delye*
Where is ...? — *abey alo ...?*
How do I get to ...? — *kemey geire naboo ... yikeid?*

Is it far/near? — *rehooq/kereba diyu?*
Can I walk there? — *baegrey kikedo yikealdo?*
Can you show me the direction? — *ket-hebreni tikealdo?*
Go straight ahead. — *ket elka kid*
Turn left/right. — *netsegam/neyeman tetewe*

Around Town
I'm looking for ... — *ne ... yenadi alekoo*
 a bank — *bank*
 the embassy — *embasi*
 the hospital — *hospital/ beit hikmena*
 my hotel — *natey hotel*
 the market — *idaga/shooq*
 a pharmacy — *farmacha/ beit medhanit*
 the post office — *beit busta*
 a public telephone — *nay hizbi telefon*
 the tourist office — *nay turist haberaita beit tsihfet*

What time does it open? — *saat kenday yikifet?*
What time does it close? — *saat kenday yi-etso?*
Do you have ...? — *... alekado?*
How many/How much? — *kenday?*
this/that — *eizee/etee*

Accommodation
hotel — *hotel*
guesthouse — *maeref agaysh/ albeirgo*
youth hostel — *nay mena-esey hostel*
camping ground — *metkel dinquan/ teinda bota*

Do you have any rooms available? — *medekesi kiflee alekado?*
How much is it per night/person? — *neha-de leiti/seb kenday yikifel?*
Is breakfast included? — *kursi mesoo hisub d'yu?*

single bed — *kelete arat*
double bed — *hadde arat*
for one/two people — *neha-de/kelete seb*
for one/two nights — *neha-de/kelete leiti*

Food
breakfast — *kursi*
lunch — *mesah*
dinner — *dirar*
restaurant — *beit megbi/restront*

I'm epileptic.	a-nne minfirfar himam aloni
I'm allergic to penicillin.	a-nne nay pencillin kute-at aloni
diarrhoea	witse-at
medicine	medhanit/fewsi
nausea	egirgir/segedged

Emergencies – Tigrinya

Help!	hagez/redi-at!
Leave me alone/ Go away!	hidegeni!/ kid bejakha!
I'm lost.	a-nne tefi-a aloku
Call ...!	... tsewe-a!
a doctor	hakim/doctor
the police	police

water	may
beer	beera
mineral water	may gas/aqua minerale
coffee	boon (Italian words like capuccino and macchiato are also used)
tea	shahee
with	mis
without	bizey
milk	tsaba
sugar	shukar
bread	banee
eggs	enkakuho
potato	dineesh
rice	ruz

Shopping

How much is it?	kenday iyu waga-oo?
I'm just looking.	nikeree tirah iye
That's too expensive.	aziyu kebiruni
bookshop	mesheta metsahifti
clothes shop	mesheta kidawenti
market	idaga/shouq
local products	nay kebabi etot/firyat

Health

I need a doctor.	a-nne hakim/doctor yedliyeni a-lo
Where is the hospital?	hospital/beit hikimina abey alo?
I have a stomachache.	a-nne kirtset aloni
I'm diabetic.	a-nne shikor/shikoria himam aloni

Time, Days & Numbers

What time is it?	saat kenday koynoo?
today	lomee/lomee me-altee
tomorrow	tsebah
yesterday	timalee
morning	niguho
afternoon	dehri ketri
night	leytee

Monday	senui
Tuesday	selus
Wednesday	reboo
Thursday	hamus
Friday	arbi
Saturday	kedam
Sunday	senbet

1	hadde
2	kelete
3	seleste
4	arba-ate
5	hamushte
6	shedushte
7	shewate
8	shemonte
9	tesh-ate
10	aserte
20	isra
30	selasa
40	arba-a
50	hamsa
60	susa
70	sebe-a
80	semanya
90	tese-a
100	mi-eetee
1000	sheh

Glossary

This glossary covers some of the local words the traveller is likely to encounter in Ethiopia and Eritrea. For information on culinary terms, see Food in the Ethiopia Facts for the Visitor chapter and in the Eritrea chapter, and the boxed text 'Food Glossary' in the Language chapter; for general information on the languages of Ethiopia and Eritrea, see the Language chapter.

abba – a prefix used by a priest before his name; means 'father'
abuna – archbishop of the Ethiopian and Eritrean Orthodox church, from the *Ge'ez* meaning 'our father'
adaï – evergreen shrub used as toothbrush
agelgil – round, leather-bound 'lunch boxes' carried by country travellers
amba (also *emba*) – flat-topped mountain
araki – grain spirit
ato – literally 'sir'; equivalent of 'Mr'
azmari – itinerant minstrel (Ethiopia)

bar girl – prostitute
beat – Amharic word meaning 'place', which is attached to the end of other words, eg, *buna beat*, *shint beat* (Ethiopia)
buluko – heaviest type of *shamma*, used in cold areas such as the Bale Mountains (Ethiopia)
buna beat – literally 'coffee house' but more often than not a bar! (Ethiopia)

chat – mildly intoxicating leaf that is consumed particularly in Addis Ababa and eastern Ethiopia; it is illegal in Eritrea
contract taxi – private, or nonshared, taxi

dejazmach – title (usually of nobility though given to any outstanding male) equivalent to duke or prince, but not as high-ranking as *ras*
Derg – Socialist military junta that governed Ethiopia from 1974 to 1991 under Lt Colonel Mengistu Haile Mariam (more commonly known as 'Mengistu'); derived from the *Ge'ez* word for 'committee'
dhow – see *sambuk*
dula – wooden staff carried by many Ethiopian highlanders when travelling

emba – see *amba*
enset – false-banana tree found in much of southern Ethiopia, used to produce a bread-like staple

EPLF – Eritrean People's Liberation Front; victorious guerrilla army in the 'Struggle for Independence'

Falasha – Ethiopian Jew
faranji – foreigner, especially a Western foreigner (Ethiopia)

gabeta – ancient board game
gabi – slightly thicker version of the *shamma*, worn by men
gada – age system of male hierarchy among the Oromo
gari – horse-drawn cart used for transporting passengers and goods in the towns
Ge'ez – a kind of Ethiopian Latin (still used in the Church today) and forerunner of modern Amharic
gommista – tyre repair shop (Italian)
gotera – granary with a little thatched roof (Ethiopia)
grocery/grocerie – more often than not a liquor shop! (Ethiopia)

hotel – often a restaurant!

jellabia – hooded cloak with wide sleeves (Eritrea)
jile – the curved knife that is carried by Afar nomads
jus beat – juice bar offering fresh fruit juices (Ethiopia)

keak beat – cake shop (Ethiopia)
Kebra Negast – Ethiopia's national epic and a 14th-century collection of legends, describing, among other things, the story of the Queen of Sheba and the origins of the Solomonic dynasty (Ethiopia)
kemis – white cotton dress worn by Ethiopian highland women
Kiddus – Saint, eg, Kiddus Mikael translates to St Michael

maqdas – inner sanctuary of a church
mesob – hourglass-shaped woven table from which traditional food is served (Ethiopia)
mies – see *tej*
muezzin – mosque official who calls the faithful to prayer

natala – women's equivalent of a *shamma*, but with a decorated border or *tibeb*
negus – king (Ethiopia)

negus negast – king of kings; the traditional and official title of Ethiopian emperors

Ramadan – ninth month of the Muslim calendar, 30 days long, during which strict fasting is observed from sunrise to sunset
ras – title (usually of nobility but given to any outstanding male) similar to duke or prince

sambuk – traditional Arab vessel (or *dhow*) rigged with a lateen (triangular) sail, plying the Red Sea and Indian Ocean (Eritrea)
sewa – see *tella*
shamma – a kind of white, light cotton toga; see also *gabi*, *natala* and *buluko*
shifta – traditionally a rebel or outlaw; today a bandit or roadside robber
shint beat – toilet (Ethiopia)
shirit – sarong-like wrap worn by men in lowland parts of eastern Ethiopia and Eritrea

tabot – replica of the Ark of the Covenant, kept in the inner sanctuary of every Orthodox church

tankwa – traditional papyrus boat used on Lake Tana among other places (Ethiopia)
tef – an indigenous grass cultivated as a cereal grain; the key ingredient of injera, a bread-like staple
tej – wine made from honey, popular in Ethiopia; known in Eritrea as *mies*
tella – home-brewed beer made from finger millet, maize or barley, popular in Ethiopia; known in Eritrea as *sewa*
tibeb – the decorative border of a woman's shawl (Ethiopia)
tukul – traditional cone-shaped hut with thatched roof; like South Africa's rondavel

VSO – Volunteer Service Overseas worker; an aid worker sent by the charity of the same name

wadi – a river that is usually dry except in the rainy season
weizerit – equivalent of 'Miss' (Ethiopia)
weizero – literally 'lady', now equivalent of 'Mrs' (Ethiopia)

Thanks

Many thanks to the travellers who used the last edition and wrote to us with helpful hints, useful advice and interesting anecdotes:

Asbjorn Aase, Noah Akiliu, Christophe Baeten, Lars Berglund, Biruk Bitew, Marcel Bon, Will Bourne, Sally Brown, Katja Budde, Rowland Burley, Mark Carter, Charles Citroen, Mark Clarke, Stewart Collis, Elisabeth Cox, John Cox, Peter Cross, Eyassu Dagnew, Philippe Delesalle, Simon Denyer, Mieke Denys, Dave Dissette, Valerie Dmaqeda, Sigrid Drage, Sally Dunsmore,

Moray Easdale, Lise Ellyin, Kari Eloranta, Angie Eng, Diana Erdmann-Sager, Guy Erricker, Ed Eurlings, Tewabe Fanta, Hanne Finholt, Andrew Fleming, Christine & Norman Foord, Tomasz & Anna Galka, Aiming Gao, Jason Garred, Yonas Gebremichael, Tewodros Getnet, Gwili Gibbon, Winnie Goedbloed, Peter Goltermann, Hamutal Granot, Guido Groenen, Brian Grove, Helen & Paul H, Tom Hall, Dana Hearn, Katherine Hobbs, Keith Holmes, NG Hornibrook, C Hoyer-Ruckstuhl, Brendon Hyde, Karl Kociper, Jon E Krupnick, Peter Kurze, Noshir Lam, Luc Lauwers, Andrew MacDonald, Bianka Madej, Jens Maertin, Edwin Martin, Arthur Marx, Simon Mason, Romà Massot-Punyet, Nora McGuigan, Colin Menzies, Thierry Michilsen, Markella Mikkelsen, AD Mills, Stephanie Mills, Jock & Janice Moilliet, David Musson,

Mark Natkin, Carlyle Joy Newman-Eden, Heidi Normann, Cecile Nouvellon, Thomas Ofcansky, Tim Otte, Irene Ouwens, Giorgio Perversi, Chris Peters, Luigi Prati, Shanti Rama, Lindsey Rees, Yuval Ronen, Darren Ross, Cathy Routhier, John Rude, Mark Sadler, Maja Sajovic, Christoph Schaaf, Deedee Schmidt-Pedersen, Getinet Seyoum, Ezra Simon, Mark Simons, Peter Smolka, Jim Sowers, Robert J Stagg, Robert Stodel, Attila Strausz,

Hisako Tajima, Maarten van ter Beek, Rene VanDam, Sally von Holdt, Karin Wandschura, B Wearne, Simon & Jennifer Wicks, Jose Wiechmann, Jeff Willner, Ulrich Winkelmann, Nachiko Yokata, Oliver Zoellner

LONELY PLANET

You already know that Lonely Planet produces more than this one guidebook, but you might not be aware of the other products we have on this region. Here is a selection of titles that you may want to check out as well:

Africa on a Shoestring
ISBN 0 86442 663 1
US$14.99 • UK£8.99

East Africa
ISBN 1 74059 131 3
US$27.99 • UK£15.99

Ethiopian Amharic Phrasebook
ISBN 1 74059 133 X
US$7.99 • UK£4.50

Available wherever books are sold

Index

Bold indicates maps.

Boxed Text

MAP LEGEND

CITY ROUTES

Freeway	Freeway		Unsealed Road
Highway	Primary Road		One-Way Street
Road	Secondary Road		Pedestrian Street
Street	Street		Stepped Street
Lane	Lane		Tunnel
	Roadblocks		Footbridge

REGIONAL ROUTES

Tollway, Freeway
Primary Road
Secondary Road
Minor Road

BOUNDARIES

International
State
Disputed
Wall

HYDROGRAPHY

River, Creek
Canal
Lake, Tank
Dry Lake, Salt Lake
Spring, Rapids
Waterfalls

TRANSPORT ROUTES & STATIONS

Train
Metro
Tramway
Bus Route
Monorail
Cable Car, Chairlift
Ferry
Boat
Walking Trail
Walking Tour

AREA FEATURES

Building
Park, Garden
National Park
Market
Beach
Campus
Cemetery
Urban

MAP SYMBOLS

✪ **CAPITAL**	National Capital	Cathedral, Church	Mine	Snorkelling
◉ **CAPITAL**	State Capital	Cave; Volcano	Monument	Spring
● **City**	City, Large Town	Cinema	Mosque	Stately Home
● **Town**	Town	Embassy, Consulate	Mountain, Hill	Stupa
● Village	Village	Dive Site	Mountain Range	Surf Beach
●	Place to Stay	Fort	Museum, Gallery	Swimming Pool
▼	Place to Eat	Garden	Pagoda	Synagogue
●	Point of Interest	Golf Course	Parking Area	Taxi
	Airfield, Airport	Hazard	Pass	Telephone
●	Anchorage	Hospital	Petrol/Gas Station	Theatre
	Animal Viewing/Hide	Information	Police Station	Toilet
●	Bank	Internet Cafe	Post Office	Tomb/Mausoleum
●	Battle Site	Islamic Shrine	Pub, Bar	Tourist Information
●	Border Crossing	Lighthouse	Ruins	Transport (General)
●	Camping Ground	Lookout	Shopping Centre	Zoo

Note: not all symbols displayed above appear in this book

LONELY PLANET OFFICES

Australia
Locked Bag 1, Footscray, Victoria 3011
☎ 03 8379 8000 fax 03 8379 8111
email: talk2us@lonelyplanet.com.au

USA
150 Linden St, Oakland, CA 94607
☎ 510 893 8555 TOLL FREE: 800 275 8555
fax 510 893 8572
email: info@lonelyplanet.com

UK
72-82 Rosebery Ave, London, EC1R 4RW
☎ 020 7841 9000 fax 020 7841 9001
email: go@lonelyplanet.co.uk

France
1 rue du Dahomey, 75011 Paris
☎ 01 55 25 33 00 fax 01 55 25 33 01
email: bip@lonelyplanet.fr
www.lonelyplanet.fr

World Wide Web: www.lonelyplanet.com or AOL keyword: lp
Lonely Planet Images: www.lonelyplanetimages.com